Memory

Phenomena and Principles

Norman E. Spear
Binghamton University, SUNY

David C. Riccio
Kent State University

Allyn and Bacon
Boston • London • Toronto • Sydney • Tokyo • Singapore

*To Linda, perfect wife, colleague and friend
and to Mandy and Jennifer
(N.E.S.)*

*To the memory of my parents, Helen Coldwell Riccio
and Leonard D. Riccio
(D.C.R.)*

Editor-in-Chief, Social Sciences: Susan Badger
Editorial Assistant: Laura Ellingson
Production Administrator: Ann Greenberger
Cover Administrator: Suzanne Harbison
Composition Buyer: Linda Cox
Manufacturing Buyer: Louise Richardson
Editorial-Production Service: Progressive Typographers

Copyright © 1994 by Allyn & Bacon
A Division of Simon & Schuster, Inc.
160 Gould Street
Needham Heights, MA 02194

All rights reserved. No part of the material protected by this copyright notice may be reproduced or utilized in any form or by any means, electronic or mechanical, including photocopying, recording, or by any information storage and retrieval system, without the written permission of the copyright owner.

Library of Congress Cataloging-in-Publication Data

Spear, Norman E.
    Memory : phenomena and principles / Norman E. Spear, David C. Riccio.
        p.   cm.
    Includes bibliographical references and index.
    ISBN 0-205-14204-4
     1. Memory   2. Learning, Psychology of.   3. Psychology, Comparative.   I. Riccio, David C.   II. Title.
BF371.S73   1994
153.1'2--dc 20   93-15722
                                                                                 CIP

Printed in the United States of America

10   9   8   7   6   5   4   3   2   1   98   97   96   95   94   93

Contents

2   Forgetting Events and Relationships: The Effects of Time   27
Absence of Forgetting in Early Laboratory Tests with Animals   28
An Orientation for Understanding Forgetting   29
Forgetting Over Time: The Effect of a Retention Interval Filled with
    Relative Inactivity   31
    Everyday Forgetting Over Time   32
        Fifty-Year Memory   32
        Remembering Unique Personal Events   34
    The Generality of Forgetting as a Steady Decline   36
    Apparent Increases in Retention Over Time: Hypermnesia   39
        Reminiscence   39
        Does Recall of Pictures and Words Improve over Time?   40
        Incubation   42
        Basic Conditioning   44
    Temporarily Impaired Retention—The Kamin Effect   46
    Multiphasic Retention Functions: Repeated Fluctuations
        in Retention   49
Chapter Summary   52

3   Significant Sources of Forgetting: Changes in Context   53
Context and Retention   53
    What Is Context and What Can It Do to Learning and Memory?   54
    Sharpening the Meaning of Context   56
        Linguistic Context   56
        Internal Context   56
    General Issues in the Relationship Between Context
        and Memory   56
Contextual Influences on Basic Conditioning and Learning   59
The Role of Context in Memory Retrieval   61
Generality and Limitations of the Contextual Change Effect   63
    The Contextual Change Effect on Human Memory   64
    Effects of Simple Context on Human Memory: The
        Smith Experiments   65
        Is the Context Effect Due to Novelty of the Test Context?   66
        Does Context Help Determine How a Word Is Perceived
            or Encoded?   67
        Is the Physical Presence of the Learning Context Essential for the
            Context Effect?   67
        Remembering the Context Itself   68
    Generality of the Contextual Change Effect   69
        A Context Effect in Deep-Sea Diving   69
        External Contextual Stimuli Control Expression of
            Basic Conditioning   70
        Summary   71
    Limits to the Generality of the Contextual Change Effect   72
State-Dependent Retention   74

Contents

Preface　xi

1　Introduction to Memory　1
How Is Memory Related to Learning?　2
Conceptual Distinctions between Memory and Learning　2
Early Ideas about Memory　4
　The Origin of Mnemonics　5
　The Art of Memory Processing　6
　The Science of Memory Processing　7
　　Memory and the Brain　7
　　The First Systematic Experiments on Memory　8
　　Increasing Breadth in the Study of Memory　10
Definitions of Memory　10
　Uses of the Term, *Memory*　11
　Memory-as-Representation　12
　Memory-as-Process　13
Retention and Forgetting: Orientation and Terminology　14
　Relationship between Learning and Retention　14
　Retention and Forgetting　16
　Storage and Retrieval　16
The Expression of Memory　16
　Measurement of Memory　17
　　Recall and Recognition　17
　　Relearning　18
　　Principles of Memory Measurement　18
　　Control Groups in Measurement of Memory　19
　Dissociation between Memories Available and Memories Expressed　21
　　The Misleading Nature of Verbal Reports of Remembering　21
　　Illustrations of Different Conclusions from Different Measures
　　　of Memory　22
　Two Features of Memory Measurement　24
Sources of Forgetting　24
Summary　25

Contents   v

      Experimental Analysis of State-Dependent Retention   75
          Design of Experiments Testing State-Dependent Retention   75
          Variables Affecting State-Dependent Retention   76
      State-Dependent Effects in Human Memory   77
      Summary Principles of Drug-Induced State-Dependent Retention   79
  Endogenous States and Memory Dissociation   80
  Chapter Summary   83

4   Significant Sources of Forgetting: Interference: Conflicting Memories Interfere with Retention   85
  What Kind of "Interference" Is Involved?   85
      Traditional Alternative to Interference: Consolidation Disruption and Decay   86
      Retroactive and Proactive Interference   87
      The Cornerstone of Interference Theory: Similarity   88
      Basic Mechanisms and Features of Interference   89
          Retroactive Interference   92
          Proactive Interference   93
      Interference and Forgetting in Animals   96
          Role of Specific Interference in Animal Memory   97
          The Kraemer Experiments   98
          Summary and Comment   100
      The Role of Nonspecific Interference in Animal Memory   100
      Summary   102
  Sleep and Memory   102
      Stages of Sleep   103
      The Function of Sleep   103
      Does REM Sleep in Normal Sleep Facilitate Memory?   104
      Can Memory Be Aided by Induced Sleep?   105
      Sleep May Promote Memory Retrieval in Human Infants   106
  Chapter Summary   106

5   Short-Term Retention   109
  Assessment of Short-Term Retention   109
      Short-Term Retention Assessed by the Delayed Response Test   110
      Improved Analysis of Short-Term Retention in Animals: Delayed Matching-to-Sample   112
  Retroactive Interference in Short-Term Retention   114
      Illumination: An Example of Nonspecific Retroactive Interference   115
      Does Retroactive Interference Depend on Sensory Modality?   117
          Symbolic versus Identity Matching   118

Retroactive Interference and Sensory Modality   119
Overt Representation for Memory   119
Proactive Interference in Short-Term Retention   121
   Three Sources of Proactive Interference   122
   Proactive Interference from Prior Processing of
      Particular Samples   123
Content of the Memory in Short-Term Retention   126
   Prospective and Retrospective Content   127
   Does Content of the Memory Determine Its Rate
      of Forgetting?   129
      Sensory Modality   129
Cognition and Short-Term Retention in Animals   132
   Rehearsal in Animals: A Consequence of Surprise   133
   Directed Forgetting   137
Short-Term Retention in Humans   140
   Capacity of Short-Term Memory   141
   Duration of Short-Term Retention   141
Comparisons of Monkey and Human Memory   143
      Rehearsal of Pictures   145
   Summary   146
   Short Note on Other Tests of Short-Term Retention   146
Chapter Summary   148

6 Memory for Stimulus Attributes and Spatial Location   151
Stimulus Generalization   152
Memory for Individual Attributes of a Stimulus   154
   Forgetting of Interoceptive (Flavor) Attributes   158
   Forgetting of Stimulus Attributes by Humans   159
   An Implication of the Forgetting of Individual Attributes of
      a Stimulus   160
Generalization Gradients and Memory for Conflicting Stimuli   161
Memory for Attributes of Reinforcers or Unconditioned Stimuli   162
   Contrast Effects   163
   Aversive Events   164
Spatial Memory   165
   Morris Maze and Cognitive Maps   168
   Memory for Caches   170
   Historical Note   173
Chapter Summary   174

7 Developmental Change in the Processing of Memories   177
Overview of the Ontogeny of Learning and Memory   178
   Assessing Developmental Changes in Memory and Learning   179

What Tests Are Needed?   179
General Issues in the Development of Memory   181
Foundations of the Development of Memory: Ontogenetic Change in
    Brain and Behavior   182
    Some Features of Brain Development   183
    General Features of Behavioral Development During Infancy   186
The Significance of Learning and Memory During Development   188
    Early Nonspecific Experience   188
    Early Experience with Specific Learning   189
Ontogenetic Change in the Capacity for Learning   191
    Ontogenetic Change in the Effectiveness of Initial Memory Storage:
        How Do We Decide When a Capacity for Specific
        Learning Emerges?   191
    The Earliest Onset of Specific Instances of Learning   194
    Systematic Analysis of Ontogenetic Differences in Learning about
        Schedules of Reinforcement   196
    Developmental Differences in Cognitive Dispositions That Contribute
        to Retention and Forgetting   197
Infantile Amnesia and the Ontogeny of Retention   200
    Theoretical Issues   202
    Memory Content and Infantile Amnesia   203
    Growth and Infantile Amnesia   207
The Paradox   208
Chapter Summary   210

8 Experimentally Induced Amnesias and Memory Modulation   213

Experimentally Induced RA   214
    Characteristics of Induced RA   216
        Interval between Training and the Amnestic Agent   216
        Interval between the Amnestic Agent and the Retention Test   217
        Type of Amnestic Agent   218
Modulation of Memory   222
    Pharmacological and Hormonal Modulation of Memory   222
        Pharmacological Modulation   222
        Memory Modulation by Hormones   223
        Memory Modulation by Neurotransmitters   225
    Postacquisition State-Dependent Effects   227
    Post-Trial Behavioral Treatments and Memory   228
    Memory Modulation through Reinforcement   229
    Modulation of Old (Reactivated) Memory   231
    Memory Modulation by the Induction of New
        Contextual Attributes   233
Malleability of Memory in Humans   234
    Issues of Interpretation: Practical and Theoretical   236

viii   Contents

        Malleable and Modulated Memories   237
    Anterograde Amnesia   238
    Chapter Summary   242

9   Recoveries from Forgetting: Retrieval Phenomena   245
    Alleviation of Forgetting in Animals   247
        Prior Cuing to Alleviate Simple (Spontaneous) Forgetting   247
    Drug-Induced Attenuation of Forgetting   250
    Alleviation of Forgetting in Humans   251
        Alleviation by Prior Cuing   254
        Spontaneous Alleviation of Forgetting   255
    Attenuation of Forgetting after Brain Damage   256
    Retrieval Deficits in Experimentally Induced Amnesia   259
        Does Retrograde Amnesia Result from Impairment
            in Retrieval?   259
            Growth of RA Over Time   260
            RA and Length of the Interval between Training and the
                Amnestic Agent   263
        Recovery from Retrograde Amnesia   263
            Spontaneous Alleviation of RA   263
            Alleviation of Anterograde Amnesia   270
    Memory Retrieval by Persons with Amnesia   272
    Test-Induced Recovery from Amnesia   273
    Recovery from Amnesia by Priming   256
        Recovery from Amnesia in Humans: Re-exposure to the
            Amnestic Agent   277
    Chapter Summary   278

10   Aspects of Human Amnesia   281
    Retrograde Amnesia   282
    Anterograde Amnesia   286
    Explicit and Implicit Memory   290
    Comment on Dissociation as a Research Strategy in the Psychobiology
        of Memory   292
    Human Anterograde Amnesia: Some Methodological Concerns   294
    Mishkin's Neurobiological Model   295
    Forgetting in Everyday Life   297
    Chapter Summary   299

11   Memory and the Principles of Learning   301
    Does Learning Establish a Memory (Representation)?   302

Representations, Memories, and Learning   305
    Representation of the Unconditioned Stimulus or Reinforcer   306
    Representation of the CS   308
    Further Evidence and Comment   309
Summary   310
Should Theories of Learning Be Theories of Memory?: Circumstances of Remembering (Memory Retrieval and Expression) Can Mask or Reveal Learning   311
The Similarity between Memory Retrieval (Remembering) and Memory Acquisition (Learning)   312
    Indication of Similarity between Memory Acquisition and Retrieval   312
    Further Illustration of Acquisition and Retrieval Similarity in Animals   313
Induced Expression   315
    Overshadowing   316
    Blocking Effect   320
    Latent Inhibition   321
    General Considerations   323
Selective Expression of Learning   323
    Backward Conditioning   324
    Somatic (Motoric) and Autonomic (Heart Rate) Learning   324
    How Learning Is Expressed Depends on the Nature of the CS   325
    How Learning Is Expressed Depends on the US   325
    Variation in How Infants Express What They Learn   326
Summary and Implications   327
    Summary   327
    Implications   328
Chapter Summary   x329

12   Structure of Memory   331

Alternatives to Multiple Memory Systems   331
Breadth of Selective Expression   334
Multiple Memory Systems   337
    Memory Systems Distinguished by Cognitive Process   337
    Some Reasons to Invoke Separate Memory Systems   339
    A Less Successful Cognitive-Process Distinction among Hypothetical Memory Systems: Short-Term Memory and Long-Term Memory   342
        Retrograde Amnesia as Evidence for a Distinction between Short-Term and Long-Term Memory   343
        Anterograde Amnesia and Short-Term Versus Long-Term Memory   344
        Cognitive Basis for Short-Term Versus Long-Term Memory   345
    Other Bases for Considering Multiple Memory Systems   346

Implications of the Ontogenesis of Sensory System Effectiveness and of Learning   346
Separate Memory Systems Associated with Separate Brain Structures   347
How Many Memory Systems Really Exist and What Are They?   350
Chapter Summary   352

References   355

Index   395

Preface

All of us are engaged daily in the processing of memories—acquiring new relationships among events and expressing them later in behavior. What goes on between acquisition and expression of a memory is unclear because it is so hard to measure directly; yet whatever occurs is of vast importance. All of us would be ill equipped to deal with the constant change in circumstances to which we must adapt if we could not remember the most pertinent relationships learned earlier. But we also would be ill equipped for survival if every relationship learned in one's past were remembered whenever behavior is required. To our good fortune, we are not constantly aware of everything we have learned and we usually can remember the most pertinent things, a circumstance that probably has a great deal to do with why we and others of our species are alive and thriving.

Yet there is an important gap between acquisition of a new memory and its expression. What is learned is not inevitably remembered, however important that remembering might be. And conversely, albeit less frequently, relationships that seem not to have been learned can later affect behavior nevertheless in a manner that verifies their previous learning.

The use of the collective "we" so far is intentional and more inclusive than you might expect. All that has been said applies to animals as well as to people. It is easiest to phrase our considerations of memory in terms of the behavior of humans—the species with which we are all most familiar in terms of memory, if only from our own experience learning and remembering. Many questions about what takes place between the acquisition of a memory and its expressions are considered, however, most readily with animals. And some questions about the neurophysiological control of memory can be considered only with animals. A reasonably thorough discussion of the memory process must therefore include evidence from both animals and humans. In this book both are included, although it is fair to say that human memory is given the lesser attention.

We wrote this book to fill a gap. Scholars seeking a broad picture of the memory process oriented along the lines of psychobiology (or if you prefer, biopsychology, or behavioral neuroscience) have few books to which they can turn. Most books on memory consider only the behavior of humans, and for the most part only verbal behavior. Although there are many collections of excellent chapters written by separate authors, those that consider memory from a psychobiology orientation are highly specialized, are not readily understood by undergraduates or even graduate students, and rarely provide an overview with continuity from chapter to chapter.

Textbooks that address the memory process from a psychobiological orientation have focused almost entirely on the first stage of the process—learning. There are good reasons for this: the empirical base of knowledge in this area historically is drawn from experimental studies of the acquisition (learning) process; the original philosophical orientation of comparative psychology severely limited consideration of later stages in the memory process (e.g., transfer, retention, forgetting, memory retrieval, expression); and quite reasonably, a good place to begin is at the beginning of the memory process, which is acquisition. It is no accident that most psychology courses dealing with behavioral plasticity are more likely to have *learning* in their title than *memory,* and if the latter term is included, the courses are likely to consider only human verbal memory. What we thought was missing—the gap we hope to fill—is a book taking a psychobiological view of the memory process, addressing principles derived from both human and animal research. Our hope is to provide a book broad enough to be useful for advanced undergraduates and graduate students, and perhaps of some value also for professionals.

A second reason for this book is more subtle and personal. We cannot escape the suspicion that the memory process will not be understood by studying only the acquisition (learning, storage) stages, and moreover, that acquisition will not be understood without consideration of later (retrieval, expression) stages. We try to illustrate these points in the book.

We begin the book with a general view of how the study of memory began and developed. Specific definitions are introduced to alleviate the conventional ambiguity that surrounds the term *memory,* and we consider how the memory process is measured, but both of these necessary, albeit dry, topics are considered in terms of fundamental issues that rest at the core of how the memory process is to be understood. Chapters 2, 3, 4, and 5 consider fundamental instances of retention and forgetting. Determinants of the course of forgetting over time and the action of general sources of forgetting, such as contextual change and associative interference, are considered for normal animals and humans. This is followed by a chapter that considers what, specifically, is retained or forgotten. This material is presented within the conceptual framework of memory as a multidimensional representation, which guides our progress through the book.

Chapter 7 begins a set of four chapters that includes increased emphasis on the biological side of our psychobiological orientation. This chapter evaluates the ontogeny of memory. Our view requires that this topic be considered in terms of neural, physiological, and behavioral ontogeny as well as the ontogeny of learning, prior to direct consideration of how memory processing changes from birth, throughout infancy, and later, into adulthood. Chapters 8 and 9 focus on forgetting (amnesia), changes in the content of a memory (memory modulation), and the alleviation of forgetting in circumstances that would not be expected in the normal course of nature. These circumstances include, for example, the administration of drugs that might increase or alleviate forgetting, severe systemic alterations such as hypothermia, and electroconvulsive shock. Yet the circumstances are nonetheless representative of what can happen outside the laboratory, and they are analytical with respect to the foundations of the memory process. The final chapter of this set (Chapter 10) includes a potpourri of phenomena, issues, and theories of contemporary relevance for analyzing the memory process within the realm of behavioral neuroscience.

Chapters 11 and 12 are more theoretical in flavor. Chapter 11 considers the relationship between learning and memory in terms of the remarkable variance observed in principles of learning, contingent upon postacquisition events and the circumstances under which the acquired memory is to be expressed. Chapter 12 discusses an issue that has been central to differences of opinion about the memory process for over 40 years and remains more debatable than ever: when we study the memory process, must we in fact study different kinds or systems of memory processes, and if so, how many are there and how do they differ? Throughout this chapter, as throughout the previous eleven, we have been guided by a particular point of view or conceptual framework, but have tried to present alternative views and avoid having theoretical biases impair communication of the facts.

Norman E. Spear owes gratitude to many people. Foremost is Linda P. Spear, a brilliant, pure scientist whose creativity and insightful scientific contributions have not only been helpful for my work but inspiring as well. Her support as wife and colleague has been superb and always dependable. My daughters, Mandy and Jennifer, have provided not only support but also inspiration, although they may not have realized it. Their scientific and personal achievements and future promise include wonderful accomplishments that I am proud of and will never match. For guidance as to how one should proceed in research and scholarship I am grateful to George Collier, Win Hill, Ben Underwood, Steve Glickman, Bob Isaacson and many others. For support as a friend and colleague who exemplifies creativity and good educational values, I am grateful to Norm Richter. For making my working life extremely pleasant with her remarkably cheerful and appealing attitude, general intellect, and remarkable memory, I am grateful to Teri Tanenhaus. Also, I wish to thank three particularly brilliant postdoctoral colleagues from whom I have learned for many years and continue to do so: Juan Molina, Phil Kraemer and Jim Miller. Finally, I am grateful to a large number of genial, creative and hardworking graduate students, postdoctoral associates, and undergraduate students who have contributed to our research and my learning. During preparation of this manuscript I benefited from a research semester and a sabbatical semester provided by SUNY Binghamton.

David C. Riccio similarly is grateful to a number of people, only a few of whom are named here. I thank Albert H. Ewell, Middlebury College, for showing me how psychology can be a science, and Byron A. Campbell, Princeton University, for (among other things) helping me to appreciate that scholarship includes far more than the assimilation of information. I would like to express appreciation to the many students who have collaborated with me and whose ideas (and findings) continuously shaped my thinking. To various collegial researchers around the country who have provided encouragement and enthusiasm, I extend a particular thanks. Special debts are owed to Diane Poston and Patricia John for cheerfully and accurately translating innumerable pages of illegible scrawl, and to Teri Tanenhaus for dealing with nearly indecipherable inserts, extensive phone messages, and hasty faxes. To my wife Brenda, and sons, Mark and Scott, I offer gratitude for their patience, encouragement and support.

Both authors are grateful to Teri Tanenhaus, who not only constructed the figures along with Jennifer Spear, but also kept in excellent order the problems of permissions, references and the construction of the book with astute computer skills. Karen Spear Harding and David G. Payne made helpful comments about specific portions of the manuscript, as did several students; they have our gratitude. Both authors are grateful to the insightful and helpful reviews of earlier drafts of this book provided by Charles Flaherty, Rutgers University; Todd Schachtman, University of Missouri; John Wixted, University of California—San Diego; Professor Louis Matzel, Rutgers University; and Professor Chuck Hinderliter, University of Pittsburgh.

Our collaboration on this book began longer ago than either of us might care to remember. The completion of the book has been anxiously awaited—at least by the authors! Since collaborative relationships on a project of this nature can sometimes prove to be tricky, we are pleased to indicate that we remain good friends.

The authors would like to acknowledge that some of the conceptualizations presented in this book developed out of research supported by grants to N. E. Spear (MH 35219) and D. C. Riccio (MH 37535).

▶ 1
Introduction to Memory

Using memory is something we all do. You have been using your memory for at least as long as you can remember. It is fairly certain that you were using memory even before that time, during infancy or even just prior to birth, but most of us cannot really remember events from that period. We will discuss later (chapter 7) when infants begin to use memory and why adults cannot remember much of their own infancy. It is such characteristics of memory that we shall emphasize in this book.

There are a number of ways to consider the topic of memory. We could consider why such a thing exists among all animals and humans. To have evolved so pervasively, memory would seem to have been a significant advantage for survival. There is growing evidence, for instance, that in foraging for food most mammals and birds depend to a large extent on memory. We could also consider the physiological basis of memory. What happens in our brain when we remember? Are specific connections between neurons activated each time we remember specific things? Is this activation due to the same chemical each time? Is what we remember coded at the cellular level, by specific sets of elicited chemicals that act selectively on a few cells, or by massive networks of cells linked neuroanatomically? A third way we could consider memory is in terms of a model or metaphor. We might be very specific and discuss how memory is like a computer or we might start with certain postulates of how we believe memory operates in specialized circumstances and then derive predictions as to how it operates in general.

Although we will have occasion to allude to the evolution or physiological basis of memory and we will consider at times specific models or theories of memory, our emphasis in this book is on none of these. We believe there are limitations to what one can learn about memory in any of these three approaches. There is as yet no clear picture of the evolution of memory nor is there a physiological basis of memory or a theory of memory that is generally acceptable to most experts in the field.

What we shall emphasize instead are the behavioral characteristics of memory: how forgetting proceeds in various circumstances; what factors or events induce forgetting or affect the speed or amount of forgetting; and how forgetting can be prevented or alleviated. To discuss these characteristics somewhat systematically we will have to consider how memory has been studied. We also will consider a framework that we find useful for thinking about memory. This framework emphasizes the remembering (we may sometimes refer to this as *retrieval*) and expression of what we have learned rather than the original learning itself.

To learn is to acquire a relatively permanent disposition to behave in a particular way in particular circumstances, including the disposition to expect certain relationships among events. There is a good deal known about how this acquisition proceeds, including some excellent textbooks on the topic (e.g., Catania 1984; Domjan & Burkhard 1986; Flaherty 1985; Gordon 1989; Klein 1987; Schwartz 1989). We believe, however, that most behavior is determined by what is remembered and expressed about what is learned. This is not to deny the importance of the characteristics of original learning; these are immensely important. We shall present and briefly consider the more important of these characteristics in this book. We have tried to do this in such a way that it would be unnecessary for you to have previously acquired a thorough knowledge of learning. But, of course, everyone knows something about learning just as everyone knows something about memory—because we all practice it. The following sections will consider certain aspects of the relationship between learning and memory.

HOW IS MEMORY RELATED TO LEARNING?

It would seem difficult to have learning without memory or vice versa. But the distinction is real, with roots in the history of our science and in theories of how behavior is affected by what we learn. Even common sense tells us that learning and memory are not the same: all things that we have learned simply are not equally accessible from memory.

We will try to establish that the transition from learning to memory is significant scientifically, and the distinctions between these two psychological processes are important. To accomplish this we will (1) sample how the concepts of learning and memory are treated in experimental psychology and some of the historical precedents for studying memory today, (2) consider how learning and memory are measured, and (3) preview how psychological issues pertaining to memory differ from those involving learning. Most of this chapter will be used to provide perspective on how memory has been understood and studied in the past, including some brief views of discoveries about memory that have emerged during the relatively short period that scientists have investigated it experimentally.

CONCEPTUAL DISTINCTIONS BETWEEN MEMORY AND LEARNING

Damage to certain locations of the brain, due to head injury, disease, surgery, or years of overindulging in alcohol, frequently causes amnesia. Physicians have described persons with this diagnosis as being quite unable to learn and remember any new episodes in their lives, whether as trivial as what they ate for breakfast or as significant as the death of a close relative. But careful application of the techniques of experimental psychology has revealed that these persons can learn and remember some things. They show new learning in terms of basic classical conditioning, solutions to mazes, mathematical rules, solutions to puzzles, new tunes, and how to be efficient in reading inverted print, to give a few examples of the fifteen or so instances discovered so far. Even while expressing in their behavior that the learning did take place, however, they cannot say when or how it occurred. They frankly assert that they remember nothing about the practice that led to this learning.

These aspects of amnesia will be discussed more fully in chapters 8 and 10. They are mentioned here to illustrate how memory can be quite separate from learning. Such facts also complicate what is meant by memory. In one sense memory means to retrieve information about discrete, datable episodes—e.g., that on October 13, 1992, I learned to play "Stardust" on the piano. In another sense, memory means a knowledge source, reference material stored in the brain that lets us know what a piano looks like, what we do with it in order to produce tones, and how to read the title of the piece and the name of the composer. We call this knowledge memory even though we probably could not tell exactly the circumstances under which we learned these bits of information. In quite another sense memory can mean either the representation of a particular event (e.g., that particular piece of music) or particular procedures (e.g., how to place the fingers for sharps and flats), or it can mean the total psychological process, the sequence of behavioral events that leads to remembering.

These are all legitimate uses of the term *memory*. Our preference is to have memory mean the representation of all that has been acquired about a particular episode (by *episode* is meant a set of events that are somehow related). But we will also use the term in some of the other senses mentioned and shall become more precise about its use.

In older textbooks and scholarly journals on the topic of learning, one rarely sees reference to memory. This is in part due to historical forces in the development of the study of learning. The forces were both empirical—the observable results of specific experiments—and theoretical. Empirical studies with animals seemed, as we shall see, to indicate that little forgetting was to be found; whatever was learned was remembered. Theoretically, scientists studying learning treated memory as a "mentalistic" term and quite unscientific. Like the soul, memory could not be seen nor readily measured. Especially for scientists using animals as their experimental subjects, the term seemed unduly anthropomorphic and not sufficiently parsimonious, i.e., not really the most efficient way to explain what was observed about learning and its consequences. Even among scientists studying forgetting explicitly in human subjects there was a reluctance to consider a process, memory, that might mediate between the behaviors called *learning* and *remembering*. What was studied was largely the identification of variables that made a difference in rates of learning and the immediate performance of that learning, with little concern for processes responsible for retention.

Yet the topic of memory has its own history independent of that of learning. Portions of this history can be used to introduce basic discoveries about memory while illustrating how memory differs scientifically from learning. After sampling this history and some long-established features of memory, we shall return to present-day conceptions of memory and its distinction from learning.

EARLY IDEAS ABOUT MEMORY

Knowledge was power 2500 years ago, as it is today. But people then were very limited in how they could record or communicate knowledge. With no libraries and few printed records of any kind, a person had to depend on his or her memory, or someone else's, in order to make use of acquired knowledge. Some, like Socrates, feared that by recording knowledge in writing, the memories of young scholars would not be properly exercised and would weaken (for elaboration on this and the following aspects of the history of memory, see Gomulicki 1953; Yates 1966).

Focus was on the practical questions of how best to remember. Issues of what a memory was or how it was processed to best accomplish remembering were given relatively little attention and of course were not tested empirically until more than twenty centuries later. A prevalent and long-lasting notion was a distinction between a person's basic capacity for memory and how well this capacity was applied. Many years later William James (1890) also emphasized the view that persons had a basic trait of retentiveness, "... a physiological quality, given once for all with his organization, in which he could never hope to change" (p. 434). James agreed that retention of acquired knowledge might be made more effective by certain mnemonic techniques, but thought these were primarily a matter of how the individual initially studied or thought about the materials that later were to be remembered, not a real advantage for remembering per se (James 1890, 435). Evidence has tended to confirm this latter opinion of James—that mnemonic techniques affect learning rather than retention—but the idea that some people are more retentive than others has been doubted (e.g., Underwood 1972).

The ancient scholars' suggestions as to how, physically, a memory might be represented or how the process of memory might work indicate that we have made some progress through science. Their suggestions remind us that only through scientific study in the past few hundred years have people come to assume that memory is actually located in the body in some physical form, rather than having a spiritual basis. To some extent the Christian Church was responsible for this ethereal approach, given its emphasis on a spiritual soul and its power during the Dark Ages to suppress contrary opinion. Previously some Greek scholars had suggested versions of a physical basis for memory.

For example, there was Plato's familiar analogy between memory and a wax tablet on which representations of events could be etched (learning) although subject later to effacement (forgetting). Plato was clear that this was merely an analogy and had no literal application.

In the second century A.D., Galen provided a somewhat more sophisticated, but still limited, account of memory. The basic idea was that animal spirits were in control. These animal spirits were believed to be manufactured in the lateral ventricles of the brain and distributed to sensory and motor nerves. As recently as the seventeenth century, Descartes viewed the pineal gland as the homunculus-like control center that emitted animal spirits through "pores in the brain" on their way to the locations of the critical memory trace. By the eighteenth century, however, some skepticism arose about the concept of animal spirits and there was a growing suspicion that some sorts of electrical forces (the computer model of the day) might be responsible for memory.

Relative to the theorizing about the nature and location of memory, pre-nineteenth century principles about the skill of remembering were fairly sophisticated. In ancient Rome, well-educated Romans studied mnemonics. With the spoken word as the major form of communication, legislators, businessmen, and theologians had to present their messages in speech form, from memory, and the accuracy of their reproduction was very important. Thus pressured, the orators clearly realized how it was one thing to recite a speech just reviewed in the privacy of one's own home, but quite another problem to deliver this speech within a context different from that in which the speech was originally constructed and studied—especially if the time between studying and reciting the speech included a long interval occupied by interfering verbal activities. Such difficulties resulted in the development of techniques for accurate recall, and these became the discipline of mnemonics that was taught within the general study of rhetoric.

The Origin of Mnemonics

One basic technique of mnemonics is symbolically to place different items that are to be remembered in familiar environmental locations. This technique of associating items with well-known locations supposedly was originated by a Greek poet named Simonides. According to one historian, Simonides was reciting his poems in front of a large crowd at a banquet hall. He was called out of the building for a brief period, which was to his good fortune because at that moment the roof collapsed, killing everyone inside. Further compounding the tragedy, the victims were smashed quite beyond recognition by the heavy stonework used in the buildings of those days. When asked to help identify the victims for their respective families, Simonides found, to his surprise, that he could identify all of the names by recalling the previous seating arrangement (Yates 1966).

This technique of pairing names with discrete objects or spatial locations is known as the *method of loci* and has been applied, under less macabre circumstances, to pairing basic ideas with distinctive spatial locations. To permit efficient retrieval of the appropriate sequential order of points in a speech, an orator first would imagine himself walking through a path in some familiar building like his home. At specific locations along these paths, concrete objects would be imagined for representing the points of his speech. For example, if the first point was to insist on a cleaner bathhouse, a huge cleaning brush might be imagined inside a tiny bathtub, all resting on the doorknob of his front door; if the second point was to urge assignment of more slaves to this job, he might imagine his foyer crowded with slaves; and so forth. At the time of the speech the orator would then imagine retracing his path and, in effect, pick up each point as its location was reached.

Many versions of this technique were employed and much polemical energy spent (e.g., on whether, for a long speech requiring more "locations," it was better to imagine two separate houses or a single larger house). Experimental tests of such issues were unknown, but the application of mnemonic techniques was passed from teacher to student for thousands of years. Even as Bacon and Descartes were establishing a scientific revolution, memory was maintained by them as an art to be practiced rather than an object for scientific study (for further discussion of these issues, see Yates 1966).

The Art of Memory Processing

Memory processing as a form of art, entertainment, or applied technique is clearly distinguishable from memory as a topic of scientific investigation. We still see a little of the former today, although the application of mnemonic techniques has been relatively deemphasized by the educational methods used in the United States during the past 50 or 60 years.

Individuals having extremely facile mnemonic skills have always been viewed with some fascination. One such individual was a Russian named Shereshevski, who applied his memory processes primarily as an entertainer. Because of his inability to forget unnecessary details, this man actually suffered from an inability to carry on normal conversation and had general difficulty in personal adjustment. Studied for many years by the Russian psychologist Luria (1968), this man had an unusually strong tendency to encode events in a sensory modality different from that used to detect and perceive the event, i.e., strong "synesthesia" (Marks 1978). For instance, to musical notes he had vivid images of colors and flashing lights, and to items he saw he might have a strong image of a taste. He seems in part to have used this unusual perception to help his memory. An individual identified as "VP" by Hunt and Love (1972) also was studied as a special case of exceptional mnemonic skill. To accomplish this he seemed not to use imagery as Shereshevski did, but instead used elaborate schemes of association to aid in remembering. Despite this difference, it is perhaps notable that both Shereshevski and VP received their early schooling in a locale in eastern Europe where memorization was emphasized for its own sake and viewed as a skill worthy of a great deal of effort.

Such case histories are indeed fascinating, but they become science only when their consideration is sufficiently systematic and the behavior studied is evaluated in the context of other knowledge about learning and memory. It was not until the late nineteenth century that information about the nature of memory processing became sufficiently systematic to qualify as a science.

The Science of Memory Processing

Among the earliest persons to consider memory processing as an object of scientific analysis was the great Russian physiologist, Sechenov. Sechenov studied "physiology" in terms that we now consider psychology. He provided a model for Pavlov, the more famous Russian physiologist whose discoveries formed the foundation for most of learning theory today. To a limited extent Sechenov was concerned with processes underlying retention and forgetting, and he suggested some mechanisms—today we might call them *memory mechanisms*—by which acquired information might be maintained following learning and how to modify subsequent behavior (Sechenov 1863, reproduced 1965, 70).

Although the work of Sechenov and Pavlov on conditioning and, ultimately, memory was conducted in departments or institutes of physiology (as is still the case in Russia), their actual experiments were precursors to much of present day experimental psychology and psychobiology in the United States and Great Britain.

Memory and the Brain

There was at the same time as Sechenov's work a growing interest, primarily among medical doctors and neurologists, in *where* memory is located in the brain. For instance, Gall suggested during the latter nineteenth century that the faculty of verbal memory must be located in the frontal cortex of the brain, just behind the eyes. Two of Gall's schoolmates who happened to be good memorizers and also had protruding eyes were a source for this notion. Gall actually made solid contributions to some aspects of neurology, and it is therefore unfortunate that he is identified today primarily for his work with Spurzheim in developing the school of phrenology. The study of phrenology considered the organization of intellectual faculties in the brain in terms of the morphological structure of the skull, i.e., that the size of a particular bump on the head would indicate one's competence in the particular faculty believed to reside in that location under the skull.

Fortunately for the development of our science, theories such as phrenology could be discarded through facts gained by laboratory research. One basic approach was to systematically cut out parts of the animal brain and observe consequent changes in behavior, setting a precedent for the later research of Lashley. Work of this kind and progress toward understanding memory in general through the study of animals were promoted by Charles Darwin's theory of evolution during this period and in particular by an influential paper read by Hering at meetings of the Imperial Academy of Science at Vienna in 1870. Hering's pertinent point was that the process of memory is more general than was believed by some scientists. Memory was not, he said, restricted only to certain aspects of the central nervous system of humans; it was in fact basic to all animal life and differed from one species to another in largely quantitative rather than qualitative ways.

This helped to encourage work on animal memory in parallel with that on the brain's control of sensorimotor behavior. Fritsch and Hitzig had begun to map out the motor area of the cortex of animals by applying electrical stimulation to certain areas and observing the animals' responses. They and other neurologists of the time believed that essentially all parts of the brain were potential sites for the location of memory. For the most part, however, the location of memory in the brain was assigned by default. For instance, Hitzig believed that the site of more abstract memories must be the frontal cortex since this area seemed to have no role in sensation or motor responses when it was stimulated. Until the work of Lashley in the early 1900s, issues of the neurophysiological basis of memory were, however, dealt with separately from those of how remembering affected behavior. This was in part because the latter sorts of questions were more likely addressed by experimental psychologists, of which there were few before 1900.

Psychologists were nevertheless well represented among the early scholars of memory processing by William James (although James was formally a medical doctor with training in physiology). James had few established facts at his disposal but nevertheless wrote about the nature of memory with extraordinary insight and eventual influence. In addition to James' judgment that individuals possess differing amounts of an inborn, physiologically based retentiveness, he was also concerned with other issues that are still with us, such as whether or not a memory ever disappears from an individual's repertoire once it is acquired (e.g., James 1890, 127).

The First Systematic Experiments on Memory

Imagine yourself in the late nineteenth century surrounded by philosophical acclamations of how the memory process functions. At this time many scholars were becoming aware that introspection cannot lead to systematic knowledge about behavior. How, then, would you objectively measure the product of memory processing? How would you assess the characteristics of behavior that depend on memory? And how would you determine those factors that cause forgetting and those that do not?

The first man to tackle this problem with sufficient tenacity and ingenuity to influence other scholars was a young German philosopher named Herman Ebbinghaus. Ebbinghaus decided that the best way to study memory processing objectively was to teach himself discrete bits of new knowledge under standardized conditions. Later he would test how well he remembered, again under standardized conditions. To force himself to learn from scratch, Ebbinghaus constructed nonwords, combinations of three letters termed *nonsense syllables.* He decided to learn ten or twelve of these nonsense syllables in order, as if they represented a string of ideas.

When Ebbinghaus was able to recite a list without an error, he would put it aside and doggedly proceed with other lists. He would come back to the list in question after a prespecified interval. He then compared the number of trials needed to relearn the list with the number required during original learning. The repetitions that he was spared in relearning, due to his efforts in original learning, were recorded as an index of retention—a savings. What Ebbinghaus (1913) found was that his retention dropped with frightening speed. After a day or so he often lost as much as 75 percent of the information he had acquired (see Figure 1-1). Although this 75 percent figure has limited generality, as we shall see, the contributions of Ebbinghaus have had a continued impact on the study of verbal memory (e.g., Slamecka 1985).

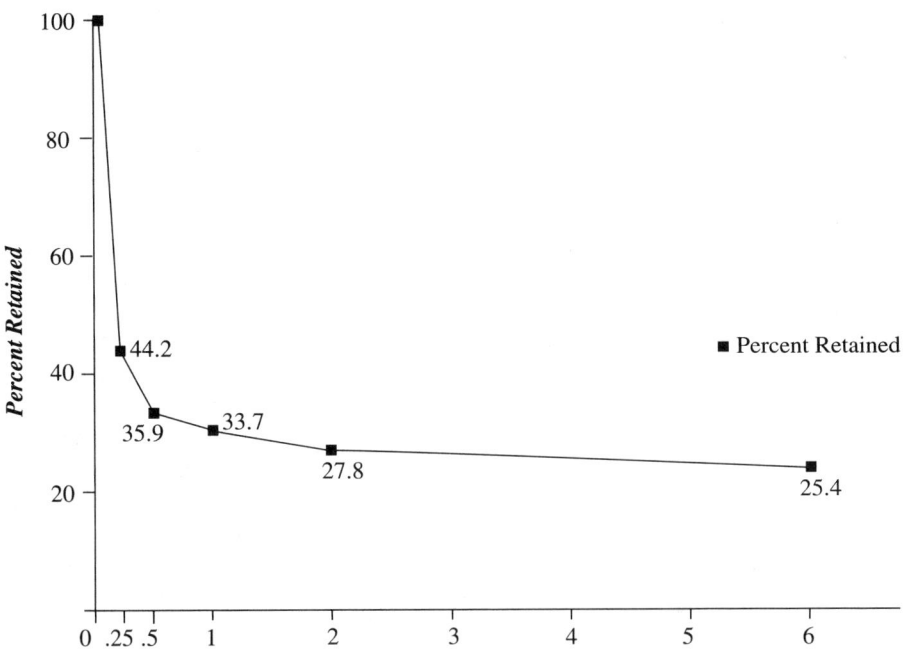

FIGURE 1-1 The conventional decrease in retention over time was illustrated in the first systematic study of the characteristics of forgetting learned information that is fundamentally verbal (nonword combinations of letters, nonsense syllables). In part of his very large study in which he served as his only subject, Ebbinghaus learned each of several lists of these verbal units and then tried to re-learn them after different intervals. This figure shows that the retention he expressed declined progressively over a 6-day interval and especially rapidly during the first 24-hour interval, in a form termed "negatively accelerated" (change in the rate of forgetting [i.e., "acceleration"] slows down over time [i.e., is negative related to time]). It was later discovered that this amount of rapid forgetting would not have occurred had Ebbinghaus learned only a single list of such verbal units (chapters 2 to 4). (Adapted from Ebbinghaus, 1913.)

The experimental study of memory thus originated with concern for retention of verbal materials. This source of information about memory continues to be of fundamental importance today. A large number of the important advances, conceptual and empirical, have evolved from the study of human verbal memory. Yet with the possible exception of processes concerned exclusively with linguistic memories—if such processes indeed exist—we may expect to find memories to be processed in similar fashion by humans and animals. Accordingly, although we will not ignore human memory studies, many of the basic principles described will come from research with animals. We elaborate on this rationale in the following sections.

Increasing Breadth in the Study of Memory
Generally speaking, there are several reasons to prefer animals for the study of memory processing, primarily due to the wider scope of experimental manipulations that are possible. One important example is the extreme experiential control that may be exerted over animals from the time of birth, including the opportunity to test after retention intervals that may vary from a few seconds to a lifetime. A related advantage exists because some animals develop so rapidly. Although even more immature at birth than is the human, it takes only a month for the rat to develop an essentially mature brain. With the rat we can therefore observe memory changes from day to day that could occur in humans only after many months. Another example is the opportunity to compare animals of selected genetic history, and still another is the experimental modification of physiological systems that may be linked to memory processes. We shall see that each of these classes of variables—environmental, subject, and physiological—has been shown to have important effects on memory processing.

The full understanding of memory requires simultaneous attention to memory in each of three types of individuals. The first is memory in normal animals, which provide the unique advantages just mentioned. The second is memory in normal humans, because of the powerful facility humans seem to have in this respect and because of the practical need to know about human memory and hence the massive amount that is known about it. The third is memory in neurophysiologically abnormal humans and animals, because memory impairment is among the most important diagnostic indicators for medical purposes, and because it is often the case that to understand the normal operation of a complex process such as memory, one must observe how it fails to operate when parts of the process malfunction.

DEFINITIONS OF MEMORY

Because many psychologists thought the term *memory* was too mentalistic for scientific use, it appears relatively rarely in older journals and textbooks. When the term *memory* began to appear frequently in scientific writing, it did so in the context of a way of thinking that was somewhat different from before. It may be that the study of learning necessarily involved, at least initially, a behavioristic stimulus-response orientation. For the sake of scientific parsimony—economy in the systemization of knowledge—the behavioristic approach was an important first attempt to map and explain the progressive change in response that anticipates (or reflects, in the case of classical conditioning) whatever is predicted by a particular stimulus.

The scientific hardware built initially for the laboratory study of learning—such as lists of verbal units for humans or complicated mazes for animals—was explicitly selected to make learning relatively difficult. The intention was that these tasks not be mastered within a single trial. By drawing out the process of learning, it could be analyzed more easily. It was important to select neutral events to be learned, those without previous association in the experience of the animal or human who was being tested, because this would provide a more pure examination of raw learning (we now realize the futility of seeking purely neutral stimuli and so consider instead their degree of neutrality with respect to past experience).

The study of memory requires a different approach. First, there is assumed in the term a need for a process beyond learning, something to maintain the learning until needed. This in itself assumes that the learning might not last, or, in other words, might be forgotten. The term *memory* also implies a process for remembering, some activity for promoting accessibility to that learning when it finally must be used. In other words, the use of the term virtually assumes cognition in the sense of mechanisms for the processing of information between its acquisition (learning) and its manifestation in behavior (remembering). The simple fact is that neither animals nor humans are machines that take in information exactly as presented and give it back in the same form. Previous learning does not inevitably affect later behavior, even when the experimenter arranges for the stimulus events to occur exactly as they seemed to during learning.

An important point is that the increase in the use of memory terminology was accompanied by a shift in the way behavior was tested. To study memory it did not matter how rapidly learning took place, only that it did. It was therefore advantageous to develop rapidly learned tasks for experimental tests. Observations from such tests, by design, promoted further conclusions and theories about memory while deemphasizing those about learning.

Uses of the Term, Memory

Memory sometimes refers to an individual's internal representation of what he or she has learned. Your memory of the party on your sixth birthday is your recorded representation of the events of that party, who was there, where it was held, what the weather was like, what games you played, what your favorite present was, and so forth.

Memory also is used with reference to the process that leads to remembering. Sometimes this means only the sequence of operations that begins after learning is established and continues until remembering is required. In other cases memory is used to encompass both the learning itself and the act of remembering. And sometimes memory is meant to include still more, beginning with initial sensory detection and perception of an episode, through learning and remembering it. For the most frequent usage, and the one we shall adopt, memory-as-process begins at some point in the perception process, presumably near the end, or just afterward.

It should be understood that the issue of exactly when perception stops and memory processing begins is difficult and not yet reconciled, if indeed it is reconcilable. We begin the processing of a memory with encoding—the individual's representation of events for convenient interpretation and memory storage—and the extent to which this overlaps with perception is not critical for our purposes. Memory-as-process is said to continue from the time of initial encoding of an episode throughout its learning and to end after remembering is accomplished.

Finally, a third way in which memory is used is as a sort of storehouse for the residual of one's experiences. This is what is meant in the writings of neuroscientists who seek the neuroanatomical location of memory.

It was not only this ambiguity in its formal meaning that made psychologists at one time reluctant to use the term, *memory*. Common words such as *memory* have the scientific disadvantage of having imprecise meanings. Not only was memory subject to misuse, it also led to weak anthropomorphic theorizing, such as this: the rat chose the correct path in the maze because of its memory of the previous trial. But to say that an animal behaves in a particular way because it has a memory to do so is really no explanation at all, unless memory can be defined independently. Hence the use of such a term was seen as a misleading hindrance to the science.

Theoretical notions about the nature of learning and remembering and how to study it also were influential in the scientist's avoidance of the term, *memory*. Early associationists viewed learning as the establishing of associations between specific stimuli and responses. This view expected, in theory, to see the responses inevitably reproduced if the stimuli were reproduced. The failure to see perfect memory in the laboratory therefore could only be a matter of the experimenter's failure to reproduce the stimulus circumstances to which the animal responded. In other words, once learning was established, forgetting could only be a matter of loss of stimulus control. There hardly seemed a need, in this view, to add a process of memory to that of learning. This view was supplemented by what Roitblat (1981) has termed the *correspondence assumption* (which sometimes has been labeled the *epistemic correlation*).

The correspondence assumption was, in essence, that the observable situational and behavioral variables responsible for learning were the same as the unobservable internal psychological processes that led to that learning. In other words, if the pairing of a bell and dog food led to a dog salivating whenever the bell sounded, what was learned was the stimulus-response connection, bell-salivate. There was no need to assume that the animal holds some other representation, or memory, of that conditioning episode. It was felt that in this way psychology could develop more objective, less mentalistic, theories, such as those in physics. This was an entirely appropriate and useful approach for the time.

Ultimately it was empirical discoveries that required use of a term such as *memory*. We briefly review some of these next in terms of the two dominant uses of the term, as a process and as a representation. Because the term *memory* is especially valuable in reference to the representation of what we have learned, this is the way *memory* usually will be used in this book. When it is used otherwise, this will be indicated. A brief mention of the use of memory-as-representation is presented next followed by a more detailed consideration of memory-as-process.

Memory-as-Representation

Just prior to 1970 it began to be recognized that a memory has multiple components. The empirical validity of this idea and its value for theories of both human and animal memory were soon established (Bower 1967; Spear 1971; Underwood 1969). Together with the increasing realization that humans typically are active rather than passive processors of material to be learned, this development encouraged great flexibility and scope in the study of memory. Investigators of human memory in particular capitalized on this notion.

Our preferred use of the term *memory* is in reference to the individual's internal representation of a particular learned episode. Such a representation is multidimensional and includes separable components or attributes to represent a variety of isolated events or event characteristics. For instance, a dog given pairings of a bell and dog food learns not only a connection between the bell and salivation, but also something about the room and apparatus in which these events took place, whether this particular experimenter treated it roughly or gently, the time of day at which this usually occurred, and so forth. A college sophomore asked to study a list of words learns not only what is on the list, but also the room in which he or she was presented the words, the time of day at which this occurred, probably a good deal about the experimenter, and so forth (for further elaboration of such a view, see Spear 1978; Underwood 1983).

This view of memory-as-representation has been useful because it reminds us that stimulus control by the discriminative or conditioned stimulus is not the only thing that determines the expression of learned behavior. This view recognizes the impact of the circumstances of context on remembering. It also discourages the misleading notion that a memory is a unitary trace located somewhere in the brain, a switch or circuit that is either activated or not to promote behavioral expression.

Memory-as-Process

What we ultimately are pursuing in research on learning and memory is how we acquire and express knowledge. As one process in the acquisition and expression of knowledge, the term *memory* is no better or worse than the term *learning*. These generally refer to different parts of the process: learning refers to the development of specific behavioral change and memory to how permanent is that change.

For a while procedures used for experiments on learning yielded little or no observable forgetting. This outcome was one reason that psychologists could believe, as mentioned earlier, that the expression of learning is merely a matter of proper experimental control of the stimulus, with no need to deal with another process such as memory. It is nevertheless undeniable now that after certain sources of forgetting, even if the conditioned or discriminative stimulus is represented in such a way as to be physically identical with that during conditioning, the acquired knowledge (what was learned) will not be seen in behavior. If one is to build theories about this, or merely to think about it or just to describe it, it is useful to label whatever the process is that determines when and to what extent the acquired knowledge will be expressed. It is entirely appropriate to label this process *memory*. We can use *learning* for the storing of new information and *memory* (as process) for maintaining that storage and retrieving it for expression in behavior.

When the representation and process senses of memory are combined, we are left with a rough concept of what memory means. This concept is partitioned in still other ways for its analysis and understanding. We turn next to some examples of this, including some relatively precise definitions of some terms you may be familiar with already.

RETENTION AND FORGETTING: ORIENTATION AND TERMINOLOGY

We have been able so far to discuss something of the background of the study of memory in a fairly informal manner. A more systematic, scientific analysis requires, however, that we be more explicit about how we use some key terms. While we do this it will be useful at the same time to provide you a few basic ideas, concepts, or miniature theories that have arisen in the field of memory. Being exposed at this time will help you to organize and understand—and yes, to remember—the rest of the book.

Relationship between Learning and Retention

If equal learning always led to equal, complete retention, the concepts of retention and forgetting would be unnecessary. Equally learned episodes may, however, be forgotten at different rates. Learning and retention are independent concepts. Degree of original learning, nevertheless, can determine degree of retention. Retention generally is more accurate and more enduring with higher degrees of learning. There has been some question as to what is meant by degree of learning, but we shall soon see that the issue is easily resolved by defining it in terms of common operations. For now, we consider three ways in which a distinction is drawn between learning and retention.

First, there is an operational difference. In tasks requiring multiple trials, we consider that retention, rather than learning, is measured whenever the interval after the last training trial exceeds the interval used between the training trials. That is, a retention interval is defined as any duration longer than the intertrial interval. In tasks acquired in only a single trial, the time between that trial and a test trial is the retention interval.

A second distinction is conceptual. Retention refers to the expression of previously acquired information at some point after an organism is removed from the physical presence of the information. The implication is that active processing of the episode by the subject has been interrupted. Conversely, testing before the interruption would assess learning.

The third, and perhaps most compelling distinction, is functional: some variables affect learning and retention in quite different ways. This lack of correspondence between how a manipulation influences learning and how it affects retention is the basis for a functional distinction. The human verbal learning literature provides clear examples of this: (1) Learning is faster when a target list of verbal items is high rather than low in "meaningfulness," as one might expect. But once the list is learned, meaningfulness has little influence on retention. (2) Some people learn very rapidly and others more slowly. This individual difference in rate of learning does not predict ability to retain the information. Once slow and fast learners have mastered the task to an equivalent degree, no differences are found in rate of forgetting. (3) In paired associate tasks, the distribution of practice (spacing of trials) has little effect on learning the response. However, under certain conditions greater distribution of practice can markedly facilitate retention (Keppel 1964; Wickelgren 1972).

With animals, too, there are cases of functional differences between learning and retention. For example, there are a variety of tasks that may be learned equally rapidly by immature and mature animals but which, after long retention intervals, are forgotten more rapidly by animals that had learned during immaturity (Campbell & Spear 1972). Another variable that influences learning but not retention is intensity of shock in avoidance learning (Feigley & Spear 1970).

The central point is that what influences learning may have no effect whatsoever on remembering after a source of forgetting, or the effects might be quite different. Conversely, factors present at the time of learning or before may not affect rate of learning but may still determine how much is remembered after a source of forgetting.

Finally, if we are to assess differences in forgetting, we must hold constant the degree of original learning. We must not allow strength of learning to vary in accord with our source of forgetting. For instance, suppose that a particular drug administered to an animal before learning reduces the amount learned by half and also increases rate of forgetting. Did forgetting increase because of the drug or because of the weak learning? We could not conclude about one independently of the other. This simply is not good science. We are not suggesting that researchers know precisely how to measure and control degree of learning; this is a complex matter indeed. Yet we are obligated as scientists to exert the best techniques available so as not to confound the effects of our sources of forgetting with differences in degree of learning.

That there are functional differences between learning and retention is not surprising. Scientists have suggested a variety of processes that may affect retention quite independently of the circumstances of learning. We have already discussed many of these. Such processes include: interference from previous or subsequent learning; hypothetical decay of the physiological underpinnings of memory; a consolidation or elaboration process occurring subsequent to learning to facilitate storage of the memory; changes in stimuli (whether subtle or obvious and whether external or internal to the organism) from those that had been present during original learning; and special cues just prior to testing that may facilitate retrieval. These are some of the features of retention and forgetting that require us to study this topic separately from learning.

Retention is evident when information previously acquired by an organism comes to influence its present behavior. When this influence is absent despite adequate perception and motivation, we say that forgetting has occurred.

Retention and Forgetting

The existence of a memory-as-representation is indexed in terms of behavior. The experimenter decides which particular behavior will best reflect what is learned about an episode, either on the basis of a particular theory or, too often, merely for convenience. At the empirical level we use the terms *retention* and *forgetting* with reference to this index.

Retention is the residual of what is learned, the difference between the behavior of individuals exposed to the specific arrangement of events that led to learning and those not so exposed but otherwise having identical experience. *Forgetting* refers merely to a decrement in retention. It implies nothing about why the decrement occurred or whether or not it is permanent. A *source of forgetting* is an event that either intervenes between the time of learning and the test, occurs during the test, or occurs prior to the point of learning and reliably is accompanied by forgetting. This concept becomes useful when such events lead to forgetting in a wide variety of circumstances, which eliminates circular definition (for further discussion, see Spear 1978). We shall return to this concept later.

While retention and forgetting are used here only to describe empirical aspects of a memory-as-representation, there are many aspects of the process of memory that require familiarity with concepts and ideas of what might constitute this process.

Storage and Retrieval

It is useful occasionally to use the theoretical terms *storage* and *retrieval*. By storage we mean the hypothetical acquisition process through which events are represented and established collectively as a memory for potential reference. Storage does *not* refer in our view to a process through which a memory is maintained over time, because in our view no such process may be needed; we are willing to assume, for now, that a stored memory remains potentially available throughout one's lifetime. Retrieval of a memory is the process through which memory attributes are taken from storage and become active, with the potential to influence contemporary behavior.

We shall have frequent opportunity to use and elaborate on these terms in the next chapters. These definitions are fundamental for studying and understanding memory as a process. These are the events that make up the process.

THE EXPRESSION OF MEMORY

To study memory we must observe it, and to observe memory it must be expressed. Suppose you are asked to express your memory (the representation) of this book. This is what teachers and professors do—they require that students express memories representing the events of a course. They usually do this by giving an examination.

The examination might consist of essays and require that you recall specific material from the course with a minimum of cues. The question of what to recall can provide some subtle cues, which might be thought of as hints or reminders. Aside from the cues given in the questions, an essay examination provides nothing to help you retrieve the memories of your course.

The other common type of examination is a multiple choice test in which you must recognize which of several alternatives correctly expresses your memory of the answer to that question. In comparison with the essay test, the greater number of specific questions in a multiple choice examination and the alternatives presented provide the student with more cues toward remembering the correct alternative.

Both types of tests are common in the scientific study of memory as well as in the classroom. Tests of recall (the essay test) require the subject to generate or produce the response, while tests of recognition (the multiple choice test) require the subject to identify the correct response from among those provided. These two tests have provided most of what we know about human memory. But there are other tests of human memory as well as many variants of the recall and recognition tests, and there is quite a different set for testing memory in animals.

The issue of the expression of memory has very important implications for the kinds of inferences that we can draw from our observations or measures. (If you have had a course on conditioning, you may have recognized this issue as a variant of the learning-performance distinction.) Usually our concern is whether the failure to perform well (express the memory) reflects lack of the information, or something quite different, like the absence of a critical retrieval cue. On some occasions, however, we may have to worry about whether good performance really reflects memory or the influences of some other nonassociative factors. A somewhat whimsical anecdote that captures the spirit, if not the exact details, of this latter concern appeared in an autobiographical incident described by R. Davies: "About 60 years ago, I said to my father, 'Old Mr. Lenex is showing his age; he sometimes talks quite stupidly.' My father replied, 'That isn't age. He's always been stupid. He's just losing his ability to conceal it.'" (Davies 1991).

Measurement of Memory

A listing of the specific means that have been used to assess memory for systematic study would not be a good use of space in this book (or of your time). The variety of specific tests is virtually endless, almost as limitless as the number of behaviors any human or animal can emit. The variety will be illustrated in a more meaningful context by specific experiments described in later chapters. We will consider next a few simple principles that allow you to generate your own measurements of memory.

Recall and Recognition
The conventional examples of memory measurement can be illustrated briefly for the general classes of tests such as recall and recognition. Suppose, for instance, that you

were asked to memorize the capitals of each province in Canada. You could be tested by *free recall* and asked simply to list all capitals of all Canadian provinces. Or you could be tested by *cued recall*—given a list of the provinces and asked to write beside each province the name of the capital. You might be allowed to recall all capitals in any order or you might be required to recall them on a geographical basis, in a west-to-east direction, or in alphabetical order. A multiple choice test might provide for each province four additional cities beyond the correct one. These alternative cities might be from the same province in Canada, from different provinces but always in Canada, or from any country in the world; evidence indicates that the last would be easiest and the first the most difficult variety of the multiple choice test.

To quantify memory, percent correct could be established by simply dividing the number correctly recalled or recognized by the total number possible and multiplying by 100. Somewhat different information about memory would be achieved if in addition to number of capitals correctly recalled, you had measured the latency with which each was recalled after presenting its province. It has frequently been shown that more accessible memories (those more likely recalled) are recalled quicker (with shorter latencies), but not all measures of memory are so well correlated.

Relearning

Another common test of memory would be to assess rate of relearning in terms of *savings,* as Ebbinghaus had done. After the capitals had been learned, suppose that a three-week interval elapsed and then subjects were asked to attempt again to learn the capitals. To the extent that they learned more rapidly the second time, we could say that a certain savings in memory occurred. If the first time around it took ten study repetitions to correctly recite the capitals and the second time it took only four, we would say that there is a 60 percent savings (obtained by subtracting the second score from the first, dividing by the first score and multiplying the result by 100).

Principles of Memory Measurement

The indices of recall, relearning, and recognition include most common measurements of memories that have been used in psychological laboratories for over 100 years, but there are many variations of these and other indices. There is a general principle, however, that covers all measurements of memory used so far: an acquired memory is indicated by any behavioral difference between subjects who have experienced a particular episode and those who have not.

An episode is a set of events, such as reading and studying a list of Canadian provinces and their capitals while seated in a particular room and being instructed by a particular experimenter. Remembering any of these events, even those irrelevant to the association between capitals and provinces—such as the color of the room or the odor of the experimenter's perfume—indicates some memory for the learning episode. To verify the memory, the possibility of being correct by chance must, of course, be eliminated. For instance, suppose that the experimenter happened to be wearing the world's most popular perfume, the subject only knew the name of that one perfume and guessed correctly; remembering the perfume may never have occurred.

Strictly speaking, a memory can be established only by comparison with control subjects who are from the same population and are given the same experimental experiences, except for the events of the critical episode. To establish an associative memory, comparison theoretically should be with control subjects given the same episode—room, experimenter, perfume, etc., including a list of the capitals and a list of the provinces—but without presenting the capitals correctly paired with their provinces.

The same general approach is used for studying memory in animals. What they are to remember is, of course, quite different from a set of words. The memory in question might be that the occurrence of a bell is followed shortly with food, or that when a particular odorant is present, a frightening, albeit mild, shock occurs to the feet, or that eating a substance with a particular taste leads to illness. Memory for each of these episodes would be achieved by measuring the animal's behavior when it is later presented with that same sound, odorant, or taste. We might expect, for instance, that the animal would become more active when the sound occurred or might run to the previous location of food whenever the sound was presented; we might expect it to avoid the location of the odorant and not to consume a substance of the same taste that previously preceded illness, regardless of how hungry the animal might be. On the basis of these behaviors alone, however, we could not claim memory for the episode. Animals not given the pairing of the sound and food might also become active upon the occurrence of that sound, and any animal might avoid that particular odorant or be unlikely to taste that particular substance. What is needed are control groups.

Control Groups in the Measurement of Memory

What control groups are used determines what can be concluded from an experiment. This issue of experimental design is in some ways the ultimate issue for experimental psychology because it determines what new information is provided by an experiment. For some conclusions the issue of what control group to use is extremely complex, but to determine merely whether or not an acquired memory has been expressed, the requirements of the control group are quite simple and follow from the general principle presented earlier. For associative learning of the kind we are discussing here, control animals would be given the same experience as the experimental animals, with all the elements of the learning episode but without the particular contingency (i.e., relationship) that defines the association to be tested. For instance, the control condition in the first example would include animals given the same number of sounds and food presentations, but given separately so the food would not follow the occurrence of the sound. In the other examples, control animals would be given the same odor and footshock or the same taste and illness, but without the same temporal relationship. For instance, they might be given the footshocks several minutes before smelling the odorant. In this sense the contingency defines the association that is to be acquired and stored in memory.

Why are such control conditions rarely mentioned in examples of human memory? The answer lies in the assumption that humans asked to recall a story or sentence or set of words will be unlikely to do so by chance. The diversity of responses possible for such verbal memories is huge. A person who does not know that the correct words for recall are the province capitals of Canada in unlikely to respond by chance with a province capital. For animals, however, even though a particular memory has not been acquired through a specific contingency, there may still be a certain level of activity in response to a sound, or a reluctance to be in the vicinity of a strange odor, or to consume a substance with a particular taste. In short, the unconditioned behavior of animals must be subtracted from the conditioned behavior if we are to assess memory for conditioning. For humans, unconditioned verbal behavior has an extremely remote chance of being the same as would be required for a particular test of verbal memory. Yet in testing nonverbal memory of humans, or any cases of memory in infant (nonverbal) humans, the same accounting for unconditioned behavior must be made as in the case of animal memory.

Another important control condition is needed for conclusions about the causal properties of the retention interval. To infer that the retention interval is responsible for some later level of performance, we have to know what level would have been achieved if that interval had not occurred. For such conclusions, it is necessary to compare performance on two independent tests of retention, one after a short interval, one after a longer interval. The short interval or immediate test usually is necessary to establish the baseline of terminal degree of learning, because retention after the interval may depend on that degree of learning.

The circumstances of the retention test also might provide quite different retrieval cues than were provided by the last training trial, which could cause behavioral differences unrelated to the source of forgetting. It is therefore important to estimate degree of learning by an immediate retention test rather than by results from the last training trial. For instance, just prior to the last training trial the person or animal was in the experimental room working on other training trials or becoming oriented to training, whereas just prior to the long-term retention test the person was walking to the laboratory and the animal was in its home cage or being transported to the testing room. The sensory consequences and the internal effects on the individual are probably quite different on a test preceded by these different events. Retrieval of the memory frequently is affected by such stimuli that accompany the test (e.g., Spear 1971, 1973). Consequently, it typically is necessary to use performance on a test given shortly after training as the baseline from which further retention decrement is compared.

The best way to learn about control conditions and measures of memory, however, is to become exposed to the wide range of controls and measures for memory that have been applied toward understanding the characteristics of memory. That is the approach taken in this book. These issues will become a good deal clearer through the examples we discuss in the following chapters.

In the meantime, we should consider two general issues of the expression of memory that actually have a great deal in common with our everyday use of memory. The first of these is that acquired memories are not always expressed when they are needed. The second point is that what persons say they can remember and what they actually express in their behavior can be quite different.

DISSOCIATION BETWEEN MEMORIES AVAILABLE AND MEMORIES EXPRESSED

It is not difficult to convince college students that wanting to express a memory does not make it happen. Students, who are constantly tested for expression of what they have learned, cannot escape this reality. Expression of a memory frequently fails even when there is no doubt that the memory is expressible—perhaps at some other time or in other circumstances, but expressible nevertheless. To say this another way, to "know" that a particular episode has occurred and that one has a memory for that episode is not sufficient to guarantee expression of that memory.

This is a very central point. What you know about a particular course is not inevitably expressed in an examination or when called upon in class. It may not matter that you know what needs to be expressed and that you need urgently to express it. During still more crucial moments, pilots freeze at the controls of an airplane if they are given only enough training to know what needs to be done. In similarly critical circumstances at home, we may be unable to remember where the fire extinguisher is kept at the moment the kitchen curtains burst into flame.

The Misleading Nature of Verbal Reports of Remembering

The independence of what we have learned and what we express is symmetrical, seen in each of two directions. Not only may we frequently fail to express what we know, we also frequently fail to know what we can express. Humans can be completely wrong about what they can express with regard to their acquired memories, which returns us to the general question of measurement of memory, i.e., what aspects of behavior indicate that a memory has been retrieved (remembered)?

The behavior we most typically encounter to indicate remembering is verbal report—our friends say they did or did not remember a particular episode. But such verbal reports can be a very poor indication of how an acquired memory might affect behavior. For instance, normal college students shown a set of words to learn may be asked later which ones they recognize as having been shown. Some items are not recognized; students say that they do not remember that a particular word was presented. Yet at another level it can be established that the students *do* remember, in spite of what they say. For example, if the word is presented for a fraction of a second, it will be identified more accurately, i.e., ability to perceive that word has been changed as a consequence of being exposed to it (Jacoby & Brooks 1984).

In short, individuals' estimates of whether they do or do not have a memory for a particular episode are not very accurate. This makes the problem of measurement of memory more difficult, but it also makes it more interesting, as can be appreciated by considering a few more concrete illustrations of how memory may be expressed in some ways but not in others.

Illustrations of Different Conclusions from Different Measures of Memory

That different measures of memory may yield different conclusions can be seen in the following studies. In one investigation, a group of psychologists at the University of Pennsylvania tested the memories of rats for a learned aversion to sweetened water (sucrose solution) (Pelchat, et al. 1983). For some of the rats, drinking of the sucrose solution had been accompanied by brief shocks to the feet. For others it had been accompanied by a drug that induces upper gastrointestinal tract discomfort (e.g., nausea), while for still others the sucrose solution had been paired with lower gastrointestinal tract discomfort (e.g., diarrhea). The rats were found to be equally reluctant to drink the sucrose, one measure of their memory of the acquired sucrose aversion. Yet in terms of other behaviors, there were important differences in the way these memories were expressed. Rats given the upper gastrointestinal tract discomfort after they drank sucrose subsequently responded to sucrose as if it were something that simply did not taste good, such as quinine. The way rats respond to such unpreferred foods (and to sucrose in this case) is by shaking their heads, rubbing their chins on the floor, and opening their mouths very wide ("gaping"). On the other hand, rats given footshock or lower gastrointestinal tract discomfort after drinking sucrose did not exhibit these behaviors when given sucrose, despite their reluctance to drink it. In terms of how much sucrose was consumed, we would conclude that memory was the same for all animals, but in terms of facial expressions in response to drinking sucrose, we would conclude that there were considerable differences.

A study of fear conditioning provides a second illustration. Rats that were either very young (21 days, weanling age) or adults learned to move from one small box into another whenever a light flashed. The flashing light signaled a footshock and by moving, the shock could be avoided. After an interval of about a month, the younger animals showed very poor memory, relative to the adults, of what to do when the flashing light and shock occurred. They required about as long to relearn as to learn originally and so appeared to forget everything about their training. Yet when presented with the flashing light without shock they behaved very differently from rats that had never learned active avoidance; they remained relatively inactive for a long period, an indication of fear. It was as if the younger animals forgot what to do but did not forget that the flashing light signaled some unpleasant event (Sussman & Ferguson 1980).

Consider the commonly accepted statement that although we may not recall a certain fact (as on an essay examination), we may be able to recognize it (as on a multiple choice examination). It is now equally clear that there are other circumstances in which the opposite is true and recall is actually easier than recognition. Studies using adjectival biasing, in which the particular meaning of a target noun is determined (biased) by the adjective employed, illustrate this apparent anomaly. For example, the target word, *jam,* may not be recognized as a previously seen noun if it were originally preceded by *traffic* but then preceded by *strawberry* at testing, even though the physical attributes are identical. Indeed, recall (of which words were in the list) is likely to be superior to recognition under such circumstances of adjectival biasing of encoding. Other variations of this advantage of recall over recognition are known, and the effect occurs frequently enough that it has become a significant factor in deciding basic characteristics of memory (Metcalfe 1991; Tulving & Thompson 1973). The main point is that measurement of a memory expressed in terms of recall may not agree with measurement of the same memory expressed in terms of recognition.

As a fourth case, memory for a list of repeated words might be expressed in several ways, such as reporting how frequently each word occurred in the list or by reciting which words occurred. These measures of memory can give quite different results, however. Hasher and Zacks (1984) reported five variables that drastically affected persons' recall of a set of words, but made no difference in their estimates of how frequently each word had occurred. These variables include practice, age, motivation, intelligence, and educational background. This indicates that remembering the frequency of an event may be independent of remembering what that event was.

Finally, persons with brain dysfunction provide some of the most striking examples of dissociation in measurements of memory. These examples also illustrate in stark fashion how persons can fail to know what can be expressed in memory. Brain dysfunction in this case refers specifically to persons classified as amnesic. Some of these persons may have had parts of their brain removed surgically or by accident, and others may have suffered diseases such as Korsakoff's syndrome that arises from excessive alcohol use or Alzheimer's disease that seems somehow linked to aging. It is characteristic of such patients to express verbally that they have no knowledge of a previous episode and yet to demonstrate, in a variety of behaviors, that they did learn about the episode and have a memory for it. A variety of examples of this characteristic will be discussed in chapters 8, 10, and 11.

These and similar examples are discussed as instances of selective expression in chapter 11, with respect to their implications for theories of memory. It is nevertheless useful at this point to be aware of the complexity these facts present whenever general principles are claimed about memory processing. Simple statements such as "X produces good memory, Y produces poor memory" should be taken with a considerable grain of salt until we know more about the circumstances under which the memory was measured and exactly how the memory was expressed. This certainly does not mean, however, that such principles cannot be obtained.

Two Features of Memory Measurement

We should keep in mind two general features of memory measurement. First, a memory acquired to represent an episode is multidimensional, and the memory's several attributes can function independently. Just as certain attributes of an episode might be learned more rapidly than others, other attributes might be forgotten more rapidly. What we do not know are specific rules to tell us when or why some attributes are forgotten more rapidly than others, and the relationship between remembering certain attributes and remembering others from the same episode. Part of the goal of the study of memory is to obtain such rules.

Second, we may measure memory in terms of any residual of one's experience with an episode that may show up in behavior, so long as the behavior differs from that of comparable individuals who have not been exposed to the same episode. This simply means that we can be creative in selecting behaviors that might have changed as a consequence of an experience and use these as an index of memory, but that we must be very certain that our measurement of memory includes consideration of the correct control groups.

SOURCES OF FORGETTING

The ultimate point of departure from the study of learning to that of memory is in the consideration of sources of forgetting. It is obvious that if everything learned were inevitably remembered, we would have no need to consider either memory or sources of forgetting. Less obvious is that the forgetting we observe does not always reflect the elimination or even the weakening of the learning. It may in fact never do so. Whatever we learn may always be with us and have a potential for being remembered.

When we determine that forgetting has occurred, we can only be sure that the target attributes of the memory, the responses that were to be measured, were not retrieved. We really can say nothing as to whether those attributes or any others of that memory are gone or still remain. In other words, we can say nothing about the integrity of that memory. If it is retrieved and so manifested in behavior, we can assert that the memory is in storage, but we can never really assert with confidence that the memory is *not* in storage. This point has important consequences for theories of memory. It is the major reason we will emphasize failures in memory retrieval when explaining forgetting.

How do we identify a source of forgetting? We do so in the same way we identify other constructs in psychology, such as a source of reinforcement. Food for a hungry animal is said to be a source of reinforcement because in a wide variety of circumstances, presentation of food contingent upon a particular response is found to increase the probability of that response. The critical point is that the same operation, providing food, has the same effect in a variety of circumstances. The effect is given the term *reinforcement* and is treated as an intervening variable for purposes of theory-building (it intervenes between the variable *food* and the other variable *response* as an explanation of their relationship). So it is with a source of forgetting, another intervening variable. It has been found that for a variety of kinds of learning, subjects, and other circumstances, allowing a relatively long interval to elapse between learning and a retention test results in forgetting. So in this respect, a long interval qualifies as a source of forgetting.

There are a variety of sources of forgetting. They include not only retention intervals but also the acquisition of competing or conflicting memories that might interfere with remembering a particular one, a variety of amnestic treatments that result in physiological trauma, and others to be mentioned later. Perhaps all such sources can be reduced to a single, common factor such as an impediment in retrieval (Spear 1978). But that is a theoretical matter and should not detract from the empirical fact that there are a variety of operationally distinct sources of forgetting.

CHAPTER SUMMARY

Memory has either of two meanings. Sometimes memory refers to the process (series of events) that carries us from the time an episode-to-be-remembered is first perceived until it is remembered later. In other cases memory means an individual's particular representation of a learned episode. A variety of distinctions between learning and memory were suggested, and will be expanded in the following chapters. Also, some technical terms were defined so we could discuss more easily the facts and theories of memory. We began to use the term *memory storage* to refer to initial acquisition of knowledge and *memory retrieval* to refer to its access and expression, realizing that these are hypothetical processes that cannot be measured directly. On the other hand, *retention* and *forgetting* were defined so as to be measured directly. It was emphasized that *forgetting* is a descriptive term that implies nothing about the source of failure to remember or the permanence of the loss.

To become acquainted with memory, we reviewed the major developments that have occurred in this field throughout history. Although not studied experimentally until the past 100 years or so, the topic of memory is very old in the sense of interest in, "What makes remembering most effective?" The skill of remembering was prized in ancient times, when permanent records of new knowledge were difficult or considered politically unwise. Techniques applied for memorizing are still used today, when they also have come to be studied scientifically.

In the early days of scientific psychology, memory was studied primarily in the context of human verbal learning and to some extent by physicians for whom abnormal forgetting was a frequent indication of disease. Progress in this field was hampered by a variety of factors, such as prejudices about the capacity of animals for anything like the memory seen in humans, emphasis on interanimal description of relative rates of forgetting rather than the processes underlying memory in animals, a scientific preference (a quite reasonable one) to understand learning before trying to understand memory, and technical limitations that failed to reveal the richness of memory in animals. Contemporary developments in the study of human verbal memory provided, however, conceptual tools that could be applied to a broader understanding of memory through the study of animals.

Perhaps the cleanest break between the study of learning and that of memory comes in the consideration of sources of forgetting. Following learning, individuals are exposed to a multitude of events that may serve to decrease the likelihood of expressing what was learned. We may consider these sources of forgetting in an empirical sense. This raises the questions of what these are, how forgetting proceeds, and under what circumstances. We begin to discuss this in chapter 2.

2

Forgetting Events and Relationships: The Effects of Time

Unlike memory in computers, memory access in humans and animals is much less certain. In some circumstances retrieving particular information from memory is actually unlikely, even if we are certain it was once stored into memory and this is verified by remembering it later. A probable circumstance for such forgetting is when an interval of time elapses since the memory was stored (learned).

In the first systematic study of memory over 100 years ago, Ebbinghaus investigated the rate of forgetting over time. After learning a list of 10 to 12 nonsense syllables (nonword combinations of three letters, such as bok) to perfection so that he could recall all items correctly without any errors, Ebbinghaus observed his own forgetting. The course of this strikingly rapid forgetting was shown in chapter 1 (Figure 1-1).

Although this figure has appeared in hundreds of psychology textbooks, it does not represent the only course that forgetting takes, or even the most common. The data represented in Figure 1-1 are not reliable; these same results almost certainly would occur today if memory were tested as Ebbinghaus tested it 100 years ago. The point is, however, that Ebbinghaus's tests were done under extraordinary circumstances. For instance, it might be difficult to convince subjects today to learn the 1,200 lists of nonword combinations of letters that Ebbinghaus himself actually learned in developing this curve of forgetting. Because these circumstances for testing memory are unusual—the learning of 1,200 lists mixed with recurrent tests for retention on many of them—the forgetting shown in this curve is unusually rapid. Rather than the 75 percent loss seen in Ebbinghaus's retention after 24 hours, individuals given only a single list without the interference from other lists would show only about a 25 percent loss. Figure 1-1 also indicates a steady, irreversible decline in retention over time, and this, too, is not always seen. Both of these features that deviate from the idealized curve of forgetting illustrated by Ebbinghaus's data are general outcomes and are seen in animals as well as humans. Historical circumstances delayed the study of forgetting in animals, however, a point we consider next.

ABSENCE OF FORGETTING
IN EARLY LABORATORY TESTS WITH ANIMALS

Studies of long-term retention in animals were, as noted earlier, of little importance during the first half of the twentieth century. Not much forgetting was observed in the few studies that were conducted, and this surprising retention among animals—considered otherwise to have little mental capacity—was so interesting that the basis of forgetting seemed secondary. In effect, the definition of learning as a *relatively permanent* change in behavior resulting from practice was read as *functionally permanent* and imperturbable, an unfortunate misconception. We illustrate this by carefully examining two of the studies that frequently were cited as evidence that forgetting rarely occurs in laboratory animals: one by Wendt (1937) and the other by Skinner (1950).

Wendt conditioned a dog to withdraw its foot upon the sound of a tone that had been paired with an electrical shock. The dog was then given considerable overtraining, including four times as many training trials as were necessary for original learning. During the last training session the dog responded appropriately on 97 percent of the trials; after a 2 1/2-year retention interval, foot withdrawal occurred on 80 percent of the test trials. This indicated that some forgetting had occurred, albeit remarkably little. However, the retention becomes less remarkable and the forgetting more so in view of three of Wendt's special procedures that we now know can slow the course of forgetting drastically. The first is the substantial overtraining. Second, the retention test was preceded by three footshocks, a treatment known to reduce forgetting in a variety of circumstances, as we shall see (cf. prior cueing and direct reactivation, chapter 9). And third, despite rapid relearning on a second test given 7 months after the first, there were no conditioned foot withdrawals whatsoever in their initial response to the tone, before repairing it with shock; prior to retraining subjects showed maximal forgetting.

A similarly remarkable instance of long-term retention by pigeons was described by Skinner (1950), but this case, too, involved a substantial degree of forgetting that was largely ignored. The pigeons were tested 4 years after they had learned to peck a "key" (a disk about the size of a quarter) whenever it was illuminated with a geometric pattern. After they were placed in the testing apparatus no pigeon responded until the pattern occurred on the key, but then they all pecked it quickly. One bird pecked it within 2 seconds after it was illuminated. This was indeed a notable feat of remembering, and it is often treated as evidence that postacquisition memory processes in animals are relatively unimportant. Yet even the pigeon that showed the most remarkable retention in terms of latency-to-respond, the bird that pecked the pattern within 2 seconds, gave only 25 to 50 percent as many pecks after the first as would have occurred without the retention interval. In other words, number of responses as a measure indicated 50 to 75 percent forgetting over the 4-year interval. This illustrates two points. (1) Some aspects (or response measures) of a learning episode may be subject to substantial forgetting while others are remembered quite well—a point of increasing theoretical importance (see, e.g., selective expression in chapter 11). (2) Instances of amazing animal memory do exist, but forgetting by animals is ubiquitous and cannot be ignored.

As our reexamination of these two famous studies indicates, the permanence of retention proved to be not so permanent after all. But it seems highly likely that retention will be determined by the nature of the learned behavior and the extensiveness and conditions of the learning—remembering how to ride a bicycle after a 20-year interval is vastly easier than, say, remembering algebra after that same interval, although it is hard to say whether this is due to the nature of these two tasks or to the amount and distribution of practice each received (for an interesting study of actual retention of algebra after 20 years or so, see Bahrick & Hall 1991). So it should not be surprising to find tasks or situations in which animal memory is very enduring, as the following studies illustrate. (1) Schwartz and Reilly (1985) required pigeons to peck each of two keys four times in any order for reward. The resulting sequences of responding were highly stereotyped and well retained over a 60-day interval. (2) Treichler (1984) examined the acquisition and retention of a concurrent discrimination task in rhesus monkeys. In the concurrent discrimination, the subject is presented with a series of two object discrimination problems. After each choice, whether it is correct (reinforced) or incorrect (nonreinforced), another pair is presented, until the list is completed. (This procedure contrasts with those in which training on each individual problem continues for a number of trials before the next problem is introduced.) The list of problems is presented in different orders until mastery is achieved, a situation that Treichler suggests is analogous to learning a foreign language vocabulary. Not only were monkeys capable of acquiring an extensive list of these concurrent discriminations, but they also showed excellent retention over a 90-day interval, even after learning other problems during that period. (3) Using a conditioned emotional response paradigm, Hoffman, Fleshler, and Jensen (1963) trained pigeons to fear a tone that predicted shock. More than two years later the birds still showed substantial conditioned suppression of key pecking for food when the tone was presented.

At the other extreme are examples showing that animals sometimes forget very rapidly. For instance, infant rats that have learned quite well to stay away from a dangerous odor that had been paired with mild footshock seem to forget this completely within 3 hours, in the sense that their behavior is indistinguishable from that of untrained animals (Miller, Jagielo, & Spear 1989).

The point is that animal memory may appear to be either extremely resistant to forgetting or extremely susceptible to it. The remainder of this book addresses the circumstances in which forgetting is more or less likely to occur.

AN ORIENTATION FOR UNDERSTANDING FORGETTING

Scientists have discovered a great deal about events that produce forgetting. These include long or short intervals of relative inactivity, interference from other learning that may be characterized as the acquisition of conflicting memories, blows to the head, electroconvulsive therapy administered to psychotic or severely depressed individuals, a variety of drugs, and, generally speaking, contextual change. Yet there is no concise, tightly woven set of principles to explain why these events, and perhaps others too, result in forgetting. There is simply no generally accepted theory of forgetting to which we can appeal for understanding or even for organizing the facts of this topic. We will use the term *forgetting* in a descriptive sense to refer to any decrement in performance that occurs as a retention test. Neither the source of impairment nor its permanence is implied by this definition.

A set of ideas about memory retrieval can provide a general conceptual framework as to how remembering is governed, however. Such a framework has been generally accepted by many psychologists and used frequently as a guide for experimentation.

The conceptual framework is built around a major assumption and three central ideas. The assumption is that whatever is learned—all memories acquired by an individual—is permanent so long as he or she remains neurophysiologically intact. This assumption is based on circumstantial evidence from a variety of sources that indicate a remarkable ability for normal animals and humans to remember episodes from their distant, sometimes obscure, past, and probably can never be tested directly by experiment. This view is understood to be extreme and no more than a working hypothesis. It is encouraged, however, by the many instances we all have known or experienced in which an acquired memory seems surely to have been lost from storage—sometimes due to temporary disruption of brain activity—yet the memory is expressed in behavior, with or without special retrieval aids. In his novel *Rabbit at Rest,* Updike (1990) captures this view with a picturesque description of old information that returns in a dream: "His dreams are delicious, like forbidden candy ... rearrangements of old situations stored in his brain cells, like ... even the nitwit Margaret Kosko, he hasn't thought of her name for thirty years, but there she was in his brain cells just as clear with her underfed city pallor as she was that night in the booth of the Chinese restaurant ..." (p. 472).

One of the three ideas is an observation common to many psychologists and philosophers for centuries: a memory is most likely expressed when the circumstances in which it is to be remembered are most like those in which it was learned originally. *Circumstances* mean not only the particular events that were associated together, such as the words that were memorized or the motor activities combined into a newly acquired skill, but also include contextual features at the time of learning that may have seemed redundant, e.g., external stimuli such as the color of the room, its temperature, and noise level, and also internal features such as the individual's mood, arousal level, thoughts, hormonal activity, degree of hunger, and so forth.

The second idea is one mentioned in the previous chapter with regard to memory-as-representation: what is acquired when learning an episode is a multidimensional memory, consisting of a group of attributes that represent specific stimuli and responses of a central, target task as well as features of the context external and internal to the learner.

So far this framework includes the notions that the major problem in remembering is in retrieving a memory and not in losing it from storage, that remembering is more likely in circumstances that mimic those when the memory was originally acquired, and that the memory we are dealing with is not a single encapsulated film of the episode, but rather is a collection of attributes that can in some circumstances function independently of one another (e.g., you might remember some aspects of an episode while forgetting others).

The final idea is a rule—at present a vague rule—to indicate when remembering can be expected: a memory will be retrieved and manifested in behavior when a sufficient number, kind, or percentage of the attributes of a memory are aroused by the occurrence of events sufficiently similar to those that had been represented by the attributes (cf. Estes 1959). The particular behavior that is taken to indicate *remembering*—such as the correct sequence of words that were to be memorized, moving toward, moving away, turning right, or choosing a particularly colored button—presumably becomes activated when the appropriate kind, number, or proportion of memory attributes associated with that behavior are activated by events that immediately precede or accompany the retention test. How this happens is unclear. A variety of possibilities are represented in existing theories, but it seems to us premature to speculate about this mechanism. When we know more about the mechanism, we may have a theory instead of a framework. For our purposes, however, the framework is sufficient to work with as it is. At the least it provides a language, albeit imprecise at this stage, for discussing the facts of memory retrieval.

The major implication is that as internal and external circumstances are modified from those of original learning, forgetting is to be expected. We know that as time passes, for instance, there is a progressively greater probability that one's external environment and one's internal circumstances will change or that what is noticed will change. Such modifications in our internal and external worlds, and in our habits as to what we attend to, may be enhanced by things such as new learning in the interim and will result in greater forgetting. Furthermore, administration of certain drugs, a general insult to the central nervous system, or neurochemically induced changes in our physiological status can alter our internal environment and also increase our forgetting. But remembering also can be enhanced, by reactivation treatments or reminders, events like those of original learning that are presented to the individual in such a way as to ensure that they will be noticed.

As we discuss the facts of memory we will appeal frequently to this general conceptual framework for considering memory retrieval.

FORGETTING OVER TIME: THE EFFECT OF A RETENTION INTERVAL FILLED WITH RELATIVE INACTIVITY

As time passes from the point of learning, is retention likely to take a regularly declining path? Might retention sometimes increase over time? Can retention ever improve by simply waiting a longer interval? Or, does retention fluctuate rhythmically, first decreasing, then increasing, then decreasing again, and so on?

A *retention interval* is an interval of relative inactivity. The interval must be longer than any interval that had separated repetitions (if any) of the learning episode (e.g., if more than one learning trial had occurred). The *relative inactivity* part merely indicates that no explicit practice occurred during this interval. There is, of course, no way to induce a complete psychological vacuum to allow assessment of forgetting after an interval of no experience. When we discuss the course of forgetting as a function of time, we really mean *time* only descriptively because it is the events taking place during that period of time that really determine forgetting; time is not causal, even though we may nominally refer to it as a source of forgetting.

Everyday Forgetting Over Time

The steady decline in retention over time is one feature of such forgetting that is observed so frequently as to seem inevitable. It is not really inevitable, however, and so its generality and characteristics are of some interest. Two examples will illustrate the decline of retention over time. Krueger (1929) had subjects learn lists of twelve nouns and tested them for retention after various intervals (1, 2, 4, 7, 14, or 28 days). Regardless of whether the material was mastered to a minimal level or with overlearning, performance declined substantially as a function of the test delay. However, retention declined more slowly in the overtrained groups.

Shepard (1967) compared recognition learning for words, sentences, and pictures. This study revealed an impressive ability of humans, immediately after exposure to about 600 stimuli, to distinguish the target items from an item to which they had not been exposed (90, 88, and 98 percent accuracy for words, sentences, and pictures, respectively). Several subjects were tested for picture recognition after various delays. Median accuracy declined only slightly after 3 days or 7 days (93 and 92 percent correct, respectively), but after 4 months, retention had declined substantially to near chance levels (57 percent correct). Despite the extraordinary ability of subjects to continue such impressive recognition for up to a week, the information was forgotten in several months. The importance of this observation should not be diminished merely because, as accomplished forgetters ourselves, we readily sympathize with this loss of retention and so tend to view any forgetting as "common sense."

Fifty-Year Memory

Of necessity, laboratory studies involve relatively limited learning episodes. Even the overlearning trials in Krueger's study constitute a pale representation of the extensive exposure we get to some events in everyday life, and these events are remembered very well indeed over long periods. But is such overlearned information retained indefinitely? Although easy enough to ask, this question is very difficult to study in a controlled experiment. We consider now, however, some research that begins to address the issue.

In the early 1970s a study was conducted in central Ohio of how well humans remember over very long intervals ranging from a few months to nearly 50 years (Bahrick, Bahrick, & Wittlinger 1975). Such intervals cannot really be accommodated in a laboratory study. For one thing, the experimenter grows old in the meantime and may retire. Another problem is the questionable validity of the memories reported. We can ask persons to describe events in their lives 20 years ago and they may do so in good detail, but this would be of no value unless we can be sure the events described in fact occurred. In the study by Bahrick et al. this problem was dealt with by assessing retention of the names and faces of high school classmates that could be verified by the yearbooks of those high school classes.

In this study about 400 people, ranging in age from 17 to 74, were given a variety of memory tests. The tests required that they recall or recognize the names or faces of classmates with whom they had graduated from high school. Gathering useful information from such a study is more difficult than it might appear, but fortunately, a good deal of experimental control was exerted in this test and sophisticated statistical techniques were used to minimize the chances for error in reaching conclusions. For instance, these investigators carefully equated each of the age groups in terms of factors such as size of their graduating class, frequency and recency of class reunions, frequency and recency with which the subjects had reviewed their yearbooks, and so forth.

The basic results are shown in Figure 2-1. The most dramatic effects occurred in contrasting simple recall of the names of everyone from the graduating class with recognition of their names or pictures. For the recognition tests, subjects were

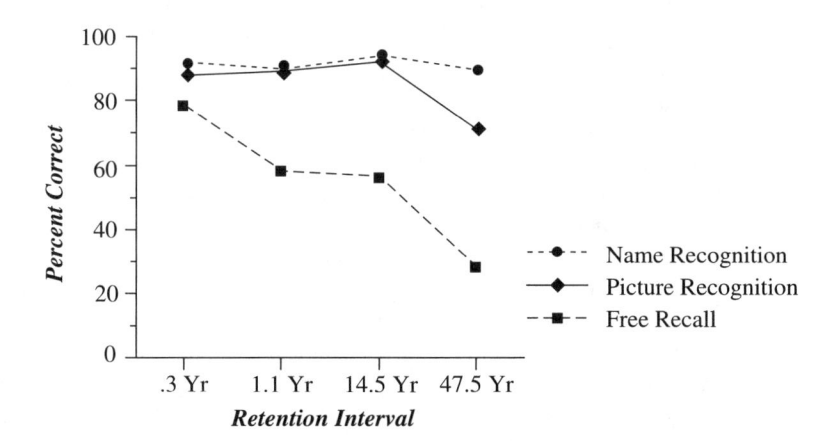

FIGURE 2-1 Rate of forgetting of the names and faces of high school classmates is shown over long intervals after completion of high school. Of the three measures forgetting was most rapid in terms of one's ability to recall, without prompting, the names of classmates. (Adapted from Bahrick et al. 1975.)

presented a set of five pictures or names, only one of which had actually belonged to the subject's graduating class (the other four pictures or names were selected from other high school yearbooks of comparable years).

Forty-eight years after graduation, recall of names had declined by about 60 percent. Yet, recognition of the names had declined by about only 15 percent, and recognition of pictures by only about 18 percent. For the first 34 years recognition of the faces of classmates in pictures did not decline at all! There was at the same time a 40 percent decline in the recall of names over this 34-year period. (The general fact of more effective memory for pictures than for words is well established.)

In more recent work, Bahrick and his colleagues have found that similarly long-term retention of memory for high school Spanish and for algebra also is remarkably effective in some ways despite clear, progressive forgetting in other respects (Bahrick & Hall 1991; Bahrick & Phelps 1987).

Remembering Unique Personal Events

Students at Kansas State University participated in an experiment to determine how rapidly they forgot relatively unique events in their daily lives (Thompson 1982). For most of an entire semester all members of a psychology class recorded daily one unique event they experienced and one their roommates experienced. Later they would be asked to remember the dates of these events. The events recorded had to be unique in the sense of having occurred only once (it would make no sense to ask "On what date did you eat lunch?"). In addition to their uniqueness, the events recorded could not be embarrassing and had to be described in three written lines or less. The sorts of things that were recorded were "found an earring on the apartment shuttle bus," "played football with Ed and Kirk," and "got elected to House Disciplinary Board." For our purposes, the results of this study illustrate the steady decline of retention and how conclusions about memory can depend on how retention is assessed.

In this experiment remembering was tested by reading each event to the subject, as it was written in the diary, and asking him or her to estimate the date on which it had occurred. As the interval lengthened between the event and the test, the subjects' accuracy in dating the event decreased in regular fashion, and rather rapidly. Roughly speaking, the average error in dating an event increased by about one day with each passing week. This unusual curve of forgetting is illustrated in Figure 2-2. The more common forgetting function is negatively accelerated in that forgetting is more rapid during the first portion of the retention interval than during the latter portion. Figure 2-2 differs from this in part because we are dealing with time estimation, but perhaps primarily because most other tests of remembering concentrate on whether an answer is correct or not, rather than on degree of correctness as is represented in this figure. When the data from this experiment are replotted in the more conventional way, counting each dating estimate as either completely correct or completely incorrect, the more conventional forgetting function emerges (Figure 2-3).

Estimates of remembering depend on how one chooses to measure memory. The answer to, "How well do high school graduates remember their classmates 34 years

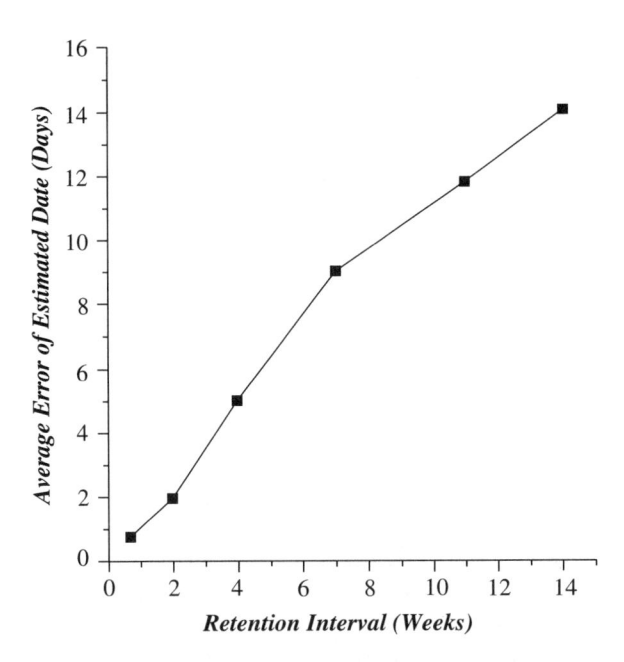

FIGURE 2-2 Rate of forgetting over several weeks following the occurrence of events significant to college students is shown for remembering of the date on which each event occurred. This figure shows the relationship between the degree of error of the date recalled and the time since the event, so that the higher the number on the ordinate, the poorer the retention. (Adapted from Thompson 1982.)

after graduation?" was very different depending on how the remembering was measured. We will see that this principle has important applications for all varieties of the study of memory. One implication is that questions about how good is one's memory for this or that episode are not useful unless we know exactly how that memory is being assessed. Equally evident, assertions about events being completely forgotten are unlikely to be accurate until we can decide how to exhaust all possible ways of measuring memory for any particular episode. Striking changes in theories of memory have occurred when apparently complete forgetting—among human amnesics with brain damage, rats given electroconvulsive shock or amnesia-inducing drugs, human infants, and so forth—turned out not to be so. In these cases either other measures of memory or different circumstances provided evidence that the memory still existed. This important point has been illustrated frequently, although perhaps not obviously, throughout decades of systematic tests of memory, as we shall see.

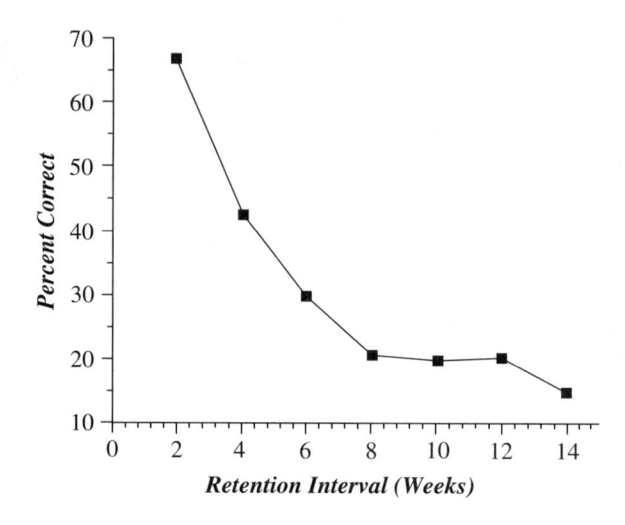

FIGURE 2-3 This figure represents the same data shown in Figure 2-2 but scored in terms of whether the date recalled was correct or not, rather than the degree of error of the date recalled. Plotted in terms of percent correct, the forgetting is seen to be negatively accelerated. (Modified from Thompson 1982.)

The Generality of Forgetting as a Steady Decline

The studies of Bahrick et al. and of Thompson verify objectively cases of forgetting we all have experienced. They also illustrate some of the complexities involved in trying to identify what actually controls forgetting. Yet, the fact that forgetting was observed in these studies is unsurprising. Forgetting is something humans expect to do; its ubiquitous nature is one of its striking features. The steady decline in accessibility of a memory over time has been observed in an extraordinarily large number of situations and for all sorts of animals. There is concrete evidence of the generality of this effect and the breadth of circumstances in which it occurs, from very simple responding to a single stimulus, to more complex variations of instrumental and Pavlovian conditioning.

Simple instrumental learning in the rat and pigeon shows a steady decline in retention during long intervals. Adult rats were trained to turn in one of two directions in a T-maze to obtain food and administered a relearning test after intervals of 1, 25, 50, or 100 days (Hill et al. 1969). A steady decline in retention occurred, although substantially more forgetting was observed in terms of latency to make a choice than in the accuracy of the choice itself (Figure 2-4). Similarly, in a systematic and thorough study of long-term retention of discrimination learning in the pigeon, Kraemer (1984) found a steady decline in retention of discrimination learning over

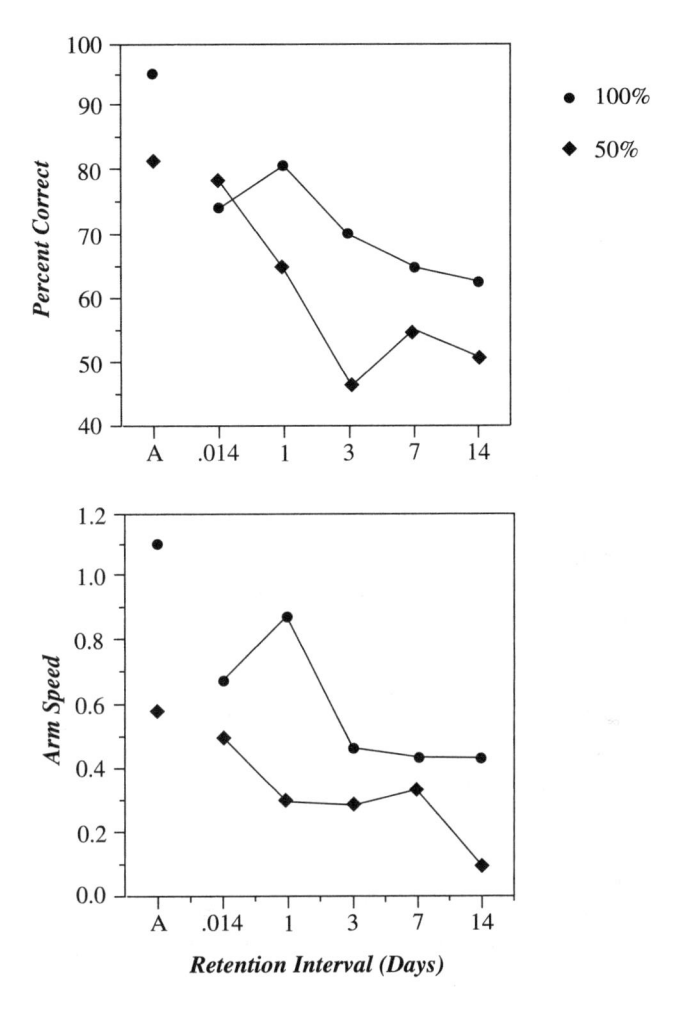

FIGURE 2-4 Forgetting over a period of 2 weeks is shown for rats that had acquired an appetitive discrimination (turning to enter a particular goal box, on the right or on the left, in order to obtain food, which was presented on 50% or 100% of the entrances). More forgetting was observed in terms of latency to make a choice and enter the goal box (arm speed, lower panel) than in terms of correctness of the choice (percent correct, upper panel). (Modified from Hill et al. 1969.)

intervals up to a month. It is notable that much more of this decline was registered for remembering what was incorrect than for what was correct (see Figure 2-5 and compare the earlier discussion of forgetting by Skinner's pigeons). In dogs a deficiency in instrumental behavior induced by prior exposure to inescapable punishment

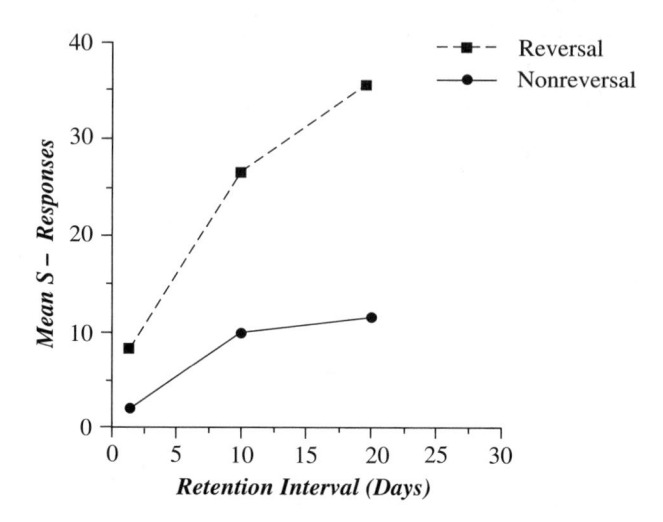

FIGURE 2-5 Forgetting of a discrimination over a period of 10 or 20 days is shown for pigeons that had learned that pecking at one stimulus (S+) resulted in food whereas pecking at the other stimulus (S–) did not. Although there was relatively little decrease in pecking to S+ over time, the probability of incorrectly pecking S– increased substantially, indicating forgetting of the discrimination. Forgetting was substantially more rapid for birds that had previously learned the reverse discrimination (in which S– led to food but S+ did not: Reversal) than for pigeons that had not (Nonreversal), indicating proactive interference (see chapter 4). There was, nevertheless, significant forgetting over time in both groups.

—learned helplessness—subsequently shows a steady decline in retention that is quite rapid under some circumstances (Overmier & Seligman 1967; Seligman, Maier, & Solomon 1971). And for monkeys, the complex learning set behavior acquired over a series of similar discrimination problems—the acquired ability to solve any discrimination problem perfectly after a single exposure to either the correct or incorrect alternatives—is forgotten progressively over a 6-year period (Bessemer & Stollnitz 1971).

This material has illustrated the generality of the steady decline rule; now we must consider exceptions to this rule. Experiments studying retention after a variety of intervals of varying length sometimes have found it to decline irregularly and sometimes apparently to increase and then decrease later. We discuss such cases next.

Apparent Increases in Retention Over Time: Hypermnesia

Reminiscence

The term *reminiscence* has been used by psychologists for many years to refer operationally to cases in which performance on a retention test is better after long than after short intervals. The term is still used today, although with increasing precision. It is now more appropriate to reserve the term reminiscence for instances of successive attempts to recall several events of a previous episode, in which previously unrecalled events are recalled on later attempts (Payne [1987] re-established this use of the term, based on its original use by Ballard in 1913). In other words, reminiscence is increased recall of previously forgotten items, i.e., items that previously were not recalled. This effect may be seen readily when people are asked to recall a set or words or the names of pictures just studied, then are asked later to try again to recall the same material. Under the right conditions, with the appropriate length of time between successive recall attempts, the number of new items recalled outstrips any forgetting of other items. The result is better retention later than sooner after learning. This effect can fall under the general term *hypermnesia* because retention is improved beyond the normal levels of original learning, a consequence of a specific treatment (additional recall tests after an interval of time).

An instance of similar hypermnesia that sometimes is (erroneously) referred to as reminiscence is the time-dependent increase in retention shown by people for tedious motor tasks they have learned, such as keeping one's finger on a dot that moves irregularly across a television screen. It has been known for years that with massed practice on such motor tasks (i.e., practice uninterrupted by rests), performance is likely to improve after a retention interval. If, instead, the person is given distributed practice with frequent periods of rest interspersed between periods of practice, the result is less improvement over a subsequent interval (or even forgetting). In other words, with distributed practice on such a task less spontaneous improvement occurs after a long retention interval. This case of hypermnesia typically has been explained in terms of the buildup of negative factors such as inhibition, fatigue, or error tendencies that continue so long as practice continues in massed fashion. Theoretically, a retention interval offers an opportunity for such negative factors to dissipate. While performance in these circumstances may undeniably be better after a long retention interval, there is no evidence that the memory has somehow gained in strength during the retention interval.

Such a facilitation in memory strength would be interesting and certainly desirable. Imagine studying for a brief period and then sitting back to rest in the knowledge that, by resting, you are somehow facilitating the processing of the memories you have just acquired, promoting later retention by doing nothing. To a degree this actually seems to occur for some instances in the recall of picture labels (Smith & Vela 1991). After a first attempt, recall is more effective after relatively long intervals even if the subject does not rehearse during the interval. This happy circumstance seems due, however, to release from sources of interference present after shorter intervals, not to an absolute increase in memory strength. We shall see later that some instances of better retention by animals after longer intervals are similarly due to something other than an absolute increase in memory strength. First, it is useful to consider the issue in more detail in terms of human memory.

Does Recall of Pictures and Words Improve Over Time?
Shapiro and Erdelyi (1974) presented subjects a list of 60 simple sketches of discrete objects (e.g., fish, key, table, football, etc.). The subjects were then asked to write the names of as many of the items they could remember, beginning either 30 seconds or 5 minutes after their presentation. Subjects tested 5 minutes after presentation recalled 12 percent more pictures than when subjects were tested after only 30 seconds. This increase was small but agreed with a similar increase seen previously (Erdelyi & Becker 1974). In the previous study accuracy in the recall of picture labels also had increased over time, but in that study successive opportunities to recall intervened. Following an initial recall attempt, subjects in two experiments were permitted a 7-minute interval to sit quietly and think about the stimulus items they had studied (the think condition in these experiments); improvement in recall after the interval was 13 percent and 10 percent for experiments 1 and 2, respectively (Erdelyi & Becker 1974).

It seemed that a slight increase in recall of picture labels occurs over time whether repeated opportunities to recall were given or not, although subjects in the Erdelyi et al. studies did spend the interval rehearsing. No increase in recall was found, however, for items presented as words and recalled as words, in any of three experiments (Erdelyi & Becker 1974; Shapiro & Erdelyi 1974). Erdelyi and his colleagues suggested that the use of visual imagery may be responsible for the increase in recall over time. This is uncertain, however. A similar increment in recall can occur with words, and it does not seem to matter whether or not the words easily form a mental image (Payne 1987; Roediger & Payne 1985).

The general effect might seem to encourage the notion that we can strengthen our memories by merely resting. The effect discussed is, after all, a net increase in retention of the complete episode to be remembered. It is common for subjects given a list of twenty or so words or pictures, to recall some items on a second test they had not previously recalled; but usually enough forgetting of other items occurs at the same time to provide a net balance of no increase in the number of words recalled on the second test (Tulving 1967). The experiments of Erdelyi et al. indicate that at least in some cases, the net balance is for better retention on the second test. They concluded that they had found a real increase in memory strength over time due, in effect, to thinking about the material in the interim between tests.

A more convincing explanation has been suggested by Roediger and his colleagues, however, accompanied by equally convincing evidence. They have shown, for instance, that recall can be significantly increased merely by allowing more time to recall a list of words. More words were recalled if subjects were allowed 21 rather than 7 minutes. The extra time does not merely let subjects say more words; an entire list of 20 to 30 words can be spoken in well under a minute, so 14 extra minutes would not matter for this. But the extra time does somehow allow subjects to generate more correct words. So, when subjects are observed to increase their recall over three successive 7-minute tests, they may recall more items on the third test than on the first merely because they had a cumulative total of 21 minutes of recall time in comparison to only 7 for their first test. If so, the time between the first and third tests should then be irrelevant to the effect. This is what Roediger and Thorpe (1978) found. When total recall time was equated for subjects given a single (long) immediate test and those given several successive (shorter) tests, there was no measurable increment in retention across time.

The most interesting question about reminiscence is whether, in the absence of rehearsal activity that might promote later recall, subjects given a single test show better retention after a long than a short interval. When Roediger and Payne (1982) tested this with procedures like those of Shapiro and Erdelyi—but with the intervals between learning and testing filled by having the subjects read prose in order to prevent rehearsal—there was no greater retention after the longer intervals. Three separate groups of subjects studied 60 pictures presented to them on slides. The group given an immediate test recalled (by naming the objects that had been pictured) an average of 25.6 items; those tested 9 minutes later recalled 25.1 and those tested 18 minutes later recalled 25.6. After this first test of each group, two more tests were given, each 7 minutes long and separated by 2 minutes each. Recall did increase by an average of about 2 to 3 items with each successive test, for an actual gain overall of 4 to 5 items. The conclusion is that prior testing improved recall, but longer intervals between study and testing did not. Although Smith and Vela (1991) applied slightly different procedures and did find that longer intervals, even without rehearsal, yielded better recall, the basis for this important effect seemed to be release from output interference after the longer interval, not a stronger memory.

The picture that emerges is that whether remembering pictures or words, we can expect no simple increase in memory strength over time. From a historical perspective of the analysis of reminiscence, the conclusions of Roediger and his colleagues are not surprising. Since the critical analysis of (apparent) reminiscence effects published over 50 years ago (McGeoch 1935), two general factors have accounted for most claims of increases in retention with increases in length of the retention interval. One is a greater opportunity for rehearsal or related processing with longer intervals. Another is the influence of multiple retention tests on the same individual. The factor emphasized by Roediger and his colleagues—time allotted for recall—can now supplement these. The factors of rehearsal, time for recall, and the effects of testing are interesting determinants of retention in their own right. But when they are controlled experimentally, there apparently are no time-related increases in memory strength in these circumstances.

This set of studies also illustrates a common finding in experiments with both animals and humans, one that will play an important role in our interpretation of memory retrieval effects: tests of retention can facilitate later retention performance, even for long-term retention over several days (Rose 1992; Runquist 1986). If the same subjects are retested several times, as in the present examples, those tested over longer intervals will have been given more tests and so their retention should be facilitated more.

The general lesson is that however appealing the concept of reminiscence might be, it is unwise to expect that an acquired memory will ever become more permanent by the mere passing of a retention interval. General hypermnesia of the kind discussed in this section can be traced either to special impairment in retention performance after short intervals (as opposed to enhanced retention after longer intervals) or to active processing during longer intervals. These sorts of ideas are useful also in dealing with a related case of apparent increase in memory strength over longer retention intervals—incubation.

Incubation
Like reminiscence, incubation refers to an increase in learned performance during a retention interval. The major difference is that incubation in this sense has been applied frequently to instances involving an emotional response such as fear, particularly when retention does not show the conventional decline. Because of the emotional context of the resultant memory, and because the term *incubation* has been applied widely in studies of both human and animal memory, separate consideration is warranted.

Incubation is really an old concept. Consider the admonition to a person who falls off a horse: get right back up in the saddle or else it will become more difficult to do so with the passing of time. Yet incubation is in some ways an unfortunate choice of terms. It implies that a seed of fear, once planted, grows spontaneously in an organism over time. This tempts one to use incubation as an explanatory concept when it is intended only to be descriptive, in the same way that we have used retention and forgetting.

Incubation in humans typically has been assessed through the measurement of responses of the autonomic nervous system such as heart rate or the galvanic skin response (a change in the electrical resistance of one's skin, for which the most familiar use is the lie-detector test). A standard experiment consists of pairing a neutral stimulus such as a letter, word, or light with the occurrence of a mild but uncomfortable electrical shock that elicits changes in the autonomic response in question (e.g., a decrease in electrical resistance of skin resistance). As we would expect from our knowledge of classical conditioning, the neutral stimulus, as a result of the pairings with the uncomfortable electrical shock, will come to elicit the change in the autonomic response. When the autonomic response is greater as the retention interval grows longer (i.e., the longer the time between acquisition and testing), incubation is said to occur.

There is some evidence that changes in arousal may modulate retention, although the relationship between arousal and remembering is not straightforward. For certain kinds of arousal-inducing words, retention has seemed to be better the longer the retention interval. Kleinsmith and Kaplan (1963) had college students study, for a short period, eight words that were "expected to produce different arousal levels" (p. 191). The words were *kiss, rape, vomit, exam, dance, money, love,* and *swim.* Each word was paired with a single digit (2 to 9), and the subjects were to learn to say the word when its paired digit appeared. As each word was studied, deflections in the galvanic skin response were measured as an index of the extent of the arousal elicited by that word. A retention test was given after 2 minutes, 20 minutes, 45 minutes, 1 day, or 1 week. Of special interest was the retention of the words to which subjects had shown high arousal and those to which they had shown low arousal.

The results, really quite striking, are shown in Figure 2-6. As can be seen, at the longer retention intervals, reminiscence occurred for high arousal words and forgetting

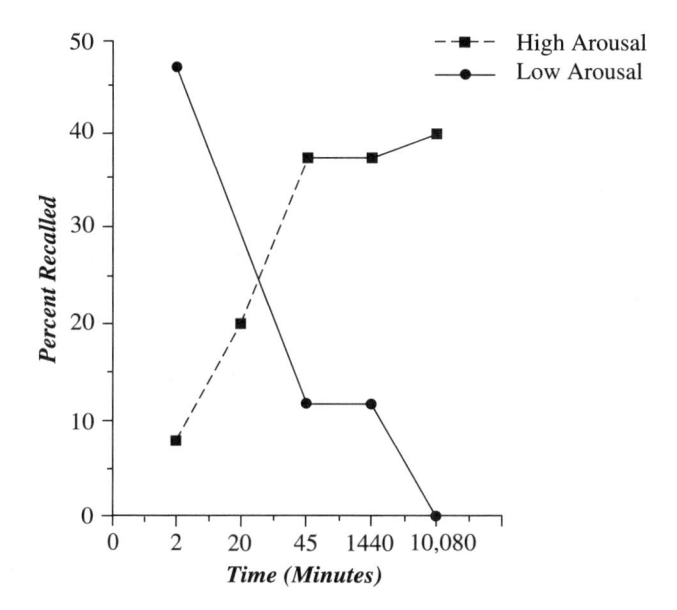

FIGURE 2-6 Change in retention of the association between a number and a particular word is shown for humans after intervals of up to 1 week following learning of the associations. The course of retention depended on the nature of the words. If the words elicited no unusual arousal, forgetting of the words in response to a particular number was quite drastic over a week's time, but if the words were arousing, retention was poor shortly after learning but increased dramatically over 1 week's time. Although the effect has not always been observed as dramatically as shown in this figure, and some experiments studying this effect have been prone to methodological error (see Keppel 1984), an effect of this kind has been observed often enough to indicate that it has generality worthy of scientific consideration. (Adapted from Kleinsmith & Kaplan 1963.)

for low arousal words. After the very short retention interval, however, the words were not equally recalled. Immediate recall was much better for low than high arousal words. In spite of methodological problems with the initial study by Kleinsmith and Kaplan, subsequent experiments using a variety of similar procedures have supported the general notion of this sort of interaction between arousal and length of the retention interval (for a critique of these studies, see Keppel 1984). There are, moreover, many studies indicating that arousal induced in other ways can have equally interesting effects on learning and recall (Eysenk 1977). For example, one way arousal has been increased is to present the subject a burst of white noise. If white noise is presented during study of a word or a set of words, immediate recall is typically impaired but less forgetting occurs over a longer interval. This effect is similar in form to that seen when the words themselves induce high arousal.

The problem is, even if one could arrive at a satisfactory way of defining arousal, it is hard to tell whether its effect is directly on memory strength or is instead the result of how much or what kind of processing is given the materials to be remembered. If emotionally loaded words or strong stimuli such as white noise induce high arousal, the items affected might be more likely to be elaborated in a semantic fashion, which is known to facilitate recall, or more likely rehearsed during a long retention interval. In other words, the subject may be more apt to think about what that word means or what it is related to than otherwise, and this might lead to better recall. But it is still difficult for such factors to explain why high arousal impairs recall after short intervals but facilitates it later (for one set of interesting explanations, see Uehling 1972).

Basic Conditioning
Following instrumental aversive conditioning with animals, there are clear instances of incubation in terms of instrumental behavior. Rats and mice show more avoidance a day or so later than immediately after training under certain conditions of one-trial passive avoidance conditioning. An example may be seen in Figure 2-7, in which the left portion shows the latency of rats to lick a water spout at differing intervals after they had been shocked while licking it, and the right portion shows the performance of mice in terms of their latency to cross over into a compartment in which they had been shocked during original training. An increase in retention also may accompany an inactive interval following multitrial active avoidance conditioning in rabbits, guinea pigs, or rats (e.g., Gabriel 1972).

The issue here, as with reminiscence studies, is whether the incubation represents a genuine increase in associative strength of the stored memory or something else. It is possible that instead, instrumental behavior is artificially depressed immediately or enhanced later due to transient alterations in the animal's disposition to express that behavior, whether learned or not. An example arises in tests of the retention of one-trial passive avoidance learning. Under some circumstances, footshock given to rats or mice results in initial hyperactivity which then decreases progressively with the passage of time. If one outlet for the increased activity happens to be entering the compartment in which the animal previously was shocked,

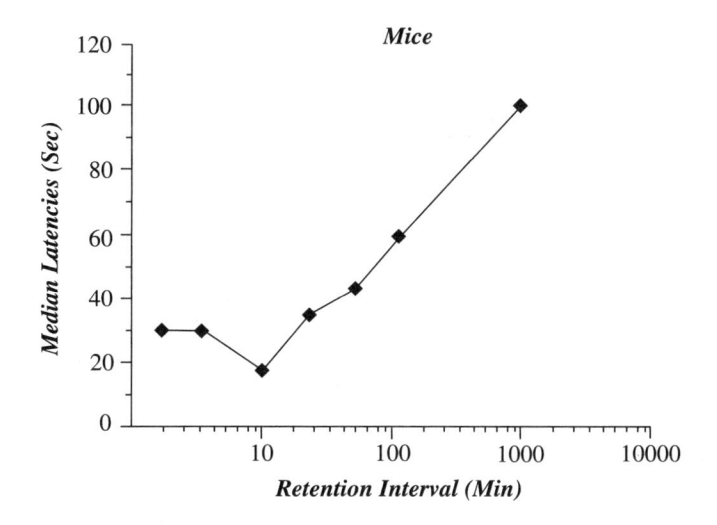

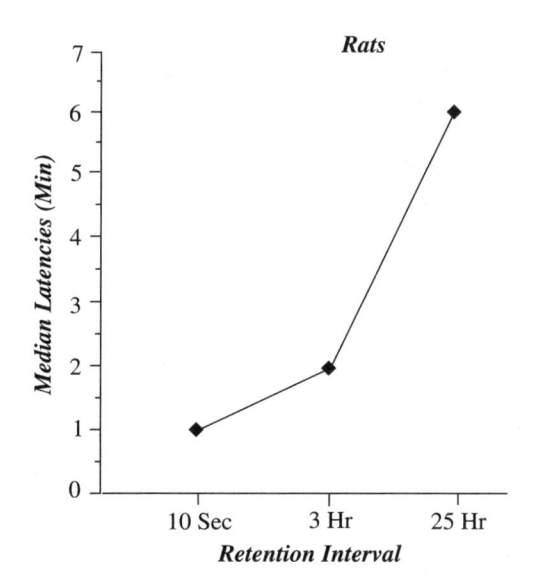

FIGURE 2-7 Performance on a retention test given after one of several intervals following passive avoidance training is shown for rats and mice (the passive avoidance task differed slightly for these two animals). This figure illustrates a result frequently observed under certain circumstances with other animals and other tasks: a pro-gressive increase in retention over time, in this case with the longest interval about 1 day. It seems unlikely that this change in retention performance represents a correspondingly sharp increase in the associative strength of what was learned. (Adapted from Pinel & Cooper 1966; Geller & Jarvik 1970.)

this will be recorded after short intervals as poor retention. This hyperactivity will have dissipated after longer intervals and retention will seem, therefore, to have improved. Also, hormonal changes associated with the stress of the learning episode (e.g., the release of epinephrine and adrenocorticotrophic hormone) may change the organism's response to or perception of the environment sufficiently to make performance on a short-term test (i.e., while the hormonal changes are still present) poorer than on a later test. Incubation under these circumstances is neither an increase in the strength of memory or in the strength of fear, but the removal of factors that hindered the expression of memory at short intervals. A finding consistent with this view is that with autonomic indices of fear, the emotional response to an aversive stimulus decreases over time and does not increase as the concept of incubation would suggest (Pinel, Malsbury, & Corcoran 1971).

Apparent instances of incubation may also represent simply an increase in the number of stimuli eliciting the response, rather than a stronger response to the conditioned stimulus per se. The idea underlying this explanation is based on stimulus generalization, i.e., the tendency to respond to new stimuli similar to the conditioned stimulus; the level of responding is a function of the degree of similarity. However, generalization is known to increase over a retention interval. The longer the interval the more likely the animal will emit the learned behavior when presented with stimuli similar to those initially associated with the aversive event. Using the example of the person falling off a particular horse, an immediate test might show the person to be afraid of that horse but to have little fear of other horses. Over time, however, a more generalized fear reaction could occur such that a later test would reveal a considerable increase in the fear of all horses. Such an explanation has been applied successfully to incubation found in terms of human classical conditioning (Saltz & Asdourian 1963), classical conditioning with animals (McAllister & McAllister 1967), and instrumental conditioning with animals (Gabriel 1972).

In summary, when retention increases with longer retention intervals, it probably is not due to a progressive increase in the strength of the memory, but is nearly always linked to an impediment to processing after shorter intervals, to performance changes over time that are unrelated to remembering, or to temporally dependent contextual change. This last factor has been analyzed in terms of the Kamin effect.

Temporarily Impaired Retention—The Kamin Effect

The Kamin effect, so-called because it was first reported by Kamin (1957), provides a clear instance of a nonmonotonic function where retention initially declines, then increases again before declining once more (the change in direction of the curve distinguishes this from a monotonic function). The Kamin effect may be described simply: following aversive conditioning, retention is quite good after a few minutes as well as a day or two later, but is relatively poor after intermediate intervals in the range of 1 to 6 hours. An example of the Kamin effect is shown in Figure 2-8.

This unusual retention function was initially viewed largely as an anomaly, and for several years the Kamin effect was not the object of much research. Subsequently, however, the Kamin effect was recognized more widely as having theoretical impor-

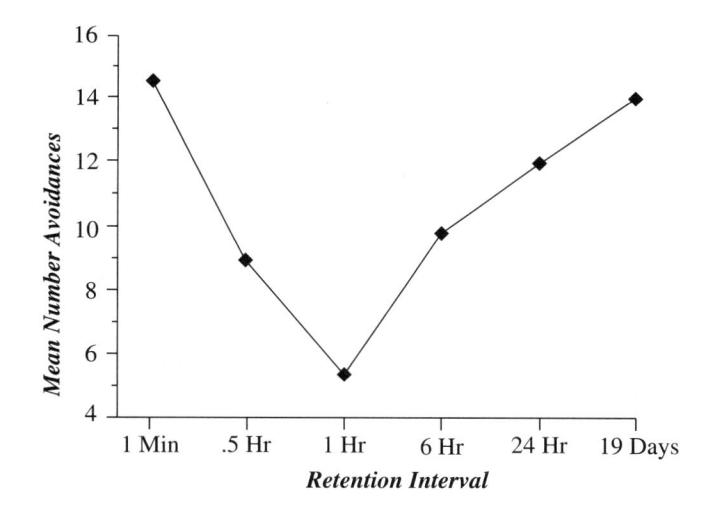

```
                16 ┐
                    ♦
                14 -
   s
   e
   c
   n
   a  12 -
   d
   i
   o
   v
   A  10 -                              ♦
   r
   e
   b                                              ♦
   m  8 -         ♦
   u
   N
   n
   a  6 -
   e
   M
                4 ┤────┬────┬────┬────┬────┬────
                    1 Min  .5 Hr  1 Hr  6 Hr  24 Hr  19 Days
                              Retention Interval
```

FIGURE 2-8 Retention after a variety of intervals following learning of two-way active avoidance is shown for rats in terms of mean number of avoidances given on the retention test. Higher numbers indicate better retention, so this figure shows a temporarily impaired retention after intermediate intervals following conditioning. (Adapted from Kamin 1957.)

tance (e.g., Brush 1971). It proved to be a reliable phenomenon and not merely due to artifactual consequences of procedure or to simple changes in the general activity levels of the animals. The intermediate-length retention intervals that yield poorest retention were found to be accompanied by temporally dependent, physiological effects on neurotransmitter activity induced by stress (including hormonal peptides now known to act also as neurotransmitters).

After an intermediate-length retention interval following a stressful learning situation, the animal is very different neurophysiologically than either immediately after learning or 24 hours later. These changes can be thought of as a regulatory device by the animal. During the stressful circumstances of something like avoidance learning, the animal must in effect shut down its efforts at metabolic regulation and recruit physiological resources to take care of the crisis at hand. After an intermediate interval (the precise length of time is dependent on the duration and extent of the previous trauma), the animal's physiological systems must get back to the business of metabolic repletion of basic energy resources. Those aspects of the neurohormonal system that were very active during the stressful learning (sometimes called the sympathetic nervous system) are shut down or even actively inhibited as the parasympathetic nervous system takes over and dominates after an intermediate interval. In this particular neurohormonal state the animal's response to new stress will be quite different from that immediately following stressful learning. When the activity of the parasympathetic nervous system has subsided 24 hours later, the animal's response to the stress of the retention test returns to the levels that had accompanied original learning and had carried over into the immediate test. The nature of the test is important; if it is not particularly stressful, retention immediately and 24 hours later may not be superior to retention after the intermediate interval, because the stress of the test determines the animal's neurohormonal state and hence the internal cues for memory retrieval.

The special neurohormonal state of the animal after intermediate retention intervals could lower retention scores in either of two ways. It could simply impair the animal's ability to perform the response. For instance, if good retention required fast movement and the state of the animal left it lethargic and slow, retention scores would be lower. This would be trivial and uninteresting insofar as memory is concerned. The second possibility is that the change in the internal state of the animal represents a new context so different from original learning that memory retrieval is impaired. An analogy may be made with a drug-related phenomenon called *state-dependent retention*—the exaggerated forgetting that occurs when organisms (people or animals) learn something while under the influence of certain drugs but later are tested for retention in a normal state. Retention is maximized when acquisition and testing occur in the same state (drug in each case or normal in each case, see chapter 3).

A large number of experiments have indicated that state-dependent retention may apply to the Kamin effect. This was established in three stages. First, it was found that the exaggerated forgetting occurs at intermediate intervals whether retention requires the animal to move slowly or rapidly, and it is also seen when speed of reactivity is irrelevant (as when retention is measured in terms of the animal's choice of a previously correct alternative). This indicates that the Kamin effect is not merely a deficit in the level of activity required for test performance.

A second set of experiments tested this state-dependent retention explanation in another way. The gist of this explanation, when applied to the Kamin effect, is that after an intermediate interval animals tend not to retrieve their memory of the learning episode because their internal state in response to the stress of the retention test differs from that of original learning. At the more extreme intervals, however, their internal state in response to the new stress of the retention test more closely approximates that of original learning. If this is correct, it should be possible to show corresponding forgetting when an animal learns the task originally under an intermediate-interval state and later is tested in a normal state. For example, the former state could be induced by stressing the animal under training-like circumstances an hour or so before learning and the latter by testing 24 hours later. Such experiments were conducted, and the predicted results were obtained. In other words, an outcome quite different from the Kamin effect—impaired retention when testing occurred 24 hours after conditioning—was obtained when animals had learned originally under an intermediate-interval state.

The third stage in this set of experiments was to show that if the neurohormonal state of the animal after intermediate-length intervals could be made more like that after shorter or longer intervals, the typically exaggerated forgetting at that point would not occur. This prediction was confirmed in a set of experiments that included three ways of manipulating the animal's neurohormonal state prior to testing: a warm-up session with other stressful stimuli, electrical stimulation of an area of the brain that controls the pituitary gland's output of stress-related neurohormones, and direct injection of the hormone itself (adrenocorticotrophic hormone; these studies were conducted by Klein, Bryan, Spear, and their colleagues; for a review see Spear 1978, 176–186). Thus, by reinstating the internal state present shortly after training, the retention deficit at the intermediate point was eliminated.

Tests of the basis for the Kamin effect have continued and support for this retrieval interpretation has grown (e.g., Seybert et al. 1979, 1982). But more important than the Kamin effect itself is the general form of its explanation. The Kamin effect illustrates a relatively minor instance of a more general phenomenon: retention deficits induced by changes in context. A change in context, which in this case is internal and termed the organism's *neurophysiological state,* can decrease the accessibility of a memory and thereby induce forgetting.

Multiphasic Retention Functions: Repeated Fluctuations in Retention

Following the initial demonstration by Kamin that there could be a decline in retention followed by a return to previous levels, researchers began to be alert for the possibility of other types of fluctuations in memory processes. If the potential exists for such a change during one time period, it seems reasonable that the change could repeat itself on a regular basis. In other words, the time course of retention might be multiphasic, with a variety of peaks and valleys in retention at various times after learning. The explanation of the Kamin effect described above suggests that such multiphasic retention functions may correspond with fluctuations in internal or external contextual stimuli. A common example is the dependence of retention on how closely the time of day of testing corresponds to that of original learning.

It has been known for a long time that a particular temporal regularity exists in the daily cycles of a variety of physiological events and also in behavior. For instance, nocturnal animals such as the rat have low levels of activity during the light portion of their cycle, with a gradual increase in activity near the end of the light portion that continues throughout the dark portion of their cycle, and gradually decreases once again as the light portion approaches. There are corresponding changes throughout each 24-hour period in physiological processes such as deep body temperature, serum content of a variety of hormones, cell mitosis, DNA metabolism and so forth. It is as if these changes, or whatever is responsible for these changes, provide the basis for a sort of internal clock that tells the animal when it is time to change behaviors. At different times of day, the internal stimuli impinging on an animal—the way the animal feels, the animal's internal state—will differ. At any given time of day an impairment in remembering an episode that had occurred at a different time of day might be expected because the contribution of the animal's internal state to the context of remembering deviates significantly from the context of learning. A striking example of multiphasic retention of this kind with the rat is shown in Figure 2-9.

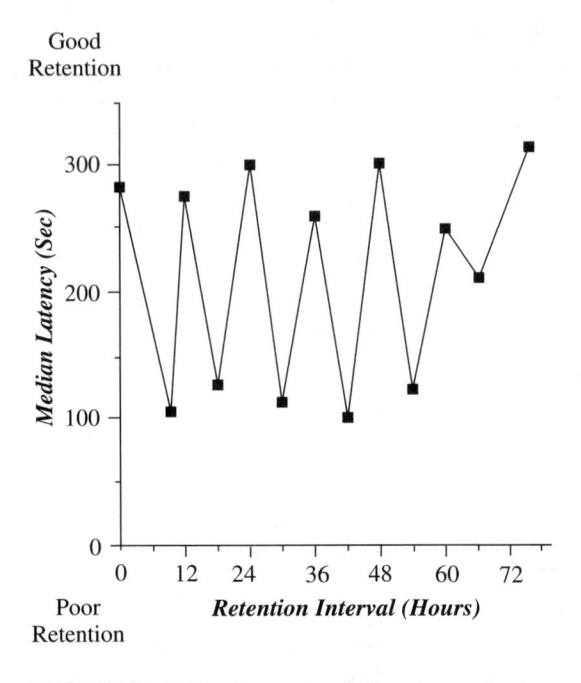

FIGURE 2-9 Retention following a single instance of training to passively avoid (i.e., withhold entering) a black compartment is shown for rats tested after an interval of specified length up to 3 days later. Retention tests were given every 6 hours following conditioning, but each rat received only one retention test. After 12 hours or multiples of 12 hours, retention was quite effective, but after 6, 18, 30, 42, 54, or 66 hours (the midpoint of each 12-hour interval after conditioning), retention was relatively poor. Although probably related to retention's dependence on the similarity of the animal's internal state between conditioning and test, which in turn depends upon the similarity of conditioning and testing in terms of the animal's circadian rhythm (sleep cycle), this example illustrates an extreme case in which retention is not monotonic, neither progressively increasing nor progressively decreasing. (Adapted from Holloway & Wansley 1973.)

In this experiment rats were given a single passive avoidance training trial—placed into the brighter compartment of a two-compartment box and given a footshock when they entered the darker compartment. After a variety of intervals, ranging between 15 minutes and 3 days, they were returned to the bright compartment, and their latency to enter the previously shocked, darker compartment was measured. When the tests were given at the same time of day as training—after intervals of 15 minutes, 24 hours, 48 hours, or 72 hours retention was excellent. But when the time of day of testing deviated from that of training, retention was poorer. This basic phenomenon has been replicated with a variety of other, more analytical tasks such as active avoidance and classical conditioning (Holloway & Wansley 1973; Wansley & Holloway 1975; Stroebel 1967).

How do we account for such multiphasic retention? One possibility is that the actual physical representation of memory in one's brain continually fluctuates in its integrity after the learning episode, so that activation of the most faithful representation is less likely at some points in the fluctuation than others. A more likely possibility is that some regularly changing physiological function unrelated to the process of memory storage may determine the effectiveness of memory retrieval by altering the similarity of the context (internal especially) at acquisition and retrieval. As indicated in the figure, the cyclic nature of retention can be quite regular and may be related to the well-established circadian rhythm. The resulting changes in the internal and external environment may provide a sufficiently large shift in contextual cues to make retrieval much easier if the conditions present during the memory test correspond to those present during training.

Finally, a study by Gisquet-Verrier and Alexinsky (1988) using an aversively motivated task provides an illustration of another type of nonmonotonic change in retention. The special feature of their investigation was the demonstration of the Kamin effect and a long-term spontaneous enhancement of memory, both resulting from the same training episode. In the first experiment, rats were trained to approach the lighted compartment of a Y-maze in order to escape shock. Retention tests, in which subjects were retrained to criterion, were administered at several intervals ranging from 5 minutes to 28 days after acquisition. The Kamin effect was obtained at a 1-hour interval; subjects required more trials to reach criterion at this time than at 5-minute or 1-day intervals. Performance was stable between 1- and 5-day tests, but then improved at 8 and 14 days. Thus, at the longer intervals, subjects showed greater savings than either immediately or 1 day after training. Finally, performance declined over still longer periods, suggesting the operation of long-term forgetting processes. A second experiment, employing a discriminative active avoidance task, found a similar pattern of temporal fluctuations in number of avoidance responses: impairment at a short interval (1 hour) followed by spontaneous enhancement at a 3-day retention test and a disruption of performance after a very long (3-week) interval. Gisquet-Verrier and Alexinsky suggest that these multiphasic variations in memory result from changes in retrievability, in which different attributes of the training episode change independently and at different rates. Different organizations of retrieval attributes after different intervals could produce the memory fluctuations.

CHAPTER SUMMARY

Retention must be considered separately from learning. Distinct differences have arisen in their definitions, but probably more important are the functional distinctions between them. Factors that influence retention may have quite different effects on learning, or no effects at all, and vice versa. To help organize what is known about retention and forgetting, a general conceptual framework was suggested. Built on broad-based ideas that are old but persist as time-tested, this framework emphasizes that aspects of memory retrieval are of basic importance to retention and forgetting.

As we extend the interval of time following one's last exposure to an episode, we can be fairly confident that forgetting of that episode will increase. This is equally true when we try to remember our specific daily activities of a few days or weeks or a month ago or if we seek to recall the names of our fellow students of a year or 5 years or even 40 years ago. This steady decline in retention also is typical for a variety of animals, all those that have been tested, in remembering single events, complex reinforcement contingencies, or fairly complicated skills. The rate of forgetting may differ depending upon what aspect of the episode is to be remembered or how it is to be remembered (such as recall or recognition), but a steady decline is the general rule nevertheless.

But steady decline is not the only course of forgetting that has been observed. The opposite effect, increases in retention with the passage of time, has been observed for both humans and animals under the heading reminiscence or incubation. Some cases of this kind seem best attributed to factors that exert a relatively trivial performance-based impairment on retention shortly after learning so that retention later on is better only relatively speaking. Other cases seem best explained by subtle extra study of the materials to be remembered or similar use of the time that elapses over an interval that can lead to better retention. There is so far no conclusive evidence that memory strength progressively grows during a period of relative inactivity. But the case is not closed, particularly for the poorly understood effects of arousal on retention.

In studies with animals that have tested retention after many different retention intervals within the same experiment, a variety of multiphasic retention functions have appeared, with retention first decreasing, then increasing, then decreasing again, and so forth. An important example of this is the Kamin effect. When such fluctuations cannot be attributed to simple changes unrelated to memory processing, such as motivation or the effectiveness of motor performance, they have seemed due to the varying degrees of similarity between the stimuli at training and testing after each of the retention intervals, resulting in differential effectiveness of memory retrieval. The primary source of stimulus change in these cases probably is within the animal.

The more general case of retention impairment due to a change in internal state between learning and testing—state-dependent retention—is considered in the next chapter when we discuss more fully the characteristics of memory retrieval.

▶ 3

Significant Sources of Forgetting
Changes in Context

Two normal, everyday sources of forgetting have special significance: contextual change and associative interference. These sources are similar in that both reduce the probability of retention for either animals or humans in a variety of circumstances and are substantial enough to be observable in everyday life without special measurement techniques. They may be effective after either long intervals or within only a few seconds following learning.

These are not the only sources that might be considered, nor even the only sources that we consider in this book. We encounter others in discussing the extreme forgetting of the events of infancy we all experience. Neurophysiological disruption or malfunction that results in amnesia provides further, relatively abnormal sources to be discussed still later. It is possible, however, that contextual change and interference might encompass all sources of forgetting in the sense that if these factors could be dismissed, no forgetting would occur. One goal of science is to reduce the number of factors needed for explanation; in this chapter as in the rest of this book, we suggest that apparently different sources of forgetting may be subsumed within the more general factor of failure in memory retrieval. This chapter focuses on the effect of context on forgetting.

CONTEXT AND RETENTION

Virtually all major theories of memory have considered context to be a major determinant of retention and forgetting. Our everyday experience confirms that the circumstances in which remembering is to occur can have a vast impact on how effective retention will be. It is probably easy to appreciate relatively dramatic instances of how a reinstated context can bring back a flood of related memories: "An individual lived for several years in China and laboriously acquired the ability to speak the Chinese language. Upon his return to this country for a couple of years' vacation, he found to his dismay that his ability to speak and understand this language had practically disappeared by the end of this time. Naturally, he expected that a considerable amount of effort and time would be required to relearn the language but to his surprise he found that he was able to speak the language quite fluently upon his return to China." (McGeoch 1942, 504; first cited by Carr 1925)

Specific experimental tests also have left little doubt of an effect of context on memory. For instance, retention frequently has been shown to be impaired if the context is changed between learning and the memory test, and there is some evidence that if a distinctive context is present during both learning and the test, retention may be facilitated. Yet the principles of contextual control are not well understood; we do not have a firm grasp on when context can be expected to improve retention and when it will not. Although this topic has been studied extensively, it continues to be an important topic of memory research.

To appreciate the effects of context and the limits of our understanding of it, we must consider a series of questions: What is context? How does it enter into our learning to become an attribute of a particular memory? Precisely how does context affect retention and forgetting? How important are these effects? How have these effects been explained and which explanation is most effective? What are the limitations or boundary conditions of the effect of context on memory? Finally, what questions remain to be answered before features of context can be applied to influence memory for practical purposes?

What Is Context and What Can It Do to Learning and Memory?

We all have some idea about what context is. Context refers to the background or setting in which an event occurs. A football game includes a cheering crowd, band music, and excited activity among players and coaches at the sides of the field, but the central event, the game itself, is the activity on the field of twenty-two players and three or four officials. Context is a setting that predicts particular occurrences. Being in China predicts that the spoken or written language will almost certainly be Chinese. Context can also determine meaning. In a forest, the term *cardinal* probably refers to a bird, in church it probably refers to a member of the clergy, and in a baseball stadium in St. Louis, it probably indicates a ballplayer. But context can determine not only our perception of what events mean or what is likely to occur; it can also affect what we learn and how well we learn it, and it can have a particularly profound effect on what we remember. To understand these and other effects of context through experimental analysis, it is convenient to separate context from the more central events of learning.

Suppose that a rat is presented a conditioned stimulus (CS) such as a tone that predicts an unconditioned stimulus (US) such as food. With enough pairings, the tone will begin to predict the food sufficiently well that whenever the tone occurs the rat will generally become active and investigate the site where the food is usually delivered. This indicates that learning has occurred. Yet we cannot understand even this simple case of learning, or the animal's memory of it, without taking into account the elementary fact that presentation of the CS and US never takes place in a vacuum but instead occurs in a particular context. For instance, the CS and US may have been presented in the context of a small dim chamber with a floor or sheet metal cloth (external context) at a time when the rat was hungry and sleepy (internal context). The rat's memory for the CS-US relationship includes information about the context in which it was acquired, just as a human's memory for a particular set of words or sentences in the laboratory is likely to include the location of the room in which the learning occurred, features of the room itself, characteristics of the experimenter who presented the task, and so forth.

What are the essential differences between the context and the target memory? There seem to be two. First, the context lasts longer and is more constant, i.e., context is a relatively long-term static event. The target occurs more briefly, often in punctate fashion at various times within the period of the context. Second, the context is accordingly a much poorer predictor than the CS of when the US will occur. In other words, although the US does occur in the presence of the context, there may be long periods of time when the context is present, but the US does not occur. These differences between the context and target memories are important because, as we shall see, these two events play quite different roles in learning and memory.

The principal ways that context can affect basic learning are by helping to predict the occurrence of a particularly significant biological event (e.g., food or an annoying or painful US) or by providing information about special relationships between certain events (e.g., a tone will predict food).

There are also two principal effects of context on memory: (1) if the context in which the memory must be retrieved differs from that in which the memory was acquired, it is likely that accuracy of retention will be impaired; and (2) if the context of both memory retrieval and memory acquisition are the same and are also quite distinctive, retention might be more accurate than if these contexts were the same but fairly common. This chapter focuses on contextual changes and retrieval, but information on a distinctive context's enhancement of retention is increasing (e.g., Concannon et al. 1978; Kraemer 1984; Lariviere et al. 1990; Riccio & Jonke 1983; Richardson, Riccio & Axiotis 1986; Schab 1990).

These general statements themselves do not convey much understanding of the effects of context on learning and memory. Their significance will become clearer after more description of the concept of context, more specific examples of how context affects learning and memory, and consideration of the role of context in theories of memory.

Sharpening the Meaning of Context

The way in which we have defined context is almost too general. Should we really expect internal context (e.g., the hormonal consequences of fear or the neurochemical consequences of a particular drug) to affect learning and memory in the same way as external context (e.g., one's physical surroundings during learning)? And isn't the case of linguistic context—the different meanings of *jam* when it is preceded by *traffic* or *strawberry*—a quite different matter than the context of conditioning for a rat? A brief consideration of linguistic and internal context is needed at this point.

Linguistic Context

The communication of meaning is an important aspect of context. We understand the meaning of many words from the setting or context in which they appear. Linguistic context in particular is something with which humans are so familiar, and which so influences us, that we are often unaware of how it affects our memory process. But the effects of linguistic context on human verbal memory are clear and powerful. Suppose you read a general story about a man walking through a forest who encounters barking dogs and the sounds of gunfire. If given a title for this story, such as "The Hunter" or "The Escaped Convict," you can more effectively recall its content later. You also will remember different events in the story, depending on which title sets the context. A variety of experiments indicate that the advantage of the title is to both allow for original encoding of the material in a meaningful fashion, and to promote efficient memory retrieval (Alba et al. 1981; Bransford & Johnson 1972; Summers, Horton & Diehl 1985).

Internal Context

In addition to external background, internal cues of certain kinds, such as the influence of drugs or some combination of hormonal activity and emotion, may function as a context. In some cases these internal contexts may be more distinctive to animals or humans than are the physical surroundings in which they might acquire one memory or another. But at another level, these different kinds of context function to influence memory in a similar way (Overton 1985; Spear 1978). Although one might maintain that linguistic context affects word meaning in a manner unrelated to anything possible with animals, context similarly can influence the meaning of stimuli for animals. For instance, an animal can readily learn that a flashing light means danger in one contextual location but safety in another or that a particular brightness predicts an annoying footshock if the animal is under the influence of barbiturates but predicts safety if the animal is in a normal drug state.

Our belief is that the principles of contextual influences on memory have broad applicability, and there seems to be some agreement about this. For instance, one effective way of viewing the influence of context on human memory, in terms of the encoding specificity principle, has seemed to work reasonably well whether the context in question is a local linguistic context (*jam* as *strawberry* versus *traffic*) or as relatively distal physical context (e.g., the particular room in which learning occurs; Spear 1976; Tulving 1974, 1983; Tulving & Thompson 1973).

General Issues in the Relationship Between Context and Memory

A decrement in retention often occurs when the context of testing differs from that of training. This is referred to as the contextual change effect. This effect has been observed in such a variety of animals and humans and an equally wide variety of types of context and learning conditions that it must be considered an important feature of memory. Yet the retention deficit is not inevitable. Untangling the necessary and sufficient conditions for the contextual change effect, while accommodating its broad basis of observation, creates quite a challenge for explanation. It is useful to present at this point some of the general issues involved in such an explanation in relation to others.

The term *generalization decrement* originally referred to the difference in response strength to a particular conditioned or discriminative stimulus in comparison to a different stimulus of the same dimension. For instance, if a bird has learned that a red light signals the opportunity to obtain food for pecking, it will peck somewhat less for purple than for red and still less for blue than for purple. If a rat has learned that a tone of 20,000 Hz is accompanied by an annoying footshock, it will work less hard to avoid the occurrence of a lower tone of 15,000 Hz and still less to avoid the occurrence of a 10,000 Hz tone. This is a universal effect, and it is appropriate to use the term *generalization decrement* to refer to the lesser response strength to a similar but untrained stimulus.

However, it is usually not correct to refer to the contextual change effect as merely a special case of generalization decrement and certainly not correct when the contextual change leaves unaltered the perceived characteristics of the conditioned stimulus. A difference in the animal's perception of the conditioned stimuli will produce a trivial, uninteresting instance of the contextual change effect. For example, changing the bird's context by decreasing illumination after it learned to peck a red key would decrease the perceived difference between a red and a blue key. The behavioral consequences in this case could be considered generalization decrement to the primary (physical) dimension of wavelength. In most instances of the contextual change effect, however, the animal's perception of the conditioned stimulus has not seemed to change enough to account for the entire effect.

If not generalization decrement, then how do we explain the contextual change effect? In a broad sense, one might conceptualize the entire array of cues, including the context and the conditioned stimulus, as the stimulus in question. Thus, changes in the context at testing, while not altering the subject's perception of the conditioned stimulus, would reduce the overall similarity to the training situation. More specifically, two consequences of contextual change seem likely to account for the retention deficit. (1) By taking away certain contextual features of learning that have been encoded as attributes of the target memory, there may be inadequate contextual support for retrieval of that memory. (2) New stimuli noticed upon a change in context may arouse competing memories that interfere with retention of the target memory. This emphasizes that one never merely removes stimulus elements; when some elements of conditioning are not present at testing, a new set of contextual events will be attended to. There may be a change in the configuration of the remaining contextual stimuli as well. New elements of a context or a new configuration of these elements may elicit previously stored memories that have these elements as attributes, which in turn may compete with the target memory for expression.

In terms of basic conditioning and learning, context has often been assumed to serve merely as another conditioned or discriminative stimulus and to become associated directly with the US. For instance, suppose that a rat in a small dark chamber smelling of mint learns that an occasional tone is always followed by food. It has been assumed that a direct association develops between the small, dark, minty compartment and food and that this association might add to or compete with that between the tone and food. If a retention test in a large, bright compartment smelling of lemon indicates that the animal does not expect food upon the occurrence of tone—the contextual change effect—the explanation has been that without the associative strength between the original context and the food, there is not sufficient associative strength between the tone and food for the tone to elicit the expectation of food.

Although sometimes associations are formed directly between the context and the US and sometimes between the context and the CS, it now appears that for the most part context does not act merely as another CS. Many of its effects, including the contextual change effect, seem to be better explained by viewing context as having a higher level of stimulus control than is held by a CS (Bouton 1991). What context does is predict for the animal the relationship between the CS and US that is to occur in those circumstances. This view links this influence of context with two well-known phenomena in human and animal learning, conditional discrimination and occasion setting.

Conditional discrimination, in which the correct stimulus in a discrimination problem is indicated by the value or presence of another (conditional) cue, has a long history in psychology. Imagine that a rat can obtain food by pressing either of two levers, one on the right and one on the left. If the rat learns that when a flashing light occurs, it is to press the right lever for food but when a tone occurs it is to press the left lever, it has learned a conditional discrimination. The solution to the right-left discrimination is conditional upon whether the light or the tone occurred. A quite similar relationship occurs in occasion setting (Holland 1985). In a common instance of occasion setting in tests with the rat or pigeon, a light predicts food when preceded by a tone, but if the light occurs without a preceding tone, no food is delivered to the animal. We know that the tone has a different function than the light in this situation, because no direct association seems to be acquired between it and the food, nor is its potential as an occasion setter affected when the food is removed in this situation; in contrast, a direct association between the light and the food is acquired and if the food is no longer delivered, the light loses its associative strength. A stimulus such as a tone seems to become an occasion setter rather than just another CS in such circumstances particularly if it is the less salient predictor of the US (by being removed from it temporally or by having less intensity than the CS [Holland 1985, 1989]). It is as if a hierarchical associative structure exists and the occasion setter determines which of two outcomes will accompany this CS.

In learning a conditional discrimination or an occasion-setting function, the animal appears to learn the meaning of a particular instruction. The instruction is in the form of a simple signal that indicates what the reinforcement contingencies are to be. We essentially ask the rat to learn a language of tones and lights. With humans much of this learning could be bypassed by a simple instruction: "On this trial, the right lever is correct," or "The next time a light occurs, it will (or will not) be followed by food." If context also acts as a simple instruction, a change in context between learning and testing offers a new instruction that is ambiguous or perhaps simply incorrect.

Yet the control exerted by context over memory is not only by way of mere instruction. The extensive training necessary for the animal to develop a conditional discrimination or an occasion-setting function is not necessary for many instances of contextual control over memory retrieval (including the contextual change effect). The contextual stimulus effect—the animal's general tendency to exhibit acquired memories in accord with the context—has been observed with minimal training and without the need to expose the animal repeatedly to contrasting contexts (Spear 1971; Spear et al. 1980). So, although context may function as an instruction, there seems to be more to it than that.

These examples are a sample of the major issues and ideas one must keep in mind when evaluating the effects of context on learning and memory. We now consider some specific instances of these effects, first through recent tests of how context can control fundamental conditioning and learning and then in the more pertinent sense of how context can control memory in a wide variety of circumstances. Finally, we will study a few examples of the role of context in theories of memory.

CONTEXTUAL INFLUENCES ON BASIC CONDITIONING AND LEARNING

Context can exert an important influence on retention and forgetting. A probable reason for this influence is that the contextual features of an episode become learned and stored as important memory attributes for that episode. The question we now consider is, how is this storage accomplished? In other words, how does context enter into learning about an episode, how does context influence what is learned about an episode, and how are the contextual features themselves learned?

There is now considerable evidence that context can become an attribute of the memory for an episode through associations formed between context and a US, between context and a CS, or between context and a particular CS-US combination. In other words, the animal can learn that context signals a particular US, or signals a particular CS, or signals that the CS will be followed by a particular US. The last feature of contextual learning—that context signals a CS-US relationship—probably is the most important for memory, but all are relevant. (e.g., Bouton & Swartzentruber 1986; Miller & Schachtmann 1985; Rescorla, Durlach & Grau 1985). To simplify matters, we will discuss only the evidence pertaining to associations between the context and the CS-US relationship.

Several years ago it was proposed that animals (or humans) use context to predict relationships amo-ng other events within that context (Estes 1973; Spear 1971). For instance, rats can easily learn that when a signal such as a flashing light occurs, they must run quickly to avoid an annoying footshock if they are in context A but should not run at all to avoid a similar footshock if in context B. This learning occurs with surprising rapidity when contexts A and B represent different locations, different noises, or different drug states (Spear 1971; Spear et al. 1980). The rate of learning about contextual significance is surprising in one sense; this form of conditional discrimination historically has seemed very difficult for animals. For example, learning typically requires many trials (comparisons) when the conditional discrimination requires the animal to learn that the left lever should be pressed for food if a tone occurs but the right level pressed if a light occurs.

It is not yet clear why context sometimes can rapidly come to control the animal's expectation about other relationships whereas conditional discriminations have seemed to be acquired relatively slowly. There are more similarities between these two cases than differences. Scientists have more recently begun to study conditional discrimination in terms of Pavlovian conditioning, with procedures that seem to reveal still more similarities. The procedures and terms are somewhat different. A rat might be presented a tone that sometimes is paired with food but on other occasions is not and preceded by a light that indicates whether the tone will or will not be accompanied by food. As when the context signaled the rat to run or not to run, or when the conditional discriminative stimuli "told" the animal to press the right or the left lever, the light tells the rat to expect food or no food when the tone occurs. In this case the light serves as an occasion-setter (Ross & Holland 1981). We mentioned earlier that an occasion setter is different from a CS. For instance, the occasion setter need not have a direct association with the US (in our example, the food) and, like context, occasion setters do not merely summate with other CSs to determine associative strength (Bouton & Swartzentruber 1986).

There is no doubt that context can serve as the controlling element in a conditional discrimination, i.e., can bias an animal to use a particular solution to a discrimination problem. For instance, Edwards, Miller, and Zentall (1985) had pigeons learn two alternative solutions to a matching problem—to select the one of two stimuli that matches a previous sample or to select the one that does not match the previous sample—based on the illumination context. The birds learned, for example, that when a plus was the sample and a circle and plus the alternatives at test, they should select the plus (match) if the test chamber was illuminated but the circle (mismatch) if the chamber was dark. Next, the birds were presented a new problem with red or green stimuli. They were to match the sample if the chamber was illuminated but to mismatch if dark (or vice versa). The previous experience helped them learn this, as if they had acquired a concept of matching and mismatching. *Concept* may not be the most appropriate term (as an alternative, Zentall and his colleagues prefer *relation-based responses*), but there is no doubt that this is a relatively high level of cognitive behavior.

The prediction of a CS-US relationship by a context is an elementary example of a hierarchical structure of knowledge. Such a structure has been favored by most theorists who have developed models of memory and the nature of knowledge. This is the familiar branching network in which a proposition leads to alternatives that in turn lead to other alternatives, i.e., a series of if-then statements. There seems little doubt that context provides a critical if portion of the statement, which in turn leads to the expectation of particular relationships. When stored as part of a memory for a particular episode, a certain context elicits the relational attributes of that memory and thereby enhances memory retrieval. We turn next to some examples of such effects.

THE ROLE OF CONTEXT IN MEMORY RETRIEVAL

There is no doubt that less retention can be expected if the context during testing differs sufficiently from that during learning. Part of a study by Gordon et al. (1981) provides a straightforward example. Rats were trained on a simple one-way active avoidance task in one room (context A) and tested 24 hours later in either the same or a different room (context B). Although the conditioned stimulus and task cues remained the same, retention performance was substantially impaired when testing took place in a different room. This effect of context change is illustrated in Figure 3-1. This context shift effect is ubiquitous, observed in a remarkably wide variety of circumstances and for different kinds of animals. One could, for instance, train a rat to run an alley rapidly or to turn one way or the other in a maze for food, or teach a pigeon that pecking at red results in food but pecking at blue does not. If the rat is then tested in a maze with walls that look different or floors that feel different or smell different from the original, or if the pigeon is tested with a slightly tilting floor or a different ambient illumination, retention performance will be poorer than if those changes had not occurred: the rat will run more slowly or tend to turn the wrong way in the maze and the pigeon will be more likely to peck at blue as well as red colors (for reviews see Spear 1978; Thomas 1985, 1991).

These effects may not tell us anything about memory, however. It is only through careful experimental analysis that we can determine if it is memory and not some other aspect of behavior that is affected by contextual change. For instance, test performance could be impaired after a change in context just because the animal is distracted from its movement by the contextual change or orients to the new context, especially if the context is novel (Thomas & Empedocles 1992). Yet, the contextual change effect still occurs when accurate retention requires passive avoidance, conditioned suppression, or simple choice—measures that do not depend on how rapidly the animal moves. The effect also occurs whether or not the change in context introduces novel stimuli (e.g., Honey, Willis & Hall 1990). Such facts indicate that these nonmemory effects of context need not contaminate the memory effects.

To understand the contextual change effect, we must identify three stages of analysis that have taken place. The first is analysis of different forms of this effect. For instance, two separable types of context may both meet the definition of being relatively weak predictors of critical events such as the reinforcer and are in turn better predicted by events within the context. There is, on the one hand, intratask

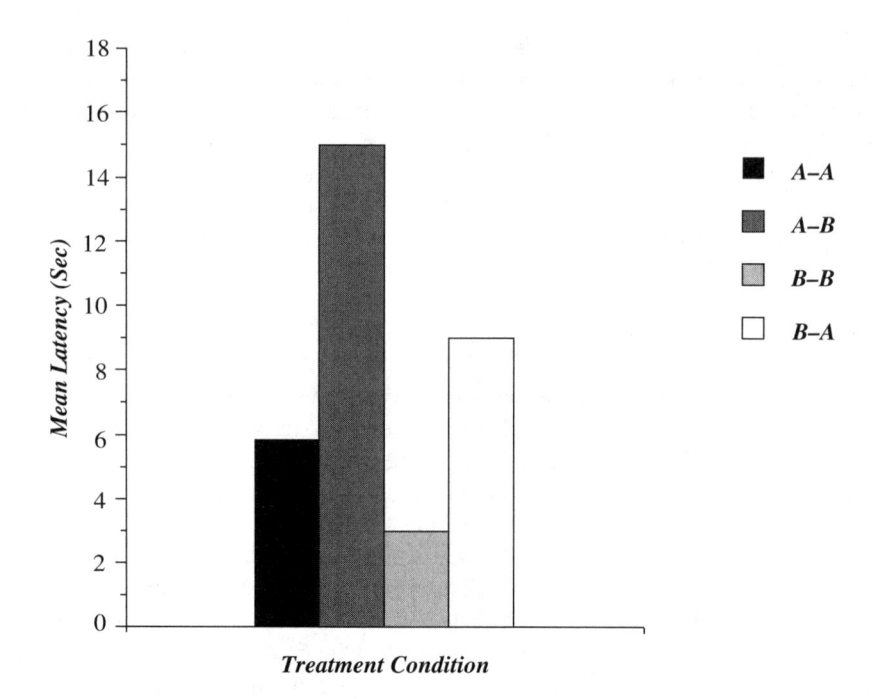

FIGURE 3-1 Retention of active avoidance is shown for animals conditioned and tested in the same context (room) or conditioned and tested in different contexts. Retention is determined by latency to leave the compartment and stimuli previously associated with the aversive US, so that higher numbers indicate poorer retention. It is quite clear that retention was poorer for animals conditioned and tested in different contexts (A-B and B-A). (Modified from Gordon et al. 1981.)

context, which refers to contextual aspects intrinsic to the task itself. These aspects would no longer be present if a specific learning episode were gone. Extratask context, on the other hand, refers to contextual events that are relatively independent of a specific episode and may remain even after the end of the episode.

For instance, suppose that a pigeon learns to discriminate a vertical line from a horizontal line. If these alternative lines, one reinforced and one not, always appear on a green disk, then green would form part of the intratask context. But if this discrimination problem also happened to be given always at 9:00 A.M. in a well-lit chamber that had a loud exhaust fan, then noisy-bright-morning would be part of the extratask context. For a word to be remembered by humans, it is conventional that other words form the intratask context. For instance, you might be required to memorize the word *bat* by studying the sentence "The second baseman dropped his *bat*" (contrast this with what is remembered given a different intratask context such as, "The vampire dropped his *bat*"). The learning of this word also could take place in either your home or classroom, which would be instances of extratask context. It is uncertain whether these two types of context have different effects on memory (e.g., Spear 1978; Thomas 1985), but this is the nature of the analysis that is required.

The second stage of analysis, the one that has attracted the most attention of scientists so far, is testing the generality and limits of the context effect on memory. We consider this stage before proceeding to third stage, which is to explain the effect.

GENERALITY AND LIMITATIONS OF THE CONTEXTUAL CHANGE EFFECT

Suppose a rat learns to run rapidly or to press a lever vigorously for food and does this during a single training session in which the air smells of lemon and there are stripes on the walls. If the rat is then tested in a context that is neither lemony nor striped, there will be relatively little fast running or vigorous lever-pressing. One interpretation is that memory retrieval is deficient in its effectiveness. It could also be argued that memory for the episode was unaffected—that access to the memory representing the relationship between running or lever-pressing and food was intact—and the rat's behavior was not directed because the appropriate instruction was missing.

That context might serve as an instruction to animals seems plausible after significant experience with a learned discrimination that is conditional upon context, of the form: if context X, then respond as if B follows A; but if context Y, then respond as if C follows A. Particularly in this case—when the circumstances are similar to those of the conditional discrimination and a large number of pairings are given with each context—it is reasonable to conclude that context may be no more than an instruction. The implication is, again, that perhaps access to the target memory is unaffected by absence of the context; if the animal could only be instructed in some other way as to which relationships were in effect, there would be no forgetting, i.e., no contextual change effect.

Although this may be an appropriate interpretation of some characteristics of conditional discriminations or occasion setters, it is unlikely to explain the more conventional contextual change effect. An important source of evidence for this comes from studies of human memory. In such studies context is not the only source of instruction as to what relationships will occur in a given situation. Language can be used to instruct humans. At a memory test humans are told which particular episodes they are to remember. Moreover, if they are not given some kind of verbal instruction, they probably would become suspicious and confused. Such a circumstance could introduce effects of emotion or of social interactions with the experimenter that have little to do with remembering, and so in this sense it is virtually impossible to test adult human memory without at least some verbal instruction. This is, as mentioned earlier, one of the unique advantages of studying memory with nonverbal animals.

The more pertinent point, however, is that the effect of context on memory cannot simply be instructional, because humans show substantial contextual change effects despite a full set of verbal instructions as to precisely what relationships they are to remember. The following studies have been conducted with humans on this topic.

The Contextual Change Effect on Human Memory

McGeoch (1942) emphasized two primary sources of forgetting: interference, which we will discuss later, and altered stimulating conditions at the time of the retention test, more relevant at this point. Despite the investigator's attempt to hold constant the stimulus situation in memory studies, inevitably some shifts occurred between training and testing. McGeoch suggested that this change in similarity of the contexts is an important factor in producing forgetting. Although anecdotal evidence supports the contention that contextual similarity is important in memory, more direct evidence comes from laboratory studies.

Experiments testing the effect of contextual change on retention of verbal materials have involved either of two procedures. With a variation in intratask context the contextual circumstances could clearly influence the perception or encoding of the verbal materials themselves. For example, stimulus words might be printed in red for learning and green during testing or presented white on black on one occasion but black on white on another. A homograph (a word that can mean different things in different settings) might be presented in one linguistic context during presentation and another for recognition. The word *pitcher* presented beside the word *water* would be learned as a kitchen utensil; if *pitcher* is represented beside the word *baseball* during a test of recognition, the difference in meaning caused by this different context has sometimes been found to impair recognition of the word.

The second general procedure has modified extratask context so that it is unlikely to alter the perception or encoding of the critical materials to be remembered. In these instances, special measures are taken to ensure that the perception does not differ across alternative contexts. Rand and Wapner (1967) used two alternative contexts for presentation and testing—the subject either stood erect or lay down on his or her back. They found that words learned in one context, physical position, were less likely to be recalled if tested in the other context than if tested in the same context. Rand and Wapner took great care to position the materials to be remembered so that perception of the items would be equal in either context. Even though the context of importance was irrelevant to the learning task with this procedure, contextual incongruity impaired retention. It is this second procedure, involving extratask environmental cues, that is of greater interest here.

Throughout a variety of tests with different kinds of context and either animals or humans as subjects, two primary experimental designs are used to assess the context effect. For the state-dependent design (shown in Table 3-1), four separate groups of subjects represent all possible combinations of learn X in context A or B and tested for memory of X in context A or B. This design permits assessment of the simple effects of each context on learning and on testing, as well as the effect of the change in context. For the alternative design (shown in Table 3-2)—the state-

TABLE 3-1 State-Dependent Paradigm (Between-Groups Design)

	Context at Testing	
Context at Learning	A	B
A	A–A	A–B
B	B–A	B–B

discrimination paradigm—subjects learn X in context A, then learn Y in context B. Later they are tested in A or B. If the context controls what is remembered, we should expect better retention of X when tested in context A and better retention of Y when tested in context B.

Effects of Simple Context on Human Memory: The Smith Experiments

Several experiments by Steven Smith and his colleagues (Smith 1979; Smith, Glenberg & Bjork 1978) addressed the scope of the influence of extratask contextual stimuli. They studied how and why common changes in context, such as learning in one room and trying to remember in another, might have an effect on retention. The experimental designs they used were variants of the state-dependent design (Table 3-1), and the results frequently indicated that when learning and testing occurred in the same room, recall could be as much as 30 to 50 percent greater than when learning occurred in one room and testing in a different room. These experiments tell us a good deal about the context effect and are partially described next.

TABLE 3-2 State Discrimination Paradigm (Within-Subjects Design)

Phase 1: Training

	Response X	Response Y
A	A–X	–
B	–	B–Y

Phase 2: Testing

Test
A ⟶ ?
B ⟶ ?

What did Smith and his colleagues use as context in these experiments? The contextual differences were multidimensional and extensive. For instance, in the above experiment one context was on the fifth floor of the Psychology Building near the animal laboratories. The experimental room itself was filled with computer equipment. During learning or testing, the subjects sat in a crowded, soundproof booth inside the room where words were presented via a tape recorder. The alternative context was a larger room in the basement of this same building with ". . . huge orange drapery hanging from the ceiling, posters and pictures on the walls, plastic plants, carpeting, a sink, books, a table, and chairs" (Smith 1979). In this context, the words were projected onto the wall by a slide projector and appeared in typed, capital letters.

Is the Context Effect Due to Novelty of the Test Context?
This possibility is especially important for context effects found in tests with animal subjects. Because the anxiety of animals cannot be quelled by verbal reassurance from the experimenter, the responses of animals to a novel context can be blatantly obvious and especially disruptive. With human subjects, this factor is more subtle and often overlooked; mild attentional disruption is not viewed as an important factor in the learning of words or stories. Also, prior experience with context is difficult to control with human subjects, unlike with animals, and this discourages attempts to test its effect, despite its importance.

To test the importance of the novelty of the testing context for humans, Smith (1979) tested the recall of subjects in a context (room and furnishings) different from the one in which they learned. There were three stages in this experiment. For the first stage all subjects were presented 80 common nouns and given an immediate test for recognition of a few of them. This was to convince them that their task was over (they were unaware that later they would be asked to recall the words in the same or a different context). The second stage was the familiarization stage in which some subjects became acquainted with the context where they were to be tested. The third stage was the critical test for recall. One group of subjects studied and recalled the words in the same context and another studied and recalled the words in different contexts. The third group was like the second—presented the words and tested for them in different contexts—but before recalling they were given familiarization experience in the testing room. The results were straightforward: recall by subjects presented the words and tested in the same context was about 30 percent greater than recall by subjects who learned and recalled the words in different contexts, and the latter subjects were equally impaired in their recall whether or not they were familiar with the testing room. In comparison to the consequences of learning and recalling in different contexts, the relative novelty of the testing context seemed unimportant.

The Smith et al. experiments are useful because they provide both a well-controlled illustration of an effect suspected and observed anecdotally by psychologists for many years: that retention can be determined by common, really mundane aspects of the context that otherwise seem quite irrelevant to what is to be remembered. The experiments of Smith et al. do more than show how substantial this effect can be, however. They also have helped us understand the context effect through answers they provided for the following questions.

Does Context Help Determine How a Word Is Perceived or Encoded?

When a word occurs twice within a single presentation of a list, subsequent recall of that word is better the greater the number of other words intervening between its first and second occurrence—the lag effect. Previous experiments had indicated that the lag effect may occur because a repeated word will more likely be encoded differently on its first and second appearances if a large number of other words are presented between these appearances. Different encodings of the same word frequently have been found to facilitate its recall. There is evidence that if a different semantic context is imposed on two repetitions of a word, for instance, *jam* paired first with the word *traffic*, then later with the word *strawberry*, recall of *jam* will be better than if the word is presented in the same semantic context each time (Light & Carter-Sobell 1970). Smith et al. asked whether a similar benefit would occur in terms of general physical context. They gave two presentations of 40 common nouns in either the same context, both in room P or both in room M or one of the presentations in room P and the other in room M. Subjects were then tested for recall in a third context, different from either P or M. The percentage of words that were correctly recalled was 61 percent for subjects presented the words once in room P and then again in room M, but only 40 percent for those presented the words in the same context on both occasions (Smith et al. 1978). These results support the hypothesis that differences in physical context may lead to significant differences in how words are encoded for later recall. Of practical significance, these results also show that repetition may lead to better recall if the material to be remembered occurs in a variety of locations.

Is the Physical Presence of the Learning Context Essential for the Context Effect?

The above results indicate that subjects associate aspects of the room with particular words they are to remember. One word might (somehow) be associated with the lamp in the corner, another with a particular chair, another with the south window, and so forth. This technique for remembering would be like the method of loci mentioned earlier, the mnemonic technique used by the ancient Greeks and Romans to remember speeches. If so, must the room where learning occurred be physically present during testing? Could a different context nevertheless allow effective retention, provided that the subject retrieves a clear memory of the room where learning took place?

For subjects who learned a set of words in room A and were tested in room B, Smith (1979) enhanced the memory for room A prior to the recall test. Some subjects were presented actual photographs of room A. Others were told they should try to remember the details of room A because it might help them in recalling the words. To help them remember these details they were asked to write down the location of room

A and ten things they could remember in that room. They were then given 2 minutes to "... think about room A, what it looked like, what sounds and smells were there, and the way it made them feel." Although tested in a different room, subjects in these two groups recalled as many words as those who learned and were tested in the same room, and about 50 percent more than control subjects who learned and were tested in different rooms but were not reminded about the room in which they learned. The general finding is that remembering the context can aid retention in the same way as the physical presence of that context. An analogous effect has been found with animal subjects (Gordon 1981).

Remembering the Context Itself
A clear memory of the context of learning seems to compensate for the disadvantage of having to recall in a different context. What determines memory for context? A reasonable hypothesis is that memory for context is governed by the same principles as any other memory. One such principle is the action of retroactive interference—impairment in remembering events due to intervening acquisition of conflicting memories. For the moment, we can consider interference as akin to confusion among memories, in this case, various contexts. Smith (1979) sought to determine whether experience with interfering contexts would influence memory for the context of original learning. Half of his subjects learned and recalled in the same rooms and half in different rooms, and within each of these groups, after subjects learned a set of words in one room, half then experienced four additional different rooms and half one additional room. After all subjects were presented the words to be recalled in one room, they were then given four other mental tasks (e.g., multiplication problems, judging the angle of rotation of letters, etc.); for some subjects all of these were given in a single different room, but others had one of these tasks in each of four different rooms. Subjects exposed to four different rooms between learning and testing were expected to have more difficulty remembering the original context than those exposed to only one room.

Subjects tested in a room different from that of learning were prompted, as in the previous experiment, to remember aspects of the learning room. This prompting was effective for those subjects exposed to only one intervening room in this experiment; these subjects recalled the critical words with about the same accuracy whether they learned and recalled in the same room or in different rooms. For those subjects exposed to five different rooms between learning and the test, however, the attempted enhancement of the learning context memory was ineffective, apparently impaired by the interference from learning about so many different rooms. Due presumably to this interference, prompting of the memory for context did not alleviate the recall deficit for subjects given learning and testing in different rooms

These experiments indicate that for recall, a clear memory of the context of learning can be as effective as having the context itself physically present. Also, retrieval of this memory for context may be subject to the same principles that govern retrieval of any other memories: interaction between the factors of contextual similarity and interference from conflicting memories.

For animals as well as humans, the factors of contextual similarity and interference continuously interact to promote or impede remembering. This interaction will be considered again in our later discussion of the ways in which interference affects memory.

Generality of the Contextual Change Effect

The message intended so far is: circumstances of context that surround learning and remembering in apparently insignificant fashion can nevertheless exert important control over what is remembered and expressed in behavior. This influence of context has both a positive and a negative side. Context can help organize our memories so that what we have learned is not inevitably emitted and associations with a particular stimulus are not inevitably elicited; expression of memories is therefore selective in accord with context and so orderly and efficient. This makes our behavior more intelligent, a positive consequence. In some circumstances, however, we are unable to retrieve a memory because the context differs from that present when the memory was acquired, a negative consequence.

To further illustrate the generality of the contextual change effect on retention, the following examples included both the positive and the negative sides of this feature of our memory process.

A Context Effect in Deep-Sea Diving

In the 1970s, it became apparent that much of the world's needs for scarce natural resources, and for oil in particular, might be met by tapping those parts of the earth that are underwater. Increasing numbers of workers spent more and more time underwater taking surveys, constructing oil rigs, etc. These people inevitably are required to remember information they had acquired on land while underwater. Conversely, they must gather information underwater that would have to be remembered later when on land. There were some suggestions of impairment in learning or remembering by persons working underwater. Because those persons who had learned underwater were tested only on land, however, it was possible that state-dependent effects might be responsible for impaired retention in these circumstances, rather than a direct effect of submersion on learning or memory.

Godden and Baddeley (1975) tested this state-dependent retention hypothesis. They conducted two experiments in which experienced divers studied a number of lists of words in either of two circumstances: sitting about 20 feet underwater, with weights to keep them stable and scuba apparatus for breathing, or seated at the edge of the water without masks, breathing air normally. Tests for recall were given either on land or underwater. In accord with the standard state-dependent retention paradigm (Table 3-1) some of the subjects learned and recalled in the same circumstances, while others did so in different circumstances—learning underwater and recalling on land, or vice versa.

Overall recall was equally effective whether the subjects had studied on land or underwater. Also, there were no differences in recall whether testing occurred on

Learning Environment

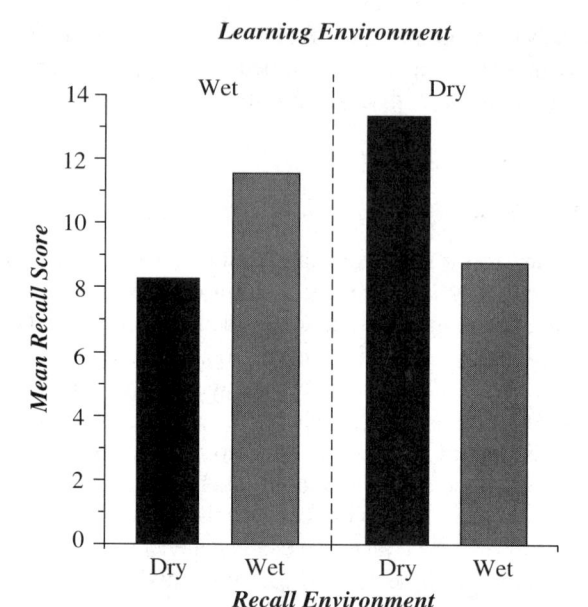

[Bar chart showing Mean Recall Score by Recall Environment, with Wet and Dry learning conditions. Wet learning: Dry recall ≈ 8, Wet recall ≈ 11.5. Dry learning: Dry recall ≈ 13.5, Wet recall ≈ 8.5.]

FIGURE 3-2 Recall of words learned by divers on land or under water is shown as a function of the context in which recall was requested. Recall was poorer when the context (wet or dry) of recall differed from that of learning. (Modified from Godden & Baddeley, 1975.)

land or underwater. As can be seen in Figure 3-2, what made a difference was whether subjects studied and were tested in the same circumstances or in different circumstances; when both the study and the test occurred on land or underwater, the number of words recalled was about 50 percent greater than if the study had been on land and the testing underwater, or if the study had been underwater and the testing on land.

The results of this undersea experiment are pertinent not only because of their practical significance. They also represent an influence on retention by a changing context that includes not only clear internal factors, like those induced by a drug or strong anxiety state, but in addition, external factors such as where the subject is, what he or she hears or sees, and so forth.

External Contextual Stimuli Control Expression of Basic Conditioning

A phenomenon termed *switching* has been studied by the Russian psychologist Asratian and his colleagues (Asratian 1965). It is defined, in our terms, by the selective expression of a response to a CS; (we are referring now to Pavlovian conditioning) in one context that differs from the response to the same CS in a different context. Switching provides a dramatic illustration that conditioned responding to a particular stimulus depends upon the context. For instance, a dog might be given several presentations of a bell followed by a mild footshock and becomes conditioned to withdraw its foot upon the occurrence of the bell. Pairings of the bell and footshock are given each morning by a particular experimenter. Each afternoon, a different experimenter conditions the same dog by presenting the identical bell, but instead of a footshock, this time the bell is followed by food placed into the mouth of the dog, to induce conditioned salivation. Before long, whenever the test is given in the morning by the first experimenter, the dog responds to the bell by withdrawing its foot but not salivating; in the afternoon when tested by the second experimenter, the dog responds to the same bell by salivating, but does not withdraw its foot. If some aspect of the context is changed—for example, if the second experimenter should test the dog in the morning or the first experimenter test it in the afternoon—then the animal is likely to both salivate and withdraw its foot in response to the bell (Asratian 1965).

This contextual control could be due to acquired associations between each context and the particular CS-US contingency in that context, promoted perhaps by separate associations between each context and the CS and between each context and the US. The general implication, however, is that the contextual stimuli—the experimenter and time of day—were the important discriminative attributes of the memories that determined the appropriate response attribute.

Stimulus context has also been shown to control the expression of memories for instrumental learning. For example, if rats are given a single session of training to turn right for food in a T-maze, and then in a different experimental room are given a session of learning to turn left, retrieval of the memories to turn right or to turn left appears to be determined by the room in which the animal is tested (Chiszar & Spear 1969; Zentall 1970). The implication is that retrieval of a particular target memory attribute (representing left alternative or right alternative) was selectively aroused by exposure to the contextual stimuli that corresponded to the context attributes of that memory.

Summary
We have seen a wide variety of instances in which the expression of learning depends on faithful reproduction of the context of that learning, even though that context might seem irrelevant to the particular associations or relationships that were learned. To say this another way, a change in contextual circumstances frequently yields forgetting.

We did not describe all aspects of context known to have this effect. For instance, Smith (1985), using college students, has reported that a shift in the auditory context (classical music versus white noise) present at training and testing can impair retention. Further, there is evidence that if learning occurs during a particular state of arousal including a particular state of sleep, optimal retention will occur only if that specific state of arousal (or sleep) is reinstated (e.g., Joy & Prinz 1969; for a review see Spear & Gordon 1981). This sort of factor might prevent us from accurately remembering our dreams, for example. Another type of internal state that can influence retention is degree of hunger or thirst. Several studies 30 or 40 years ago strongly hinted that retention is relatively poor when testing occurs under a degree of hunger or thirst different from that of learning, and more recent studies by E. D. Capaldi and her colleagues have verified and further analyzed these effects (e.g., Capaldi, Viveiros & Davidson 1981). An impressive body of research by Rovee-Collier and her colleagues has demonstrated the importance of context for memory retrieval in human infants only 3 to 6 months old (e.g., Borovsky & Rovee-Collier 1990; see Rovee-Collier 1990 for review). Taken together, the evidence for this context effect is sufficiently pervasive throughout nature that whenever forgetting is observed, we might look first to subtle contextual change as a likely cause.

Limits to the Generality of the Contextual Change Effect

You might now be concerned about whether your examinations will be given in the same room where lectures are held. The context effect suggests that recall (and hence, your grade) for an examination would be relatively poor in a classroom other than that in which the course was taught. Although a few experiments have indicated such an effect, a study by Saufley, Otaka and Bavaresco (1985) indicates instead that the contextual change effect is not important for college students in these circumstances.

Over a period of 3 years, Saufley et al. tested about 5,000 students in twenty-one experiments that included examinations for several sections of each of five different courses (Introductory Psychology, Advanced Psychology, Computer Science, Physical Anthropology, and Introductory Biology). At the time of each exam some students were selected at random from the class and given their examinations in a room quite different from their usual lecture hall, while the others took their examinations where their lectures had been given. This did not arouse suspicion among the students because, "Students were told routinely that additional room space was being used to relieve crowding in the lecture room and permit more thorough monitoring of the exam. This is a usual procedure in many courses, and there was no indication that the students considered the move as being out of the ordinary" (Saufley et al. 1985, 523). The contexts were nevertheless distinct physically. For example, for the course in Advanced Psychology some students were given the examination in the same large auditorium in which their lecture was given, whereas others were given the examination in a chemistry demonstration room that contained sixty movable desks on two levels and more windows, and still others in a room that held twenty-five movable desks on a level floor and had no windows.

The results indicated that the students' scores did not depend on where the examination was taken. In none of the twenty-one experiments did subjects in the changed-context condition score significantly lower than those in the same-context condition, and in some experiments the scores of the changed-context subjects were numerically higher than those of the same-context subjects.

It seems clear for practical purposes that neither students nor professors need worry about the similarity between examination rooms and lecture rooms. There are good reasons for this. First, much of the learning tested on an examination for a course does not take place in the room where the lectures are presented. A good deal of the learning for any course takes place when the students study or discuss the course material away from the classroom, in a context such as their dormitory rooms or the library. We have seen from the studies by Smith that the contextual-change effect diminishes if learning has taken place in a variety of different contexts. Second, we have also seen that the contextual-change effect is reduced by giving experience with a variety of testing rooms, and of course college students have had experience with a variety of testing rooms in their various courses. Third, although some previous experiments had reported contextual-change effects in classroom situations, these effects were either relatively weak (Abernathy 1940) or were based on tests with younger subjects (Jensen, Harris & Anderson 1971). There is some indication that relatively immature animals or children may be more susceptible to the contextual-change effect (Spear 1984a). For the contextual change effects that have occurred in a classroom situation, it is perhaps more difficult to understand why the effect was obtained (Metzger et al. 1979).

In the laboratory, too, there remains some question as to what determines the contextual-change effect in human memory. The problem is that with different rooms to represent context change, as in the experiments discussed by Smith, the contextual-change effect has not always been found. A particularly thorough set of experiments failing to find this effect was published by Fernandez and Glenberg (1985). Glenberg had participated with Smith in some of the early experiments that showed substantial contextual-change effects in similar circumstances.

Fernandez and Glenberg conducted eight separate experiments and were unable to find a consistent disadvantage in recall for subjects given their recall test in a room different from that in which they had learned a set of words. Fernandez and Glenberg concluded that although the contextual change effect in general is an important determinant of retention and forgetting, probably for real life situations as well as laboratory experiments, manipulating the differences between study and test rooms for human verbal memory "... does not capture the critical features of natural changes in context that produce the same-context advantage" (Fernandez & Glenberg 1985, 344).

What is not clear is when a change in external contextual features may be expected without fail to disrupt retention. One condition contributing to this effect has been suggested to be when persons specifically encode aspects of their environment along with the materials to be learned (Eich 1985). This may be a sufficient condition, but it is probably not necessary in view of the large number of instances of the contextual-change effect in circumstances in which perceptual or associative links between context and the target memory seem obscure and unlikely to be learned. It is nevertheless certain that a change in external context will remain an important source of forgetting for humans and animals in a wide variety of circumstances.

We turn next to another case of a contextual change effect, that associated with changes in internal context corresponding to chemically induced state changes in animals or humans.

STATE-DEPENDENT RETENTION

We anticipate retention, i.e., the expression of acquired information, rather than forgetting, when the circumstances of remembering include events that correspond to the attributes stored as the original memory for the episode. Significant deviation in this correspondence could lead either to a failure to retrieve the memory of that episode or to retrieval of a conflicting memory that happens to have similar attributes. The previous discussion emphasized that change in the external contextual environment can induce forgetting. What about our internal environment, our neurophysiological context? If internal contextual stimuli also influence remembering and forgetting, we should observe state-dependent expression of memory—the waxing and waning of retention in accord with either drug-induced changes in state or with internal state changes that occur from relatively natural circumstances.

A common instance of state-dependent retention is the effect produced if one learns something when intoxicated with alcohol but is asked to remember it when in a sober state, or vice versa. This effect is easily appreciated and frequently is a topic in folklore or entertainment. It was illustrated, for instance, in two classical silent movies. In *The Covered Wagon,* a film about the Wild West produced over 60 years ago, an old geezer is given a critical message while he is heavily intoxicated with alcohol. Later he attempts to deliver the message when sober but cannot remember it. Then at a critical moment later in the movie, he becomes re-intoxicated and promptly recites the saving message. The other film is a Charlie Chaplin classic, *City Lights.* Charlie is invited to be a guest in the home of a wealthy, but heavily intoxicated, man. When sober the next morning, the man fails to recognize Charlie and has him thrown out; then he becomes drunk again and invites Charlie as a guest once more, then becomes sober and throws him out again, and so on. Classical literature also alludes to state-dependent retention. In *The Moonstone,* an early and important detective novel by Wendel Collins, published in 1868, the mystery of the missing gem hinges around opium-induced state-dependent memory in one of the characters. (For a fascinating description of the author and his prescient psychopharmacological insights see Siegel [1983].) Furthermore, Charles Dickens, in his novel *The Mystery of Edwin Drood,* first published in 1870, writes, ". . . in some cases of drunkenness . . . there are two states of consciousness which never clash, but each of which pursues its separate course as though it were continuous instead of broken (thus, if I hide my watch when I am drunk, I must be drunk again before I can remember where). . . ." (Dickens 1870, 20). Effects of this kind are readily observed in laboratory studies of either animals or humans, although humans have seemed resistant to the effect when moderate doses of drugs are used (e.g., Mueller, Lisman & Spear 1982; Spear & Mueller 1984). Because high doses are difficult or impossible to administer to humans for experimental purposes, analysis of the effect may have to proceed with animals.

In state-dependent retention (SDR), learning acquired under one state (typically drug-induced) fails to transfer to a retention test conducted in the absence of that state. Such an outcome by itself could reflect impairment of long-term storage—except that the learning reappears if the state is re-induced at the time of testing. Since storage impairment precludes recovery of performance, the memory lapse in changed states is attributable to the lack of necessary cues, hence, state-dependent retention.

Experimental Analysis of State-Dependent Retention

Although several studies of drugs and learning in the 1950s suggested that drugs might have important stimulus properties, Overton (1964) provided one of the first definitive demonstrations of SDR. Because many centrally acting agents have general depressant and other motivational effects that could complicate interpretation of tasks measuring the strength of a response, Overton used a discriminative task where accuracy of choice to escape electrical shock was the dependent variable. Rats first were trained to escape shock by turning left (or right) in a T-maze; during training trials the incorrect goal box was blocked by a barrier. A single daily training trial was given for 10 to 15 days. Prior to training rats were injected with sodium pentobarbitol or saline (control injection), so for the first training the rat was in either a drugged or a nondrugged condition. In the critical part of the experiment the rats received a series of daily test trials, some while in the drugged condition and some in the nondrugged condition. The results revealed a substantial degree of dissociation: subjects made virtually no errors when tested in the same state as training, but performed at a random level of choices when in the state different from training. Apparently the presence of the training state, whether pentobarbitol or saline, was a necessary condition for retrieval of the memory at testing. Although other experiments in Overton's study used a somewhat different paradigm (see below), they collectively implicated changes in the brain rather than in the peripheral nervous system as critical to the effect. Drugs that affected the rest of body without entering the brain were not very effective as discriminative stimuli, and direct manipulation of external stimuli (e.g., lights, etc.) seemed less effective than the pentobarbitol state as a contextual change. While these control experiments helped to restrict the generality of drug-induced SDR, the major impact of Overton's study was in providing a striking demonstration of stimulus control over retention by internal contextual cues.

Design of Experiments Testing State-Dependent Retention

A great many studies of SDR have been completed. Most of these have used the 2×2 design in which four conditions are generated by crossing the state at training (drug or no drug) with the state at testing (D or N) (see Figure 3-1). Thus, two groups are trained and tested in the same condition (D-D, N-N) while the other two are tested in a condition different from training (D-N, N-D). With some agents, the dissociation is readily apparent; the two mismatched groups perform more poorly than either of the same-state groups. It is common, however, to find agents that yield dissociation only with one set of switched conditions, asymmetrical SDR. When SDR is asymmetrical, the impaired performance is almost always in the group trained with the drug but tested in the nondrugged condition. In this case, adding a new context (D) at testing is less detrimental than removing a special context (D) that had been present at training. This imbalance in conditions necessary for SDR generates some puzzling theoretical issues (Berger & Stein 1964; Overton 1978, 1984).

Although the 2×2 design has inherent limitations, especially when drugs exert multiple effects on performance (Overton 1978, 1985), it has gained considerable popularity not only because of its simplicity, but also because the four conditions permit investigators to evaluate contributions of nonmemorial factors. Let us examine this feature more closely. Although our interest is in the same versus switched states, including only two groups would be inadequate. Had the comparison been between only one switched condition (D-N) and a same state group (N-N), the performance difference obtained might be interpreted as failure to learn in the presence of the drug. This problem is not corrected by comparing the mismatched group (D-N) with the other same state group (D-D), because now we have the possibility that the drug enhances performance at testing, and the savings would be achieved even in the absence of any prior learning. Notice, however, that poor performance in the mismatched group given saline at training and drugs at testing can control for the latter concern. As these considerations imply, interpretation is much simpler in symmetrical SDR, where both mismatched states are similar to each other and inferior to the two same state groups. The issue becomes more complex when only one of the changed-state groups is inferior to the same-state control groups, i.e., asymmetrical SDR. Moreover, as mentioned earlier, the asymmetrical SDR, in which a drug or another agent at testing only (N-D) has no detrimental effect on retention, is fairly common (Overton 1985). Even this situation, however, may represent a type of selective memory retrieval failure in the D-N condition. Although the 2×2 design continues to have appeal, certain patterns of outcomes are difficult to interpret, and some investigators have opted for more complex designs and tasks.

Variables Affecting State-Dependent Retention
Several variables appear to be critical in terms of their influence on SDR. Type and amount of drug certainly determine whether or not SDR occurs. The effective drugs are those known to act directly on the central nervous system—alcohol, amphetamine, atropine, and the barbiturates, all centrally acting agents, are among the drugs inducing SDR. Drugs that produce only peripheral changes without entering the brain are either not effective or less effective than centrally acting agents. Central versus peripheral effects can clearly be demonstrated with certain drugs that have two chemical forms, one of which acts both centrally and peripherally and the other only peripherally. For example, scopolamine has both central and peripheral influences and can induce dissociative learning. In contrast, methylscopolamine, a closely

related compound having only peripheral effects, does not produce SDR. This indicates that it is the central action that is responsible for SDR. Drug dose is important as well. Typically, the intensity (dose) of an SDR agent has to exceed some threshold level before it is effective. But even very high levels of peripherally acting drugs do not allow them to function as dissociative agents.

SDR appears quite sensitive to the strength of learning of the target task. Studies have shown that extensive training (overtraining) will attenuate or completely eliminate SDR. Whereas weakly learned responses will not transfer across drug states, a more strongly learned response may occur regardless of the drug state. Perhaps a corollary of this principle is that SDR is best obtained when the retention task does not provide extensive retrieval cues. It is a fairly common observation in SDR research with humans that a drug that produces memory dissociation with a free recall test will have no effect on retention in terms of a recognition test, which presents the actual item to be remembered as an alternative and hence includes a good retrieval cue (e.g., Eich 1980). Apparently, if a sufficient number of retrieval cues are provided to the subject, the importance of the internal drug context is greatly reduced.

An important but not yet fully resolved question is whether the stimulus conditions produced by a drug state are special or unique. For example, decrements in performance resulting from a change in drug state (mismatched groups) share an obvious resemblance to findings with changes in external features of context. Is state-dependent retention simply another example of the general consequences of contextual-change, but with drug-related cues rather than manipulation of external stimuli? Or, is there some unique process—perhaps the nature of the brain state—that is involved when various drugs produce SDR?

It is difficult to draw a firm distinction between internal or interoceptive, and external or exteroceptive events. All experience is mediated in the brain whether the source is inside or outside the body. Some early theories of state-dependent retention claimed that this effect represents a unique action of drugs, unlike anything producible by natural stimuli. The drugs were thought to act, in effect, by switching on and off separate areas of the brain; when one brain area was turned on during training but off during testing, or vice versa, retention could not be expected. An alternative view is that to induce state dependence, drugs merely alter neurotransmitter activity in much the same way as events in our environment alter neurotransmitter activity when they are processed in the brain. At this point, however, we consider it best to take the view that the mechanisms of state-dependent retention are the same, whether induced by drugs or external stimuli (also see Overton 1982; Spear 1981).

State-Dependent Effects in Human Memory

Like many of the other memory phenomena described in this book, state-dependent retention is seen in humans as well as animals. Alcohol, which is often consumed because of its effects on the central nervous system, has been widely investigated as a dissociative agent with humans. An early study by Goodwin et al. (1969) confirmed the presence of SDR with alcohol. Volunteer subjects were assigned to one of the four combinations of alcohol (A) or placebo (P) at training and alcohol or placebo at testing (A-A; A-P; P-P; P-A). A battery of tasks was employed, ranging from avoidance learning to verbal recall to picture recognition. Generally, subjects given alcohol at training but saline at testing did more poorly than either of the same-state groups. There was some evidence that alcohol depressed performance at acquisition (see also Birnbaum & Parker [1977] for a similar finding), but this cannot account for the fact that the alcohol-alcohol group was superior to the alcohol-saline group. As in many of the animal SDR studies, the disassociation in humans has tended to be asymmetrical; the mismatch group receiving alcohol at testing only (S-A) performs about as well as the two matched groups.

Is alcohol-induced SDR attenuated in people with extensive drinking experience, such as alcoholics? The experience would seem to afford them repeated opportunities to become familiar with the drug state as well as shifts in that state. Some evidence suggests that the opposite may be true: SDR may be slightly more pronounced in alcoholics. Weingartner and Faillace (1971) compared directly the performance of alcoholic and nonalcoholic subjects under the four conditions resulting from being intoxicated or sober at training or testing. Both types of subjects showed a modest SDR effect on free recall tests; the magnitude of the difference between the same-state and incongruent-state conditions was somewhat greater in alcoholics. While this exacerbation was not very strong in the alcoholics, the important point is that the SDR was not lessened by their previous drinking histories, and there is no doubt that the effect can occur in alcoholics (Lisman 1974). It may be, as Weingartner and Faillace suggest, that the cognitive response to verbal items in alcoholics during drinking is qualitatively different from that when they are sober, while such a difference in response is less marked in nonalcoholic drinkers.

Another popular psychoactive drug, marijuana, has at least modest state-dependent properties. In one study, college students were given either marijuana or a placebo cigarette prior to studying a list of words (Eich et al. 1975). The word list comprised a number of categories with four instances of each. The test session, some 4 hours later, was preceded by administration of the drug or placebo. Two types of tests were given: free recall of the items, followed by cued recall in which the category names were presented. The interaction between drug condition at training and that at testing was clearly seen in the uncued recall condition, demonstrating that marijuana can induce SDR. However, another important aspect of the study was the finding that the SDR effect was eliminated under the cued-recall condition. Recall was equally effective under all drug conditions so long as intratask cues were available. This study, then, also relates to the important question of sensitivity of different tests to SDR effects. As mentioned above, there is now substantial evidence that recognition and cued-recall tests, which provide a number of retrieval stimuli for the subject, are less apt to reveal dissociative learning than those in which subjects must generate their own retrieval cues (Eich 1980).

State-dependent retention in humans can be an important practical matter. For instance, when a mentally ill individual is given psychotherapy while under the influence of drugs prescribed for his illness, will the therapy be of any value when the individual no longer is taking the drugs? Will what is learned in therapy while under drugs be remembered by the individual when he or she is in everyday life, no longer under the drug treatment? As another example, is alcoholism promoted because drinking helps the individual to forget some unhappy circumstances of his or her sober life? Do people continue to drink in spite of embarrassing or damaging behavior when drunk because such unfortunate consequences of drinking are forgotten upon the return to sobriety?

On the practical side of science, studies of state-dependent retention in humans are very difficult to conduct. They require a great deal of time and special care of subjects. It is always a difficult and complex matter to conduct experiments with any sort of physiologically intrusive treatments such as drug or alcohol administration with humans. Progress in understanding state-dependent retention is therefore slow, but it can be facilitated by the more analytical experiments possible with animals and is in any case important both for medical purposes and for understanding the processing of memories in general.

Summary Principles of Drug-Induced State-Dependent Retention

The forgetting that accompanies a change in drug state—state-dependent retention—is a particularly important context effect. The topic really warrants more discussion than can be provided here. However, some general features of these effects are offered in the following summary:

1. By tapping a wide variety of drugs a rather amazing number of discriminable states, approximately two dozen or so, can be identified in animals alone. For drug states that are discriminable, a change from one during learning to another during testing nearly always impairs animal memory.

2. The drugs most readily discriminated and most effective in inducing state-dependent retention are those that readily pass the blood-brain barrier to directly alter chemical neurotransmission in the brain. Drugs that do not do so have not seemed to have state-dependent effects, even though their peripheral consequences might be detectable by human subjects.

3. State-dependent retention depends on what is to be remembered and how the memory is to be expressed. There are indications with animal subjects that discrimination learning is less subject to state-dependent retention than is learning expressed by particular behaviors (Bindra, Nyman & Wise 1965). Furthermore, a good deal of data on human memory indicates that the recognition and cued recall of learned materials are less subject to state-dependent retention than is free recall of those materials, presumably because of the greater number of retrieval cues implicitly provided by a recognition test in comparison to those provided by a free recall test.

ENDOGENOUS STATES AND MEMORY DISSOCIATION

The phenomenon of SDR appeals to many individuals besides those studying memory processes. What drugs are effective as SDR agents? What are the relative potencies of these drugs? If one drug yields SDR, are there related pharmacological agents that are functionally equivalent (or nearly so) if substituted for the first drug at testing, i.e., does drug B at test act like drug A by producing good retention even though A was the agent present at training? While there is an almost endless array of pharmacological or chemical treatments that can be evaluated, some investigators recently have chosen to focus on the more limited issue of whether naturally occurring states can be a source of SDR. The obvious importance of such a question is that all of us undergo various shifts in internal states, some periodic but others not. If these types of changes can be shown to influence memory in a state-dependent manner, the implications would have considerable practical as well as theoretical value.

One naturally occurring change involves daily biological rhythmicities, termed *circadian rhythms*. We mentioned earlier the research by Holloway and Wansley (1973a, 1973b) and Wansley and Holloway (1975) that illustrates nicely the sensitivities of memory to mismatches in these rhythms. Rats trained on a passive avoidance task did well when tested immediately, or 12 or 24 hours later (or multiples thereof), but not when tested at 6, 18, 30, or 42 hours after training (Holloway & Wansley, 1973b). Could it be that the performance changes merely reflect a direct effect of the time of day at testing? To evaluate this possibility, a control experiment was conducted in which subjects were trained at one of four times during the day and then tested at the various intervals. The results indicated that the retention patterns were determined by the training-testing interval, rather than the absolute time at training or testing. Similar effects have been reported in adult animals for a variety of learning tasks and occasionally for humans or infant animals as well (for review, see Spear 1978).

Another source of fluctuations in endogenous stimuli is the female reproductive cycle and related hormonal changes. Although these hormonal alterations are thought to affect several nonreproductive behaviors such as mood and emotionality, their role as contextual cues for memory retrieval appears to be negligible or weak at best. Ebner, Richardson, and Riccio (1981) were unable to obtain a reliable effect on retention of Pavlovian conditioned fear when female rats were trained in estrus and tested in anestrus (or vice versa), confirming a similar observation with active avoidance made by Gray (1977). Although shock may be an unusually salient US, similar negative results have been obtained in tasks which have used other types of reinforcers (Morilak et al. 1983), even when hormonal injections have been used to allow precise specification of the estrous state. In an attempt to determine if the extreme hormonal and bodily changes associated with pregnancy might not exert a more readily detectable state-dependent influence on memory, Ebner et al. (1981) compared several groups trained at one stage of pregnancy and tested at a later stage or even postpartum. Again, there was no indication that retention of conditioned fear was impaired by such mismatches.

Yet there is little doubt that pharmacological levels of certain reproductive hormones can be effective as SDR treatments. Stewart, Krebs, and Kaczender (1967) administered high doses of progesterone to ovariectomized rats and reported dissociated learning in a choice response to escape shock in a T-maze. Using a lower but still nonphysiological level of this steroid hormone, Ebner et al. obtained an asymmetrical SDR effect in Pavlovian fear conditioning: rats injected with progesterone prior to learning but injected with saline at testing showed poorer retention of fear than either of the same-state conditions. It is clear that certain hormones can act as SDR agents, but the high pharmacological dosages employed beg the original question of whether dissociative memory results from naturally occurring fluctuations in hormones.

The question of whether endogenous cycle changes modulate memory in animals is paralleled by the issue of whether mood levels or affective attributes can serve as sources of SDR in humans. Interestingly, the findings are similar to those obtained in animal studies: mood-related SDR may exist, but it does not appear to be a very robust effect. In one study, Macht, Spear, and Levis (1977) used threat of electric shock to induce a negative affective state in college undergraduates. After learning a list of words either in a neutral or shock condition, subjects were tested in the congruent or mismatched condition. While evidence of an SDR outcome was obtained in the initial experiment, the finding failed to occur with a slightly changed procedure (experiment 2) or with an exact replication (experiment 3). One possible interpretation of this outcome is simply that the mood induction technique failed to elicit a reliable and salient affective state.

Bower, Monteiro, and Gilligan (1978), using hypnosis to induce sad or happy moods, found evidence of reduced recall when their subjects were tested in the opposite state. However, as Bower (1981) noted, a critical feature of the experimental paradigm was the presence of a source of interference. For example, two lists of words were learned prior to testing: list 1 might be learned while happy and list 2 while happy or sad. When subjects were tested for recall of list 1, those tested in the sad condition (associated with list 2) did more poorly than those returned to the original happy state. When the second list was acquired in the changed mood, later induction of that same mood (opposite of list 1) at testing may have provided a source of interfering or competing responses. In contrast, list 2 items (sad) would remain isolated from interference (compartmentalized) if subjects were returned to their original list 1 mood (happy). Under this set of interference conditions, incongruent moods at training and testing impaired retention relative to same-mood groups. Bower et al. suggested that the failure to obtain SDR when only a single list was used could be due to the distinctiveness of the list. Furthermore, learning conflicting information under varied emotional states may provide an analog to naturally occurring events. Mood-related SDR has also been found by other investigators using this conflicting-learning paradigm in circumstances yielding no SDR with the single-list, more conventional test of SDR (Schare, Lisman & Spear 1984).

The issue of whether affective states in humans serve as a significant basis for dissociated learning is far from settled. Ellis and his colleagues (Ellis 1985; Leight & Ellis 1981; Ellis et al. 1985), in addition to presenting evidence for state-dependent effects of mood, have also argued that a depressed mood can impair retrieval. For example, using an incidental learning paradigm with college students, Ellis et al. (1985) gave an unexpected recall test 25 minutes after presentation of the target material. When the test was preceded by having subjects read a series of statements designed to induce depressive mood (Velten technique), their performance was inferior to that of control subjects who read neutral statements. While this retention deficit might be attributable to a state-dependent effect (from a neutral to a depressed context), Ellis et al. suggest that a more appropriate interpretation is in terms of allocation of resources in the cognitive demands of the task. According to this view, negative mood states reduce performance either because fewer resources are available at retrieval or because the associated cognitions compete directly with retrieval efforts.

If moods do exert an influence on retention, it appears to be constrained by highly defined boundary conditions, or is simply elusive. Yet most tests of the effect have employed relatively mild affective states that are within the range of almost everyone's experience. More extreme mood states, such as those associated with clinical pathological conditions, may be more potent in inducing SDR. In agreement with this possibility Weingartner, Miller and Murphy (1977) found dissociated retention in hospitalized patients who were subject to major mood swings. Patients whose behavior cycled between manic and normal served as subjects in a series of retention (retrieval) tests. The subjects' task was to recall self-generated events, i.e., their previous free-associated responses to stimulus words. Thus, training consisted of presenting nouns and asking subjects to produce a number of free-associated responses. At testing the subjects were again presented the stimulus words and asked to recall their previous responses to those items. Since the subjects' mood states were not under experimental control, the procedure was repeated at 4-day intervals in order to obtain samples of congruent and incongruent mood states between training and testing. The principal finding was that the associative responses were recalled better when the patient's moods at training and testing were matched than when they were disparate. Furthermore, clinical evaluation of the intensity of mood states suggested an inverse relationship between the recall of associations and the degree of mood change—as the size of the mood disparity increased, the number of items reproduced decreased.

This finding of Weingartner et al. may have interesting implications for personality theory and understanding of psychopathology; individuals may be more likely to recall episodes that are concordant with their current mood states. Indeed, there is some evidence to support this hypothesis (for a review see Johnson & Magaro 1987). Thus, depressed patients appear prone to recall unhappy events and less able to recall pleasant events. Such selectivity of memory could then contribute to intensifying the depressive episode.

Finally, from an evolutionary perspective, the lack of SDR effects with routine hormonal fluctuations hardly seems surprising—after all, it would not appear adaptive for organisms to suffer memory impairment as they move through their reproductive cycles. Evolution, however, is not a logical or rational plan, but the results of a myriad of selection pressures. Predictions about processes that should (or should not) have evolved sometimes go astray, so it would be unwise to dismiss the possibility of endogenous SDR effects on this basis alone.

CHAPTER SUMMARY

This chapter discussed circumstances in which context affects retention. In comparison with other stimuli in a learning episode that an individual might learn in association with a reinforcer, contextual stimuli last longer and are more constant, and hence are relatively poor predictors of the reinforcer. A fairly safe general prediction is that the more similar is context during learning and a test for retention, the better the retention. When the same context is present during learning and the retention test, its absolute distinctiveness also may promote retention.

With regard to central issues of how context influences learning and memory, it was suggested that the most important function of context is its exertion of a higher level of stimulus control than is held by more predictive stimuli such as a CS. The context indicates the conditions under which other associations may hold, or, in other words, sets the occasions for particular relationships. This function does not preclude the formation of associations between the context and other events in the learning episode, but it might work against them when there is a limit to how much can be learned about a learning episode. Finally, it was concluded that the contextual change effect is not a special case of generalization decrement.

Using Pavlovian conditioning as a model learning episode, we described samples of the concrete evidence that context may serve as a predictor for a relationship between a CS and US as well as having the potential to become associated directly with the CS and/or US. Evidence for the primary effect of context on retention—that retention is proportional to the similarity of the learning and testing contexts—was considered in terms of human and animal memory and for internal and external context. We favor the view that state-dependent retention induced by drugs is no different in kind from conventional effects of external context on retention, and so a review of state-dependent retention was presented.

▶ 4

Significant Sources of Forgetting

Interference: Conflicting Memories Interfere with Retention

The second major determinant of retention and forgetting is interference. Compared with contextual change, interference probably is more pervasive, influential, and widely accepted as a source of forgetting.

WHAT KIND OF "INTERFERENCE" IS INVOLVED?

Interference can be thought of as the effect produced by conflicting memories. Memories that share attributes conflict if the attributes contain opposing information critical to behavior: if, for example, a tone that signals food later signals footshock in the same circumstances, the memories representing the two episodes are conflicting memories.

The action of interference has been viewed as largely associative, with identifiable associations disrupted by particular kinds of interference. An alternative view of interference is a nonspecific, neurophysiologically based noise in the organism's information processing system. Such a neurophysiological source of interference has been suggested to be a cause of impairment in retention associated with intense physiological trauma (e.g., Weiskrantz 1966). This idea has received little empirical support, however, and does not seem to be useful theoretically. A more specific version might yet be needed to account for the full array of memory deficits that can accompany brain trauma, but in the meantime our focus is on associative interference.

Analysis and understanding of interference effects do not require a formal theory, but a general theoretical framework is useful as a basis for interpretation. This analysis is fundamentally associative and has been identified historically with J. McGeoch, B. J. Underwood, and others.

Traditional Alternatives to Interference: Consolidation Disruption and Decay

The basic notion of interference is that associations are best remembered if competing associations are not established. For instance, remembering the association between A and B is especially difficult if an association between A and C or between C and B also is learned. In other words, if A and C share an association with B, forgetting is more likely than if A or C had an unshared association with B.

Alternative theories of forgetting that are not based on associative interference, such as consolidation or decay, are more general in terms of the processes considered responsible for forgetting. When first introduced nearly a century ago, *consolidation* referred to the neurophysiological activity presumed to be necessary after study if a memory is to be solidified into relatively permanent form. At that time it was thought that the reason verbal materials were quickly forgotten when learning of a second set of materials followed that of the first was because the second set disrupted consolidation of the first (Muller & Pilzecker 1900). Subsequent studies found, however, that it did not matter how closely the learning of one set of verbal materials followed that of another. This and more complex factors have caused consolidation to be a relatively unimportant consideration in the study of human forgetting (Keppel 1984; Weingartner & Parker 1984).

What about decay of memory? If *decay* is meant merely to describe the steady decline in learned performance as time passes since learning, there could be no debate. But decay in this sense is only a description, not an explanation. The difficulty arises when decay is meant to imply the gradual deterioration of an acquired memory. There are two problems with this. First, there is no evidence that acquired memories do in fact disintegrate in the sense of being lost forever, nor is it clear what would constitute proof of such a proposition. Moreover, given the abundant evidence for the retrieval of all sorts of memories over entire lifespans, a more reasonable working assumption might be that memories do not decay but are at least potentially accessible. The second difficulty with decay was noted by McGeoch: it can be useful scientifically only to the extent that it refers to identifiable events that occur during a retention interval, because time alone explains nothing. Although decay theory most often implies a sort of deterioration of the brain's representation of an experience, the critical events responsible for such decay of a memory have not been identified, and it seems unlikely that they could be without first identifying the neurophysiological substrate responsible for a particular memory (which has yet to be accomplished).

In 1932 McGeoch suggested interference theory as an alternative to consolidation theory or decay theory. The mechanism of interference had a distinctly different locus than that of either consolidation or decay. For consolidation the events critical to forgetting occurred just after learning. For decay they occurred throughout the retention interval, from the point of learning onward. The associative interference originally suggested by McGeoch occurred at the time of memory retrieval (or more precisely, at the time the appropriate memory was to be expressed). The critical factor was reproductive inhibition, the impossibility of simultaneously emitting two conflicting responses that had been associated with a common stimulus. If you first learn to say *rat* when *chair* appears and then learn instead to say *mouse* when *chair* appears, you will be able to give only one of these responses at a time when tested as to the first word that went with the stimuli, *chair*. If the interfering response happened to be more dominant by virtue of a stronger association than the one to be remembered, forgetting would be observed. It was soon discovered, however, that while a mechanism very much like the one McGeoch suggested could account for a great deal of forgetting, there were others at least equally important and apparently more interesting in terms of the scope of forgetting accounted for. We discuss these after distinguishing again the two major sources of interference.

The principles of interference are most readily appreciated in terms of memories for verbal materials in accord with our own personal experiences. We therefore introduce these principles in these terms first, before considering the more general case of interference in animal memory.

Retroactive and Proactive Interference

Forgetting arises from either of two sources of interference, retroactive interference and proactive interference. *Retroactive interference* refers to forgetting caused by conflicting memories acquired between acquisition and testing of the critical memory. The conflicting memory acts retroactively (backwards) to affect retention of the critical memory. (Schematically we can think of a memory as an A-B relationship, consisting of two events to be associated, stimuli A and B, responses A and B, or stimulus A and response B. A typical situation for inducing retroactive interference is when the acquisition of one response to a cue is followed by the acquisition of a different response to the same cue; this arrangement is symbolized A-B,A-D to indicate the same stimuli but different responses.) Under these conditions, retention in the group with the interpolated (second phase) learning is usually inferior to that of a control group not given the competing learning.

Suppose that A corresponds to the English word *white* and B to the French equivalent, *blanc*. Learning *white-blanc,* and then learning a German equivalent, *white-weiss,* constitutes an example of the type of conflicting memories we are describing. To the extent that retention of A-B is impaired relative to subjects who learned only A-B, retroactive interference is observed (in this case, there would be forgetting of the French word for *white*). A simple incident related by a friend will help to illustrate what is meant by the notion that competing learning can render the original target information inaccessible in a retroactive manner. Our friend recently purchased an expensive pair of brand-name ski boots. In keeping with the psychological principle of cognitive dissonance, upon arriving home he immediately began to examine the ski boot ads in several skiing magazines to justify to himself that the brand he had chosen was really among the best. When he called one of us a while later, he found to his chagrin that he could no longer recall the name of the boots he had bought! Despite the fact that he certainly knew what boots he had chosen when he got home only a few minutes earlier, the intensive examination of the names and information about a series of other boots served as a potent source of retroactive interference.

Proactive interference is less intuitively apparent as a source of forgetting, since the loss of the target memory is based upon previous learning. If we take A-B as the target information to be retrieved, then proactive interference is based on prior A-D learning. Referring to the foreign language example just presented, imagine subjects learning the German equivalent (A-D) first, and then the French (A-B). Although the A-B association is learned last, and so is not followed by competing information, the earlier learning of A-D can impair retention of A-B after a period of time has elapsed. This is easily demonstrated by comparing the retention of A-B in the A-D,A-B condition with that of control subjects not previously given the conflicting information (—,A-B). Assuming that conditions are arranged to permit equivalent degrees of learning A-B, better retention in the control condition reveals that prior learning can act as a source of proactive interference.

While writing his classic textbook McGeoch (1942) barely mentioned proactive interference; he focused on retroactive interference. This turned out to be the wrong emphasis. Proactive interference probably is the more important determinant of most forgetting, as we shall see.

The Cornerstone of Interference Theory: Similarity

Interference theory rests on the notion that interference in retention depends on the similarity between materials to be retained and interfering materials. Specifying what we mean by similarity is where the difficulty arises.

We can be fairly certain that acquiring the proper motion for the forehand and backhand in tennis is unlikely to interfere with retention of the words to your favorite popular song. But what about the effect on remembering appropriate movements in squash or handball? What about the effect of learning one new song on remembering another? Could similar sounding words be a source of interference, even if their meanings are different? If you are to remember a list of words like *pear, lion,* and *match,* each paired uniquely with a specific stimulus, will the subsequent learning of a list including *peer, lying,* and *mask* be more likely to cause forgetting than a list like *apple, tiger,* and *lighter?* In other words, is acoustical similarity more important than semantic similarity for determining interference in retention?

Such complexities are important, but should not detract from the more general implication of interference theory: if the respective contents of two memories are not at all similar, there is no reason to expect that learning one will influence retention of the other. A quite different view is illustrated in this quote from a treatise written in the sixteenth century: "To sleep hosed and shoed especially with foule socks, doth hinder the Memorie, because of the reflection of y (the) vapours." (Marshall 1991). Although we would not quarrel with the author's esthetic and personal care sensibilities, his view of memory impairment is unfounded. While it is true that events subsequent to our learning something may impair, or more accurately, interfere, with retrieval of that information, we know that these interpolated events must share some degree of similarity to the original information. Unless the "Memorie" we hope to recall later involved something like the fragrance of perfume, we probably need not worry about the presence of even "killer sneakers" in our bedroom. (Parenthetically, we might note that the research literature on retroactive interference with odors as the stimulus materials is sparse indeed!)

Basic Mechanisms and Features of Interference

The basic mechanisms of Interference Theory can best be appreciated if we remember why the theory was developed: to account for the forgetting of lists of paired verbal units, typically words or nonword combination of letters. For the experiments with human subjects that led to, and tested, this theory, these sorts of instructions were given: "When a word appears, try to say the word previously paired with it." Such a list was considered the prototype of much learning undergone by humans. Whether it is or not, this probably was the most analytical procedure with which to begin.

Although the mechanisms of interference can account for a variety of our common difficulties in remembering, they typically have been tested experimentally when subjects learned two similar lists in which the first member of each pair of words is the same, but the second member is different (Table 4-1). The A-B,A-D combination mentioned earlier is not the only form such conflicting memories could take. Other differences between the pairs also are of analytical interest, such as the A-B,A-B' (stimuli are the same, responses are different but somehow related) and A-B,A-B$_r$ (stimuli and responses are the same but re-paired randomly—hence the "r" subscript) (Underwood 1966; Jung 1967; Spear 1970).

TABLE 4-1 **Paradigms of Interference**

Condition	List 1	List 2	Test
A-B, A-D	Cup/desk	Cup/lock	Cup/?
A-B, C-D	Cup/desk	Box/home	Cup/?
RI control	Cup/desk	—	Cup/?
PI control	—	Cup/lock	Cup/?

Learn list 1; learn list 2; interval; test either list 1 (retroactive interference) or list 2 (proactive interference).

One question is, Why is retention for the first list impaired by having learned the second (i.e., why does retroactive interference occur)? The other question is, Why is retention of the second list impaired by having learned the first (i.e., why does proactive interference occur)?

There are two sets of interference mechanisms. The first set is addressed, essentially, to considerations of how an organism might get mixed up about which environmental event belongs to which memory. In the case of humans having learned two lists of the A-B,A-D type—in which the stimuli of two successive lists are identical but must be associated with different responses (e.g., *dog-chair, dog-kite*)—this mix-up might occur as response competition, an extension of McGeoch's reproductive inhibition. Although two different responses have been learned in association with the same stimulus words (one pairing in the first list and another in the second list), only one response can be given if only one list is tested for retention. So, if the incorrect response happens to be dominant at the moment of the test—the first response expressed—forgetting is observed.

Another example of the mix-up mechanism is list differentiation, or, more accurately, a lack of differentiation among the potential sources of a learned word. Forgetting may be attributed to a failure in list differentiation when a human recalls an item correctly, as learned within the context of the experiment, but recalls it with reference to the wrong list of items. In other words, interference with retention of one word list by another could occur if one of the memory attributes lost were identification to which list the particular item belongs. This mechanism has been important for explaining proactive interference. It has the advantage of being directly testable—you can easily measure how many words are recognized incorrectly as belonging to the other list. It also is generalizable in terms of sets of events other than lists of words. For instance it can apply to a situation in which an animal must remember that responses A, B, and C are appropriate in context X but D, E, and F are given only in context Y (for an analogous consideration of abnormal forgetting of the source of a memory, see chapters 10 and 11, source amnesia).

Response competition also was thought initially to be directly observable. The extent of response competition seemed measurable in terms of the number of times the incorrect responses were given. But there were two problems with this reasoning. First, when forgetting occurs subjects most often give no response at all. Second, the number of intrusions from that list—responses from list 2 mistakenly given when recalling list 1—is a poor indication of the forgetting of list 1; these intrusions can be quite independent (Melton & Irwin 1940; Melton & Von Lackum 1941).

The first experiment to test this possibility made the point quite well (Melton & Irwin 1940). Subjects studied an ordered list of 18 nonsense syllables (nonword combinations of letters, such as *pos* or *tuk*) on 5 occasions, then studied a different list of this kind on either 5, 10, 20, or 40 occasions. Correct recall of the first list was less the more the second list was practiced. The number of intrusions in recall exhibited the opposite relationship, however. Generally speaking, more practice on the interfering list led to fewer intrusions. For example, subjects given 20 interfering (second list) trials in relation to those given only 5 had retroactive interference in recall that was about 30 percent greater, yet they gave only about half as many intrusions; their mistakes, in other words, were largely omissions or misplaced responses from the same list, not incorrectly recalled items from the interfering list. You can see in Figure 4-1 that as practice on the interfering list was increased, forgetting of the first list also increased.

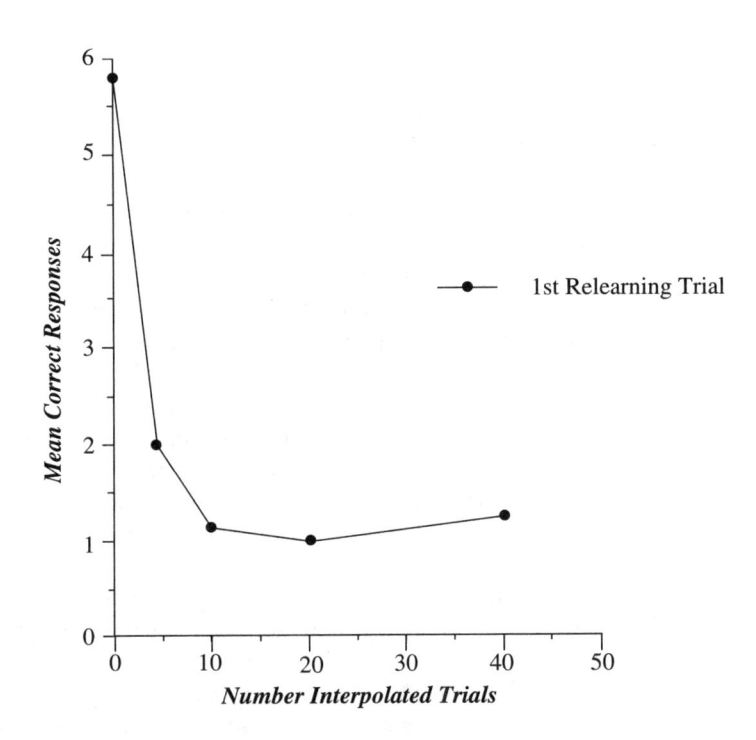

FIGURE 4-1 Number of correct responses recalled in the same order as they appeared during learning is shown for subjects given different amounts of interpolated practice learning a different list (also in serial order). The greater the number of practice trials on the interpolated list, the poorer the recall of the first list. Despite this, the number of second-list responses incorrectly given when recalling the first list (i.e., intrusions) decreased with greater numbers of second-list trials. This indicates that forgetting of the first list induced by the second (retroactive interference) could not be attributed to simple response competition reflected by intrusions. (Adapted from Melton & Irwin 1940.)

If intrusions reflected the mix-up factor, some other factor was responsible for the increase in retroactive interference when more practice on an interfering list was given. Apparently this unaccounted for factor made the responses less accessible in an absolute sense. This influence, first termed *factor X,* was soon considered to represent a type of extinction of specific responses and their associations. Extinction of responses in the first list would occur because producing these responses would be incorrect during learning of the interpolated list. Understanding of retroactive interference required analysis of this extinction factor, which was frequently referred to as *unlearning.*

Retroactive Interference
To obtain a solid index of the amount of unlearning, it became clear that consideration of intrusions did not help because so few occur in these situations. For instance, in the Melton and Irwin experiment the average number of intrusions given by each subject was less than one, and still fewer intrusions typically are observed with paired associate lists involving words rather than nonsense syllables.

A better estimate of unlearning was obtained by Barnes and Underwood (1959). We will focus here on their tests with the A-B,A-D paradigm (Table 4-1), Subjects learned the A-B list, then studied the second (A-D) list on 1, 5, 10, or 20 occasions. Using a new testing procedure intended to eliminate the mix-up factors, subjects were presented with the stimulus items and given several minutes to write down the correct responses from either list. Subjects given the A-D list correctly recalled only 6.7, 5.4, 5.0, or 4.1 responses from the A-B list, depending on whether they had studied A-D list 1, 5, 10, or 20 times. The magnitude of this effect is significant. Here we have bright young college students who had completely learned a set of 8 common adjectives only 15 minutes earlier. Yet, after studying a list with different responses, they were unable to remember about one-half of the items they had just recited perfectly. You can be sure that they wanted very much to remember them all. Subjects in these experiments go to great lengths to avoid appearing stupid to the experimenter, and you can bet also that had they been offered $5.00 for each additional correct response, they could have done no better; motivational factors have a negligible influence on remembering in these situations. Such is the power of retroactive interference.

The loss of responses need not represent an actual unlearning or extinction effect, however. The impaired expression of such recently acquired memories may be considered instead to be an active suppression of the entire set of responses associated with the first-list memory, or response set interference (Postman, Stark & Fraser 1968; for an excellent review see Postman 1976). The notion of response set interference is based on a powerful and intriguing phenomenon of human memory, the selector mechanism: subjects tend to restrict their responses to those contained in the particular list of items being learned. This mechanism—not only useful for understanding the above effects of retroactive interference, but also interesting in and of itself—permits humans to be superbly proficient in remembering what they did not learn in a particular situation. For instance, you would be highly unlikely to respond on a recall test with a word that was not presented to you for learning. In one large study requiring learning and recall of lists of 16 relatively familiar nouns, less than 1 percent of the words recalled were not in the list presented. In a slightly different experiment testing learning of pairs of common words, only 1 of 1,424 errors was a word that did not appear somewhere in the list; a subject imported the word *yellow* when the correct response was *canary*. This ability to remember what was not on a list of words is striking. We know, for instance, that these college student subjects had a vocabulary of about 75,000 words that could be given erroneously in such tests of recall (these and similar data were reported by Underwood 1964).

If the selector mechanism were used to suppress responses from a previously learned A-B list while an A-D list is learned, this might be responsible for the inaccessibility of responses from the A-B list. From this reasoning it was established that the bulk of the retroactive interference in these circumstances tends to be in accessibility of the responses—a failure in the expression of a memory, not loss of the associations or responses from memory (Postman 1976).

Proactive Interference

If there is a single factor responsible for most forgetting observed over long intervals, it probably is proactive interference. People or animals usually have acquired more potentially interfering memories prior to learning something they wish to remember than between learning and the time of remembering. But this source of forgetting was almost totally ignored during the first 50 years of scientific tests of the memory process. An important exception is a report by Whitely and Blankenship (1936) that indicated powerful effects of proactive interference after a 48-hour retention interval. Subjects with proactive interference recalled in this study only about half as much as the control group in one experiment and about 60 percent as much in another (reviewed by Underwood 1983).

In his quest to understand the power of proactive interference, Underwood (1957) was inspired by a simple but basic question: why was there was so little agreement among experimental tests of how much forgetting can be expected by humans over a 24-hour interval? The estimates ranged from more than 80 percent forgetting in some tests to less than 20 percent in others. Underwood (1957) matched the estimates of forgetting in these experiments with the number of previous lists of verbal materials the subjects had learned in that same laboratory. When he did this, the vast differences in estimates of forgetting made perfect sense: the greater the number of previous lists of verbal units learned in a particular laboratory, the less was recalled of the materials used to estimate forgetting (Figure 4-2). In other words, the differences in amount forgotten were due to uncontrolled differences in proactive interference from prior learning.

The accumulation of proactive interference can have devastating consequences for long-term retention. This is illustrated by a long and difficult experiment that involved, however, a simple procedure. Subjects learned 10 pairs of common words until they could correctly state the response to each stimulus on a given trial. Recall was tested 48 hours later. After this test a second list was learned and this too was

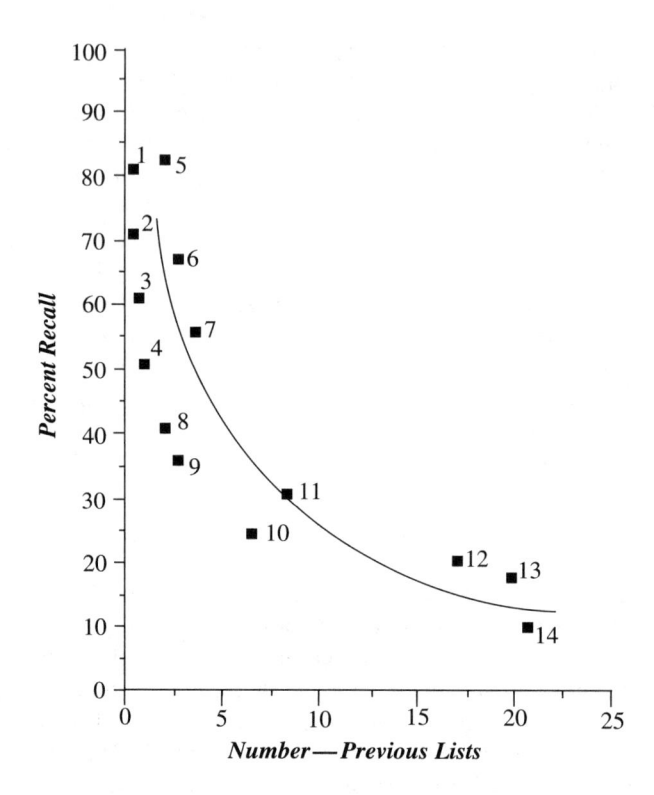

FIGURE 4-2 Rate of forgetting of verbal materials found after a 24-hour retention interval is shown for each of fourteen experiments that differed in the number of lists of verbal units the subjects had learned in the laboratory prior to learning the critical list for which retention was tested. This dramatic suggestion that rate of forgetting of verbal units in the laboratory might be impaired by prior learning in the laboratory (proactive interference) subsequently was corroborated in a variety of direct experimental tests. (Adapted from Underwood 1957.)

tested 48 hours later; then a third was learned and tested 48 hours later; and so forth, for 36 lists. In spite of a progressive improvement in rate of learning the lists (learning to learn), a dramatic decline occurred in recall, from 70 percent accuracy on the first list to only 4 percent on the 36th. In the face of such massive proactive interference, virtually nothing was remembered about a set of words that had been learned perfectly only 2 days earlier (Keppel, Postman & Zavortink 1968).

A similar buildup of proactive interference also can drastically increase forgetting over intervals much shorter than 48 hours, in fact, for intervals as short as 18 seconds. We discuss in chapter 5 the Brown-Peterson paradigm that requires that after studying a word or nonword (e.g., *csp*), subjects be occupied during the retention interval by counting backwards by threes from a three-digit number (e.g., beginning with 658, 655, 652, 649, etc.; this paradigm and the rationale for it will be discussed further in chapter 5). It was found that in such tests, subjects forget more over an 18-second interval the greater the number of previous trigrams learned and tested (Figure 4-3). This was clearly more rapid forgetting and not due merely to a lower degree of learning the original trigram; the effect of number of prior syllables was greater with the 18-second than the 3-second interval. In other words, forgetting increased between 3 and 18 seconds after study of an item, the greater the number of previous items studied and tested. (In our later discussion of short-term retention [chapter 5] we will see that pigeons also forget much more rapidly over intervals of this length, the greater the number of previous items studied and tested [Wright, Urcuioli & Sands 1986]. Probably this principle applies to all animals.)

The source of the proactive interference in the short-term retention test with the Brown-Peterson paradigm seems to be the similar, yet conflicting, letter sequences on previous tests. Without the similarity among the items tested, less buildup of proactive interference would be expected. Wickens (1972) provided a clever test of this interpretation by shifting to a different class of target items after the initial trials. He showed that the interference is attenuated by changing to items from a new category (e.g., from letters to numbers, or from one category of words to another). Short-term retention returns to a higher level when, for example, the fourth trial involves a target from a different class of stimuli. For instance, an individual tested for retention of *apple,* 15 to 20 seconds after studying it, then given the same study-test sequence for *orange,* then for *pear,* and then *banana* shows much more rapid forgetting of *pear* and still more of *banana* than if the previous items had been unrelated, nonfruit words. And if the fourth word *(banana)* had instead been *France* (or some other nonfruit word), it would have been released from proactive interference and so forgotten less rapidly than the third word, *pear* (Wickens 1970, 1972).

There can be no doubt about the generality of the importance of proactive and retroactive interference in laboratory experiments. We will see later, in this chapter and also in chapter 5 how these factors can determine forgetting and retention by animals as well as by humans in a variety of circumstances. In the case of humans in particular, are the effects and specific factors of Interference Theory likely to influence our remembering in everyday life, which only rarely involves isolated sets of words? An experiment involving memory for everyday language illustrates that these interference effects and factors probably have general importance for all of our remembering. The effects of retroactive interference were tested in a situation that involved remembering meaningful sentences rather than pairs of unrelated words (Bower 1978). Thorough tests led to this conclusion: "It appears that nearly every prediction of interference theory for this experiment has been confirmed. All in all, the results suggest that interference theory and interference paradigms apply just as

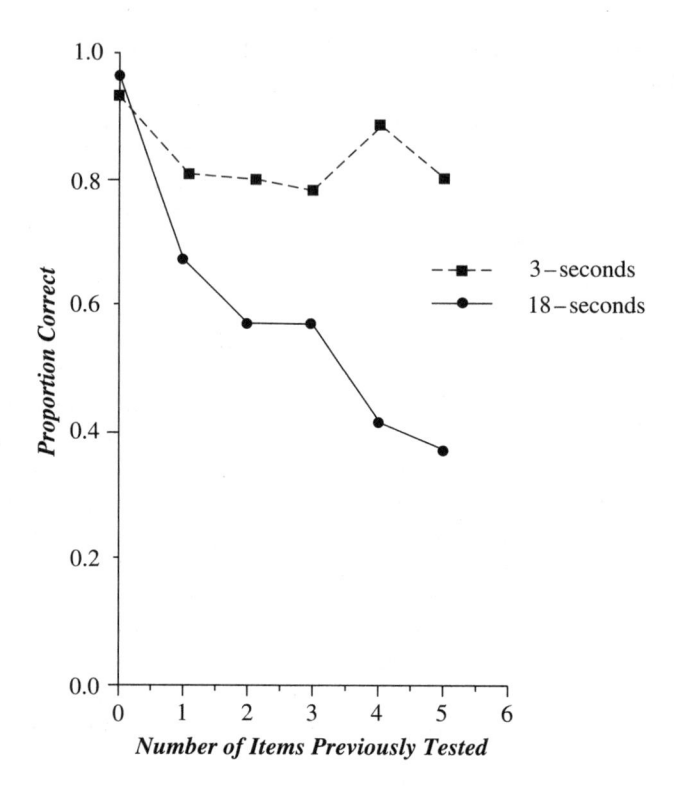

FIGURE 4-3 Forgetting of a single three-letter unit is shown to increase more rapidly between 3 and 18 seconds after learning when a larger number of similar verbal units had been learned and tested previously. This verifies the same effect for short-term retention as illustrated for longer term retention (24 hours) in Figure 4-2. (Adapted from Keppel & Underwood, 1962.)

readily to meaningful propositions as they do to verbatim learning and standard verbal learning tasks." (Bower 1978, 583)

Interference and Forgetting in Animals

Interference from conflicting memories is surely an important source of forgetting in animals. One can appreciate this simply by changing the location in which you feed your pet dog or cat. Initially the animal will learn and remember to eat in this new location, even if distracted briefly from doing so or if removed a bit from that location. But the next day at feeding time the pet will probably be waiting at the old location of feeding. One might think of this, loosely, as an A-B,A-D interference paradigm in which the A term is the signal that dinner is available and the B and D terms indicate the animal's response in running to where the food is expected.

But the analogy with tests of interference in human verbal memory is not tight; it is in fact a bit strained. The major difference to be emphasized, again, is that in the laboratory the human is instructed which of the alternative memories is requested. People become pretty suspicious, even confused or irate, without that instruction. Animals, however, neither receive nor expect instructions and must depend on aspects of the context to determine what is to be remembered. Because so little of the memory retrieval people do under natural circumstances is in response to specific verbal instruction to do so, tests of animal memory are in this sense more representative of real-life memory. You were not instructed this morning to put the toothpaste on your toothbrush rather than your comb, to use a fork rather than a spoon to eat your breakfast eggs, to turn right rather than left at the corner to get to the University, or to say "good morning" rather than "good night" when greeting your neighbor. Instead, the great majority of the memories we retrieve each day—from among the many potentially conflicting memories we have acquired—are determined by what is appropriate, which in turn depends on nonverbal context.

Role of Specific Interference in Animal Memory

The major differences in studying this topic with animals rather than humans are what is to be learned and remembered. The schematic representation of the paradigms for testing the effects of interference (Table 4-1) could in principle apply to either animals or humans, but we must be careful. For instance, suppose the rat first learns that food can be obtained by turning right in a T-maze, but then learns that food can be obtained only by turning left. How one describes this as an interference paradigm depends on what one thinks the animal learns. We might view the entire T-maze as stimulus A, turning right as response B, and turning left as response D (hence an A-B,A-D paradigm). Or, the paradigm might symbolize the supposed instruction to the rat—when at the right-hand alley (A), run to get food (B), and later, when at the left-hand alley (C), run to get food (B) (hence, an A-B,C-B paradigm). There are circumstances in Pavlovian conditioning in which the stimuli and responses are more clearly defined and the A-B,A-D type of abstraction might be useful (Wickens et al. 1977). The point is, however, that for most tests of interference and forgetting in animals, simple schematic representations will not be particularly useful until we determine precisely what the animal is learning and the content of the memories that represent these tasks.

What kinds of tasks are used to study interference and forgetting in animals? The list is too long to state completely, but the basic approach has been to present one set of reinforcement contingencies in association with A (which could be a stimulus such as a colored light or a response such as turning left) and then to present a different set of reinforcement contingencies in association with A. At some later point the test is whether behavior associated with A is more like that expected from the first or the second set of reinforcement contingencies. Sometimes A involves a discrimination and sometimes it does not. For instance, a hungry bird first learns that if it pecks the red key but not the green, food will be delivered, but then later is taught that pecking of green but not red results in food. Or, the rat first learns to make a left, not right, turn to obtain food. Or, the rat first learns that footshock is delivered in the black compartment and not in the white compartment, but then learns that the white compartment is associated with shock and not the black.

It is important to realize that animals in such tests of interference have a particularly strong tendency to perform behaviors most recently reinforced. Animals are in fact trained to do so in typical laboratory experiments; once they have emitted the response the experimenter had in mind, they are thereafter rewarded whenever they repeat it. Whatever the reason, animals that acquire two conflicting memories in succession are more likely to express the more recently acquired of these memories. This fact suggests that retroactive interference typically will be strong and proactive interference weak in experiments with animals. The history of work in this area plainly confirms this. For years retroactive interference was so strong and common as to be uninteresting, and the occurrence of proactive interference was virtually nonexistent. This was especially so in tests of long-term retention, which follow high degrees of learning and, perhaps not coincidentally, a good deal of reinforcement for performing the most recently correct behavior. Variation in the temporal relationships and contextual similarity among the interfering episode, the episode to be remembered, and the retention test can strongly influence this state of affairs, however. Retroactive interference is more likely with a short interval between the second episode and the test, but proactive interference is more likely with a long interval at this point and a short interval between learning of the two episodes. In both cases, more similarity between the contexts of the interference episode and the retention test leads to more interference with retention of the target episode (e.g., Dekeyne & Deweer 1990; for reviews see Gleitman 1971; Spear 1971, 1978).

We considered in chapter 3 a related example in which animals first learned to move slowly (passive avoidance) and then to move quickly (active avoidance), and then were tested in a context like that of either the first or second tasks. This type of effect has been confirmed and explored analytically with different procedures in a particularly elegant set of experiments by Thomas and his colleagues (e.g., Thomas 1981). One valuable feature of Thomas's experiments is that the strength of memory is measured within each subject by obtaining generalization gradients for the stimuli involved in conflicting memories, a procedure that has appreciably aided our understanding of animal memory. The general conclusion is that proactive interference can markedly accelerate forgetting, particularly when the context of the test is more similar to that present when the subject acquired the conflicting prior memory than to that of the target memory.

The Kraemer Experiments
Proactive interference in animals does not, however, require explicit changes in context. An especially thorough example is a study by Kraemer (1984). This study tested pigeon memory in an extensive experiment that illustrates the influence of interference after long intervals. The pigeons learned a discrimination between an

array of 3 green dots and another of 2 green dots that appeared on separate occasions on the pecking-key disk. For some animals the pecking of 3 dots was followed by access to food but pecks to 2 dots were not, and for other animals pecks to 2 dots were rewarded but those to 3 dots were not. The array of dots followed by food is called the S+, and the array not followed by food is called the S–.

Discrimination training continued until about 9 of every 10 pecks were to the S+. Half of the animals were then simply removed to their home cages to wait for a retention interval of 1, 10, or 20 days. The remaining birds immediately began learning the reverse discrimination. If 3 dots had been rewarded before, 2 dots were now rewarded, or vice versa. These birds thus acquired a new memory that was in clear conflict with the memory they had previously acquired in these circumstances. After this reversal they went back to their home cages to wait until their retention test 1, 10, or 20 days later. Their test was relearning of the most recent discrimination (in this case, the reversal discrimination).

In summary, all birds were tested after 1, 10, or 20 days for the most recent discrimination learned—e.g., that 3 dots were followed by food but 2 dots were not (as it turned out it did not matter which of these two stimuli was the S+). Half of the animals previously had acquired a conflicting memory—e.g., that 2 dots signaled the availability of food but 3 dots did not—whereas the other birds had no such source of proactive interference.

Two details of the results are important. First, the major indicator of learning and memory was number of errors—responses to the incorrect stimulus (S–). Birds tended to respond to S+ regardless of their condition. Second, degree of learning prior to the retention interval did not differ for birds that previously had acquired the conflicting memory and for those that had not, although of course it took the former birds longer to achieve that learning. This allowed a clear test of forgetting independent of degree of learning.

The retention data (shown in chapter 2, Figure 2-5) indicate two main features: a good deal of forgetting, even without the prior conflicting learning; and apparently more forgetting if a conflicting memory previously had been acquired (the reversal group). The latter effect was small and its significance could be questioned, so Kraemer repeated the study with a somewhat different design. He found that a single source of proactive interference did indeed significantly increase rate of forgetting over the 20-day period.

Generally speaking, this pattern of results has been common in animal studies of proactive interference effects over long intervals; the tendency for more rapid forgetting given the proactive interference frequently is small statistically and overshadowed by the retarding effect on learning after the source of proactive interference. More complex discriminations seem more susceptible to proactive interference's effect on forgetting (Spear 1978), and in view of the similar studies with short-term retention (see chapter 5) multiple sources of proactive interference might be more effective than the single source used in studies like Kraemer's.

Nevertheless, major points from Kraemer's work are that pigeons do show a good deal of forgetting over a period of several weeks even for well-learned problems, a feature that had seemed to be denied earlier (e.g., Skinner 1950, chapter 1), and that proactive interference can further increase that forgetting.

Summary and Comment
What do we know about interference and forgetting in animals? Generally speaking, most of the basic phenomena of retroactive and proactive interference observed in humans have, when properly tested, been observed also in animals. This generalization has been confirmed for long-term retention in a broad range of circumstances, including cats tested with Pavlovian conditioning procedures, rats in a variety of tests responding for food reward or to avoid footshock, and pigeons or monkeys responding for food by selecting the appropriate visual stimuli. Similar evidence about short-term retention will be discussed in chapter 5. There is clear evidence that with increasing length of the retention interval, retroactive interference decreases and proactive interference increases, the general result to be expected from the human data. More specific effects also have been observed. For instance, experiments with different kinds of animals in different circumstances have shown that the effect of proactive interference on forgetting can be decreased by either increasing the interval between acquisition of the two conflicting memories or by having the second of the two conflicting memories acquired under more distributed practice or in a different context than the first (for a review, see Spear 1978).

In experimental settings, certain effects of interference and forgetting can be observed more readily with animals than humans. One example already mentioned is the contextual control of conflicting memories. Another is the influence of nonspecific retroactive interference. Human subjects have displayed substantial forgetting in the laboratory only when the source of retroactive interference is specifically related to an event to be remembered or is the same class of event. In some cases verbal materials may interfere with the retention of other verbal materials that do not share an associate (e.g., learning C-D may impair remembering A-B [Underwood 1983]), but a loud noise or a bright light will not affect retention of verbal materials or vice versa. Yet in animals, relatively nonspecific sources of retroactive interference, sources quite different even in form from what is to be remembered, have been found to result in considerable forgetting.

THE ROLE OF NONSPECIFIC INTERFERENCE IN ANIMAL MEMORY

An animal's memory for a particular episode may be impaired by events that have little or no relation to that episode. Although two of the examples refer to short-term retention, which we will cover more thoroughly in the chapter 5, it is useful to mention them here. These examples involve the retention of visual events within several seconds or a few minutes after they occur. The task is termed *delayed matching-to-sample* and the subjects in these two examples were monkeys or pigeons. For this test the animal is first presented the sample, which might be a green light or an X projected on a small screen. After the retention interval the animal is rewarded with food if it correctly chooses the sample rather than an alternative that also is presented—for instance, it must choose green rather than red or the X rather than a +.

Monkeys have been found to forget visual samples more rapidly if they are required to attend closely to tones during the retention interval. They attended closely to the tones because a preferred food accompanied a particular tone. The main point, however, is that the tones interfered with visual memory, and it did not matter whether they were presented early or late in the retention interval (Moise 1970).

The other source of nonspecific retroactive interference in short-term retention is illumination during the retention interval. In tests of delayed matching-to-sample with both monkeys and pigeons, animals left in the dark during the retention interval remember visual events more effectively than if left in the light, and the difference is substantial. More specific details and qualifications about this effect will be discussed in the next chapter, but for now it is worth noting that the degree of nonspecific interference produced by illumination during the retention interval depends in part on the illumination to which the animal is accustomed in the experimental situation (Tranberg & Rilling 1980).

Another source of nonspecific interference may be a general opportunity for varied perceptual and motor experience. Forgetting of acquired avoidance behavior was increased among rats exposed to an enriched environment (large cages containing a number of rats and toys for the rats) during a long retention interval of several weeks (Parsons & Spear 1973). This result later was replicated in a test of memory for a brightness discrimination acquired with food reward (D. Hurst and N. E. Spear, unpublished observation). It was not clear what aspects of these enriched environments were responsible for the retroactive interference.

Finally, an experiment with cats found impaired retention of an A-B association following acquisition of a relatively unrelated C-D association (Wickens et al. 1977). Using Pavlovian conditioning procedures, either of two conditioned stimuli (light or tone) was paired with a footshock to either the left or the right forepaw. After training with stimulus A (e.g., a tone) paired with a response B (e.g., withdrawal of the left forepaw induced by a mild electrical shock), the second (C-D) task was pairing of stimulus C (light) with response D (withdrawal of the right forepaw; all stimuli were counterbalanced). While nonspecific retroactive interference of the A-B,C-D paradigm is known to induce forgetting in humans, as mentioned earlier, it has never been observed to be greater than that found with the A-B,A-D paradigm; yet in this study with cats, retention of A-B was impaired more by subsequent learning of C-D than by subsequent learning of A-D.

Although the evidence for nonspecific interference in animals appears to undermine the major principle that similarity determines interference, and so seems discordant with the human memory literature, we think consideration of the role of context helps to resolve the dilemma. As we have discussed, context provides animals with instructions for what to expect and what to do. We might think of context as a superordinate stimulus within which the specific training cues are presented. Consider for example the test with cats just discussed, in which interpolated irrelevant (C-D) conditioning interfered with the retention of the target (A-B) associations. All of this training existed within the same distinctive context (e.g., the stimuli of the testing room, restraining harness, etc.). Further, the auditory and visual conditioned stimuli share a sudden appearance or onset, a common amodal property. It is reasonable to suppose that the conditioned cats might respond rapidly to the abrupt appearance of any cue presented in this context. When the cue (and shock location) changes, the initial conditioned responses previously given (e.g., withdraw left paw) have to be suppressed before the new conditioned responses (e.g., withdraw right paw) can be established. But the background context is, in a sense, associated with both conditioned responses, and thus may mediate the interference (impairment) obtained on the subsequent retention test.

Summary

Acquired conflicting memories have been found to be a profound source of interference that causes forgetting in animals in much the same way as it occurs in humans. It seems likely that these effects of interference in animals may be more closely modulated by aspects of context than is the case with humans, but it is difficult to test this directly. What can be asserted is that associative interference is one of the two most potent sources of normal forgetting for animals and humans (the other is contextual change).

SLEEP AND MEMORY

If you can sleep between learning and a test for memory of that learning, your retention will be greater than if you do not sleep. One interpretation of how sleep protects us from forgetting is that it prevents the acquisition of conflicting memories that occur while we are awake, i.e., it limits retroactive interference. This topic therefore should be considered in the context of the effects of interference on memory. But might not something about sleep actually promote remembering, aside from just protecting us from interference? To answer this we must know a little bit about what sleep is, what it is for, and what sorts of effects it can have on memory.

A well-known study showing that sleep slows forgetting was conducted by Jenkins and Dallenbach (1924). Their careful reading of Ebbinghaus's studies indicated that his forgetting was less rapid during periods when he (probably) was asleep. They tested this directly with two subjects. Each subject learned a number of lists of 10 nonsense syllables each. The learning of some lists occurred in the evening just before sleep and that of other lists occurred in the morning just at the beginning of their waking day. Retention was tested 1, 2, 4, or 8 hours after learning. When the subjects slept for 4 to 8 hours between learning and testing, retention was two to three times as effective as when they were awake during that period.

Although the procedures used by Jenkins and Dallenbach preclude a strong conclusion about the effect of sleep on retention and methods required to study this effect properly are difficult and expensive, the general phenomenon of lesser forgetting when one is asleep than when awake has been firmly replicated, particularly by Ekstrand and his colleagues (e.g., Ekstrand 1967, 1972). The question is, why does less forgetting occur during sleep?

Stages of Sleep

For scientific purposes the term *sleep* is imprecise. Being asleep and being awake are not so discretely different as we typically think. There is in fact a continuum of arousal differences between the beginning and end of our nightly rest. These differences are readily measurable with physiological measures such as the brain waves shown on an electroencephalogram. What we usually think of as sleep consists of at least four stages through which we cycle about every 90 minutes or so. For memory, some stages seem more important than others.

The stage of sleep most extensively studied probably is the one termed *paradoxical* or *active* sleep. In this stage brain wave patterns from the electroencephalogram are very much like those when we are awake, but our muscle tone is too loose to support normal posture, hence the term paradoxical. During parts of this stage of sleep the eyes move back and forth rapidly under the lids, so it is sometimes termed *rapid eye movement* (REM) sleep. Persons awakened during such REM sleep usually report having been dreaming. Dreaming also occurs to some extent in all other stages of sleep, so far as can be determined.

All stages of sleep are accompanied by important neurophysiological changes. Changes in the activity of some brain neurotransmitters (e.g., catecholamines) linked to memory processing have been identified in particular with REM sleep. For this and other reasons the stage of REM sleep has been hypothesized as important for memory processing (Fishbein 1981; Drucker-Colin & McGaugh 1977).

The Function of Sleep

Is one purpose of sleep to allow us to restore somehow the physiological basis of our memory processing? Does this restorative activity slow down our forgetting? Probably not. There is in fact good reason to believe that sleep is not restorative in its function. Contrary to what most people believe, there is surprisingly little evidence that sleep has evolved primarily to help us replete physiological resources spent during the day.

It is particularly difficult for a restorative theory to account for the wide variation in the time various animals spend sleeping. For instance, the bat and the shrew, although very much alike in many physiological characteristics such as their high metabolic rates, occupy opposite ends of the sleep scale; the bat sleeps about 19 of every 24 hours while the shrew apparently does not sleep at all. Even among normal humans there is wide variation, with several valid reports of persons who get by quite well with only 1 or 2 hours of sleep during every 24-hour period. And although people obviously show negative consequences from sleep deprivation, the additional sleep undergone to compensate for prior deprivation rarely exceeds 10 percent of the sleep missed.

An interesting alternative theory by Meddis (1975) is that sleep evolved primarily to immobilize animals during certain vulnerable periods. This allowed them to avoid being eaten during periods when predators were very active or when the animal itself could not succeed in acquiring food (such as night, for visual animals such as ourselves).

Does REM Sleep in Normal Sleep Facilitate Memory?

Some theories have suggested that sleep promotes the storage of memories and, in particular, that paradoxical or REM sleep promotes memory consolidation (Fishbein & Gutwein 1977). One general variation of such a notion is a theory that REM sleep aids in the integration and elaboration of the components of complex and instinctive behaviors (Jouvet 1961). How can we test such ideas?

Fortunately, REM sleep is subject to experimental manipulation. Certain drugs affect REM sleep selectively (although having side effects that can make experimental analysis difficult), and REM sleep can be increased by depriving the individual of it during previous sleep episodes. After REM sleep deprivation there is a rebound effect in which a greater percentage of the individual's sleep is spent in REM. Humans can be deprived of REM sleep by merely waking them whenever this stage is indicated psychophysiologically. The rat or mouse can be deprived of REM sleep by placing it on a small pedestal at the surface of a body of water, a 2- or 3-inch island. The loss of muscle tone that accompanies REM sleep causes the animal to slip into the water. So, whenever REM sleep occurs the animal is awakened and so is selectively deprived of it.

Some experiments in which rats or mice have been deprived of REM sleep immediately following learning have found poorer retention later on, which has been interpreted as caused by a deficit in the consolidation that would have occurred if REM sleep had occurred. Others have used the rebound feature of REM (animals deprived of REM engage in it quickly when given the opportunity) to increase it just after learning, which has seemed to facilitate retention (Fishbein & Gutwein 1977). Tests with human subjects have indicated, however, that "... REM sleep is not particularly beneficial to memory or memory consolidation." (Fowler, Sullivan & Ekstrand 1973, 304) The contribution of REM sleep to memory processing, if there is any at all, is generally unclear and may depend on specific neurochemical activity associated with REM sleep (Fishbein 1981).

Particular stages of sleep, not necessarily REM, may nevertheless have special importance for the basic effect of sleep on forgetting by humans. By varying the time during the night at which learning and testing were given, one extensive study arranged for the retention interval for some subjects to occur during their first half of a night's sleep and for the others during the second half (Ekstrand 1972). Some subjects did not sleep at all during the retention interval. There was as usual less forgetting for subjects who slept than for those who did not, but this alleviation was greatest for subjects whose retention interval was in the first half of their sleep than for those in the second half. Although retention was best for subjects who slept during the first half of the night's sleep, this half included only about 7 percent REM sleep and 31 percent another stage (IV) of sleep. The relationship was reversed during the second half of the night when sleep helped retention less, with 30 percent REM sleep and 6 percent Stage IV sleep. If sleep provides some benefit to memory storage, it does not appear to be based on the REM phase.

There is reason to doubt that any particular stage of sleep has special benefit to something like a consolidation process. It seems more likely that the benefit of sleep on retention is due to a decrease in retroactive interference or perhaps to special effects on memory retrieval, although the proper tests have yet to be conducted (Spear & Gordon 1981).

Can Memory Be Aided by Induced Sleep?

In order to determine whether memory might be enhanced by induced sleep, it would be desirable to control directly the onset and duration of sleep. Subjects, whether human or animal, are not always able to sleep upon request, nor to stay asleep for the desired duration. One approach that can be used with animals involves administration of anesthetics. Although sleep induced by anesthesia may not share all the same characteristics as normal sleep, it does offer the distinct advantage of manipulability.

Experimenters have found it difficult to keep animals under anesthesia for intervals long enough to permit forgetting in control animals. An alternative approach has been to examine memory for the conditioned stimulus in long-delay conditioning—the learning of an aversion to a flavor that is followed by illness, even though there is a long delay between the flavor and the illness. Such conditioning sometimes has been assumed to serve as a test for retention of the flavor. If the flavor becomes aversive despite the delay, it is assumed that the flavor was remembered when the illness occurred (Revusky 1971).

From this perspective, retention of the flavor at the time of the illness was compared for rats that did or did not sleep between ingestion of the flavor and the illness (Rozin & Ree 1972). After rats had ingested a novel flavor (any of three flavors had the same effect), they were maintained under anesthesia for about 9 hours. Soon after the rats awoke from the anesthesia, lithium chloride was intubated intragastrically (i.e., into their stomach) to induce toxicosis. The question was whether the association of the flavor and the illness would be more likely when the animal was asleep during most of the interval between the flavor and the illness. From previous experiments with the same conditioning procedures, it was estimated that the maximal interval the rat could be awake and still show conditioning would be 3 hours. On this basis one would expect no conditioning for rats awake during the entire 9 hours between the flavor and illness. In contrast, effective conditioning was found for rats anesthetized throughout that 9-hour interval. The conditioned aversion in this case was comparable to that found in nonanesthetized rats given only a 30-minute interval between the flavor and illness. One possible conclusion is that the sleep under anesthetization slowed forgetting of the flavor.

Sleep May Promote Memory Retrieval in Human Infants

Finally, a particularly intriguing effect of sleep on memory processing has been reported for 3-month-old human infants by Rovee-Collier and her colleagues (e.g., Fagen & Rovee-Collier 1983). These investigators employed a prior cueing treatment to alleviate forgetting of learned kicking. After intervals long enough that the infants would be expected to show complete forgetting (i.e., as much forgetting as could be measured), they were exposed to the cueing or reminder treatment and then tested after intervals of either 15 minutes, 1 hour, 2 hours, or 8 hours (in previous experiments of this kind only intervals of a day or more had been used). The surprising result was that the longer the interval between the cueing treatment and the test, the better the retention. This is surprising because with intervals longer than 24 hours, retention of such learning declines with more time between the cueing and test (see chapter 9).

Why should the effect of a reactivation treatment grow over several hours after it is given? We still do not know, but one incidental bit of data reported by Fagen and Rovee-Collier (1983) may lead to interesting answers. They had asked the mothers of these infants to record how much time their child spent sleeping between the reactivation treatment and the test. Infants of this age spend a great deal of time asleep. For infants given an 8-hour interval between the reactivation treatment and testing, there was a direct relationship between the amount of time spent sleeping and the subjects' retention scores: the correlation between these measures was +.87, nearly perfect. The more time spent sleeping, the more effective was memory retrieval.

In view of Ekstrand's conclusion that paradoxical sleep may not be crucial to slowing forgetting, it is unclear what role this stage of sleep might have for the alleviation of forgetting following prior cueing. Nevertheless, because infant altricial mammals such as the human and the rat spend so much of their time in paradoxical sleep, this may prove a valuable setting in which to investigate the influence of this stage of sleep on memory processing.

CHAPTER SUMMARY

The second primary cause of change in remembering after initial memory storage is associative interference from conflicting memories. Conflicting memories have some degree of similarity to the target memory, but also have critical differences. Conflicting memories can have devastating effects on retention whether they have been acquired prior to (proactive) or subsequent to (retroactive) initial memory storage. The basis of proactive and retroactive interference has seemed to differ, however. The latter has seemed to be due to factors such as unlearning or response set interference that drastically impairs access to or retrieval of a memory. Proactive interference seems attributable primarily to the mixup factors and perhaps to some extent to effects on the specific encoding employed during initial memory storage. The influence of interference on retention is quite general, occurring for essentially all animals that have been tested and regardless of what is to be remembered. The basic mechanisms of interference discovered through experimental tests apply nicely to a variety of cases of human learning, from the learning of individual letters to the learning of stories or entire sets of text, as well as to animals. One aspect that may be more powerful among animals than humans is nonspecific interference.

It has been suspected for some time that retroactive interference might be decreased by sleeping during the retention interval, in view of the better retention shown when individuals sleep during this interval compared to when they are awake. This conclusion today may be too simplistic in view of what is known about the separable stages and physiological correlates of sleep, but there can be no doubt about the importance of some aspects of sleep for remembering. It is unclear which stages of sleep, if any, have special importance in remembering. Although some studies with animals have suggested that REM sleep might be particularly conducive to remembering, this has not been confirmed in careful studies of this effect with human subjects.

▶ 5
Short-Term Retention

The instances of memory discussed so far in this book have dealt essentially with long-term retention. Our discussions have involved tests of memory that occur after hours, days, or weeks following, usually, a number of repetitions of a learning episode and a fairly solid degree of learning. We now turn to instances of short-term retention—memory for very recent episodes that (usually) have occurred only once, a few seconds or minutes earlier. A major question is whether such short-term retention is governed by the same memory processes responsible for long-term retention. We will not focus on that question, although we will devote some discussion to it.

We will focus on what is known about short-term retention. The similarities between short- and long-term retention will emerge, if only because important differences have not been established with certainty. The operational distinctions are nevertheless important, because some experimental issues can be solved only with tests of short-term retention and others only with tests of long-term retention. This will become clear as we discuss how short-term retention has been studied and what has been learned about it. We begin with a somewhat historical discussion of how short-term retention is measured in animals, starting with a story about an ape.

ASSESSMENT OF SHORT-TERM RETENTION

Long before television, and even before the widespread availability of radio, an exciting opportunity for entertainment in many parts of the country was provided by the traveling circus. Of these, the Ringling Brothers and Barnum & Bailey Circus combination was perhaps the most well known and featured a young gorilla named Congo. Very little was known of ape behavior at that time, but the eminent psychologist R. M. Yerkes was rapidly adding to this knowledge by studying Congo while the circus wintered in Florida. It was during tests conducted in February and March of 1928 that Yerkes intended to study Congo's memory.

Yerkes had some rough indications of the gorilla's long-term retention capacity. Congo seemed to recognize Yerkes after the 10-month interval that had elapsed since the last set of tests. Yerkes also assessed this memory capacity systematically in terms of Congo's efficiency in obtaining food from a box outside his cage by using a long wooden pole to retrieve it. By apparently recognizing Yerkes, Congo showed good general memory capacity; by showing almost a complete failure to solve the box and pole task in three daily sessions of 30 minutes each, a problem that Congo previously had been able to solve within 1/2 minute 10 months earlier, there were indications of substantial forgetting as well.

Yerkes did not wish to wait another 10-month interval in order to further assess Congo's memory (and it is a good thing he did not, because Congo died soon afterward from a gastrointestinal ailment). So, Yerkes sought to study short-term retention and forgetting over periods of minutes or hours. The reward for a correct response was ample (for one test a single reward included two big bananas, a large orange, and two sweet potatoes [Yerkes 1928, 36]) and could be found by Congo in a container on a turntable that also held empty containers. Congo watched as the food was placed in one container, but was prevented from reaching any of the containers until a particular interval had elapsed. During this interval the turntable was rotated to prevent Congo from remembering the correct container by physical orientation alone. Congo accurately remembered the correct container after intervals as long as 10 minutes.

This turntable memory test is one version of a widely used experimental paradigm in which the animal is provided information as to the location of reward, but is prevented from responding to obtain it until a particular delay has elapsed—the delayed response test.

Short Term Retention Assessed by the Delayed Response Test

The delayed response test was first applied scientifically by W. S. Hunter, although as is the case with many scientific techniques, it had been developed largely by two enterprising young graduate students (Tinklepaugh 1928). Hunter applied the delayed response task toward resolution of a major and enduring issue in the field of memory in animal behavior: do animals carry with them representations of what they learn? Presumably, such representations would be stored in the brain. Horses were the dominant form of travel in 1913 when Hunter published his paper, so this animal provided an appropriate illustration of the issue: will a horse that has mastered a particular route from farm to town without guidance somehow think over some representation of that route in its memory while back in its stable?

Hunter was a leader of the behaviorist revolution that sought to analyze behavior without resorting to mentalism, or, in the case of animals, anthropomorphism, and even more reluctant to explain the horses' travel routes in terms of unobservable mental operations such as ideas, thoughts, or memories. He preferred the term *sensory recognition* to explain why the horse increased its speed as it encountered objects closer to home. Although this term implies, paradoxically, a sort of mental state of familiarity, Hunter probably found sensory recognition preferable because it emphasized the need for sensory information to guide behavior and precluded consideration of the voluntary production of a memory presumed by many persons then (and even now) to occur in active recall by humans. The emphasis on sensory information is reasonable, but the presumption that humans spontaneously produce memories in the absence of eliciting stimuli is misleading if not flatly incorrect, in the same way that it would be for animals. All memory retrieval is cued by some source, internal or external, specific or contextual. The source might be the test itself or, for example, instructions to recall (for human tests). There is no more of a factual basis for entirely self-induced, intentional recall by humans than by animals, without exposing oneself to such cues. This is asserted a little strongly, perhaps, for an issue that has not been tested satisfactorily (and may not be testable). Yet the alternative working assumption—that humans can somehow will that a memory be retrieved—seems unreasonable to us.

Although addressing these major issues was the overriding purpose of Hunter's study, the more specific aim was to assess discriminative responding after a delay had elapsed since the animal was first given information about the correct response. His initial version of this test was more complicated than that used later to test Congo. Hunter's first step was to train hungry animals (rats, dogs, raccoons) to obtain food by entering only the lighted door of three possible doors. Hunter then began trials in which the light was shown as before but turned off before the animal was able to complete its response.

The training procedure that prepared the animal for the critical delayed response test was a long and tedious affair. At first the light was turned off when the animal was en route to its location, then it was turned off just prior to the animal's initiation of the response. Finally, after several hundred shaping trials, delays were introduced between light offset and the opportunity to respond. Since the animal was not permitted to respond until after removal of the stimulus that signaled the location of food, reliable correct responding could hardly be caused by sensory recognition of the signal-location solution. Hunter, however, also had to account for (and eliminate) overt response orientation similar to the pointing response that an Irish setter might make toward a bird in the field, if he was truly to test memory. Aside from these factors, the only remaining control over the delayed response had to be within the animal itself, the sort of "ideation" or mental process for which Hunter sought objective measurement. One of Hunter's goals was to study this ideation in comparative fashion, comparing its efficacy for animals of different phylogenetic status.

For subsequent comparative studies, Hunter used the simpler method applied for Congo. The subject saw the location of the reward object before the door of the container was closed and the retention interval began. Hunter measured the longest retention interval that each of his subjects could tolerate before their choice behavior fell to chance. For rats, he estimated this to be about 10 seconds, for raccoons 25 seconds, for dogs 5 minutes, for his 13-month-old daughter about 24 seconds, for 2-1/2-year-old children 50 seconds, and for a 6-year-old child 20 minutes. Hunter felt that the rat and sometimes the dog used physical orientation during the delay and for them ideation was discounted, but something like ideation seemed to him possible for raccoons and children, even preverbal children, who did not seem to depend on physical orientation for accurate retention.

One might think that Hunter's creative work would have led to conceptual breakthroughs about animal memory through tests of delayed responding, but it did not. Psychologists were at that time deeply influenced by behaviorism and not ready for systematic consideration of the role of cognition in memory. The issue of how animals represent events they are to remember is fundamental to understanding the processing of memories, however, and a good deal of progress on this issue has been made recently with new techniques for measuring short-term retention with computer-controlled instrumentation.

Improved Analysis of Short-Term Retention in Animals: Delayed Matching-to-Sample

The technique that formed the basis for most tests of short-term retention in animals today is termed *delayed matching-to-sample*. Matching-to-sample is by no means new as a psychological test or teaching device. Applying the delayed matching-to-sample procedure to a normal adult human would be a simple matter: show the subject an apple, then show an apple and an orange, and simply ask the subject to point to the one that matches the first object shown; next, present a fork, then a knife and a fork, still with the understanding that the subject was to select that member of the pair that matched the object previously shown. Retention is tested by introducing a longer delay between the first object and the pair of objects. The only assumption is that to correctly select the item that matches the first object, the first object must be remembered to some degree.

To apply this test to animals is a good deal more difficult. One cannot merely tell the animal that it should select the item of the pair that matches the previous item. Without the advantage of verbal instructions, animals must undergo a laborious shaping procedure to teach them that by matching, they will earn some preferred food.

The animals most frequently tested with this procedure are the monkey and pigeon because they respond so readily to a broad variety of easily presented visual stimuli. For either of these animals the same or similar shaping procedures and apparatus may be applied. Both monkeys and pigeons can operate the same keys (quarter- or half dollar-sized disks that act like electrical switches); monkeys push them and pigeons peck them. Increasingly, touch-sensitive computer screens are used to allow any picture to be touched directly to indicate which one the animal chooses as the match. Figure 5-1 illustrates the four basic steps required to train an animal to match to a sample before any delays are introduced between removal of the sample and the matching test. The sample pictures that appear on the keys or computer screen typically are colors or geometrical forms such as a vertical line or a cross, relatively complex pictures of real events, or everyday objects. This training procedure is more complicated than the delayed response task, in which the monkey need only learn to observe food being placed into a container and then to select one container over another in accordance with where the food was placed. This is significant because once trained on delayed matching to sample, an animal is so valuable that it is tested in many different experiments. This means that the subjects in many of these experiments are more sophisticated in laboratory experiments than are those in other memory tests, which can have special effects that we discuss later, such as proactive interference.

Delayed matching-to-sample has special analytical advantages over the delayed response task. More rapid presentation of stimuli and a larger number of tests are readily achieved, so important effects such as rate of processing the critical stimuli and amount of study can be tested with relative ease. Also, a large variety of samples

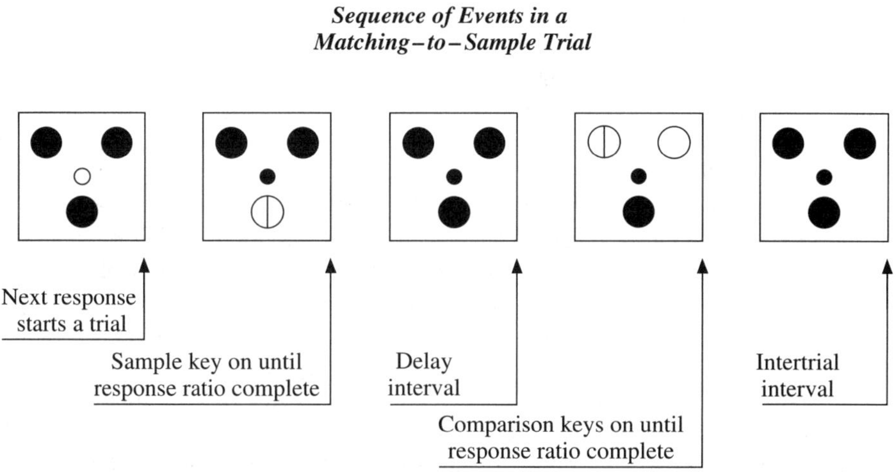

Sequence of Events in a Matching–to–Sample Trial

FIGURE 5-1 This figure exemplifies the sequence of events with which the monkey must become familiar for tests with delayed matching-to-sample procedures. This particular procedure involves four major steps. Throughout the monkey is presented a panel consisting of three round disks (keys) upon which symbols may be projected. In this case there also is a lamp in the center that may or may not be lighted. At the beginning of a trial (1) the three keys are darkened and the lamp is lighted to indicate that the next response to the sample key (i.e., pressing of the lower key) will initiate a trial. When the monkey presses the sample key, the lamp goes off, and the sample stimulus appears on the sample key (2). The monkey may then be required to complete a particular number of presses of the sample key, and when these are accomplished, the delay interval begins (3). The entire panel is darkened during the delay. Following the delay, the two comparison keys become illuminated with alternative symbols (4), one of which is the sample that was lighted before the delay. The monkey's task now is to respond to the key on which the sample is projected. If correct, the monkey typically receives a preferred food (raisin or peanut), followed by the intertrial interval during which the entire panel is darkened. If the monkey responds incorrectly, the intertrial interval begins immediately. (Adapted from Mello 1971.)

can be presented easily, first in one position and then in another, so that correct responding cannot be based on the animal's postural orientation toward a particular location.

A study by Grant provides a convenient illustration of delayed matching-to-sample and of several of the important parameters that affect performance in this task. Pigeons trained to match color stimuli received trials in which duration of the sample stimulus and length of the retention interval were systematically varied. Specifically, pecking on a white (neutral) key produced the sample stimulus (e.g., a blue key) for 1, 4, 8, or 14 seconds. The test stimuli, consisting of the matching sample stimulus and one other color (e.g., yellow), were presented on separate keys 0, 20, 40, or 60 seconds later. Both the sample duration and length of the delay (retention interval) affected retention. As the duration of the sample exposure increased, so too did accuracy of choice; conversely, as the length of the retention interval increased, the pigeons' accuracy diminished. A very long interval combined with very brief exposure to the sample resulted in nearly chance levels (50 percent) of correct choices. These facts are shown in Figure 5-2.

This type of finding and some others like it (Grant & Roberts 1976) support trace-decay explanations of short-term forgetting. The notion is that presentation of the sample establishes for the animal a representation which, through inherent biological processes, decays or fades with time. Longer exposure to the target stimulus permits a stronger representation or trace to be formed, and this is more resistant to decay. It is dangerous to rely too heavily on such a passive decay process for explanation, however, because the basis of decay is still less certain than that of other mechanisms of forgetting that are more testable, such as interference. The tests have indicated several other factors that make a difference in how effectively the animal remembers a sample, which we consider next.

RETROACTIVE INTERFERENCE IN SHORT-TERM RETENTION

In chapter 4 we discussed how events between learning and testing can impair long-term retention, an effect known as retroactive interference. Retroactive interference also has proven to be important in short-term delayed matching. But unlike the situation with long-term retention, in which the role of stimulus similarity is a paramount feature of retroactive interference, significant sources of interference in delayed matching seem to be nonspecific—unrelated to the similarity between interpolated events and the sample-to-be-remembered. This point was raised in chapter 4, and we now elaborate on it.

We focus on nonspecific retroactive interference for two reasons. First, its analysis has produced interesting surprises. Second, some tests in delayed matching deal with a trivial form of specific retroactive interference that represents merely a failure of communication about the target stimulus. Suppose that on a particular trial a target (red light) is presented, but shortly afterward, an interfering event (a green

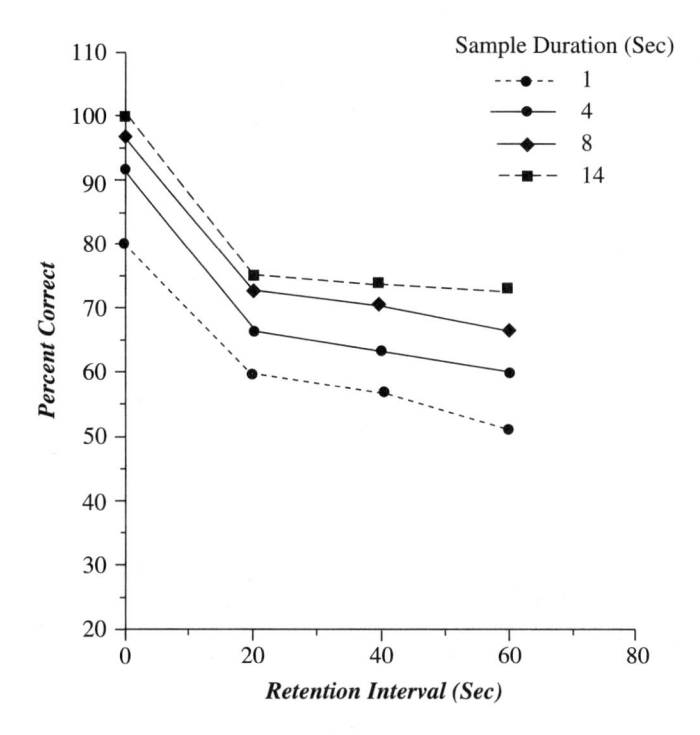

FIGURE 5-2 Rate of forgetting, by pigeons, of a color that had appeared 0, 20, 40, or 60 seconds prior to the test is compared when the duration of exposure of the color varied between 1 and 14 seconds. Forgetting of the color occurred in all conditions and with equal rates. (Adapted from Grant & Roberts 1976.)

light) is presented. It is easy to see that if the interfering stimulus is also one of the choices at testing, the failure of an animal to choose the proper target (red) probably indicates confusion about which stimulus is the target—after all, each had been presented before, with little or no designation as to which was the target. We consider next instances of retroactive interference that are not trivial.

Illumination: An Example of Nonspecific Retroactive Interference

Retention by monkeys or pigeons is improved markedly when they spend the retention interval in darkness rather than in normal illumination. The term *normal illumination* needs defining here. Retention may depend on how illumination during the retention interval compares with that during the experimental situation, as well as on the absolute level of illumination during the retention interval. Most studies have been concerned with only the absolute level of illumination, and so that is our initial topic.

The effect of illumination on retention is substantial. Mello (1971) found that monkeys regularly responded correctly after a retention interval as long as 232 seconds, whereas Jarrard and Moise (1971), using very much the same delayed matching task, estimated the longest retention interval their monkeys could master to be only 1/15 of that length. Probably the most important procedural difference was that the monkeys in the Mello study spent their retention interval in darkness; those in the Jarrard and Moise study spent theirs in light. D'Amato and O'Neill (1971) found that for each of their three monkeys and for all four different samples tested, retention after a 2-minute interval was always above chance if that interval was spent in darkness but never if it was spent in light. A 2-minute interval in the circumstances of the tests of D'Amato and his colleagues is a very long interval over which to maintain accurate retention. Yet, D'Amato subsequently found reliable instances in which, with darkness during a retention interval, monkeys were reliably accurate in their retention 9 minutes after presentation of a sample (D'Amato 1973).

The retention of pigeons, too, was facilitated if the retention interval was spent in darkness rather than illumination. The dimmer the illumination during a 5-second retention interval, the better the retention (Grant & Roberts 1976) (Figure 5-3). Illumination seems to affect retention in this way almost without regard to what is to be remembered. This effect occurs in retention for remembering either of three kinds of events: visual stimuli, particular behaviors emitted by the pigeon prior to the retention interval, and whether food had or had not been presented prior to the retention interval (Maki, Moe & Bierley 1977).

The total amount of illumination throughout the retention interval seems to be the most important factor in the impairment in retention. Relatively little impairment in retention occurs for either monkeys or pigeons when brief durations of illumination are interpolated during a dark retention interval—whether these bursts of illumination occur just after the sample, just before the test, or somewhere in between. Pigeons do seem a bit more disrupted when the illumination occurs just prior to the test than if just after the sample. Although this and other effects of relative amount or temporal locus of illumination have been observed, their magnitudes are small and depend on the animal's experience with these particular circumstances (Grant 1988). The absolute benefit from a darkened retention interval (i.e., more rapid forgetting in light) is quite clear.

In all experiments mentioned so far in which illumination impaired retention, the samples-to-be-remembered were explicitly visual events (even the behavioral and food samples tested by Maki et al. [1977] required vision). Is illumination detrimental only when the major attributes for memory are visual? Or, is relative darkness beneficial to retention generally, regardless of what is to be remembered? The latter is not implausible; sleep facilitates long-term retention and our eyes are closed during sleep, and persons sometimes close their eyes when trying to remember. A question that immediately arises is whether auditory memories—for episodes made up primarily of acoustical signals such as tones—would be subject to impaired retention if

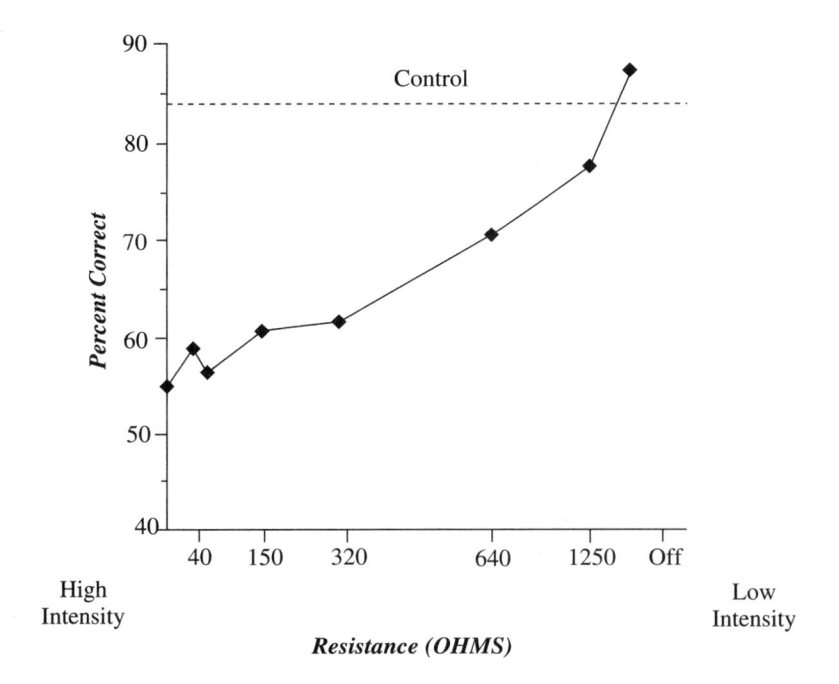

FIGURE 5-3 Forgetting of a simple visual stimulus is shown for pigeons exposed to different amounts of illumination during their 5-second retention interval. This figure shows the pigeons' accuracy in choosing the correct stimulus as a function of the amount of electrical resistance placed in series with the house lights; the higher the resistance, the darker is the chamber during the retention interval. In other words, the brighter the light to which the pigeon is exposed during the retention interval, the greater the impairment of retention. (Adapted from Grant & Roberts 1976.)

illumination rather than darkness were presented during a retention interval. If separate systems of memory exist for vision and audition—which is sometimes suggested—we might expect little interference from one to the other. This issue is hard or impossible to test with humans, who can use verbal labels to equate visual and auditory events.

Does Retroactive Interference Depend on Sensory Modality?

In studies with the dolphin, a mammal very effective in processing information presented acoustically, auditory memories in delayed matching were found to be susceptible to retroactive interference from other sounds. Dolphins showed impaired retention of a sound in a delayed matching-to-sample task when sounds unrelated to the sample occurred during a retention interval (Herman 1975). But is memory for sounds impaired by illumination? To test this with monkeys required that they be trained to match to an acoustical sample. This turned out to be a very difficult matter with monkeys, apparently more so than with dolphins.

The most important work on this problem has been done by D'Amato and his colleagues (D'Amato 1973; D'Amato & Salmon 1984), who initially had great difficulty in getting monkeys to learn and remember acoustic signals. It was as if the monkey were such a visually oriented animal that it simply could not process memories of sounds. This seems unlikely, however, because it is not reasonable to expect that any animal's sensory modality would be given such a low priority not to be used at all in the processing of memories. Even the albino rat with its notoriously poor visual acuity can learn and remember a great deal about visual events and does so readily in laboratory tasks. Moreover, the vocalizations of other monkeys are very important to alert them to general dangers and to specify actual sources of danger; even the infant monkey produces distinctively different distress calls depending upon the circumstances of its isolation from its mother (Levine 1987).

The more probable reason for the difficulty in getting monkeys to learn and remember acoustical signals was that D'Amato and his colleagues were testing monkeys that had for years been trained to respond only to visual signals in the laboratory. How could these monkeys be tested visually for what they had heard? D'Amato's solution was to apply an important technique, symbolic matching-to-sample. A good many of the breakthroughs in understanding short-term retention in animals have been made possible by the use of this technique, so it should be noted carefully.

Symbolic versus Identity Matching

The meaning of symbolic matching-to-sample can be understood when we realize that the task we have been discussing so far is identity matching to sample—the animal must select at the test the same, identical stimulus that was presented as the sample. In symbolic matching-to-sample the animal must select at the test the stimulus that is only equivalent to the sample, not necessarily identical. The animal is taught the equivalence by the experimenter. For instance, suppose the samples are the colors *green* and *red*. The animal first learns, for example, that *red* and a *triangle* (black triangle, against a white background) mean the same thing because the animal is rewarded if it selects *triangle* when *red* is the sample. Similarly, the animal will be taught that *green* is equivalent to a *vertical line*. The animal would be rewarded by selecting *triangle* after the retention interval if *red* had been the sample, or by selecting *vertical line* after the interval if *green* had been the sample. Monkeys and pigeons are quite adept at this. Their retention with symbolic matching-to-sample can be as effective as that with identity matching-to-sample.

More important, with this method scientists answer questions not previously answerable, simply because with symbolic matching-to-sample, the physical characteristics of the alternative stimuli at the test can be completely independent of those of the sample. This is a great advantage for tests of animal cognition. For interpreting such tests, however, it is useful to be aware that the term *symbolic* can be a little misleading. For instance, the pigeon does not use symbols in these cases as we humans might. Although quite able to learn to respond to *triangle* whenever *red* was the sample, the pigeon will not then respond accurately to *red* if *triangle* were the sample. Because the acquired equivalence is not symmetrical, experts do not view this as involving a truly symbolic relation and prefer the term *arbitrary* matching (Catania 1987).

Retroactive Interference and Sensory Modality
D'Amato and his colleagues found that monkeys could be tested for retention of acoustical signals—short tunes—if each of the two tunes used was made equivalent to a visual symbol, for example, *white dot* and *plus* (D'Amato & Salmon 1984). In other words, when the animal had heard *tune A* as the sample, it was to select *white dot* at the test, and if it heard *tune B,* then *plus* was to be selected. D'Amato and Salmon (1984) found that illumination during the retention interval impaired memory of a visual sample but not that of an acoustical sample.

What about the effect of interpolating acoustical stimuli during the retention interval? To provide a direct test Columbo and D'Amato (1986) developed techniques that allowed their *Cebus* monkeys to learn identity matching with auditory stimuli. With a careful and detailed study, they found that with either monkey vocalizations or simple tunes as a source of nonspecific retroactive interference, forgetting of either of two other simple tunes was enhanced over a 28-second delay. Forgetting of the tunes was not enhanced by visual stimulation. This complements the results of the D'Amato and Salmon (1984) study which had indicated that retention of a visual event is more likely impaired by subsequent illumination than by subsequent acoustical stimulation. These studies suggest that for monkeys, unrelated visual events interfere retroactively with visual but not auditory memories, and unrelated acoustical events interfere retroactively with auditory but not visual memories. The implication is that although specific similarity may not be necessary for memory interference (monkey vocalizations have little specific similarity to a tune), nonspecific similarity—within versus between sensory modalities—is important. This is interesting because usually it is specific similarity that is more likely to induce interference (chapter 4) and because of the possibility that separate memory systems exist for each sensory modality (chapter 12).

OVERT REPRESENTATION FOR MEMORY

Before moving on to discuss another source of interference, we must briefly consider how the animal's overt behavior could provide a potential nonmemory aspect of delayed matching.

Although postural orientation toward a specific location cannot be the basis for good performance in delayed matching, it remains possible that the animal might use some aspect of its motor behavior as a physical mediator to allow accurate performance. For instance, the pigeon is adept at representing samples in terms of its own peculiar movements during a delay in order to enhance its retention performance. If pigeons could do this well enough, they might show accurate test performance even without the use of the internal processing that we typically associate with memory. The first to study this systematically was Blough (1959).

Four pigeons were presented with either a flickering light or a steady light through a vertical aperture centered between two circular response keys. One or the other of these lights provided the sample-to-be-remembered. Zero, 2, 5, or 10 seconds later, both the flickering and steady lights were presented, one through each key. If the pigeon pecked the key illuminated like the original sample, grain was briefly made available to the hungry bird. Otherwise, no food was presented.

Two of the four birds performed with remarkable accuracy, one choosing correctly on more than 90 percent of the trials for all retention intervals. This accuracy is unusual, because 10 seconds is a long interval for a pigeon in these circumstances and typically yields a great deal of forgetting. Blough noticed, however, that both of these birds performed certain ritualistic behaviors during the retention interval, depending on which stimulus had served as the sample. When the sample had been the flickering light, one of the pigeons with good retention scores would step back from the keys and slowly wave its head back and forth; when the sample had been the steady light, the same bird would spend the interval pecking at the top of the vertical aperture. The other of these two pigeons spent the retention interval biting at the top of the vertical aperture when the flickering light had been the sample, but pecked directly at the center of this aperture when the steady light had been the sample. It was as if these pigeons had selected one response to represent the flickering light and another to represent the steady light.

Blough also found that if these representational responses did not occur, or if they became less distinctive when he attempted to photograph the bird through an open window (which, it might be noted, modified the stimulus context), performance following the retention interval declined accordingly. Thus, loss of the sample-specific behaviors during the retention interval seemed to be accompanied by loss of the memory of the sample. Like the setter-orientation behavior in the delayed response task, the sample-specific behavior seemed to provide a version of overt rehearsal, somewhat more complex than mere bodily orientation toward the correct alternative but nevertheless unlike the representative memory process presumed to take place internally.

An even more subtle form of mediating behavior was studied by Kendrick and Rilling (1984). The pigeon had to learn that when a light was over food, pecking produced food; but if dark, the food was unavailable. Then a retention interval was introduced between the sample (lighted food or darkness and no food) and the opportunity to peck for food. When required to remember the occurrence of illuminated food, the pigeon exhibited different behavior during the interval than if it was to remember that darkness and no food had occurred. After the food-light sample, the pigeon began pecking a response key immediately and continued to peck at a rate of

46 pecks per minute throughout the delay. When the sample was darkness and no food, the bird immediately retreated to a far corner away from the key and did not return to peck until the house light came back on, then gave a relatively high rate of pecking at the response key (63 pecks per minute) throughout the delay. One might reasonably think, therefore, that for this pigeon initial movement into the corner followed by fast pecking actually meant that no food and darkness had been the sample, whereas relatively slow but continuous pecking meant that food and illumination had been the sample. If this were so, most psychologists, like Hunter when he first observed this type of behavior, would not think of it as reflecting a true memory process.

The more important function of the mediating behavior itself might not be the animal's representation of the sample, however. Kendrick and Rilling (1984) view the behaviors that occur during a delay as the context in which the animal covertly rehearses information about the sample. This approach is especially appealing because it can account for the data, and it employs a conceptual framework that has successfully encompassed many other memory effects in the past—that context controls memory retrieval.

Kendrick and Rilling (1984) found that after a delay of 5 to 8 seconds (a substantial delay for a pigeon) retention could be disrupted whenever the pigeon was induced to engage in atypical behavior during the delay. This was accomplished by presenting, during the delay, stimuli to which the bird had been conditioned to respond (peck a key) at unusually high or low rates. In this way the experimenter could provide a particular mediating behavior (a rate of responding) to represent each particular sample.

Retention was clearly influenced by the similarity between the pigeon's rate of responding during an ordinary retention interval and that when the rate was modified by presenting one of the conditioned stimuli. When this stimulus resulted in a rate of responding that differed from that to which the animal was accustomed during the delay, retention was disrupted. Rate of responding provides the animal a distinctive context. It is as if retrieval of the memory for the sample depends on the occurrence of the same context in which the pigeon previously had remembered the sample.

We do not completely understand the function of sample-specific behavior and how its presence or absence affects retention performance. The evidence suggests that it is unnecessary for retention and probably not sufficient either. Despite such sample-specific behavior, therefore, the animal might nevertheless be engaging in memory processing. It remains a topic well worth studying, however, because it may tell us something about how animals symbolically represent their world.

PROACTIVE INTERFERENCE IN SHORT-TERM RETENTION

Just as retroactive interference from events between the sample and the retention test may lead to impaired retention, proactive interference from events prior to presentation of the sample may similarly lead to impaired retention. You will remember from chapter 4 that proactive interference in retention should be distinguished from negative transfer. Negative transfer occurs when prior events impair perception or initial learning of the sample and is reflected by impaired performance after short as well as long retention intervals. Proactive interference in retention is more than negative transfer; it refers to an accelerated rate of forgetting due to prior events. In other words, proactive interference is indicated when retention after an interval is impaired despite relatively little impairment in retention immediately after presentation of the event-to-be-remembered.

We also saw in chapter 4 how Underwood (1957) corrected the underestimation of proactive interference as a source of forgetting in human memory; he demonstrated that previous learning in a similar experimental setting could triple the forgetting of a single set of verbal units over a 24-hour interval. A similar evolution of thought and discovery about proactive interference has appeared in the study of short-term retention in animals. In the considerable struggle to understand such effects, the amount of proactive interference to be accounted for seemed quite small (Roberts & Grant 1976; Spear 1978, 198–203). In other words, in spite of the theoretical importance of proactive interference, it originally had only a small effect in tests conducted on short-term retention in animals. This perspective has changed, as we shall see.

Three Sources of Proactive Interference

With delayed matching-to-sample, there are three sources of potential proactive interference. The first is intertrial. A trial in delayed matching-to-sample is considered to be the entire sequence: presentation of the sample, the retention interval, and the test of the animal's choice between that sample and an alternative. If *triangle* was the sample on a preceding trial, and if the animal was then presented *circle* as the sample and tested for a choice between *circle* and *triangle,* the immediately preceding experience with *triangle* would be a source of (intertrial) proactive interference. Such proactive interference has impaired retention by about 5 to 10% (Wright, Urcuioli & Sands 1986).

The second potential source of proactive interference, intratrial, occurs when a single sample-like event is presented prior to the occurrence of the sample on an otherwise conventional delayed matching-to-sample trial. For instance, a few seconds before *triangle* occurs as the sample, *circle* might be presented. Retention of *triangle* might then be tested in terms of a choice between *triangle* and, say, *plus.* In some experiments the test choice was between a *triangle* and *circle,* in which case we would have another potential instance of the communication failure referred to earlier with respect to retroactive interference. In any event, the influence of intratrial proactive interference also has been relatively small, again on the order of a 5 to 10% reduction in retention.

The third source of proactive interference, more general and perhaps most pervasive of those tested experimentally, is the animals' vast experience of, and memory for, specific samples presented during shaping or in previous experiments. Such prior learning is analogous to that of the prior memory tests in an experimental situation given to human subjects, which Underwood identified as a powerful source of proactive interference. Scientists studying short-term retention in animals are well aware of this. If general experimental experience is a source of proactive interference, one might expect progressively more rapid forgetting as animals serve in more and more experiments of this kind. This has not been found, however. There has instead been the opposite tendency, a learning to remember effect such that with increasing experience with delayed matching-to-sample—literally thousands and thousands of trials—forgetting gradually becomes slightly less rapid (D'Amato 1973; Grant 1981). The possibility remains, however, that both factors occur. The basis of learning-to-remember could actually be, in part, learning to counteract proactive interference. Such a basis would have different implications than absolute learning-to-remember, albeit interesting and generally adaptive.

A better test would be to compare, as Underwood did with humans, the forgetting observed among animals with prior experimental experience and those without it. Such a comparison is not possible with animal subjects, however. Animals' behavior must be carefully shaped for them to respond in such memory tests and this shaping requires experience with a number of samples, at least with all procedures employed so far.

An alternative way to test this general notion is to arrange to have animals tested on samples they have never seen before. Until relatively recently, most tests of short-term retention in animals used a complete set of only 2 to 5 alternative samples in all the experiments in which an animal serves. The above indications of improved retention after huge numbers of tests were based on repeated experience with few samples. Suppose that instead of a few alternative samples there were several hundred alternative samples, so that the probability of being tested for retention of a sample experienced before by the animal is relatively low. The proactive interference effect should then be relatively low also.

Such variation in terms of sample set size has revealed a great deal about how powerful the influence of proactive interference can be on short-term retention in animals. The strength of this effect was emphasized in an excellent and thoughtful review by Wright et al. (1986). Much of the following discussion was suggested by these authors.

Proactive Interference from Prior Processing of Particular Samples

An early assessment of how proactive interference might impair matching to sample was contributed by Mishkin and Delacour (1975). These investigators asked why monkeys perform so poorly on matching-to-sample tests even with short delays, yet show good retention for tests involving the spatial location of objects. Their analysis led them to suggest that the difficulty might lie with the fact that in many previous studies, only a small number of alternative stimuli had been used as samples, whereas many alternative spatial locations are possible. The samples not only were repeated frequently during testing, they also were changed from being the target sample on some trials to the incorrect alternative on others. If monkeys were instead given a series of matching-to-sample trials with relatively unique samples and comparison stimuli at each test, their retention might be markedly superior to that of animals given the same tests with only a few alternative samples or test items. Mishkin and Delacour (1975) conducted precisely that type of comparison and obtained the predicted outcome. For animals given the large sample set, some 200 different junk objects were used. Since most monkeys received over 100 trials (2 items per trial), a given stimulus might not be absolutely unique, but certainly more so than for monkeys given only 2 different objects.

Delayed matching performance in monkeys given the large sample size and in those that repeatedly were to remember 1 of only 2 alternative junk objects did not differ for the first 200 trials. By the end of 400 trials, however, retention after a delay was nearly 50 percent greater for monkeys given the large sample set than for monkeys with a sample set size of only 2.

It was as if animals that acquired a large number of competing memories involving only 2 alternative samples had a buildup of proactive interference that dramatically increased the rate with which those animals forgot the sample over a 10-second interval. One difficulty with this interpretation is that Mishkin and Delacour included no animals given a relatively short retention interval. Perhaps the small sample size would have impaired matching performance even without a delay, and the effect was on perception or original learning—negative transfer of learning rather than proactive interference of retention. Or perhaps the effect was due to a deficit in general attention caused by progressive boredom with the same objects. Overman and Doty (1980) showed that either of these is unlikely to have been the case.

The samples and test alternatives used by Overman and Doty were pictures, and the procedure was delayed matching-to-sample. Monkeys first were tested with a trial-unique procedure, which means that each of a large number of pictures was used once and not repeated as samples or alternatives at the test. This beginning ensured rapid acquisition of matching behavior. The training continued in the same way for some monkeys, but for others tests repeatedly used the same pictures from a small set. The delays varied between 5 and 180 seconds, and the results are shown in Figure 5-4. Not only did the monkeys given the larger sample set show much greater accuracy in matching at all retention intervals, but this difference also increased with longer retention intervals. The retention of monkeys with the small sample set size was no better than chance at intervals of 50 seconds or longer, whereas responses of animals given different samples and alternatives on each trial remained at about 70 percent accuracy after even a 3-minute interval.

Based on earlier tests that had involved very small sample set sizes, the memory capacity of monkeys in such delayed matching-to-sample task had been thought to be quite limited, extending only to 20 to 30 seconds. But, as expressed well by Wright et al., this apparently limited memory capacity was ". . . not because subjects forget the samples over the retention interval . . . but rather because, in some sense, they remember the samples too well and are unable to distinguish *which* memory item was presented at the start of each trial...." (Wright et al. 1986, 109)

Finally, the effect of proactive interference with small versus large sample sets has been studied with another technique worth describing because of its general

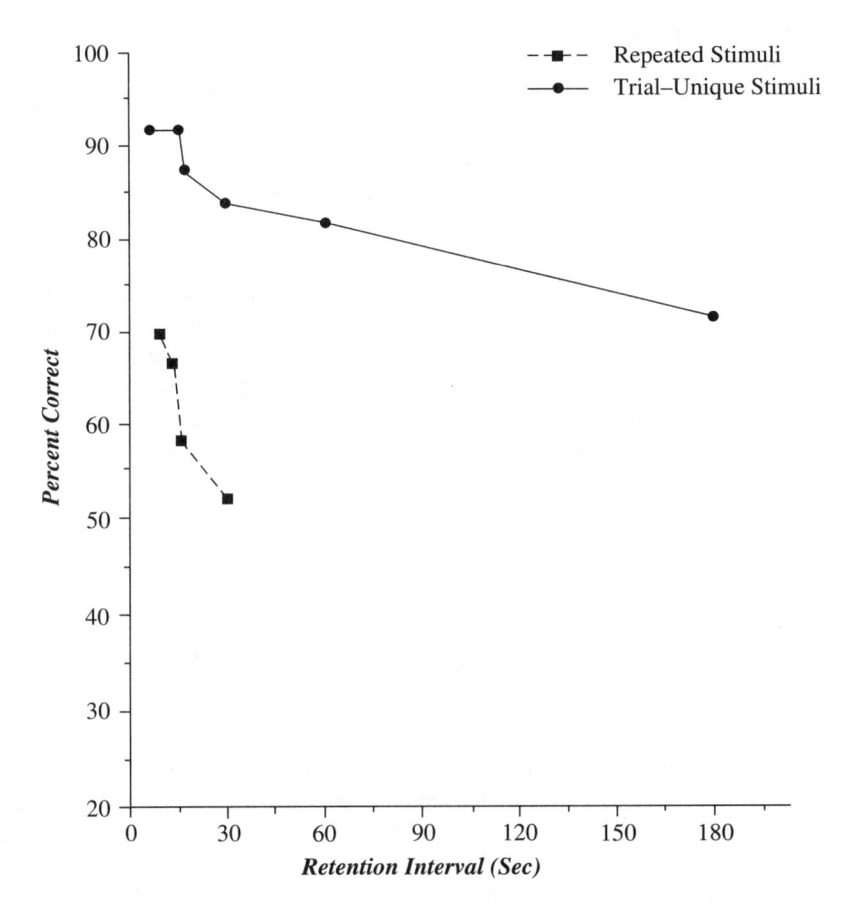

FIGURE 5-4 The rate with which pictures are forgotten by monkeys is shown in terms of their accuracy in choosing that critical picture over another presented at the test. In the case of trial-unique stimuli, the alternative picture at the test as well as the critical picture had not previously been seen or reinforced, but in the case of repeated stimuli, both stimuli presented at the test probably had been presented earlier for other tests given to these monkeys. The greater rate of forgetting in the case of repeated stimuli indicates proactive interference. (Adapted from Overman & Doty 1980.)

value—the serial-probe recognition task. Instead of a single object or picture as a sample, the monkey is presented on each trial with three objects (or three pictures) that are to be tested for retention after the retention interval. At the test, the animal is presented a single object (or picture) and moves a lever to the right if the test item matches one of those presented among the three samples (same), or to the left if it does not (different). Wright et al. (1986) compared retention for animals given a large sample set (211 different items; low proactive interference) with that of monkeys given a small sample set (6 different items; high proactive interference). Retention accuracy in the former case was higher by more than 30 percent. Retention with this larger sample set also was more than 30 percent higher than that reported in any of five other published experiments that had used the more conventional small sample set procedure. Three other studies reviewed by Wright et al., one with a chimpanzee, one with a rhesus monkey, and one with a dolphin, found similar results.

It would appear that most studies of short-term retention in animals have underestimated memory capacity by using relatively small sample set sizes. This underestimation is due to proactive interference, although exactly how proactive interference exerts its effect in these cases is unclear. What is clear is that the influence of proactive interference is quite strong. It is equally clear that the magnitude of intertrial and intratrial proactive interference reported in most studies probably has been underestimated by comparing the consequences of these sources of proactive interference against a baseline of relatively poor retention. The low baseline is caused by the use of too few samples and alternatives. Proactive interference is an important and powerful source of forgetting in delayed matching-to-sample, as well as in the serial-probe recognition test of short-term retention.

CONTENT OF THE MEMORY IN SHORT-TERM RETENTION

Among the memory attributes that may be stored by animals to represent sample presentation in delayed matching-to-sample are two aspects of the sample itself: its physical characteristics and its encoded characteristics. Collectively these characteristics constitute the content of an animal's memory for the sample; these combine with contextual characteristics to form the memory of the sample's occurrence.

What the animal detects at the sensory level and how it would perceive the sample in isolation from other components of the task constitute the initial registration of information about the physical stimulus. The immediate meaning of the sample to the animal—its relationship to other aspects of the learning episode and to the animal's own history—determines the encoded content of the sample's memory attributes. The encoded content of the memory becomes especially pertinent when its symbolic equivalent and not the sample itself is an alternative at the retention test. Consideration of encoded content is also useful when the sample is a compound of two or more events, such as a sound and a color, because the color could be encoded by the animal and the sound ignored, or vice versa, or the compound could be encoded in some integral fashion (e.g., as a red tone or a shrill blue circle). The issue of encoded content arises later when the ontogeny of memory is discussed, and it is relevant also to two ways remembering can proceed in short-term memory, prospectively or retrospectively.

Prospective and Retrospective Content

In recent years investigators have recognized and addressed an important distinction with respect to the encoded content in symbolic matching-to-sample—the distinction between prospective and retrospective content of the memory. These terms reflect the fact that an experienced animal could do well in delayed matching-to-sample by remembering either of two things. It could remember prospectively in the following way: when the sample is presented the subject could instruct itself as to what alternative must be selected at the later test, and then remember that self-instruction at the test. Or, the animal could remember retrospectively by encoding and remembering the actual sample and using that to guide its selection at testing. In other words, in the prospective case the transformation of information—from encoding of the sample to that of its symbolic equivalent (the correct alternative)—occurs at the time the sample cue is presented initially. In the retrospective case the transformation is at the time of presentation of the test stimuli. Although retrospective memory may seem intuitively to be more obvious, both ways of remembering symbolic equivalents are viable. The distinction and its general implications were elaborated on originally by Honig, Grant and others (e.g., Honig & Thompson 1982; Grant 1981).

The distinction between retrospective and prospective content is an idea that has some empirical support, and it seems useful in trying to understand short-term retention. Wasserman (1986) pointed out that the idea was first asserted concretely by Konorski (1967). The early evidence for the distinction was largely indirect, albeit based on rather ingenious experiments. Three of these will illustrate how the distinction between retrospective and prospective content of a memory has been tested, as well as the fact that evidence for both types of encoding has been obtained.

In one study, Roitblatt (1980, experiment 3) assessed memory content by examining the errors made by pigeons during symbolic matching-to-sample tests. After one of the three possible samples (red, orange, or green) was presented and a particular delay had occurred, the three symbolic equivalents of the samples were presented (lines that were either horizontal, 12.5 degrees off from vertical, or exactly vertical, respectively). Note that although red and orange are very similar as samples, their symbolic equivalents differ considerably (horizontal, and 12.5 degrees off vertical), whereas the two symbolic equivalents for the very different samples of orange and green are quite similar, 12.5 degrees off vertical and exactly vertical.

Suppose a pigeon is presented orange as the sample and makes an error after the delay: instead of selecting the correct symbolic equivalent of the 12.5-degree line, it selects either the vertical or the horizontal line. The basic question is whether the pigeon was really remembering orange or instead had transformed orange into its symbolic equivalent (the 12.5-degree line) prior to the retention interval and so was remembering the line. If retrospective processing had occurred, the color more likely mistaken for orange would have been red, and the animal would have mistakenly selected the horizontal line at the test. But if the memory content was prospective, i.e., if transformation to the nearly vertical (12.5-degree) line was made just prior to the retention interval, then the erroneously selected line at the test would be expected to be the more similar alternative, the exactly vertical line.

The results suggested that with relatively long retention intervals (up to 5.6 seconds, which is long for pigeons under these circumstances) the confusions were more likely to be among test stimuli (orientations of the line) rather than among sample cues (the nature of the color). This suggested that prospective content—the transformation of the actual sample at the time of initial presentation—was employed.

In another study, Stonebraker (1981) signaled his pigeons during a retention interval as to whether they would be tested with the actual sample (e.g., *red*) or its symbolic equivalent (e.g., *vertical lines*). For instance, if *red* was the sample and the alternatives at the test were to be *red* and *green,* a triangle would appear prior to the test; but if *red* were the sample and its symbolic equivalent were to be tested (*vertical lines* versus the alternative of *horizontal lines*), then a circle would be presented prior to the test. Occasionally Stonebraker would give the birds the wrong signal, e.g., present the circle prior to the test but then present the actual sample as one of the test alternatives. If the bird always used retrospective encoding and remembered the sample up to the time of the test, this sort of misleading signal should not affect retention performance. The misleading information impaired retention performance, however, suggesting that prospective encoding was used to at least some extent.

A third example is provided by the finding that pigeons are more accurate in delayed matching-to-sample when the sample and test stimuli are colors than when they are vertical and horizontal lines. Urcuioli and Zentall (1986) trained pigeons to treat a particular color as the symbolic equivalent of a particular line orientation *(red = vertical; green = horizontal).* The birds then were given either *red* or *green* as the sample in a symbolic matching test or *vertical* or *horizontal lines* as the sample in an identity matching test (the birds always were tested with the alternatives of *vertical* and *horizontal lines*). If the animals given color as the sample encoded prospectively, they would remember lines throughout the retention interval just as was required by the birds that were presented lines as the sample. The results showed, however, that the birds given color as the sample forgot less rapidly than those given lines. This indicated that what they had encoded and held in memory was the color (retrospective encoding) rather than its symbolic (prospective) equivalent, the more poorly retained lines.

These examples illustrate not only the creativity of some experimental psychologists, but also that the distinction between prospective and retrospective encoding might be a valid and useful one (see also Santi & Roberts 1985; Linwick et al. 1988; Urcuioli & Zentall 1992; Zentall, Steirn & Jackson-Smith 1990). In spite of these excellent experiments, however, limits on what we really know about short-term retention in animals preclude firm conclusions about whether retrospective or prospective encoding is employed. For instance, what happens to the memory for the sample in prospective encoding? Might not its physical content also be remembered throughout the retention interval? And, what does it mean for a particular event or symbolic equivalent to be remembered throughout a retention interval? Is the animal actively aware of and rehearsing that memory attribute during each second of the interval? Or, if the animal's awareness lapses, will retrieval of that memory be triggered by the alternatives at the test? Finally, you will see in the literature reference to retrospective processing and prospective processing, as if the memory process involved is different as well as the encoding; are there really two separate memory systems at work here (chapter 12) (for some empirical evidence, see Linwick et al. 1988)? When questions of this sort are answered, the distinction between retrospective and prospective encoding will become still more useful.

Does Content of the Memory Determine Its Rate of Forgetting?

Are events perceived through one sensory modality forgotten faster than those perceived through another modality? For instance, are events seen forgotten faster than events heard? This is one form that our question about the content of memory can take. Obtaining the answer to this would seem to be a simple matter. Why not just measure the rate of forgetting in a delayed matching-to-sample paradigm when samples are, say, visual events in comparison to when they are, say, acoustical events?

This approach has not always led to clear conclusions, however, due to two factors we have already considered. One is that animals might employ prospective encoding and remember how to respond at testing rather than what was actually presented to them as the sample. The physical content of the sample might then be irrelevant. The other factor is differences in degree of learning (i.e., differences in matching accuracy before the retention interval). Some animals presented with certain samples may show so little accuracy in matching before the interval that relatively little forgetting can be observed until chance performance is reached. Also, degree of learning by monkeys or pigeons may be so much lower with acoustical than visual samples, for example, that it is difficult to separate differences in forgetting from differences in degree of learning. Such differences in matching accuracy could also be due to differences in sensory detection, but we can make the simple assumption that if they learn, they have detected; equivalent learning would in a rough sense imply equivalent detection. Neither of these factors is insurmountable, but we must keep them in mind.

Sensory Modality

Columbo and D'Amato (1986) found more rapid forgetting by monkeys for acoustical than for visual samples, over intervals up to 32 seconds. This was the case even when the acoustical discrimination required at the test seemed quite easy in relation to the visual discrimination. In these experiments matching accuracy was 100 percent with the shortest delay (0.5 second) for both visual and acoustical events. This certainly equates them mathematically, although we should not discount the possibility of overlearning in the case of the visual stimuli to a degree not measurable (i.e., beyond the point of 100 percent accuracy, cf. Underwood [1964]). In view of the consistency of this effect with different levels of discrimination difficulty at the test, however, overlearning is probably not a problem in the Columbo-D'Amato experiment. It is notable that these monkeys had a good deal of previous experience working with auditory stimuli, which might have increased their proactive interference in auditory retention.

A difference in the rate of forgetting visual and acoustical stimuli has been found for the rat (and perhaps for the pigeon) that is exactly opposite the effect seen with monkeys. The rat has been found to forget visual samples more rapidly than acoustical ones (Wallace et al. 1980; Cohen, Galgan & Fuerst 1986). Wallace et al. found this effect with each of two procedures. The first is similar to symbolic matching-to-sample. The rat learned to press a single lever at the rear of a box, which initiated a trial by presenting the sample to be remembered. The sample was either onset of a 7.5-watt bulb located in the ceiling or onset of a white noise (82 dB) that also came from the ceiling. There were two other levers on the front wall of the box, opposite the wall that held the single lever. After the sample terminated and a certain delay had elapsed, a light above one of the two levers was illuminated as a cue. For some animals the lighted lever was correct if the acoustical sample had been presented and the unlighted lever correct if the visual sample had been presented; the opposite was the case for the remaining subjects. Figure 5-5 shows that with no delay between the sample and the test, the rats' responses were equally accurate for the visual and auditory stimuli but not perfect with either (hence avoiding the possibility of overlearning with one or the other of the samples). With longer delays there was essentially no forgetting following the acoustical stimulus (up to a maximum of 4 seconds) but very rapid forgetting following the visual stimulus.

The second procedure of Wallace et al. was similar to one developed by Konorski (1959). The animal is rewarded for responding after the retention interval only if the stimulus presented is the same as the sample. For this experiment the stimuli were a little different than before—a tone was the acoustical sample (4,000 kH$_z$, 72 dB) and a somewhat brighter light was the visual stimulus (15 watts). Each rat was given four kinds of trials. Following the tone and the retention interval either the same tone or the light occurred, and following the light either the same light or the tone occurred. In this experiment retention did not differ for the auditory and visual samples either immediately or after a 2-second delay, but as with their first experiment, the visual sample was forgotten more rapidly after a longer interval, a 5-second delay, than was the auditory sample.

If rats and monkeys forget visual and acoustic samples at different rates, what about pigeons? Kraemer and Roberts (1984a) tested pigeons in delayed matching-to-sample for visual stimuli (red versus green) and acoustical stimuli (a high-pitched tone of 3,000 Hz at 68 dB and a low pitched tone of 300 Hz at 78 dB). More rapid

Short-Term Retention **131**

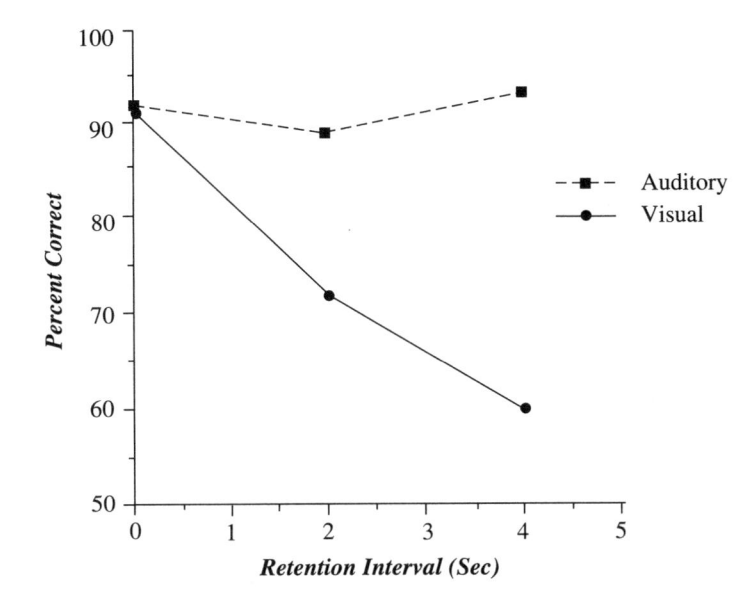

FIGURE 5-5 Rate of forgetting by rats of an auditory (white noise) or visual (onset of a ceiling light) stimulus is shown over a period of a few seconds following the occurrence of that stimulus. (Adapted from Wallace et al. 1980.)

forgetting occurred for the visual than the acoustical sample. Interpretation of this result by Kraemer and Roberts was made somewhat difficult because of the poor matching performance for the acoustical stimuli, even at very short intervals (Figure 5-6). Fortunately, the auditory sample presented with a long duration (8 seconds) yielded matching on an immediate test equivalent to that of the visual sample presented for a 1-second duration (sample duration itself did not affect rate of forgetting). In other words, degree of learning prior to the retention interval was equivalent. Comparison of these two conditions suggests that forgetting was considerably more rapid for the visual sample.

Taken together, the data indicate that for rats and pigeons visual events are forgotten more rapidly over a short interval than acoustical events, but for monkeys the opposite holds. This conclusions must be tentative, however, even though the experiments described above are perhaps the best available so far on this topic. It is uncertain psychophysically how other, amodal attributes (e.g., subjective intensity, familiarity) might differ between the visual and acoustical events to affect how rapidly they are forgotten.

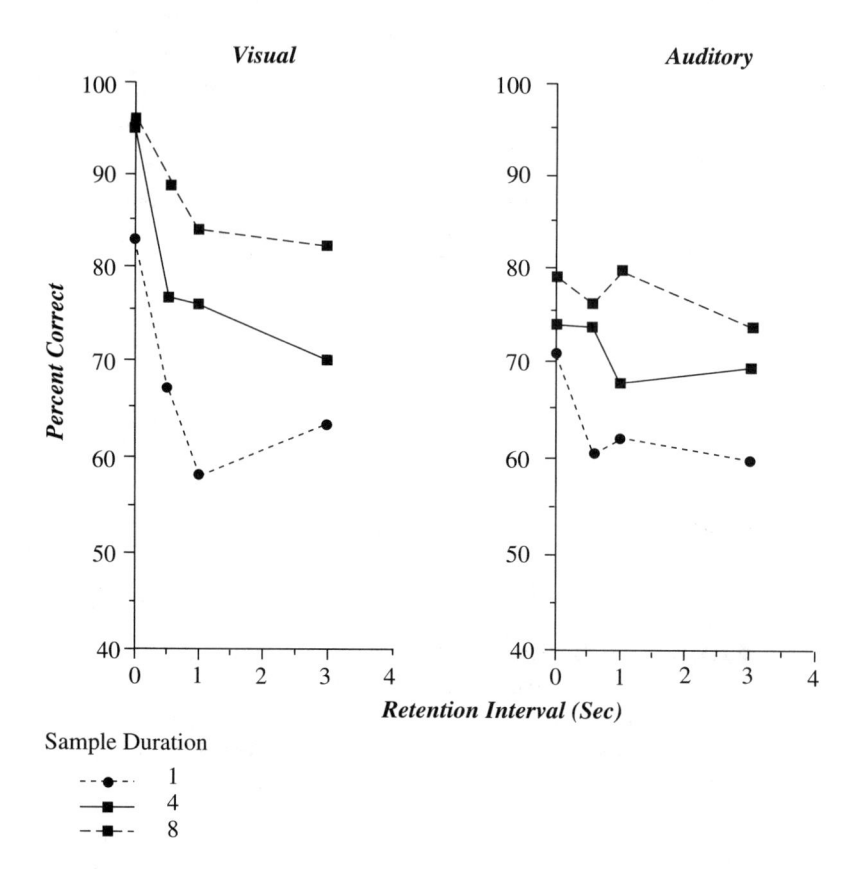

FIGURE 5-6 Forgetting by pigeons of an auditory (low versus high pitched tone) or visual (red versus green) stimulus is shown over a period of a few seconds as a function of the duration of the stimulus when it was originally presented for study. (Adapted from Kraemer & Roberts 1984.)

COGNITION AND SHORT-TERM RETENTION IN ANIMALS

As long as there have been systematic tests of memory, there has existed the idea that how a person or animal operates on what is to be learned—cognitively, behaviorally, or neurophysiologically—will determine how well that learning will be remembered. Muller and Pilzecker (1900) were among the first to express this idea. In attempting to explain why retroactive interference occurs in memory for words when a new set of words is learned afterward, they suggested that consolidation of the memory for the critical words was disrupted by studying the new words. Consolidation was one version of how the processing of words to be remembered might continue after the words were no longer visually perceived. Memory consolidation implied a different, less behaviorally active process than common rehearsal (e.g., simple repetition of the words to oneself after they are removed from sight), and it was thought to depend on perseveration of neural activity.

A process as basic as consolidation did not prove to be the best way to explain retroactive interference in humans. The notion was applied later, nevertheless, to explain retrograde amnesia, the drastic forgetting of immediately preceding events upon severe concussion or other insult to the brain (chapters 8 to 10). This form of consolidation is taken to be an automatic process that begins upon the receipt of new information and runs its course unaltered in the absence of severe neurophysiological disruption. Simply distracting the animal by having it notice, learn, or remember some other event is, in this view, insufficient to alter the consolidation process.

It took a long time for scientists to concede that in the course of memory processing humans are active processors of information rather than passive recipients of some automatically occurring mechanism of memory. For an even longer period animals were assumed not to process actively—not to think about or otherwise engage in cognition about an episode they recently experienced. Animals, too, were assumed to be passive recipients of whatever permanent changes occur in the brain as a consequence of noticing and learning specific episodes. Available evidence has forced a change in this view. It now seems likely that animals do engage in some postepisode, cognitive processing of what is to be remembered.

Rehearsal in Animals: A Consequence of Surprise

In order to explain some observations about animal memory, three types of rehearsal have been proposed (Maki 1979; Wagner 1981; in particular, Grant 1981, 1984). The theory of Wagner (1981) (also see Wagner & Brandon 1989) is perhaps clearest about the properties of what we might term *associative rehearsal*. A basic aspect of Wagner's view of rehearsal is that learning the associative relationship between two events, such as a buzzer that predicts food, depends directly on the length of time during which the animals' representations of these two events are somehow linked by the animal—rehearsed simultaneously—after those events themselves are no longer present. Wagner emphasizes that the animal does not decide to initiate such a rehearsal process. This form of rehearsal is instead an integral part of the memory process that occurs automatically, and once initiated, the animal is required to do nothing special to maintain it. This rehearsal process is different from consolidation in that its disruption does not require a massive neurophysiological insult; instead, the processing of other information may detract from and compete with rehearsal. Rehearsal is particularly likely to be disrupted by the competing processing of surprising events.

Although outside the realm of short-term retention, an initial test of these ideas about rehearsal is nevertheless worth mentioning because it illustrates the concept of surprise (Wagner, Rudy & Whitlow 1973). The question was how conditioning of the rabbit's nictitating membrane (a sort of eyelid) to a mild electrical shock near the eye would be affected by following the pairing of the conditioned stimulus (e.g., a flashing light) and the unconditioned stimulus (the shock) with a surprising event. The surprising event intended to disrupt conditioning was a clicking noise or a vibration on the animal's chest accompanied by an unexpected consequence. For instance, a familiar clicking noise not previously followed by shock was made into a surprising event by now having shock follow the click, or a vibratory stimulus to the chest previously paired with shock would be followed by no shock. If the surprising event occurred within 3 seconds of the critical conditioned stimulus and unconditioned stimulus, then conditioning was impaired by about 25 percent; if presented 10 seconds or 60 seconds afterward there was less, but still significant, impairment; but if presented 5 minutes after the critical pairing, there was no impairment and conditioning proceeded normally (Figure 5-7). This study focused on how surprise could impair retention of a preceding event, presumably by disrupting processing or rehearsal. But what about the surprising event itself? Might an unexpected stimulus be remembered better than an anticipated stimulus? This possibility has been studied most effectively with pigeons in delayed matching tests.

Rehearsal by pigeons may or may not be different in kind from the associative rehearsal hypothesized by Wagner, but its assessment has depended upon somewhat similar experiments. In a symbolic matching task, the sample consisted of either the occurrence or nonoccurrence of food. If *food* had been presented as the sample, the pigeon had to peck the green alternative (in order to get more food), but if *no food* had been the sample then the pigeon had to peck the red alternative (Maki 1979). These same pigeons were also taught something else, a simple discrimination between horizontal and vertical lines. For example, pecking *vertical* was rewarded with food and pecking *horizontal* was not. This discrimination learning permitted presentation of the following sequence of events: one of the discriminative stimuli (the lines), then the reinforcer (food or no food), and then the test (color) stimuli. Food had a dual role: it served both as the reinforcer in the discrimination task and also as the sample stimulus to be matched (symbolically). At this point Maki could ask how well the occurrence of food would be remembered when it was not expected (i.e., if it followed *horizontal*) compared to when it was (i.e., if it followed *vertical*). Maki found that after a delay, matching accuracy was about 20 percent greater if the sample had been a surprise than if it had not.

To test whether surprise might affect the rate at which a sample is forgotten—rather than, or in addition to, an effect on the general accuracy of identifying it soon after presentation—pigeons were tested either immediately after presentation of the sample or 6 seconds later (Roberts 1980). This method was a little different from that just described. The samples were either particular colors or particular line orientations, and the schedule was arranged so that on a few selected trials color samples preceded a trial with line samples, although usually line samples were preceded by

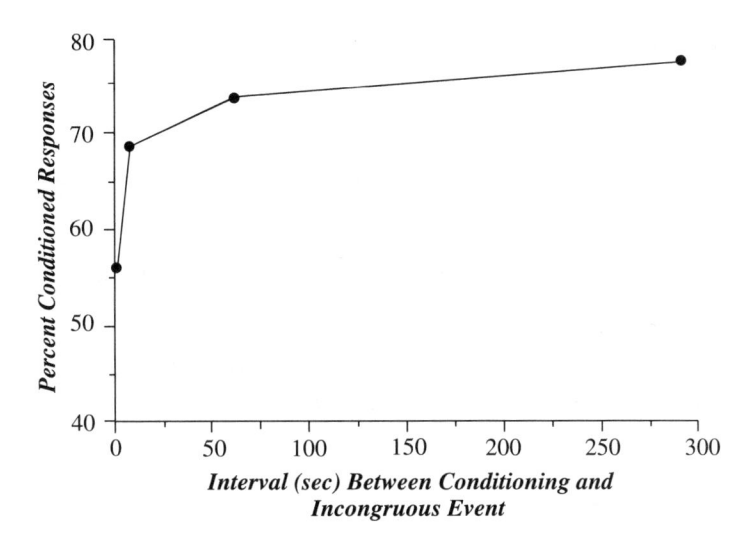

FIGURE 5-7 Mean percentage of conditioned responses is shown to be an increasing function of the time between the conditioning trial and the introduction of an incongruous, post-trial event. The sooner the incongruous event occurred after the reinforcer, the less effective was subsequent retention of conditioning. (Adapted from Wagner et al. 1973.)

trials with other line samples. Rate of forgetting a sample was slower when the sample was such a surprise. There was no effect on matching immediately after the sample, but after the longer (6-second) interval, accuracy was significantly higher when the sample had been a surprise than when it had been expected. This experiment seems to indicate that surprising events are forgotten more slowly than expected ones, an intuitively reasonable fact. It might be argued, and at least as reasonable by intuition, that the element of surprise primarily influences perception or degree of learning rather than directly affecting rate of forgetting. Given no effect of surprise at a very short interval, however, perception or degree of learning seems not to have been facilitated, and yet the surprise effect occurred more strongly after a longer interval.

That the effect of surprise on forgetting is solid can be illustrated by one final experiment (Grant, Brewster & Stierhoff 1983, experiment 3). An intricate sequence of training sessions led pigeons to expect 2 seconds' access to their food (grain) if a *large triangle* had appeared for 10 seconds, but to expect a 2-second blackout (house lights turned off) if a *small triangle* had appeared for 10 seconds. The pigeons also were trained with *food* or *no food* as samples: if *food* had been presented, a peck on a red disk was rewarded with more food, but if *no food* (blackout) had occurred, a green disk was rewarded. The final step was to measure delayed matching of the *food* or *no food* samples when food was expected and when it was a surprise. Remember that the birds had learned to expect food after a *large triangle* but not after a *small triangle*. The test for memory of the occurrence of food was given either immediately after the sample or 5 or 10 seconds later. Results were fully in accord with those above: when the food had been surprising (i.e., followed a *small triangle* instead of a *large triangle*) its occurrence was forgotten more slowly. Figure 5-8 shows that there was no detectable forgetting over a 10-second interval for samples that were surprising, and yet if these same samples were expected, the usual rapid rate of forgetting occurred.

Although the effect of surprise on retention is firm, it is less clear how surprise induces in the animal a rehearsal-like process, if this is indeed the process responsible for the effect. Although conceivably a cognitive effect of some kind, it probably does not resemble the rehearsal commonly thought of in humans as verbal in nature (even though there may be more to rehearsal than the verbal aspects for humans as well). It seems likely that surprise is accompanied by the same sort of hormonal and neural activity observed to modulate the effectiveness of memory processing in other

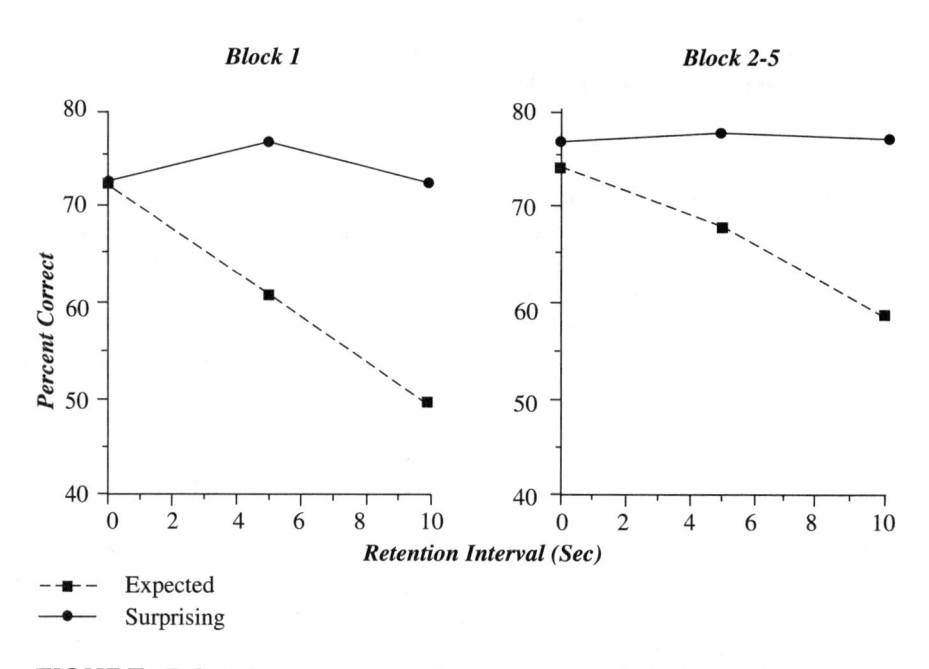

FIGURE 5-8 The forgetting of pigeons over a period of several seconds following the occurrence of an event is shown to be more rapid if the event had been expected than if it was a surprising event. (Adapted from Grant et al. 1983.)

circumstances, particularly catecholamine activity involving epinephrine (see chapter 8) (Gold 1989; McGaugh 1989a).

Directed Forgetting

The phenomenon of directed forgetting provides further evidence in both humans and animals that processing of memories persists after acquisition. Indeed, tests of forgetting have provided a useful strategy for inferring the presence of rehearsal. By rehearsal is meant, again, no more than an internal cognitive process that is perhaps cognitive with neurophysiological components, but is not an automatic consequence of perception and is instead under the control of the animal or its environment.

The general idea of directed forgetting is to signal the subject when remembering of certain events will be required and when it will not. If the signaling takes place after the events occur, any difference in retention could not be because the organism simply ignored those samples that were signaled to be forgotten. A difference would indicate instead that the animal somehow operated differently on equally perceived events-to-be-remembered and events-to-be-forgotten, presumably through a rehearsal-like mechanism.

Let us first consider this idea with respect to human memory. What happens to information if, after its presentation, subjects are instructed to forget it? Several studies have shown that this instruction alters the subsequent accessibility of the material, even though the instruction is not given until after the material is presented. For example, subjects were presented a list of 24 words, half of which were to be remembered and half of which were to be forgotten. Immediately following each item a cue was given indicating the category to which it belonged, R (remember) or F (forget). When tested later for recall of all of the items, subjects were able to produce many of the R words but very few of the F items. This and other studies have shown also that the poor performance with respect to F words reflects lack of memory processing (e.g., less organization, rehearsal) rather than some form of active suppression of these words (e.g., Davis & Okada 1971; Bjork & Woodward 1973).

If rehearsal-like activities are involved, one might expect that retention would improve as a function of the delay between learning and the F cue, since processing should continue until directed otherwise. Accordingly, when the experimenters allowed subjects to maintain the target stimulus in memory for variable durations by delaying the instructional cues (F or R), recognition increased systematically with the amount of potential rehearsal time (i.e., the more time that elapsed before the instructional cue was presented, the better the recognition of F words [Woodward, Bjork & Jongewand 1973]).

Does a similar type of control over memory processing exist in animals? Can differential environmental signals (analogous to verbal instructions to remember or forget) influence how well target information is retained? The answer is affirmative—poorer retention occurs if a forget signal is given than if a remember cue appears. The initial discovery and elaboration of this effect was with pigeons, although similar effects have been found also with the rat (Grant 1982) and the monkey (Roberts, Mazmanian & Kraemer 1984). Experiments with pigeons illustrate the effect nicely.

A form of conditional delayed matching was used to investigate directed forgetting in pigeons (Maki & Hegvik 1980). *Food* or *no food* served as the sample stimuli to be matched symbolically after an interval by the selection of one of two arbitrary color stimuli (e.g., if *food,* peck *red* and if *no food,* peck *green*). The cuing stimuli were presentations of a houselight (e.g., forget) or darkening of the chamber (e.g., remember). The roles of the stimuli were counterbalanced for the birds, so that for half the birds houselight meant remember and for the other half it meant forget. How can one assess whether the birds are, in fact, following their instructions to forget or remember? After the birds were trained extensively under these conditions, they were given occasional probe trials. On the probe trials the test stimuli (red versus green) were presented and retention tested after the delay interval, even though the pigeons had been instructed that this was a forget trial. (Obviously, one can only occasionally lie to pigeons in this way before the F signal begins to lose its meaning. This type of minor deception, incidentally, appears no more disruptive to pigeons than to humans.) Choice of the correct comparison stimulus was generally impaired on the F cue trials compared with the same subjects' performance on R cue trials.

A second example of directed forgetting in pigeons is a study by Grant (1981) using a method similar to that of Konorski (1959) mentioned earlier. A single stimulus was presented at the test; responding to it was rewarded with food if the test stimulus matched the sample but was not rewarded if there was no match. To the extent that the pigeon pecked more at a matching than a nonmatching stimulus, retention was established. The samples were either *red* or *green.* After the sample was removed, a *vertical* or a *horizontal* line appeared on the same illuminated disk. *Vertical* indicated that memory for that sample would be tested later, but *horizontal*—the forget cue—indicated that there would be no test and that instead, a *black dot* on a white background would appear. This *black dot* had no real significance (it was followed by food on an unpredictable half of the trials regardless of whether the pigeon pecked it or not), but it did serve to keep the animal working at the problem. Some trials were no cue trials in that neither *vertical* nor *horizontal* appeared, and testing proceeded exactly as after the remember cue. Retention performance also did not differ in these two conditions, suggesting the possibility that the remember cue did not really add anything to the animal's processing. Alternatively, this could mean merely that the absence of a cue was interpreted as the absence of the forget cue, and hence so far as the pigeon was concerned, a signal to remember. More important, however, is the fact that with the forget cue, retention after the short interval was poorer, and the decrease in retention was more rapid between that point and the longer interval (Figure 5-9).

Finally, an important extension of the directed forgetting phenomenon was studied by Stonebraker and Rilling (1981). They varied the time at which presentation of the F (or R) cues followed the sample and preceded the test. Varying the interval between sample and forget cue permits examination of the effects of re-

Dot Test

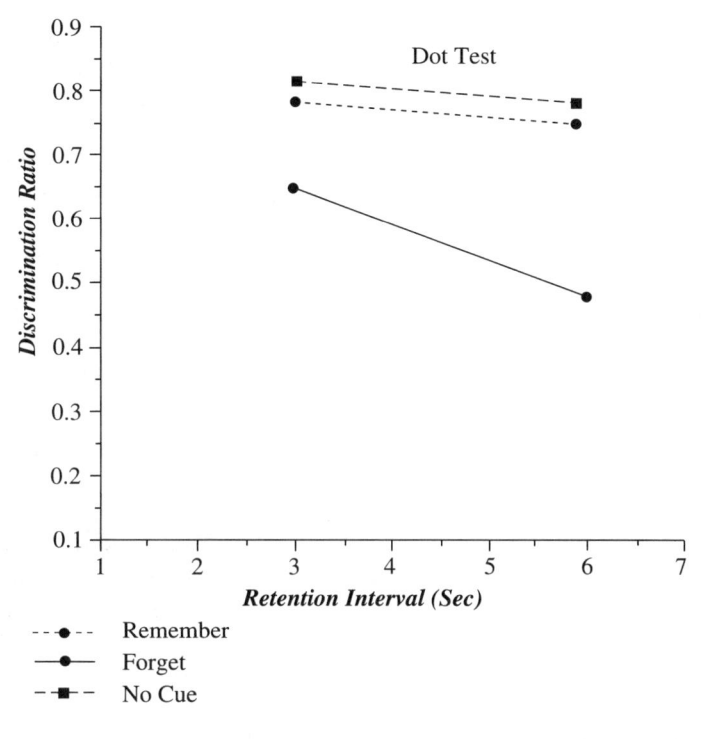

FIGURE 5-9 Forgetting by pigeons over a period of a few seconds is shown for colors that were signaled as to whether they would be tested later for retention (remember) or not (forget). The no-cue condition indicates trials on which neither the remember nor the forget signal was given following the occurrence of the critical color. (Adapted from Grant 1981.)

hearsal duration. As had been found with humans, longer delays before presentation of the R or F cues should enable the subject to process the sample information while awaiting instructions. The Konorski test for short-term retention was used as above. The sample was followed after the desired interval by a single comparison stimulus. The subjects' task was to respond only if the comparison stimulus matched the earlier sample. The interval between the sample comparison stimuli was held constant at 4 seconds, but the R or F cues were introduced either immediately (0 seconds), 2 seconds, or 3.5 seconds after termination of the sample. The F cues produced poorer retention in a time-dependent fashion. As the delay before introduction of the F cue increased, the effectiveness of the F cue decreased. This suggests that processing (rehearsal) of the target stimulus was stopped or interrupted by the F cue, with greatest effect when the F cue occurred immediately. In contrast, when the F cue was presented at the end of the interval (just prior to comparison stimulus), sufficient processing had already taken place to make the information available. The nature of the time-dependent effect is in opposition to an alternative theory: that the F cue disrupts matching because its occurrence prior to the test changes the stimulus context of the sample at test from that during its initial appearance. F cues had the least effect when they occurred 3.5 seconds after the sample and 0.5 second before the test, the condition in which the F cue should alter test context most because of its close temporal contiguity with the comparison stimulus. This would have provided the best opportunity for a disruptive effect by changing the context of the sample's appearance; instead, facilitation rather than disruption occurred.

Such experiments on the surprise effect and on directed forgetting have formed much of the basis for considering the role of cognition in animal memory (Wasserman 1993). These basic observations have been elaborated in interesting ways that further encourage the notion of such cognition. For instance, Grant (1984) has been able to decrease the effects of proactive interference on retention by selectively signaling when the interfering stimulus was to be forgotten and when it was to be remembered. Also, qualitative differences in the cognition (rehearsal) associated with memory may occur. Results by Maki (1979) may be taken to imply that the sort of rehearsal in which an animal engages for delayed matching may be of a different kind than that used for the associative learning observed in Pavlovian conditioning (Grant 1984). Generally speaking, we expect such discoveries of how cognition and memory interact to be increasingly interesting and important.

SHORT-TERM RETENTION IN HUMANS

Having considered a variety of techniques and findings for studying short-term retention in animals, we now focus on some of the literature on human memory. One might expect that research on transient forms of retention in humans would have had a long history. After all, people have been looking up phone numbers since the invention of the telephone, to say nothing of the length of time we have used momentary memory for other needs. For the most part, however, such a supposition would be incorrect. The experimental paradigms used in the first 50 years of studying human learning and memory were not suitable for investigating short-term retention, and a prevalent research theme during that period was an examination of forgetting over long intervals. Major systematic investigation of short-term retention did not begin until the late 1950s. Two papers, one by Brown (1958) and one by Peterson and Peterson (1959), initiated an investigation of memory over brief intervals that rapidly became an area of tremendous interest.

Before turning to their work, however, we consider a notable historical antecedent. At the turn of the century, William James identified two aspects of memory which he labeled primary and secondary. In contrasting primary (immediate) with secondary memory, he wrote: "But an object of primary memory is not thus brought back; it never was lost; its date was never cut off in consciousness from that of the immediately present moment." He went on to relate primary memory to the issue of how, in a world in which time flows continuously, humans seem to experience time in chunks such as moments or episodes: ". . . the portion of time which we directly intuit has a breadth of several seconds, a rearward and forward end, and may be called the specious present." (James 1890, 608–9)

Capacity of Short-Term Memory

That there are limits on the amount of information that can be encoded or apprehended during one brief presentation has long been recognized. Ebbinghaus observed, with himself as the subject, that a relatively short list (up to about 7 nonsense syllables) could be remembered after a single reading while longer lists required several repetitions. More direct examinations of short term storage capacity came from apprehension span tasks. For example, a series of randomly ordered digits might be presented to subjects instructed to repeat the sequence. It turns out that the maximum number of items that can be recalled correctly is 7, give or take a couple of items. This observation, and many others like it, led Miller (1956) to suggest that 7 ± 2 is the magic number characterizing human immediate memory span. This limited capacity of primary memory can be conceptualized as a bottleneck, restricting the flow of information for further processing. This restricted capacity provides a sound behavioral reason why 9-digit zip codes (or phone numbers) are cumbersome, since they are at (or beyond) the limit of what can be maintained in memory after a single glance. However, as Miller and others have shown, the limitations can be loosened to some extent by combining bits of information into more meaningful chunks. For instance, a long-distance phone number can be remembered not as a 10-digit number, but as a 3-digit area code followed by a 7-digit number. While the total amount of information held is expanded by chunking, the limit on the number of chunks (7 ± 2) still applies. Unfortunately, in many cases, a simple code or rule for successfully chunking arbitrary information (e.g., 9-digit numbers) is not immediately apparent.

Duration of Short-Term Retention

The studies by Brown (1958) and Peterson and Peterson (1959) focused on the duration, rather than capacity, of primary memory. Duration of retention is not a meaningful concept if subjects are free to rehearse material; continuous rehearsal could maintain information indefinitely. The question that Brown and the Petersons asked was how long information is retained in the absence of rehearsal. To assess this issue, the investigators adopted a distracter task. The idea was to prevent subjects from rehearsing by giving them an attention-demanding task that was unrelated or irrelevant to the target material. The interpolated task had to be independent of the target material, because the investigators did not want to introduce information that would produce retroactive interference.

With that general strategy as background, let us examine the Peterson and Peterson (1959) study in more detail. The subjects, college students, were presented the target item, a verbal nonsense term of 3 consonants (e.g., txk) that was followed immediately by a 3-digit number (e.g., 506). Subjects were instructed to begin counting backward by three from the number until signaled to recall the target item. To ensure that subjects were actively engaged in the distraction task, they were to count aloud. Thus, subjects counted backwards aloud until the retention interval ended, at which point the experimenter signaled them to recall the verbal item. The retention intervals ranged from 3 to 18 seconds in 3-second intervals. A single new verbal item was used for each test, and subjects were tested several times (in various orders) at each of the intervals. It should be noted that this experimental strategy was in sharp contrast to that used in traditional studies of retention (long-term), in which a number of items are presented repeatedly during the acquisition or learning phase.

Under these special conditions, which prevented or severely restricted the opportunity for rehearsal, subjects showed a precipitous decline in retention over the 18-second interval. Although the 3-letter target items were well within the span of apprehension, recall was substantially impaired with retention intervals longer than 3 seconds; by 15 seconds retention was near chance levels. In contrast, at the shortest interval performance was nearly perfect. This latter outcome is important and informative, as it rules out the otherwise plausible interpretation that the brevity of the presentation prevented subjects from fully encoding the target. Had that been the case, of course, the poor performance would simply reflect a deficit in perception rather than in memory.

Initially, the Brown-Peterson findings were taken as direct evidence of decay of information. The idea was that material that is encoded but not rehearsed dissipates or fades rapidly with the passage of time. While this is a convenient and appealing interpretation, we now know that other mechanisms are involved. For example, we discussed in chapter 4 how Keppel and Underwood (1962) found that proactive interference from preceding items could account for the short-term memory loss in the Brown-Peterson experiments (in a manner directly analogous to the similar effect described earlier for monkeys; see Figure 4-3). The proactive interference develops rapidly, as indicated by the course of the forgetting curve; the rate of memory loss as a function of the delay intervals is markedly steeper for the third (and succeeding) target items than for the initial one or two items.

The development of the Brown-Peterson paradigm led to a veritable explosion of research on short-term retention, now more generally called working memory. These elaborations are beyond the scope of this book, but a useful overview can be found in more specialized texts (e.g., Baddeley 1990; Greene 1992).

While the Brown-Peterson paradigm for humans may be quite different from the delayed matching used with animals, in both cases we see the operation of a common process, interference from prior learning acting on short-term retention. Attempts to compare the characteristics of short-term retention in animals and humans more directly have indicated other similarities as well as differences. A few examples are presented next.

COMPARISONS OF MONKEY AND HUMAN MEMORY

It should be clear by now that retention after short intervals can differ in ways other than rate of decline in accuracy over time. Retention may differ also in terms of its functional characteristics. A common example is the serial position curve, in which the first few and last few items presented among a set (list) will be more accurately recalled later than items from the middle of the list. The characteristics of memory may be said to differ also if variables such as study time or length of retention interval have different effects on retention in different circumstances.

Roberts and Kraemer (1981) directly compared retention of abstract symbols in humans and monkeys (e.g., white triangle against background of a black circle; white stripes against a black circle; white triangle against a striped circle, etc.). For both the monkeys and humans the task was delayed matching 0.5 or 5 seconds after the sample or samples were shown. On various trials either 1, 3, or 6 samples appeared. When 3 or 6 samples were presented, one immediately followed another. Each sample appeared for a duration of either 0.25 or 1 second. The major differences in the procedure were that the monkeys were confined in a standard test chamber and, when they responded correctly were rewarded with a sweet banana pellet plus the brief sound of a 2,900-Hz tone, whereas for the humans the display apparatus was placed on a table and correct responses were rewarded with only the tone.

There were some striking similarities in the characteristics of monkey and human memory, but some differences also. Both the monkeys and humans showed conventional serial position effects in remembering lists of 3 or 6 samples. These included primacy and recency effects—superior retention for those items presented first (primacy) and those items presented last (recency) relative to items presented in the middle of a list.

The biggest differences were in retention accuracy, with humans being more accurate (Figure 5-10). Sample duration did not affect retention accuracy for either monkeys or humans. There was clear forgetting over the 5-second interval by the humans, but the small amount of forgetting by the monkeys during this period was not statistically significant.

Finally, memory for a sample presented alone was generally better than that for any sample presented in lists of 3 or 6 items, for both humans and monkeys. In comparison to the single-item list, the relatively poor retention observed for the last items of a longer list may be attributed to proactive interference from previous items in the list, the relatively poor retention of the first items on the list may be attributed to retroactive interference from subsequent items in the list, and the poorest retention

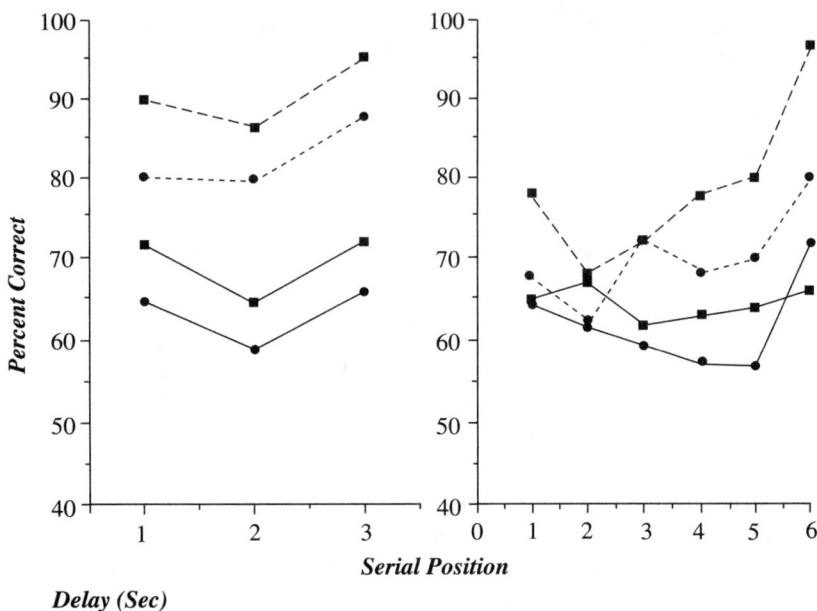

Delay (Sec)
- ─■─ Humans–.5
- ─●─ Humans–5.0
- ──■── Monkeys .5
- ──●── Monkeys 5.0

FIGURE 5-10 Retention of visual stimuli by humans and monkeys tested either 0.5 or 5 seconds after they observed the stimulus is shown as a function of the order in which the stimulus occurred in a list (serial position). Although the accuracy of the monkeys obviously was poorer than that of the humans, in both cases retention was more effective for items that had occurred at the beginning or end of the list than for those that had been presented in the middle of the list. (Adapted from Roberts & Kraemer 1981.)

among mid-list items to both factors. Although statistical evaluation of all of these effects was not presented by Roberts and Kraemer (this was not the focus of their study), it seems clear that when ceiling effects do not impair measurement, both retroactive and proactive interference effects are evident for both monkeys and humans.

One way to explain the primacy effect is by assuming that the initial items in a list will be subjected to more rehearsal than items presented later. There is a variety of fairly good evidence for this notion, for which the first systematic application to human memory may be attributed to Atkinson and Shiffrin (1968). It has been used to explain such interesting effects as the relatively small primacy effects observed among preschool children (who do not rehearse in the same way as adults [e.g., Ornstein 1977]). On this basis, it might appear that the primacy effect observed in monkeys by Roberts and Kraemer (obtained also in studies by Sands and Wright 1980) implies that the monkeys were rehearsing the pictures. It has been established that humans can rehearse pictures without using language (Graefe & Watkins 1980; Watkins & Graefe 1981). Whether monkeys do so is considered next.

Rehearsal of Pictures

To assess the possibility that monkeys might rehearse pictures to enhance their later retention, Roberts and Kraemer (1984) varied the time between pictures. More time between pictures would allow more time for rehearsal of the preceding picture. A previous experiment with humans illustrates this effect nicely (Intraub 1980). This experiment tested recognition for pictures that had been presented for a brief duration of 0.11 second. In different conditions, the remaining 5.89 seconds of a 6-second period was filled in either of three ways of interest here. Either the picture remained on, the picture was replaced by a blank homogeneous field, or the picture was replaced by the next rapidly presented picture to be remembered. Retention was strikingly accurate (83 percent) for those subjects that merely looked at a blank field for the remainder of the 6-second period after the 0.11-second picture had appeared. This high level of performance was only a little less accurate than when the picture itself remained on throughout the entire 6-second period (97 percent). In contrast, when additional pictures to be remembered were presented at a rapid rate instead of the blank field, retention accuracy dropped to 37 percent. It was as if the period following a picture is used by humans for rehearsal to promote remembering of it.

Roberts and Kraemer (1984) tested monkeys in an analogous experiment. Rather than abstract geometric figures, this study used as samples a large set of pictures of objects belonging to particular categories, such as fruits, flowers, people, animals, and so forth. Each monkey was given three pictures before each test, with either of three kinds of presentations: (1) a picture presented for 6 seconds, followed immediately by another picture presented for 6 seconds; (2) a picture presented for 0.3 second followed immediately by another picture for 0.3 second; or (3) a picture presented for 0.3 second followed by 5.7 seconds spent in darkness prior to presentation of the next picture. The longer duration of exposure of the picture (5.7 seconds versus 0.3 seconds) resulted in significantly better retention after the only delay tested (1 second). But there was no indication whatsoever from the second condition that adding 5.7 seconds of rehearsal opportunity in darkness facilitated retention. Monkeys did not show the enhanced retention observed in humans permitted a similar period of rehearsal following sample presentation. This suggests that monkeys either do not rehearse pictures, do not rehearse pictures in the same way as humans, or do rehearse pictures but it does not affect their retention.

A final example addressed an issue of content of memory: Do monkeys and humans encode and remember the same things about pictures? Roberts, Mazmanian and Kraemer (1987) tested the delayed matching accuracy of monkeys and humans for the same sort of pictures used in the Roberts and Kraemer (1984) study. The task of these subjects was to identify a picture 1 or 10 seconds after it had been presented, on the basis of only part of the picture. Sometimes the subjects saw at the test only the central portion of the picture with the remainder obscured by a peripheral mask (blackened portion of the periphery). On other trials the animals saw only the peripheral part of the picture (center mask) and on still other occasions they saw obscured portions of both the peripheral and central features of this picture in which randomly selected, 1-cm squares were blackened out (noise mask). For each type of mask either 25, 50, or 75 percent of the picture was obscured. Although humans tended to be more accurate and to respond with shorter latencies in essentially all conditions, their similarity to monkeys in the effects of the type and amount of masking was striking. For both monkeys and humans, accuracy was poorest with the central mask, intermediate with the noise mask, and best with the peripheral mask. This suggests that what was noticed and remembered about the samples was similar for monkeys and humans.

Summary

Comparisons of short-term retention in monkeys and humans have revealed similar effects of the length of time allowed to study pictures and of the primacy and recency positions in memory for serial lists, and similar results in what portion of the sample is most likely noticed and remembered. Humans are more accurate in retention—no surprise—but so far the only difference between monkeys and humans that may tell us something about differences in their memory processing is that human retention is facilitated by a postsample rehearsal opportunity whereas that of monkeys is not.

Short Note on Other Tests of Short-term Retention

There are many ways to test short-term retention in animals other than delayed matching or delayed response tasks. A common test with the rat is termed *delayed alternation.* For this test the rat first is allowed to enter one of two alternative goal boxes. After a prescribed delay, the rat is given a choice between the two and must select the alternative goal box in order to obtain the reward. A slightly complicated variation of this is the radial maze test in which there are many alternative goal boxes, typically 8 or 16, and the rat learns that reward can be obtained only by entering a goal box that it has not previously entered on that trial. One can then test the rat's memory for where it has been. This is a useful paradigm for assessing spatial memory, as will be discussed in chapter 6, and also may provide a model for how animals forage for food in the wild.

Still another way to measure short-term retention is by varying the interval between a conditioned stimulus and the unconditioned stimulus that it signals, or what has been referred to as *associative memory* (Revusky 1971). The most striking example of this is the retention of information for a novel taste. If such a taste is followed after 6 or perhaps even 12 hours by an illness, an aversion to that taste will be acquired by the rat. The conditioning of such an aversion becomes weaker the longer the interval between the taste and the illness, which might be an indication that retention of the taste is required at the time of the illness and declines with time just as do other memory attributes. When memory for taste is assessed in this way, one can observe both retroactive and proactive interference (impairment in conditioning observed when the critical taste is followed or preceded by a different taste) and poorer retention by immature animals, the sorts of phenomena common to memory generally. This lends credence to the view that such long delay learning can be taken as an approximate index of memory for taste.

Using an analogous strategy, the memory for responses in the rat (or monkey) has also been assessed by variation of the delay between that response and the reward for that response (e.g., Lett 1974; Salmon & D'Amato 1981). Special circumstances are necessary for such a test, however, because in most procedures reward will not affect responding if the delay is more than a few seconds. Generally speaking, these tests lose many of the analytic advantages shown in the delayed matching test. A primary difficulty is that such tests do not permit a clear separation of processes responsible for forgetting and motivational effects linked to different lengths of delays before reward is obtained. At best they provide a modest alternative that can be applied to rodents, which are otherwise unsuitable for efficient application of the delayed matching procedures.

Is there any critical observation indicating that the processes mediating short-term retention differ from those responsible for long-term retention (the latter tested over periods of days, weeks, or a lifetime rather than seconds or minutes)? This question has been stated in different ways throughout the history of psychology. During the 1960s the hypothetical distinction between short-term memory and long-term memory was used so frequently that even today they are spoken of as if they represent different brain and behavior processes (see chapter 12). Yet the functional distinctions that seemed then to argue for such different processes were not substantiated. At present there is still no single observation, or even a convincing set of observations, that one can point to to justify such a distinction. The distinction remains possible, nevertheless, on the same vague basis as that conjectured by William James 100 years ago: that, shortly after exposure to an episode, the memory representing that episode remains in something like conscious awareness, or to say that another way, the memory remains active. As such the memory would require no retrieval process for it to be manifested in behavior. Otherwise, if the memory became inactive like all other memories that we have acquired and stored, some special event-driven process would be required for retrieval of that memory. While we have not the space to speculate further on this point, chapters by Grant (1981, 1984) and Honig (1984) may be studied for thoughtful reviews on this subject.

CHAPTER SUMMARY

The study of short-term retention in animals focused until about 1970 on the delayed response task—a test of what response is given when there is a delay between the signal as to which response is correct and the opportunity to respond. A different type of test—delayed matching-to-sample and its variations—has analytical advantages over the delayed response test that have been exploited since then to increase more rapidly our knowledge about short-term retention. Delayed matching requires that the animal identify a previous event, such as a picture, as the same or different from a test picture. This task permits wide variation in what is to be remembered and experimental control over the relationship between the target memory and other events experienced by the animal that could influence responding.

Short-term retention is influenced by events experienced during the retention interval (retroactive interference) and those occurring prior to the event that is to be remembered (proactive interference). If a visual event (picture, color, symbol) is to be remembered, short-term retention in monkeys and pigeons can be drastically improved if they spend the retention interval in darkness. Retention also is determined somewhat by relative illumination during the three phases of learning, retention interval, and test. But when illumination occurs during learning and during test, retention is proportional to the amount of darkness experienced during the retention interval. In monkeys, degree of illumination during the retention interval does not seem to influence memory for sounds, although memory for sounds is impaired by nonspecific acoustical events during the retention interval. Surprisingly, however, more specific similarity between the target sound and subsequent sounds has not seemed to affect retention of the target in any simple manner.

Despite early indications that the amount of proactive interference to be accounted for in short-term retention by animals is quite small, it is now known that this source of forgetting can have massive effects. Tests of short-term retention in animals have also provided answers to the old question of whether rate of forgetting depends on what is to be remembered. Tests with rats, pigeons, and monkeys have all indicated clear differences in the forgetting of visual and auditory events. The meaning of such effects of memory content on forgetting remains uncertain, however. We do not yet know, for example, whether these differences are intrinsic to the sensory systems or whether they might disappear or be different if the stimuli were equated for other psychological factors such as subjective intensity or familiarity. Uncertainty remains also in the meaning of memory differences attributed to prospective versus retrospective processing, which seem more realistically to reflect differences in encoded content than in memory processes. For this distinction the issue is whether the animal holds in memory a representation of the sample item presented initially or the symbolic equivalent of the sample item that is presented only at the test. Substantial experimental creativity has been exhibited in establishing this distinction, and we may anticipate similarly creative tests in the future to determine the importance of this distinction.

It is within the context of short-term retention that the cognitive processes of the animal following critical events have seemed to determine subsequent retention of those events. In both rats and pigeons there appears to be a type of rehearsal that occurs rather automatically after a learning episode but is disruptable by relatively innocuous psychological events such as surprise. Such a process has been suggested further by experiments showing that retention can be determined by signaling the animal, following an event, whether to remember it or not. The similarity between this hypothetical rehearsal process and the mechanisms applied by humans in remembering may be fortuitous. Yet there are an increasing number of phenomena in short-term retention that have seemed similar when compared relatively directly for monkeys and humans. These similarities have, however, been accompanied also by the observation of important differences in the short-term retention of monkeys and humans.

▶ 6

Memory for Stimulus Attributes and Spatial Location

Studies of animal memory traditionally have defined retention in terms of the fate of the learned response. Does an animal remember to turn left to obtain food or to escape shock? Do rats that have received avoidance training continue to make the avoidance response, or make it as swiftly, following a retention interval? These and related questions characterize in simple form what is often considered under the topic of simple forgetting or spontaneous forgetting, and the focus is often on whether subjects retain what to do.

As we have indicated, however, memories are likely to be represented as a collection of attributes associated with the target event. Thus, not only responses but also conditional stimuli (CSs), discriminative stimuli, and even background stimuli (contextual cues) ought to constitute some of the features of memory for a particular episode. Organisms may forget when (or where) to make the responses. Suppose that subjects retain information about the general relationships or contingencies (e.g., tone was followed by shock), but forget the specific attributes of the critical stimuli (e.g., frequency of tone, intensity of shock, elements of context). In this case, the continued occurrence of the response under the original training conditions would tell us little about these other aspects of memory. What is needed is a different type of assessment procedure to address this issue. In a sense, we would like to be able to sort out whether the subject remembers not only what to do (i.e., which response to make) but also when to do it (i.e., under which stimulus conditions should the response occur) and why to do it (i.e., what is the value of the reinforcer or unconditioned stimulus [US]).

One strategy employed to answer the latter two questions has been to determine if behavior is changed when the conditions at testing are altered. If the alteration is sufficient to disrupt responding at a short interval (and is therefore detectable or perceivable) but fails to impair performance at longer retention intervals, then we can infer that at the longer intervals forgetting has occurred for those specific stimulus features. Paradoxically, memory is said to be impaired when responding increases in the presence of changed stimuli. But this paradox disappears when it is recognized that the memory in question is for stimulus attributes. If the organism no longer can distinguish or remember the features of the training situation, it is unlikely to be disturbed by changes in those cues. We will consider some specific examples that may help make this point clear.

STIMULUS GENERALIZATION

To understand more fully the strategy for investigating stimulus memory, we need to review stimulus generalization, a fundamental and very robust learning phenomenon. Basically, generalization refers to the tendency of subjects (human and animal) that have been conditioned to one stimulus to respond to new stimuli which are similar to the training stimulus. Generally speaking, the strength or probability of responding decreases as the novel stimuli become more dissimilar to the original. In effect, stimulus generalization means that subjects will respond to stimuli to which they have never been trained, albeit less to these stimuli than to the training stimulus.

One of the earliest and most striking demonstrations of stimulus generalization was seen in Watson and Raynor's (1920) study of Little Albert. In that classic study, Albert, a 2 1/2-year-old boy, was conditioned to be mildly fearful of a white rat. Prior to conditioning, Albert reacted to the rat with signs of approach, such as reaching out to touch the animal. This positive affect changed to fear, however, after a few trials in which presentation of the rat was followed shortly by the noxious clamor of a loud gong behind Albert's back. Not surprisingly, the gong elicited visible startle reactions and crying from Little Albert, and conditioning occurred: after the pairings he began to cry and display other signs of distress at the mere sign of the rat.

In the stimulus generalization aspect of their study, Watson and Raynor found that a Santa Claus mask and cotton would also now upset Albert, although not as strongly as the rat. Since he did not cry at the sight of opera glasses or toy blocks, the reaction appeared to be based upon similarity among the stimuli—the common features of white furriness shared in various degrees by the rat, the Santa mask, and the cotton. Not only can a relatively neutral environmental stimulus (the rat) come to acquire properties or hedonic value (fear) through association with unpleasant events, but these conditioned responses can transfer, as it were, to related cues. Importantly, the related cues themselves were never paired with the aversive event.

Despite serious methodological and ethical objections raised about Watson and Raynor's procedures in recent years, this study had a profound intellectual importance that remains with us today. Clearly, Pavlovian conditioning was not limited to dogs, nor to salivary reactions. Important and strong emotional responses can be readily conditioned even in very young humans. Watson and Raynor were quick to point out how such an associative process could provide a mechanism by which early experiences might influence our later behaviors, as well as provide a source of irrational fears or phobias and how they might transfer to new cues. While conditioning in children and even newborn infants is now well known (Rovee-Collier 1984), Watson and Raynor's finding constituted a serious challenge to many of the genetic and psychoanalytic assertions of their era.

Although the stimulus generalization seen in Watson and Raynor's study was based upon Pavlovian conditioning, generalization is also an important characteristic of instrumental and operant learning. In fact, several methodological considerations have made the free operant task a particularly attractive paradigm for investigating generalization. For example, pioneering work some years ago by Guttman and Kalish (1956) demonstrated that the strong resistance to extinction produced by schedules of reinforcement permitted assessment of generalization gradients within individual subjects. This study opened the way for investigations using the free operant paradigm, and orderly inverted V-shaped generalization gradients have subsequently been obtained in many species and with a variety of stimulus dimensions.

In most instances stimulus generalization is adaptive for an organism. Just as we "never step into the same river twice," stimuli are seldom exactly the same from moment to moment. If generalization did not occur, every perceptibly different variation on a stimulus theme would constitute a new situation requiring further conditioning to acquire new properties. Generalization permits responding to occur despite "slop" in the stimulus situation; learning transfers to related stimuli.

But there are limitations on generalization to new stimuli, and as the similarity to the original situation decreases so too does responding, which is equally adaptive because it helps prevent inappropriate responses. It is this feature of stimulus generalization, generalization decrement, that has attracted particular attention over the years. For one thing, reliable changes in responding as stimuli are varied physically indicate that subjects must be able to perceive or detect these alterations—otherwise, responding should be about the same among the various test stimuli. (If an animal trained to respond to a red disk cannot distinguish pink from red, then substituting a pink disk should make little difference.) Thus, generalization decrement phenomena afford a convenient technique for evaluating the sensory/perceptual capacities of nonverbal organisms. In essence, differential responding to stimuli can reveal an animal's sensitivity to various sensory characteristics. In addition, the lawful relationship between amount of responding and degree of physical change in stimuli has intrigued investigators. While there is no a priori reason, for example, why pigeons should see relationships between wavelength (hue) as we do, the shape of the generalization gradient suggests that their phenomenological experience of color is rather like ours—orange is closer to red than to blue, etc. Shepard (1987) has suggested that stimulus generalization is as basic a learning phenomenon as the associative process itself. For these reasons, there are now hundreds of published studies in the area of stimulus generalization, exploring a variety of physical stimulus dimensions as well as various experimental manipulations that can influence the generalization gradient.

MEMORY FOR INDIVIDUAL ATTRIBUTES OF A STIMULUS

A decrement in responding to test stimuli different from the training stimulus indicates that subjects must be able to distinguish perceptually among the values—otherwise, responding should be similar across the test continuum, i.e., a flat gradient should be obtained. If the same test conditions producing a generalization decrement shortly after training yield a flat gradient following a longer retention interval, then it would appear that information about the characteristics of the target stimulus have been forgotten. Certainly the sensory/perceptual acuity already demonstrated could not have deteriorated in a few days. Imagine a situation in which we are shown a red patch and asked to remember it. If tested with a higher similar but slightly pinker color a few minutes later, we might correctly reject the new stimulus. After a week, however, we are likely to mistakenly accept the similar stimulus as if it were the original. Note that we haven't forgotten the response (it's a reddish patch), but only the precise quality of the attributes.

With these considerations in mind, we can turn to some of the experimental evidence concerning memory as it pertains to attributes of stimuli. In one of the earliest studies examining the effects of retention interval upon stimulus generalization gradients, Perkins and Weyant (1958) trained rats to run down a black (B) straight alley for food and later tested them with the same color condition (e.g., B-B) or under a switched condition (e.g., B-W). When testing occurred shortly after the end of training, rats ran much more slowly in the new (generalized) stimulus alley than in the alley of the original color. This generalization decrement, in which subjects responded to altered stimuli with less strength than to the training situation, provided clear evidence that the rats recognized the differences between the two situations. Despite this physical discriminability, subjects tested 1 week after training no longer performed differentially, i.e., they responded vigorously in the presence of either the original or shifted stimulus condition. Thus, the running response was well retained, but the differential behavior to the two test conditions (B versus W) disappeared. These outcomes are summarized in Figure 6-1. Why did subjects come to respond equally to either stimulus situation after a long interval? One likely view is that they no longer remembered the particular characteristics of the training situation; the common aspects of the context (the physical structure of the alleys, similar odors, etc.) were sufficient to support the behavior of running for food. Or, as Perkins and Weyant (1958) put it: "forgetting the color of the runway occurs more rapidly than does the general tendency to run on elevated runways" (p. 599).

A few years later Thomas and Lopez (1962), using pigeons in a free-operant appetitively reinforced task, replicated the basic finding that generalization gradients

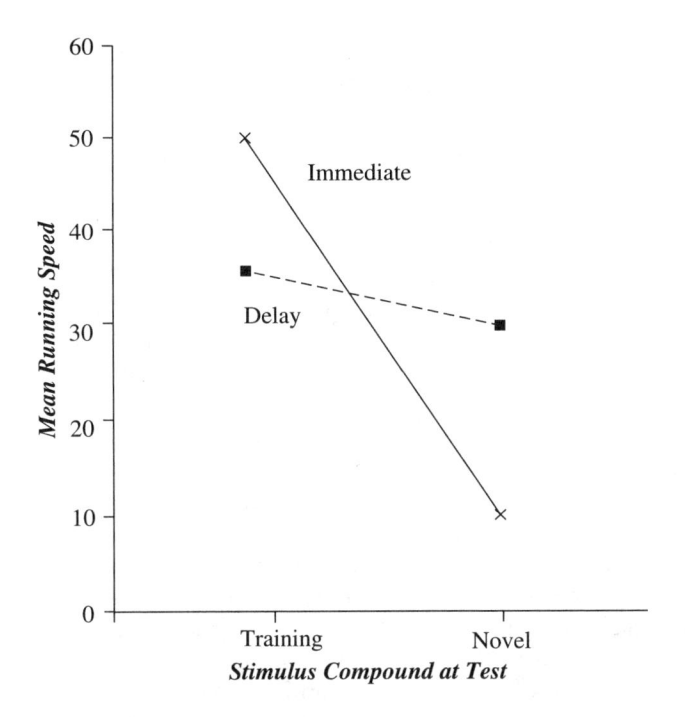

FIGURE 6-1 Running speed in a straight alley under the original training (T) or altered (N) stimulus conditions at testing. (Adapted from Perkins & Weyant 1958.)

flatten as the retention interval increases. After being trained on a variable interval schedule of reinforcement to peck at a key of one color (550 μ, or bluish-yellow), birds were tested for their tendency to respond to the disk when it was illuminated with the original wavelength or one of several other wavelengths. Subjects tested in a 24-hour delay condition had significantly flatter gradients than those tested with only a few minutes delay. Flat gradients might represent an artificial effect (artifact) if, for example, responding to the original stimulus had fallen to a low level after 24 hours. In that case, poor responding to the original stimulus would produce a floor effect so that any changes in response rates to generalized stimuli simply could no longer be observed. Such a finding would not be of much value with respect to assessing the influence of a retention interval on the slope of the gradient. Fortunately, no such artifact was involved; indeed, Thomas and Lopez (1962) observed that the subjects in the delay condition actually emitted slightly more responses than did the immediate test group. Thus, the flatter gradient appears to reflect loss of information about the particular stimulus correlated with reinforcement during training. More recently,

Thomas et al. (1985), using either wavelength or line tilt as stimulus dimensions, have shown that generalization gradients continue to flatten when the retention interval is expanded from one day to one week.

Explicit discrimination training is known to produce sharper (steeper) gradients than single stimulus training. One interpretation is that differential reinforcement (e.g., one color pays off, another color doesn't) results in better attention to stimuli, or more precisely, to differences among stimuli. Would such training eliminate the flattening of the generalization gradient that occurs with delayed testing? Apparently not—Thomas and Burr (1969) found the gradient to flatten over time even following discrimination training. In that study, pigeons were reinforced for pecking at one of two colored disks (the S+) and not reinforced (extinguished) for pecking at the other (S–) until subjects restricted almost all of their responses to the correct stimulus (S+). As expected, subjects showed quite steep gradients immediately after training, but the gradient became flatter when testing was delayed.

Evidence that stimulus attributes are forgotten is not limited to operant tasks with appetitive reward. McAllister and McAllister (1963) found a similar effect in rats given Pavlovian fear conditioning. Their procedure also provides another illustration of the often pervasive effect of context. The McAllisters had developed an avoidance paradigm in which the acquisition of Pavlovian fear and the instrumental response were separated (cf. Miller 1948). In phase 1, subjects received a number of light-shock (CS-US) pairings in a small compartment. No programmed instrumental response was available to prevent or terminate shock. In phase 2, a barrier was removed and the subjects could leave the compartment when the CS was presented. No shocks were delivered in this stage. Learning was measured by the increasing quickness (shorter latencies) with which subjects escaped from the CS over trials. Because the motivation and reinforcement for such responding would reasonably appear to be the emotional state of fear (in the absence of any further shocks), the McAllisters have argued that such an escape from fear task has important advantages over traditional avoidance tasks where escape from shock and escape from the CS may be intermingled.

But the finding of particular interest to us here concerns the effect of subtle changes in the compartment where CS-US pairing occurred. The McAllisters had two apparently identical chambers, although only one of these was connected to a shock source. To facilitate testing, however, some subjects were tested in the original training chamber (A) and others in the identical second chamber (B). An unexpected outcome was observed when subjects were tested immediately after training: although all subjects learned to escape from the light (CS), responding was significantly poorer in the alternative (B) chamber. Since the animals were escaping from the CS and the compartments appeared interchangeable, this disruptive effect of a change in the background contextual stimulus was striking. A comparable finding has also been obtained in a study in which rats received fear conditioning to static cues (the black side of a black-white box) and were then tested for their tendency to avoid the shocked side. Avoidance of the black compartment was significantly higher when subjects were tested in their own training apparatus than in another matching black-white box (Rohrbaugh & Riccio 1968).

In the McAllister's investigation, responding to the light (CS) differed depending on whether or not the very same apparatus was used for both training and testing. This outcome indicates that subjects were able to distinguish between two very similar background (apparatus) contexts. (How this was done, i.e., what stimuli the subjects attended to, is an interesting issue but not relevant to our immediate concerns.) But impressive as this feat is, subjects do prove to be fallible—if a delay is introduced between training and testing. In the McAllisters' study, following a 24-hour interval rats still showed excellent escape from fear performance, but now responding was equally good in either test apparatus. This outcome is illustrated in Figure 6-2. Desiderato, Butler, and Meyer (1966) extended this finding to a situation in which an explicit and physically specifiable change was made in the training

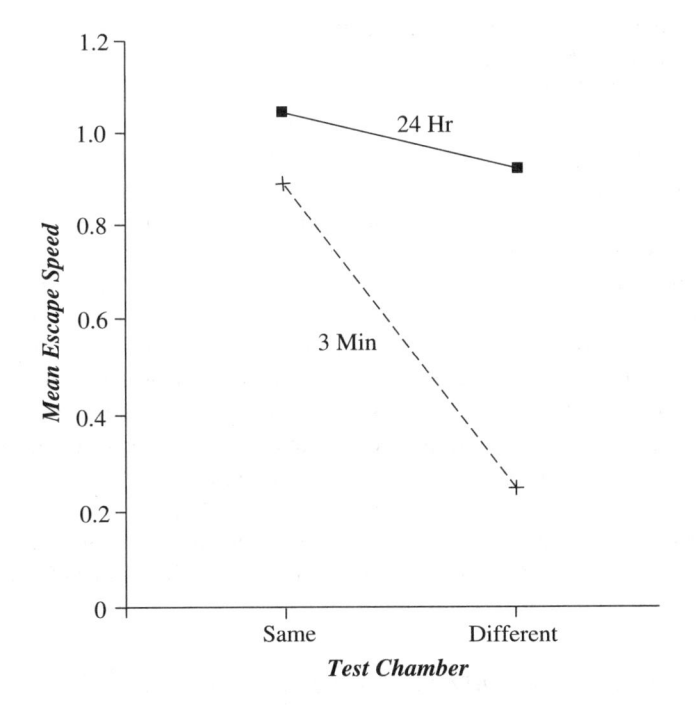

FIGURE 6-2 Performance in an escape from fear test when the context (chamber) was either the same as or slightly different from that in training. Light was the CS in all conditions. (Adapted from McAllister 1963.)

stimulus. They gave rats Pavlovian fear conditioning in which the color of the apparatus cues (white panel) was paired with shock. Rats were tested with the original color or with new stimuli (black panels) either immediately or at several intervals during a 24-hour period. Response levels to the training CS (white) remained similar across the retention intervals. In contrast, responding to the generalized stimulus was poor at the short intervals but improved with longer delays.

Several other examples of forgetting of attributes of signals will illustrate the pervasive nature of the phenomenon. One study (Thomas & Riccio 1979) took advantage of the Kamin blocking effect to assess temporal changes in memory for stimuli. Kamin (968) and others had found that prior conditioning to one stimulus (A) will prevent or attenuate conditioning to a second stimulus (B) presented in compound with the first element (A + B together). Thus, if tone and shock are paired for several trials, whereupon a light is added to the tone and the compound is paired with shock for several more trials, separate assessments of the individual stimuli will reveal strong conditioned fear to the tone, but little fear to the light. One interpretation of this blocking of learning is that the added stimulus (light) is redundant—subjects have already discovered that tone predicts shock, the addition of the light provides no new information about the impending event, and only informative stimuli are conditionable.

Thomas and Riccio reasoned that if some feature of the original CS (element A) were changed in the second phase of the training (compound CS-US pairings), the blocking effect might not occur because both elements of the compound would now be novel (more or less). Indeed, this is exactly what happened when rats received a 3,000 Hz tone paired with shock on initial conditioning trials, followed 1 day later by training trials with a compound stimulus in which a light (element B) was combined with either the original (3,000 Hz) or one of two different tones (1,000 or 10,000 Hz). Subjects showed substantially more conditioning to the light when it was combined with the different tones than when the light was combined with the original tone. However, when the same manipulation (combining the light and a different tone) was made 21 days rather than 1 day after initial training, little learning conditioning occurred to the light. Why should a tone different from the conditioned tone block learning to the added element after the long retention interval? Presumably subjects had forgotten the precise aspects of the original tone, so that they failed to recognize the new tone as different. Forgetting of stimulus attributes led to the functional interchangeability of several tones that were perceptually distinguishable from each other at short intervals.

Forgetting of Interoceptive (Flavor) Attributes

The preceding studies all involved exteroceptive signals such as lights and tones. Do similar changes in retention of stimulus features occur for other classes of stimuli, such as interoceptive cues? There is reason to suspect that differences might exist, since interoceptive (e.g., taste) and exteroceptive cues differ in their associability with various unconditioned events. Garcia and his colleagues (e.g., Garcia & Koelling 1966) provided a now classic demonstration of this effect by showing that taste-illness pairing produced much better learning than did comparable tone-illness pairings; conversely, a tone-shock correlation resulted in stronger conditioning than comparable taste-shock pairings. This differential associability of particular signals with particular types of events (USs), often referred to as the Garcia effect, in conjunction with the finding that taste aversions can be acquired with extraordinarily long delays between the CS and US, have led some to believe that conditioned taste aversion is a unique form of learning. The argument has been made that conditioned taste aversion represents a very specialized and adaptive form of learning (cf. Logue 1979). Accordingly, perhaps there would be very little degrading of the memory for stimulus (taste) attributes. Although evidence on this topic is limited, at least one study has examined retention of a feature of a flavor CS (Richardson, Williams & Riccio 1984). Their study took advantage of the fact that conditioned taste aversions are very enduring. Thus, the indicator response (for assessing stimuli) should still be available after a long retention interval, and a generalization test could be conducted. Adult rats were made slightly ill by administering lithium chloride after they drank a 10% sucrose solution. When tested after a short (2-day) interval, the rats showed much less aversion to two novel sucrose concentrations than to the original. After 1 or 3 weeks, a different picture was seen: the aversion to the original flavor (CS) remained strong, as expected, but now the subjects avoided the novel solutions almost as much as the CS. This flattening of the gradient is consistent with the conservative behavior of rats reported in other studies of aversively motivated behavior (Hendersen 1985). It appears that the rat initially attributes the cause of its illness to a particular sweet flavor, but with the passage of time comes to play it safe by avoiding a wide range of sweet solutions.

Forgetting of Stimulus Attributes by Humans

Do humans also show forgetting of stimulus attributes, or is this effect peculiar to animal studies? There is no doubt that humans are equally susceptible; entire books have dealt with how humans process separately individual attributes of verbal units such as words (Underwood 1983).

In a study that parallels many of the experiments just described, Bahrick, Clark, and Bahrick (1967) examined visual recognition of drawing in humans after retention intervals of 0 hour (immediate), 2 hours, 2 days, or 2 weeks. The subjects' task was to choose the original target item (e.g., a drawing of a coffee cup) from an array of 11 choices (e.g., other styles of cups). The false alternatives, or foils, were scaled with respect to their similarity to the prototype object. The tendency for humans to pick incorrect but similar stimulus objects is not unlike an animals' tendency to respond to new (but related) stimuli. Viewed this way, orderly and fairly steep generalization gradients were obtained at the shortest interval, i.e., subjects chose mainly the correct object or one or two similar items. With increasing time between exposure to the target and the test, the distribution of errors changed—foils increasingly different from the target were now also incorrectly chosen as matching the original. The distinctive features of the target were no longer remembered very well, although the generic response (choose cup) was certainly not forgotten.

Forgetting of the precise features of stimuli can be seen in more complex cognitive processes as well. In one condition, Sulin and Dooling (1974) gave a sentence recognition test to college students who had read a passage about a famous person (e.g., Adolph Hitler) either a few minutes or 1 week earlier. The subjects were to decide whether the test sentences were in fact in the original passage or not. At the short retention interval subjects were quite accurate in discriminating even highly related thematic foils from the target sentences. However, false positive errors increased significantly at the 1-week test interval. Sulin and Dooling interpreted this outcome as evidence of reconstructive processes at work in memory in that prior knowledge about Hitler distorted judgments about what particular statements had been present during the episode of reading the passage. However, their finding is certainly consistent with our view that the forgetting of stimulus attributes is a pervasive principle of memory.

An Implication of the Forgetting of Individual Attributes of a Stimulus

The finding that discriminability of stimuli and stimulus situations diminishes as a function of the retention interval poses something of a dilemma for interpretations of retention loss (forgetting) that emphasize the role of subtle changes in contextual cues at testing. In its simplest form, the problem is that if contextual changes cannot be detected after a long interval, the stimulus changes present at a retention test should have no adverse consequences for retrieval (Riccio, Richardson & Ebner 1984). Indeed, just as responding increases to generalized stimuli following a delay, one might expect memory retrieval to be enhanced with the passage of time—an outcome which, sadly, seldom occurs. Gisquet-Verrier and Alexinsky (1986) have bolstered the analysis of this paradox by showing that reminder treatments that are effective in alleviating spontaneous forgetting of a runway task provide no benefit when the response decrement is induced by a deliberate shift in context. Yet if spontaneous forgetting is based upon a change in context (albeit an implicit one), how could the reminder outcomes be so different? The suggestion is that two quite different processes must be involved. Although further consideration of the apparent paradox is beyond the scope of this text, we should note that the decreased discriminability of stimulus situations over time may result in increased opportunities for other processes, such as proactive and retroactive interference to impair responding (see Riccio et al. 1984; Riccio, Ackil & Burch-Vernon 1992).

GENERALIZATION GRADIENTS AND MEMORY FOR CONFLICTING STIMULI

In the preceding section, we described studies employing generalization gradients to assess spontaneous or simple changes in memory for stimulus attributes. But the phenomenon of generalization can also provide a means for investigating memory for conflicting information, as Thomas (e.g. 1981) has shown in a series of elegant studies. Using changes in the slope of gradients and in the location of the peak of the gradient, Thomas has extended the traditional analysis of interference to the domain of interactions between stimuli. For example, Burr and Thomas (1972) asked whether distributed practice on a second, conflicting, task would reduce proactive interference, as has been found with human memory (Underwood & Ekstrand 1966). In the proactive interference condition, pigeons on a simple color discrimination (task 1) subsequently learned the reversal (task 2) of the original problem with either massed (one session) or equal but distributed (daily 30-minute sessions) exposures. On an immediate test, little proactive interference (PI) was obtained; all groups showed similar sloping gradients with peaks at the second S+ (recency effect). However, on a delayed test, the massed practice group showed substantial PI, as reflected in a relatively flat gradient of responding across several test stimuli. These differences at the two retention intervals are shown in Figure 6-3. Consistent with other research on PI the gradient in the distributed group continued to reflect a recency effect, i.e., retention of the second S+ was not disrupted by the prior (opposite) training.

Using similar strategies in a series of rather complex experiments, Thomas and his colleagues (see Thomas 1981) also examined the influence of general attentional sets as sources of PI. In one study, pigeons trained to peck at a vertical line were later trained on a discrimination problem where green was reinforced, but the vertical line was not. When tested to stimuli on the wavelength dimension after a retention interval, these subjects showed a flatter gradient than control subjects, apparently reflecting PI from implicit nondifferential experience, i.e., both line and green had been rewarded. Conversely, PI from discrimination training on an irrelevant dimension produced a steepening of the generalization gradient over time. After being trained to peck at a green key, experimental birds received discrimination training between two values of line angularity. (Since line angularity is orthogonal to color, this is an extradimensional task.) The extradimensional discrimination training (task 1) is known to steepen the gradient along an unrelated continuum (in this case, color), presumably by increasing a set to attend to differences between stimuli. The second, competing training (task 2) involved reinforcing responses to both the S+ and S– line values. This nondifferential or equivalence training typically exerts a flattening effect on the generalization gradient, even across dimensions (line to wavelength). The intriguing outcome here was that the gradient was steeper in the delayed than in the immediate test, an effect opposite to the change usually seen over a retention interval. Controls not exposed to task 1 (line discrimination training) as the source of PI

162 *Chapter Six*

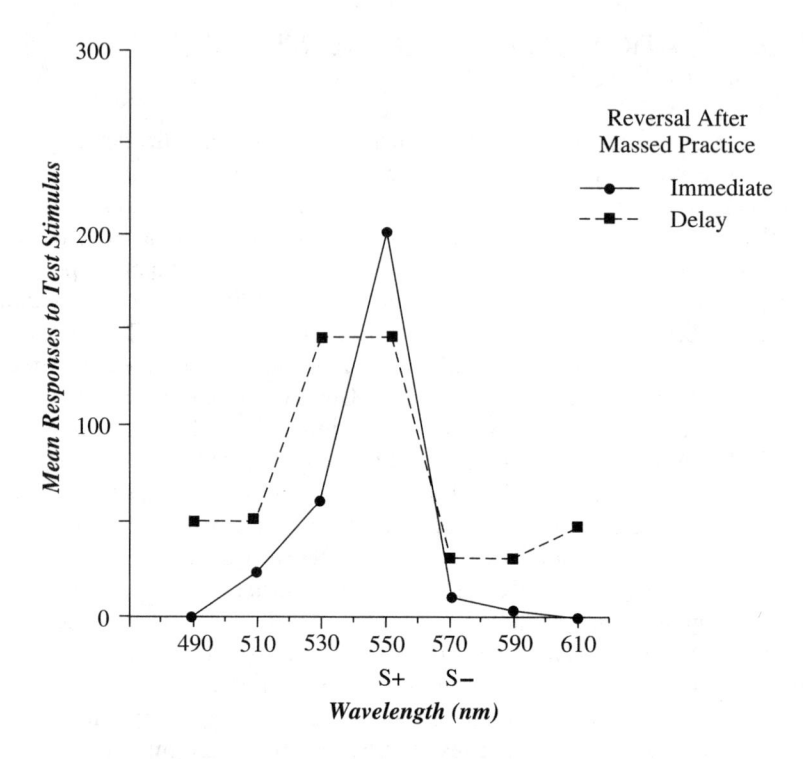

FIGURE 6-3 Flattening of the slope of a stimulus generalization gradient reflects an increase in proactive interference after a delay interval. Both groups were trained on a simple color discrimination followed by reversal training under massed conditions. (Adapted from Burr & Thomas 1972.)

showed the usual flattening of the gradient. A plausible interpretation is that in the experimental group the effect of initial discrimination learning (sharper gradient) comes increasingly to interfere with the tendency for the nondifferential training on the second task to flatten the slope of the gradient. The result was more discriminative behavior—more differentiation.

MEMORY FOR ATTRIBUTES OF REINFORCERS OR UNCONDITIONED STIMULI

As we have seen, the evaluation of memory for characteristics of conditioned stimuli, discriminative stimuli, or contextual cues is simple, at least in principle—measure the extent to which change in some feature of the stimulus disrupts performance after various retention intervals. As forgetting occurs, the severity of disruption diminishes. But what about memory for the US or reinforcing stimulus? Here the situation is more difficult because the reinforcer (or US) itself, whether original or altered, can directly affect performance. If a change in the reinforcer modulates responding, this may merely reflect the effect of the present level of reward upon responding rather than reveal anything about memory. Nevertheless, there are several studies suggesting that animals forget the attributes of reinforcers. To circumvent the difficulties described, one approach has involved tracking of the contrast effect, a phenomenon associated with a change in magnitude of reinforcer.

Contrast Effects

Over a wide range of values, there is a direct relationship between the magnitude of reinforcement and the vigor or strength of responding. When groups of animals receive different amounts of reinforcement, performance is a direct function of the magnitude of reward (e.g., Crespi 1942; Flaherty 1982). This finding, obtained in a variety of tasks and for quality as well as quantity of reward, is known as the magnitude of reinforcement principle. While it may seem like an obvious outcome, it is not. One could just as easily have predicted that after the reward size exceeded some minimal level, or threshold, performance would be independent of reward magnitude. Since such all-or-none behavior does not occur, it is clear that organisms are sensitive to features of the reinforcer. But by itself this does not allow an evaluation of memory; performance is simply controlled directly by the reinforcer that is present. A change in reinforcer magnitude proves instructive, however. In many cases subjects trained at one level of reinforcement and then shifted to a new reinforcer magnitude will show an exaggerated responsivity to the new conditions.

For example, Crespi (1942) trained rats to run in a straight alley for either a large or small portion of food. Half of each group was then switched to the opposite reward level; the other half remained under their original conditions as baseline control subjects. Speed of running not only changed in the shifted groups, but also tended to overshoot or undershoot the baseline. Thus, animals switched to a larger reward ran faster than those always given the large reward, and those moved to a smaller reward ran more slowly than their counterparts maintained on the small reward. These changes are referred to as *contrast effects*. For a variety of reasons, negative contrast, the exaggeratedly poor performance when a large reward is reduced in size, has been the more robust effect. In an important variant on this paradigm, Flaherty and Largen (1975) have shown that consummatory behavior (lick rates) is also subject to contrast effects. Rats shifted from a very sweet sucrose solution (32 percent) to a much weaker sugar concentration (4 percent) lick at significantly lower rates than subjects which have consistently received the 4 percent reward. A thorough review of the now substantial literature on incentive contrast has been presented by Flaherty (1982).

Clearly, these findings reveal that the effect of reward magnitude is, in part, relative rather than absolute. Past experience with reward influences the efficacy of the present level of reward; otherwise, subjects' responses should change in accordance with a new reinforcement condition but should not differ systematically from a group exposed to only that level of reward. Furthermore, and of particular relevance for memory assessment, the contrast effects imply some type of comparison process—that the new reward is being compared with earlier reinforcement in the same situation. It is this implicit comparison of hedonic values that provides the key to the usefulness of the contrast phenomenon for investigating memory of reinforcer attributes. As the reference (original) value of reward is forgotten, then the contrast effect should be reduced. In the extreme case, only the magnitude of reward effect would remain; performance would correspond to the level expected by the absolute size of the test reinforcement.

Just such a pattern of changes has been reported. Gleitman and Steinman (1964) found a contrast effect when rats were trained in a runway for a large reward and shifted to a smaller reward 1 day later; however, no contrast occurred with a 2-month interval between the end of training and the test phase with the smaller reward. In the latter condition, subjects performed in accord with the small reward (magnitude of reinforcement principle), but failed to show the further depression of running speed (contrast) that characterized the short retention interval. What these findings seem to indicate is that animals have forgotten the particular attribute (size) of the previous reinforcement in the task. Without this reference point, the learned response occurs (and get reinforced), but the organism fails to perceive a disparity. Similarly, when negative contrast in consummatory behavior is induced by shifting from high to low concentrations of sucrose solution, the contrast effect diminishes with increasing retention intervals between the pre- and postshift manipulations (e.g. Ciszewski & Flaherty 1977; Gordon, Flaherty & Riley 1973). These and related consequences of variation in retention of reinforcer magnitude (Spear 1967) indicate the importance of memory for attributes of positive reward.

Aversive Events

With respect to memory for features of aversive or noxious reinforcers, the contrast effect paradigm appears not to have been used. This may reflect the view that contrast effects in shock-escape learning are difficult to obtain, although there is some evidence that such contrast effects do occur (Nation, Wrather & Mellgren 1974). An alternative strategy, involving modulation of aversively motivated behavior by a qualitatively different aversive US, has been used by Hendersen, Patterson, and Jackson (1980) to assess memory of US attributes. These investigators capitalized on the finding that a Pavlovian conditioned stimulus can modulate the rate of responding in an unsignalled avoidance task (Sidman avoidance). Hendersen et al. (1980) initially found that rats acquire what appear to be global expectancies followed by more specific anticipations of the US predicted by a Pavlovian signal. Thus, a CS that had been paired with an airblast (US) for only a few trials would enhance responding when added as a signal for *shock-based* Sidman avoidance. However, with more extensive CS-US pairings the CS no longer enhanced avoidance responding. Why should further conditioning reduce the effectiveness of the CS? Hendersen et al. proposed that the features of the airblast (predicted by the CS) began to be differentiated from those of shock (the source of motivation for Sidman avoidance). Subjects initially learned that the CS indicates that something unpleasant will occur, but after further Pavlovian conditioning they acquire the more specific expectancy that a particular event, an airblast (not a shock), will occur. Since airblasts and electric shocks are different kinds of aversive events, the CS for airblast comes to have less effect on avoidance behavior motivated by shocks.

Of particular relevance to memory issues is the fact that Henderson et al. went on to show that this specificity of expectations breaks down after a long retention interval. A CS which had extensive pairings with airblasts and which would not influence Sidman avoidance at a short interval had a strong effect 45 days after pairings were completed. Again, the apparent paradox that a stronger effect occurs after a long delay seems explainable in terms of forgetting of the precise attributes of the predicted US. Just as subjects had only a general expectation of a bad event following a few pairings, so too after a long retention interval the precise anticipation had degraded into a more global form. In both cases, the CS interacts with other fear-motivated behavior to alter the rate of responding.

SPATIAL MEMORY

Several tests developed in recent years appear to simulate some of the demands on memory posed by environmental circumstances in the natural world. Apart from the interesting issue of ecological validity, these paradigms have provided important information on hitherto neglected aspects of the ability of animals to process separable attributes of a memory.

The radial maze task developed by David Olton and his colleagues at Johns Hopkins provides a case in point (e.g., Olton & Samuelson 1976; Olton 1979). Consider a situation in which an animal can perform efficiently only by keeping track of where it has already been. This is the essence of Olton's task. A number of arms (e.g., eight) radiate out of a central compartment, and all goal boxes are baited with food at the beginning of a trial (session). A rat can hardly go wrong on the first trial—wandering down any of the arms is bound to be rewarded. But since the food eaten is not replaced, the game becomes tougher with successive trials—tougher if energy is not to be expended unnecessarily by returning to empty goal boxes. After a little practice, rats become amazingly adept at keeping track of which arms they have visited. With the eight-arm maze, there are virtually no errors—no returns to an old arm where food has been consumed—and even with a larger seventeen-arm task, error rates remain on the order of one to two. No wonder that Olton, with the literary work of Proust in mind, dubbed an article on the phenomenon "Remembrances of Places Passed."

This task can be viewed as incorporating both working memory and reference memory (e.g., Honig 1978). Working memory refers to the organism's retention of information about where it has been recently in the maze, and this information changes, or is updated, during the course of choices during the trial. Further, the working memory must somehow be reset at the start of a new session, since the information about previous choices is no longer relevant. In contrast, reference memory pertains to the enduring, more general, retention of information about the task—for example, that food can be found at the end of the arms but that edibles will not be found when visits to an arm are repeated. Reference memory has much in common with instrumental learning that learning researchers initially studied in mazes; working memory is the added twist that provides the special interest.

Rats are so good at not repeating visits to arms in such a maze that one might (should) justifiably ask: is this really memory, or can it be accounted for by other mechanisms involving sensory tracking or perhaps learning of simple rules or algorithms (e.g., move clockwise through the arms of the maze)? There is substantial evidence showing that these alternative explanations are not adequate. Leaving an odor trail to mark where it has been would be a plausible sensory tracking process (for the rat). However, the addition of strong masking odors fails to impair normal rats. Also, rats do perfectly well following destruction of their olfactory sense. The clincher is that altering the position of the maze (e.g., rotating the entire maze by 90 degrees) results in an increase in re-entries into incorrect arms. Since any marking odors or stimuli would still be present in a given arm, such an error is informative in indicating that sensory marking cannot be the basis for the behavior. By the same token, this manipulation also eliminates an explanation in terms of animals tracking the smell of food in the goal boxes. If that were true, responding should continue unimpaired. Rather, the disruption of performance with changes in maze orientation suggests that extra-maze cues provide the markers for this type of spatial memory.

Another impressive feature of rat's working memory in the radial maze is its durability. One might expect that if a subject were interrupted after having had an opportunity to choose only some of the arms, and a delay were introduced before maze running could continue, then accuracy of performance would drop off rather precipitously. But such is not the case. Rats interrupted after entering half the arms are able to resume where they left off with virtually no loss of accuracy even with delays of 4 to 6 hours (Beatty & Shavalia 1980a). Since short-term retention in humans is typically measured in terms of seconds, it seems unlikely that the rat's task is analogous to the human one. Thus, while the retention of the radial maze locations is relatively short term, it is probably misleading to lump this phenomenon in the same category as the short-term retention studies with humans.

The durability of memory for spatial locations of food is seen in at least two other ways. One finding comes from studies employing electroconvulsive shock (ECS), a neurophysiologically disruptive treatment known to produced forgetting (amnesia) for recently learned information. However, ECS administered shortly after the subject makes the first four choices in the eight-arm maze has relatively little effect on subsequent accuracy (Shavalia, Dodge & Beatty 1981). Indeed, the temporal gradient of susceptibility to ECS appears to be just the opposite of that in traditional learning tasks, where information is much more vulnerable to an amnestic treatment immediately after training than some minutes later. Instead, rats receiving ECS several hours after being interrupted in the radial maze task show greater impairment than those given the amnestic agent immediately after the interruption (Shavalia et al. 1981).

A second way in which spatial memory shows durability is in its resistance to interference from related memory episodes. For example, Beatty and Shavalia (1980b) allowed rats to make four choices in one radial maze (maze A). The rats were then placed in another, apparently highly similar, radial maze (B), and again permitted to make four choices before being removed. The question of interest was how well rats would do if tested in maze B after various intervals. This is an instance of the proactive interference paradigm. Would the prior choices made in maze A become a source of confusion when the rat has to remember the arms chosen in B? Moreover, since mazes A and B were in the same experimental room, subjects did not have distinctive contextual or locale cues to help sort out their behaviors. Nevertheless, performance was intact—most subjects managed to pick up where they had left off in maze B. Thus, the two working memories were somehow maintained separately despite the opportunity for confusion between the two.

The investigators subsequently took this approach one step further. If several choices were permitted in maze A, and then additional choices in B, what would happen when subjects were returned to the first task (maze A)? In this example of a potential source of interference from the interpolated behavior (i.e., retroactive interference), rats still managed to perform with very few erroneous entries into empty arms. Thus, memories for places visited initially were somehow segregated from those made in the second task, and little interference was obtained when subjects were given the opportunity to complete the first task.

Earlier, we saw that a U-shaped function characterized memory for serial lists of items in a probe recognition task. Serial position effects in animals have also been observed in the radial maze. Modifying the typical free-choice procedure used in studies of working memory, Kesner and his colleagues (Kesner & Novak 1982; DiMattia & Kesner 1984; Kesner et al. 1984) permitted rats access to the eight arms of the maze in a predesignated sequence. All arms except the correct one were momentarily blocked to manipulate the sequence. Thus, each arm can be viewed as an item in an eight-item list. Following this training phase, rats were tested on pairs of arms corresponding to responses 1 and 2 (initial), 4 and 5 (middle), and 7 and 8 (terminal). The rule for a correct choice was that the subject should now choose whichever of the two arms had been entered earlier in the original sequence, i.e., arms 1, 4, and 7. With a relatively short delay (e.g., 20 seconds) between the training phase and testing, a serial position effect was obtained: correct choices were higher for the initial (primacy) and final (recency) pair of arms than for the middle ones.

What would happen to the retention curve if a delay were introduced following the list learning phase? A number of studies of serial learning in humans have found that a delay of testing impairs the recency effect while leaving the rest of the curve largely intact, a finding sometimes taken in support of the concept of separate (and separable) short- and long-term storages. Interpolating a 10-minute delay in the radial maze situation resulted in a decrement in performance to near chance levels for the final two items but no change in accuracy for the initial pair. Thus, analogous to human memory, rats show intact primacy but impaired recency when the retention interval is lengthened after list learning.

In chapter 5 on short-term retention, we discussed prospective as well as retrospective strategies in delayed matching-to-sample tasks. An elegant study by Cook, Brown, and Riley (1985) provides evidence that rats can (and do) employ both strategies in the radial maze. The basic approach used by Cook et al. was to interpolate a brief delay (15 minutes) following varying numbers of choices (2, 4, 6, 8, or 10) in a 12-arm radial maze. A consistent finding was that fewer errors were made when the interruption occurred early or late in the sequence than when the delay was in the middle. Since a retrospective strategy should produce more errors with increasing numbers of arms visited (i.e., the memory load increases), the nonmonotonic function obtained suggests that rats have a flexible, dual memory system. Apparently choices are based on retrospective representations for the early arms but on prospective (arms yet to be visited) representations toward the end of the sequence.

Morris Maze and Cognitive Maps

A rather different form of spatial memory seems to be implicated in several other situations. One of these is the so-called Morris maze, which is not a maze in the usual sense, but does involve the ability to remember where a hidden goal is located (Morris 1981). Like the radial maze, the Morris maze provides a good example of a task that is elegant in its simplicity. A small platform is submerged just below the surface of the water in a small tank of water (e.g., something about the size of a young tot's wading pool). The animal's task is to escape from continuously swimming by finding the hidden platform, on which it can perch. To prevent solving the problem merely by visually locating and homing in on the target, Morris simply added milk to the water to produce an opaque medium. Thus, a rat released into the pool could initially find the safety ledge only by trial and error—swimming in different directions until by chance stumbling, as it were, upon the platform. Not entirely surprisingly, rats soon learned to swim directly to the hidden ledge. (The reinforcement is presumably the escape from water as well as the rest from swimming.) More interestingly from a spatial memory point of view, when subjects were released into the pool from a new location or quadrant they also went with almost unerring accuracy to the platform. This effect is clearly shown for six subjects in the top panel of Figure 6-4. Since a direct path to the goal from a novel starting point necessarily involved a new route, the findings suggest that rats had learned about the general location of the platform with respect to environmental cues. That is, the subjects seem to acquire a cognitive map of the surroundings and their relationship to the hidden platform. Indeed, the use of a rather heterogeneous laboratory room, with windows, shelves, posters, etc. appears to have provided a rich source of extra-maze cues.

If the subjects are locating the target by some memorial representation rather than through subtle visual, tactile, or other stimuli revealing its location, then surreptitiously moving the platform to a new place should disrupt behavior. This manipulation is, of course, very different from keeping the platform in one place while releasing the subject from various locations, and it does severely impair performance. As in other situations, the nature of errors made are informative. By and large, immediately following such a change, rats spend a good deal of time swimming in the vicinity of the former location of the platform, a kind of searching behavior strongly suggesting an expectancy for the now missing target. The middle panel of Figure 6-4 provides a striking illustration of the disruption and searching resulting from moving the underwater platform to a new place. Restricting their swimming to the old area also seems to reflect learning; in previous trials such behavior would have corrected any slight errors in approaching and allowed them to find the target. Eventually, in the face of continued lack of success, rats begin to swim throughout the pool until once again they encounter the ledge in its new location.

Like Olton's radial maze, the Morris maze task taps into what can be viewed as spatial memory. Both seem to depend on a representation of places in the environment. However, whereas the radial maze has been particularly useful in revealing information about working memory, the Morris maze fits better into the category of

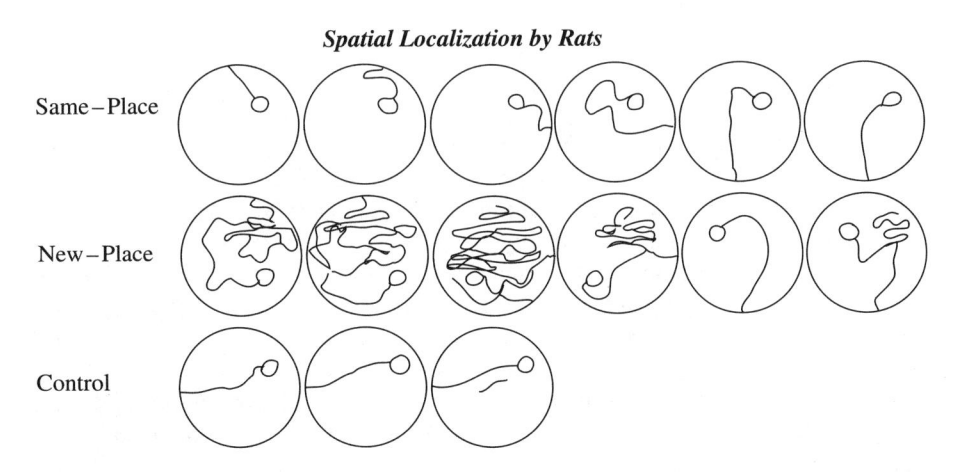

FIGURE 6-4 The tracking patterns (as seen from above) of individual rats in the Morris water maze when released from new positions. In the upper row, the hidden platform remained in the same place as training. (Adapted from Morris 1981.)

reference memory. Learning and remembering the location of safe places in a dangerous or threatening environment is an important part of the behavioral repertoire of animals.

If rats are acquiring maps of their environment, perhaps the act of swimming to the hidden platform is not critical to the formation of learning about a specific location. Sutherland and Linggard (1982) observed that rats spent a considerable amount of time rearing and rotating on the platform after emerging from the water, as if sampling the distal visual cues in the environment. To test the notion that information about location was gained during the time on the platform, these investigators placed some rats directly on the platform. Control rats received similar exposure except that their preexposure platform was in an incorrect position—a quadrant opposite the hidden platform for testing. Although both groups had comparable amounts of preexposure to (and thus familiarity with) the environment, the group given the correct placement showed markedly superior performance on the initial test trials (after a few trials, of course, all groups mastered the task). This transfer of learning indicates that information acquired during the stimulus exposure could be used to guide navigation during the instrumental swimming test.

Just how well retained is the spatial mapping in the Morris maze? Perhaps because of the many other interesting questions generated with this paradigm, examination of long-term retention has received relatively little attention. However, at least one study indicates that the memory for specific place location is quite durable. Sutherland and Dyck (1984) gave rats 5 days of training with a fixed invisible platform. After a 2-week retention interval, these rats performed just as well as on the last day of training. Indeed, other data in that study suggest that there is little forgetting of the place navigation even with a 3-month delay until testing.

Memory for Caches

In addressing the issue of whether spatial memory is limited to mammals, Gould (1986) has provided an intriguing demonstration of spatial memory in honey bees. In order to determine whether bees could efficiently navigate to a particular feeding station out of direct sight, individually marked bees were released from various points in a familiar environment. Both the bearing of the bees as they disappeared and their flight time indicated that they chose a direct (bee-line?) path to the feeder. Since the bees' success presumably involved a novel path, rather than part of a route-specific pattern of navigation, the findings suggest that a spatial or locale map may also exist in these invertebrates. In addition to such studies with invertebrates, a great deal of exciting work on spatial memory has been done with another nonmammalian species—birds.

Reference memory for spatial loci should be important in foraging as well as in defense, and several studies with birds attest to such a conclusion. Although it is widely assumed that some animals hide food which they can later recover (e.g., dogs bury bones; squirrels hide acorns), until recently there has been little experimental examination of such capacities. And in the absence of careful and controlled observation, what is common knowledge may in fact be no more than old wives' tales. For example, squirrels might not actually remember where nuts were buried, but by random digging (or perhaps digging in preferred sites), may find acorns, whether hidden by themselves or others.

This kind of issue clearly is of interest to both biologists and behaviorists. From an evolutionary perspective, information on hoarding and finding hidden food is relevant to the question of how animals solve problems posed by nature. At the same time, knowledge about the extent to which foraging is dependent on memory, and about the characteristics as well as limitations of such memory, is of value in gaining a more comprehensive understanding of memory processes.

Shettleworth (1983) has recently summarized some of the fascinating controlled observations that point to memory for cached food in food-hoarding species such as the marsh tit. Although earlier work suggested that marsh tits find food stores they have hidden, the evidence was rather indirect and subject to other interpretations. Also, the global nature of the earlier procedure precluded precise information about the accuracy of memory. Accordingly, Shettleworth and Krebs (1982) devised a scheme for assessing food-hoarding memory directly. Taking advantage of the fact that marsh tits will hoard in captivity, they placed individual birds into a room with several tree branches along with a small supply of 12 seeds. The experimental situation is shown in Figure 6-5. About 100 holes just large enough for 1 seed had been drilled in the branches as caching places. Since the number of available locations far exceeded the number of seeds, a bird attempting to recover the seeds without remembering their locations would be expected to make many errors searching in empty holes. However, when tested several hours after hiding seeds, the marsh tits made relatively few errors in recovering seeds, often gathering 3 or 4 seeds consecutively without a mistake. This ability to locate seeds could not be attributed to tracking by smell, as performance dropped to chance levels if the seeds were rehidden in new places by the experimenters during the waiting interval.

A more subtle but important alternative explanation of the caching behavior is that the birds were not remembering where to go, but had hidden the seeds in preferred locations on the branches, and then merely returned to those preferred spots. (This problem is instructive with respect to seminaturalistic observations of memory behavior and controlled laboratory arrangements. In the laboratory, the target information can be provided by the experimenter in a way [e.g., random selection of correct location] that minimizes or eliminates the subjects' preferences. In contrast, in the wild, as in this study, the target information [location] is under the control of the subjects, so that favored locations have to be considered in evaluating the purity of what appears to be memory.) To determine whether the birds were merely returning to favorite haunts, the experimenters made a simple but clever change in the test procedure: birds were given an additional supply of seeds to hide. If they had previously recovered seeds by returning to preferred locations, their errors would now be revealed by trying to hide the new seeds in these same places. Instead,

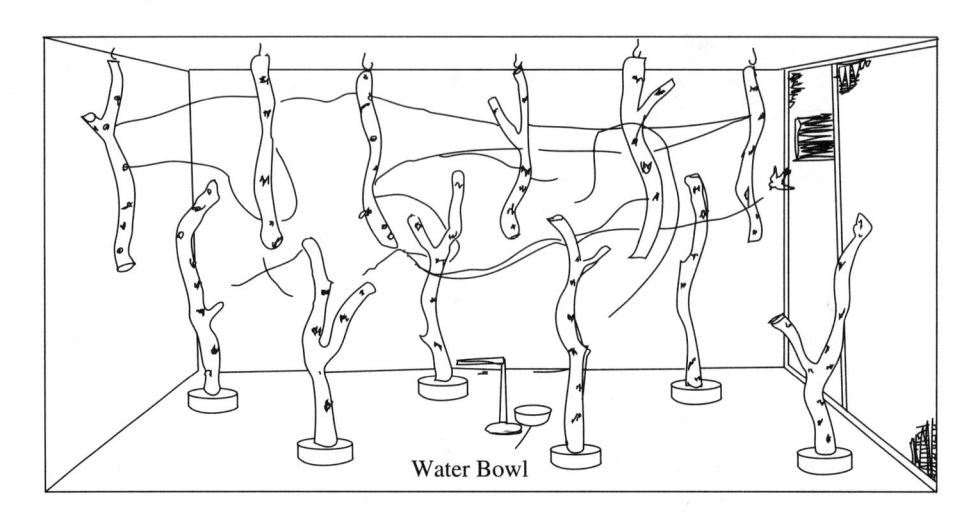

FIGURE 6-5 The seminaturalistic laboratory situation used by Shettleworth and Krebs to investigate cache memory in marsh tits. Birds stored seeds in some of the holes drilled in the tree branches. (Adapted from Shettleworth 1983.)

birds correctly avoided the holes where they had already cached food and chose new locations.

Given that marsh tits remember where they have hidden food, do they also remember which location they have already visited during the recovery test? This question is very similar to that asked in radial maze experiments and illustrates the combination of a reference memory task (where have the seeds been cached?) and a working memory problem (from which cache locations have the seeds been removed?). While performance was not perfect, it was far better than chance for the birds avoiding sites they had visited previously.

That cache recovery represents spatial memory rather than the return to preferred locations is also demonstrated in a study by Kamil and Balda (1985). In one of their experiments, captured Clark's nutcrackers, a bird about the size of a bluejay that is found in the western United States, were permitted to hide seeds in a naturalistic laboratory environment. Of 180 possible hiding sites, only 18 were available to the birds; the other 162 were capped by the experimenters. Subsequently, the nutcrackers were removed from the caching area for a 10-day retention interval. At testing, the birds were able to locate the seeds successfully among all 180 possible sites, even though the available cache locations had been chosen by the experimenter.

While early studies of retention of food-hiding behavior often tested birds after a few hours or days, there is evidence that the memory can be quite enduring. For example, Hitchcock and Sherry (1990) reported black-capped chickadees were able to recover seed caches after retention intervals up to 28 days, although with longer intervals performance was not distinguishable from control levels.

In the preceding studies, the mini-caches of seeds were established by the birds themselves, as part of their natural food-hoarding behavior. What if the food locations were established by the experimenter while being observed by the subjects? Would memory for hidden food locations still be possible? As you can imagine, such a procedure would be difficult to implement with marsh tits—not the least of the problems would be ensuring that these active creatures ever attended to the baiting of different locations. But data from such a paradigm are available, although the subjects were primates. Menzel (1973) asked whether chimpanzees were capable of efficiently gathering a number of hidden objects. For example, would they take a route which required the least traveling distance? Chimps were allowed to watch while an experimenter hid different kinds of foods in various locations throughout a large field. When released later, the chimps clearly demonstrated observational learning and cognitive mapping by gathering up an average of 12.5 of the 18 hidden pieces of food. How do we know that the chimps success was not merely due to random searching in various likely spots? The answer is simple: control subjects that had not witnessed the baiting were also allowed to search for food, but had markedly less success (an average of less than 1 piece was found). Further, a very revealing feature of the chimp's performance was that they gathered much of the food not in the order it was baited but in terms of adjacent locations. Thus, if the 2d and 7th pieces of food hidden were closer to each other than pieces 4, 5, and 6 (the experimenter crisscrossed the area in laying out the food), then items 2 and 7 were likely to be collected together. This kind of geographical efficiency suggests that the chimps were by no means retracing the experimenter's initial route, but were using an organizational scheme (location) to remember where food was. Re-arranging or encoding information into some form of organization is, of course, a major characteristic of memory for many species, including humans. An interesting variation on the organizational principle was found when several types of foods, differing in their preference value for the chimps, were hidden. By and large, most of the preferred foods (fruits) were gathered before any of the less preferred items (vegetables) even though the order of distribution of foods was completely intermixed by the experimenter. The efficiency of food gathering extended to quantitative as well as qualitative dimensions. When 2 pieces of food were hidden on one side of the field, and 3 on the other side, chimps almost always gathered the larger food cache first. These outcomes suggest that representation can be quite specific and can include information about amount as well as types of food.

Historical Note

Although the work on spatial navigation is attracting considerable interest these days, it is worth noting that 40 years ago a very eminent learning theorist, Edward Chase Tolman, called attention to such phenomena. In a charming article titled "Cognitive

Maps in Rats and Men," Tolman (1948) described some of the work from his laboratory supporting the notion that rats learned more than stimulus-response associations. Tolman suggested that through exposure to the environment organisms actively construct a tentative map of environmental relationships. The way one could determine whether this map was "narrow and strip-like or relatively broad and comprehensive" (p. 193) was to alter the environment at testing and determine the ability of the subjects to reach the goal under these new conditions. Accordingly, in one experiment, rats learned to cross an open area and enter an elevated maze in order to reach a goal box with food. When the original starting path was blocked and a sunburst array of radiating pathways was provided, rats tended to choose a pathway leading very near to the goal box or, alternatively, a pathway at least leading to the appropriate side of the room. This spatial orientation of the rat toward the location of food was also seen in a different type of task where rats were initially trained to find food at one end of a simple T-maze. Did subjects learn to go left (or right), or did they acquire a representation of where food was located in their environment? To address this question, Tolman reversed the starting point of the maze (e.g., from North to South) and replaced the single arm of the T-maze with an array of ten pathways spanning 180 degrees. Although the rats were not terribly accurate with respect to choosing the most direct pathway, they correctly selected a pathway leading perpendicularly to the correct side of the room, even though this choice required a turn opposite from what they learned in training.

While Tolman's work was addressing a hotly debated theoretical issue in his day about the nature of learning, certainly his strategy and his conceptualizations have a very contemporary ring to them! We might also note that he anticipated later developments in this area by identifying four variables that he believed would tend to prevent the development of broad cognitive maps: brain damage, impoverished cues in the environment, overtraining on a particular pathway, and the presence of very high motivation or severe frustration.

CHAPTER SUMMARY

Memory includes information not only about what response to perform but also about the characteristics of the stimuli associated with the learning episode. To assess memory for the attributes of conditioned or contextual (background) stimuli, researchers have utilized stimulus generalization tests after various delay intervals. At short intervals, decremental gradients of responding are typically obtained, indicating that the novel test stimuli are perceptually distinguishable. Forgetting of attributes is reflected in a flattening of the gradient, i.e., discriminative control over responding diminishes and subjects treat different stimuli as functionally equivalent. Changes in the characteristics of generalization gradients have also been used to investigate retention of conflicting memories, such as those produced when the correct and incorrect stimuli in a discrimination task are reversed. A different research strategy involving magnitude of reward contrast effects is necessary for investigating the memory for attributes of reinforcers (or unconditioned stimuli). When a small reward is substituted for a large reward shortly after acquisition, performance of subjects declines below the level of control subjects that were trained on only the smaller reward. This negative contrast suggests a memory attribute representing reward size; conversely, a decline in the extent of the contrast effect reveals that the organism has forgotten the specific reinforcer attribute (reward size).

Several intriguing tasks have been developed to evaluate what animals learn and remember about their spatial environment. In the Olton radial maze, a number of arms (e.g., eight) radiating out from a central arena are baited with food. Rats readily learn and remember not to re-enter arms from which they have already eaten the food. Their accurate performance is not attributable to artifacts such as odor trails or specific response sequences. Cognitive representations of spatial arrangements are also tapped by the Morris maze. After learning to swim from one location to a platform hidden under opaque water in a large tub, rats continue to locate the platform with little error even when they are started from different points in the tub. Contemporary studies of memory for spatial location were preceded historically by Tolman's conceptualization of cognitive maps.

Hiding and recovering food or caching behavior provides an opportunity to examine memory for spatial locations under naturalistic conditions. Food-hoarding birds such as the marsh tit can recover seeds they have hidden in tiny holes with a high degree of accuracy. The behavior does not reflect simply visiting preferred locations, as the birds will avoid the already occupied places when hiding a second set of seeds. Chimpanzees permitted to observe an experimenter hiding pieces of food in a large field not only remember the location of the pieces, but demonstrate organizational strategy by gathering pieces located near one another, rather than retracing the original random order in which they were hidden.

7

Developmental Change in the Processing of Memories

In the area of Boston, Massachusetts, people were questioned about their memory for a particularly significant event that had occurred when they were much younger. The people included children from 4 to 12 years of age as well as college students. The event they were questioned about was the birth of a younger brother or sister. They were asked about a variety of details of that event: Who told you that your mother was leaving to go to the hospital? Who went with her? Did you go? How long did she stay in the hospital? What did you do when your mother arrived at home? Twenty questions in all were asked, and the facts related to these questions were verified by information provided from the mothers of the children and the college students.

The results were remarkable. Although college students whose siblings were born when they were older than 3 years exhibited substantial memory for verified events of their sibling's birth, those younger than 3 at the time remembered essentially nothing of the events (Figure 7-1). Despite an average of nearly 12 items recalled correctly if their siblings had been born when the students were 3 to 5 years old (or older), none of the events could be recalled correctly for 86 percent of the sibling births that took place when the students were younger than 3 years old. It is as if even the most important events experienced before the age of 3 left little or no record in memory. Retention of the events of infancy is extraordinarily weak not only for us, but for other animals that also are born with an immature brain. This effect is commonly referred to with a term invented by Freud, *infantile amnesia*.

All that has been discussed about learning and memory so far in this book has been about normal adults. But a great deal of learning and remembering takes place by other kinds of humans or animals, as we shall see in this and following chapters.

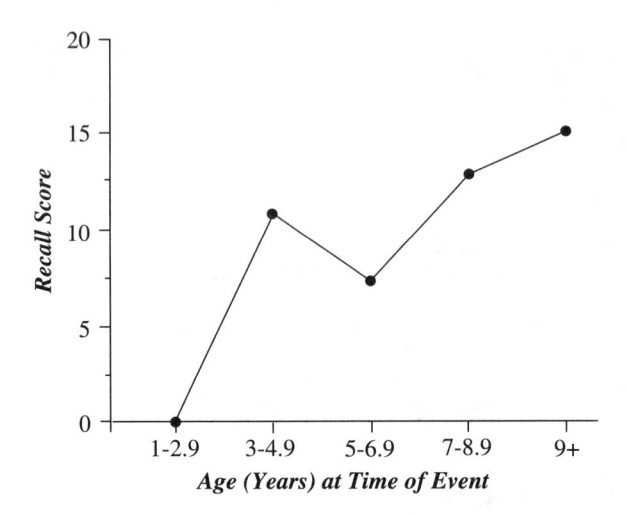

FIGURE 7-1 Recall of events associated with the birth of a younger brother or sister is shown for college students that differed in age when their younger brother or sister was born. If younger the age of 3 years at the time of their sibling's birth, recall was almost nil. (Adapted from Sheingold & Tenney 1982.)

This chapter will focus on developing animals and humans, particularly infants. It would seem that learning and memory early in life must have special importance. For animals early learning can determine adaptation as an adult and even whether adulthood will be reached! For humans it has seemed so critical for later psychological well-being that most psychotherapies require the retrieval of childhood memories for their success. Understanding how memories are processed by young children and animals is therefore a high priority.

OVERVIEW OF THE ONTOGENY OF LEARNING AND MEMORY

We now know a good deal about three general principles of the ontogeny of learning and memory that were barely evident 10 to 15 years ago and were not appreciated, or mistaken, 50 years ago.

The first principle is that mammals are capable of substantial learning very early in life. Not only can the newborn rat or newborn human learn the relationship among specific events in their new world, but even before birth such learning can take place and can be expressed prenatally or postnatally (Fifer 1987; Smotherman & Robinson 1987). Second, early experience is vitally important for adaptation during development and as an adult. It is likely that prenatal experience is important for this purpose, and it is certain that early postnatal experience, whether specific or general, is important. Third, despite the remarkable capacity for learning in the earliest stages of life and despite the significance of the infant's experience for later adaptation as an adult, the memory of adults is strikingly deficient with respect to events of infancy, as was discussed at the beginning of this chapter. Such infantile amnesia seems paradoxical in view of the infant's good abilities for learning and the established importance of the infant's experience for later success as an adult. We shall consider this paradox later.

Infantile amnesia is particularly interesting because its influence is so widespread and pervasive. It seems to occur in all altricial mammals, so it is not merely an artifact of the human's use of a language that develops after the early stages of infancy. Nor is it primarily, as Freud suggested, a consequence of society's inhibitions as to which infantile memories are or are not suitable for remembering. The effect becomes especially interesting when it is realized that (1) memories of infancy are remembered less effectively than those of adulthood even when degree of their learning is carefully equated, and (2) forgetting generally is more prevalent among infants than adults, whether considered over very short intervals of a few seconds or minutes, or over longer intervals. It is not only that adults have difficulty remembering the events of their infancy; infants also have difficulty remembering the events that occur during their infancy.

Assessing Developmental Changes in Memory and Learning

It has been convenient to contrast the cognitions and behaviors of two extreme periods of ontogeny—infancy and adulthood. This is, of course, a gross simplification because a variety of important changes in learning and memory occur between infancy and adulthood and also following adulthood into old age. The major issues are nevertheless understood most readily in terms of the extremes of infancy and adulthood, so that is the comparison emphasized here. The questions we shall entertain are simple ones, but the answers are more complex than you might suspect. The question of description comes first: how do infants and adults compare in a wide variety of instances of learning?

What Tests Are Needed?

Generally speaking, adults have been found to learn more rapidly than infants. But tests of learning differ in how much the newly acquired memories depend on transfer from other learning. To take an extreme example, you can bet that almost any adult could learn to recite the Declaration of Independence or to ride a motorcycle more rapidly than most any 3-year-old—even if the Declaration were read aloud to the person for learning or if the motorcycle were a foot high or so, scaled down to 3-year-old size. Such a comparison would not be useful analytically because so much of the adult's other learning about the source of language used in the Declaration of

Independence and about skills used for riding a motorcycle have not yet been experienced by the 3-year-old. Transfer of previous learning to a new task is of vast importance. It is difficult to imagine anything adults learn that does not depend on transfer from some previous learning. If we want to understand ontogenetic differences in capacity for new learning or ontogenetic changes in the processes applied and we are not explicitly testing age-related differences in transfer, we must use learning tests that minimize age-related differences in specific transfer from past learning experiences. To accomplish this we test animals, such as the laboratory rat or monkey, so that we can know or control precisely what prior learning has occurred.

But even tests that minimize transfer from previous learning may not clearly determine the comparability of infants and adults in new learning and memory. We will soon see, for instance, that although adults may learn more rapidly most of the time, infants in some circumstances learn more rapidly than adults. Which age learns faster depends on the learning test. This may not be surprising, because there is such a variety of instances of learning possible. It would make little sense, then, to concentrate on only one kind of learning test. There would be particular impediments to understanding if we were to study only memory for words or verbal symbols, because much of what is learned by the infant human (and the adult human) has little to do with language (and this is certainly true for infant animals!) Another advantage in using animals is that a much broader array of truly significant learning instances can be tested, from learning where to go for food and home to learning how to avoid danger.

The conclusion is that the tests most useful for understanding the ontogeny of learning and memory should minimize transfer from other learning and should include a variety of different events and life experiences. Both of these factors suggest that it is essential to study the ontogeny of learning and memory with animals as well as humans.

Must the type of learning we study be very simple? We do not believe so. If too simple and elemental, a learning test may not be representative of ecological experience and, moreover, might be unlikely to reveal any differences in the ontogeny of learning and memory. It does not take much of a brain for the simplest instances of conditioning and learning. For example, adult animals and humans can show basic conditioning quite effectively even though they may have very little cerebral cortex, and basic conditioning has been established both within low-level animals that have only a few neurons as a brain and within individual synapses between two neurons in an isolated piece of the brain from more advanced animals (long-term potentiation [Bliss & Lomo 1973]).

The simple question of whether the capacities of infants and adults for learning differ must therefore be answered with experiments that test learning of a variety of events in circumstances with reasonable control over transfer from other learning. These learning tests should vary in complexity to take into account the fact that the potential for dealing cognitively with more complex events is especially likely to change ontogenetically. An important caveat about method needs to be mentioned, although we cannot discuss it here in the depth it deserves. To compare the learning and memory of animals (or humans) at different ages, we must take steps to ensure that apparent differences in rate of learning or forgetting did not arise merely because the animals perceived the event differently at the different ages tested, or the motivation of the younger animals differed from that of the older animals, or the reward or unconditioned stimulus had a different value for the infants than for the adults. The general rule is that if we want to attribute learning differences to age differences, we must control all other factors: we must be certain that the differences in learning are not due to differences in perception, motivation, or incentive scores or the animal's motor capacity to express the learning at the test.

These aspects of method must be kept in mind in evaluation of tests of the ontogeny tests of learning and memory. In this chapter we will not emphasize this matter further but will consider only those studies that have been careful and scientifically responsible in comparing learning and memory at different ages.

General Issues in the Development of Memory

If children are given lists of objects or pictures of objects such as cars, animals, or toys—things that can be identified by children of all ages over 2 years or so—the number of objects correctly recited later will increase quite regularly from preschool to age 16 to 18 or so (Figure 7-2). Among developing monkeys given discrimination problems in which they must decide which of two alternative objects to select in order to receive food, there is a similar progressive increase in the effectiveness of this discrimination learning between infancy and adulthood (Figure 7-3). If rats of different ages are taught to turn a particular way in a T-maze to escape a mild footshock or to obtain food, there will be a progressive increase between infancy and adulthood in the effectiveness of learning this discrimination. Hundreds of such examples are available in the literature (for a review, see Spear & Rudy 1991). The question we must consider is, what do such findings imply?

One possibility is that in comparison with adults, infants are less capable of learning merely because their immature brain allows less "machinery" to be devoted to learning. Another is that infants could learn as rapidly as adults but do not know how, i.e., the learning processes they apply are ineffective at the behavioral level. A third is that the learning tests are biased for the older animals or people because they require past knowledge not yet learned by the younger ones. And there are, of course, other possibilities.

How can we maximize learning and retention by children? Do they have basic limitations in neurological capacity that are significant for education, and if so what are the corresponding limitations on cognition and behavior? Can learning by infants and children be improved by teaching them to apply the processes used by older children and adults? And once learning is established, is it inevitable that younger organisms will forget an extreme amount through infantile amnesia?

Answers to questions such as these require knowledge of the fundamental characteristics of the ontogeny of learning of memory. A complete description of these characteristics must consider development of the major events that constitute

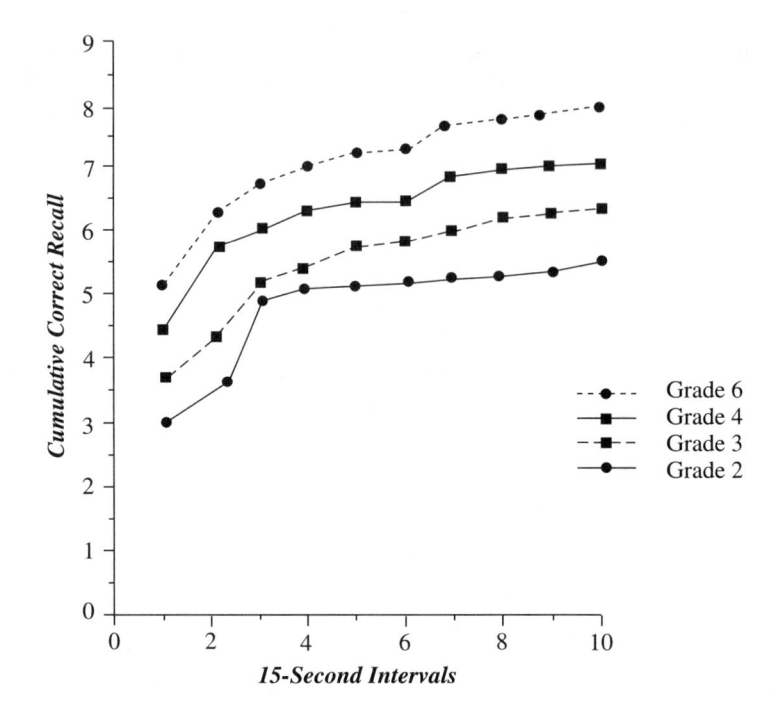

FIGURE 7-2 Recall of a list of common words is shown for children in primary grades 2, 3, 4, and 6. Recall was timed; this figure shows cumulative recall according to each 15-second interval. More effective final recall in older children is shown in terms of bin 10 on the abscissa, although this age-related difference is constant throughout. (Adapted from Heckleman & Spear 1967.)

the memory process—the brain, sensory detection, perception, memory storage (learning), and memory retrieval (retention). Only then can we begin to analyze what features contribute to differences in learning and memory by infants and adults. For our description we shall focus on the developing rat and the developing human.

FOUNDATIONS OF THE DEVELOPMENT OF MEMORY: ONTOGENETIC CHANGE IN BRAIN AND BEHAVIOR

For altricial mammals such as the human or the rat, the brain changes dramatically between birth and adulthood. The temporal sequence of these changes is similar from species to species, although the length of time required for their completion may

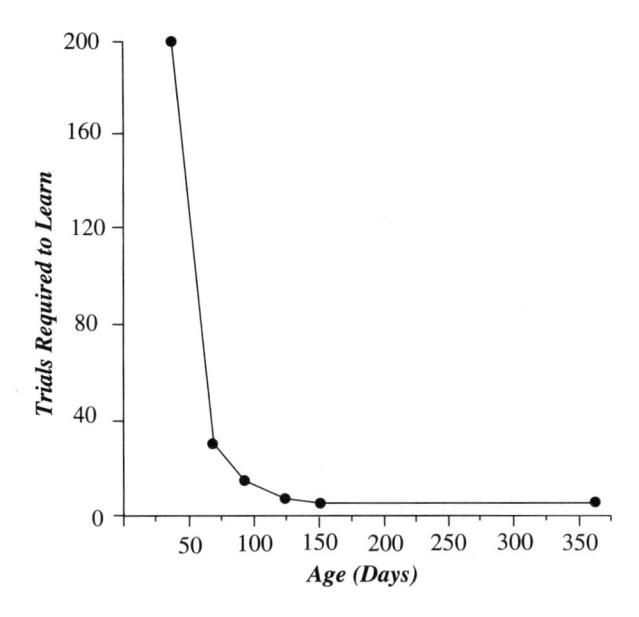

FIGURE 7-3 Number of trials required for monkeys to correctly recall (on an immediate test) the correct object in a discrimination task is shown as a function of the age of the monkey. (Adapted from Harlow 1959.)

differ. For instance, prenatal development of the brain takes over half a year for humans but only about 2 weeks in the rat, and after birth the rat's brain becomes adult-like in most respects within a month whereas the human's brain does not reach a corresponding level for several years. This rapid brain development makes the rat particularly useful as a model system—a good deal can be learned about brain development over a relatively short time in the rat. The primary value of such a model system is, however, that experiments to understand brain development—by selectively influencing the action of certain portions of the brain and evaluating the effects on behavior, or by direct manipulation of behavior and observation of effects on brain development—can be accomplished only in such model systems and never in humans.

Some Features of Brain Development

The human brain at birth weighs 300 to 350 grams, about one-quarter of its adult weight. By 6 months of age the brain weight is 50 percent of adult weight, by 2 years it is 75 percent, by 5 years 90 percent, and by 10 years of age the child's brain is 95 percent the weight of an adult's. The increase in brain weight after birth is not so much due to increasing numbers of neurons as to an increase in their size, complexity, and myelinization.

Myelin is the white fatty-like substance formed by a particular kind of support cell called glia. Myelin is visible to the naked eye upon inspection of a brain. Because it is so easily detected, myelin was one of the first indices of brain growth. Today the use of electron microscopes and the increasingly fine-grain assays of molecular biology permit direct observation and calculation of the most minute properties of neurons. Myelinization is significant; it forms an insulation-like coating for neural processes that facilitates the rapid conduction of neural impulses. Its absence in adults is debilitating and is labeled as the disease multiple sclerosis. Generally speaking, there is a positive correlation between degree of myelinization and the mature action of neural conduction in the brain. Myelinization occurs in the primary motor areas of the brain before the primary sensory areas; the latter catch up at about 2 years of age in the human. The cerebellar-cerebral cortex connections needed for fine motor control are not fully myelinated until a child is 4 years old. At this age some critical areas—the reticular formation, which services general arousal, and the hippocampus, which has some central role in attention and memory—are still developing in many ways and will not be fully myelinated for 6 to 8 more years.

The brain of the adult human has been estimated to contain as many as 10^{12} neurons (a million million). Based on this figure and the time required for full brain development, a conservative estimate is that new neurons appear in the developing human brain at the rate of 250,000 per minute (Cowan 1979). Most neurons are formed before birth, during the third, fourth, and fifth months of pregnancy. Maturation of these neurons differs from area to area of the brain, and the timing of this maturation differs from species to species. For instance in the human, which can see (poorly) at birth but uses vision as one of its primary sources of information from then on, cells in the visual cortex have their greatest spurt of maturation prenatally during the eighth month of pregnancy.

Each neuron in the brain has itself a good deal of growth to accomplish. The average cortical neuron has about 30,000 nerve processes that terminate on it from about 3,000 other neurons. Each neuron therefore must develop a number of offshoots to receive messages as well as to carry them onto thousands of other neurons. It has been estimated that in the developing rat brain such new neurites develop at the rate of 500,000 per second (Schuz 1978; from Doty 1984).

The increasing complexity of neurons during development in terms of new branches of neurites is accompanied by a corresponding increase in the number of synapses, i.e., the number of connections between one of the processes that grow out from a neuron onto another neuron or its processes. The synapse is the site of much of the chemical activity responsible for memory storage. The increase in number of synapses during development in the rat is shown in Figure 7-4. In these morphological respects, and in chemical respects as well, the rat brain is practically mature (adult-like) by 30 days of age. Analogous to the human brain, however, there is some later development still to be completed in areas such as the hippocampus and the reticular formation. It can be interesting to keep these aspects of brain growth in mind when considering the development of learning. For instance, it is striking that the 15-day-old rat has use of all of its sensory modalities, moves with remarkable quickness and physical dexterity and can learn a variety of things as rapidly as an adult, and yet has in its cerebral cortex only about one-tenth the number of synapses found in the adult.

A particularly significant feature of the growing brain is that all neurons that are formed do not contribute later on. About 3 percent of the neurons generated in the brain migrate to an abnormal location and die (Cowan 1979). To account for this, more neurons must be produced than are actually used. Similarly, more synapses are formed than are ultimately used. As an example from the peripheral nervous system, most muscle cells in the adult rat are innervated with one synapse from a single axon. The neonatal rat, in contrast, may have five or six axons that form synapses with a

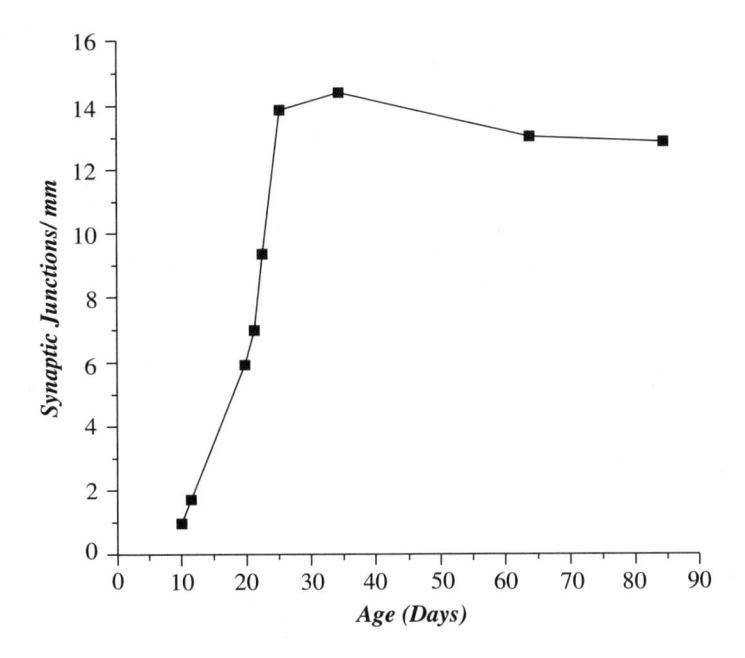

FIGURE 7-4 Synaptic density in the neocortex is shown for rats at several ages during ontogeny. Based on a count of synapses using an electron microscopic technique, this figure provides a reasonable estimate of age-related changes in number of synapses in the neocortex of the rat. (Adapted from Aghajanian & Bloom 1967.)

single muscle cell. All but one of these will be eliminated during the following first 2 or 3 weeks of the rat's life, however, probably by cell death.

The number of neurons and synapses produced and then lost in developing animals is striking. Much of the measurement has taken place in the striate cortex, one of the major primary receiving areas for vision. It has been estimated in the monkey, for instance, that the total number of synapses in this area of the brain increases from 389 billion at birth to 741 billion 6 months later, and then decreases again to about 381 billion in adulthood (Boothe, Vassdal & Schneck 1986). This is accompanied by a 16 percent decrease in the number of neurons in this area between birth and adulthood (from 192 million to 161 million). In the cat, the fluctuation with development in number of synapses in this area is especially dramatic. At 8 days of age there is only 1.5 percent of the adult synapses present in this area, which is increased by 70 days of age to a maximum far above that of adulthood, but then decreases a full 30 percent into adulthood

This overproduction of neural connections and their selective loss or pruning with development is now known to take place in many parts of the brain. Although the precise basis of this process is uncertain, it seems likely that correct synapses may be established by some combination of indiscriminate growth of many connections and elimination of all but those that are correctly formed. By analogy, a computer may be built by hard-wiring only those connections needed or by first making all possible connections and then snipping off the unnecessary ones; the latter mechanism is the sort that seems to contribute to brain development. This description may seem to imply that the unnecessary connections involve mistakes, but this method probably evolved for more positive reasons. It may simply be the most efficient strategy for normal brain development to function in this way; this strategy requires less genomic information than if the correct point-to-point connectivity were completely specified in the genome. It would be easier in this sense to overproduce nonprecisely characterized neurons than to produce just the number needed and specify them completely.

General Features of Behavioral Development During Infancy

Careful consideration of the behavioral capacities of developing animals and the infant's special abilities in adapting to its world is critical for testing and understanding their learning and memory. It is useful to describe briefly some features of behavioral development during infancy.

At birth the human is quite adept at sucking, at rooting with its head in order to acquire the opportunity to suck and feed, and at swallowing. If it loses bodily support, its arms flail upward quite reliably (Moro reflex); it grasps objects with its hand quite effectively and blinks to a light shown in its face. By 6 weeks of age it will move its head as if to look upward when lying on its stomach, carefully observes its mother's face and follows objects visually as they move. By 3 months the sucking and grasping abilities are less reflexive and more selective. Its head is held upright more often and longer, and the infant turns its head toward objects that appear in the periphery of its visual field and responds to sounds in the same way. By 6 months of age both hands are used to grasp objects, and the infant can roll over, sit up briefly, and even stand for a short time. Articulation of various sounds increases and so does laughter. By 9 months of age the infant will pull itself to a sitting position and remain in that position, has good dexterity in using its thumb and forefinger, and moves about by crawling. When 12 months old the child is effective in releasing as well as grasping objects in timely fashion and will walk either by itself or with one hand held by an older person. Communication skills increase at this age in the form of waving bye-bye, imitating sounds, saying a few words, and understanding many.

The main features of the infant rat's behavioral development take quite a different form but follow a similarly progressive increase in adaptiveness toward more independence throughout infancy. Like the human, the infant rat's primary job is to maintain its growth rate and to process information for learning and memory. Although the human infant may seem to have more help from its caretakers in achieving these goals than the rat, under normal circumstances both animals receive all that they need. A description of specific aspects of behavioral development in the rat can help us appreciate the tests and theories of memory development that apply to this animal.

Beginning the first week after its birth the newborn rat is in many ways relatively less mature than the newborn human. It is hairless and wrinkled, cannot see or hear, cannot regulate its body temperature neurophysiologically (nor through external behavioral means without parental help), and is apparently quite helpless. Yet it is quite adept at the two activities essential for its survival—getting nutrients from the milk obtained at its mother's nipple and conserving the calories acquired by keeping warm. And like the human, the infant rat exhibits reflexes (such as sucking) that will not be apparent later on in life.

During the second week after birth the rat has some hair and loses body temperature less rapidly. It is more likely to wander a short way from the nest, but is adept at getting back home on the basis of the odors of the nest alone. At the end of this period its ears and eyes open. By the beginning of the third postnatal week the pup is very active, walks and runs much like an adult, and is intent on exploring its world. Part of this exploring leads to alternative foods, which is a good thing because by the beginning of this third postnatal week the pup needs more nutrients than mother's milk can provide. The mother initiates fewer feedings when the pups are this old, and anyway, the pups at this age begin to find the milk less attractive, in part because they are less able to digest it. This introduction to adult sources of food and an improved regulation of its own body temperature make it possible for rat pups in the laboratory to be weaned at 21 days of age despite a good deal of continued maturation of the brain over that takes place largely over the next 9 to 10 days.

THE SIGNIFICANCE OF LEARNING AND MEMORY DURING DEVELOPMENT

We have already seen that from very early in life, even prior to birth, animals and humans are capable of some learning. We can now consider two basic questions: what is the nature of the changes that take place, as maturation occurs, in the capacity to learn and to remember relatively complex episodes? And second, are there also changes in the efficacy of the simple learning that can occur very early in infancy? In other words, why are relatively young organisms apparently less able to learn and remember the complex events that adults regularly learn and remember, and if we could test learning and remembering of the simplest, most elemental association, would younger animals and humans still be less effective at it than adults?

Before addressing these questions we can consider whether altricial infants such as the rat (or human, dog, cat, ape, etc.) need to learn and remember as well as adults in order to survive and thrive in their ecological circumstances. It is common to believe that learning and memory are important early in life to prepare for adulthood. This is not entirely correct. Much of what the infant does at that age, including what it learns to do, does not apply at all to its adjustment as an adult. Instead, these early acquired behaviors are needed for the infant's solution to problems unique to infancy. A variety of evidence has convinced developmental scientists that much of early experience, learned or not, is more important for allowing the infant to adapt during that stage of life than for preparing it for adulthood.

Another fact suggesting that early learning could be of little use in adulthood is infantile amnesia. The events of infancy simply are not remembered in adulthood. What specific incidents can you recall from your first 2 or 3 years of life that have helped you as an adult? If you can recall any particular incident from that period of your life you are unusual. We will return later to this topic.

Early Nonspecific Experience

Despite these points, a variety of experiments have verified everyone's intuitive conviction that early experience of some kind, which would seem to include early learning, is important for adulthood. These effects, however, are more indirect than is ordinarily supposed, and more complicated. A large set of studies has investigated the consequences of general early experience—experience that is not directed toward specific learning. Studied in this category are the consequences of: early exposure to gonadal (sexual) hormones such as testosterone (which can determine sexual differentiation in the developing animal); early exposure to stress or the internal consequences of stress such as norepinephrine or corticosterone (which will alter this animal's response to new stress later in life); deprivation of the opportunity for vision (which can result in an animal that later is unable to see visual patterns of which they were deprived in infancy); or enriched early experience that includes more sensory, social, or motor experience than otherwise is available (which can increase the number of synapses in the brain and facilitate a few, but not many, instances of learning). Space does not allow elaboration of these consequences here. We shall consider next the consequences of early experience with specific learning, because this is closer to the focus of our book. The long-term consequences of both classes of early experience are relevant, however, to a paradox involving infantile amnesia that we discuss later in this chapter.

Early Experience with Specific Learning

An important issue is whether environmental enrichment affects learning by making the animals generally more competent in cognitive skills or by providing them with specific experiences that transfer directly to the learning test. Does early exposure to a variety of stimuli and experiences generally strengthen the mind, making the animal or child more capable in any situation of intellectual challenges such as learning? Many educators have believed this and used it as a justification for having children study Latin and Greek or a particular choice of subject such as philosophy in the core curricula in colleges. Such nonspecific transfer also is expected by classic theories such as that of Hebb (1949). Yet, because the early enrichment in rats has facilitated only some kinds of learning (e.g., complex mazes) but not others (e.g., discriminations based on lever-pressing or passive and active avoidance), most of the benefit seems specific to the particular stimuli and events experienced during the enrichment.

Specific transfer of learning from early experience is nevertheless an important feature of the development of learning and memory. Probably this is obvious. What is not obvious is the extent to which new skills that arise during development are due to specific earlier experiences or, alternatively, would emerge regardless of what was learned earlier. This is one version of the nature/nurture question—the extent to which new behaviors that arise during development (walking, interacting socially in terms of aggressive, sexual, and play behaviors, appropriate vocalization, and so forth) are "hard-wired" into the brain through genetic disposition and would occur regardless of experience.

About 50 years ago a variety of experiments were conducted with human infants to determine whether early training techniques could facilitate the onset of muscular skills such as walking. Scientists drew very definite opinions about this from their research, often in sharp disagreement with others. Based on a good deal of close observation of developing infants, McGraw (1943) concluded that "training in any particular activity before the neuromechanisms have reached a certain state of readiness is futile" (p. 130). Experiments with humans frequently involved twins: one trained from an early age for the components of skills such as walking, roller-skating, swimming, or toilet training; the other not trained. The relative speed of emergence of these skills in the twins was recorded.

Although the effects of such training were surprisingly small, the existence of some benefit from the early learning indicates that it was an overstatement to suggest that it is irrelevant. Hunt (1979) pointed out that, in fact, the data that had led to the general conclusion that early learning had no effect actually indicated statistically significant, albeit small, advantages from early toilet training, rollerskating, or swimming. Said Hunt (1979, 111), "Experience clearly plays a major role in the rate of psychological development."

There remains, however, a good deal of credibility in the general notion of learning readiness—that despite the presence of all the environmental circumstances needed for learning a particular association or skill, a certain degree of neurophysiological maturation is required for learning. This fact, hardly surprising in this general form, becomes interesting in light of the different levels of such maturation apparently required for different kinds of learning. We discuss in the next section some modern tests of this issue.

First, however, suppose that early specific experiences benefit later learning of more complex problems. Suppose also that nonspecific experience might change the physical character of the brain to enable, potentially at least, more effective cognition later. Would it not be reasonable, then, to flood infant humans with massive experiences involving early learning? There might be some risk in this procedure, however; there are indications that early learning of a particular type can impair later learning.

For instance, Harlow (1959) found that infant monkeys exposed to relatively difficult discrimination problems had an especially hard time later on acquiring a learning set. A learning set is a progressive improvement in the solution to a class of discrimination problems with increasing practice on such problems and is thought to represent a relatively high-level cognitive skill. The younger the monkeys when exposed to the initial discrimination problems, the more difficulty they had in acquiring the learning set. Similarly, Papousek (1969) found that humans exposed to a difficult discrimination problem soon after birth had special difficulty in ever mastering the problem, even at an older age; they did not perform the discrimination as well as those who began 44 days after birth until they were twice as old. In other words, it was as if the early discrimination experience impaired their later ability to learn the discrimination. Similar negative consequences of early learning in the rat have been reported (Spear & Hyatt 1993).

In summary, studies have not indicated that memory capacity can be increased or learning generally made more effective by appropriate early experience. These studies have shown, however, that some early experiences are critical for appropriate and efficient adaptation for infants and later in life. Included among these helpful early experiences are several cases of specific kinds of early learning, particularly those involving specific aspects of communication such as language in humans or songs in birds and social skills. If nearly all of our infancy is forgotten through infantile amnesia, it is puzzling how this could be. We shall return to this paradox later.

ONTOGENETIC CHANGE IN THE CAPACITY FOR LEARNING

Does the capacity for learning change with development? The effectiveness of learning certainly seems to change. Hundreds of experiments have found poorer learning by infants than adults, or more generally, better performance on learning tasks among older developing animal and humans. Almost no experiments have found the opposite relationship ("almost" is a significant adjective here, as we shall see). The expectation of improved learning as development proceeds is strong. For instance, Henderson (1980) suggested that a particular task (the Hebb-Williams maze) may not yield useful information in certain studies because learning in this task does not seem to improve with age. The implication is that a learning test should be considered valid only if it is learned more slowly by younger animals!

If improvement in learning during development is a fact, as indicated by so much of the data, then it is inevitable that we might consider when certain kinds of learning are at all possible during development. We already know that learning of some kinds is possible prior to birth. We mentioned earlier how evidence clearly indicates that some learning is possible without much of a brain at all, in fact with only a few neurons or only a single one. Given that at least some learning is probably possible in the earliest prenatal stages of brain development, it does not seem useful to consider the onset, during postnatal development, of a capacity for learning in general. We may consider, however, the onset of specific types of learning and subsequent changes in its effectiveness. The concept of learning readiness and its application in education suggests value in determining for specific tasks at what age learning is possible. It is especially interesting when it is determined that despite established competence in the individual components of a learning task, the association of these components is not possible until a particular age. We consider such cases next.

Ontogenetic Change in the Effectiveness of Initial Memory Storage: How Do We Decide When a Capacity for Specific Learning Emerges?

Deciding at what age learning of even specified events is possible is more difficult than it might seem. A major problem is deciding for infants whether they cannot associate two events that they see or smell, or if instead they are simply not very effective at seeing or smelling these particular events. We have seen that there is a change in the effectiveness of most or all sensory capacities after birth for all altricial mammals. Yet for all such animals the somatic (tactile) and olfactory (smell) senses can be used very early. Even prior to birth the rat (and probably most other mammals) can use these two and probably does so (Smotherman & Robinson 1991).

It is usually difficult to separate the influence of olfaction from that of gustation (taste). What is known is that at least some forms of olfaction and tactile detection develop a little earlier than gustation, that all three occur before audition, and that audition precedes vision. This sequence is remarkably consistent across all animals, whether mammals or not and whether altricial or precocial, although the rate of development of each sensory system can differ markedly. For instance, it is fairly certain that the human and certain birds such as the duck or chicken can and do hear prenatally, but it is unlikely that the rat, cat, or dog do so. Yet in each case the tactile, olfactory, and gustatory senses are effective before audition.

Given this order of sensory development, it should not be surprising that learning involving these sensory systems would follow the same order. One could hardly expect to see the emergence of learning in a sensory system with which there is no detection. This has been studied along with related, more interesting facts in a report by a Russian scientist, Volokhof (1970). From a large number of studies Volokhof determined the ages at which animals such as the dog and rabbit seemed capable of simple learning involving each of the major sensory modalities. The results illustrated in Table 7-1 were obtained with young dogs and rabbits that were required to learn to approach a stimulus where food was acquired. The onset of such learning follows the same order as the onset of the basic detection of events by that particular sensory system, but in each case the learning within a particular sensory system did not occur until a substantial period after detection with that stimulus was established. In terms of the animal's basic orienting reflex (a primitive indication of detection, sometimes referred to as the what-is-it response), the dog on postnatal day 1 seemed

TABLE 7-1 **Appearance of the Alimentary Motor Conditioned Reflexes in the Dog and Rabbit During Ontogeny (Days after Birth)**

	Dog		Rabbit	
	(Troshikhin 1957)		(Ivanitsky 1958)	
Analyzer	Conditioned stimulus	Days after birth	Conditioned stimulus	Days after birth
Olfaction and taste	Aromatic oils	1	Camphor oil	1
Tactile temperature	Fan with hot air	7–9	Fan with hot air	10–11
Vestibular	Swinging	10–12	—	—
Auditory	Bell tone 800 cps	15–16	Tone 500 cps	11–13
Visual	Lamp 40 watts	22–25	Lamp 40 watts	13–15

Source: Spear 1978.

to detect both olfactory and some somatic events, on days 9 to 15 it detected auditory events, and on days 15 to 19 after birth visual events. This work suggests that learning to associate two events comes at a later age than does perceiving them.

Volokhof reviewed data pertinent to a number of other points of interest. These include the observation that the age at which the developing animal becomes effective in learning depends on certain features of the task. For instance, if there is a delay between the occurrence of the stimuli that are to be associated, younger animals are at a special disadvantage for learning. In most cases this probably reflects the younger animals' greater susceptibility to forgetting, which readily translates into a greater difficulty in integrating events separated by a delay. But perceptual factors may also influence this age-related difference, as we shall see.

Volokhof's review consisted of both classical or Pavlovian conditioning—learning that event A predicts or is accompanied by event B—and instrumental or operant conditioning—learning that in a certain situation a particular response will lead to a favorable outcome such as acquiring food or avoiding pain. Although both classes of learning have been studied ontogenetically, the former (Pavlovian) has been more studied in very young infants because their responses are so limited. Pavlovian conditioning also is in many ways more analytical, because the stimuli actually learned can be identified more accurately. There is no doubt, however, that animals such as the rat are capable of both classes of learning in some form before or just after birth.

A few days before birth the rat is capable of Pavlovian conditioning of an aversion to a flavor that is paired with an induced illness. A technique was developed to allow the fetus to consume a novel flavor such as apple juice, after which the fetus was administered an illness-inducing drug, lithium chloride (LiCl) (Smotherman 1982). It is known that all embryos drink their amniotic fluid. A flavor, apple juice, put into the fluid therefore was consumed and apparently detected by the fetus. To administer the LiCl, cesarean-like surgery was conducted several days before birth to open the uterus. Some of the fetuses then could be given LiCl and others a neutral control substance. More than 3 weeks after this conditioning, when the pups were old enough to be weaned, the animals that had been made ill after consuming apple juice displayed an aversion to it. Interestingly, those that had not been made ill after consuming apple juice showed a preference for that substance relative to rats of the same age that had never tasted apple juice. This finding indicates retention of the taste experience, since rats generally prefer more familiar tastes.

Operant conditioning has not yet been established before birth, but it has within the first day after birth. One-day-old pups in a relatively cool location learned to turn their head in a particular direction, always to the left for some pups and always right for others, in order to obtain a burst of warm air (Pfister & Alberts 1983). Hungry rat pups of about this same age learned to push, mostly with their heads, a specially scented ball of cotton in order to receive a squirt of milk into their mouths (Johanson & Hall 1979).

The Earliest Onset of Specific Instances of Learning

Not all instances of Pavlovian and operant conditioning are possible before birth or just afterwards. For many cases of Pavlovian conditioning, it has been determined that the earliest age of effective learning depends on which sensory modality is involved, but in a more interesting respect than merely whether or not it is possible for the infant to perceive what is to be learned (Rudy, Vogt & Hyson 1984). This question was asked: for specific events such as a flashing 6-watt bulb and a brief footshock, to what degree will their capacity for perception of these events precede the animal's capacity to learn the association between them? In other words, will an animal's ability to learn the association between two events develop at the same time as the ability to perceive each of them separately or, alternatively, is more development required for the events' association than for their individual perception?

This approach and some important questions of control in tests of the ontogeny of learning can be illustrated by an experiment (Moye & Rudy 1985). Preweanling rats were presented 25 pairings of a flashing light and footshock when they were 15, 17, 19, or 21 days old. The acquired memory for the association between the flashing light and the footshock was tested 24 hours later. The index of learning was conditioned suppression, the extent to which the animal would suppress its ongoing activity when the flashing light occurred. The tests indicated clear and substantial memory for conditioning in animals 17 days or older. The 15-day-old animals seemed not to have learned: behavior in those given light-shock pairings did not differ from that of control animals presented only the lights or presented an equal number or lights and shocks distributed randomly over time (i.e., not explicitly paired).

The first control question was whether the 15-day-old rats knew that the light occurred—whether they would respond to the presence of light differently than to the absence of light. It was found that the pups were less active during a session when the flashing light alone was presented than when it was not. The second question was whether the 15-day-old rats were capable of responding to the footshock; they were, because when pairings of a clicker and a footshock were presented, the pups conditioned quite well to the clicker. So, the pups were capable of responding to both the light and the footshock, although they apparently could not learn to associate them.

A third possibility was that the 15-day-old pups did learn to associate these two events but could not express them 24 hours later (because the retention interval was too long) or when 16 days of age (because the pups were still too young). These hypotheses also were rejected; there was no expression of conditioning when 15-day-old pups given light-footshock pairings were tested only 1 or 6 hours after the pairings nor when they were tested when 18 days of age. The former result indicates that the absence of conditioned aversions was not due to forgetting over the 24-hour period, and the latter indicates that it was not due to their immaturity in expression when 16 days of age.

The conclusion is that learning of the association between a light and a footshock requires, in these circumstances of conditioning and testing, more maturation than is necessary to respond to either of the events individually. The same conclusion was reached about the age at which the association between a tone and a sweet taste could be acquired (Hyson & Rudy 1984). More generally, the results agree with those of many other experiments in showing that the capacity for simple Pavlovian conditioning develops progressively after birth. Pavlovian conditioning of detectable events that may not seem possible at early ages does occur, and becomes more effective, as the animal matures physiologically. We shall encounter exceptions to this more general conclusion, however.

For the case of instrumental or operant conditioning, there also are many experiments to indicate that learning improves with development. One of the simplest kinds of instrumental learning is how to escape from unpleasant events. The development of this kind of learning was investigated among infant rats and mice (e.g., Misanin et al. 1971, 1973). Developmental changes in the animal's effectiveness in learning to escape a mild footshock were studied for each of three types of escape behavior: crawling onto a surrounding ledge; moving from one end of an alley to another; or turning in a particular direction (right for some animals, left for others). The climbing task, in which escape could take place in any direction, could be learned by 5-day-old rats. Rats seemed unable to learn the direction-specific runway task before 7 days. The turning discrimination task could not be learned before 10 or 11 days of age.

Like most tests of Pavlovian conditioning, these and similar studies of instrumental learning have suggested that learning simply is faster as the infant grows older. This is the sort of result one might expect if the maturation of some basic physiological feature determines the effectiveness of learning. The notion would be that the more of X, where X might be number of synapses or concentration of a particular neurotransmitter or receptor sensitivity or whatever, the better the learning. Perhaps, such a notion might continue, maturation of these or similar physiological mechanisms also determines the developing animal's increasing capability for remembering over long intervals. Unfortunately, this simple model alone does not work. For instance, it cannot account for the several instances in which young infants not only learn as well as older animals but learn more rapidly, a point to which we shall return.

Studies that tell us at what age a particular task can be learned are useful but, paradoxically, understanding what these studies do not reveal is important for understanding the ontogeny of memory. Such studies cannot tell us why learning effectiveness changes developmentally, nor can they explain apparent differences in the rate of development of different kinds of learning. For instance, despite indications from the above studies that some of the simplest instances of associative learning may not take place until the second or third postnatal weeks of the rat's life, there is clear evidence that within a few days of birth, the rat can learn to associate two tastes, a taste and an illness, and an odor and a taste, can learn a discrimination between two odors, and can learn to withhold a response that would be punished if emitted (Spear & Rudy 1991). There is apparently more to the development of learning and memory than the development of a unitary physiological process that makes learning and memory possible.

Systematic Analysis of Ontogenetic Differences in Learning about Schedules of Reinforcement

An alternative to testing directly the age at which certain kinds of learning can occur is to investigate ontogenetic change in more complex consequences of learning. From the unspoken assumption that some learning will be possible at all ages, the question in such investigations is, what are the qualitative differences that occur in learning as the infant develops? This is the approach taken in a systematic study of how the effects of certain schedules of reinforcement change as the rat develops (Amsel 1986).

The basic learning that occurs for all of the infants in these experiments is that movement from one end of a short alley to the other gains access to an anesthetized mother rat. From the mother rat the pup can obtain tactile comfort and can suckle on a nipple that may or may not yield milk (but is reinforcing nevertheless). The interesting question pursued in these experiments is how learning about the schedule of reinforcement in this situation changes ontogenetically to affect the animal's behavior in traversing the alley. *Schedule of reinforcement* means that according to a prescribed schedule, reinforcement is only sometimes obtained: sometimes access to the mother rat is permitted after the pup traverses the alley, and sometimes it is not. After this learning-to-approach is well established, all reinforcement may be discontinued (by permanently closing the door to the compartment holding the mother rat) and resistance to extinction assessed. A long series of experiments determined the age at which the adult-typical response to reinforcement conditions (involving a different reinforcer, of course), well-established from previous research, was first observed in the developing rat. We consider four examples:

1. An adult rat given reinforced and nonreinforced experiences on alternate trials (R N R N R N . . .) will soon come to exhibit what is called single patterned alternation, running slowly on the trials in which no reward will be found in the goal box and more rapidly on trials in which reward will be found in the goal box. In other words, the animal learns to anticipate what will be found in the goal box on the basis of what was there on the previous trial (they cannot otherwise know what is in the goal box until they reach it). Infant rats show this patterning quite well by postnatal day 11 and fairly well at earlier ages also. We will see that this fact is especially important.

2. Adult rats given a reward on only a partial set of their acquisition trials, with nonrewarded trials interspersed among them at random so that their occurrence is not readily predictable, will continue to respond for a longer period during extinction (after reward is taken away entirely) than will animals given reward on every acquisition trial in which they responded. This is the familiar partial reinforcement extinction effect that is so prevalent in every mammalian species, including humans. Amsel found that rats do not begin to exhibit this until 12 to 14 days postnatally.

3. Behavior of adults given a large number of trials in which a substantial reward is present in the goal box (e.g., ten 45-mg pellets of food) subsequently will extinguish more rapidly than that of adults given a small reward in the goal box (e.g., one pellet). This magnitude of reinforcement extinction effect is not observed in the developing rat until postnatal days 20 to 21.

4. As a final example, adults given a large reward in the goal box on several trials followed by a small reward in the goal box on additional trials, will run more slowly to obtain this small reward than will adults that had received the small reward all along. This successive negative contrast effect was not observed by Amsel and his colleagues until postnatal days 25 to 26.

Results such as these help determine what processes are responsible for certain learning effects at particular ages. For instance, it has been suggested that for adults, single pattern alternation behavior (see 1 above) indicates memory for the reward on the previous trial. An elegant theory based on this interpretation has been described by Capaldi (1971). It accounts for all four of the above effects in adults in the same way, in terms of the interaction among memories for different reinforcers. Yet, the above results indicate that these effects—partial reinforcement extinction, magnitude of reinforcement extinction, and successive negative contrast—may not occur for infant rats until several days after the animal has the capacity to remember the reward event that occurred in the previous trial. If the Capaldi theory is correct for all ages, then why should the ability to remember something about the previous reward not be sufficient for adult-like expression of the other reinforcement-conditioning effects? A simple explanation might be that the memory of the 11-day-old for the prior reward, although somewhat effective, is not nearly as effective as that of the adult which makes possible the other reinforcement condition effects. There are, of course, alternative explanations (e.g., Capaldi's theory might apply only to adults) but which is more correct is not at issue here. This particular interpretation helps illustrate that the mere occurrence of a learning or memory effect in infants by no means establishes that the strength of the effect is equal to that in older animals. This is particularly true for retention, which, we will find shortly, is drastically inferior in younger infants in comparison with older animals.

Developmental Differences in Cognitive Dispositions That Contribute to Retention and Forgetting

Finally, there is still another viewpoint from which to consider the basis of apparent developmental increases in learning. Although it may appear to introduce a further complication, the basic notion is quite simple, perhaps deceptively so. The core of the idea is that infants have a different perspective on the world than do adults. Even aside from their inferior detection of some sensory events, they perceive objects and events with, literally, naïveté. And they have a different agenda of motivations and activities than adults, which is accompanied by different priorities as to what to notice and how to encode what they notice for storage in memory. We considered these factors earlier in a general fashion and now ask how they might influence the ontogeny of learning and memory.

An example may help. Suppose that you hide your 8-month-old daughter's toy under the center of the couch near the flowerpot that is on the coffee table in front of the couch. She finds the toy, you hide it there again after she has left the room, and she tries to find it once more when she returns. Assuming that she has encoded the previous location of the toy, how would that encoding differ from the way we adults encoded it verbally in the description above? The most obvious difference is that older children or adults probably would use a similarly verbal encoding, whereas the 8-month-old infant would not.

There are other differences aside from the use of verbal representations, however. The infant would be unlikely to view the flowerpot as separate from the coffee table, particularly if it has always been there in her experience; for the infant the flowerpot and table are one object. And the toy might not be represented (nonverbally) as under the couch but rather on a spot on the floor one cannot crawl over. Slightly older infants who could encode verbally might do so in a different way. Rather than "under the couch" the toy might be remembered as "on the floor near where Daddy takes his nap" or "near the flowers I am not allowed to touch." A still younger infant, during the first month or two after birth, might represent the flower+table "object" that she has smelled, tasted, and touched, as an intense sensory experience that is arousing and reasonably pleasant without reference to how it smelled, felt, or tasted or even that the smell, touch, and taste were different sensations.

Like an adult, all of these infants might have, in some sense, different representations of the location of the toy, and all of these are likely to differ from that of an adult. The two older infants might even have learned the location of the toy as effectively as an adult and might remember it later. The infants would not be as able to remember the location several months or a few years later in part because the location of the toy comes to be encoded differently from before. A few years later the child would be representing things in verbal form, would have learned that the flowerpot was an object separate from the table, and would not reference objects on the floor as things they do or do not crawl over. For the older infant the location of "under the couch," will have taken on many different meanings and would not be the best reference as to "where Daddy sleeps." The representations and encodings of 1- or 2-month-old children would change even more over a period of a few years, and there would then be even less contact with the way they originally had encoded the events surrounding the location of the toy.

Although based on some known dispositions of human infants at these ages, all of this is hypothetical. It does serve to emphasize two points, however. First, the drastic changes in encoding from one point of development to another may make retrieval of early memories difficult. Second, we will have to find out a good deal more about what is in fact learned at each age, beyond a single target memory that is chosen for measurement, in order to understand age-related differences in learning and memory.

Like infant humans, infant rats also develop quite different encodings of events than do their older counterparts. To say that another way, the attributes an infant rat uses to comprise the memory of an event may differ considerably from what comprises the adult's memory for that same event. Three examples, for which there is good empirical support, will be useful:

1. If required to learn what outcome is associated with a taste and an odor that occur together, or two tastes, or a texture and an odor or a light and a tone, infant rats tend to treat the two events as if they inevitably go together—inseparable or equivalent parts of a larger whole. Adults tend to concentrate their attention and learning on one of the two events at the expense of the other, to use one of them to form the association, and to neglect (at least temporarily) the other.

2. The context of learning is less likely to be noticed and encoded into memory by adults than by infants and may play a more important role in the retention of the younger animals.

3. Sensory modalities of the infant that are relatively weak or less critical than others for their survival while in the nest, such as vision or audition, may be less likely to be used by them than by adults in encoding a learning episode. Infants seem less likely than adults to differentiate events in terms of sensory modality. Infants can detect the differences if required to do so, but they are otherwise disposed to treat a tactile stimulus and a taste or a light and a tone as if they were equivalent. This disposition may be increased if the two events both happen to be novel, are pleasant (or aversive) events, have comparable intensities, occur simultaneously in the same place, or are each associated with a common third event.

These samples illustrate how infantile perception and ecological circumstances might lead infants and adults to learn quite different things from the same episode (for further consideration, see Spear & Molina 1987; Spear et al. 1988; Spear & Hyatt 1993). This difference in what is encoded has two significant implications. First, we should expect that some events will be learned more readily by infants than by older animals. In general we would expect this for events that are especially amenable to infantile perception or critical for the infant's momentary adaptation, but the basis for more specific prediction is not yet apparent.

There have been several observations to confirm that in some circumstances infants may learn more rapidly than older animals. We list five (for further elaboration see Spear, McKinzie & Arnold 1993): (1) When a taste aversion is to be acquired by pairing that taste with a startling mild shock to the animal's feet, rats learn more rapidly when 5 or 10 days of age than when 15 days or older (Hoffmann & Spear 1988). (2) Rats 12 days of age learn a conditioned aversion to the odors of their home nest more rapidly than do rats 16 days of age (Corby, Caza & Spear 1982). (3) Preweanling rats learn olfactory context more readily than do adults (Lariviere, Chen & Spear 1990). (4) Rats 8 to 16 days of age learn the association between two odors presented simultaneously (sensory preconditioning) more rapidly than do older rats (e.g., Chen et al. 1991). (5) When a stimulus conditioned to evoke fear and aversion is paired with a second stimulus (second-order conditioning), preweanling rats learn the association between the two stimuli more readily than do adults (Smoller, Serwatka & Spear 1987).

Although the precise connection between these results and infantile perceptual dispositions or ecological circumstances is unclear, these samples do illustrate that basic conditioning is not inevitably more effective later in development and that in some circumstances—presumably those in which infantile encoding is especially amenable to the learning conditions—young infants learn more rapidly than older infants or adults.

A second consequence of infantile encoding is the expectation of great difficulty in remembering specific events of infancy later in life. The discrepancy between what is noticed at the time of retention later in life and what was encoded for memory storage in infancy is presumably sufficient to virtually preclude memory retrieval. That the episodes of infancy may be especially susceptible to forgetting leads us to the topic of infantile amnesia and, more generally, ontogenetic changes in rate of forgetting. This will be covered in the rest of this chapter.

INFANTILE AMNESIA AND THE ONTOGENY OF RETENTION

The difficulty humans have in remembering the events of their infancy (infantile amnesia) was of central importance to psychoanalysis. Freud's idea was, essentially, that the infant's concepts and behaviors deal with sexuality in a socially unacceptable way and so these events become pushed out of consciousness—made difficult or impossible to retrieve from memory storage—when the developing human becomes aware of what is and what is not socially acceptable.

Infantile amnesia occurs for all altricial mammals in which it has been tested, including wolves, monkeys, and rats, whose social standards about sexual behavior are a good bit more lenient than those of humans. So it is obvious that Freud's interpretation of infantile amnesia was wrong in this respect. Yet his observation that the events of infancy are especially susceptible to forgetting remains important. There is today an increased appreciation of the generality and impact of this effect.

The paradigmatic observation suggesting infantile amnesia is that a typical 20-year-old human remembers nothing of his or her life when 1 year old and yet a 40-year-old remembers a great deal of his or her life at age 21. Confirmation of this particular observation with solid experimental evidence from human subjects is virtually impossible, however, and other sources of evidence, clinical or anecdotal, are inconclusive.

Rare reports of memories for infancy are somewhat interesting. One could, of course, merely ask a group of 20-year-old humans what they remembered of their infancy, and a significant number of studies have done just that. Such studies were fairly common 50 to 75 years ago, involving either direct questioning of persons or the study of their autobiographies. The earliest memories reported usually were for events that occurred at about age 3 (for a review of early studies, see Dudycha & Dudycha 1941). Investigators in these studies claimed some fairly specific conclusions, for instance, that only 10 to 20 percent of one's fearful memories seem to occur before the age of 6 and that women seem to recall earlier memories better than men, including more minor details and more pleasant events.

Yet there are two major problems with such studies that limit the scientific value of their conclusions. First, there were few attempts to confirm the veracity of these early memories—little or no confirmation that specific events actually happened the way they were reported. Second, there were no data, aside from the individual's verbal report, to confirm that the subject really remembered experiencing as an infant the events reported. For instance, a few people in these studies reported that they remembered being born. It is admittedly unlikely that any of these subjects were not born, but on the other hand, saying so does not confirm that they actually remembered it. The third problem is, how can one know that what was reported as a memory of infancy is not instead a repeated story learned from pictures or conversations to which the subject was exposed after infancy? Studies of this sort are still conducted today, but although they typically deal more effectively with these methodological problems, they have added little information of analytic value.

Experimental tests have tried to avoid these problems of interpretation and to draw more substantial conclusions. Although no one as yet has systematically recorded specific learning in infants and tested its retention 20 years later, the more general question of how long infants of different ages can remember specific events has been studied with humans. Most experimental investigations of retention in human infants have tested their recognition memory for pictures (usually geometric designs) or their repetition of what they have learned to do. To test recognition memory, infants are first shown the target item, such as a picture of a triangle. Then, after different intervals of time, they are shown that item again along with a new item, such as a picture of a number of small circles. Based upon the observation that infants of particular ages always spend more time looking at a new item than at one they have seen before, retention of the memory for the triangle is said to be stronger to the extent that the infant looks at the circles longer than at the triangle.

To test remembering for what an infant has learned to do, as well as what it has seen, infants with a ribbon tied from their ankle to a mobile above their crib learn that kicking will make the mobile move. They increase their kicking accordingly. After differing retention intervals, memory for what they learned to do is measured in terms of the number of kicks the infant gives when the kicks do not result in movement of the mobile. Memory for what they saw is assessed by the infant's response to replacing the old mobile with a new one. This technique has been developed and employed with extraordinary profit by Rovee-Collier and her colleagues (e.g.,

Rovee-Collier 1989). This work has led to a substantial proportion of the new knowledge gained about infant memory during the past 10 years. Like the evidence from the picture recognition procedures, this work also has led to the general conclusion that forgetting is more rapid in young than older infants. It is somewhat surprising that when memories with much more verbal content are measured in young children after their infancy, from 2 years of age and older, the forgetting rate does not seem to change ontogenetically, at least to the degree observed in the infant humans and developing animals (Perlmutter 1987).

Aside from the experiments by Rovee-Collier and her colleagues, most of the experimental analysis of infantile amnesia has taken place with animals as subjects, and most of this has been with rats (and to a lesser extent, mice). A broad range of issues has been tested in this way, and this approach allows direct tests of fundamental issues of theory. The theoretical issues are fairly straightforward, although the theories are by no means specific.

Theoretical Issues

A fundamental issue for theory is whether the source of the forgetting labeled infantile amnesia is unique to infancy. Perhaps it is not. Perhaps the rapid forgetting for the events of infancy has the same sources as forgetting of the events of adulthood, and infants are simply more susceptible to them. For instance, retroactive and proactive associative interference, generally acknowledged to provide a major source of forgetting at all ages, might be especially detrimental to infants. There is in fact some evidence to support this, e.g., previously acquired conflicting memories increase the rate of forgetting a position discrimination in both preweanling (16 days old) and older rats but have greater effect on the preweanling rats (Smith & Spear 1981).

Yet, infantile amnesia is such a strong effect and so widespread that it lends itself to explanation in terms of circumstances unique to infants. There have been two major classes of theories developed from this view. One set emphasizes the consequences of the rapid growth that takes place during and after infancy, and the other emphasizes the consequences of an infantile brain or behavior for memory storage.

Theories emphasizing growth as a relatively unique source of forgetting within infantile amnesia have emphasized several factors: psychoanalytic (Freudian) repression of infantile amnesia due to growth from one stage of social development to another; exaggerated changes in the perceived context or details of the episode to be remembered, due to growth-induced changes in perception between learning and remembering; the immense morphological development that normally occurs in the central nervous system, including a dramatic increase in the number of synapses in the brain (especially neocortex) and the complexity of their organization, which might render memories laid down during infancy inaccessible later, after such growth; and, corresponding changes in the chemical milieu, including increasing amounts and turnover rates for a variety of neurotransmitters as well as changes in receptor sensitivity and other cellular characteristics that could well disrupt the electrochemical code associated with memories stored prior to these changes.

Theories emphasizing the uniquely infantile character of original storage of the memory have generated a different set of hypotheses, such as the following two: (1) Infantile encoding leads to the treatment of many separable events as if they were unitary, yielding perceptions inconsistent with those that occur for the older animal when remembering is acquired. This is thought to impair memory retrieval by decreasing the congruity between the attributes of the stored memory (coded, perhaps, in unitary fashion) and what is perceived by the animal at the test (coded as separate events). (2) The limited number of potential storage sites (synapses) in the infant's brain precludes redundant storage of the memory (if such is to be expected in older animals). It should be noted that growth during a retention interval and immaturity during initial storage of a memory normally are quite confounded. Some creative research designs will be needed to untangle the contributions of growth and infantile storage to the net effect of infantile amnesia.

The basic empirical observation critical to infantile amnesia is that despite equivalent retention soon after learning, retention becomes progressively poorer for infants than for older animals the longer the retention interval. This experimental finding, first documented most clearly by Campbell and Campbell (1962), has been made for a number of instances of instrumental learning. Examples include active avoidance, in which the rat learns to move from one location to another upon a specified signal in order to avoid a footshock (Figure 7-5), and passive avoidance, in which the animal learns not to move from one location to another in order to avoid a similar footshock (Figure 7-6). Other examples include discrimination learning in which the animal learns to turn in a particular direction to escape an annoying footshock (Figure 7-7) or to press a particular lever to obtain food.

These developmental changes in memory have been found to include habituation (nonassociative learning). For instance, although 16-, 30- and 75-day-old rats showed equally rapid habituation (decline in responding) to an auditory stimulus, they differed strikingly in retention. Adults continued to display habituation after a 1-week retention interval, while the youngest subjects had forgotten after only a few hours (Richardson & Campbell 1991; for a similar result with a different class of habituation, see Parsons, Fagan & Spear 1973).

Memory Content and Infantile Amnesia

Retention of the above instances of instrumental learning required the retrieval of memory attributes for responses—what the animal has learned to do—as well as of memory attributes for specific signals as to when to respond. There are circumstances of Pavlovian conditioning in which relatively little forgetting occurs for a simple stimulus (e.g., a single tone) that provides a signal function, such as a conditioned stimulus, even for infants. A memory representing Pavlovian conditioning need not include the level of response attribute intrinsic to that for instrumental learning. That

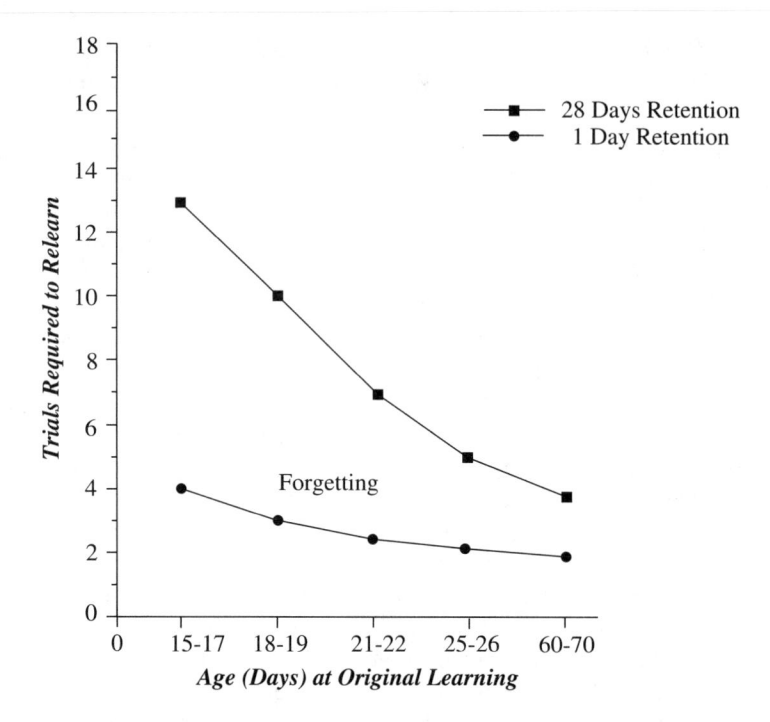

FIGURE 7-5 Retention of learned one-way active avoidance is shown 1 or 28 days following the attainment of a learning criterion (three consecutive avoidances) for rats of several ages. This illustrates that the retention loss during the interval between 1 and 28 days is greatest at the youngest age and progressively decreases among older rats. (N. G. Richter & N. E. Spear, unpublished data.)

there might also be relatively little infantile amnesia for such events has been suggested by evidence. For instance, when a single taste is paired with an illness to induce an aversion to that taste or a single tone is paired with a footshock, retention after long intervals seems almost adult-like for older preweanlings (17 to 22 days of age) that do, however, show infantile amnesia in terms of the instrumental learning tasks (Campbell & Alberts 1979; Coulter, Collier & Campbell 1976). Younger preweanlings, however, show infantile amnesia even in these tests of Pavlovian conditioning. Moreover, subsequent experiments have confirmed that in different circumstances older preweanlings also show infantile amnesia for single events such as a taste, as well as for an odor, visual event, or tactile event (Markiewicz, Kucharski & Spear 1986; Steinert, Infurna & Spear 1980). Whether the degree of infantile amnesia is generally lower for Pavlovian than for instrumental conditioning is unclear; to accomplish an appropriate test would require not only truly comparable

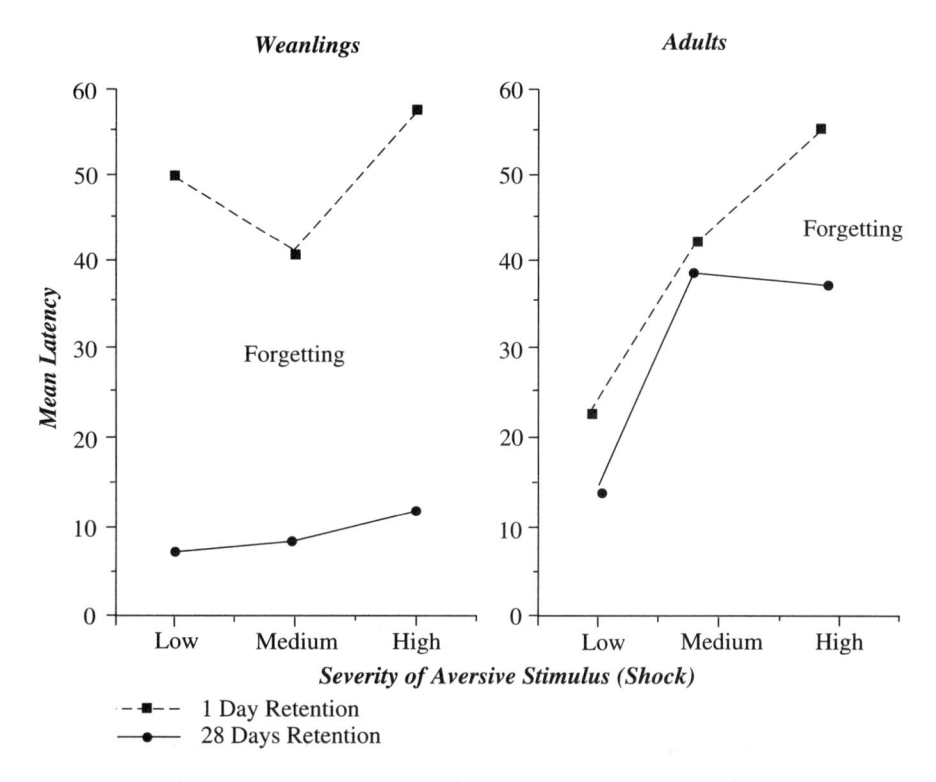

FIGURE 7-6 Retention of passive avoidance 1 or 28 days after achievement of the learning criterion is shown for weanling rats (21 to 25 days old) and adults (60 to 90 days old) as a function of the severity (intensity and duration) of the footshock delivered if the animal failed, during acquisition, to passively avoid. Sometimes referred to as *inhibitory avoidance,* the animal learns to avoid shock by remaining on the white side of a two-compartment apparatus (the other side is black). The measure of retention was latency to cross from the white to the black compartment when the animal was returned to the white compartment 1 or 28 days after conditioning. The results indicate more forgetting between 1 and 28 days for the younger animals than for the adults (and no significant effect, on forgetting, of the magnitude of the negative reinforcer). (Adapted from Feigley & Spear 1970.)

Pavlovian and instrumental tests of learning, but also equivalent learning for the two cases and for all ages tested, altogether a formidable challenge.

The age at which such infantile amnesia is most severe might nevertheless depend on aspects of memory content such as the specific stimuli to be remembered and their configuration (i.e., the task). One aspect might be response attributes that

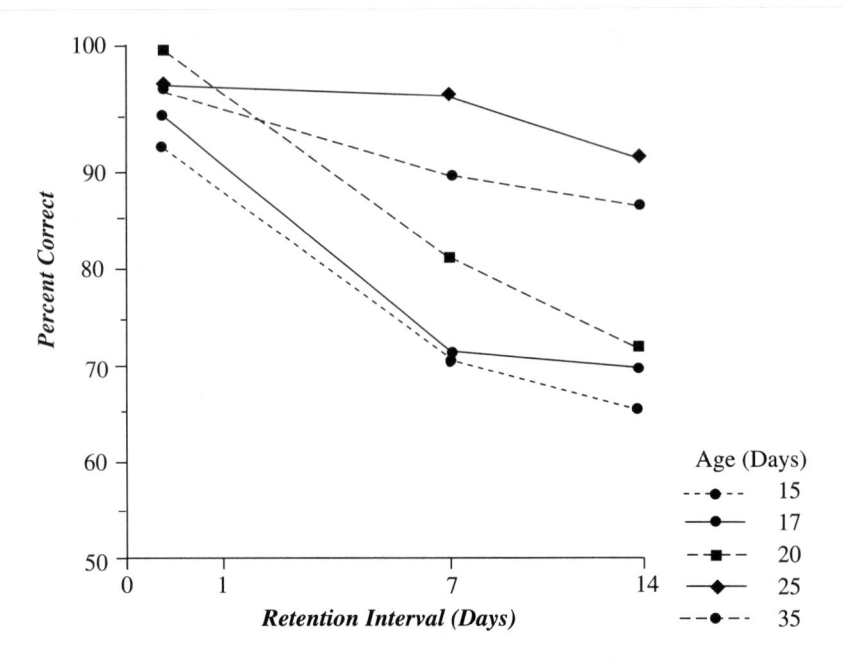

FIGURE 7-7 Retention of a simple spatial discrimination is shown in terms of the percent correct responses given 1, 7, or 14 days after the discrimination was learned by developing rats of five different ages. The figure shows more rapid forgetting in the younger animals. (Adapted from Campbell et al. 1974.)

could form an important part of the memory, and another might be the stimulus modality used for perception during learning. Although response form is likely to change with development during a retention interval, it seems unlikely that response attributes are especially resistant to infantile amnesia. Memory for a response in a situation even simpler than Pavlovian conditioning—habituation to the response of poking one's nose into a hole—has seemed quite susceptible to infantile amnesia over short periods (Parsons, Fagen & Spear 1973). The extent of infantile amnesia may depend on the sensory modality involved in the memory, but the difficulty in testing this properly has discouraged attempts to do so. Preliminary results indicate that sensory modality does not alter the relative rates of forgetting shown by infants and older rats (Markiewicz et al. 1986), but the evidence to date is inconclusive.

The conclusion is that some degree of infantile amnesia seems to be present for Pavlovian as well as instrumental conditioning, regardless of the particular conditioned stimulus employed during Pavlovian conditioning. If degree of infantile amnesia nevertheless depends on the nature of the events to be remembered, this would support the idea that an infant-unique source of forgetting might be the character of initial encoding and memory storage during this period.

Growth and Infantile Amnesia

Guinea pigs are precocial, even more so than cows or horses, and their adult-like motor capabilities within minutes of birth are matched by a relatively mature brain. This contrasts with the extreme immaturity of the newborn rat's brain. The infant guinea pig therefore has relatively little brain growth to undergo prior to adulthood whereas the infant rat has a great deal. When retention of discriminated escape learning or passive avoidance learning was measured in infant and older guinea pigs, there seemed to be no important differences (Campbell et al. 1974). This suggests that guinea pigs do not undergo infantile amnesia and supports the notion that amount of brain growth during a retention interval helps determine the amount of infantile amnesia. It also suggests that infantile amnesia is in part due to a source of forgetting unique to infancy—rapid growth between learning and testing.

Conclusive interpretation of such comparative studies is fraught with difficulties, however. The reasons were noted in our earlier discussion of the comparative problem and include the difficulty of equating memory context, procedures, degree of learning, etc. from one species to another. Unfortunately, no analytic studies have appeared to clarify the interesting effects with guinea pigs or other precocial animals. Moreover, it is now clear that extensive growth during a retention interval is not necessary for the appearance of more rapid forgetting by younger infants. Infant rats have been found also to forget more rapidly than older rats over periods of minutes, and a duration of minutes does not allow for extensive growth. For instance, retention of the memory for either the pairing of a black compartment and a mild footshock (Miller & Spear 1989) or for a white compartment alone (Kucharski, Richter & Spear 1985) decreases more rapidly within a 30- to 40-minute period for 16-day-old rats than for 21-day-old rats or adults. Similarly, the rat's retention of the memory for an odor-footshock pairing or for the occurrence of the odor alone increases drastically between the ages of 8 and 12 days postnatally on tests given within an hour of learning. Less rapid forgetting over such short intervals is observed for 18-day-old animals (Figure 7-8) (Miller, Jagielo & Spear 1989).

For theoretical purposes, then, there is some support for the notion that an infant-unique source of forgetting due to growth or to immaturity during initial memory storage might be responsible for infantile amnesia. But the evidence to date is minimal and barely suggestive. What is clear is that with infantile amnesia, we are dealing with a very powerful effect that also is quite general, not only covering a variety of species but also a variety of circumstances. The robust nature of this phenomenon encourages scientists to study further the extent to which infantile amnesia might be due to infant-unique sources such as growth and infantile memory storage.

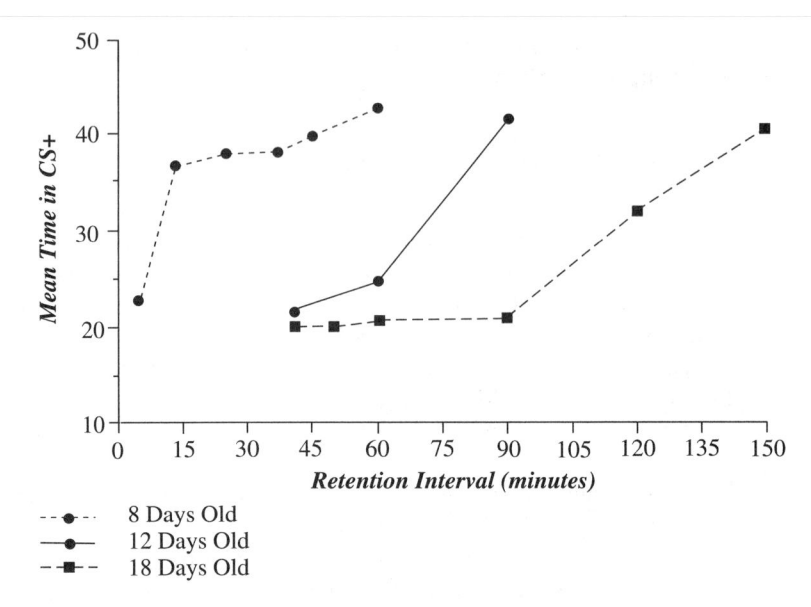

FIGURE 7-8 Retention of an acquired aversion to an odor (CS+) is compared over relatively short intervals following conditioning, for three ages of preweanling rats. The test for retention is a 1-minute assessment of the preference for the aversively conditioned odor relative to a novel odor. The less the time spent in the proximity of the aversively conditioned odor (the CS+), the better the retention. This figure shows more rapid forgetting the younger the animal. Control animals not given pairings of the odor and the aversive stimulus spend between 40 and 45 seconds in the CS+ (not shown). If we define this level as complete forgetting, it is reached within 45 minutes for the 8-day-old rats, within 75 minutes for the 12-day-old rats, but not until 150 minutes after conditioning for the 18-day-old rats. (Adapted from Miller et al. 1989.)

THE PARADOX

This chapter contains a paradox. On the one hand, we have considered evidence that the particular experiences one undergoes during infancy and the specific learning that takes place has great significance for one's adaptation and general behavior later in life. Yet we have the apparently contrary fact of infantile amnesia, which indicates that specific learning derived from particular experiences during infancy is forgotten rapidly and unlikely to be remembered at all during adulthood.

How can these apparently contrary facts be reconciled? First, it now seems clear that many consequences of early experience are mediated by organismic changes that need not involve memory for specific events. For instance, it is established that an apparently innocuous treatment like placing a neonatal rat into a tin can for 3 minutes can influence that rat's behavior in an open field or active avoidance learning as an adult. This experience influences permanently the animal's adrenal-pituitary response to stress, however, a response that helps determine open field behavior and avoidance learning. A more extreme early experience such as long-term deprivation of visual stimulation (such as living in total darkness) substantially alters the neurophysiological structure of eye and brain and, of course, later visual behavior as well (Hubel & Wiesel 1963). Effects like these do not require behavioral retention of the early experience responsible for them.

What about those aspects of specific learning early in infancy that must be remembered for later adaptation? How is this retention accomplished? It now seems likely—this is the second point to reconcile the paradox—that little or no infantile amnesia occurs for specific events of infancy that recur periodically between infancy and adulthood. In some circumstances, the recurrence of some part of that episode may be sufficient to reactivate the memory and prevent infantile amnesia even though the entire episode is not repeated. For an infant rat that has learned that a flashing light predicts a novel and annoying footshock, for example, the periodic recurrence of only the footshock has seemed sufficient to reduce forgetting of the avoidance learning. More generally, periodic exposure to an abridged form of the conditioning paradigm, insufficient to produce learning by itself, can nevertheless maintain memory in infant rats. Procedures for this instance of reduced infantile amnesia have been termed *reinstatement* (Campbell & Jaynes 1966; Rovee-Collier & Hayne 1987; Spear & Parsons 1976).

The third point of reconciliation rests on the fact that not all infantile memories that are measurably forgotten are lost irretrievably. Instead, the observed forgetting is due in some way to difficulties in retrieval and expression that often may be overcome. It is, of course, an assumption of psychoanalysis and most other psychotherapies that infantile memories can be retrieved given the appropriate treatment, and the success of therapy is thought by many to depend on how effectively this is accomplished.

A number of experiments have studied the alleviation of forgetting in developing rats (e.g., Hinderliter & Misanin 1988; Spear & Parsons 1976; Richardson & Riccio 1986; Miller et al. 1991) and in human infants (primarily tests by Rovee-Collier and her colleagues [e.g., Rovee-Collier 1984, 1989]). These experiments have left no doubt that the rapid forgetting of infants can be alleviated by providing reactivation or prior cuing treatments just before the retention test, as support for retrieval (chapter 9). These treatments consist basically of providing to the subject some fractional part of the learning task prior to the retention test. A variety of control conditions are needed to establish that forgetting is indeed alleviated and that the prior cuing treatment did not merely yield new learning similar to the forgotten learning.

A number of significant features of infant memory have been determined with such experiments, primarily by Rovee-Collier and her colleagues (for a review, see

Rovee-Collier 1991). We do not have the space here to elaborate on these issues and facts, but we can point out the three most salient features of this effect: (1) There is no doubt that the prior cuing treatments can alleviate forgetting to a remarkable extent. As a result new respect has emerged for the memory systems of immature animals and humans. For instance, despite the previous insistence of some theorists that human infants have little capacity for memory before the age of 8 months or so, Rovee-Collier has established that at the age of 3 months substantial retention occurs after an interval of a month, given the administration of a prior cuing treatment. (2) There are definite limitations to this effect. There seem to be retention intervals that are so long that the prior cuing treatments—at least those attempted so far—no longer can alleviate forgetting, and the length of these intervals may be shorter for younger infants (Spear & Parsons 1976; Rovee-Collier & Hayne 1987). (3) These effects so far have provided no strong confirmation that infantile amnesia is due to a source of forgetting that is unique to infants. If a unique source of forgetting were involved, and if this source were associated with the retrievability of memories, we might expect that prior cuing treatments would alleviate forgetting to a greater extent in infants than in adults or in younger infants than in older infants. So far such interactions have not been observed.

CHAPTER SUMMARY

Understanding how memory processing changes between infancy and adulthood will allow insights into how experience and neurophysiological growth contribute to memory generally. It may also provide critical practical information for education and for clinical therapy, which depends to a large extent on the patient's recall of childhood events.

Meaningful comparison of memory among animals at different stages in development presents a difficult methodological problem, analogous to that encountered in comparisons among different species. Generally speaking, the tests that would be most useful for understanding the ontogeny of learning and memory should minimize transfer from other learning and include a variety of different events and life experiences.

Although it has most often been found that developing animals learn more slowly than adults, several instances of the opposite result may be cited. In contrast, experimental results are virtually unanimous that when differences in retention are observed, the youngest infants show the most rapid forgetting.

The dramatic development-induced changes in the brain and in the animal's requirements for adaptation must be considered for effective analysis of memory development. What can be learned and how it will be encoded at any moment may depend on previous experiential and neurophysiological development, and memory may depend further on such development between learning and remembering.

Despite extremely poor memory for specific events of infancy, experience during infancy is vitally important for neurophysiological development and for the effective use of sensory mechanisms, perception, and the expression of a variety of species-specific behaviors later in life. The effect of early experience on later learning and memory, particularly the effect of nonspecific early experience, is less clear. Although early environmental enrichment has sometimes influenced later learning, the same effects have been obtained when the enrichment is given later in life, indicating nothing special about the experience being early.

A capacity for learning of some kind is no doubt present even in the early stages of embryonic development, which might seem to make questions of the development of a general process of learning rather uninteresting. There is nevertheless value, albeit limited, in determining the age at which specific types of learning first appear and their efficacy subsequently develops. The most important marker for when a particular type of learning will emerge during development is the animal's sensory capacity, but this is not really of interest for the ontogeny of learning per se. Prior to development of the capacity for sensory detection, learning of events processed through that sensory modality will not occur, which is no surprise and trivial. Yet the learning of an association between two events has been found to lag, developmentally, behind the capability for sensory detection of those two events. This lag, if substantial, is important. Similarly, the developing animal's capacity for certain cases of instrumental learning may be present before the animal exhibits mature, differential behavior to different conditions of reinforcement or to relatively complex discriminations involving such learning.

Special difficulty in remembering the events of infancy has been observed in all animals tested, such as the rat, mouse, or monkey, that are, like the human, born with an underdeveloped brain and require extensive parental care (i.e., altricial animals). Theories to explain this effect have focused on either how growth following learning might lead to especially rapid forgetting or how an underdeveloped and inexperienced brain might yield learning that is especially susceptible to forgetting. The latter approach tends to be favored by evidence indicating that the events of infancy are especially susceptible to forgetting over short intervals, during which little growth would be expected, but growth theories remain viable nevertheless.

Generally speaking, why infantile amnesia should occur despite the importance of early experience remains a paradox. One resolution is in the discovery that given the appropriate environmental circumstances prior to testing, learning that took place during early infancy may be remembered after long intervals. Although not necessarily true for all infantile memories, such cases of the alleviation of forgetting agree with a vast array of similar effects (to be discussed) which collectively indicate that a great deal of forgetting and retention may be controlled during the stages of memory retrieval and expression.

▶ 8

Experimentally Induced Amnesias and Memory Modulation

Late one rainy evening, John X., driving home from an evening of study at the university library, hit a slick spot on the road. His car slid into a tree and John, who had not been wearing a seatbelt, was thrown against the windshield and knocked unconscious for a brief period. Fortunately, he sustained only minor injuries and after being treated in the hospital, was released. When questioned by the police and friends about the accident, however, another kind of problem came to light. John cannot remember the events immediately preceding the accident. He does not recall leaving the library nor much else of what he was doing for about half an hour before the crash. But he has no trouble remembering events somewhat earlier in the evening and no difficulty with mundane questions such as who and where he is, the names of his friends, and the college courses he is taking.

Most of us are familiar with, or have read about, episodes not totally unlike this one. The failure of memory following a concussive injury is referred to as retrograde amnesia, since the forgetting is for events prior to (or backward from, in a manner of speaking) the traumatic insult. Since John was stone-sober when he left the library, we have every reason to believe that he was fully cognizant of the events through the evening up to the moment of the crash. But somehow that concussive blow has produced a substantial memory loss for relatively recent events.

This selective memory loss, with impairment of recent information but sparing of older memory, is a hallmark of retrograde amnesia (RA). One might expect the importance of the event, rather than time, to be a determinant of recall, but this is not the case. Memory for recent but important episodes is impaired, while trivial but earlier episodes are quite intact. Summarizing studies on a number of RA victims, Russell and Nathan (1946; see also Russell 1971) noted that the memory loss seldom extended backward for more than 30 minutes, except in cases where an unusually profound concussion had been received. Some amnesic victims who suffer what appears to be much more extensive forgetting will gradually recover memory for earlier events until only the information from a relatively brief span of time remains "lost." (This shrinkage of RA will be discussed in more detail in chapter 9.)

EXPERIMENTALLY INDUCED RA

Although accounts of naturally occurring RA are fascinating and can be of heuristic value in suggesting interpretations, it should be obvious that, for a number of reasons, amnesias based upon accidents are not an ideal way to study memory processes. To determine more precisely the processes involved in RA, researchers have used some simple procedures to induce amnesia in animals under controlled laboratory conditions. An early study by Duncan (1949) investigated the effects of electroconvulsive shock (ECS) on a recently learned response in rats. ECS, which induces electrical seizure activity in the brain, was (and is) used in the treatment of severely depressed humans; in that function it is referred to as electroconvulsive therapy. Whether improvement in patients is related to the effects of ECS on memory or on other processes is not yet known. Duncan's procedure involved administering ECS to rats following training in an escape/avoidance task in a runway. In this situation, mild footshock was delivered through the grid floor of the start chamber and runway until the rat reached the safe compartment (goal box) at the opposite end. However, rats could prevent (avoid) footshock by scampering to the goal box within a few seconds after being released from the start box. With this arrangement, early trials typically involve escape responding in which rats learn to run down the alley to terminate the unpleasant footshock. Avoidance emerges in later trials; the running response becomes anticipatory, and no shock is actually received. Presumably, through Pavlovian conditioning, the cues associated with footshock come to elicit fear; the running behavior is maintained because these stimuli are removed (and fear is thus reduced) when subjects reach the goal box, a location where shock has never occurred.

Duncan asked whether the memory for a trial would be disrupted by administration of ECS after the trials, and whether this disruption would diminish as the interval increased between the trial and the ECS. He found that ECS at short intervals (a minute or less) after each daily training trial impaired the subject's ability to acquire the avoidance response, but that ECS after a long interval (an hour or more) had relatively little effect. The temporal gradient relating test performance to the delay of ECS is shown in Figure 8-1. This time-dependent effect of ECS is consistent with clinical observations and at the same time rules out debilitation or other general impairment as the source of the impairment. Thus, if ECS were simply acting on the subject's ability to traverse the runway on the following day, those receiving the delayed ECS should also have shown impairment.

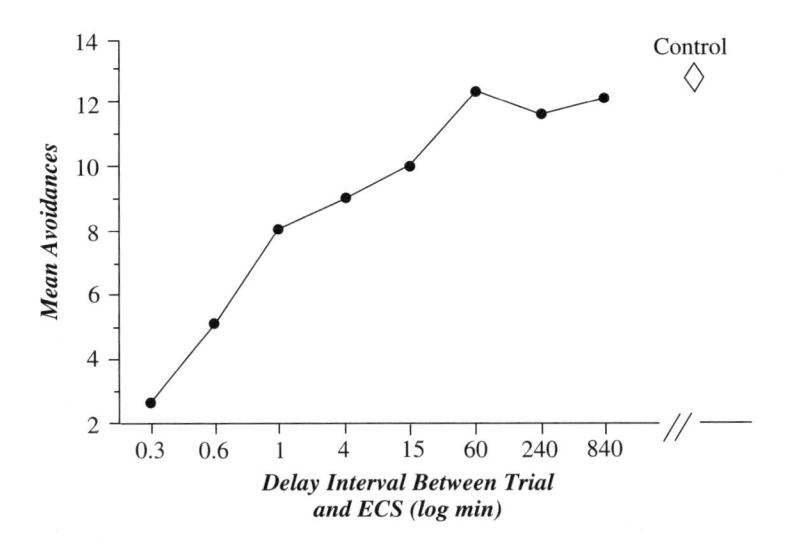

FIGURE 8-1 Temporal gradient of retrograde amnesia in rats. Electroconvulsive shock was administered at the designated interval after each training trial. Memory impairment is reflected in fewer anticipatory running responses. (Adapted from Duncan 1949.)

However, Duncan's study included another, more subtle methodological problem: the possibility that the ECS acted as a punishing agent. Although ECS renders subjects unconscious almost instantaneously, perhaps for just a fraction of a moment there was some unpleasant sensation. At the same time, it is well known that delivery of an aversive stimulus following a response can suppress that response, a contingency commonly referred to as punishment. Moreover, the extent of suppression is an inverse function of the interval between the response and the punishing stimulus, i.e., a delay of punishment gradient. Recall that the ECS was presented at various intervals after the response. Does the gradient of performance change reflect loss of memory (amnesia), or simply a delay of punishment effect? These two alternatives imply radically different interpretations, of course. Yet how are they to be differentiated, since both predict the same type of function?

One way would be to run an explicit punishment condition as a baseline. If the gradient were different from that produced by ECS, one might infer different processes at work. This was essentially Duncan's approach to the potential confounding. He included a control experiment in which groups of rats received an explicit punishment (footshock) at one of several intervals following the avoidance response. Although the two curves differed, with avoidance performance much less affected by footshock in the goal box than by ECS after the same delay, this outcome did not convincingly rule out a punishment interpretation of ECS effects.

A more compelling experimental refutation of the punishment interpretation is possible, however, by employing a different type of learning task. Rather than escape or active avoidance, the task involves suppression of ongoing behavior. The essential strategy is to arrange a situation such that the memory or punishment effects of the amnestic agent would lead to differential outcomes. More specifically, if the amnestic treatment (ECS, etc.) were having a punishment effect, the learned response would be enhanced, but if the treatment were affecting memory the performance would be impaired. Suppose a rat receives mild footshock contingent upon stepping off a platform onto a grid floor. A simple way to assess what is learned (and remembered) is to place the subject back on the platform the next day and measure the time (latency) until the animal steps off the platform. Normal subjects are very hesitant to return to the place where they received shock, and latencies are very long. Now suppose that we administer ECS to some subjects immediately after their training trial. Since the amnestic agent follows the footshock on the grid floor, a punishment interpretation predicts that these subjects would also have long step-off latencies at testing, because two aversive events (footshock and ECS) have been associated with moving onto the floor. But if ECS impairs memory, then subjects should not remember much about the consequences of their behavior and should readily return to the grid floor. Madsen and McGaugh (1961) were among the first to show that it is the latter outcome that occurs—ECS-treated subjects return quickly to an area that control subjects will passively avoid for a prolonged period of time. Thus, we can reasonably infer that the amnestic agent is affecting memory rather than acting as a punisher to change performance. Not surprisingly, such passive avoidance tasks (also termed inhibitory avoidance) are now employed extensively in studies of RA. Technically, the term *passive avoidance* refers to the response requirement at testing. However, the term is now widely used to encompass a variety of simple tasks in which training involves aversive consequences contingent upon a response, i.e., punishment training, and for convenience we will use this broader terminology.

Characteristics of Induced RA

What are the characteristics of this experimentally induced amnesia? As mentioned earlier, one salient feature is the time-dependent nature of the memory impairment—memory for a recent event is much more vulnerable than that for an older event. In the laboratory this is easily demonstrated by varying the interval between the passive avoidance training trial and the administration of the amnestic agent, using separate groups of subjects at each delay.

Interval between Training and the Amnestic Agent

In a now classic paper, McGaugh (1966) summarized a number of studies, many from his laboratory, demonstrating that severity of amnesia diminished as the training treatment interval increased. The time-dependent effects of various treatments are well established, but the slope of the RA gradient depends upon a number of parameters, such as the strength of conditioning, the intensity of the amnestic treatment, the type of task, and so forth. Although gradients of memory loss under laboratory conditions do not usually exceed 30 to 60 minutes, evidence of RA in mice extending back for several days has been reported (Squire & Spanis 1984).

The time-dependent function has attracted considerable attention among investigators since it promised to provide information about the psychobiological dynamics of information processing. Further, the outcome is tantalizing because it suggests that even in nonverbal organisms such as rats and mice some sort of processing of information continues after the physical events have actually terminated. And since the nominal learning episode is completed before the ECS is delivered, investigators need not worry that subjects' associative, motivational, or sensory processes were impaired during the trial. The status of the information changes over time, as reflected in the gradient of decreasing memory impairment. Were the amnestic treatments merely producing a dysfunctional brain system, the memory impairment should occur regardless of the delay interval. Indeed, with a constant retention interval (e.g., 24 hours), general impairment of brain function should show up best with a long training-treatment delay, because then the interval between treatment and testing is relatively short. Intriguingly, memory loss in amnestic situations follows a time course quite opposite to everyday forgetting, where older information is more likely to be unavailable than newer learning. As Rozin (1976) has noted, the principle governing amnestic memory loss seems to be more like that of the rule of thumb for computing taxes on sales of stocks: last in, first out.

Given the time-dependent nature of retrograde amnesia, it is hardly surprising that theoretical interpretations focused on the need for information to consolidate or gel following training. In an earlier chapter we mentioned a concept proposed by Muller and Pilzecker (1900) to explain retroactive interference. Their idea of neural activity perseverating in order for memory to consolidate seemed particularly applicable to the time-dependent feature of RA. According to a consolidation interpretation, the massive electrical seizure pattern (central nervous system [CNS] "storm") interrupts the neurochemical changes necessary to establish a long-term memory trace. Thus, with short delays between an episode and ECS, little if any storage of memory takes place. However, as the delay interval increases, more of the information becomes consolidated and stored, and the severity of disruption is diminished. This interpretation meshed nicely with an influential idea proposed by D. O. Hebb in 1949. In his book *Organization of Behavior*, Hebb speculated that during learning (and perception) patterns of neural activity persisted as reverberatory circuits. This reverberatory activity established semipermanent changes at synaptic junctions, which facilitated activation of the same circuit in response to similar inputs at a later time. In the case of RA, it appeared reasonable to assume that the reverberatory circuit mediated consolidation and that by disrupting the reverberatory circuit an amnestic agent blocked storage of information.

Interval between the Amnestic Agent and the Retention Test
Another characteristic of RA involves a different temporal dimension—the time until onset of the amnesia. Surprisingly, memory is often quite good shortly after the

amnestic treatment, but then declines rapidly. This delayed onset of RA was not recognized initially because many studies interpolated a 24-hour recovery period between administration of the amnestic agent and the retention test. Substantial amnesia was obtained at the 24-hour test, and so it was assumed that a similar loss would be found throughout the interval.

Experimental investigation revealed that this assumption was incorrect. In one early study using ECS, Geller and Jarvick (1968) asked whether the incomplete RA they obtained at 24 hours might represent partial recovery from a more profound loss at intermediate intervals. Mice received ECS immediately after a single passive avoidance training trial and were tested 1, 2, 6, or 24 hours later. Only the 6- and 24-hour control groups showed reliably poorer performance than the training-only control groups, an outcome that was the opposite of the predicted results. Additional control groups indicated that the good retention at short intervals was not a spurious effect from ECS acting on performance variables such as decreased activity level. Observing that rats recovered their motor abilities within minutes after ECS, Miller and Springer (1971) tested rats at even shorter post-treatment intervals. Retention was better at a 15-minute interval than at 30 to 120 minutes, thus replicating the pattern of Geller and Jarvik's findings.

Kesner and his colleagues (e.g., Kesner & Conner 1972), using electrical stimulation of the hippocampus to produce amnesia, have also reported that performance is intact at short retention intervals (e.g., 1 minute) but is substantially disrupted at longer test intervals (e.g., 1 hour).

Although the particular curves obtained for the onset of amnesia depend on a number of parameters (e.g., shock level, training-ECS delay, strength of ECS, etc.) as well as species of subjects, a particularly slow onset of amnesia has been observed with hypothermia as the amnestic agent (Hinderliter, Webster & Riccio 1975). In one study rats showed little forgetting up to 12 hours after treatment although by 16 hours substantial amnesia was present (Mactutus & Riccio 1978).

The delayed onset of amnesia found in the laboratory has a counterpart in the naturally occurring accidental amnesias of the everyday world. In addition to anecdotal reports of amnesia where memory was present immediately after the traumatic insult, a field study by Lynch and Yarnell (1973) provides an instructive example. Football players suffering a concussive head injury were queried about the preceding events at several intervals after they were removed from the field. While recall was good at the immediate test, retention had deteriorated drastically a few minutes later. In contrast, the control subjects, i.e., individuals removed for other types of serious injuries (dislocations, fractures, etc.), showed no such decline in memory with delayed testing. This study provides a nice illustration of an unexpected and somewhat counter-intuitive laboratory finding receiving confirmation in the messy and often difficult to investigate circumstances of real life amnesia.

Type of Amnestic Agent
What are the types of treatments that yield experimentally induced RA? A number of manipulations have been employed, and although they differ in many ways, all seem

to disrupt the normal functioning of the brain. Electroconvulsive shock is by far the most widely used agent, but it is not unique in producing memory loss. Post-training administration of convulsive doses of certain drugs (e.g., Metrazol) can induce a time-dependent memory loss (Palfai & Chillag 1971). It should be noted that overt (behavioral) convulsions are not a necessary condition: mice lightly anesthetized with ether prior to ECS administration in order to eliminate motor seizures showed as much RA as nonanesthetized control animals, even though seizure activity in the brain still occurred (Zornetzer & McGaugh 1971). Although the ether itself did not produce amnesia, under certain conditions this inhalation anesthetic does function as an amnestic agent (Pearlman, Sharpless & Jarvik 1961). Carbon dioxide (CO_2), another gas that can produce anesthesia, has been shown to impair memory in rats and mice. Although the severity of amnesia resulting from immediate post-training administration of CO_2 was less than for ECS under generally similar conditions, the temporal gradient of memory disruption extended longer with CO_2 (Paolino, Quartermain & Miller 1966).

Direct suppression of electrical activity in the cortex is another experimental means for inducing RA. Application of potassium chloride to the cortex is known to produce a spreading wave of depressed cortical activity, i.e., a functional but reversible decortication. Using this technique following training, Bures and Buresova (1963) found time-dependent memory loss in a spatial discrimination escape task as well as a passive avoidance situation.

One potential analytic advantage of spreading depression is that, in contrast with the extensive brain involvement in ECS seizures, the disruption appears limited primarily to the cortex. However, even more precise localization of neural structures mediating memory processes can be achieved by subthreshold stimulation of specific structures in the brain. An early study using this strategy was conducted by McDonough and Kesner (1971). Although Kesner and Doty (1968) had previously shown that electrical stimulation of the amygdala following passive avoidance training produced RA, the intensity of the stimulation was relatively high. Thus, although the seizures were localized, it was probable that they spread to other neural systems and disrupted normal activity for a prolonged period. Accordingly, in the McDonough and Kesner study, the level of electrical stimulation used in cats was carefully chosen to be below the threshold for inducing seizure activity. Immediately following a single punishment trial, subthreshold electrical stimulation was applied briefly to the amygdala. In contrast to control animals, the stimulated group quickly resumed eating, the previously punished response, when tested the following day. Thus, disruption of the functioning of a relatively discrete subcortical area was sufficient to impair memory. A similar outcome was obtained when subseizure stimulation was delivered to the hippocampus.

Other, less direct, ways of modifying normal brain functioning can also yield RA. Disruption of the thermoregulatory system is a highly effective amnestic treatment. Although early studies reported that deep body cooling (hypothermia) produced profound changes in electrical activity of the CNS, amnesia was not obtained when the hypothermia occurred following multitrial training task (see Grossman

1967). This negative result may have been related to the particular learning tasks, however, as several subsequent investigations demonstrated a robust RA induced by deep body cooling (Beitel & Porter 1968; Jacobs & Sorenson 1969; Riccio, Hodges & Randall 1968). A threshold level of hypothermia was required, as slight reductions in body temperature failed to affect memory. The RA was clearly time dependent; in one study, memory disruption occurred when hypothermia exposure began immediately, 5 or 15 minutes after training, but not when the cooling was delayed for 60 minutes. In the latter condition, retention was comparable to that in training-only control subjects.

The other side of the thermoregulatory coin, of course, is elevated body temperature, or hyperthermia. A study by Misanin and his colleagues (1979) provides a particularly clear demonstration of the amnestic effects of mild hyperthermia in rats. Although hyperthermia itself had no effect on passive avoidance latencies, as seen in a sham-trained group receiving hyperthermia, the same treatment following training produced a marked impairment of performance. Furthermore, as Figure 8-2 shows, the degree of memory loss increased as a function of the level of hyperthermia, which was manipulated by varying the duration of partial immersion in warm water. Even a very mild increase in body temperature (about 3°C) from the briefest exposure produced some amnesia. The amnesia was selective for recent memory, following a time-dependent relationship quite similar to that obtained for hypothermia. The temporal gradient of hyperthermia-induced forgetting was also obtained by Mactutus, Ferek, and Riccio (1980), who suggested that raised body temperature may be an unusually potent amnestic agent since manipulations known to attenuate the severity of RA induced by ECS or hypothermia did not seem to protect memory from hyperthermia treatment.

Could these amnestic treatments, particularly those that do not produce unconsciousness, be acting as distracters or surprising events that interfere with processing of information? The analogy here would be to the forgetting we experience when an event intrudes just after we have looked up a phone number and we find ourselves having to look it up again! While there are circumstances in which memory seems to be impaired by surprising episodes in animals (see chapter 5; also discussed later in this chapter), such a process does not seem to be responsible for most cases of experimentally induced amnesia. For example, under conditions where deep body cooling produces forgetting, other rats exposed to the same chilling environment immediately after training but for a short duration of time showed no impairment of retention. Had the onset of the cold treatment served as a surprise, then these animals should also have shown some memory loss.

The question of whether unexpected or surprising events might disrupt memory for immediately preceding events has a counterpart in research on human memory. For example, Tulving (1969) presented lists of common words to college students in a single-trial free recall paradigm. In various locations in each list was the name of a famous person (e.g., Freud, Aristotle). Subjects were directed to pay particular attention to these names so that they would be sure to remember them. The major

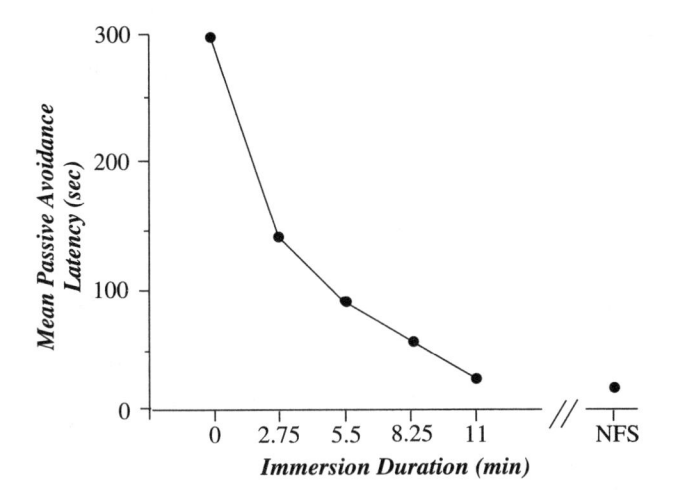

FIGURE 8-2 Passive avoidance performance as a function of duration of exposure to warm water, i.e., hyperthermia treatment. Animals in NFS condition were not trained or immersed. (Adapted from Misanin et al. 1979.)

finding was that the presence of the special item in the list depressed the recall of the immediately preceding word in the list. The memory impairment was primarily retrograde. This retrograde amnesia, as Tulving referred to it, was time dependent, in that a longer interval between presentation of the individual words (2 seconds rather than 1 or 0.5 second) prevented the impairment. Presumably, the attention afforded the high-priority famous names disrupted the encoding of the previous item. Others have obtained a similar effect; the finding can be produced by a salient physical event (e.g., shouting the word) as well (Detterman & Ellis 1972; Saufley & Winograd 1970). There is also some evidence of an anterograde amnesia for the word that follows an unusual event (Detterman 1975; Detterman & Ellis 1972). The retrograde finding is clearly in keeping with the general theme that processing of information in man and animals extends beyond the time in which the target stimulus (or training situation) is physically present.

A dramatic example of the disruptive effects of a surprising event comes from a study of eyewitness testimony by Loftus and Burns (1982). College students viewed a film depicting a bank robbery. To induce mental shock, one version of the film ended with a violent episode in which a young boy was shot in the face. Control subjects saw a nonviolent ending for the same film. Several experiments indicated that subjects in the mental shock condition remembered fewer details of events in the film than did control subjects. This retrograde amnesia for incidental information was obtained whether recall or recognition tests were used to assess memory. Loftus and Burns suggest that the shocking event may have prevented adequate storage of information by disrupting the lingering process that continues following removal of the physical stimulus.

MODULATION OF MEMORY

The research on retrograde amnesia illustrates that memory can be modified, and in this case impaired, by a traumatic insult occurring shortly after a target episode. Memory also can be altered by other types of retrograde events or treatments. In some cases these treatments lead to enhancement rather than impairment of memory, so we will use the more general term *modulation of memory* to describe these changes. Modulation of memories by reducing or inflating the value of the reinforcer or unconditioned stimulus in basic conditioning, supported by many experiments, has been reviewed quite effectively elsewhere (e.g., Delamater & LoLordo 1991), so this case will not be discussed (a small sample of these experiments is considered in chapter 11).

The notion of modulatory effects is rather general and does not depend on identification of specific mechanisms. Further, the period of memory susceptibility may not be identical to that for the formation or consolidation of memory. Although the analysis shifts from when memory is formed to how it can be modified, the time-dependent nature of the modifiability of memory is a theme which remains in common with the RA research. Studies of memory modulation, like those of RA, serve to further emphasize the importance of postacquisition processes in the establishment of memory (e.g., McGaugh 1983).

Pharmacological and Hormonal Modulation of Memory

It would be beyond the scope of this book to catalog and examine all the agents that have been found to modulate retention. Instead, we have selected a few representational examples that give the flavor of this approach to memory processing. A more extensive review of the pertinent literature can be found in McGaugh (1983, 1989b).

Pharmacological Modulation
In the same article that summarized laboratory evidence for selective loss of recent memory, i.e., retrograde amnesia, James McGaugh (1966) also presented evidence that "memory storage can be facilitated" by post-trial manipulations. Central nervous system stimulants such as strychnine and picrotoxin were reported to enhance retention of maze learning. Such enhancement of memory (and perhaps memory storage) was obtained if the drugs were administered shortly after training, but not if they were given after long delays. As with RA, post-training administration of the

agent eliminates alternative interpretations such as altered perceptual or motivational states during the learning session. Similarly, because the drug is not present at the time of testing, improved responding cannot reflect some irrelevant effect of the agent on performance. These considerations have made the retrograde modulation of memory a very appealing paradigm for investigators.

The exact nature of any modulatory effect is a central question for memory investigators. To determine whether post-training administration of strychnine facilitated memory of specific attributes, such as the response-reinforcer contingency, or whether the effects were of a less specific nature, Gordon and Spear (1973b) used a conflicting task, or negative transfer, paradigm. Subjects were trained on a passive avoidance task but were later tested for their ability to learn an active avoidance response in the same apparatus. That is, the original cues now required a different response. In original learning, the requirement may have been to stay on the white side to avoid shock; in testing, however, the requirement would be to leave the white side quickly to avoid shock. As one would expect, such requirements establish conflicting response tendencies. In this arrangement, memory for specific attributes of passive avoidance should be reflected in poorer test performance, since better retention of a "no-go" response interferes with the acquisition of the "go" response. Consistent with other findings, Gordon and Spear found that administration of strychnine immediately after training enhanced memory. Strychnine-injected rats took roughly twice as many trials as the saline control group to master the new, competing demands of the active avoidance task, indicating greater interference from the specific requirement of the "no-go" task. This outcome suggests that the memory enhancement was for a relatively specific set of attributes.

Memory Modulation by Hormones

Although strychnine and other pharmacological agents provide a useful approach to examining retrograde memory modulation, another question of interest is whether naturally occurring or endogenous substances might influence memory. In this connection, Gold and VanBuskirk (1975) asked whether the nonspecific sequelae of an experience, such as variations in hormonal levels, might serve as biological modulators of memory. Rats were injected with one of several dose levels of epinephrine (adrenaline), a hormone released from the adrenal glands and the sympathetic nervous system during stress. Subjects were trained with a relatively weak footshock in a passive avoidance task, and the drug was administered either immediately or 10, 30, or 120 minutes afterwards. As Figure 8-3 illustrates, an intermediate dose of epinephrine were found to enhance performance on the 24-hour test in a time-dependent manner: The facilitation of memory diminished as the interval between training and hormone administration increased. Presumably, the epinephrine injections mimicked some of the internal consequences associated with the training footshock, thus potentiating normal memory processes. The dose of epinephrine is quite critical, as higher levels can induce an opposite effect, i.e., amnesia. Additional research indicates an important interaction between level of footshock and dose of

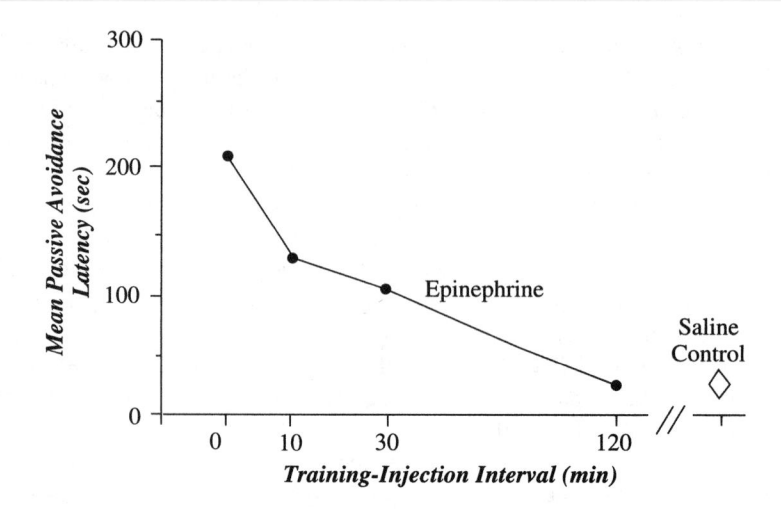

[Figure 8-3: graph showing Mean Passive Avoidance Latency (sec) vs Training-Injection Interval (min), with Epinephrine curve and Saline Control point]

FIGURE 8-3 Time-dependent retrograde enhancement produced by epinephrine for memory of a punished response (licking). (Adapted from Gold & VanBuskirk 1975.)

epinephrine. The same amount of hormone that facilitates retention after a weak footshock can produce impairment (amnesia) after a strong training footshock (Gold & VanBuskirk 1976a). Gold (1987) has recently presented a very readable summary of this research.

The generality of this modulatory memory effect was extended by employing adrenocorticotrophic hormone (ACTH), another endogenous substance released during stressful events. (One important role of this peptide hormone, released from the anterior pituitary, is to stimulate the synthesis and release of corticosteroid hormones from the adrenal cortex. The term *trophic* in ACTH refers to action toward another target, in this case the adrenal glands. For some time, this trophic activity was considered to be the only major function of ACTH.) Earlier work by deWied and Bohus (Bohus & deWied 1966; deWied 1966; Bohus & deWied 1981) had demonstrated that ACTH influenced resistance to extinction and retention. Subsequently, Gold and VanBuskirk (1976b) found that administration of ACTH has effects that seem to parallel those described above for epinephrine. Memory is modulated in a time-dependent manner; whether the modulation is enhancement or impairment depends upon the dose of ACTH and the intensity of the training footshock.

The role of adrenergic hormones in modulating memory has been further elaborated on in a series of studies by McGaugh and his colleagues (1984). For example, they have shown that the altered retention by post-training administration of epinephrine is not limited to inhibitory passive avoidance. In one study, injection of epinephrine following training in an aversively motivated Y-maze discrimination enhanced retention, as reflected in greater interference with learning the reversal of the original discrimination at the time of testing. Furthermore, consistent with the notion that the adrenergic hormone acted much like additional training trials and should have long term effects, the modulating influence was obtained at 1-week and 1-month retention intervals as well as after 1 day (Introini-Collison & McGaugh 1986).

These findings are consistent with the view that the time-dependent susceptibility of memory serves an adaptive function: "The period of susceptibility allows hormones released by experiences to influence memories of the experiences." (McGaugh et al. 1985, 253) That hormones released during an episode of emotional significance have memory-modulating effects has become a topic of considerable interest to many investigators. The spirit of this conceptualization of affective influences on memory is succinctly described by the musings of a character in one of John Updike's novels, *Rabbit Is Rich:* "Funny about feelings, they seem to come and go in a flash yet outlast metal." (Updike 1981, 163).

The exact mechanism by which adrenergic and other hormones act to modulate memory is not yet fully understood. However, several lines of evidence suggest that adrenergic effects may be mediated by feedback from peripheral systems rather than by any direct action on the CNS (see McGaugh, 1983, 1989b). For example, post-training administration of amphetamine influences retention, an effect assumed to be due to alterations in catecholamine levels in the brain. (Amphetamine, unlike epinephrine, readily passes the blood-brain barrier.) However, in one study injection of amphetamine directly into the ventricles of the brain influenced locomotor activity levels but had no effect on memory, while systemic (peripheral) injections enhanced retention (Martinez et al. 1980). Furthermore, a metabolite of amphetamine that does not easily cross the blood-brain barrier also enhanced retention (Martinez et al. 1980). Also, surgical removal of the adrenal medulla in rats reduces the modulatory effects of amphetamine on both active and passive avoidance. These findings appear to implicate an important role for peripheral adrenal influences in the postacquisition modification of memory.

Other research from McGaugh's laboratory has begun to examine the interaction of endogenous hormonal systems with the central nervous system in the modulation of memory. It has been known for some years that post-training stimulation of the amygdala can impair retention, but it now appears that an intact adrenergic system is important for this outcome (McGaugh et al. 1985). This type of finding provides an important illustration that what might appear to be direct brain effects may actually be mediated by, or along with, other systems. A review of recent developments in research on post-training administration of hormones and drugs can be found in White and Milner (1992).

Memory Modulation by Neurotransmitters
Earlier we discussed the memory-enhancing effect of strychnine, an agent producing CNS arousal or excitation by blocking inhibitory impulses. Agents that block or antagonize endogenous opiate-like substances (endorphins) have also been found to

improve retention. For example, an opiate antagonist, naloxone, injected directly into the amygdala immediately after training increased memory of a passive avoidance response; the same treatment after a delay of several hours was without effect. Conversely, injection of an opiate agonist, levorphanol, impaired retention in a time-dependent manner (Gallagher & Kapp 1978). Injection directly into the brain proves not to be a critical condition: Gallagher (1982) has found a similar retrograde enhancement with naloxone and several other opiate agonists when they were administered systemically (intraperitoneally). Since the endogenous opiate-like substances are closely linked to systems involved in the perception of pain, it is worth noting that Gallagher, Bostock, and King (1985) have shown a time-dependent effect of naloxone on working memory in a food-rewarded radial maze task. Using a long interval between the fourth and fifth trials to reduce performance below maximum (ceiling) levels, they obtained an enhancement of accuracy on the delayed trial when various opiate agonists were administered. These observations suggest a broader role of the endorphins in memory process than has been generally recognized (for reviews see Gallagher 1984; Gallagher & Kapp 1981; Messing et al. 1981).

Cholinergic agents provide another example of a neurochemical which exerts retrograde modulatory effects on memory. Central cholinergic systems have long been considered to play a role in learning and probably in memory as well. Evidence that the cholinergic systems are impaired in Alzheimer's disease highlights the potential importance of this neurochemical system. In a study done to obtain more precise information on the potential memory effects produced by cholinergic activity, Haroutunian, Barnes, and Davis (1985) administered several different classes of cholinergic agents to rats immediately following acquisition of a passive avoidance response. Subjects were tested for retention 72 hours later; thus, the pharmacological agent was not present during the training trial itself or during testing. Nevertheless, drugs that augmented cholinergic function were found to improve performance on the retention test. This enhancement of memory indicates that the cholinergic system is an important contributor to postacquisition processing of information.

As we indicated earlier, these findings represent only the "tip of the iceberg" with respect to the rapidly burgeoning area of research on the role of neurochemicals in memory. Almost any current issue of journals such as *Behavioral Neuroscience, Behavioral and Neural Biology,* and *Psychobiology* (to name a few) includes articles investigating the effects of endogenous chemicals on memory. For example, Gold (1986) presented experimental evidence suggesting that the epinephrine-induced enhancement of memory (see above) may be mediated by increased blood glucose levels, an interpretation that may help explain how adrenaline could be effective without crossing the blood-brain barrier (see also Gold 1987). Gold's work is complemented by evidence that administration of insulin, which reduces the level of blood sugar in the blood, can produce memory impairment in rats (Santucci, Schroeder & Riccio 1990). Other topics attracting considerable research include the role of the peripheral nervous system in mediating the influence of opioid peptides (Martinez et al. 1981; Messing et al. 1981) and the effects of pituitary hormones such as vasopressin and oxytocin on memory storage (e.g., deWied 1984).

Postacquisition State-Dependent Effects

A small but growing body of research has shown that under some conditions memory can be modified by inducing a distinctive state following the training session. Except for their retrograde nature (a small but important difference), these studies are similar in conceptualization to state-dependent retention experiments. Using a passive avoidance task, Chute and Wright (1973) injected rats intravenously with sodium pentobarbitol or saline immediately after a single learning trial. Twenty-four hours later subjects were tested for retention after receiving either the drug or saline. The findings were quite consistent with traditional state-dependent retention studies in which the drug is administered prior to training: performance was impaired in the mismatched conditions groups (ND-D; D-ND) but not in the same state groups (ND-ND; D-D). Of particular interest here is the D-ND condition, since impaired retention represents the modulation of memory by a treatment administered after acquisition.

In a subsequent study, amnesia for an appetitively reinforced bar press discrimination was produced by post-training injection of pentobarbitol, thus extending the findings to a measure involving choice rather than latency (Wright, Chute & McCollum 1974). A retrograde state-dependent effect of pentobarbitol has also been obtained with attenuation of neophobia as the task (Richardson, Riccio & Steele 1986). In the latter study, rats were given a brief opportunity to drink a novel fluid, apple juice, and then were injected with either the drug or saline. Two days later subjects were given another opportunity to drink the apple juice. Prior to this test session, animals were injected with the agent that was either the same or different from that administered after the training session, thus forming two same state groups (D-D; S-S) and two mismatched state groups (D-S; S-D). It was reasoned that if rats remembered their original taste experience, then their consumption should increase on the second exposure, i.e., there should be an attenuation of neophobia to the previously novel taste. However, forgetting would be reflected in low levels of consumption, as the flavor would again appear to be novel and hence elicit neophobia. Consistent with this expectation, subjects receiving pentobarbitol after training and saline at testing drank less than the other groups, indicating a retrograde (asymmetrical) state dependency.

A state-dependent examination of the role of epinephrine and ACTH in modulation of memory has been provided by Izquierdo and Diaz (1983), Taking advantage of the training parameters and post-training hormone levels, which impair retention of a step-down passive avoidance task, these investigators were able to reverse the deficit by readministering the hormone shortly before testing. That is, the amnesia resulting from post-trial administration of either epinephrine or ACTH was eliminated if the subject received the same hormone at testing. Some degree of interchangeability between the two hormones in reversing the amnesia was also found, such that epinephrine at testing would attenuate the deficit produced by post-trial ACTH and vice versa. However, higher doses were required for this crossed state effect. As Izquierdo and Diaz (1983) note, the reversibility of the loss induced by post-trial hormone injection argues strongly that the original storage of memory was not impaired (see also Riccio & Concannon 1981).

Post-Trial Behavioral Treatments and Memory

Modulation of memory by events after training has been achieved by behavioral as well as pharmacological manipulations. We have already discussed the study by Wagner, Rudy, and Whitlow (1973) that used an unexpected outcome (surprise) as a post-trial manipulation following Pavlovian conditioning trials (see chapter 5). Without going into the details of that experiment, let us consider the general strategy. In an initial phase, rabbits received differential Pavlovian conditioning: one stimulus, call it CS_A, predicted shock while a second stimulus (CS_B) predicted the absence of shock. After this discrimination training, subjects received simple Pavlovian conditioning of the eyeblink response to a third stimulus (CS_C). It is important to note that in this phase each trial was followed by either the old CS_A or CS_B; however, for some subjects the CS_A was no longer followed by shock; for others the CS_B was now followed by a shock. This change in the predictive outcome of the post-trial stimuli (CS_A and CS_B) constituted surprise. For comparison, the control subjects received CS_A and CS_B in their original predictive relationship, i.e., they continued to predict shock or no shock, respectively. Acquisition was substantially impaired in the groups when CS_A and CS_B led to unexpected (surprising) outcomes. It is important to recognize that the impairment of conditioning was not based upon any single stimulus component (e.g., shock presentation), but the incongruency of stimulus events. Thus, conditioning in subjects receiving the CS_A and shock (a congruent set of events) was not disrupted, but it was in those receiving CS_A without shock (incongruent).

Since the surprise occurred after the target training trial, the impaired acquisition appears to reflect a disruption of post-trial processing, i.e., a retrograde effect on memory. Moreover, as with other retrograde treatments, the surprise effect was time dependent. When Wagner et al. (1973) varied the interval between the acquisition trial and surprise, they found less disruption at longer intervals. This effect, shown in Figure 8-4, is consistent with the view of a time-limited period of rehearsal-like processing of information. At the same time, the functional relationship between retention level and the length of delay is not consistent with an interpretation that the surprise worked proactively to alter processing on the subsequent trial.

Another postacquisition behavioral manipulation that can lead to memory disruption is extreme stress. Rats receiving a number of unpredictable shocks immediately following exposure to a novel taste (apple juice) subsequently responded to the flavor as if it were still novel; in contrast, unstressed subjects increased their test

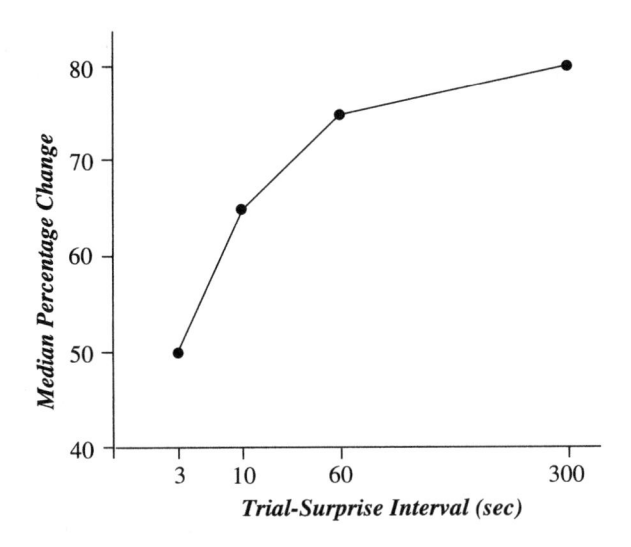

FIGURE 8-4 Retrograde impairment of classical conditioning as a function of the interval between training trials and delivery of the surprising post-trial events. See text for further details. (Adapted from Wagner, Rudy & Whitlow 1973.)

intake, reflecting an attenuation of neophobia (Richardson et al. 1986). In view of the work by Izquierdo and Diaz (1983), it seems likely that the effect was mediated, at least in part, by changes in epinephrine and ACTH levels. This interpretation is bolstered by another parallel with the hormone manipulations—the memory loss was attenuated by re-exposing the rats to the stress treatment shortly before testing.

An important implication of studies showing reversible memory impairment is that some modulatory effects may reflect changes in retrieval cues rather than storage failure. Obviously, where post-training treatments produce facilitation (e.g., Gold & VanBuskirk 1975), such a concern is moot. But evidence for post-training state-dependent retention effects suggests that experimental designs in which some treatment is administered only after acquisition may not be adequate to permit inference about disruption. To determine the source of the memory deficit, inclusion of same state conditions at testing are needed (see Richardson et al. 1986).

Memory Modulation through Reinforcement

Several studies have taken a reinforcement approach to the modulation of memory. The central proposition is that a post-trial reinforcing stimulus can act to maintain the memory (trace) of immediately preceding instrumental learning (Mondadori, Waser & Huston 1977). For example, food given shortly after an appetitively reinforced response should strengthen the memory representation for that response. When the two reinforcing events are positive, as in this hypothetical case, improved test performance could more simply be explained in terms of the additive (summative) effects of the reinforcers, rather than in terms of altered memory processes.

A summation of reinforcers interpretation cannot easily account for enhanced responding when the reinforcers are of opposite hedonic value, however. For example, Mondadori et al. (1977) reported improved passive avoidance performance when the training trial was followed by a 1-minute access to food. The effect was time dependent, with improvement when food was presented 10 or 30 minutes after training, but not when given after 60 or 90 minutes. In the same study, post-trial punishment, consisting of a brief swim in ice water, impaired later test performance. However, the peculiar time function, in which the deficit was obtained with a long interval between training and punishment at longer (60 seconds) but not at shorter intervals (10 or 30 seconds), makes the outcome difficult to interpret. Using self-stimulation of the brain as a positive reinforcer, Coulombe and White (1980) reported an enhancement of memory for aversive conditioning. In that study, in order to reduce floor effects, rats received a number of conditioned stimulus (CS) pre-exposures prior to conditioned emotional response training, i.e., a latent inhibition paradigm. At various intervals following the CS-unconditioned stimulus (US) pairings, subjects were placed in a separate apparatus and allowed to bar press for lateral hypothalamic electrical stimulation. Testing was done 1 day later. Suppression of bar pressing was greater (an enhanced conditioned emotional response) in the self-stimulation groups with relatively short delays (0, 15, or 30 minutes).

The issue of reinforcement of memory (as distinguished from reinforcement of a response) is complex and even the existence of the phenomenon is far from agreed upon. Kesner and Calder (1980) have pointed out that the memory reinforcement concept runs counter to many of the findings obtained with brain stimulation as the reinforcer. In those studies, test performance more commonly depends upon the hedonic quality of the training reinforcer and the type of brain stimulation. Thus, rewarding brain stimulation following aversively motivated learning would impair retention, not strengthen it, as the work of Mondadori et al. (1970) suggests. This very different interpretation is nicely illustrated by Kesner and Calder's (1980) extensive study using electrical stimulation to the area of the periacqueductal grey (PAG) in the brain. The PAG was chosen because stimulation in that area can have rewarding, punishing, or neutral effects depending on the choice of parameter values. The training consisted of punishment for a licking response. When rats received rewarding stimulation following the aversion conditioning trial, retention performance was disrupted; conversely, when the brain stimulation was aversive, retention was improved. Neutral stimulation, a condition which failed to support responding for self-stimulation, had no effect on retention. The modulatory effects of rewarding and aversive PAG stimulation on the suppression of licking (the target behavior)

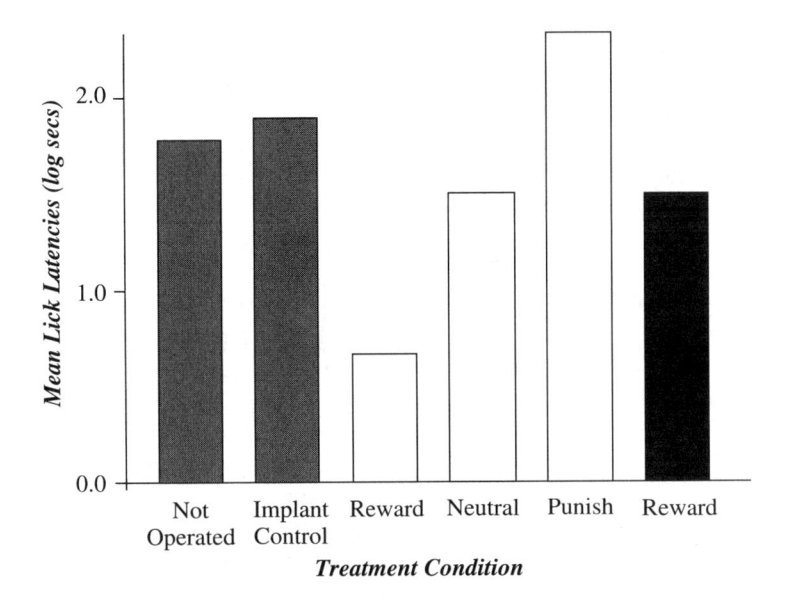

FIGURE 8-5 Retention of a punished response is impaired by rewarding brain stimulation (periacqueductal grey) but enhanced by punishing brain stimulation immediately following training. No effect is seen with the delay condition. Memory strength is indexed by severity of lick suppression (latency). (Adapted from Kesner & Calder 1980.)

were time dependent, as the same manipulations after a 3-hour delay failed to alter retention performance. These several outcomes can be seen in Figure 8-5. Another noteworthy observation was that the memory impairment resulting from rewarding PAG stimulation was reversible. To determine whether rewarding stimulation prevented consolidation, some rats were given a reminder cue (noncontingent footshock in a different apparatus) and tested 24 hours later. Since the reminder treatment restored normal performance, the original memory was presumably successfully stored but overlaid or distorted by the competing hedonic information.

Modulation of Old (Reactivated) Memory

Another facet of modulation of memory research focuses on changes induced in old but reactivated information. The rationale for this approach originated with research on retrograde amnesia for old memory such as that initially described by Misanin, Miller, and Lewis (1968). Their study showed that ECS could produce RA for an event well beyond the limits of the temporal gradient, provided that subjects were re-exposed to the CS shortly before the amnestic treatment. Presumably, the CS exposure primed or reactivated a representation of the original learning, making the information vulnerable to amnesia. Strictly speaking, then, it is not the age but the activity status of memory that determines its modifiability. As Lewis (1979) has observed, age and activity of memory are typically confounded—as the interval following acquisition lengthens the activity of the representation diminishes. This relationship can be altered, however, by presentation of conditioning cues to activate the memory.

Might a reactivated memory be impaired by treatments other than amnestic or pharmacological agents? Can stored information be altered by providing new and different information at the time memory is reactivated? One approach to this issue of memory malleability has involved presentation during memory reactivation of a stimulus that is opposite in hedonic value to the original training reinforcer. Thus, the strategy is akin to Pavlovian counterconditioning, with the important difference that at the time the counter US is presented, the conditioned stimulus is not physically present, although its representation presumably is. For example, in one study (Richardson et al. 1982) rats were conditioned to fear the black compartment of a black-white shuttlebox. Twenty-four hours later subjects were re-exposed briefly to the fear (black) cues (without further shock) in order to reactivate memory and then returned to their cages. A group which immediately received maltose solution, a highly palatable substance with a strong positive affective valence, showed less fear when tested 24 hours later than groups either with memory reactivated but not given maltose or with memory not reactivated. Presumably, the positive reward value of maltose interacted with the memorial representation of conditioning to attenuate the fear. That the counterconditioning effect represented changes in a memory representation, rather than a more general retroactive interference by the interpolated maltose exposure is revealed by a time-dependent relationship obtained in another experiment. As the interval increased between the cuing exposure and maltose delivery, the strength of the counterconditioning effect diminished, i.e., fear remained high. Also, presentation of the maltose without prior reactivation exposure did not attenuate fear to the CS. Apparently, reactivation also can be achieved by evoking various attributes of the conditioning session, since a modulating effect of an appetitive stimulus (sucrose solution) has been obtained when the training US (footshock), rather than the CS, served as the cuing procedure (Richardson, Riccio & Smoller 1987).

As is the case for modulation of newly acquired information, enhancement as well as impairment of old memory can be produced. An example of enhancement is provided by Gordon and Spear (1973). These investigators extended their finding that strychnine improves memory when administered shortly after training by showing a similar outcome for old (72 hours) but reactivated learning. Rats were trained to criterion on a passive avoidance task; 3 days later this memory was reactivated by placing the animal in the start chamber for 1 minute with the nominal CS (flashing light) activated. Some subjects received strychnine immediately afterwards while others received saline. Subjects now had to actively avoid stimuli associated with the previously safe area. The strychnine-injected rats showed enhanced memory for the original response, as reflected in greater difficulty in acquiring the competing task than the saline injected group. The memory modulation could not be attributed to nonspecific drug effects since another group given strychnine 24 hours prior to testing but without the cuing or reactivation treatment did not show memory enhancement. Presumably, the drug treatment improved subsequent retrieval of the reactivated memory, leading to greater interference in the learning of a competing task.

Memory Modulation by the Induction of New Contextual Attributes

The preceding studies illustrate that the strength or intensity of a particular target memory from earlier learning can be increased or decreased by manipulations following a reactivation exposure. There is also evidence that memory can be modified with respect to the cues that are effective in retrieving information. In this paradigm, memory is modulated in the sense that stimuli that fail to produce expression of memory can be induced to serve as retrieval cues. As one might imagine from the importance assigned to contextual cues in retrieval, the focus of this research has been on adding new contexts to the attributes of the target information. If mismatches between training and testing contexts contribute to retention loss, then incorporation of training stimuli into the testing context might attenuate memory deficits.

Following this strategy, Gordon et al. (1981) trained rats on an active avoidance response task in one context (room A) and later tested them in a distinctly different context (room B). The response deficit resulting from this context shift was alleviated by a brief cuing exposure in the test context (room B). The cuing consisted of exposure to the apparatus stimuli associated with footshock during conditioning. Importantly, the cuing or reactivation treatment was not effective unless given in the test context. Cuing in a context not present at testing (room C) did not improve performance in room B, nor was familiarity with the test context sufficient by itself to alleviate forgetting. Subjects placed in the shifted context (room B) without the cuing treatment and then tested continued to show poor performance. This outcome and others like it (e.g., Wittrup & Gordon 1982) suggest that new contextual cues present during the reactivation treatment become added to, or incorporated into, the original memory. The addition of these new contextual stimuli reduces the disparity between the mismatched context (A versus B) at testing, resulting in improved memory retrieval.

Admittedly, there are two puzzling features in this intriguing finding. Gordon et al. noted one of these: since testing involved multiple trials, why does the first trial in the new context not serve as a cuing exposure to facilitate performance on the succeeding trials? A second puzzle concerns reactivation in the new context: if avoidance is poor because the mismatched context does not support retrieval, how can a cuing exposure in the same mismatched context function to reactivate memory?

Although the answers to these questions are not yet entirely clear, differences in some of the temporal parameters between cuing and testing trials may explain why memory is not ordinarily reactivated during a test in the mismatched context. With respect to the second issue, potential differences in thresholds for emitting a locomotor avoidance response and for activating a memory representation could play an explanatory role, although this interpretation is clearly ad hoc at the present time.

MALLEABILITY OF MEMORY IN HUMANS

The retrograde alterations in animal memory we have described have a (rough) parallel in research on malleability of memory in humans. All of us are familiar with instances in which several people have very different recollections of the same episode. When the facts of the matter are contested by the observers at a later time, this variability in retention can be infuriating—especially if the other accounts differ from our own version. Quite apart from such things as heated family discussions of what really happened at the July 4th picnic, differences in recollections of an event can be matters of great concern, particularly if a legal decision or other major judgment hinges on the outcome of the witnesses.

Consider the implications of the title of Thomas Wolfe's famous novel, *You Can't Go Home Again*. At one level this alludes to our disappointing discovery that over time our recollections of home have often become transformed into something of a more idyllic nature. Consequently, what we remember and what we find upon returning may not be at all the same. As one recent example (making due allowance for political posturing), consider the differing memories for certain crucial episodes among various participants in the so-called Iran-Contra Affair. Was there a deal in which military arms were sold to Iran in exchange for the return of American hostages? Who knows about, and who authorized, an illegal diversion of funds to the Nicaraguan rebels (contras)? These and related questions became the subject of a Congressional investigation, but substantial conflicting testimony developed. While some of the discrepancies reflect political chicanery or sheer dishonesty, at least part of the conflict is attributable to differing memories (as well as perceptions) among various participants. Clearly, distortions of memory can occur with respect to extremely critical information as well as for more trivial events.

A number of studies by Elizabeth Loftus and her colleagues have provided a laboratory paradigm for investigating memory distortions and have helped to increase our understanding of some of the principles involved. A basic theme underlying this work is that memory can be supplemented or, more radically, transformed by information presented after the target memory is encoded and stored. Thus, distortion of remembering does not depend upon misperception or impaired encoding of an event, but is a genuine memory phenomenon (Loftus 1979).

Two examples will illustrate this phenomenon of memory malleability. In one study described by Loftus (1975) college subjects watched a film of an auto accident (staged, of course). Subsequently, one group was asked a question which presupposed the presence of a background object (barn), e.g., "How fast do you think the car was going when it passed the barn along the road?" Another group viewed exactly the same film but was asked a neutral question, e.g., "How fast did you think the car was going as it went along the road?" Although a barn was never actually shown in the film, on a later retention test a sizable proportion of the subjects in the former condition answered "yes" to the question of whether they had seen a barn. Presumably, the misleading information inherent in the question became incorporated into the old memory, causing subjects to recollect an item that, in fact, had never existed in the movie. Notice that the biased question could not have distorted the perception of the film, since it was not asked until after the viewing was over. (If you have identified these procedures as a special case of the retroactive-interference paradigms mentioned in chapters 4 and 5, you are correct.)

Another study indicates how subtle differences in the wording of a question can result in distortion of memory. In this case, the question itself provides the source of distorting information. After viewing a film depicting a car accident, subjects were asked a set of questions about events in the film. The critical question—the experimental manipulation in this paradigm—asked of one group of subjects was, how fast were the cars were going when they *smashed* into each other? Control subjects were asked a similar but more neutral form of the same question, in which the verb *hit* was substituted for *smashed.* On a retention test 1 week later, a substantially greater number of subjects who heard the verb *smashed* reported seeing broken glass at the site of the accident—even though no broken glass had been shown in the film. One plausible interpretation is that the verb *smashed* connotes a higher speed than *hit,* and the incorporation of this implicit information into the memory distorts later recollection. Further, the memory becomes modified in a way that is consistent with the new facts—higher rates of speed when two cars crash are more likely to result in broken glass at the scene of the accident (Loftus & Palmer 1974).

These findings are consistent with Bartlett's (1932) early suggestion that long-term memory in humans is reconstructive, such that remembering is a matter of interpreting past events in light of other knowledge, rather than recollection of a stored, relatively unaltered representation of the events. In this view memories should be susceptible to distortions from the acquisition of subsequent information. Thus, our recollection of an incident that we have seen may be substantially colored by accounts of the event that we later read in the newspaper. One version of this problem is nicely illustrated by the insight of a character in the novel by William Kennedy, *Billy Phelan's Greatest Game* (1978). On being asked if he remembered his father who had abandoned him at age 9, Billy replies: "I don't know if I remember his face from seeing it, or from the picture. There's one (at) home in a box of snapshots. . . ."

Although the focus in memory malleability studies is typically upon interpolated information (such as an eyewitness might be exposed to), distortions can arise from proactive sources as well (Lindsay & Johnson 1989). At an informal level, some of former President Reagan's personal reminiscences may illustrate this point. It has been noted that certain of Mr. Reagan's autobiographical stories had an uncanny similarity to various movie roles he had portrayed in his earlier career. There is certainly no reason to believe that Mr. Reagan would lie about those events, but there is good reason to assume that his memory, like that of everyone else, could undergo distortions and transformations. In this case, the sources of misleading information would come from salient earlier episodes, rather than interpolated events.

ISSUES OF INTERPRETATION: PRACTICAL AND THEORETICAL

It is important to recognize that subjects may have no conscious recognition that their memory is distorted. If given an opportunity to rate their confidence in the accuracy of their reports, subjects indicate a high degree of confidence in their recollection. Even when pressed in an interview, many are completely convinced that they saw broken glass in the film. A more general aspect of this finding is that the correlation between a person's confidence in his/her recollection of events, and the actual accuracy of their memory, is quite poor (see Zechmesiter & Nyberg 1982, for review of the confidence-accuracy relationship). The implications are disturbing. The eyewitness who is confident and self-assured in his/her testimony is no more likely to be correct than the more tentative and hesitant witness, although the former is more likely to be believed by a jury! One can readily see from these studies on the misleading question effect why some people in the legal system are concerned about the nature of interrogations and their relationship to the accuracy of eyewitness testimony. Information inherent in questions posed by lawyers or police may well result in a subtle but critical (and genuine) change in what a witness later remembers about an event.

If adults are susceptible to distortions of what they remember, then how much faith can we put in the accuracy of children as eyewitnesses? Yet court cases involving sexual abuse and other violations, whether at home, school, or day-care centers, often depend heavily on just such testimony. Are 5-year-old children's memories less suggestible than those of adults? Or might they be more so? In the absence of experimental data, decisions on this matter represent speculation or beliefs (whether true or not). Understandably, the issue of susceptibility of memory in children to other sources of information is a matter of great interest and importance to psychologists and lawyers alike, and the American Psychological Association's Science Directorate has recently sponsored a conference on the topic (Doris 1991). Further, if the modification reflects what Loftus has referred to as an "erase and update" operation, there may be no way to recapture the original information.

The correct interpretation is debatable, however. Some evidence suggests that the memory distortion can be interpreted in terms of coexistent competing information, rather than an elimination (erasure) of the original information (see, for example, Bekerian & Bower 1983; Christiansen & Ochalek 1983). The issues will be recognized as similar to those associated with the interpretation of retroactive (or proactive) interference effects (see chapter 4). This should be no surprise. These memory distortion experiments are the same experimental designs applied earlier to tests of retroactive or proactive interference, except that quality or content of the interference-induced forgetting is emphasized rather than quantity of interference-induced forgetting.

Although much of the research on memory malleability has focused on how new information distorts and impairs recollection of an episode, memory can also be enhanced with appropriate manipulations. This represents a further departure from conventional studies of retroactive interference. For example, in one study the interpolated information presented in a questionnaire was made consistent with the observed incident. Compared to subjects in a neutral condition who received no interpolated treatment, subjects in the consistent condition showed superior performance on a 1-week recognition test (Loftus 1979).

Malleable and Modulated Memories

The findings indicating that a target memory in humans can be distorted by new information clearly represent a type of modulatory effect. However, it should be noted that the phenomenon differs in several respects from the research described earlier on modulation of animal memory. Quite apart from the different procedures used to establish and to assess a target memory in human and animal studies, a major difference is that a time-dependent decrease in susceptibility does not characterize the human malleability findings. If anything, the latter effect is the other way around—distortions are better induced as the original memory weakens over time—in contrast to the greater susceptibility of more recently acquired memories to modulation in studies of animal memory. Loftus, Miller, and Burns (1978) introduced inconsistent or misleading information at various intervals after subjects had seen a series of slides depicting an accident. The interval between the presentation of the information (treatment) and testing was held constant, with all subjects being tested shortly after the interpolated treatment. Accuracy of recognition of the original (correct) slides was much poorer when the presentation of misleading information was delayed for 2 to 7 days than when it was introduced after a shorter period. Presumably, as a result of the naturally occurring weakening of retention at the longer intervals, inconsistent information was more readily incorporated into the target memory.

Another important distinction between animal and human studies of memory modulation concerns the centrality of the event. Studies of misleading questions and other forms of interpolated information have found that incidental information is most subject to distortion (Loftus 1979). Thus, it is not the main event, such as the car accident or a theft, that is altered, but rather a detail associated with the event, e.g., presence of broken glass, color of the car, etc. In contrast, modulation of memory in animals centers around the target itself, even when the aim, as in the work of Gordon et al. (1981), is to add new contextual attributes to the memory representation.

Finally, we should note that an insightful critique by Zaragoza and her colleagues (McCloskey & Zaragoza 1985; Zaragoza & Koshmider 1989; Zaragoza, McCloskey & Jamis 1987) has called into question certain aspects of the methodology used in a number of memory malleability experiments. The essence of the criticism is as follows: ". . . some of the errors are due to misled subjects who have forgotten the original detail even before they were misled, and are selecting the misleading item because it is the only response that is familiar to them." (Zaragoza 1991, 29) More generally, the rationale is this: in the standard procedure, subjects receive a recognition test in which the original and misleading items are included. But if subjects simply forgot the original item and happened to remember the more recently presented misleading stimulus, their errors would not reflect a distortion of the original information. The contrast is between malleability of the target versus replacement of missing information. To eliminate this potential problem, McCloskey and Zaragoza (1985) developed a modified test procedure in which the misleading item is not one of the choices on the test. Quite different pictures of malleability of memory emerge in comparing the results of the standard and modified tests. While discussion of the intricacies of this debate are more appropriate for specialized texts, we should note that a central conceptual issue which emerges is whether the new information actually distorts an earlier representation, as malleability or plasticity would imply, or whether the new material merely supplants already forgotten information, i.e., fills a gap in memory (see Loftus et al. 1978, experiment 4; Zaragoza et al. 1987). This distinction is critical, as two very different processes in memory are implied. In any event, understanding the conditions that promote (or diminish) distortions of memory remains an important and intriguing goal in contemporary cognitive research.

ANTEROGRADE AMNESIA

While playing a hotly contested game of soccer, the goalie, Jane Smith, dives for the ball just as her opponent attempts to kick a goal. Her heroic effort prevents the score; unfortunately, the kick lands solidly on her head. Jane is momentarily stunned, but soon returns and finishes the final 30 minutes of the game. The next day, Jane remembers virtually nothing of the several hours following her accident—not her game-saving deflection of the ball, nor the ride home, nor the movie she and her husband saw that evening. Happily, she does remember events from the following morning on; her memory loss is restricted to a period of several hours following the traumatic blow to her head.

This fictitious but not unrealistic vignette captures some of the essential aspects of one form of anterograde amnesia. Anterograde (forward acting) amnesia (AA) indicates a forgetting of events that follow an amnestic agent. There is a memory deficit with respect to events subsequent to traumatic insult to the brain, even though the subject may appear to be functioning normally, cognitively and physically. It would not be surprising if Ms. Smith also suffered from some difficulties remembering events prior to being kicked in the head, i.e., retrograde amnesia. Both types of amnesia often occur together, but for simplicity of exposition here we will only be concerned with the forward, or anterograde, amnesia.

In this section, we focus on the anterograde-related forgetting resulting from relatively acute and reversible insults to the CNS, such as those that occur with closed head injury or electroconvulsive therapy. It should be noted that there is extensive research literature concerning the effects of chronic brain dysfunction on memory. Enduring brain damage, as may occur with strokes, wounds, surgery, or long-term alcoholism (Korsakoff's syndrome), is most often simulated and investigated under laboratory conditions with animals by carefully specified brain lesions. Because the issues, paradigms, and methodological problems in these latter studies are rather different from the work with acute insults, we will consider the findings later under the rubric of the pathology of memory (see chapter 10).

The major methodological issue that confronted us with respect to retrograde amnesia—whether the amnestic agent might have suppressed responding because of punishment-like effects rather than true memory loss—is not an issue in AA. The reason, of course, is that in AA the insult occurs prior to the to-be-remembered events, whereas punishment must follow behavior if it is to be effective in suppressing it. There are other methodological problems, however, and as one might anticipate from our consideration of punishment, these problems are the flip side of the coin from those in RA. Because the anterograde amnesic agent occurs prior to training, it is possible that subjects simply fail to learn or that the learning is inadequate. Obviously, a failure to acquire the target information should not properly be regarded as forgetting, at least not for a useful experimental analysis of memory processes. As Supreme Court Justice O. W. Holmes once remarked in another context (and prior to the use of nonsexist language): "A man must *get* a thing before he can forget it." To take an extreme example, if a subject were stunned or unconscious following a concussive blow, we would not wish to call the failure of remembering during this period amnesia. It is more reasonable to conclude that learning failed to occur; the information never registered.

Obvious as this difficulty may seem, it has not always been fully appreciated. Perhaps the most straightforward way to handle the problem is to train subjects to some criterion, or in cases where performance is not measured during conditioning, to test immediately after training in order to assess the strength of learning (e.g., Bresnahan & Routtenberg 1980; Richardson, Riccio & Morilak 1983). An early example of the latter approach is seen in a study investigating the effects of hypothermia on learning and memory in mice (Essman & Sudak 1963). Under the conditions of their experiment, hypothermic mice given a simple passive avoidance training trial performed poorly on an immediate test—a finding that clearly cautioned against interpreting poor performance on longer term retention tests as evidence of anterograde amnesia.

If deficits are found in original acquisition in the AA condition, it may be possible to adjust the training conditions to bring the AA group to the same level as control subjects. One example of this approach is seen in a study by Huppert and Piercy (1978), who called attention to evidence suggesting that on a given trial (exposure to visual slides) amnesiacs with Korsakoff's syndrome failed to acquire the same amount of information as normal subjects, and hence necessarily should have lower retention scores. To correct this disparity, Huppert and Piercy substantially increased the trial duration (length of slide exposure) for subjects with Korsakoff's syndrome. Thus, a physical imbalance in training conditions was used to achieve a functional constancy—that both groups were matched with respect to amount learned prior to the start of the retention interval. Under these conditions, no differences in rate of forgetting were found between the subjects with Korsakoff's syndrome and control subjects.

A study by Bresnahan and Routtenberg (1980) illustrates the basic principle of AA. Rats received electrical stimulation to a subcortical region of the brain during punishment training on a step-down task. To ensure that the task was in fact learned, subjects were trained to a criterion—they had to remain on the safe platform for 2 minutes. Although there were no differences between the stimulated and unstimulated groups in achieving the learning criterion, groups in the two conditions differed markedly on a 24-hour retention test. While most control subjects continued to remain on the platform, rats receiving brain stimulation during training stepped down to the grid floor with short latencies, indicating they had forgotten the previous consequence (footshock) of the response. Similarly, Richardson et al. (1983) found a striking loss of memory over 24 hours when rats were mildly cooled (hypothermia) prior to receiving a single passive avoidance training trial in a cross-through task. The design included a within-subjects comparison where subjects were tested twice: immediately after training (to assess strength of original learning) and again 1 day later (to assess forgetting). Responses of subjects trained while hypothermic (experimental group) or at normal body temperatures (control group) were equivalent on the immediate test, as measured by achieving the maximum test scores of 600 seconds, i.e., never re-entering the shocked compartment. However, after 24 hours the anterograde group showed very poor test performance, while control subjects continued to remain in the safe compartment. In both of these studies, acquisition appeared intact following a manipulation (e.g., brain stimulation, hypothermia), but forgetting was much more rapid than in control subjects, i.e., experimentally induced AA was obtained.

With respect to acute traumatic episodes, AA typically shows a time-dependent characteristic: memory loss is greater the shorter the interval between the insult and the target event. Kopp, Bohdanecky and Jarvik (1968) administered ECS to mice at intervals from 1 to 6 hours before one-trial passive avoidance training. Test performance 24 hours later was directly related to the interval that elapsed between ECS and training, with no deficit seen with intervals longer than 4 hours. Although the study did not clearly differentiate whether the proactive effect of ECS was on learning or on retention of what was learned, it demonstrated that the performance decrement was not due simply to any prior exposure to ECS, i.e., a general proactive effect. But unlike the case in RA, where a time-dependent gradient reflects the role of post-training processes, the time-dependent changes in AA presumably reflect simply the dissipation of the mild insult to the organism. For example, in their study on hypothermia-induced AA, where tracking of body temperature provides a convenient index of physiological disruption, Richardson et al. (1983) cooled two groups equally but introduced training after short or long recovery intervals. With the longer interval and warmer body temperature anterograde amnesia was not obtained, while substantial forgetting did occur when subjects were trained shortly after the cold treatment.

In humans, the effect of varying the treatment-to-training interval on AA can be seen with electroconvulsive therapy (ECT) as the amnestic agent. One study tested patients receiving ECT for relief of severe depression (Squire & Miller 1974). The learning materials consisted of visual items, ranging from drawings of common objects to simple words. The learning sessions were scheduled either 20, 50, or 180 minutes after an ECT treatment, and recognition tests were given 1/2 hour or 24 hours after the session. Regardless of the retention interval, memory improved as the interval between ECT and training increased. The Squire and Miller study also illustrates the learning versus memory issue described earlier. When only 20 minutes elapsed between ECT and learning, test performance 1/2 hour later was extremely poor, with subjects having 10% (or less) correct recognitions. While this outcome could reflect very rapid forgetting, it more likely reflects a failure to acquire the information in the first place. In that case, the equally poor performance at the 24-hour retention interval would not be viewed as a true memory loss.

It should be noted that anterograde amnesia may also result from chronic or enduring insult to the brain, as would be the case with Korsakoff's syndrome, gunshot wounds, and a variety of other sources of brain damage. In these instances, the temporal relationships we have been discussing become irrelevant—the dysfunctional condition of the brain does not dissipate but is more or less permanent.

Because punishment is not a viable interpretation of the performance deficits in AA paradigms, a broader range of tasks is potentially available. Other constraints do exist, however. In particular, the use of appetitively reinforced tasks may not be feasible due to the general systemic disruption resulting from many amnestic treatments (e.g., ECS, hypothermia). A second consideration, at least with respect to transient amnestic treatments such as ECS, is that the target task must be acquired within a relatively brief session, i.e., before the functioning of the brain has returned to normal. Among the other learning situations used to assess acutely induced AA in animal research are a two-way active avoidance task in goldfish (Springer et al.

1975), an aversively motivated brightness discrimination in mice (Boyd & Caul 1979), and a positional discrimination based on escape from shock in a T-maze with rats (Santucci & Riccio 1986).

It should be clear from the studies described that a variety of sources of insult to the brain can produce AA, just as was the case with RA. If anything, there are probably more agents that can produce AA than RA, simply because rapidity of onset of the CNS effect is not a critical factor. In the AA paradigm, if a particular treatment does not affect the CNS for several hours, the investigator simply waits longer before introducing the target task. By contrast, the temporal gradient of susceptibility in the retrograde arrangement means that an agent that does not have a rapid impact on the CNS may be ineffective in disrupting memory—its influence will miss the window of susceptibility. These considerations indicate why the AA situation may prove useful in assessing whether relatively commonplace disruptions of homeostatic balance might also impair memory. Thus, heat prostration, fever, and hypoglycemia are among the naturally occurring bodily malfunctions that warrant exploration for their potentially detrimental effects on memory (Ahlers & Riccio 1987; Santucci et al. 1990).

It is worth noting that memory loss resulting from acute anterograde episodes shares a number of similarities with the phenomenon of state-dependent retention. For many years, the emphasis in AA studies was on the finding that various treatments produced memory loss, and it was often implicitly assumed that the memory failure was permanent. However, with the recognition that the impairment is often reversible following re-exposure to the amnestic agent (see chapter 9), the similarities to state-dependent retention became more apparent. One way to determine whether these two classes of memory loss are manifestations of the same processes is to determine whether they are affected in the same way by various manipulations (e.g., prior exposure to the agent or drug, etc.). At this point it is too early to draw any final conclusions.

CHAPTER SUMMARY

Traumatic disturbances of the central nervous system can result in loss of memory for events that occurred shortly prior to the disturbance. This backward-acting or retrograde amnesia can be induced in the laboratory with animals in order to investigate memory processes. A variety of treatments, including ECS, thermoregulatory disruption, and drugs can act as retrograde amnestic agents.

Learning per se is considered to be unaffected, as the amnestic agent follows the learning episode. The use of one-trial passive avoidance tasks demonstrated that the performance deficit is a true memory impairment, rather than an artifact of the treatment. A central characteristic of RA, in the laboratory as well as in the natural world, is the time-dependent change in loss of memory. Severity of amnesia decreases as the interval between learning and the amnestic agent increases. In addition, a delayed onset of amnesia is often found in which the loss of memory does not develop until shortly after the amnestic treatment. Although surprise or psychological shock does not seem to be the basis for most RA in animal studies, some evidence suggests that these manipulations can be effective with humans.

A second type of time-dependent effect on memory involves postacquisition treatments that can enhance or impair retention, i.e., modulation of memory. Exogenous administration of stress-related hormones such as epinephrine and ACTH following training can modulate memory, as can drugs such as strychnine, naloxone, and cholinergic agents. Different mechanisms appear to underlie impairment versus facilitation of memory, as the former is often attributable to a state-dependent effect, but the latter is not. Although in a few cases modulation may represent a reinforcement-like effect of treatment, findings from research with positive or negative brain stimulation typically are inconsistent with such an interpretation. An apparent exception to the time-dependent rule is that old memories can be modified by amnestic or Pavlovian counterconditioning treatments. Importantly, however, such changes are only brought about if memory is activated (by cuing) prior to treatment. Thus, degree of memory activation rather than age of memory may be the underlying basis for the time-dependent relationship. Modulation of representations in humans is most strikingly seen in research on malleability of memory. Information acquired from witnessing a naturalistic episode (e.g., staged accident) can be distorted by subsequent presentation of inconsistent information, which can even take the form of misleading questions. Whether this represents a true plasticity, or whether new information merely fills a gap of forgotten details, is debatable, but the phenomenon clearly has great importance for eyewitness testimony.

Exposure to a traumatic insult prior to a target episode can result in unusually rapid forgetting of that information, i.e., anterograde amnesia. Material reviewed in this chapter focuses on acute or transient amnestic treatments, as contrasted with enduring conditions such as brain damage. In contrast with RA, research on AA must confront the major methodological concern of whether learning has been prevented or impaired by the prior treatment. Poor memory could be an artifact of poor learning. However, several studies have now shown that under conditions where degree of learning in the anterograde groups appears comparable to that of control subjects, amnesia is still obtained. In many respects, AA from acute insult appears similar to the state-dependent retention induced by centrally acting drugs (see chapter 3). Because they are not restricted to the time-dependent window of vulnerability, anterograde treatments may provide useful models for determining the effects of naturally occurring homeostatic disruptions on memory.

9

Recovery from Forgetting: Retrieval Phenomena

The term *forgetting* is neutral with respect to the permanence of the loss. Some forgotten information conceivably might be gone forever, but more commonly the material or item could be remembered again at another time under appropriate circumstances. Most of us have had the annoyance of being unable to recollect a name (or fact), only to have the desired item suddenly pop into our awareness at another time. Clearly, the target information was inaccessible at one point but ultimately available (e.g., Tulving & Pearlstone 1966).

A more formal demonstration that material can apparently be completely forgotten while remaining available comes from studies using relearning (savings) techniques. It has been known since Ebbinghaus' pioneering work (see chapter 1) that items no longer recallable can usually be relearned more rapidly than they were learned originally. This faster relearning is often measured or expressed as a savings relative to original acquisition. Since substantial savings occur even when any gains from processes such as learning to learn have been eliminated, the engram (or however the information is represented) could not have been totally destroyed or eroded. Rather, some residual information must have been present to facilitate the relearning.

It could be argued that the savings technique is primarily of theoretical value or limited to academic-type settings. Admittedly, for many episodes, the prospect of savings is simply irrelevant—the opportunity to re-experience the event will not again occur. In these circumstances, if memory is to be regained, some other way of jogging memory or eliciting the information is necessary. In the following sections, we consider some of the various treatments, short of actual retraining, that have been found effective in facilitating retrieval.

Before we present some of the findings on retrieval of memory, however, we briefly look again at the notion that memories consist of representations of various attributes of a target episode. In this connection, the tip-of-the-tongue phenomenon provides a simple but instructive illustration of the encoding of multiple attributes of information. Most of us have suffered at one time or another from the annoyance of not quite being able to remember some item—perhaps a name, the title of a book or movie, or a familiar incident—while having the feeling that we have almost got it, "it's on the tip of my tongue." Experimental study of this phenomenon might seem unlikely—how shall we find enough people in the act of this memory lapse? However, as Brown and McNeill (1966) cleverly showed some years ago, it is possible to induce such a tip-of-the tongue (TOT) effect for study in the laboratory by reading definitions of relatively rarely used words to a group of subjects.

For the study of the TOT effect, subjects might be asked, what does this describe?: "Any of various small boats of the Far East, as one propelled by a single scull over the stern and provided with a roofing of mats" as defined in *The Random House College Dictionary* (Stein 1984). Of course, some subjects will not recognize the description at all, while others will immediately identify the target word as *sampan*. But some proportion will be likely to experience the TOT effect, and these cases provided the basis for an analysis, by asking subjects about various features of the elusive item. For our purposes, the intriguing aspect of the TOT phenomenon is that many of the attributes of the target are retrieved. Thus, subjects tend to recall characteristics such as the initial letter, or the length of the word, or something about how the word sounds; they might even be able to generate terms with similar meaning.

These bits and pieces of the sought-for information illustrate what W. James meant when he remarked that a "wraith" of the name seemed to be present during this type of memory lapse. At the same time, the nature of the wraith reveals that we encode not simply the meaning of the target word, but also a number of other features pertaining to the item (Underwood 1969, 1983). Happily, in many instances retrieval of these various attributes culminates in recall of the target word itself. (Brown and McNeill noted that some people report attempting to cue themselves by going through the alphabet searching for the initial letter.)

Although the TOT may be a unique human verbal experience, in some ways it provides a prototype of retrieval processes generally. In many of the studies we will describe, the experimenter presents some component or attribute of the learning episode in an attempt to remind the subject of some forgotten responses. In animal research Pavlovian conditioning has proven very attractive as the source of the target information, since for analytic purposes the conditioned stimulus (CS), unconditioned stimulus (US), and context can be manipulated not only relatively easily but also independently of each other.

ALLEVIATION OF FORGETTING IN ANIMALS

Prior Cuing to Alleviate Simple (Spontaneous) Forgetting

One of the most common sources of forgetting is a long interval of time following acquisition of the target information. We are all familiar with the annoying outcome that as retention intervals increase many kinds of information become increasingly difficult to retrieve. As we have seen earlier, a variety of mechanisms may be involved in such spontaneous forgetting, including proactive and retroactive sources of interference and shifts in internal or external contextual cues. Although simple decay of the memory trace is not easily ruled out, we noted earlier that so far, the concept of decay has not proven very useful for either biological or psychological analyses of memory. Further, the various instances in which forgetting is reversed without new training tend to undermine the easy appeal to decay or erosion of engrams as a reason for forgetting.

Given the ubiquity of forgetting over long intervals, and the variety of contributing factors, is there reason to believe that any simple treatments can lead to recovery of memory? It is encouraging that several experiments have now shown that forgetting associated with a long retention interval can be alleviated by treatments shortly before testing. In one early study, Hamberg and Spear (1978) investigated the effects of prior cuing treatments on retention of a choice response. In their first experiment, rats learned a shock-motivated brightness discrimination in a T-maze and were tested 28 days later. As Figure 9-1 shows, subjects exposed to a noncontingent footshock 1 day prior to the test made fewer errors than a control group given no prior cuing. Since choice rather than vigor of performance constituted the dependent variable, the outcome is not attributable to performance artifacts. A second experiment involved a simple spatial discrimination for food reward. Again, substantial forgetting occurred over a 28-day retention interval unless subjects received a prior cuing treatment the day before testing. In this case, the prior cuing consisted of three trials with food reward in a straight alley. Even though the prior cuing treatment did not involve differential reward, retention of the choice response was enhanced. Taken together, these two experiments suggested that providing a component or attribute of the original learning is sufficient to alleviate forgetting of a learned discrimination.

This prior cuing effect has been extended to other complex learning situations involving multiple choices. For example, Deweer, Sara, and Hars (1980) trained rats to locate a food reward in a relatively complex (several choice points), maze and then tested for retention some 25 days later. Substantial forgetting, as measured by increased errors and slower running times, occurred in control animals. For subjects receiving a prior cuing treatment, however, test performance was comparable to their terminal acquisition level. The prior cuing manipulation consisted simply of placing

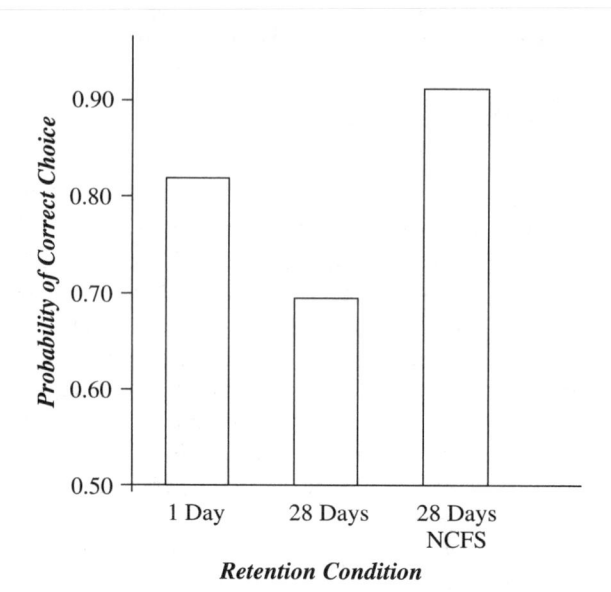

FIGURE 9-1 Retention of aversively motivated brightness discrimination is enhanced by noncontingent footshock (NCFS) prior to testing. (Adapted from Hamberg & Spear 1978.)

subjects in a holding cage next to the maze for 90 seconds just prior to testing. Several aspects of the prior cuing treatment are noteworthy. First, by its very nature the holding cage exposure could hardly have provided the subjects with new learning about the maze task. Further, a control condition indicated that the 90-second exposure by itself did not have any facilitative effect on maze learning in naive animals, thus ruling out a non-memorial explanation (e.g., general arousal, systemic effects) for the improved retention. The study of Deweer et al. (1980) provides an illustration of the potency of context as a retrieval cue, although the extra maze cues to which subjects were exposed could be viewed as somewhat more directive or discriminative in guiding behavior than some other contexts.

Subsequently, Deweer and Sara (1984) examined several aspects of this contextual reactivation effect. Both the duration of the exposure and the temporal proximity of the prior cuing treatment to the test session proved to be important. A very brief (10 seconds) exposure treatment had no effect on retention, as performance was similar to that of untreated control subjects. Intermediate durations (30 and 90 seconds) were both effective reminders, but a still longer duration (300 seconds) produced only partial alleviation of forgetting. It seems likely that with prolonged exposures some extinction-like process may counter the retrieval benefits (see also Deweer et al. [1980] for a similar outcome with multiple exposures during the retention interval). When testing was delayed by 1 or 24 hours after an otherwise effective exposure duration (90 seconds), the benefits of the prior cuing treatment were found to diminish.

If memory is represented as a collection of attributes, prior cuing with several features of the training episode might be even more effective as a reactivator (or reminder). Testing this notion, Deweer (1986) found a mild synergistic effect when cuing included exposure to the training reinforcer as well as environmental context. The basic paradigm was similar to that used in previous studies (e.g., Deweer et al. 1980). Rats were trained for several days in a complex maze for a food reward. Following a 25-day retention interval, retention was measured in terms of number of errors made in traversing the maze. The data of special interest are from the initial trial before re-exposure to the training contingencies has occurred. Placing subjects in the training room for 90 seconds enhanced retention if the test was given immediately thereafter. However, no reactivation effect was observed if the test was delayed for 1 hour. On the other hand, exposure to another attribute, the food reinforcer itself, had little effect on retention performance whether the test followed immediately or after the 1-hour delay. An intriguing synergistic effect was obtained when both treatments were administered: retention was improved even with the 1-hour delay between cuing and the test session. Thus, the reactivation effect of exposure to environmental background cues was extended when a second manipulation, exposure to the food US, was included.

An issue beginning to attract research attention concerns the changing effectiveness of retrieval cues as the retention interval progressively increases. That is, the contribution of a particular attribute to the retrieval process may be a dynamic one that varies as a function of time. An important demonstration of this concept comes from the work of Gisquet-Verrier, DeKayne, and Alexinsky (1989). Using a discriminative avoidance task, these investigators examined the effects of cuing with the CS, the US, the context, or combinations thereof. The cues were presented just prior to testing, either 1 hour, 3 days, or 21 days following initial training. The major finding was that the various cues were differentially effective at the different retention intervals. Thus, a prior cuing treatment that had little effect in alleviating forgetting at a short retention interval might be highly effective after a longer interval and vice versa. Gisquet-Verrier et al. (1989) suggest that internal representations can change over time, so that the effective reminder cues are those matching the representation at the time of testing.

An illustration of the generality of these effects is shown by results obtained using a very different paradigm to investigate the rapid forgetting of Pavlovian conditioning in infant rat pups (Miller, Jagielo & Spear 1991). These rats (18 days old) were given a brief treatment to induce a conditioned odor aversion that is forgotten rapidly. Within 2 to 3 hours after conditioning, conditioned animals in this experiment behaved no differently than animals not given the conditioning treatment—

complete forgetting occurred. But if after a 3-hour retention interval conditioned animals were given either of three brief (30-second) prior cuing treatments, they behaved on the retention test as if conditioning had occurred only a few minutes before—no forgetting was evident. The three prior cuing treatments included exposure to only the context of conditioning, exposure to an odor presented during conditioning but not paired with an aversive event (CS–), or the aversive event itself (US).

Other experiments in this study tested retention at different intervals following either of the prior cuing treatments, which yielded three interesting facts illustrated in Figure 9-2. First, and in some ways most remarkable, forgetting following either of the three prior cuing treatments was a great deal slower than that following original learning. In contrast to the extreme forgetting observed within 2 to 3 hours after original conditioning (Figure 9-2A), substantial retention of the conditioned aversion was found after intervals as long as 48 hours following the prior cuing treatment (Figure 9-2B; illustrated with CS– as the prior cuing treatment). Note that this increased retention occurred despite the fact that no additional conditioned aversion to the critical odor could have occurred as a consequence of the prior cuing treatment. One viable interpretation is that the mere reactivation of the memory in this case made it more resistant to forgetting. Second, the increased resistance to forgetting following a prior cuing treatment differed depending on which prior cuing treatment was used; resistance to subsequent forgetting was least following exposure to only the context as the prior cuing treatment (Figure 9-2C). Finally, the prior cuing effectiveness of a novel odor (the animals had not previously experienced it) increased the longer the interval between original conditioning and the prior cuing treatment (Figure 9-2D). The increased effectiveness of this novel reactivation cue with increased retention intervals may reflect loss of stimulus differentiation (Miller et al. 1991; Riccio, Richardson & Ebner 1984). The more general point, however, is that retrieval of information may depend on different attributes as time passes following original learning (as indicated also in the study by Gisquet-Verrier et al., discussed on page 249).

Drug-Induced Attenuation of Forgetting

In addition to exposure to various attributes of training as a prior cuing treatment, the attenuation of spontaneous forgetting has been achieved by administration of pharmacological agents (e.g., amphetamine) at the time of testing. In one study, mice were trained in a Pavlovian fear conditioning situation (Quartermain & Judge 1983) One month later, shortly before retention testing, the mice received either saline or amphetamine. The amphetamine improved retention whether the measures of retention was passive or active avoidance. Since the motor response demands are opposite in these two tasks, alternative explanations in terms of increased (or decreased) locomotor activity are not tenable. Also, with the dose level used the drug had no effect on acquisition (another type of evidence that learning and retention involve separate processes). Using rats, Sara (1984) has also shown that administration of amphetamine prior to testing improves retention of conditioned fear. It is worth noting that in a quite different study examining the detrimental effects of cortical lesions on retention of a learned discrimination, Braun, Meyer, and Meyer (1966) similarly found that retrieval was enhanced by an amphetamine treatment. Thus, amphetamine appears to alleviate retention deficits resulting from different sources of forgetting. This conclusion receives support from recent work with this drug in which several types of forgetting were compared directly (Quartermain, Judge & Jung 1988).

Because amphetamine stimulates catecholamine release, which also occurs naturally during fear conditioning, and these studies tested retention of fear conditioning, it might appear that the similarity of internal contexts at learning and test played a role in the reactivation effect. This may be so, but amphetamine has also been found to improve retention based upon appetitively reinforced learning. Sara and Deweer (1982) trained rats for food reward in a complex maze containing a number of choice points. A 3-week retention interval was sufficient to induce considerable forgetting, but this was alleviated by administration of amphetamine at the time of testing. The improved performance was not attributable to changes in activity. In another experiment a second test was given in which two groups continued to receive the drug or saline and the other two were switched to the opposite treatment (e.g., test 1, drug—test 2, saline). The improvement produced by the drug remained even with only saline present in the second test, suggesting that recovery was not a state-dependent retention effect.

The maintenance of recovery from forgetting after the drug apparently was no longer present in the animal's system is an intriguing outcome. It implies that once the target information has been reaccessed with the aid of the drug, the reprocessing involved results in a more durable memory, consistent with the study with infant animals described above. Unfortunately, the finding in this case is actually somewhat more difficult to interpret because testing involved reinforced training trials. Thus, all four groups showed improvement and did not differ from each other on the second test, indicating that testing (relearning), with or without amphetamine, provided a potent reminder. But apart from issues of the durability of recovery when the drug is no longer administered, these findings, in conjunction with others, suggest that amphetamine acts on some fairly general mechanism, perhaps arousal or attention, to facilitate retrieval.

ALLEVIATION OF FORGETTING IN HUMANS

The demonstrations that exposure to contextual stimuli can enhance retrieval of otherwise forgotten information have some interesting parallels in recent investigations of human memory. The facilitating role of contextual cues in human memory

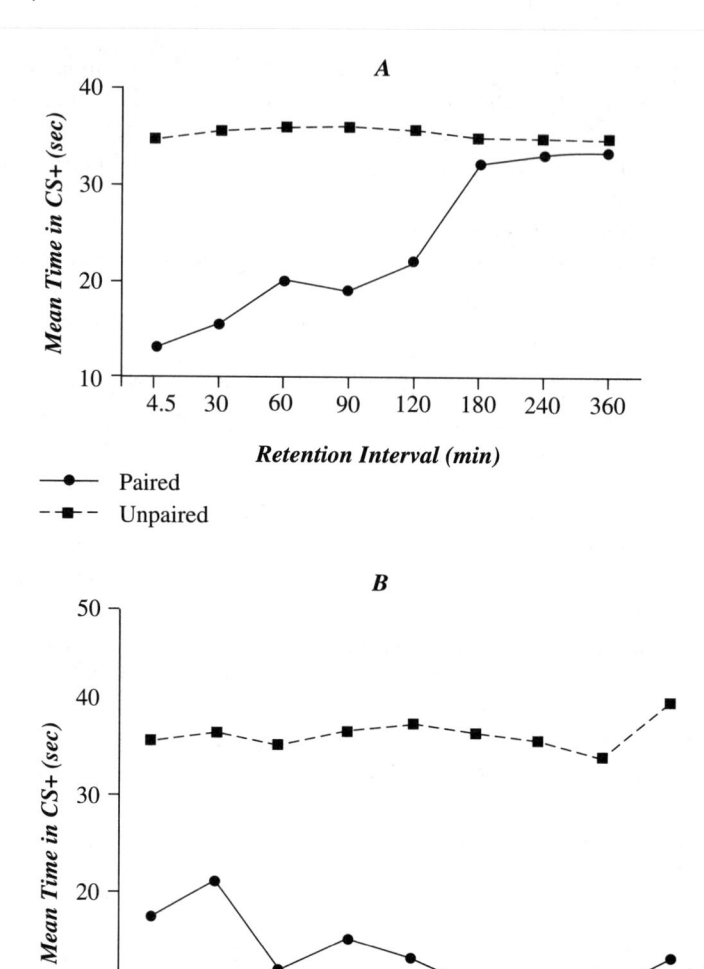

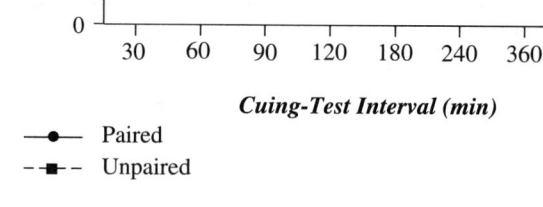

A

Retention Interval (min) — Paired / Unpaired

B

Cuing-Test Interval (min) — Paired / Unpaired

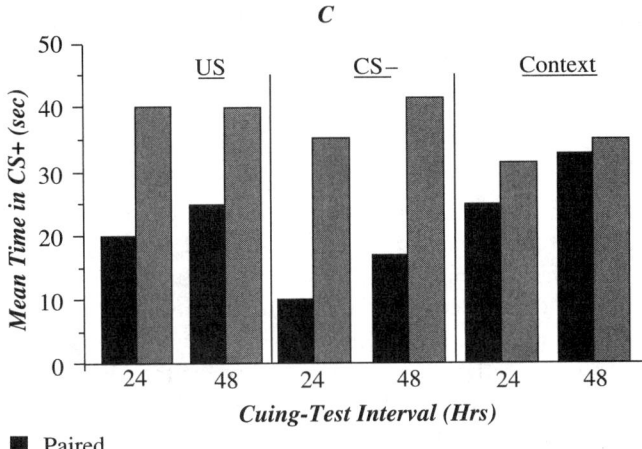

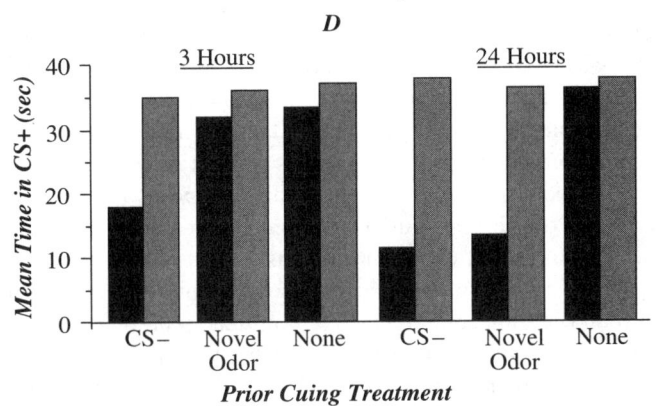

FIGURE 9-2 A. Loss of aversion to CS+ over a several hour retention interval in 18-day-old rat pups. The unpaired group provides a control for nonassociative effects on performance. B. Prior cuing with the CS– as a reminder; conditioned aversion is retained for many hours. C. Differential effectiveness of three types of prior cuing (reminder) on retention of a conditioned aversion to CS+. D. Increased effectiveness of a novel odor as a reminder with a longer interval between training and cuing. The conditioned aversion had previously been established to another odor cue (CS+). (Adapted from Miller, Jagielo & Spear 1991.)

retrieval is nicely illustrated in a study by Smith (1979), which we also considered in chapter 3.

Alleviation by Prior Cuing

Having shown that a change in environmental (room) context between acquisition and testing disrupted retention of a list of words in college subjects, Smith (experiment 2) examined the possibility that reinstating the mental representation of the training context would alleviate the deficit. Prior to a free recall test of a word list in a room different from that where the list was studied, two groups were given instructions intended to activate a representation of the training context. One group was asked to recall and think about the room where they had learned the list; another group received similar instructions supplemented with the presentation of slides of the room. These constituted two different prior cuing treatments. To control for the effects of instruction and imagining activities, another group was given placebo instruction in which they were asked to remember and think about an irrelevant location (a room at home). While the latter condition, as expected, had no beneficial effect on retention, retention in the two groups receiving information to reinstate the original context was significantly better than that of the baseline condition of context change without reinstatement. Indeed, their retention was comparable to that of subjects without a context shift, i.e., trained and tested in the same room. Thus, some form of representation of the stimulus attributes of the training room was sufficient to alleviate the impairment produced by a physical change in context.

The advantages of the prior cuing treatments were offset, however, if subjects were exposed to a number of different contexts so that recall of the target environment was impaired. Subjects given distracter tasks in four different rooms following training did more poorly, despite the prior cuing treatment, than those receiving the same distracter tasks in one different room (Smith 1979). Presumably, the additional room exposures resulted in confusion or interference with the subjects' ability to implement the prior cuing treatment by recalling the training context.

At a more applied level, there is evidence that manipulations designed to reestablish the context present at the time a person witnessed an important event can enhance memory in eyewitness accounts (Geiselman et al. 1985, 1986; Malpass & Devine 1981). In order to simulate, or at least approximate, the fast pace and complexity of events that happen during an eyewitness episode, films of violent crimes are often used as the target material. Assessment of memory for various aspects of the incidents shown on film is then obtained 1 or 2 days later. As a prior cuing treatment, some subjects were given a "cognitive interview." The major elements of the interview were instructions, the gist of which was: "Try to reinstate the context (weather, feelings, etc.) at the time of the incident; report everything you can think of; try to recall the events in different orders and from different perspectives." At a more general theoretical level, these instructions can be viewed as a way to help re-establish a representation of the stimulus complex present during the event.

Such prior cuing has been quite successful in improving retention of critical events witnessed earlier. The ability of subjects to recall various elements of the eyewitnessed episode was substantially greater with the prior cuing cognitive interview procedure than without it. As Geiselman et al. (1986) point out, one potential advantage of this behavioral technique for improving recall is that it avoids the legal problems associated with hypnosis in eyewitness accounts.

Finally, an unusual but intriguing application of contextual cue reinstatement has been reported recently for memories associated with aircraft mishaps in the Air Force (Levy 1987). In each instance, the eyewitnesses, either pilots or a ground controller, were amnesic for critical events preceding the mishaps. Although in the report of this study the author's emphasis is on a relaxation technique as an alternative to hypnosis (which is forbidden by the Air Force in these situations), it is clear from the protocols that efforts were made to reinstate as many of the critical contextual cues as possible. In one case, the pilot "entered the cockpit of an aircraft identical to that lost in the mishap," complete with a "stand-in for the deceased flight member, in full flight gear" in his usual seat. As the imaginary final phases of the fatal approach sequence began, the pilot, "visibly startled by the realistic appearance of the stand-in, began to recall the entire cockpit routine...." (p. 258) In another case, in which the flight controller could not recall whether the landing gear had been lowered, "The entire RSU crew was placed in their unit at the same time of day that the mishap occurred while a similar aircraft flew a similar pattern of the mishap aircraft." (p. 258) Although the very nature of these difficult situations precludes determination of the absolute accuracy of the recovered memories, their recovery was later indirectly supported by other types of corroborating physical evidence.

Spontaneous Recovery of Memory

Not all instances of remembering an item after a memory lapse need involve explicit reminders. Most of us have been unable to recall a needed piece of information (such as someone's name or the title of a movie), only to have the answer come back to us at a later time. A particularly clear laboratory test of spontaneous remembering was conducted by Buschke (1974). Adult subjects were presented with a list of verbal items and then tested repeatedly for recall. Words that were not recalled initially (i.e., forgotten items) were likely to be recalled on one of the subsequent tests. Buschke ensured that words were learned in the first place by a *restricted presentation* procedure. After each recall test, the list was presented again, but only with the words that had never been recalled. Thus, the training ensured that subjects had encoded the information as demonstrated by at least one successful recall. The finding that an initially recalled item would be forgotten on one test but remembered on a later test with no further presentations of the item was obtained whether subjects were asked to recall orally or in writing and whether the target list consisted of animal names or unrelated words. Thus, this spontaneous recovery of memory implicates retrieval deficits, rather than loss or degrading of the original information, as the source of the retention decrement.

ATTENUATION OF FORGETTING AFTER BRAIN DAMAGE

Most behavioral scientists assume that there is a physical locus for the changes in performance we identify as learning and memory. The search for the physiological substrates of learning and memory, let alone more molecular processes, has proven elusive, although recent work by Thompson and his collaborators seems especially promising (e.g., Thompson 1986).

For many years the neocortex of the brain received the most attention as the area where associations should be formed and memories would be stored. By extirpating particular areas of the brain one might hope to map the geography of memory locations as represented in the brain, or *engrams,* a term used by Karl Lashley, a particularly influential scientist in this area. If retention of an episode were impaired by a particular brain lesion, then presumably the engram was stored in that region (taking care to rule out possible artifacts such as sensory or motivational deficits, of course). If subjects subsequently were able to reacquire the task, this would suggest that intact areas of the brain were capable of replacing the functions of the lesioned regions (equipotentiality of the brain).

The classic work by Lashley (1950) provides an illustration of this approach. Lashley demonstrated that destruction of the posterior cortex in rats resulted in total loss of a previously learned brightness discrimination. Rats with posterior brain lesions could reacquire the discrimination, so clearly the lesion did not obliterate the ability to learn. However, subjects required just about as many trials to reach criterion the second time as they did in their initial acquisition. This complete lack of savings or transfer contrasts with normal animals (controls) that required far fewer trials on the retention test. When these unoperated rats were trained on a discrimination problem and later tested for retention, they required only a few trials to achieve criterion—savings on the order of 90 percent or better. The interpretation seemed straightforward: The cortical lesion destroyed the tissue where the engram for the discrimination was stored, so operated subjects had to start from scratch at the time of the relearning test. Presumably the remaining intact regions of the brain were capable of supporting the discrimination learning and came into play with the primary location gone.

That the substantial memory failure seen in posterior lesion studies does not necessarily reflect loss or destruction of stored information was indicated in an important study by Braun, Meyer, and Meyer (1966). Perhaps because Meyer and his colleagues had long worked in and been identified with the Lashley Tradition, the Braun et al. finding was particularly startling, since it challenged the apparently obvious and compelling interpretation of brain damage effects on memory. Braun et al. reported that administration of amphetamine at testing substantially eliminated the deficit in lesioned rats. Consistent with previous studies, performance of lesioned animals receiving saline instead of amphetamine was comparable to that of naive animals when confronted with the discrimination problem test; no retention was evident. However, lesioned rats given amphetamine relearned with considerable savings. These findings are summarized in Figure 9-3.

If the locus of memory in the brain had been destroyed, how could any treatment make subjects behave as if they remembered the problem? One possibility would be that amphetamine directly enhanced the rate of learning of the discrimination problem. If this were the case, the apparent savings during relearning would represent not memory, but an artifact of the drug's effects on acquisition. To test this alternative, the study included rats given amphetamine at original training. Since these animals learned no faster than their nondrugged counterparts, Braun et al. concluded that amphetamine must have facilitated retrieval of memory in their lesioned subjects. If amphetamine permitted access to an engram, then wherever else the information might be stored, it was not exclusively in the cortex. One could imagine information being represented redundantly at both cortical and noncortical sites. The important point is that what appeared to be located only in the cortex was available somewhere else.

Further support for the view that information about a brightness discrimination is not necessarily destroyed by posterior decortication comes from research by LaVere (1984). In one study using a brightness discrimination task similar to that of Braun et

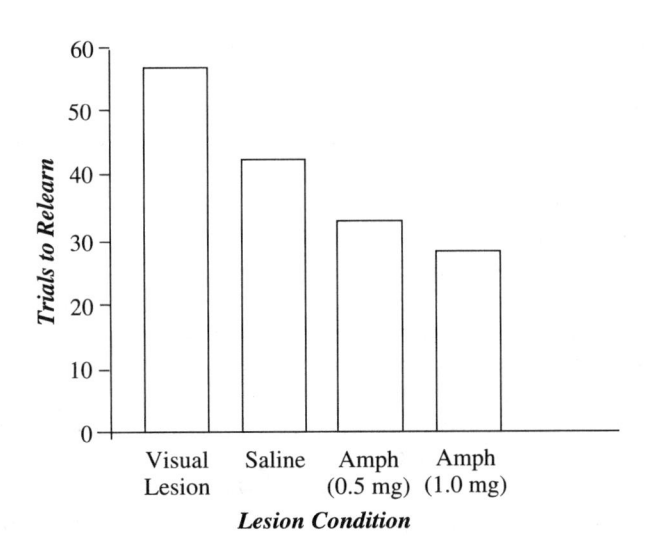

FIGURE 9-3 Relearning of a brightness discrimination habit in animals with destruction of posterior cortex is enhanced by administration of amphetamine (Amph). (Adapted from Braun, Meyer & Meyer 1966.)

al. (1966), LeVere and Morlock (1973) trained rats to criterion and then performed the posterior cortical lesion. At the time of testing, rats were trained on a reversal of the original discrimination. In the reversal task, of course, the formerly correct cue was now incorrect and vice versa. The rationale here was that if the lesion destroyed the original memory, then from the perspective of the lesioned rat, the reversal would simply be a new task. However, the lesioned rats showed substantial negative transfer; like normal animals, they required more trials to learn the reversal than control animals not given the original (now conflicting) learning. Since conflicting response tendencies should not exist if there were no information present about the original contingencies, the fact that the preoperative learning impaired the postoperative reversal task reveals that some memorial representation remained despite removal of the posterior cortex.

To address the possibility that changes in preference for brightness cues resulting from the brain lesions might have produced this outcome, LeVere and Morlock (1973) undertook a second study using a successive (go-no go) brightness problem. In the successive task, as the name implies, the discriminative stimuli are presented one at a time, in succession, and the subject's task is to learn to respond (or not) to that stimulus. In this arrangement a preference for one of the two stimuli is less likely to distort performance than when the two stimuli are presented together (simultaneous discrimination) and subjects must choose between them. Again, performance of rats undergoing posterior decortication following initial acquisition was severely impaired when they were retrained on the reversal task, a finding inconsistent with the belief that the engram was destroyed. While it is not entirely clear why memory in posterior decorticated subjects is expressed in a reversal task but not in relearning of the original problem, perhaps the answer lies in differences in the sensitivity of these two tests.

How are we to account for the recovery of the negative transfer in lesioned animals? The size of the lesion, as well as the apparent absence of memory under ordinary circumstances, makes it unlikely that the engram persisted in spared neocortex. Meyer and Meyer (1982) have argued vigorously that storage therefore must be in subcortical regions. More germane to our present concerns, they have advocated the view that lesions suppress the expression of memory but that under appropriate circumstances organisms again can gain "access to [these] engrams." The problem thus shifts to one of accounting for the initial retrieval deficits and conversely, their subsequent alleviation.

The interpretation of Meyer and Meyer has been developed and extended in interesting ways by LeVere and his collaborators. The essence of their explanation is that memory failure (or suppression) occurs following a lesion because other neural systems come to direct the behavior of decorticated subjects. The lesion creates an imbalance in neural systems and as a result there is a shift to other systems. Thus, the neural system associated with the earlier learning is bypassed, and the memory is not expressed. Indirect support for this view comes from studies using redundant sensory cues in discrimination problems. Rats given extirpation of the visual cortex were found preferentially to use haptic (touch) cues, in contrast with normal rats, which relied about equally on haptic and brightness cues (LaVere 1984). This conclusion was reached on the basis of the ease with which subjects acquired a new problem in which only one of the two original stimuli was present. LeVere has proposed that the original memories are neither destroyed nor altered by cortical insult. Rather, it is the shift to different neural/behavioral strategies as the altered (brain-damaged) organism encounters its environment that results in performance decrements. Interestingly, a rather similar argument has been developing with respect to infantile amnesia. For example, several studies have focused on how ontogenetic changes in encoding and other processing dispositions and capacities could translate into retrieval failures when subjects are later tested at a more mature stage of development (Spear 1979, 1984b; see chapter 7).

It should be apparent why these kinds of findings (for reviews, see LeVere 1984; Meyer 1984) provide a powerful impetus to the view that many instances of memory impairment might reflect deficits in retrieval. Destruction of brain tissue produced what appeared to be total loss of memory, yet other techniques revealed that the target information was still present. Retention losses resulting from less traumatic types of insult to the organism seem equally unlikely to be based upon disruption of storage.

RETRIEVAL DEFICITS IN EXPERIMENTALLY-INDUCED AMNESIA

In an earlier section we described some of the findings that characterize amnesias induced by events such as electroconvulsive shock (ECS), electrical stimulation of various areas in the brain, drugs, and extreme body temperature. Here we focus on presenting evidence for the modulation or reversibility of amnesia and try to show how these findings indicate retrieval dysfunctions.

Does Retrograde Amnesia Result from Impairment in Retrieval?

The original demonstrations of time-dependent memory loss when traumatic insult occurred following training were generally taken as evidence that a consolidation process was interrupted (e.g., McGaugh 1966). Presumably, the electrical "storm" and drastic modification of neural transmission of other kinds generated by ECS and other amnesic treatments prevented the establishment of a long-term memory trace. This view dovetailed nicely with Hebb's important speculation that the uninterrupted continuation of specific neuronal activity (the reverberating circuit) was a critical ingredient in the development of all cell assemblies. These cell assemblies were viewed as the substrates for a variety of experiential based changes (roughly, learning and perception). Even 20 years after Duncan's (1949) report (chapter 8), investigators attempting to explain how disruption of body temperature produced retrograde amnesia appealed to the fact that deep hypothermia shared with ECS the ability to alter electrical activity of the central nervous system and thus destroy or damage the storage of the memory. Accordingly, they concluded that the retrograde amnesia (RA) produced by lowered body temperature was most likely attributable to seizure discharges preventing consolidation of memory traces in a manner similar to that of ECS (Vardaris, Gaebelein & Riccio 1973).

What phenomena challenged this reasonable and comfortable understanding of experimentally induced amnesia? Probably no single finding by itself, but the cumulative impact of several different outcomes raised serious questions about the disruption of storage interpretation and helped shift attention to the role of retrieval deficits in RA.

Growth of RA over Time

A simple but striking observation concerning the onset of amnesia was made some years ago: amnesia was not present in subjects tested shortly after ECS administration, but required a period of time to develop (Geller & Jarvik 1968). Most experiments had used a 24-hour retention interval after ECS before the test was administered. This interval allowed subjects ample time to recover from any disruptions in sensory, motivational, or locomotor abilities that might mask retention. Furthermore, this interval was usually convenient from an experimenter's point of view—a 12-hour retention interval might require trekking back to the laboratory at 2:00 A.M.! But it turned out that any debilitating effects of ECS treatment were quite transient and that testing could be done within a relatively short period.

When such short-term testing was done, retention was found to be intact. It was only at longer intervals that retention began to decline, and by 24 hours the memory loss was, of course, severe. In short, there was a delayed onset of amnesia. While the exact function describing the time course for the onset of RA varies depending on the particular parameters used in training, the intensity of the amnestic agent, and other variables, the reliability of the finding is well established and has been obtained with different amnestic agents, such as hypothermia (e.g., Mactutus & Riccio 1978). Some of the studies included a repeated measure procedure so that subjects tested at a short interval were also tested at the traditional 24-hour point. These data are particularly striking, since the same animals showing excellent retention at one interval were strongly amnestic at 24 hours. The decrement was not due simply to repeated testing (extinction effects), as control animals (trained but not given amnestic treatment) maintained excellent retention when tested at the same two intervals. The relatively slow onset of amnesia with hypothermia is illustrated in Figure 9-4, where it can be seen that strong RA (short latencies) does not occur until about 16 hours after training and an amnestic treatment episode.

It is useful to recall the nonlaboratory study of amnesia in human head-injured subjects mentioned in chapter 8 that reported a comparable and parallel finding (Lynch & Yarnell 1973). The subjects were football players removed from the game because of a severe blow to the head. Control subjects were players removed for other

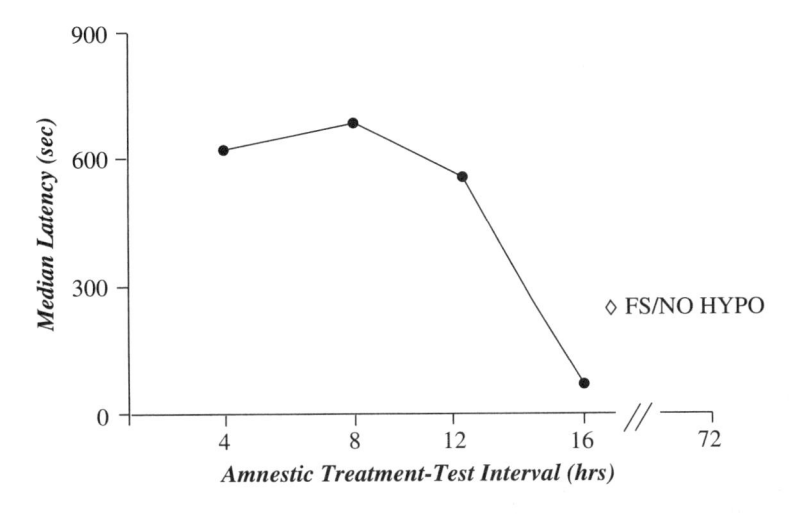

FIGURE 9-4 Decline in passive avoidance test performance as a function of time following exposure to retrograde amnesia treatment. (Adapted from Mactutus & Riccio 1978.)

types of injuries (e.g., twisted ankle, bruised shoulder). The measure was a verbal report of a target incident (the preceding play), and investigators queried the players immediately following their injury or 30 or 60 minutes later. Both head-injured and control subjects showed excellent retention immediately after the injury. As more time elapsed, however, the head-injured subjects showed substantial loss of recall of the information, while players with other injuries showed little change across all time intervals.

The problem raised by the delayed onset of amnesia is straightforward: If brain insult interrupts the consolidation process and prevents the further establishment of memory, should not retention be about the same at all the test intervals? Stated another way, if amnesia involves the destruction or prevention of storage, then the memory loss seen at 24 hours should be found also at shorter test intervals. It is still possible to defend a storage view, however. For example, one could assume that long-term but not short-term traces are affected by the amnestic treatment. Yet the ad hoc nature of such explanations and the evidence from some studies that amnesia onset can be delayed for many hours, well beyond usual conceptions of short term (see chapter 5), tends to detract from such a two-trace view.

To anticipate our later discussion, we might consider the status of internal cues as they relate to the onset of amnesia. Perhaps the target memory is accessible at short intervals precisely because the effects of the amnestic treatment have not worn off. Rather, they are still present as part of the complex of stimuli associated with the target episode. With the passage of time, however, and the organism's return to its more normal state, these internal stimuli are no longer available as retrieval cues. As you can see from even this brief sketch, a retrieval view focuses on the role of cues permitting access to memory. From this perspective, amnesia (and other memory losses) need not be due to storage impairment but can reflect the lack of relevant internal or external stimuli.

RA and Length of the Interval between Training and the Amnestic Agent

Another finding considered problematic for a consolidation-disruption model of RA concerns an exception to the time-dependent characteristic of amnesia. The often demonstrated gradient for obtaining amnesia—less RA the longer the interval between training and the amnestic agent—was long taken as evidence that as a memory becomes older it also becomes less susceptible to the effects of amnestic agents. Even earlier, Ribot (1882), on the basis of extensive clinical observations, had formalized this relationship in his law of regression, i.e., older memories were impervious to the same insult producing profound loss of newer memories. Given the historical and empirical status of this law, the outcome reported by Misanin, Miller, and Lewis (1968) seemed almost startling. As discussed in chapter 8, this study showed that if rats were re-exposed to the fear cues (CS+) just prior to administration of ECS, substantial memory loss resulted even if this occurred 24 hours after learning. Without the cuing, ECS 24 hours after learning failed to affect memory, an outcome consistent with the RA gradient (see chapter 8). Whereas old information was resistant to RA (the typical result), amnesia could be induced after reactivation of the target memory.

But how can old well-consolidated information become susceptible to ECS? If consolidation is complete, as suggested by the total lack of amnesia in the group receiving ECS delayed 24 hours without cuing, how can re-exposure alter this? Even if the consolidation process restarts at cuing, should it not continue to add to an already established trace?

One resolution of the dilemma would be to show that amnesia for an old, reactivated memory was a fluke, one of those chance occurrences that are bound to happen occasionally. Indeed, several studies that failed to obtain the phenomenon were reported. On the other hand, there have now been sufficient successes to establish the reality of amnesia for reactivated old memories. In one paradigm (Robbins & Meyer 1970; Howard, Glendenning & Meyer 1974; Meyer 1972), rats were trained in mazes on a series of three discrimination problems. The motivation, which was either hunger (food reward) or shock (escape), alternated for each problem. Thus, some subjects learned a pattern to escape shock (S_1), then another maze task to obtain food (F_1), and then the original escape task again (S_2). Others were assigned to the converse order $= F_1, S_1, F_2$. What Meyer and his colleagues found was that ECS after the last learned task produced amnesia for the earlier task learned in the same motivational state. In the S_1, F_1, S_2 arrangement, for example, ECS following the third problem (S_2) disrupted retention for the S_1 problem, even though the F_1

task was temporally much closer to the amnestic treatment. This selective amnesia for old memory seems understandable in terms of an implicit cuing of the earlier task produced by the motivation and reward conditions of the last learned task. Thus, while CS exposure was the reactivation manipulation in the Misanin et al. (1968) experiment, the work of Meyer et al. suggests that exposure to the reinforcer (or motivational state) can have similar effects. Indeed, other experiments using simple fear conditioning paradigms have found that exposure to the previous US makes old learning susceptible to amnestic treatments (DeVietti & Holliday 1972; Gerson & Hendersen 1978; Richardson, Riccio & Mowrey 1982).

Several studies have examined other aspects of amnesia for old memory. With hypothermia or ECS as the amnestic agent, there is evidence that old memory is in one respect more vulnerable than new memory: old reactivated information was disrupted by a relatively weak treatment that failed to induce amnesia when administered immediately after training (Mactutus, Riccio & Ferek 1979).

A temporal gradient relating the interval between reactivation and administration of the amnestic agent has been obtained. Mactutus et al. (1982) gave punishment training for entering the black compartment of a black-white chamber. One day later brief exposure to the black cues (CS) was used to reactivate the memory, and subjects received hypothermia either 0.5, 5, 10, or 30 minutes later. After a 24-hour retention interval, the rats were tested. Severity of amnesia decreased as the delay interval increased. A similar outcome has also been obtained when US—rather than CS—exposure provided the reactivation episode (Richardson et al. 1982). Whether the slope of the delay gradient is the same for a new and an old memory is an interesting question, although difficult to answer because of differences inherent in the two types of paradigms (Mactutus et al. 1982).

Recovery from Retrograde Amnesia

Spontaneous Alleviation of RA

If RA represents the failure to store information about an episode, then one certainly would not expect to find recovery of the target memory under any circumstances. While new training (relearning) can re-establish the memory, this does not address the issue of recovery, but indicates that the capacity for further learning has not been lost.

An early study by Zinkin and Miller (1967) appeared to challenge the storage view by reporting evidence of spontaneous recovery from ECS-induced RA. Rats showed significantly better retention scores 2 and 3 days after ECS than after a 1-day interval. However, that finding appears to represent something other than true recovery, and the methodological problem is instructive. The design of the experiment called for repeated testing of the subjects rather than separate groups for each retention interval. Thus, each rat was tested at all of the retention intervals. It was soon recognized that under these conditions, if RA was not complete (and it seldom is), then any residual learned fear could serve as a conditioned punishment. The conditioned punishment effect would be reflected in a longer latency on the following trial, and so on. More specifically, in the passive avoidance task when a partially amnesic animal crossed into the previously shocked compartment at testing, the cues (including those from the response itself) were still capable of eliciting a mild fear response. This negative reinforcement cannot influence the latency measure already obtained, but could make the animal more hesitant to make the same response on the next trial. While the pattern of performance change would appear to represent memory recovery, the effect could more correctly be described as a type of new learning, based on secondary reinforcement.

In defense of Zinkin and Miller's use of this experimental design, we should note that the choice of a particular design can reflect many considerations, practical as well as theoretical. The within-subjects design is efficient and economical and is the design of choice for studying many phenomena. At the same time, these two basic designs (separate groups versus repeated measures within subjects) may yield very different outcomes, so that facts are not independent of the design used to obtain them. As we have just seen, findings (and interpretations) can be strikingly influenced by the researcher's choice of procedures.

Although serious questions have been raised about the validity of spontaneous recovery from induced amnesia, at least one study using separate groups at each test interval appears to have found a reduction in amnesia as the retention interval increased. Deutsch, Hamberg, and Dahl (1966) injected an anticholinesterase drug into the hippocampal area of rats shortly after they were trained on a Y-maze escape task in which illumination was the discriminative stimulus for the correct arm. Relearning scores were greatly impaired when the animals were tested 1 day later. This impairment was reduced in groups tested 3 or 5 days after injection, indicating a recovery of the training memory. To ensure that poor performance was not due to the effects of the drug on testing at the 1-day interval, one group of control subjects did not receive the drug until several days after training, and then was tested 24 hours later. Since the long delay interval should eliminate any retrograde effect on memory, an impairment in performance would reflect consequences of the drug at testing. However, these animals responded as well as animals given a placebo treatment following training. Perhaps the spontaneous recovery seen here represents some unusual feature of the pharmacological amnestic agent, since the fact remains that such recovery has not been clearly documented with ECS or thermoregulatory disruption, two of the more commonly used treatments.

While recovery from experimentally induced amnesia does not often occur spontaneously, several types of treatments have been shown to alleviate the memory loss. Each treatment involves presentation of some attribute of the training-amnestic episode. Some of the prior cuing treatments that have been effective are exposure to the reinforcer (US), or to the training stimulus (CS), or to the amnestic agent itself. Consider exposure to the US. While administration of the reinforcer within the original training context might induce improved performance, how would we distinguish this recovery from the possibility (or likelihood) that the subjects simply acquired the necessary information during the prior cuing? This problem of new learning can be reduced, if not entirely removed, by providing the reinforcer exposure in an environment very different from training. Thus, for memory of an aversive-conditioning task motivated by mild footshock, the footshock as a prior cuing treatment is presented noncontingently. There are actually two ways in which the reinforcer is noncontingent. First, unlike punishment training, the footshock is delivered independently of the behavior of the subject. Second, of course, the footshock is administered in an apparatus very different from that of training; hence, it is noncontingent with respect to the original training stimuli.

Almost any two pieces of apparatus share some similarities and the phenomenon of stimulus generalization indicates that subjects transfer what they learn in one situation to other similar situations. Some investigators have judged that the delivery of the reinforcer in a situation different from that of training does not rule out improved performance based on generalization of new learning, so the reinforcer could be much more than just a prior cuing treatment (Gold & King 1974). However, in one particularly well-controlled and convincing study, Miller and Springer (1972) showed that noncontingent exposure to the footshock reinforcer reversed impairment of memory produced by ECS, when new learning was apparently precluded. The study included groups of rats receiving ECS following one-trial punishment training; some of these subsequently were exposed to the training footshock in an apparatus unlike that used for training. The ECS was effective in producing retrograde amnesia, but the memory loss was reversed in the reminder condition. To evaluate the possibility that the recovery reflected generalization of new learning from the reminder apparatus to the test apparatus, Miller and Springer included untrained control subjects given the footshock prior to the test. Presumably, any learning produced by the footshock would be reflected in long latencies at testing. However, these rats showed no tendency to display the passive avoidance response when placed in the test apparatus, so the contribution of any new learning appears negligible. These findings over three test trials are presented in Figure 9-5.

DeVietti and Hopfer (1974) were similarly able to attenuate ECS-induced amnesia for conditioned fear by exposing subjects to the training footshock. A tone paired with footshock served as the conditioned stimulus which produced suppression of licking. Subjects receiving ECS after training later showed little evidence of suppression. Recovery of memory, measured by increased suppression of licking, occurred in subjects given any of three reminder treatments: tone followed 1 hour later by the footshock (the long interval was to reduce the possibility of direct reconditioning to the tone); footshock alone; and tone alone. None of these manipulations significantly increased lick suppression in control animals that had received ECS following pseudotraining.

How can memory be restored after it has been destroyed? Presumably, of course, it cannot—unless the amnesia represented a deficit in retrievability rather than degraded storage. Pursuing this line of reasoning, we might conjecture that the amnestic treatment blocked or suppressed the representations of events at training.

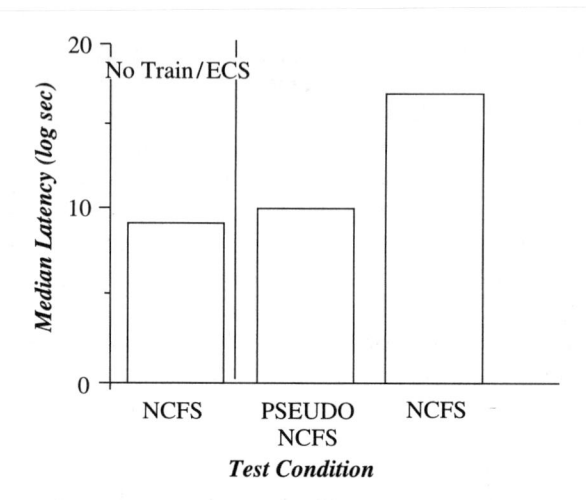

[Bar chart showing Median Latency (log sec) vs Test Condition, with bars for NCFS (~8), PSEUDO NCFS (~10), and NCFS (~17). A marker labeled "No Train/ECS" appears near the top.]

FIGURE 9-5 Alleviation of electroconvulsive shock-induced amnesia in animals receiving noncontingent footshock (NCFS) prior to passive avoidance testing. (Adapted from Miller & Springer 1972.)

Delivery of the punishment (response-contingent footshock) was one of those events. Administration of the footshock noncontingently activates a representation of this critical attribute, permitting retrieval of memory and the expression of target behavior. By the same token, an effective prior cuing treatment for a positively reinforced response should be the appetitive reinforcer. This was confirmed after rats received a single training trial in which they obtained access to a sucrose solution upon locating a drinking spout in one area of a large chamber. Delivery of ECS after the trial produced amnesia for the approach response; however, the performance was restored in animals permitted to drink the sucrose solution in a different apparatus prior to testing (Miller et al. 1974).

Since the noncontingent delivery of the reinforcer could not provide relevant information about the locus of the goal, this outcome (and others like it) raises some interesting questions about the nature of the memory loss. Did ECS impair memory for what happened (sucrose available) or where it happened or both? While one might think in terms of loss of memory for the hedonic quality of the event, it is likely that the representation of the taste of sucrose and its location are linked such that activation of one attribute facilitates retrieval of the other. This same study also reported that numerous attempts to reverse the memory loss for appetitive learning, i.e., approach to sucrose, were totally unsuccessful when only footshock was used as the reminder treatment. This is an important negative finding, as it suggests that the retrieval of memory depends upon specific cues associated with training, rather than the general arousal induced by the administration of the sucrose or the footshock.

Finally, in this study alleviation of the ECS-induced memory loss was also achieved by exposing subjects to the training CS and/or context. In addition to using the appetitive reinforcer (sucrose) as a prior cuing treatment, a second experiment was conducted in which ECS-treated rats were returned to the training environment prior to testing. During this exposure to the apparatus cues, the sucrose tube was removed and the opening to the chamber was blocked to preclude any relevant new learning. With the proper duration of exposure, however, these reminded subjects were quicker to locate and drink from the sucrose delivery tube than nonreminded animals; the context alone served as an effective reactivation treatment, confirming and extending earlier work (Sara & Remacle 1977). In the latter study, mere detainment in the apparatus (safe compartment) for a brief period prior to initiation of a trial (opening the door to the previously shocked compartment) attenuated ECS-induced amnesia in rats.

Gordon and Mowrer (1980) have used exposure to a discrete CS to alleviate experimentally induced amnesia. Their study employed an active avoidance paradigm with a flashing light as the warning signal (CS) and ECS as the amnestic agent. In this situation, memory loss is reflected in longer latencies to respond to the warning signal, i.e., impaired active avoidance. However, animals subsequently given a 60-second exposure to the CS while confined in the start box showed recovery of the active avoidance response. An important finding was that the same CS exposure impaired performance in subjects not given ECS after training. This latter outcome confirmed that the CS-only exposure was sufficient to produce extinction in controls. The particular importance of Gordon and Mowrer's study is the obtaining of memory recovery where any new learning from the reminder treatment would be incompatible with the original task, i.e., learning that the CS no longer predicts shock impaired avoidance behavior. Presumably, for amnesic animals, the value of the cue as a reminder is greater than its role as an extinction treatment.

In the same year the Gordon and Mowrer paper appeared, a similar result was published from a different laboratory and produced by different techniques. Wittman and DeVietti (1980) conditioned fear to a tone (CS) and followed this training by ECS for some groups. ECS produced a strong amnesia, reflected in continued lick responding when the tone was presented. Mere placement of subjects in the training apparatus along with a brief presentation of the tone between training and testing alleviated the amnesia and re-established fear to the tone. However, in animals trained but not given ECS, the same prior cuing treatment reduced (extinguished) fear to the tone.

Although exposure to the CS or the reinforcer is an effective way of alleviating experimentally induced RA, treatments that mimic or recreate some of the internal stimulus attributes associated with the amnestic episode can also produce memory recovery. It may seem surprising, but re-exposure to the amnestic agent prior to testing can attenuate RA. For example, Thompson and Neely (1970) delivered ECS to rats immediately following a single punishment training trial in a step-down task. The next day, 20 minutes prior to the retention test, half the subjects received a second ECS administration. A small but significant improvement in performance was observed in these animals, and the authors suggested that recovery might have been stronger if it were possible to test subjects immediately after the second ECS, i.e., when the ECS state more closely resembled that which followed training.

Several subsequent investigations of the amnestic treatment as a prior cuing treatment have employed lowering or increasing body temperature as a source of RA. The rationale is straightforward. Because changes in body temperature provide at least a rough quantitative index of the severity of the treatment, it is possible to monitor and control the correspondence between the amnestic episode and test conditions in a way that is not easily accomplished with agents such as ECS. Hinderliter, Webster, and Riccio (1975) rapidly reduced body temperature in rats following a single punishment trial in a step-through task. Subjects that were later recooled shortly prior to testing showed much less RA (i.e., longer latencies) than non-recooled animals. As we saw when the reinforcer is used as a reminder treatment, it is very important to take into account any effects that the hypothermia might have on test performance. Hinderliter et al. (1975) showed, accordingly, that cooling prior to the test had virtually no effect on the responding of untrained rats. Thus, the longer step-through latencies of the recovery group reflected recovery of the punishment memory rather than an artifact of systemic stress. Figure 9-6 summarizes the basic findings of the study.

The critical role of body temperature (and associated internal cues) in reversing memory loss was further demonstrated in several other studies. In one (Mactutus & Riccio 1978), rats given deep body cooling after training were tested 1 or 7 days later. Some were tested shortly after recooling, while they were moderately hypothermic; others were allowed to rewarm more completely until only slightly below normal body temperature. Attenuation of RA was obtained at both retention intervals, but only in the groups with moderate hypothermia. Because duration of rewarming time was confounded with body temperature (i.e., those tested while at higher body temperature had required a longer time to reach this level), a subsequently study manipulated temperature at testing more directly and confirmed the previous observations (Mactutus, McCutcheon & Riccio 1980). An additional experiment used a within-subject paradigm with repeated tests to demonstrate that recovery was controllable by body temperature at testing. On days when testing was preceded by recooling, subjects performed well; when testing was in the normal body state, the same subjects showed amnesia.

Taken together, the studies using ECS and hypothermia suggest that the magnitude of recovery from amnesia depends upon the extent of congruence between the animal's state at training and at testing. Unlike re-exposure to the US, which appears to produce a durable attenuation of RA, re-exposure to the amnestic agent induces a

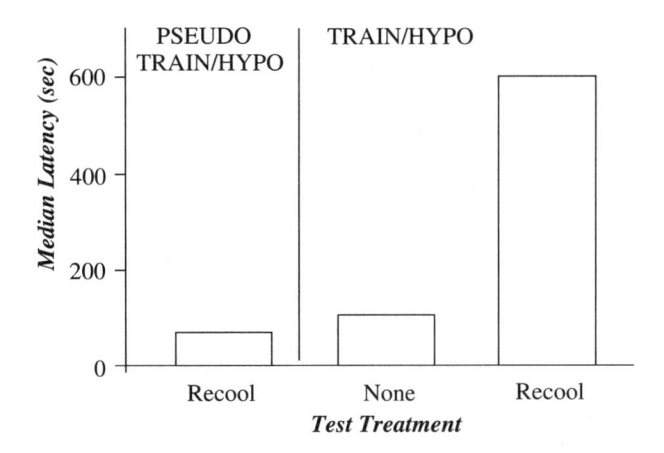

FIGURE 9-6 Alleviation of hypothermia-induced retrograde amnesia through re-exposure to the amnestic treatment prior to passive avoidance testing. (Adapted from Hinderliter, Webster & Riccio 1975.)

more transient recovery. In the latter case the internal attributes of the amnestic treatment apparently have to be in an active state to facilitate retrieval. Finally, it should be noted that problems of new learning as the source of recovery from amnesia are obviated by use of the amnestic treatment as a reminder. It is difficult to imagine how the administration of ECS or hypothermia can produce learning that is at all relevant to performance on the original task.

If the internal cues induced by an amnestic treatment constitute part of the encoding environment for the target information, then we might expect that administration of stress-related hormones at testing would reinstate some of the attributes necessary for memory retrieval. (A similar strategy was discussed with respect to the Kamin effect in chapter 3.) Consistent with this interpretation, several studies have found that administration of the pituitary neuropeptide adrenocorticotrophic hormone (ACTH) (or certain fragments of the string of amino acids that make up the ACTH molecule) can attenuate RA. Rigter, Janssens-Elbertse, and van Riezen (1976) were able to reverse ECS-induced amnesia by injecting a form of the ACTH molecule. Moreover, as with those studies employing re-exposure to the amnestic agent, the recovery of memory was time dependent. As the delay between hormone injection and the test session increased, the degree of recovery diminished. Similarly, Mactutus, Smith, and Riccio (1980) were able to partially reverse RA resulting from hypothermia by injecting rats with ACTH prior to the test session. The recovery did not occur when a delay between injection and testing was introduced. An exception to this transient recovery was found if the subjects were re-exposed to the conditioning cues and ACTH together, as in a Pavlovian pairing. Under this arrangement, where the presumed reactivation of memory can become reassociated with the original external cues, testing even several days later revealed a diminution in the severity of amnesia.

Another class of hormones that increases during stressful episodes are the catecholamines, norepinephrine and epinephrine. Epinephrine is ordinarily released by the adrenal medulla and sympathetic nervous system when an organism is confronted with danger. Concannon and Carr (1982) showed that injection of epinephrine in rats prior to testing was sufficient to reverse the RA induced by a pharmacological agent (diethyldithiocarbamic acid). By implicating retrieval processes at testing, the finding extends previous work showing that manipulation of catecholamine levels following training and the amnestic treatment could modify RA (Martinez, Jensen & McGaugh 1981; Quinton & Bloom 1977).

Alleviation of Anterograde Amnesia

As we indicated earlier, anterograde amnesia (AA) has received substantially less attention in the laboratory than retrograde amnesia, a disparity related to the methodological difficulties inherent in AA studies. Nevertheless, there is some evidence that AA, like RA, may be a reversible loss. Conceptually, AA is very similar to state-dependent retention, so it is not surprising that much of the research on recovery employs a design in which the same state is present at training and testing. This idea will become clearer with some examples.

Perhaps the first study to examine whether an amnestic agent such as ECS would both induce AA and the recovery from that AA was conducted by Thompson and Neely (1970). Rats were trained in a simple step-down task (given a mild footshock after stepping down from a platform) 25 minutes after ECS or sham ECS. Twenty-four hours later, ECS was administered to half of each group 25 minutes before testing. Strikingly, step-down performance did not depend upon whether subjects were trained after ECS, but rather upon whether the training and testing states were the same. Animals receiving ECS prior to training and again prior to testing did as well as those never receiving ECS; forgetting (anterograde amnesia) was seen in subjects trained after ECS but tested without ECS. A second experiment explored further the role of state similarity by manipulating the interval between the second ECS and retention testing. Animals trained 25 minutes after the first ECS were tested 24 hours later; the second ECS treatment occurred 15, 25, 35, 45, or 55 minutes prior to the test. Although all groups showed some recovery from AA, by far the stronger reduction in amnesia was obtained in the 25-minute group, i.e., the testing condition which exactly matched the relationship between ECS and original learning. Gardner, Glick, and Jarvik (1972) confirmed that a second ECS administration prior to testing alleviated anterograde amnesia. Their study also explored some of the neurochemical conditions necessary for recovery by introducing pharmacological agents in lieu of ECS at testing.

The importance of close congruence between the anterograde state at training and at testing in order to obtain memory recovery is illustrated in a study using lowered body temperature as the amnestic treatment (Richardson, et al. 1984). Rats were trained after mild hypothermia was induced. When subjects were recooled prior to testing 24 hours later, those tested at the same level of hypothermia at testing present at training displayed little amnesia. However, for subjects tested while hypothermic but at a somewhat higher body temperature, the amnesia was as strong as that in the non-recooled amnesia baseline group. Furthermore, test performance was intermediate in a group whose test temperature differed only slightly from that at the time of training. This evidence of stimulus control over recovery from AA is displayed in Figure 9-7.

Recovery from AA in the laboratory is not restricted to the passive avoidance task. Mildly hypothermic rats trained to escape shock by turning left or right in a T-maze performed better when returned to the hypothermic state at testing than those tested at normothermic levels (Santucci & Riccio 1986). Thus, as with many state-dependent retention studies using pharmacological agents, loss and recovery of memory for a discrimination can be seen.

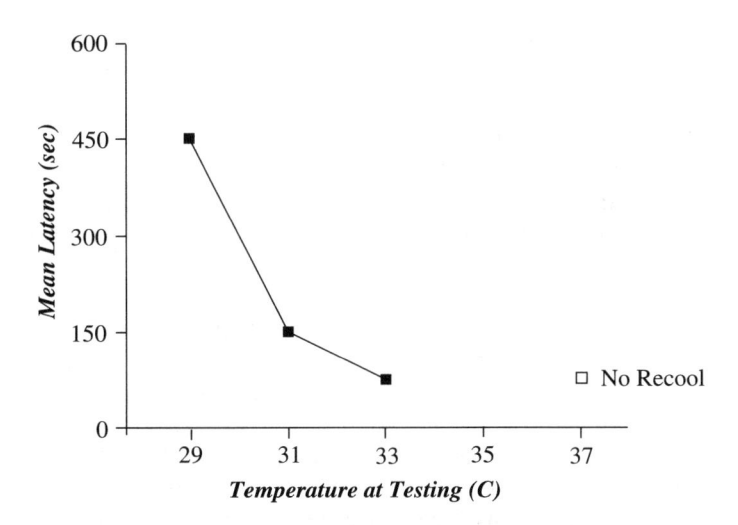

FIGURE 9-7 **Stimulus control over recovery of memory from hypothermia-induced anterograde amnesia. Retention is strongest when testing and training temperatures are similar (29°C). (Adapted from Richardson et al. 1984.)**

MEMORY RETRIEVAL BY PERSONS WITH AMNESIA

We have reviewed a variety of evidence showing that experimentally induced amnesia in animals is often reversible. A critical question, from both a theoretical and practical standpoint, is whether comparable outcomes occur when humans suffer from amnesia. One suggestive finding comes from observations of what appears to be spontaneous recovery of memories in RA from closed head (concussive) injury. As there appears to be a progression of recovery in which older information returns first, followed by memory for events closer to the amnesic event, the phenomenon has been referred to as shrinking RA.

Benson and Geschwind (1967) provided a fascinating case study of shrinking RA. The patient, a 34-year-old man who had apparently suffered a severe blow to the head, initially showed confusion, impaired use of language, an inability to remember new information, and retrograde amnesia for events within the preceding 2 years. After several weeks many cognitive functions improved, but he still showed profound retrograde amnesia. For example, he insisted that he was a bus driver in Washington, D.C., although it was known that he had given up that job and moved to Boston 2 years earlier. The patient's recovery is described as follows:

> *During the remaining period in hospital, the retrograde amnesia consistently improved. Thus when he first returned to the Neurology Service he was unable to remember living in the Boston area. Three or four days later he spontaneously recalled separating from his wife and moving to Boston. Several days later he remembered the job in Boston. Within a few days, however, he recalled the second and last job but was still vague as to how long he had worked there. Before discharge the retrograde amnesia had cleared to the point that he remembered quitting work on the day before the injury, approximately 24 hours before admission to the University Hospital.* (p. 540)

Given the history of alcohol use in the patient, there was suspicion that the inability to recover memory for the 24 hours before the injury may have been related to a bout of heavy drinking. The investigators suggested that shrinkage of retrograde amnesia implicates a failure of retrieval rather than failure of consolidation as the mechanism underlying retrograde amnesia, although they also proposed that a "permanent post-traumatic retrograde amnesia of seconds, to minutes duration does, however, probably represent the true abolition of memories not yet consolidated" (p. 542).

Unfortunately, the question of whether there is genuine recovery of memory in human amnesics, while obviously important, has been difficult to answer definitively. In many cases, a variety of non-memorial contributions to the recovery cannot be ruled out. A patient's conversations with friends or other people about the events preceding an amnesic episode (e.g., car accident) can result in a new memory (based on the conversations) which is indistinguishable from the original. Similarly, the patient may read various accounts of events in newspapers and incorporate the information into memory as if it had been directly witnessed and remembered. Even apart from these sources of relearning, factors that initially depress performance and produce poor memory may diminish over time. This, of course, could give the misleading impression that memory has recovered. If events responsible for the amnesia also impair motivation, attention, or other cognitive processes, then memory may appear to be poorer than it really is. As the patient recovers, improvements in these important processes may produce gains in performance that look like a return of memory. These difficulties in determining whether recovered memory in such clinical circumstances truly reflects the original memory are a counterpart of the methodological concern for new learning and other performance variables that we considered with respect to reversals of experimentally induced amnesia in animals.

Test-Induced Recovery from Amnesia

There is evidence, primarily from studies of chronic anterograde amnesia in advanced alcoholics at the stage of Korsakoff's syndrome and other brain-damaged patients, that acquired information which apparently undergoes complete forgetting actually is partially spared and can be retrieved under appropriate conditions. One of the more striking illustrations that amnesic loss can be reversed has been provided by Warrington and Weiskrantz (1968, 1970). A graded series of fragmented drawings or words (Figure 9-8) was presented, starting with the most incomplete form. The subject's task was to learn the target item on the basis of the most fragmented representation; errors were scored when closer approximations were required to cue the correct response. The materials were chosen in such a way that guessing, with or without experience on other fragment items, did not improve performance; correct responding thus depended on information specific to the target. Training on a series of items occurred for 3 successive days. Despite the fact that the patients were severely amnesic and unable to recall events from day to day, they acquired the task to the same level as normal control subjects, although at a slower rate. Intriguingly, in addition to within-session improvement, the amnesic subjects showed substantial transfer of learning from day to day during the 3 days of training, suggesting the presence of a capacity for long-term retention.

The fragmented-item technique was used next to examine the retention of amnesics in more detail (Warrington and Weiskrantz 1970). After subjects learned the most incomplete version of the target, they were tested for retention in 3 ways: recall of the items from the list; recognition (yes-no) of the 9 correct responses from an 18-item list; partial information, in which the test trial, like training trials, consisted of a fragmented word. Control subjects did substantially better than amnesic subjects on recall (48 percent versus 14 percent) and recognition (94 percent

PORCH

FIGURE 9-8 Examples of fragmented (degraded) stimuli used by Warrington and Weiskrantz (1968) to study retention in human amnesiacs. (Adapted from Warrington & Weiskrantz 1972.)

versus 59 percent) tasks. While results for both groups appear to have improved on the recognition test, it should be recognized that since the base rate is 50 percent on the yes-no task, the amnesic group's score of 59 percent correct hovers around chance, hardly a gain over their recall performance. In contrast, control and amnesic subjects show excellent and similar levels of retention (96 and 94 percent, respectively) on the fragmented words test. In a second experiment, lists of words were presented in the ordinary manner (not degraded) during training, and retention was assessed using recall, recognition, and two partial information tests. In one of the latter tests, the items were presented as fragmented words; in the other the partial information was provided by the initial letters of the words. (To eliminate the possibility that the partial information would be sufficient to produce correct guessing in untrained subjects, the lists were constructed on the basis of pilot tests.) On recall and recognition tests, performance of control subjects was superior to amnesics. Also, the recognition test produced improved performance over the recall condition, but only in control subjects. However, the amnesic subjects benefited significantly from the partial information test procedure, which raised their scores roughly to the level of control subjects. Thus, with appropriate cuing, severely amnesic humans show evidence of long-term retention for information acquired under controlled laboratory conditions.

As in the cases of recovery from amnesia in tests with animals, these findings raise important questions about the process involved in amnesia. A failure of consolidation during learning, or rapid deterioration of the engram, would not easily predict that recovery from forgetting would be achieved. Given the precautions taken to rule out new learning in the form of successful guessing based on the partial information, it appears that much of this particular memory loss reflects some form of a retrieval deficit.

Although the exact nature of the patients' retrieval problem is not defined by these studies, one possibility is suggested by the paradox inherent in the outcomes. As the investigators recognized, it seems peculiar that amnesics do so well with fragmented items when they do so poorly at recognizing the complete item. Warrington and Weiskrantz suggested that interference is a major source of memory loss in amnesics; errors occur because subjects are unable to sort out or discriminate various lists of items and have difficulty rejecting incorrect (false-positive) responses. The value of tests with fragmented words or initial letters would be that they necessarily restrict or eliminate other alternatives (e.g., few other choices would fit the pattern represented by the fragmented word). Tests of recognition, in contrast, include distractor items, which are not included in fragmented-word tests, but provide the potentially interfering alternatives that amnesics find so difficult to deal with. The apparent retrieval deficit in amnesics subsequently was characterized as reflecting a disconnection between memory systems, such that a cognitive mediational system is no longer integrated with their semantic memory (knowledge of the world) (see Warrington 1985).

Recovery from Amnesia Induced by Priming

Evidence of memory representations in severely amnesic subjects can also be seen in certain tasks involving priming. *Priming* is a special case of prior cuing; it refers to the finding that a particular target item may be retrieved (accessed) faster when that item, or a related one, has recently been presented to the subjects. Consider a study by Freedman and Loftus (1971) in which subjects were asked to produce an example of a category (e.g., animal), with the restriction that the example begin with a particular letter (e.g., H). While college subjects obviously can do this task accurately and rapidly, their response time is slightly but reliably shorter if the category is given first, followed by the restrictive letter, rather than the other way around (e.g., "animal—H" produces a faster answer than "H—animal"). Presumably, having the category presented first primes or prepares the subject's representation of items in that domain and allows quicker access to an exemplar when the designating letter is given.

In another early study involving priming, college students were asked to name an example of a category as quickly as possible after being shown the category title (Loftus 1973). The task was made more difficult by the fact that a restrictor rule was included, as we saw above. That is, the example had to start with the particular letter also presented with the category (e.g., for "tree—O," "oak" would be an appropriate response). The question of interest was the speed with which subjects responded correctly on a second trial with the same category but a new initial letter: "tree—M"). In that case, latency to respond (reaction time) was faster on the second trial. The facilitation diminished, however, as a function of the number of tests with other categories (plus the time required for these tests) interpolated between the first and second presentation of the same category. Presumably, the first trial initiated a semantic activation of words related to types of trees which then facilitated access to names of trees on a subsequent trial, provided that other categories or a long interval of time did not intervene (see Collins & Loftus 1975).

An extensive literature has developed on priming effects, which seem to constitute an example of memory without conscious awareness and bring us back to our focus on memory in amnesics. Several experiments by Jacoby and Witherspoon (1982) offer evidence of priming effects in amnesics with Korsakoff's syndrome (an advanced stage of alcoholism). In one experiment, the spelling of a homophone (word having the same sound but different meanings, depending on their spelling, such as *bare* versus *bear*) was used to examine the influence of previously presented material on memory in these amnesics. Subjects initially heard the homophone as part of a question to be answered; the answer was such that the representation of the word would be biased toward the infrequent spelling of the word (What is a musical instrument that employs a *reed?*) Later the subjects heard the critical words presented (along with control words) and were asked to write them down. The critical question was how the subject spelled the words. If a previous question about musical instruments had primed a representation of *reed* in memory, then the spelling should reflect this influence. If there was no residual effect of the pre-exposure, then spelling should conform to baseline levels. Jacoby and Witherspoon found that the patients with Korsakoff's syndrome were indeed susceptible to this type of priming effect; their spelling was affected by their memory for the sentences read to them earlier. A striking aspect of this study was that while priming clearly revealed a memorial influence of the earlier information, the amnesiacs not only appeared unaware that they had remembered anything, but did no better than chance in a recognition task. This dissociation of performance between two tasks is not unique to amnesia; normal subjects show the same pattern of responding.

A second experiment by Jacoby and Witherspoon used a perceptual identification task as the critical measure of memory priming. A list of words to be studied was presented visually to subjects. Subjects were tested later by flashing the studied words or new (control) words very briefly (a fraction of a second) on a screen. Identification of words was enhanced by their prior presentation, indicating that some memorial representation of the target items existed. As in the priming study, performance on the identification task was independent of that on a recognition task; again, this dissociation obtained for normal subjects as well as Korsakoff patients. The more general point made by these studies is that humans often show retention without being conscious (aware) of the information.

There is an important theoretical issue also addressed by Jacoby and Witherspoon (1982). The issue concerns thresholds for the expression of memory. If various tests require different amounts of information for successful performance (e.g., recognition versus recall), then perhaps success (or failure) represents different thresholds among the tasks rather than the quality of the task itself. As Tulving and others have pointed out, however, such an interpretation implies that success on a difficult or high threshold task (recall) would predict success on an easier or low threshold task (recognition), but it does not. It seems reasonable therefore to conclude that the dissociated performance obtained by Jacoby and Witherspoon reflects the nature of the tasks. We shall return to this issue in chapter 11.

While vigorous discussion about the interpretation of the word fragment and primary findings can be found in the literature, such phenomena are consistent with the view that memory stores may be intact (or partially so) even in amnesic humans and can be tapped with appropriate retrieval techniques. It would be overly facile to view the priming effects as tantamount to the prior cuing effects with amnesic animals; nevertheless, both manipulations point to a recoverability of information assumed otherwise to be lost.

Recovery from Amnesia in Humans: Re-exposure to the Amnestic Agent

Earlier we described the apparently paradoxical finding that the very same amnestic treatment that impairs memory can be effective in restoring memory. It was suggested that reinstating the internal context associated with the amnestic episode could provide necessary retrieval cues to reverse experimentally induced amnesia. This interpretation sometimes is referred to as the "two-bump theory" in recognition of certain mystery-novel plots where the amnesic victim, unable to identify the culprits due to a blow to the head, suddenly recovers his or her memory following another, accidental head injury. While the literal two-bump notion is not exactly the sort of thing one can demonstrate in the laboratory with humans, occasionally there are anecdotal reports consistent with the view.

The *Washington Post* recently reported the case of a 60-year-old man, James M., who reappeared in Larchmont, New York, 15 years after suddenly leaving home in an amnesic fugue. The precipitating event seems to have been a car accident that gave him a mild concussion and left him unconscious for a brief period. Several days later, suffering from a headache, Mr. M. went out for a walk. He reported that the next thing he knew, he was in Philadelphia, with no recollection of who he was, where he came from, or any of the other attributes of identity that we all take for granted. The 15-year amnesia period ended when he accidentally received a severe bump to his head while working. This second bump was followed by the return of his memory, and he took the next train home to Larchmont. While this fascinating incident appears to provide a nice illustration from real life of a second insult to the central nervous system reversing the original amnesia, the event should properly be viewed as illustrative rather than as evidence. Not the least of the peculiarities here is that the amnesia extended to Mr. M.'s own identity—an outcome hardly in keeping with the selective loss of memory for relatively recent information that so often characterizes RA.

CHAPTER SUMMARY

Not uncommonly, we fail to recall information (e.g., someone's name) at one moment, only to recall it later. This anecdotal example illustrates that forgetting does not necessarily imply that information was destroyed or erased from storage; rather, the target item temporarily may simply not be retrievable. Tulving has characterized such information as inaccessible but available, and a major focus of contemporary memory research is on determining the various cues that control retrieval.

This chapter examined several types or sources of forgetting with respect to the reversibility of the memory deficit. In animals, so-called spontaneous forgetting of either aversive or appetitive tasks has been reversed by manipulations just prior to testing. These prior cuing treatments have included exposure to the training reinforcer (US), to the conditioned stimuli (CS), to background or contextual stimuli present at training, or to certain pharmacological agents. Contextual cuing has also been effective in alleviating spontaneous forgetting in humans and has been applied to enhance eyewitness memory.

A provocative early finding on retrieval effects in the psychobiology of memory came from studies of cortical lesions in animals. Classic work by Lashley had long been interpreted as showing that extensive brain lesions destroyed memory; lesioned animals not only failed to perform previously acquired discriminations, but also exhibited no savings in relearning. However, evidence that the lesion effects could be attenuated by drug treatment implicated retrieval deficits rather than loss of storage as the basis of the impairment. Related work suggested that the lesions block expression of memory by shifting control of behavior to other neural systems.

The role of retrieval deficits in experimentally induced amnesias has received extensive research attention in recent years. The findings that the onset of retrograde amnesia is gradual and that amnesia can be induced for old (reactivated) memories are problematic for traditional interpretations that emphasize an impairment in memory storage (e.g., consolidation). More direct evidence for the role of retrieval comes from investigations testing treatments that alleviate amnesia. Re-exposure to components of the training episode (i.e., the CS or US) can reduce amnesia, as can re-exposure to the original amnestic agent itself, or administration of stress-related hormones such as ACTH or epinephrine. To account for the characteristic temporal gradient of retrograde amnesia, retrieval models emphasize that processing of information following training can become associated, or otherwise tagged, with the special amnestic state. State-dependent-like effects are seen in anterograde amnesia, where reversal of loss is most frequently achieved by readministering the amnestic agent (e.g., ECS, hypothermia) just prior to testing. Stimulus control over memory retrieval is suggested by the finding that degree of recovery increases as the correspondence between the training state and the test state increases.

With respect to human retrograde amnesia, the temporal boundaries following concussive accidents have been reported to diminish or shrink over time. Although consistent with the view that the amnestic episode did not destroy storage, this finding is difficult to interpret because of the possibility that the recovery is actually based on new learning about the old events. However, laboratory evidence reveals that some of the memory impairment in chronic anterograde amnesic patients is attributable to difficulties in retrieval. Failure to recall or even recognize items from a previously presented list can be substantially eliminated with certain cuing techniques that involve presentation of partial information (e.g., perceptually fragmented words, initial letters) about the target. Amnesic subjects are also responsive to priming effects, a phenomenon widely studied in normal subjects as well. Thus, after presentation of information that activates a representation of the less common spelling of a homophone (e.g., *reed* rather than *read*), amnesics are biased at testing to produce *reed*. Like normal control subjects, amnesic subjects show this residual influence of priming despite being unable either to recall or to recognize the same items in other tests. This and related findings have stimulated considerable interest in dissociation of memory and the fact that remembering may occur independently of any conscious awareness of the information.

10
Aspects of Human Amnesia

In earlier chapters we presented some examples of anterograde and retrograde amnesia and in chapter 9 we focused on how the experimental induction of amnesia could be used to explore memory principles. In this chapter we examine in more detail some of the characteristics of the amnesias that occur in some unfortunate persons due to accident, biological dysfunction, or the violent acts of other humans, among other misfortunes. In addition, we will consider some laboratory research, based mainly on using nonhuman primates (monkeys), that attempts to delineate the psychobiological mechanisms that underlie the human amnesias.

As an overview, let us look at the status of memory in an imaginary, but characteristic, patient, M.K., who suffered from a catastrophic head injury several years ago and now exhibits the following characteristics with respect to memory. M.K.'s score on a standard intelligence test remains well above average and pretty much the same as before her illness. Her vocabulary is unimpaired, she recognizes all her old friends, and her performance in a standard test of short-term retention is perfectly normal. Indeed, our initial impression might be that this individual does not need to be considered as a patient at all. But further interactions reveal some interesting, if unfortunate, anomalies. M.K. does not remember a number of important and salient world events that occurred in a period of 3 months or so preceding her illness, although as a competent citizen she usually followed the news avidly. The latter characteristic is borne out by the fact that her memory for newsworthy events that occurred several years ago is largely intact. Always somewhat aloof in interpersonal relations but socially adept, M.K. retains these features, but her inability to remember for more than a few seconds the names of new people she has met, despite repeated introductions, is frustrating to her, especially as she dimly recognizes that these individuals are important to her. As it happens, this deficit in learning names is part of a much more devastating impairment in acquiring many kinds of new information. The location of her hospital room, the city sights that she was taken to see yesterday, the golf and tennis she played the day before, and the novel she read this morning all elude her recall. Her inability to form new memories deprives her of the threads of continuity that give people a sense of self and of the events that constitute the warp and woof of their lives.

There are some other interesting features of M.K.'s otherwise unfortunate situation. As a competent pianist, she has learned several new classical pieces that she plays very well, although when asked she denies knowing any of them. Her tennis game has improved during her hospital stay; more strikingly, she shows a strong command of the appropriate strategies (e.g., when to rush the net or to lob against her opponent, when to use a delicate drop shot) as well as the standard but peculiar nomenclature of scoring in tennis (e.g., thirty-love; deuce; add-in). On the other hand, she is quite likely to forget the score during a game even shortly after announcing it, and were it not for a convenient blackboard, M.K. would have no idea of whether she is winning or losing the set.

Finally, there is the matter of M.K.'s aversion to one of the staff, P.L., a burly man who playfully squeezed her hand too hard when they were introduced. Ever since, M.K. has avoided P.L., although she cannot remember what he did that makes her dislike him.

In brief, although M.K. has a relatively intact short-term or working memory, she is largely unable either to transfer newly acquired information into long-term storage or to demonstrate evidence of such storage. This failure to remember events (episodes) is not absolute, as we saw with the incident involving the painful handshake. But notice that M.K. is unable to verbalize the episode that gave rise to the learning—she seems to have an implicit, but not explicit, memory for the event (Graf & Schacter 1985; Schacter 1987). We see a similar peculiarity when she learns to play a new song, but is subsequently unaware that she knows or has learned the piece. On the more positive side, although M.K. has a retrograde memory loss for many events prior to the traumatic insult, the impairment diminishes with events more remote in time. Thus, her autobiographical memory up to some months before the accident is intact, as is her general knowledge of the world, i.e., semantic memory. And her motor skills, such as tennis, are well preserved.

This vignette, although fictitious, provides a reasonably accurate portrayal of the kinds of memory problems seen in many amnesic patients. It might be considered a composite of the descriptions provided by a number of investigators (Cohen & Squire 1980; Milner, Corkin & Teuber 1968; Rozin 1976; Schacter 1983; Schacter & Crovitz 1977; Squire & Cohen 1984). With the example of M.K. in mind, we can now proceed to consider some of the observations and interpretations with respect to retrograde and anterograde amnesia in humans.

RETROGRADE AMNESIA

As we saw in an earlier chapter, temporally graded memory loss for episodes that precede insult to the central nervous system is one of the hallmarks of retrograde amnesia. In their analysis of a large number of human traumatic amnesias, Russell and Nathan (1946) found that the memory loss usually extended back for some minutes or hours, although much longer retrograde impairment has also been reported (for reviews, see Schacter & Crovitz 1977; Squire & Cohen 1984). Over 100 years ago, Ribot (1882) formulated the principle that vulnerability of memory to traumatic insult decreased as the memory grew older. Rozin (1976) has neatly rephrased this principle as the "last in, first out" concept, a contemporary phrasing that invokes accounting terms familiar to taxpayers who sell stocks. As there is also some evidence that the temporal extent of retrograde loss depends upon the severity of traumatic insults (Rozin 1976, 21), age of the target information is not the sole determinant of the memory impairment.

Clinical impressions and anecdotal reports of the time course of memory loss for events prior to a mishap can leave something to be desired in terms of the accuracy and systematic description of the retrograde gradient. One attempt to circumvent some of these difficulties makes use of a questionnaire technique (Sanders & Warrington 1971; Warrington & Sanders 1971). The essence of the procedure involves asking subjects to recall public events or recognize particular faces from a specific era; that is, to remember certain kinds of information that were uniquely salient during different time periods.

Squire and Slater (1975) modified the technique in an attempt to eliminate sampling bias and to equate the difficulty of questions from different time periods. Using normal subjects they found that information faded gradually for several years. Subsequently, Squire and his colleagues used this modified approach to examine retrograde amnesia resulting from various causes. In one study, patients receiving electroconvulsive therapy (for depression) were tested for recall of aspects of TV programs that had been broadcast for only one season during each year of an 8-year period. As Figure 10-1 shows, for the electroconvulsive therapy group selective memory impairment was revealed in the better recall of information about earlier (3 to 8 years old) programs than more recent ones (Squire & Cohen 1984, 44). This outcome is clearly different from the gradient of forgetting seen in normal subjects, where older information is more difficult to recall. With regard to theoretical issues, it can be noted that some recovery from the retrograde amnesia was also seen (Squire & Cohen 1984).

A similar retrograde amnesia involving differential disruption of memories of different ages was also seen in patients with Korsakoff's syndrome, which you will recall from chapters 8 and 9, is related to long-term chronic abuse of alcohol and usually reflects the combined effects of alcohol as a toxin and vitamin deficiencies from inadequate nutrition. Compared with control groups consisting of alcoholic or nonalcoholic subjects, Korsakoff patients showed much greater impairment in recognition of faces made famous in more recent years. Although performance of Korsakoff subjects appeared somewhat inferior to control subjects even at very remote intervals (30 to 40 years), the disparity was much greater for the more recent past. One potential interpretative difficulty is whether the loss is truly retrograde. Thus, in the

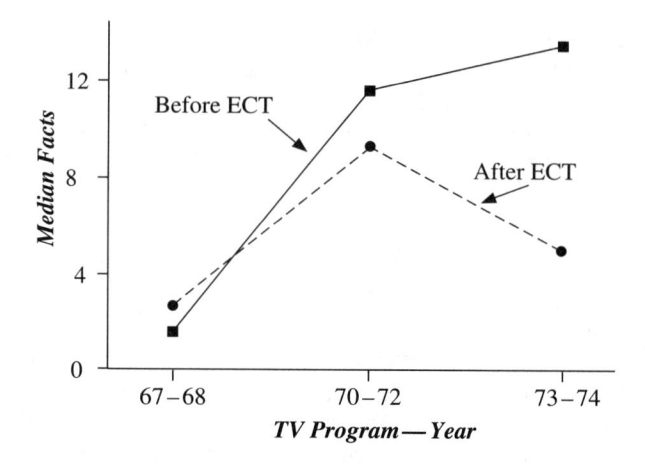

FIGURE 10-1 Performance in psychiatric patients tested for recall of information about single season TV programs occurring over 8-year period. Following electroconvulsive treatment (ECT) memory is better for older programs (1970–72) than for more recent ones (1973–74). (Adapted from Squire & Cohen 1979.)

case of diseases of gradual onset (such as those produced by abusive drinking), the memory loss may not be truly retrograde but rather may reflect some subtle impairment in acquisition processing at the time of the event. Thus, periods of heavy drinking may have altered patterns and effectiveness of TV viewing, as well as impaired establishment of memory for the episodes. At least in some cases, however, this concern seems negated by evidence suggesting that the impairment extends backward to a time period that precedes the onset of drinking (Squire & Cohen 1984).

Evidence for remote retrograde memory impairment is problematic for most models of forgetting. Clearly, the information was encoded adequately, stored successfully, and presumably was used (or at least was usable) at earlier points in time. It seems unlikely that information from events of months or years ago would continue to undergo consolidation, as that term is usually used. But retrieval views do not have a satisfactory explanation, either. While the unusual context or state produced by some retrograde insults may be the critical (missing) source of retrieval cues on certain occasions, the temporal remoteness of the memory loss is again troublesome in much the same way as it is for storage accounts. It is extremely improbable that the old information was being processed at the time of the insult, as would be required from the view that a memory that is active just before an amnestic event becomes more susceptible to be rendered inaccessible by that event. Alternatively, if the

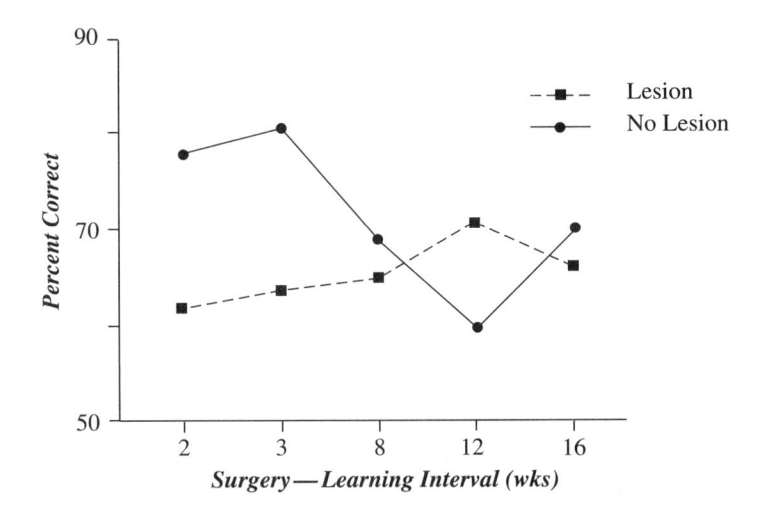

FIGURE 10-2 Retention of an object discrimination problem in monkeys as a function of the interval between learning and hippocampal surgery. Unoperated control animals were tested after comparable retention intervals. (Adapted from Zola-Morgan & Squire 1990.)

retrieval process itself were somehow disrupted (a view we argued against earlier), then it is not clear why a temporal gradient of retrograde amnesia should exist. While some memories might be more resilient and have a higher threshold of vulnerability, this effect should be independent of the age of the memory.

This theoretical impasse has received little clarification from experimental research with animals. Although there is a voluminous literature on experimentally induced retrograde amnesia, most of this is based upon amnestic agents such as electroconvulsive shock, thermoregulatory disruption, or other convulsive agents, rather than explicit destruction or disturbance in specific areas of the brain. However, with the development of an animal model of anterograde amnesia in primates (Mishkin & Appenzeller 1987; Mishkin, Malamut & Bachevalier 1984), we can expect an extension to retrograde phenomena. In this connection, Zola-Morgan and Squire (1990) have now reported an important demonstration of time-dependent retrograde memory loss in cynomolgus monkeys following bilateral lesions of the hippocampus. Prior to surgery, the animals were trained on five different sets of two-choice object discrimination problems of comparable difficulty. The training was arranged such that the different problem sets were presented 16, 12, 8, 4, and 2 weeks prior to surgery. Thus, it was possible to assess whether differential loss occurred as a function of the age of the discrimination memory. As can be seen in Figure 10-2, performance in unoperated control subjects diminished as a function of the length of the retention interval, i.e., they showed normal forgetting, while performance in the subjects with hippocampal damage followed a nearly opposite pattern. For these subjects, retention of the discrimination sets learned a few weeks before surgery was worse than for stimuli learned 12 or 16 weeks earlier. Indeed, at the longest interval the two conditions yielded comparable performance, although at the short intervals performance of the lesioned subjects were markedly inferior to that of control subjects.

ANTEROGRADE AMNESIA

As we saw earlier, anterograde amnesia is characterized by relatively rapid forgetting of information learned following insult to the brain. An important assumption, often a presumption, is that the target information was in fact processed—one can hardly have forgetting unless something was at least momentarily acquired.

Perhaps the most famous neuropsychological case of anterograde amnesia is the patient H.M., discussed earlier. Following surgery for intractable epileptic seizures, H.M. suffered a debilitating failure of memory for new information or episodes. Although his memory for events some years prior to surgery remains largely intact, H.M. is unable to remember from one day to another the names of the new people around him (e.g., nurses, physicians, psychologists), the location of his room, and a myriad of other commonplace but important bits of information (for recent discussion of H.M., see Ogden & Corkin 1991). His immediate memory is within normal limits, so it is clear that the information registers—most of it just does not stick. The magazines or novels he reads today are again new to him a day or so later.

Given that initial registration of information takes place, how can we account for the rapid forgetting that characterizes anterograde amnesia? That, of course, is the big question (or one of them) in the psychobiology of memory, and no entirely satisfactory answer has yet emerged. In a useful review, Stern (1981) has delineated six theories of human amnesia. Several of these interpretations, not necessarily mutually exclusive, will be mentioned here. One interpretation emphasizes deficits at the time of encoding or initial input. According to this view, proposed by Cermak and Butters (1972), even though registration of information takes place, perhaps the processing of the information is impoverished or less elaborate relative to normal subjects. (We considered a similar concern with respect to experimentally induced anterograde amnesia in chapter 8.) For example, amnesics may ordinarily encode information about the sound of a word (phonemic processing) rather than its meaning (semantic processing).

A study by Cermak and Reale (1978) illustrates one approach to this issue. The logic was straightforward: if amnesics fail to use appropriate coding strategies, then perhaps instructions that encourage better processing will improve retention. To manipulate processing, the investigators utilized the levels of processing approach developed by Jenkins (e.g., Hyde & Jenkins 1973) and Craik and Tulving (1975).

Thus, for each item in a list subjects would be asked to answer a question that required either physical analysis (appeared in uppercase letters?), phonemic analysis (rhymes with pen?), or semantic analysis (usable in a particular sentence?). For normal subjects, this levels-of-processing manipulation is known to enhance performance on an unanticipated retention test; a higher level of processing (e.g., semantic analysis) promotes better recall or recognition later on. Will it have a similar effect on alcoholic patients with Korsakoff's syndrome? This reasonable hypothesis failed to be supported in two initial experiments, even with variations of the instructional questions designed to enhance further the processing during encoding. The patients seemed unable to use a semantic level of processing to help their later recognition. However, when the target lists were shortened to 12 items (from nearly 60) the hypothesized pattern was obtained: recognition of words increased as a function of type of analysis required by the question, with best performance in the semantic condition. Presumably, the greater ease of the shorter list permitted the effects of differential processing to be revealed. By implication, then, the anterograde amnesia typically seen in Korsakoff patients reflects, in part, their failure to encode information with respect to semantic characteristics (but see also Cermak 1982).

Another interpretation of anterograde amnesia suggests that it is based on unusually rapid forgetting. While this may seem like a circular explanation, the notion was tied (weakly, perhaps) to the concept of consolidation and the idea that a short-term memory must be preserved long enough for it to enter the hypothetical long-term memory. According to this reasoning the memory trace otherwise fails to be consolidated into long-term storage; thus, the patient with whom you have an interesting conversation in the morning no longer remembers it later in the day. Interestingly, the data do not support this view. In several studies, Huppert and Piercy (1977, 1978) exposed subjects with Korsakoff's syndrome and control subjects to a series of distinctive pictures. With relatively brief and fixed exposure durations, the control subjects were superior in retention after a long interval. However, because performance in control subjects was also better even with an immediate retention test, initial encoding of information in the Korsakoff patients may simply have been deficient. When Huppert and Piercy increased exposure times for the Korsakoff group so that their acquisition level on an immediate test matched that of control subjects, then the rate of forgetting over longer retention intervals was nearly identical in the two groups. Perhaps attentional or motivational factors impaired the Korsakoff patients' ability to rapidly encode the pictorial information in the first place, but once the material was encoded the memory representation was not lost any faster than in control subjects. Similar findings have been obtained in other tasks. These outcomes, then, are contrary to the proposition that an unstable trace fails to consolidate (or decays more rapidly) in amnesic subjects.

A third interpretation of memory deficits in amnesic patients has focused on the role of interference from other learned responses. The proposition is that amnesics have difficulty screening out competing responses and thus suffer more interference from other learning than do normal subjects (Warrington & Weiskrantz 1970).

Although this approach may seem paradoxical in implying that amnesics have too much memory (albeit of competing information), it has the appeal of assigning the deficit to a set of principles extensively investigated as sources of forgetting in normal subjects (chapter 4). Thus, the amnesic patients' difficulty might be seen as an exaggeration of normal processes of forgetting rather than as a unique property, a quantitative rather than qualitative difference.

An example of this approach is derived from the evidence that partial cues (e.g., fragments of a target word or picture) can alleviate memory loss in amnesics (Warrington & Weiskrantz 1968; Weiskrantz & Warrington 1970a, 1970b; see chapter 9). This effect was believed to be due to a reduction in one form of interference in retention—response alternatives that might be given for a particular item.

The general idea that amnesic patients are particularly susceptible to interference has been tested often and received some support. Warrington and Weiskrantz (1974) compared proactive interference effects in amnesic (of mixed etiologies) and control subjects. Having shown in an initial experiment that amnesic subjects whose performance was markedly impaired in a recognition (yes-no) test performed as well as control subjects in a cued recall test in which the first 3 letters of the target word were presented, these investigators explored the effects of proactive interference on cued recall. In one experiment proactive interference was produced by having subjects learn two lists of words that shared a common property, i.e., items in the second list were from the same taxonomic category as the first. Under this condition, amnesic subjects showed greater impairment (more proactive interference) than control subjects tested on the second list. This differential effect was seen even more strikingly in a further experiment using a type of reversal learning. By judicious selection of stimuli, Warrington and Weiskrantz provided subjects with a list of 30 words whose first 3 letters were the beginning of only 2 English words (e.g., *eno* yields only *enormous* or *enough*). The idea is that such words restrict responses to only two possibilities and provide a situation where reversal learning (analogous to that in animals) might be tested. After being taught and tested by cued recall on one list, subjects were trained on the reversal (the alternative word beginning with the same 3 letters; note that this is merely a special case of the A-B,A-D negative transfer paradigm mentioned in chapter 4). Although performance of both control and amnesic subjects was impaired on the first reversal test trial, with further tests performance in control subjects recovered while retention scores in amnesic subjects remained poor and at near chance levels. This persistence of proactive interference (in this case, negative transfer) in amnesics under conditions where restriction of response alternatives should enhance response competition is generally consistent with the interference interpretation of the amnesic syndrome.

Another aspect of the interference interpretation involves the contribution of contextual cues. Winocur and his colleagues (e.g., Winocur & Kinsbourne 1978; Winocur, Kinsbourne & Moscovitch 1981) have called attention to the implications of the evidence that amnesics have difficulty in utilizing subtle contextual information. If the ability to use context to differentiate between (or among) learning episodes is deficient in amnesics, then one would expect interference to become especially pronounced. Conversely, interference might be reduced by enhancing the distinctiveness of the contexts in which two potentially competing sets of items are learned. Winocur and Kinsbourne (1978) found such a result when they manipulated the environment (e.g., type of lighting, color of background for the cues, and quality of ambient auditory stimulation) present during learning of two semantically related lists of paired associates. Although performance in amnesics was not brought to the level of control subjects, they did show substantial benefit from the contextual differentiation, whereas control subjects were relatively unaffected by the manipulation. In an experiment using the converse strategy, these investigators showed that when competing learning was not introduced, then the presence of the same distinctive context at training and testing served to enhance recall of a list of items in amnesic subjects (a similar contextual salience approach has been used to decrease forgetting in infant animals, see chapter 7). This contextual salience effect in amnesics seems to imply that in a typical recall situation the presence of familiar stimuli can trigger implicit competing responses. The resulting interference is more disruptive to amnesics who are deficient in utilizing contextual information to differentiate sources of learning. Providing highly distinctive backgrounds that do not contain competing associations can facilitate retention in the amnesic subjects.

The case for greater susceptibility to interference in amnesics is not without problems, however, as Warrington and Weiskrantz (1978) were among the first to acknowledge. As we mentioned above, in their earlier (1974) study using a verbal reversal learning task, the difference between amnesia and control conditions emerged only across repeated test trials on the second list. This is somewhat puzzling, as an interference interpretation would predict a difference on the very first trial. However, the predicted outcome may have been obscured by a floor effect; because PI was very strong and performance in both groups was at (or near) chance levels, differential effects may have been precluded simply because there was no room to detect the difference. In order to explore this issue, Warrington and Weiskrantz (1978) carried out a replication in which conditions were slightly altered to avoid floor effects. Thus, subjects might learn that *cyc* means *cyclone* in list 1, while in the reversal phase *cyc* stands for *cycle*. Although PI was clearly evident in both groups on the first test, once again performance of the amnesic subjects was not significantly more impaired. The differential influence of prior learning still was only seen with repeated test trials, despite the absence of floor effect.

In a related experiment, the procedure attempted to avoid response competition and assess item availability by asking for both responses to the cue. Under this arrangement, the momentary dominance by one item (e.g., the first list response over the second list response) is relatively unimportant; an opportunity is provided to produce both items. Shortly after list 1 training, subjects were presented with a second list of words (starting with the same 3 letters). The cued recall procedure (initial 3 letters) was then used to test retention, except that subjects were instructed to try to recall both words. Despite the opportunity to give two responses, suppression of response availability was evident, i.e., subjects failed to recall the second item. However, the pattern of interference obtained was very similar in both groups (although the amnesics showed numerically more PI than controls, 33% versus 22%, respectively). The conclusion seems to be that despite the greater susceptibility to interference exhibited by amnesics in some situations, the effect probably is not sufficiently robust or general to account for all of their memory problems.

EXPLICIT AND IMPLICIT MEMORY

Although individuals suffering from anterograde amnesia seem unable to recall or recognize new information, it is now clear that at some level memory for certain aspects of an episode often exists—that some attributes of the memory are accessible (see Schacter 1987). In the opening vignette, we saw that M.K. could learn to play new songs although she could not remember that she knew the piece. Similarly, she had remembered something about the nature (unpleasant) of her interaction with the staff aide, although she was unable to state the basis for her dislike of him. In both cases, based on documented evidence, we see evidence of a memory influencing behavior, although the individual has no apparent awareness that she had acquired the memory; this has been termed an implicit memory. Schacter and his colleagues have distinguished between implicit and explicit memories. Implicit memories are revealed by facilitated performance on a task from previously acquired target information without the subject's conscious awareness of the acquisition. In contrast, explicit memory refers to intentional and conscious recollection (e.g., free recall, recognition) of the target material itself.

There are many more formal instances of this distinction in the expression of memories. The documentation includes findings that anterograde amnesic subjects can learn to solve efficiently a difficult parlor puzzle known as the Tower of Hanoi, while at the same time they cannot recall ever having seen the puzzle before, let alone verbalize the strategies or rules they use in solving the problem (Squire & Cohen 1984). Similarly, amnesiacs show substantial improvement across daily sessions in the acquisition of new tasks such as tracing a form presented in a mirror or reading inverted type and in a Pavlovian conditioning paradigm, acquiring an eyeblink response to a signal that predicts an impending puff of air to the cornea (see chapter 11). Strikingly, however, these patients have no explicit recognition of having been confronted by these tasks earlier (Weiskrantz & Warrington 1979)! This discrepancy between what subjects report knowing and what they can actually do has been characterized in different ways (see Squire 1987, p. 168). With respect to learning rules and motor skills (e.g., mirror tracing), a distinction between procedural and declarative memories seems apt (Cohen & Squire 1980, Squire 1992). Thus, declarative memory involves the ability to verbalize (or declare) what one knows and one's own awareness of this information. It is knowing about an event, or knowing that. In contrast, procedural memory, or knowing how, involves carrying out behaviors (procedures) that one need not be conscious of, and often includes integrating new sequences of motor skills (see Squire 1987, 1992).

Memory for new information that can influence behavior without the amnesiacs' conscious awareness is not restricted to perceptual-motor skills or tasks, however. Earlier we discussed work by Jacoby and Witherspoon (1982) in which amnesic patients were asked to spell certain words that sound alike but have different spellings and meaning (homophones). If subjects were exposed to information about one form of the homophones ("What is a musical instrument that uses a reed?") before being asked to spell the word, they tended to use that particular form of the homophone. Since this choice was for the less frequent form of the spellings, the shift in bias appears to represent memory for information activated by the prior questions. That subjects are not consciously aware of the information is indicated by the fact that in a separate test subjects are unable to recognize the items they have heard. Depending on the nature of the task, the expression of information about a particular episode (e.g., the biasing question in this case) without awareness has been characterized as involving implicit memory or perceptual fluency as opposed to explicit memory. The distinction from procedural and declarative memory, while not hard and fast, is that the concept of implicit and explicit memory is generally applied to an event or episode, rather than a task involving a rule or motor skill learning.

This selectivity of memory impairment even in so-called global amnesia is an important and illuminating phenomenon. Clearly, some system or systems must be spared to permit new information to be acquired and to influence subsequent behavior, even if subjects are unaware of (i.e., unable to verbalize) what this information is. Perhaps the concept of awareness in memory, while not always easily defined operationally, should not be entirely surprising. Some years ago studies in the area of perception revealed what appeared to be levels of awareness with respect to certain stimuli. For example, when normal human subjects were asked to identify words that were presented very briefly (tachistoscopically) on a screen, they were typically unable to do so. However, when the stimulus item was a sexually explicit or emotionally charged term, subjects often showed subtle emotional responses, as reflected in changes in their galvanic skin response (an index of electrical resistance of skin) (McGinnies 1949). How could a stimulus that is not recognized give rise to an emotional interpretation? While many methodological criticisms were raised against some of the perceptual defense studies (e.g., Howes & Solomon 1950), it now seems clear that in many cases the findings represented expression of information at a different level of awareness. As with implicit memory, information could affect behavior even though the target item could not be recognized or recalled.

One of the major ways in which implicit memory is revealed is through the technique of priming. In an earlier chapter we discussed the phenomenon of priming with respect to retrieval processes. Here we will briefly consider priming in the context of selective memory impairment in amnesic subjects. One of the major points to emerge has been that priming can benefit the implicit memory of amnesic subjects

292   *Chapter Ten*

much as it does with normal subjects. In one study (Graf, Squire & Mandler 1984), normal and amnesic subjects were given a list of words to study under different orienting instructions. Some subjects were to decide whether successive words shared vowels, a task that promotes orthographic or phonemic processing; others were to evaluate how much they liked or disliked the words, a task that promotes semantic processing. Immediately after studying the list, all subjects were given an explicit memory test in which they were asked to recall as many of the words as possible. Not surprisingly, normal subjects performed substantially better than the amnesic subjects. However, when implicit memory was assessed by presenting the first few letters of each item and asking subjects to respond with the first word that came to mind, both amnesic and normal subjects did well, and their performance levels were comparable. Since the initial 3 letters did not uniquely predict the target word (e.g., *def* could be *default, deface, define, defense,* etc.), the improvement apparently reflects priming or activation of a memory of the word seen earlier. The priming effect had a limited and similar time course for amnesic and normal subjects; after a 2-hour retention interval performance declined to chance levels for all subjects.

Although evidence of substantial retention in amnesics could be seen by priming, the same could not be said for recognition. Even though recognition is usually a sensitive indicator of memory, amnesics asked to recognize the target word when presented in a list that included two distracters beginning with the same initial letters (*marker* versus *Mary* or *marble*) showed substantial impairment. That the requirements of the memory test can be quite critical is supported by evidence from a related experiment (Graf et al. 1984, experiment 3). Telling subjects to use the first few letters to help remember the word, i.e., a cued recall task, did not help the amnesic subjects. The instructions imposed a constraint akin to explicit memory tasks, with the result that the beneficial priming effect was prevented. Presumably recognition tests invoke similar constraints.

The notion of activation seems central to the findings just described, as well as those on word fragmentation and perceptual recognition fluency tasks (Graf et al. 1984; Rozin 1976). Successful performance in these tasks can be based upon activation of a trace or representation. Rozin has suggested that priming might be thought of as a hot tubes effect. The priming event activates a representation that can persist for a period of time and facilitate a response, just as vacuum tubes (pretransistor era) would stay warm after a radio was turned off.

COMMENT ON DISSOCIATION AS A RESEARCH STRATEGY IN THE PSYCHOBIOLOGY OF MEMORY

The selective impairments of memory that we have described may appear puzzling, but this reaction is probably due to an unwarranted, if implicit, assumption that memory is a unitary process. It might be preferable to think in terms of a number of separate but related memory systems, some of which can function relatively independently of others. From this perspective, as Rozin (1976) and many others have pointed out, pathologies of memory can reveal aspects of the psychobiological organization of memory—some systems may be compromised by brain injury, while other components remain intact. We will ignore for now the more subtle theoretical issue of whether these systems represent different processes and operations or different stores of information (on this issue see, for example, Tulving 1985; Kinsbourne 1989; also see chapter 12).

Weiskrantz (e.g., 1985, 1989) has been particularly eloquent in arguing for the importance of studying selective impairments, or more specifically, dissociation. The idea is to determine which deficits are obligatory following a lesion, and which simply co-occur. For example, temporal lobe damage can impair both memory and vision. Are these defects part of the same system? Not if we can find a case where only one occurs: "If a temporal lobe memory loss can occur in the absence of a visual field defect, then the two need have nothing to do with each other except that they are cerebral roommates, or worse, components in a psychological broth." (Weiskrantz 1989, p. 105)

Any given task, no matter how simple, has a variety of aspects that may be disrupted and lead to impaired performance. As a start, Weiskrantz argues that the effects of a given lesion need to be assessed across a range of behavioral tasks. What is lost and what is preserved, i.e., selective impairment, can then guide our inferences about the role of the lesioned structure. But any lesion may also have a multiplicity of behavioral consequences. Furthermore, different behavioral tasks may have different sensitivities, that is, they differ not only in terms of what they measure, but they also vary along some unspecifiable scale of difficulty. To circumvent these problems, Weiskrantz proposes looking for double dissociations: "If a task is affected by one treatment (e.g., lesion), is unaffected by a second treatment, and if that second treatment does affect some further task that is unaffected by the first treatment . . . we now have reasonable grounds for suggesting that the two tasks in question can be assigned to different and potentially independent pathways. . . ." (1989, p. 105) The logic of double dissociations is applicable even when impairments are relative rather than absolute.

Finally, the issue of differential memory effects has practical as well as theoretical implications. Baddeley (1990) provides an amusing (albeit disturbing) anecdote about a psychiatrist who was apparently unaware of the possibility of selective impairment in memory. Confronted by a patient whose short-term or working memory was fine, the psychiatrist diagnosed her impairment of longer term memories as a result of hysteria. Presumably, the psychiatrist assumed that both immediate and long-term retention should be disrupted if the problems were due to an organic amnesia. (In chapter 11 we discuss further the perplexing fact that conclusions about the effectiveness of memory processing can depend significantly on which attributes of a memory are tested for retention.)

HUMAN ANTEROGRADE AMNESIA: SOME METHODOLOGICAL CONCERNS

As you might suspect, the anterograde amnesia seen in nearly all clinical patients with brain damage seldom represents an instance of pure memory failure. Whatever injury led to impaired memory may have resulted in other types of cognitive deficits as well. Impairments of reasoning, language, perception, and general planning can all contribute to the performance deficits referred to as amnesia. And just as was the case with animal research, inadequate motivation can reduce performance, quite apart from memory failures. A disinterested amnesic patient is unlikely to show stellar performance on even modestly demanding memory tasks.

In addition to the methodological issue that nonassociative (or non-memorial) factors can impair performance on a retention test (and thus distort an assessment of memory), interpretation of human anterograde amnesia is often complicated by other issues. Consider the following general questions. Does chronic brain damage produce anterograde amnesia through the same mechanisms as does transient insult? That is, is the anterograde memory loss resulting from tissue destruction, Korsakoff's disease, surgery, and missile wounds based on the same processes as that resulting from more transient insult, such as a concussive blow and closed head injury? Perhaps even more obvious, does the amnesia depend upon what areas of the brain are afflicted? Can we classify the characteristics of amnesia on the basis of the site of brain damage? Although there certainly are articulate proponents of the affirmative view, there are other competent neuropsychologists who have raised serious questions about whether there are qualitative differences in the memory processing of patient with different types of brain injury (e.g., Corkin et al. 1985). Even if location of damage is critical, how precise is the assessment of injury while the patient is still living, i.e., in vivo? While computed tomographic and positron emission tomographic scans, which provide computerized images of one's brain without opening the skull, have greatly enhanced information on the location of injury in patients, a definitive assessment of damage still often depends on an autopsy. Even then, does the behavioral effect result from destruction of an area or of the fibers and pathways from other areas that pass through the area of damage? Furthermore, the disruption of function resulting from identical lesions can vary depending upon whether the damage occurred suddenly or developed slowly, as in tumor growth, i.e., the momentum of lesion effect (e.g., Finger & Stein 1982). Because of this momentum of lesion effect, some individuals with slow growing tumors may suffer substantial brain damage before dysfunctions become apparent, while the impact of a stroke to a much smaller region of the same area may be immediately noticeable.

Quite apart from this sample of neurobiological questions, there are numerous equally important behavioral considerations in trying to extract principles of memory from human amnesic patients. Typically, careful assessment of premorbid abilities is lacking (since the injury was not planned, of course). So the preinjury versus postinjury evaluation of behavior that can be obtained in animal studies is not available. While comparison can certainly be made implicitly with respect to data from normal subjects, this can yield only relatively gross conclusions. Unlike the random assignment of subjects to conditions in an experiment, which in the long run results in groups relatively comparable with respect to all variables, accidents of nature provide no such methodological nicety.

Let us consider the problem from a slightly different perspective. Is the motorcyclist who roars down the mountain road at 80 mph without a helmet a little different from most of us? And if she sustains a brain injury and memory problems after skidding into a tree, what are the implications of this "difference" for drawing general conclusions? Or, to return to H.M. for a moment, it is easy to forget that as a victim of severe epilepsy, his brain functions could hardly be considered normal or typical. Could the inferences about memory drawn from H.M. be biased? We certainly have to recognize such a possibility in clinical cases, although in this instance substantial converging evidence from other sources makes serious bias unlikely as a problem. Obtaining convergent findings from different patients, different paradigms, and so forth is one way out of the dilemma.

These comments are not meant to denigrate the many important contributions of case studies. Indeed, with the all-too-plentiful and increasingly abundant supply of brain-damaged victims from biological failures, accidents, wars, and other assorted sources, it would be wasteful to ignore the information potentially available. However, we wish to emphasize that there is still plenty of need for thoughtfully designed animal research using classic experimental methodology, and we consider one such example in the following section.

MISHKIN'S NEUROBIOLOGICAL MODEL

An animal model that captures some of the features of global amnesia that we have seen in humans has been described by Mishkin and his colleagues at the National Institute of Mental Health (e.g., Mishkin & Appenzeller 1987; Mishkin et al. 1984). Their extensive investigations with monkeys have led to a description of the types of damage that may be responsible for profound memory impairment along with sparing of other memory-related functions. As is often the case, these studies originated with a slightly different aim—in this case, to understand the neural mechanisms of visual perception and learning. Attempts to disentangle various factors contributing to disruption of visual processes led to a detailed examination of learning and memory mechanisms.

Bilateral removal of a portion of the limbic system, the amygdala and the hippocampus, proved to severely impair retention for an object seen only a few seconds before. To illustrate this, monkeys were trained in a nonmatching-to-sample task (see chapter 5). In the learning phase, one object is presented over a well containing a food reward, and the subject is rewarded for choosing (displacing) the item. In the test phase, which can be immediate or delayed, the original and a new object are presented together and the monkey is now rewarded for selecting the new stimulus. This nonmatching-to-sample can be viewed as a recognition test; recognition of a previously seen stimulus provides the basis for rejecting it. An important aspect of the paradigm in this case is that new stimuli are used on each trial. This permits an assessment of memory for the stimulus independent of interference caused by previous experience with a stimulus. Monkeys with damage to the amygdala and hippocampus perform normally with an immediate test, indicating that perceptual mechanisms are intact. Relative to intact control subjects, however, they show a rapid loss of memory as the delay intervals are increased to several seconds. While this anterograde amnesia may not be perfectly parallel to that in humans, for whom short-term retention is often unaffected, it shares a critical conceptual similarity: information that is available immediately after an episode is not retrievable at a later time.

In contrast with the impairment on the delayed nonmatching-to-sample task seen in these limbic-damaged monkeys, learning of a two-choice discrimination task proceeds at pretty much the same rate as in normal animals. In the discrimination task subjects are rewarded for choosing one of two objects simultaneously displayed, and they are given a number of trials with the same items. The ability of amnesic monkeys to learn to choose the previously rewarded stimulus is not based on a lingering trace between closely spaced presentations of the object; their performance is equally proficient when trials are spaced 24 hours apart. Moreover, the discrimination task may consist of a list of 20 different pairs of objects that are to be learned during daily presentations.

Mishkin et al. (1984) have noted that this dissociation of memory abilities presents an even more striking paradox than that seen in humans, since the stimuli, responses, and general rules remain the same in both tasks in the animal paradigms. To resolve this paradox, they propose two types of memory systems. Recognition memory, which involves the ability to recognize stimuli seen only once (as in the nonmatching-to-sample test), depends on the integrity of the limbic system, in particular the amygdala and hippocampus. A second system mediates the development of stimulus-response associations (as Mishkin characterizes the discrimination learning task), habit memory. This latter process is viewed as similar to the historically important notions of Thorndike and Skinner in which responses are stamped in or strengthened through reinforcement contingencies. Habit memory is viewed as entirely independent of the limbic circuit and as representing a noncognitive control over performance. In contrast, recognition memory presumably is based on a more cognitive representation of the stimulus items. The development of this and other animal models with many of the characteristic features of human anterograde amnesia have proven valuable in elucidating the nature of this disruptive phenomenon (Squire 1992). Although the underlying neuroanatomy remains somewhat indefinite, albeit well proscribed, striking dissociations in the effects of brain damage on the two classes of memory problems identified by Mishkin and colleagues frequently have been reported (e.g., Bachevalier 1991; Gaffan & Murray 1992). We consider later whether this implies separate memory systems (see chapter 12).

FORGETTING IN EVERYDAY LIFE

For the reader, this discussion of the memory problems in amnesics may have produced something like the proverbial medical student's disease—a sense that many of the symptoms studied are applicable to oneself and that perhaps he/she is also amnesic. Accordingly, it may be useful to recapitulate briefly some of the processes affecting normal memory and its failures.

A wide variety of contextual stimuli are present and potentially noticeable during any event; shifts in some of these cues can impair our ability to retrieve that information. Did you ever see someone who seems familiar but find yourself unable to recall his or her name, only to realize later that the person was someone you knew mainly in a different context? Our inability to recognize the butcher when he or she shows up at a classical music concert would illustrate this type of contextual shift effect on memory.

Although the experimental evidence for mood states and other naturally occurring internal environments as retrieval contexts is limited (see chapter 3), these special states may well have a modulatory influence on retrieval. The notion that a change in emotional state can impair recall was succinctly captured by John Updike in *Rabbit Is Rich*. Harry (Rabbit), relaxing with his buddies following a round of golf, finds himself unable to remember the name of his friend's date, "What the hell was this one's name? She had been introduced around not a half hour ago, but then everybody was still drunk on golf." (Updike 1981, 58)

Interference, whether from information acquired prior to or following the target item, is of course another common source of everyday forgetting (see chapter 4). Once the central focus of students of human memory, proactive and retroactive interference no longer attract the same amount of research attention. Nevertheless, despite limits on what interference theories can account for, there is little doubt that interference contributes significantly to retention loss. An old anecdote illustrating the notion of interference goes something like this: a college president, by professional training a specialist in nomenclature and classification of fish, was said to have complained that every time he learned the name of a new species of fish he forgot the name of a faculty member! (The implicit message here, given the importance of stimulus similarity in interference, was that this president must have viewed his faculty simply as "more fish.") Most of us have had the experience of trying to recall someone's last name ("George _____?") only to find ourselves stymied when we retrieve the name of another George. The latter, we recognize with annoyance, is incorrect but momentarily represents the only name we can generate. Yet both

Georges are available in storage, as indicated when the sought-for name belatedly springs to mind. While interference can occur in other more subtle ways than intrusion errors, having a temporarily dominant response inhibit or interfere with retrieval of another response is a phenomenon with a familiar ring, sometimes labeled *output interference* (see Roediger 1974).

Some of our forgetting is attributable to lack of encoding, as can happen when we carry out some routine task or do one thing while attending to something else. Thus, if I quickly put down my sunglasses somewhere because the exciting tennis on TV caught my eye upon entering the house, it is not surprising that I end up wondering where my sunglasses went. There are innumerable simple responses (e.g., setting down one's keys) that can be performed without paying much, if any, attention to our own behavior. Unfortunately, the corresponding failure to encode this simple piece of information makes it unlikely that the item will be retrieved by searching our memory—a physical search is more likely to be necessary. This simple principle underlies much of what we often refer to as absent-minded behavior with its attendant and exasperating consequences. Active processing of the details of our own actions is a good rule if we hope to remember where we have placed something.

While attentional and encoding activities are important, they are not always sufficient. At one time or another, most of us have had difficulty in locating things that we carefully (even thoughtfully) stored in special places for later use. Winograd and Solloway (1986) have provided an insightful analysis of this type of memory failure. They note that people often choose unlikely places for items so others will not easily find them (e.g., hiding one's passport or extra car keys). These special places presumably have high memorability or distinctiveness at the time of storage, and people fully expect to recall the location. To examine this memory phenomenon, Winograd and Solloway had college subjects imagine hiding various objects in specified locations in their home. Based on ratings provided by another group of subjects, the locations varied in terms of likelihood of their use for storing the objects in ordinary life. Subjects were then asked to rate how memorable they believed that object was in that particular location. An unexpected recall test for each item was given a few minutes later. The central and intriguing finding was that for any given level of memorability, items in low likelihood places (rated independently by other subjects) were recalled more poorly regardless of their rated memorability. In the extreme case, although subjects reported being highly confident of their ability to remember all object locations, they were in fact still more than twice as likely to forget the location of items in unlikely than in likely places.

Winograd and Solloway suggested that given some forgetting after an interval of time, subjects must try to generate the correct location. But if the original episode of placing the object is not remembered, then by definition the unlikely places should have a low probability of being produced. To test an implication of this interpretation, a similar experiment was conducted except that a recognition test replaced the cued recall test. Under this condition, in which subjects no longer had to generate the location, the performance associated with uncommon places was as good as with more likely locations.

Why then do people choose distinctive but unusual hiding places when they are unlikely to later remember the location? Winograd and Solloway propose that, in part, this strategy represents a common misunderstanding of the importance of distinctiveness. The distinctiveness that memory theorists have emphasized involves recall or recognition of items rather than the relations between them. However, remembering locations is an associative task—the item is known (e.g., I need my passport; where is it stored?)—and the distinctiveness strategy is not appropriate: "Putting things in unusual places apparently does not lead to integration of object and location, even when one element, or the relation itself, appears to be distinctive." (Winograd & Solloway 1986, 371).

Finally, we need at least to mention the likely role of motivational forces in some instances of forgetting. Freud's (1938) analysis of the psychopathology of everyday life (e.g., slips of the tongue, memory lapses) may not have been based on direct experimentation, but few would quarrel with the power of some of his insights. That competing motivational forces might distort memory processes seems no stranger to us than the more firmly established concept that motivation can affect perception. Specifying the principles and boundary conditions of motivational influences on memory is yet another matter, of course.

There seem to be few among us who have not accidentally forgotten an appointment that we had reluctantly made or agreed to. At least one of the authors has been known to forget an unwanted appointment despite several reminders (which were somehow overlooked). While Freud's motivational concern had more to do with powerful unconscious conflicts than the minor anxiety of, say, a dental appointment, it is possible to view these events as points along a continuum. Some behavioral approaches would interpret repression or related memory lapses in terms of avoidance learning. Thus, thoughts (or impulses) that have become associated with discomfort either directly or indirectly (e.g., dental visits through prior experience, sexually related thoughts through parental admonitions) can serve as conditioned cues in fear. As with other avoidance situations, a response that removes the subject from the cue (or vice versa) is strengthened. In this case, the incipient thought presumably becomes suppressed immediately and the fear-provoking stimulus is avoided by actively not thinking of the topic. Admittedly, there are problems with this interpretation, but it may provide a useful first approximation to certain types of memory lapses.

CHAPTER SUMMARY

This chapter focused on human memory dysfunctions. The characteristics of memory loss in naturally occurring retrograde and anterograde amnesias were described, and some of the important models (storage loss, encoding deficits, retrieval impairment) were presented. In addition, consideration was given to some of the methodological issues and problems associated with interpreting human amnesias. A final section reviewed how principles described previously could affect everyday memory in normal individuals and considered briefly several other sources of forgetting that can contribute to the lapses of retrieval that plague all of us.

▶ 11
Memory and the Principles of Learning

In this chapter we focus on how memory is related to topics covered in conventional courses in learning, usually entitled something like "Principles of Learning" or "Conditioning and Learning." In our view, courses that concentrate on the acquisition phase of the learning process are an absolutely essential part of psychology and biology. In a sense we have devoted our professional lives to these topics: we earn our living by teaching them and conducting experiments to understand them better. So maybe we put our livelihood in jeopardy by asserting that these topics cannot be covered thoroughly without considering material like that presented here under the heading, "memory."

The preceding chapters in this book convey this major message: expression of what has been learned is extremely variable, albeit lawful and regular. This message in turn has a major implication for the study of learning, which is obvious yet profound: we cannot predict learned behavior solely on the basis of the circumstances of learning. In order to know whether learned behavior will be or could be expressed and which aspect of behavior will occur, we need to know also the relationship between how the learning occurred and the general circumstances encountered by the learner prior to and since the learning. Further, we especially need to know the relationship between the conditions at the time of learning and those present when expression is desired.

For psychology it is the expression of behavior that is of interest. However fascinating might be certain operations of the central nervous system and the cognitive processes that arise from them, if they cannot be shown to affect immediate or subsequent behavior, they are irrelevant to psychology. Psychology has an ultimate concern and it is behavior.

The expression of behavior can be controlled by many things. Factors like motivation and simple motoric capability are not considered here because they are controlled experimentally in tests of learning and memory. Changes in behavioral expression that are of interest are those relatively permanent changes linked to associative experience—learning and its residue, memory.

General distinctions between learning and memory were discussed in chapter 1. We now consider the relationship between learning and memory in a more substantive sense: the concrete manner in which the major phenomena of learning—those effects for which learning theories are developed—depend on the process of memory. We also shall consider how the understanding of learning phenomena is aided by concepts derived from the study of memory. We will illustrate how the occurrence and nature of major effects of learning depend on variables usually considered to be in the domain of memory, such as length of the retention interval.

As the central content of the study of learning, we have effects that cannot be fully described without reference to parameters that control memory and cannot be understood without considering separable aspects of the memory process, particularly postacquisition processes. To say this another way, concepts from the study of memory are now needed to consider major puzzles—complexities, contradictions, anomalies—that have arisen at the core of knowledge about the learning process.

One of these concepts is the multidimensional nature of the memory that results from the process of learning and may be said to serve as a representation of what is learned. However, a memory is not in any literal sense a copy of a learned episode. At the neurophysiological level the representation is no more than the product of the brain's activities during learning of the episode; even this representation will depend on the animal's prior experience and perception for what actually is encoded.

With this in mind, this chapter considers three general topics. The first is evidence that an important part of what is acquired in learning is a memory representation, the second is how conventional principles of learning depend on the memory process, and the third is the temptation to conclude that we must in fact deal with many different memory processes or a variety of memory systems.

DOES LEARNING ESTABLISH A MEMORY (REPRESENTATION)?

The idea of a memory representation is controversial. But it also has practical significance for directing the questions we ask in experiments and hence for the understanding of basic learning, so we must discuss it.

It is worthwhile first to consider what we are talking about when we refer to basic learning. The fundamental features of learning are common to all animals and humans. Although there is good reason to consider nonassociative learning, which includes the changes in response to an individual stimulus as a consequence of having experienced it, it is associative learning that is most widely studied and probably most widely implemented. Associative learning, you will recall, is analyzed in terms of instrumental (or operant) conditioning or Pavlovian (or classical) conditioning. Instrumental conditioning refers to the learned changes in responding that occur when that responding has some special consequence, a reward or punishment. Pavlovian conditioning refers to learning that occurs when one event signals another regardless of any responding that takes place by the animal. It has been described as "... the learning that results from exposure to relations among events in the environment" (Rescorla 1988, 152) and is "... a primary means by which the organism represents the structure of its world" (Rescorla 1988, 152).

A good deal of debate about these matters still exists. You may already have been exposed to arguments whether Pavlovian or classical is the better adjective or whether operant or instrumental is better, or whether instrumental and Pavlovian conditioning involve the same underlying processes. Our view is that the two cases of associative learning have few, if any, significant differences; learning generally is the fundamental acquisition of relationships among events or objects. There is now a fair amount of agreement also about other fundamental features of basic learning, and they are worth mentioning because some misunderstanding about them still exists.

We begin with the role of contiguity. The mere contiguous occurrence of two events that are detected, perceived, and recognizable does not guarantee that the relationship between them will be learned, even for an alert, motivated animal. For instance, learning of a relationship between a light and food by a hungry rat may not be observed if a tone also occurs at the same time as the light, especially if that tone was previously paired with food. In this case, contiguity of stimulus presentation is not sufficient to produce learning. Learning, moreover, can occur when events are not contiguous. For instance, learning of the relationship between a particular taste and illness occurs for many animals even when the taste precedes the illness by hours. So, contiguity is generally deemed neither sufficient nor necessary for learning. The jury is still out on this matter, however, for reasons associated with the memory process. As to the above example of compound (light and tone) conditioning conventionally used to argue that contiguity is not sufficient for learning, there are now indications that the effect reflects differential expression of what was learned rather than differential acquisition (see sections on overshadowing and blocking effects, this chapter). For the example suggesting that contiguity is not necessary, there remains the possibility that the memorial representations of the taste and illness are to some degree contiguous even though experimental presentation of the events themselves are not.

Another general point is what basic learning actually accomplishes. There is a widespread misconception about Pavlovian conditioning, held even by some psychologists and biologists, that Pavlovian conditioning applies only to the training of a reflex that is activated automatically when a conditioned stimulus is presented. This misconception, based on general nonscientific literature, folklore, or an incomplete reading of Pavlov, views basic learning as quite mechanical and mindless: that when a bell (conditioned stimulus) is paired with food (unconditioned stimulus), the salivation (unconditioned response) to the food has its control taken over by the bell and it becomes a conditioned response that is quite reflexive in the sense that whenever that bell occurs the salivation must also occur. This is very wrong.

Most conditioning studied during the past 30 years is not about reflexes in the sense of involving inevitable and uncontrollable responses to stimuli. Pavlov and his students were well aware that even in the case of conditioned salivation, there might be no evidence of conditioning to a bell in one context but quite clear conditioning in another. Even more pertinent is the misconception of substitution of the conditioned response for the unconditioned response. These two responses are always differentiable and usually quite distinct. For instance, a rat responds to a mild footshock by jumping and scurrying around, but to a tone that had been paired with footshock it responds by crouching and being very still. Quite unlike a mechanical view, the precise behavior that is actually learned and expressed depends on a number of features, including the nature of the conditioned stimulus. For instance, the unconditioned response of a hungry rat to food is to eat it; the response to a tone that had predicted that food is to crouch and move its upper body from side to side. To a light that had predicted the same food the response learned is to rear, stand on its hind legs, and look around.

The misconceived view of conditioning as a process through which reflexes (unconditioned responses) become involuntarily controlled by a conditioned stimulus includes the idea that conditioning is a slow, gradual, and ultimately permanent process. In fact, conditioning can take place almost immediately, within a second or two, among even the simplest or most immature animals. With the possible exception of the conditioning of a type of blink of the eye in a rabbit (by closing the nictitating membrane over its retracted eyeball), most of the conditioning studied today is complete within only a few pairings and often only one, and in many cases the entire procedure may require only a few minutes or even seconds. However slowly or rapidly it occurs, though, conditioning is not permanent and is subject to forgetting, as we have seen throughout this book.

Finally, Pavlovian conditioning probably never involves a single association between, say, a conditioned stimulus and a conditioned response. The consequence of conditioning is instead a number of associations between the context and the unconditioned stimulus, for example, or the context and the conditioned stimulus. These multiple associations might involve many separable aspects of context as well as many separable aspects of the unconditioned or conditioned stimuli themselves. This notion that a learning episode is represented multidimensionally, as an ordered array of memory attributes representing separable events of the episode, is consistent with the theoretical orientation of this book as well as an established fact of Pavlovian conditioning.

These generalizations reflect the contemporary view of the evidence, as summarized by Rescorla (1988) and others (e.g., Flaherty 1985; Gordon 1989; Domjan 1993; Klein 1987). The gist of the message is that Pavlovian conditioning and other basic forms of learning are the means through which animals and people determine the relationships that exist within their environment and between their behavior and the events in their environment. Our point is that how this information is used, and indeed whether it is used, depends upon the memory process.

Representations, Memories, and Learning

It is difficult to discuss contemporary investigations of learning without reference to some sort of mental representation held by the animal for environmental events, such as the animal's memory for a tone or for the relationship between a tone and food. It is not impossible to do so, however, and some first-rate scientists studying learning believe it is a distortion to think in terms of the animal's representations or memories. We take the view that reference to a memory can at least provide a useful metaphor for designing experiments that will allow us to understand the consequences of learning. We also take this opportunity for a few brief comments about our reasons for referring to memories in this way.

The rationale is in part due to the phenomenon of implicit reactivation (see chapter 9). A relatively old memory can become vulnerable to modification if it is reactivated implicitly by a prior cuing treatment (implicitly, because the memory need not be fully expressed in behavior). For instance, drugs or environmental events that ordinarily affect retention—disrupt or enhance it—only if given very soon after learning, can be effective even long after learning if they are preceded by a prior cuing treatment. Amnesia for old memory (see chapters 8 and 9), would be a case in point. It is difficult to consider such results without reference to a memory (representation) that is activated by the prior cuing treatment.

Reference to memory (representation) is also difficult to avoid in considerations of encoding. There is now overwhelming evidence that animals and people act on stimuli in accord with their own past experiences as well as contemporary environmental and physiological influences. What is learned about a particular stimulus may differ from subject to subject or from circumstance to circumstance, and it is often quite different than what is intended by the experimenter. In discussing the ontogeny of memory, for instance, we alluded to evidence in which, unlike adults, infants might encode a tone as an intense event, a novel event, or an unpleasant event rather than as an auditory event—as something disruptive or different rather than something they heard.

There is a huge body of literature on stimulus selection confirming differential use, and hence representation in at least some sense, of selected attributes of a stimulus from among the many that could be identified (e.g., Lawrence 1963; Underwood, Ham & Ekstrand 1962). This research was begun over 30 years ago, many years after initial attempts by scientists to test experimentally the memory representations of animals. Among the first was Hunter (1913), whose work we discussed in chapter 5. Hunter's experiments, using the delayed response technique, established that even nonverbal organisms could learn and remember the location of a previously baited goal in the absence of differential (discriminative) cues. This finding, when coupled with appropriate control manipulations to rule out mediation by motor (interoceptive) cues, suggested that some type of representation of events persisted after the removal of the physical signaling stimuli. The Zeitgeist in Hunter's era was not receptive to interpretations involving internal representations that could not be observed directly, so this conceptualization remained largely dormant for several decades. The introduction of delayed matching-to-sample techniques helped rekindle interest in memory representations in animals. Particular advances have been made, also, in the analytic realm of Pavlovian conditioning, discussed next.

Representation of the Unconditioned Stimulus or Reinforcer
Although focused on Pavlovian conditioning and more specifically on the associative relationship between a signal (conditioned stimulus [CS]) and the outcome (unconditioned stimulus [US]) that the signal predicts, experiments conducted by Robert Rescorla have turned out to have an important bearing on animal memory. He asked whether postconditioning modifications of the perceived value of the US could alter the strength of previous learning about the CS-US relationship. Such an outcome would hardly be expected if Pavlovian conditioning represents only an association between the CS and the response elicited by the US, because altering the US value after conditioning is completed should have little impact on that stimulus-response association. On the other hand, the conditioned response might be modified if the critical connection is between the CS and some central representation of the US that determines the response. According to this interpretation of Pavlovian conditioning, post-training manipulations designed to alter the US, and thus the representation later evoked by the CS, should produce a change in the responses that had been conditioned.

A light was paired with a very loud horn, to induce conditioned suppression of behavior whenever the light appeared (Rescorla 1973). For some rats, the horn was then repeatedly presented by itself, following the pairings, in order to devalue it as a US. (An independent test indicated that subjects actually habituated to the horn during these repeated exposures.) Although the CS was never presented during these US devaluation exposures, on a subsequent test these animals showed less conditioned suppression to the CS than control animals. Presumably, the US exposures reduced its functional severity; the weaker suppression corresponded to the animals' new, deflated representation of the predicted event.

A subsequent study (Rescorla 1974) examined the converse change in the representation of the US—an increase in value. Following conditioned suppression training in which a tone was paired with a shock of moderate intensity, rats received a series of unsignalled shocks. For two groups the shocks were more intense than during conditioning, a treatment intended to inflate the perceived value of shock. A third group was administered the same level of shocks used in conditioning, and a fourth received no shocks. Both groups in the inflation conditions showed greater suppression than either the group given the same level shock as acquisition or a group without any interpolated shocks. These findings are congruent with the view that subjects form a representation of what the CS is associated with and that information about the US is stored independently of its associations with other events.

The studies on deflation and inflation of the US set the stage for a number of subsequent investigations on postconditioning modulation of the hedonic value of the US or reinforcer. In many cases the US was revalued by pairing it with another stimulus having different hedonic significance. Following conditioning, for instance, food as a US might be paired with events that induce illness, such as the toxin lithium chloride (LiCl) or a motion sickness-inducing rotation, to reduce the value of the animal's representation of the food. The general strategy has now been extended to explore representations in instrumental as well as Pavlovian conditioning (e.g., Adams 1980; Adams & Dickinson 1981).

A demonstration of the effects of devaluing a reinforcer in an instrumental task is seen in studies by Colwill and Rescorla (1985, 1990). Rats learned to make two different instrumental responses; one response permitted the rat to obtain one kind of food (Noyes pellets), while the other led to a different food (sucrose pellets). After training was completed, half the subjects were fed Noyes pellets and made ill with LiCl; the other half were made ill after eating the sucrose pellets. The important outcome was that the subsequent depression in operant responding was selective—rats poisoned in connection with Noyes pellets made very few of the responses that had produced the Noyes pellets, but continued to make the response reinforced by sucrose; the opposite was true for the sucrose-poisoning condition. Moreover, the testing was conducted in extinction, so changes in response levels could not have been mediated by sensory feedback from the delivery of pellets. It would appear instead that the rats not only had acquired instrumental responses, but also had acquired a rather specific representation of the reinforcer associated with each class of response. When the value of the reinforcing stimulus was later deflated, so too was the animal's willingness to perform the responses leading to that reinforcer.

Evidence for representation of stimuli also can be seen in studies in which the magnitude of reward is drastically increased or decreased. These contrast effects have long been viewed as implying an expectancy about stimulus values mediated by the animal's representation in memory of the previous reward, and their influence on behavior depends on factors associated with memory, such as proactive and retroactive interference (Flaherty 1982; Spear 1967).

Similar inferences about an animal's representation of a reward may be made from the role of distinctive attributes of reinforcers (USs) as mediators in discrimination learning. Trapold (1970) compared rate of discrimination learning when reinforcer expectancies associated with each alternative were distinctively different or not. Subjects learned to press the left lever for reinforcement during one signal (e.g., tone) and the right lever when another signal (clicker) was presented. For the experimental group, one of two distinctive reinforcers, sucrose solution or grain-based food, was uniquely associated with each lever. Presses on the left lever when the tone came on produced a few drops of the sucrose solution; responses on the right lever (to the clicker) resulted in food pellets. Control subjects also received reinforcement for correct choices, but the reinforcing stimuli were intermixed so that no specific expectancy was established with respect to responding on the left or right lever. Learning of the discrimination was more rapid when a specific reinforcer was associated with each of the stimulus-response relationships than when the reinforcers were varied.

In another experiment Pavlovian conditioning preceded instrumental learning of a discrimination between signals A and B (Trapold 1970). During the Pavlovian conditioning, signal A predicted one reinforcer (e.g., sucrose) and signal B predicted the other reinforcer (e.g., food pellets; the signals and reinforcers were, of course, counterbalanced across conditions.) The animal was conditioned to expect different outcomes for A and B. The question of interest was whether learning was faster in a task requiring A versus B discrimination when the previously established stimulus-reinforcer relationship was maintained (e.g., choice of A produces sucrose) than when it was changed (e.g., choice of A produces food pellet). A changed relationship would mean that in the presence of signal A, a response was reinforced with food rather than sucrose and vice versa. Since acquisition of the discrimination was more rapid with the consistent relationship, Trapold suggested that the rats had developed an expectancy (representation) of the specific quality of a particular reinforcer. Presumably, by providing additional distinctive cues in the consistent arrangement, the representation of the reinforcers helped the rats learn which response to make when the two different signals were presented as discriminative stimuli. Although this evidence for stimulus representations is rather indirect, the general conclusions have been confirmed in a number of transfer designs (Linwick et al. 1988).

Although the above studies focused on the conditioning process rather than on retention, their implication that organisms form representations of the associated events is clearly relevant to memory research. The research suggests that conditioning and memory processes may interplay in a way that goes beyond operational distinctions, in terms of the animal's memory representation for exhibiting conditioned behaviors.

Representation of the CS
Finally, some striking experiments by Peter Holland and his colleagues (e.g., Holland 1983) emphasize the action of memory-as-representation in studies of basic Pavlovian conditioning with the rat. These experiments illustrate how one event can come to represent another with which it has been associated, with the consequence that a memory involving that first event can be changed directly without recurrence of the first event. It is as if what is being manipulated is the animal's memory (representation) of specific events.

For instance, a tone was paired with a particular flavor of food. Conditioning continued until the tone reliably elicited from the rat the characteristic response to a tone in anticipation of the food—crouching and swaying the upper body near the food cup. The flavor of that food was then paired with a toxin that induces illness, LiCl, so that the flavor itself subsequently was rejected by the rat and expressions of disgust were emitted (rats regularly elicit specifiable facial expressions and other disgust responses to a food that has been paired with an illness). The interesting point is that the tone itself—which was never directly paired with illness—now elicited the behavioral expressions of disgust. Also, the tone no longer elicited responses indicating the anticipation and acceptance of the food.

At the same time, however, a different tone to which the rat had learned to anticipate a different flavor continued to elicit responses that were anticipatory to food, with no disgust reactions. This showed that it was not merely the general experience of illness that produced the disgust reactions to the first tone. Moreover, direct pairing of a tone and illness did not itself yield disgust responses to the tone, in accord with cue-consequence specificity (mentioned in chapter 7).

A familiar example of cue-consequence specificity is that whereas rats readily condition to tones paired with food or footshock, they do not condition to tones paired instead with illness. Food, of course, is readily conditioned by pairing with illness. Holland (1990) found, however, that a tone that had been paired with food would readily condition to illness, as if the tone was now represented in part as a food (incidentally, the food that had been paired with the tone also became aversive in this case).

In other experiments with the same sort of conditioning procedure—pairing a tone with a particular flavor, then pairing the flavor with LiCl—the tone was presented alone to extinguish the tone-food associations. As a consequence the association between food and LiCl tended to extinguish, i.e., the aversion to the food also decreased (Holland & Forbes 1982).

Further Evidence and Comment

It is difficult to explain such results without reference to the animal's internal representation (memory) for specific stimuli. Reference to an animal's memory or representation of a learned episode makes it easier to understand other instances of learning and memory in animals as well. This is so whenever learning of a particular episode is manifested by behaviors other than those that had actually occurred in the original episode or when the behavior is to occur in a quite different situation than the original episode. A simple example is provided by the conditioned emotional response paradigm used commonly to study conditioning in animals. If a tone that was once paired with mild footshock is presented when an animal is drinking, eating, or just generally moving about, such behaviors will dramatically decrease. Yet this same tone-footshock learning can also be expressed by a tone-induced increase in the vigor of a previously learned avoidance response or in startle to a novel sound. Obviously the tone in this case is not conditioned directly to a particular response; it is instead associated with the animal's representation of the US (footshock).

Reference to a memory or representation also seems needed to discuss the alleviation of forgetting that can be produced by a prior cuing treatment, when the treatment is not otherwise related to the behavior used to indicate learning. We mentioned earlier that it is especially difficult to avoid consideration of an animal's representation of an event when considering the effects of implicit reactivation (discussed in chapter 9). An example is the dramatic decrease in retention of a learned episode by presenting an amnestic treatment or the increase in retention by presenting a hypermnestic treatment, long after learning, if and only if the treatments are preceded by a cue to remind the animal about the original episode. Given the control procedures used and the nature of the prior cuing treatments, there is no way that these dramatic changes in the appearance of an acquired behavior can be due to new learning that somehow resulted from the prior cuing treatment. In this situation we are almost forced into considering that the animal's representation or memory of the episode is made active by the prior cuing treatment and that whenever memories are active they become susceptible to change.

The nature of a representation or memory also can readily be changed without retraining of the animal, in circumstances beyond those mentioned above (a particularly thorough review of studies like those mentioned above was written by Delamater and LoLordo 1991) For instance, a rat that has learned active avoidance in context A ordinarily will not exhibit much active avoidance in context B, but if a prior cuing treatment for the active avoidance memory is presented in context B—i.e., if the memory for avoidance learning is made active in context B for only a short time—the active avoidance subsequently is readily exhibited in context B (Gordon 1983). It is as if the memory for avoidance behavior has been changed to allow the incorporation of context B, as well as that of context A, as part of that episode being represented.

What is the nature of the representation the animal uses? It is not necessary that the representation be a copy of the real world or a blueprint-like transformation of the events of the episode. It is in fact unlikely that the representation takes this form. A more reasonable possibility is that what is represented is a sort of recipe for neural action and consequential behavior (Catania 1987; Holland 1990). What is stored in memory may be procedures for particular temporal and spatial neural patterns and neurochemical action. What is stored is a means for reproducing or simulating the neurological response to the original event rather than the simulation itself, and reproduction will occur contingent upon other neural events that may be tied to more general circumstances of a contextual nature.

Summary

The purpose of this section was to consider what basic learning accomplishes. We established that even classical, Pavlovian conditioning does not merely involve the automatic activation of a reflex nor a mere substitution of the conditioned stimulus for the unconditioned stimulus, nor substitution of the conditioned response for the unconditioned response. Simple conditioning is not always a slow, gradual and ultimately permanent process—it usually is not—and for vertebrates like rats, monkeys, or people, it probably never involves the formation of a single association between a conditioned stimulus and a conditioned response. Instead, what basic conditioning accomplishes is a representation of how one's environment is structured.

The evidence that what is acquired in basic learning is a representation (a memory) was discussed briefly, including the phenomena of revaluation, implicit reactivation, and stimulus selection. Within the realm of basic Pavlovian conditioning we considered experiments by Rescorla, Holland, and others to illustrate how difficult it is to consider basic learning without reference to a memory that is acquired with such learning but is modifiable through postlearning experience.

SHOULD THEORIES OF LEARNING BE THEORIES OF MEMORY?: CIRCUMSTANCES OF REMEMBERING (MEMORY RETRIEVAL AND EXPRESSION) CAN MASK OR REVEAL LEARNING

The issue we need to discuss is closely related to a simple question that might occur to anyone about their own memory processing: what is more important, the circumstances under which I learn originally or those present when I need to remember what I learn? For convenience we refer to the first factor as memory storage or acquisition and the second as memory retrieval or expression. This is certainly not the only way to view the memory process, it may not be the best, and, as we shall discuss shortly, the processes that occur during memory storage and retrieval are probably very similar. This view has nevertheless provided a useful characterization for organizing the facts throughout this book and elsewhere.

Most books on learning and probably most experiments testing learning have taken the view that the more important events occur during memory storage. This has helped to make theories simple and economical. And it was perfectly reasonable when, as we mentioned earlier, there was little indication that what happened after memory storage was important for memory. Now that we know what a substantial impact on memory later events can have, it is appropriate to reconsider the emphasis on memory storage that has been given by theory.

An extreme, yet plausible view is this: whatever events an animal encounters and detects are registered relatively permanently in the brain, so memory storage of detected events always occurs and so might later remembering, depending on how the memories stored are organized and circumstances at the time remembering is required (cf. Johnson 1983, 1989). We need not adopt such a view, though, to recognize the significance of postacquisition events for the memory process. A general consideration of the similarity between the processes of memory storage and memory retrieval also can be persuasive.

New learning for storage in memory must be built on what one already knows; this old idea about teaching is nearly a truism. A child engaged in her first basic arithmetic, how to add and subtract, makes use of words she has learned before, the concept of numbers, counting, and so forth. When you learn to operate a new computer you make use of what you have learned from other computers, from typing, and from prior learning about how to follow rules; when you learn French you use what you have already learned about English syntax and general linguistic structure.

These elementary points emphasize that all learning involves the use of previously acquired memories. The process of acquisition of a new memory includes retrieval of memories of previous knowledge, to which is added the new information encountered in the relationships that are to be learned. The process of remembering is basically the same. Previously acquired information is retrieved and, as such, becomes subject to modification by new relationships encountered at that time (see chapter 8 on memory modulation).

These intuitive similarities between the processes of memory acquisition and memory retrieval are buttressed by the ideas of many scientists and some empirical evidence, which we briefly review next. The similarity between these processes is emphasized at this point because it helps us appreciate how one might readily confuse the consequences of postacquisition events, including memory retrieval, with the consequences of events associated with acquisition (we may refer to acquisition, learning, or memory storage interchangeably).

The Similarity between Memory Retrieval (Remembering) and Memory Acquisition (Learning)

Although truly general principles of learning are elusive, they seem attainable, but only with qualifying statements about the entire process of memory. These qualifiers would deal primarily with postacquisition processes. For this topic we consider two facts that have been particularly difficult to deal with from the conventional perspective of the study of learning: (1) fundamental learning phenomena may change in strength, disappear, or even be reversed by variables associated with the processes of memory that follow acquisition (induced expression); and (2) major effects of learning observed in some measures of learning frequently do not exist or are quite different with other measures (selective expression). We consider induced and selective expression in detail after a brief review of the similarity between memory acquisition and retrieval.

Indication of Similarity between Memory Acquisition and Retrieval

The similarity between characteristics of a recently acquired memory and one acquired long ago but recently reactivated was discussed in Chapter 9. This similarity supports the idea that the processes underlying initial storage and subsequent retrieval are similar. For instance, both recently acquired and recently reactivated memories are initially susceptible to the disruptive effects of an amnestic agent such as electroconvulsive shock (Misanin, Miller & Lewis 1968) or the facilitative effects of a hypermnestic agent such as strychnine (Gordon & Spear 1973a); with decreasing susceptibility as time passes since storage or retrieval, both interfere proactively with the retention of later learning (Gordon, Frankl & Hamberg 1979; Gordon & Spear 1973b); and both are susceptible to increased forgetting as the interval lengthens between the acquisition or retrieval of a memory and a retention test (e.g., Rovee-Collier & Hayne 1987, J. Miller et al. 1991).

A variety of scientists studying memory with either animals or humans have assumed such a similarity to good advantage. In the view of Jacoby and Craik (1979), "Retrieval is regarded as being quite analogous to a second encoding; just as study processing (in our terms, processing for memory storage) is under the control of task demands, so is retrieval processing." (p. 18) The experiments by Jacoby and Craik showed how subsequent retention is better when encoding during initial memory storage is harder, and similarly, subsequent retention after retrieval of a previously acquired memory is better the more difficult was retrieval.

We discussed earlier how a previously acquired memory can be modified by events that occur at the time of its retrieval (see chapter 8) (e.g., Gordon 1981; Loftus 1979). There is reason to believe that when a new memory is acquired and stored for the first time, related information previously acquired may similarly be retrieved and become accessible for modification. This notion is supported by research on human memory observing that tests for the recall of previous learning may facilitate later recall of that learning, apparently in the same way that initial memory storage facilitates later recall (i.e., retrieval). Several treatments have been found to influence later retention in the same way when they occur during a memory test as when they occur during original acquisition of a memory (e.g., Jacoby & Craik 1979). Although this evidence sometimes is prone to interpretative difficulties that make conclusions difficult, it can stand nevertheless as another strong indication of a similarity between the processes of memory acquisition and memory retrieval (for review, see Spear & Mueller 1984).

Further Illustration of Acquisition and Retrieval Similarity in Animals
Some basic experiments with animals also address this similarity. Trial-to-trial improvement in the learning of a new task is usually thought of as reflecting the development of new associations. The less than maximum performance on early trials presumably reflects incomplete learning. In principle, however, forgetting or retrieval impairment can occur immediately following a trial, so intermediate levels of performance could reflect, in part, a failure to retrieve already acquired information. To investigate this issue, rats were trained in a complex four-choice maze using either escape from footshock or approach to an incentive (sucrose) as reinforcers (Miller 1982). When acquisition was still incomplete, rats received intertrial exposure to the appropriate reinforcer. This prior cuing treatment was given in a different apparatus and independent of any response. Such noncontingent, pretrial exposure to

the reinforcer could not have provided any new information about the solution to the maze. Yet it did enhance performance, as measured by an increased number of correct choices on subsequent trials.

The use of choice behavior to index learning in this study reduced or eliminated the possibility that the prior cuing reinforcer had its effect by increasing motivational level. On the other hand, a measure such as latency to reach the goal would have been subject to this alternative interpretation. The facilitation effect was obtained with prior cuing from either the appetitive or aversive reinforcers, indicating the generality of the finding. Moreover, the effect was specific to the training reinforcer—intertrial footshock failed to enhance acquisition when sucrose was the reinforcer during training trials and vice versa. This helps rule out a number of trivial performance factors as explanations for the improvement.

This study also found that acquisition was facilitated by intertrial reinforcers even when they and the training trials were separated by a long interval (24 hours), at which time active memory processing from the preceding trial presumably had terminated. Finally, a second class of prior cuing treatments—mere nonreinforced exposure to the startbox stimuli between two trials—also was sufficient to facilitate the acquisition of this discrimination (maze) learning.

Similar improvement in acquisition by the interpolation of reinforcing events outside of the learning episode was reported many years ago for human subjects tested with Pavlovian conditioning. Kimble, Mann, and Dufort (1955) paired a tone with a puff of air to the eye, a procedure known to induce a conditioned eyeblink upon presentation of a tone. Kimble et al. found that presenting air puffs to the eye between acquisition trials facilitated acquisition of the conditioned eyeblink. Although such results might be interpreted in terms of a change in value of the unconditioned stimulus (e.g., perhaps giving a large number of air puffs increased the subjects' sensitivity to an air puff), an interpretation consistent with the variety of experiments by Miller (1982) is that the air puff presentations served as a reactivation treatment. That acquisition can be enhanced or otherwise altered by memory of the reinforcer has been established in other types of experiments as well (for a review see Spear 1967).

An illustration of how interspersed nonreinforced exposures to the context of learning can facilitate acquisition (memory storage) in the same way that it can facilitate memory retrieval is found in a series of tests with instrumental learning by Cotton and Jensen over 30 years ago. These experiments were designed to show that in the context of instrumental responding for food reward, presenting an interpolated series of extinction trials (no reward present) had almost the same effect as presenting further conditioning trials (with reward). The test for learning was a further set of trials in which reward was present. These effects were found in a variety of experiments with rats that measured acquisition of rapid running in a straight alley runway (Jensen & Cotton 1960), position discrimination in a T-maze (Cotton & Jensen 1963), or free operant lever pressing (Jensen 1961). This facilitation of acquisition by nonrewarded re-exposure to stimuli associated with the learning episode is similar to the enhanced memory retrieval that has been observed after the same sort of treatment (Gordon 1981).

The similarity between the processes of memory acquisition (storage) and memory retrieval is worth emphasizing, even though the evidence so far is largely indirect. It also provides an introduction to our consideration of whether learning effects conventionally believed to be due to factors associated with memory acquisition might instead be a consequence of postacquisition events and perhaps linked to memory retrieval. Yet it should be clear that although similar, these processes are not identical. Storage and retrieval are likely to incorporate quite different sources of information (e.g., Johnson 1985). Also, if they were identical we might expect that all fast learners would be correspondingly good at remembering, but in fact the correlation between the rates of learning and forgetting is a good deal less than perfect in normal humans (Underwood 1954) and obviously low or nonexistent in certain brain-damaged persons whose retention can bear little relation to their learning (e.g., see chapter 9).

Induced Expression

In this section we consider learning that seems not to have been accomplished, but can in fact be expressed in special circumstances. This is a serious matter for theories of learning or even for the evaluation of individual principles of learning. For these, it is crucial to know precisely what has and what has not been learned.

Within the past 25 years new discoveries about Pavlovian conditioning have forced a reconsideration of the principles of learning. New theories were needed to replace those summarized by the learning theories of the previous 40 years and expressed most articulately by Hull (1943), Spence (1956), Tolman (1932, 1959), Miller and Dollard (1941), and Mowrer (1960). The new theories that became conventional were quite successful in accounting not only for the basic features of Pavlovian conditioning but also for the characteristics of stimulus selection, a particularly important issue (e.g., Mackintosh 1975; Rescorla & Wagner 1972; Pearce & Hall 1980).

The issue of stimulus selection is: how do we decide which particular stimuli, among the large number that might possibly be noticed and learned by an animal in a learning episode, are in fact learned? The new theories that emerged within the past 25 years had to accommodate this increasingly clear observation: neither contiguity (the mere occurrence of two stimuli in close temporal proximity), nor reinforcement (the occurrence of an event that is significant for the animal's biological needs), nor both together are sufficient for the immediate expression of learning. This observation required a sharp break from earlier theories, which had focused on how contiguity and reinforcement determine learning.

What is learned, from among the many stimuli that could be learned, seemed to depend instead on the information value of the stimulus or the extent to which the animal attended to or dedicated associative processing to that stimulus. Although the new theories that evolved did not agree on which of these three processes was the most important, they did agree about which of the new facts about stimulus selection were most important. They also agreed—this is the punch line—that the consequences of stimulus selection were due to processes operating at the stage of memory acquisition.

The most important new effects of stimulus selection were termed overshadowing, blocking, and latent inhibition. There were other related effects that these new conventional theories accommodated as well, in ingenious fashion, such as learned irrelevance, US inflation or US deflation, and superconditioning, but the first three are more basic and especially important for theory. For instance, they seemed to demonstrate quite easily that neither contiguity nor reinforcement is sufficient for learning. The analysis ignored postacquisition factors of the memory process, though. When these factors were considered, a new picture emerged. We turn now to specific examples.

Overshadowing

If stimulus A and stimulus B are presented in compound to serve as the CS paired with a US, do they share equally in controlling conditioned behavior? As Pavlov showed years ago, the answer is often "no." For example, by testing with either stimulus element alone one might observe that A elicits a strong conditioned response, but stimulus B produces little if any response. Termed overshadowing, since one stimulus seems to dominate or overshadow the other in controlling the conditioned response, the effect apparently is not due to generalization decrement based on changing the compound CS, since the differential response strength to the two stimuli would not be expected if one were simply splitting the CS into each of its components (but see Pearce 1987).

Overshadowing occurs most reliably when the two stimuli differ in intensity or some other aspect of saliency. Accordingly, although the details of theoretical explanations vary, overshadowing has been widely assumed to be an associative phenomenon in which the more salient stimulus is more likely attended to or otherwise processed, and so acquires most of the associative strength to the detriment of the CS value of the weaker element.

In recent years, however, several findings have challenged the view that the overshadowed stimulus suffers from an acquisition deficit. Consider the situation in which compound conditioning results in A overshadowing B. If subjects then receive nonreinforced exposures to the A component, later testing of stimulus B reveals expression of more associative strength than before (e.g., Kaufman & Bolles 1981). Learning of B that was not evident after acquisition was revealed by a postacquisition treatment. If the presence of A during compound conditioning had in fact prevented element B from being fully acquired in association with the US, it is very difficult to see how weakening A through nonreinforcement would in any way strengthen B.

We might make more sense of this outcome in terms of a postacquisition memory phenomenon, such as a retrieval failure. For instance, suppose that element B had acquired associative strength during compound training, but the information was not retrieved during testing with B because its retrieval was blocked by a disposition first to retrieve and express information about the more salient A. Repeated exposure to A alone extinguished the association to A, making it less salient relative to B, and perhaps also primed the representation to B.

In support of the latter part of this interpretation is evidence that prior cuing could significantly decrease overshadowing (Kasprow et al. 1982). Rats conditioned to a compound stimulus were later exposed to the overshadowed (B) stimulus outside the test context. Even though the stimulus exposure involved no further training (i.e., no CS-US pairings), these subjects showed greater suppression (less overshadowing) when tested with element B than control subjects. As with other examples of prior cuing effects that we have considered, presentation of a portion of the training complex facilitated later test performance, i.e., a reactivation effect. The reversibility of the deficit associated with the overshadowed stimulus implicates retrieval processes as a contributing factor; treatments that improve retrieval attenuate overshadowing.

In support of the former part of the interpretation—that it is relative dominance of two elements at the time of retrieval that determines overshadowing, not their relative dominance at the time of conditioning—are experiments showing that this relative dominance changes over time. Overshadowing of conditioning to a taste by the presence of an odor was found to decrease with time after conditioning in each of two studies (Kraemer, Lariviere & Spear 1988; Miller, Jagielo & Spear 1990). In these studies rats were made ill by LiCl after they had consumed chocolate milk in the presence of the odor of banana. Either 1 day after conditioning or 21 days later, all rats were tested for their aversion to drinking chocolate milk or to drinking water in the presence of banana odor. Other animals made ill after drinking only chocolate milk (with no odor present) or after drinking water in the presence of banana odor did not differ in retention of their conditioned aversions 1 or 21 days later (no significant forgetting occurred). There was, however, a very interesting change over time in the learning expressed by animals that had been conditioned with the stimulus compound; their aversion to the taste of chocolate milk was weaker 1 day later than that of animals conditioned only with the chocolate milk (thus indicating overshadowing after the short interval), but this aversion became stronger over time so that 21 days later it was equal to that of animals that had been conditioned with only the chocolate milk (thus, no overshadowing at this point).

Yet it is not the case that all overshadowing simply decreases over time. The opposite effect occurred in these experiments in terms of the conditioning expressed to the odor: the aversion to drinking in the presence of banana odor was equally strong 1 day later, whether the animals had been conditioned with the taste-odor compound or with the odor alone (indicating no overshadowing), but 21 days later the odor aversion expressed by animals conditioned with the taste-odor compound was less than that expressed by animals conditioned only with the odor (indicating overshadowing). Whereas the overshadowing of taste by odor had decreased over time, the overshadowing of odor by taste had increased over time, in essentially reciprocal fashion. These results are summarized in Figure 11-1.

Chapter Eleven

A

Retention Interval: 1 Day | Retention Interval: 21 Days

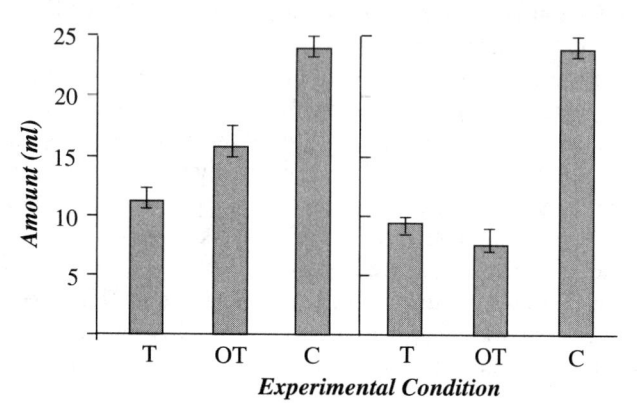

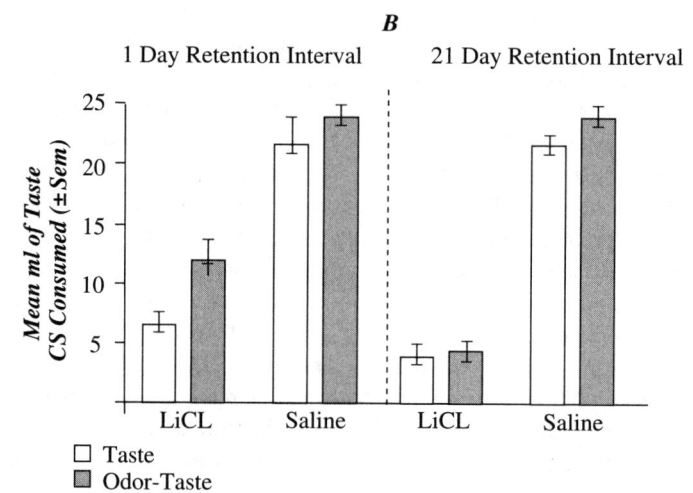

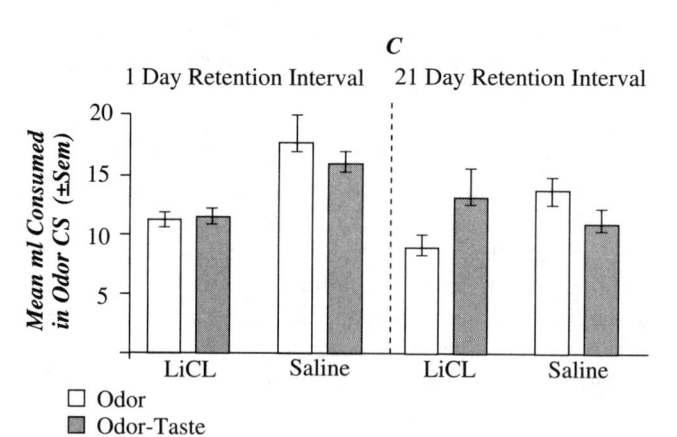

Experimental Condition — Amount (ml); conditions: T, OT, C

B

1 Day Retention Interval | 21 Day Retention Interval

Mean ml of Taste CS Consumed (±Sem); conditions: LiCL, Saline

☐ Taste
■ Odor-Taste

C

1 Day Retention Interval | 21 Day Retention Interval

Mean ml Consumed in Odor CS (±Sem); conditions: LiCL, Saline

☐ Odor
■ Odor-Taste

FIGURE 11-1 A. This figure illustrates that changes in overshadowing occur over time, contrary to the conventional view of overshadowing as a phenomenon attributable to a deficit in acquisition of the less salient stimulus element. This figure suggests instead that overshadowing is attributable to postacquisition processes of memory. The left half illustrates conventional overshadowing observed 1 day after conditioning. Rats in group T (taste) were injected with illness-inducing LiCl after ingesting chocolate milk; rats in group C (control) experienced both the illness and the taste but not paired. The reduction in consumption of chocolate milk by group T relative to C indicates the conditioned aversion. Group OT consumed their chocolate milk during conditioning in the presence of a novel odor; more consumption during the test by this group than group T is termed overshadowing of taste by odor. This overshadowing clearly was not present 21 days later, as shown in the right panel, even though the level of conditioning in group T was undiminished. The consequential increase in the aversion to T exhibited after the longer interval in group OT suggests the dissipation of overshadowing over time. (Adapted from Kraemer et al. 1988.) B. The left panel shows the intake of chocolate milk that had been paired alone or in the context of a novel odor with either LiCl or saline. Overshadowing of the gustatory stimulus by the olfactory stimulus was indicated 1 day later by the greater aversion (less consumption) among animals conditioned with only the chocolate milk relative to those that also had the presence of a novel odor. The right panel shows that this overshadowing no longer occurred 21 days later, due to an increased aversion to the gustatory stimulus among those animals conditioned with an olfactory as well as a gustatory event paired with the LiCl. This experiment replicates and substantiates, with different procedures, the results shown in A. (Adapted from Miller, Jagielo & Spear 1990.) C. This figure illustrates the results of a test of the aversion acquired to a novel odor when it was accompanied or not accompanied by the ingestion of chocolate milk and paired with LiCl or saline. The left panel indicates that 1 day after conditioning, expression of the aversion to the odor was not overshadowed by the concurrent presence of the taste of chocolate milk. Yet after a 21-day retention interval (right panel), overshadowing of this olfactory component by the gustatory component emerged. The results constitute a mirror image of the time-related changes observed in the overshadowing of the gustatory component by the olfactory component. (Adapted from Miller, Jagielo & Spear 1990.)

Similar results subsequently were obtained in terms of conditioning to a compound consisting of a light and a tone relative to conditioning to a tone alone or a light alone (Miller et al. 1993). Testing to the light or tone alone was conducted after a short or long interval following the pairing of each element or of the compound with footshock. The results indicated overshadowing of the light by the tone after a short interval but not after a long interval, while the tone was overshadowed by the light after a long retention interval but not after a short interval.

It is as if when two elements are conditioned in compound, both are learned and compete for dominance after learning is achieved, perhaps at the time of retrieval in a manner similar to output interference (see chapter 4). Although the full explanation remains uncertain, it is clear that overshadowing is not merely a matter of differential attention or learning, but depends significantly on postacquisition memory processes.

Blocking Effect

The blocking effect is a phenomenon akin to overshadowing in that one stimulus of a compound appears to have acquired the preponderance of associative strength. Unlike overshadowing, however, the difference in salience between the two stimuli is produced experimentally rather than assumed prior to the experiment. The blocking comes about because one stimulus (A) is repeatedly paired with the US prior to the addition of stimulus B to form an AB compound. This prior conditioning to one element of the compound impairs (blocks) the ability of the new element, B, to control responding. When B is tested following compound training, there often is no evidence that it was conditioned. In these tests A and B are selected to be of about equal salience to allow good conditioning to each element when only the AB compound is paired with the US, and control conditions also are tested to ensure that this deficit is specifically related to the prior conditioning of element A.

The blocking effect has attracted a great deal of theoretical attention because it illustrates that the contiguity of B and the US is not sufficient for conditioning (even though the same US led to conditioning of A). Like overshadowing, explanations of blocking have centered around mechanisms underlying the presumed attentional or associative impairment of memory storage. The phenomenon seems so obviously to be an acquisition problem that one might be surprised that it could be viewed differently. However, Balaz et al. (1982) challenged the acquisition impairment notion by showing that blocking was alleviated by any one of several traditional prior cuing treatments. In their study, stimulus A was initially paired with the US (shock) for a number of trials, after which stimulus B was introduced to form a compound (AB) and stimulus-shock pairings were continued. As intended, this paradigm resulted in blocking, i.e., little conditioning was seen when subjects were tested with the B element. A very different picture emerged, however, for groups that were exposed, just prior to testing, to either the US (outside the training context), the blocked stimulus (B), or the training environment by itself. All three of these treatments attenuated blocking; in each case, conditioning to B was revealed by manipulations after acquisition was completed. Apparently the associative relationship had already been acquired but not expressed, presumably because of a retrieval deficit. Given the efficacy of the prior cuing treatment used by Balaz et al. in alleviating known instances of memory loss (see chapter 9), it seems likely that a similar principle is involved in alleviating blocking.

Other experiments have confirmed that blocking is not due solely to attentional or associative processes at the time of memory storage. Two sets of experiments were analogous to the tests for change in overshadowing over time. Conditioning in one set was to either a taste, an odor, or a taste-odor compound with LiCl-induced illness as the US; in the other set conditioning was to either a light, tone, or a light-tone compound with footshock as the US in the other set. In both sets of experiments blocking was seen to depend on length of the retention interval in such a way as to force a conclusion that the expression of the blocked stimulus is somehow dependent on postacquisition memory processes (Miller et al. 1993).

Latent Inhibition

When organisms are repeatedly exposed to the to-be-conditioned stimulus (CS) prior to the pairing of the stimulus with a US, acquisition of conditioning is impaired. This is an extremely robust phenomenon, obtained in a variety of tests with different species, and studied frequently for well over 30 years (for a review of early studies, see Lubow 1973). Although termed latent inhibition, this label is something of a misnomer; subsequent research has generally failed to find evidence that the CS has clear inhibitory properties. We will not elaborate on the issue here, except to note that while the pre-exposed CS does appear inhibitory with respect to retardation of new learning of another stimulus with which it is compounded, it fails to demonstrate an inhibitory influence in a summation test in that its presence does not detract from the associative strength of a previously conditioned stimulus. Essentially all interpretations of latent inhibition have focused on decreased attentional or associative processing of the CS due to the pre-exposure treatment, and a consequential impairment in the acquisition of associative strength.

While it seems reasonable to think of latent inhibition as representing some form of acquisition impairment, several recent studies suggest that the basis of the deficit may lie elsewhere, perhaps in the effect of prior nonreinforced exposure on later retrieval of the memory for reinforced exposure.

Kraemer and Roberts (1984) examined retention of the effects of latent inhibition on conditioned taste aversion. This kind of conditioning is very sensitive to the effects of stimulus pre-exposure and accordingly is widely used in investigations of latent inhibition. Rats given several daily exposures to apple juice alone and then given a pairing of saccharin solution and illness showed virtually no aversion to the saccharin flavor when tested the next day. Since the pre-exposed and training stimuli were not identical, this is actually generalized latent inhibition. Presumably, some attribute(s) common to both tastes provided the basis for generalization of latent inhibition. But the critical observation occurred when the testing was delayed for 21 days. Subjects in the latent inhibition condition showed, at this point, substantial aversion to the saccharin.

An additional experiment replicated this paradoxical phenomenon with somewhat different flavors. The generality of the findings was further extended in a replication which employed a briefer pre-exposure treatment and a modified (single bottle) test procedure after 1- and 21-day retention intervals (Kraemer & Ossenkopp 1986). The basic effect—less effect of CS pre-exposure on the expression of conditioning, the longer the interval between conditioning and test—has now been replicated in several laboratories with both pre-exposure to the same CS that is conditioned or to only a similar CS (Kraemer, Hoffmann & Spear 1988; Kraemer, Randall & Carbari 1991; Bakner et al. 1991).

Clearly, the attenuation of latent inhibition over a long interval is puzzling. If subjects did not learn the relationship between taste and illness, as the 1-day test suggests, why do they show a strong conditioned taste aversion 3 weeks later, with no further conditioning experience? Kraemer and Roberts (1984) tentatively proposed that two independent memories were formed with respect to the consequences of tastes (e.g., safety and illness) and that the likelihood of retrieving each shifted over time. This form of interpretation remains viable and is consistent with other views of how alternately rewarded and nonrewarded experiences are processed in memory (Bouton 1991, Capaldi 1971; Kraemer & Spear 1993; Spear 1971).

A different type of experiment also supports the notion that latent inhibition is due to postacquisition processes such as retrieval (Kasprow et al. 1984). Rats received several presentations of white noise before noise-shock pairings, then were tested for suppression of licking in the presence of the noise. As expected, pre-exposure to the noise CS retarded acquisition of conditioned suppression. However, when testing of the pre-exposed subjects was preceded by a prior cuing treatment—shock-alone presentations in another context following conditioning—the severity of the impairment was significantly reduced. These subjects showed less latent inhibition, i.e., more complete suppression to the CS at testing. To avoid the problem that the prior cuing treatment (noncontingent footshock) might have produced learning that generalized to the training or test contexts (see chapter 9 for discussion of this issue), Kasprow et al. tested all subjects in a third context which differed from that used for training or for the reactivation treatment; other control conditions further verified the interpretation that latent inhibition was alleviated by the reactivation treatment.

Precisely why latent inhibition can be reduced by postacquisition treatments is not specified by these experiments. It seems clear, however, that despite the CS pre-exposures an association was formed during conditioning and that with circumstances that apparently act on memory retrieval, the learned information can be expressed in behavior. Ironically, then, the latent aspect of latent inhibition might more appropriately refer to the unseen conditioning in the paradigm and the effect could instead be termed latent excitation.

General Considerations

It should be noted that the recovery of responding from overshadowing, blocking, or latent inhibition has often been incomplete. That the reversibility is only partial could indicate that some impairment of memory storage did occur. Under such circumstances any treatment would have limited effectiveness in restoring the presumably acquired memory to full strength. On the other hand, the incomplete recovery may simply reflect the use of less than optimal circumstances for revealing the full memory storage that did in fact occur. Since there is no way to know in advance the optimal conditions (e.g., intensity and duration of the reactivation treatment, length of CS exposure, interval between reminders and testing, etc.), it would be premature to conclude that in principle the deficit is only partially reversible. Such a conclusion would gain viability, however, if a variety of parametric manipulations repeatedly failed to fully re-establish responding.

A second issue is that of new learning. This is not an issue when expression is induced by merely allowing a long interval to pass, but it does arise when the inducement is by prior cuing. As we have emphasized, the possibility that any prior cuing effects are simply due to new or generalized learning is an alternative interpretation that must be considered in each case. If new learning were involved, postacquisition memory processes would be unnecessary and so questionable as contributors to expression of the memory. Certainly one could hardly invoke retrieval of memory as an interpretation if the same performance were generated in subjects that never acquired the target task. Most investigations have, however, included control groups to discount any contribution of generalized learning to test performance. The basic approach involves exposure to the components of conditioning (CS and US) in an unpaired or noncontingent relationship in lieu of training. If there are any systemic or cumulative effects of exposure to stimuli per se, that feature is equated in controls. So if a prior cuing treatment improves their test performance as much as that of animals previously given the pairings needed for conditioning, new learning induced by the prior cuing treatment would be indicated and the results discounted. Some types of prior cuing treatments, however, inherently control for any new learning. For example, exposure to the CS only, or to the context alone, cannot constitute excitatory conditioning since no reinforcer or US is present. If anything, these treatments would be expected to reduce response strength, since they are nominally extinction exposures. Behavior involving choice responses, although used only occasionally (Hamberg & Spear 1978; Miller 1982), provides another good way to assess prior cuing effects uncontaminated by new learning, because in this case new learning would require differential reinforcement by a prior cuing treatment, which is especially unlikely.

Selective Expression of Learning

Here we are referring to learning that seems not to have occurred in terms of some behaviors but is evident in others. The following provides a few examples dealing with issues of fundamental importance to the topic of basic learning. The wide-spread realization of selective expression has created a major revolution in the field of memory in general, however, and we shall return to it and its implications after these examples.

Backward Conditioning

Backward conditioning is a term used for changes in response to a CS that has been preceded by a US. This is opposite to forward conditioning, the standard ordering of a CS followed by a US. Backward conditioning is seldom found. It sometimes is observed if one or only a few pairings of the US and CS are given (Shurtleff & Ayres 1981), but in most experiments with multiple pairings it has not been.

Other evidence suggests, however, that backward conditioning may occur more often than is usually assumed but is expressed selectively, in some kinds of behaviors but not in others. This evidence was provided in a test with rabbits given pairings of a mild shock delivered in the vicinity of the eye (the US) and followed by a tone (the CS) (Tait & Saladin 1986). Learning was measured in two ways: in terms of the nictitating membrane response and in terms of conditioned suppression of drinking, i.e., the cessation or slowing of drinking by a thirsty rabbit in the presence of the tone CS. Despite the backward nature of the conditioning procedure (mild shock first, tone second), the rabbit stopped or slowed its drinking whenever the tone occurred. This learning of the tone's excitatory characteristics was not seen, however, in terms of the nictitating membrane response, for which the rabbits exhibited acquired inhibitory properties; the tone apparently acquired the capacity to inhibit fear. If a tone always follows the shock as it did with this backward conditioning procedure, the animal could learn that the tone indicates safety from shock: the shock stops occurring when the tone comes on. Such a tendency for conditioned inhibition (of fear) was shown by a lower occurrence of the nictitating membrane response in the presence of the CS for animals that had been given the backward conditioning procedures than for control animals (for these controls the CS and US was not paired). This study showed, therefore, that conventional (excitatory) backward conditioning occurred in terms of conditioned suppression, which happens to be the behavior used in other studies to indicate backward conditioning (e.g., Shurtleff & Ayres 1981), but it did not in terms of a different behavior, reflexive closing of the nictitating membrane. Given that backward conditioning was expressed quite differently for different modes of its expression—excitatory when expressed by conditioned suppression, inhibitory when expressed by closing the nictitating membrane—it is easy to imagine that for some ways of expressing the learning, no learning would be evident.

Somatic (Motoric) and Autonomic (Heart Rate) Learning

It has been known for many years that the rate with which the heart beats in the presence of a conditioned stimulus can change relatively permanently as a consequence of conditioning. This form of learning, which involves the autonomic nervous system, is sometimes compared with learning involving somatic responses, which seem more voluntary—e.g., pressing a lever, running, or standing very still. Conclusions about the characteristics of learning have sometimes differed depending on whether the learning is expressed in terms of a change in heart rate or in terms of a change in somatic responding.

These differences have been illustrated in several ways. (a) Discrimination learning has seemed relatively rapid in terms of heart rate but relatively slow in terms of the nictitating membrane response in rabbits (Schneiderman 1972). (b) Learning sometimes has seemed not to occur at all in terms of heart rate, even though occurring quite clearly in terms of conditioned suppression (Schneiderman 1972). (c) In some circumstances retrograde amnesia induced by electroconvulsive shock has been absent in terms of conditioned heart rate, even though quite clear in terms of conditioned suppression; i.e., as expressed in terms of heart rate, the memory was more stable and resistant to forgetting than as expressed in terms of conditioned suppression (Springer 1975). (d) At certain points during ontogeny, developing animals clearly exhibit conditioning in terms of somatic behavior but not heart rate, although at a later age conditioning is observed with both measures (Campbell, Hayne & Richardson 1992).

How Learning Is Expressed Depends on the Nature of the CS

How learning is expressed or if it is expressed at all in terms of the response the experimenter has chosen to measure, can depend on what the CS is. A hungry rat given pairings of a food pellet preceded by a light will come to respond to the light by standing up and looking around, whereas if the food had been preceded by a tone, the rat will come to respond to the tone by raising its head, moving it from side to side, and approaching the food cup. An experimenter who unknowingly decides to measure learning about a tone in terms of the frequency of raising the head or learning about a light in terms of frequency of a head jerk is likely to conclude that the rat will not learn in these circumstances (for an important elaboration of these effects, see Holland 1984; for interesting earlier consideration, see LoLordo 1979).

A hungry pigeon will readily learn to peck at a lighted disk (key) on the wall if illumination of that disk is paired with food, but will not learn to peck the disk when a tone occurs if the tone is paired with food. Yet the noise-food association clearly is learned because the pigeon's general activity increases upon its occurrence (Nairne & Rescorla 1981). Learning the relationship between a light and food is expressed by pecking and not by a general increase in moving about the chamber, whereas learning the relationship between noise and food is expressed by an increase in the bird's movement about the chamber and not by increased pecking.

How Learning Is Expressed Depends on the US

What is expressed about learning depends on the US as well as the CS. This is shown best in tests of learning an aversion to a flavor consumed just prior to an unpleasant event. Frequently the existence of learning has been quite clear in terms of a reluctance to consume food or drink with that flavor but not with other behaviors, although in other circumstances there may be little or no decrease in consumption despite other indications that learning had occurred. Which result occurs depends on the nature of the unpleasant event that had followed consumption of the flavor. For instance, there have been reports that people stop eating food when it has led to one type of illness, but not if it has led to a different type.

Such reports convinced Pelchat et al. (1983) to do a series of experiments with rats to test this effect. People had reported finding a particular food less pleasurable if it had been followed by distinct nausea and vomiting, but if it had made them feel uncomfortable by causing other symptoms such as diarrhea they reported that the food still tasted good (even though they would not eat it). Toward understanding the basis of this distinction Pelchat et al. allowed rats to ingest sucrose solution and then induced either of two kinds of illness: upper gastrointestinal tract discomfort induced by LiCl, or lower gastrointestinal (GI) tract discomfort induced by high levels of lactose. Other rats ingested sucrose followed by a quite different source of discomfort, footshock. Different amounts of training were given with each of these USs until learning was equated in terms of the animal's reluctance to consume sucrose solution (this required hundreds of pairings of sucrose with footshock, to reach the level of reluctance found after only one or a very few pairings of sucrose with the illnesses).

The question was whether other ways of expressing this apparently equivalent learning would instead indicate differential learning depending on the US. To answer this, Pelchat et al. measured responses that rats characteristically make when they ingest relatively preferred foods (e.g., tongue and mouth movements) and those they make when tasting aversive or unpreferred food (e.g., gaping, head shaking, chin rubbing). Responding of this kind to the drinking of sucrose solution differed depending on whether it had been paired with footshock or one of the illnesses. If the US had been upper GI tract discomfort, a large number of the aversion-characteristic facial responses were given by the rats, but essentially no responses of this kind were given for rats that had lower GI discomfort or footshock paired with the sucrose. If only these facial responses had been used to express learning, one might conclude that learning occurred only with upper GI discomfort and not with either lower GI discomfort or footshock. But if the expression of learning had been measured only in terms of how readily the rat would drink sucrose solution, the conclusion would be that equivalent learning occurred regardless of the US.

Variation in How Infants Express What They Learn
Conclusions about the effectiveness of conditioned taste aversion at different points in the animal's development also depend on how that learning is expressed. Infant rats 10 or 15 days old expressed equivalent learning of an aversion to sucrose solution in terms of sucrose ingestion, whether induced (upper GI) illness or footshock served as the US. Yet only the 10-day-old rats expressed learning about the pairing of sucrose and footshock in terms of orofacial responses; the 15-day-old rats, like the adults in the Pelchat et al. experiment just described, did not express footshock-induced learning with orofacial responses. Rats of these two ages differed also in the nature of the orofacial responding through which learning of the sucrose-illness association was expressed (Hoffmann, Hunt & Spear 1991).

Other important instances of learning by infant rats also are easily overlooked depending on how that learning is measured. Learning not observed in terms of conventional measures frequently has been found to be expressible in other terms. Infant rats seem to have special difficulty in learning about a black compartment or a particular odor that has been paired once with footshock, if that learning is measured by changes in the animal's preference for black in comparison to white or in preference for the conditioned odor compared to a second odor. Yet in circumstances in which no learning at all was expressed in terms of this preference measure, direct observations of the animal's behavior when confined in the black compartment have indicated, in terms of freezing behavior, that learning of the relationship between that compartment and footshock had indeed occurred (Miller et al. 1989).

Finally, the consequences of pairing a particular odor and induced illness for infant rats during the first or second postnatal weeks frequently is unclear in terms of a test of preference for that odor versus another. Infants given pairings of the odor and the illness frequently show no less preference for the odor than those not given the pairings. That an aversion to the odor is acquired when paired with an illness can be shown, however, in terms of the capacity of that odor to induce a second-order acquired aversion. In second-order conditioning, you will recall, if a CS1 that previously was paired with a US is now paired with a second, relatively neutral CS2 (CS1-US followed by CS2-CS1), CS2 acquires the conditioned properties of CS1. Following pairings of an odor and induced illness for 4- and 8-day-old rats, the odor was paired with a particular texture (soft flooring). The question was, to what extent did the animals come to find the texture to be aversive? In circumstances in which learning was not expressed in terms of decreased preference for an odor relative to another, it was expressed in terms of decreased preference for the particular texture with which the odor had been paired (Miller, Molina & Spear 1990). Learning that was not expressible in terms of odor preference was expressible in terms of texture preference.

Summary and Implications

Summary

The relationship between memory and learning was emphasized first by discussing the similarity between processes involved in memory retrieval and those involved in memory storage. This similarity was illustrated in theory and also with reference to specific experiments. The learning-memory relationship was then discussed in terms of induced expression and selective expression. For both cases we referred to a variety of specific experimental results that converged on a single general phenomenon: learning that seemed not to have been accomplished was later shown to actually have been accomplished, because in special circumstances this learning could be expressed. Instances of induced expression included experiments in which aspects of the learning episode that seemed originally not to have been learned by the subject were shown to have been learned; the learning was expressed in behavior upon the occurrence of postacquisition events such as a long retention interval or a prior cuing treatment. The phenomenon of selective expression is somewhat different. These are cases in which learning expressed by a particular response measure is not expressed by another, equally sensitive and equally reasonable response measure. In these cases learning is shown clearly to have occurred, although expressed selectively, in one behavior but not in another.

Implications

The most general implication of the evidence sampled in this section could stand as the theme of the entire book: if we are to understand learning—how new information is acquired—we must also understand why the expression of what is learned varies so drastically. We can only understand what we can observe, and we can only observe learning that is expressed. What the evidence in this chapter suggests so far is that phenomena conventionally used in learning textbooks to characterize the acquisition process actually depend on postacquisition circumstances—those parts of the memory process that occur after learning is assumed to have taken place. Paradoxically, then, postacquisition processes such as cataloging, referencing, retrieval, or expression seem more likely to determine the characteristics of learning than the events that actually take place during the learning (acquisition) phase.

It is useful to consider separately the two sets of evidence reviewed in this section. The first set discussed the consequences of learning that depend on postacquisition events. For experiments contributing this evidence, the circumstances of acquisition and the test for expression of the learning are held constant. Termed induced expression, reference is to learning that is expressed only after special postacquisition treatment such as a retention interval or cuing. The instances mentioned are interesting because learning that theoretically did not occur is shown nevertheless to have actually occurred. These effects have been observed largely in tests of basic conditioning with animals, in the context of fairly circumscribed theories of learning.

The basis of induced expression may be different from that of selective expression, learning expressed in one behavior but not in another. For experiments contributing evidence of selective expression, the circumstances of acquisition and events preceding the test are held constant. The interest in selective expression is in the observation that different ways of expressing an acquired memory (different kinds of memory tests) have led to different conclusions about the characteristics of learning. The evidence for this is extensive—really quite massive in relation to the few examples presented here. Much of it has arisen in tests of human memory, normal and abnormal, with implications that are relatively broad (we discuss some of this in the next chapter; also see chapters 9 and 10). This evidence has led to intense discussions about the nature of memory as a process—whether there is one memory system or many, and if many, how they might be related—which in turn have had implications for the nature of cognition in general. It is primarily these consequences of pervasive selective expression that form the basis for the remainder of this book.

CHAPTER SUMMARY

The importance of memory for understanding basic learning was illustrated in terms of memory treated both as a representation and, separately, as a process. While specifying the nature of basic learning and correcting persisting misconceptions of what it is, the value of reference to acquired memory representations of environmental events was emphasized in terms of several phenomena. These included implicit reactivation, stimulus selection, and postacquisition revaluation of events that had been learned. The importance of appreciating the full memory process (including especially postacquisition processes) for understanding basic learning (i.e., acquisition) was illustrated by considering the effects of induced expression and selective expression on basic phenomena that have incorrectly been attributed solely to acquisition effects. Evidence was presented to support the notion that, at present, central principles of basic learning contain fundamental anomalies that can be resolved only by considering postacquisition memory processes.

12

Structure of Memory

To entitle this chapter, "Structure of Memory," may be pretentious because it suggests that we know what the structure of memory is. We do not.

A general description of the memory process is easy. It surely consists of the detection and perception of events to be learned, encoding and learning of the relationships among the events, and the later retrieval and expression of this learning. Anyone could tell you this upon a little reflection, although probably using different words.

What is usually meant by the structure of memory, however, is much more theoretical, less descriptive, and generally vague. It is how different kinds or components of memory fit together: anatomically in the case of neuroscientists; conceptually, in terms of how different kinds of information are treated and organized for later use, in the case of cognitive psychologists. In this book we have referred to both approaches.

What neuroscience and cognitive psychology have in common in this case is a disposition to take evidence for selective expression as an indication that there are different forms or systems of memory. The different memories are thought to handle different kinds or sources of information, and in some cases are believed to function more or less independently. Vast differences of opinion exist on this topic, however, even within the areas of neuroscience and cognitive psychology. What we shall do is to present some of the evidence and issues involved in considering multiple memory systems, but the full scope of the arguments for and against their existence is more than can be discussed here.

ALTERNATIVES TO MULTIPLE MEMORY SYSTEMS

There is a significant cost associated with an orientation or theory based on the existence of multiple memory systems: it can cause scientists to ignore simpler explanations that might indicate the need for only a single memory system or relatively few such systems. Remember that a fundamental rule of theory-building is parsimony—economy in assumptions—which in this case can translate into economy in the number of memory systems supposed.

Another cost is that the notion of multiple memory systems can discourage experiments that test ideas more fundamental to the understanding of memory. In the extreme case, assigning each unexpected observation about learning to a separate memory system that has its own peculiarities would lead to a ridiculous number and detract from tests of the basic characteristics of learning and retention. For instance, when it was found that a rat made ill an hour or so after consuming a new flavor would acquire an aversion to that flavor, the result seemed so anomalous relative to previous tests with other conditioned and unconditioned stimuli—given the length of the delay between the flavor and the illness—that it was tempting to assume a separate memory system involving flavors and illnesses. Although this remains a possibility, depending on one's criteria for a separate system, if everyone had believed it we would not have learned of the many similarities between flavor-illness conditioning and conditioning involving any other stimuli (e.g., Domjan 1985; Logue 1979).

Before considering multiple memories, we should first ask whether selective expression and induced expression have a common basis. If they do, evidence of induced expression might be applied to this issue in the same way that evidence for selective expression is conventionally applied. You will recall from the previous chapter that selective expression refers to learning that is readily observed in terms of changes in behavior A but not in an equally plausible behavior, B. Induced expression refers to instances of learning that seem not to exist but are revealed by treatments given after termination of the learning, such as cuing prior to the retention test or events during a lengthy retention interval. In our view either of these phenomena might conceivably be used as an argument for multiple memory systems. For instance, it might be assumed that selective expression reflects a memory system associated with behavior A that is quite separate from a system associated with behavior B. Or it might be asserted that instances of learning that are susceptible to induced expression are controlled by a different system of memory than those that are unaffected by circumstances that induce expression. Selective and induced expression might therefore be a shared consequence of multiple memory systems (although there is as yet little evidence to support this conjecture).

Perhaps, moreover, the selection of what is expressed also is determined by postacquisition events, in the same sense as induced expression. For instance, suppose that the test for retention were a relearning test. This would include presentation of the unconditioned stimulus or reinforcer as well as all the other features present during original learning. Presentation of the reinforcer is a powerful way to promote memory retrieval (see chapter 9). So in the present example the presence of the reinforcer at the test will not only help to measure retention, it also will promote and shape what is remembered. In the same way that they serve induced expression, particular cues of this kind lead to selective expression. If the reinforcer attribute of the memory is associated closely with a particular behavior, for example, that behavior might be expressed to the exclusion of others. Selective expression seems likely to be a consequence of such competition. If this competition is eliminated by presenting some other cue associated more closely with another behavior or a stimulus leading to another behavior, we would have induced expression. It should be clear that selection of the response actually activated by an associate (such as the reinforcer) is not the only response rule that might be used. A good deal of the competition probably occurs among stimulus attributes that are acted upon at retrieval, quite independent of the responses exhibited during learning. This is not to suggest that the nature of selective expression depends capriciously on the circumstances in which retention is required; there is instead good reason to assume that selective expression is a biologically adaptive feature of the memory process (Lennartz & Weinberger 1992).

We nevertheless find attractive this simple explanation: expression is selective depending upon what behavior is measured, because different tests provide different retrieval cues (for empirical consequences, see Spear 1971). Yet we must deal also with the fact that a memory may be expressed in terms of a behavior that was never given during acquisition and so had not been encoded as an attribute of the memory. An example is the freezing behaviors (standing motionless) exhibited by rats exposed to stimuli previously paired with the footshock, to which freezing was never exhibited during learning. In this view, again, the events at the retention test can still be expected to promote selection of what is expressed as well as to induce what is expressed. This is accomplished in each case by selectively activating a subset of otherwise equally accessible attributes.

An even simpler way to account for selective expression is to appeal to differential sensitivity in the measurement of alternative ways of expressing the memory. We think that this rarely applies to the important phenomena, but it is a technical point that requires mention. By sensitivity of measurement is usually meant variance in measurement. It can be illustrated in terms of the decision about whether learning is expressed. This is, of course, decided by the difference between animals given the events and circumstances needed for learning and those given the same events but in circumstances that would not permit the learning. For learning that a tone signals food, for example, responding to the tone after the paired presentation of tone and food would be compared to responding after unpaired experience with the same tone and food. Insensitive measurement would occur if the response chosen to measure learning about the tone were too variable among animals given the same treatment— if the probability of the response for some animals on some trials was very small, but that for other animals or on other trials was very large. With so much variance within each condition, a statistical difference is unlikely to be detected between these two conditions, and so the test is termed insensitive. Measurement might also be insensitive if variance is too low. If all animals are certain to exhibit a response or have almost no chance of exhibiting a response, learning will not be detectable in terms of that response. But although it is a factor of concern in designing experiments, such measurement sensitivity is rarely or never a problem for interpreting the results of selective or induced expression that have occurred in the literature. For such reports the editorial review process usually eliminates experiments that fail to attend to the relatively trivial issue of measurement sensitivity.

BREADTH OF SELECTIVE EXPRESSION

Observation of selective expression in normal and abnormal humans since the early 1970s has provided striking, dramatic examples that have shaken fundamental beliefs about memory processing. It is the breadth of these examples and the magnitude of many of them that have provided the strongest argument for the existence of multiple memory systems. We now review a sample of these effects. Because such effects have been mentioned previously in this book and may also be familiar from other sources, they will be described briefly.

1. Source amnesia is among the most frequent instances of selective expression in human abnormal memory. Source amnesia is self-descriptive; it occurs when new learning is evident, but the individual cannot remember the source of the new learning—cannot remember the experiences that led to his or her change in behavior. The posthypnotic suggestion that hypnotists commonly apply for entertaining on stage can be an instance of induced source amnesia. Subjects exhibit a bizarre behavior but forget that they have been told to do so by the hypnotist. They are said to exhibit the bizarre behavior unconsciously, in the sense that they do not acknowledge that the behavior was suggested by the hypnotist earlier.

Amnesic patients show source amnesia spontaneously. For instance, a group of brain-damaged persons with good intelligence but severe impairment for acquiring most new information were found quite capable of Pavlovian conditioning (Weiskrantz & Warrington 1979). The conditioning involved pairing a tone with an air puff to the eye, which induces a blink. After several such pairings, these patients exhibited an eyeblink whenever the tone occurred, even when they were not tested until 24 hours after the conditioning. This was surprising because at the time these experiments were conducted, it had seemed that these patients could retain no new learning for more than a few minutes. For the procedures used in such conditioning, an elaborate apparatus was required: machinery to present the tone and the air puff and special headgear to indicate when the eye does and does not blink. It was an imposing and intrusive procedure. Yet when interviewed these patients said they did not remember having been exposed to this elaborate apparatus before. They did not, for example, acknowledge any special significance in the part of the apparatus that actually delivered the air puff to the eye. But they nevertheless exhibited retention of the conditioned eyeblink.

The well-studied amnesic patient, H.M., has shown source amnesia in several situations. In tests performed in the 1960s, not long after his brain surgery, it was confirmed that despite his profound inability to express new memories if more than a few minutes elapsed since their acquisition, he could show relatively permanent learning in several perceptual-motor tasks. These included learning to complete a drawing while looking at the paper only through a mirror (which gives a reverse image, so such drawing is not easily accomplished at first) or discriminating between different geometric forms. Despite the evidence of learning these behaviors, H.M. consistently indicated from session to session that he had no recollection of having performed in that kind of task before, as has often been the case despite impressive remembering of the perceptual-motor skill. An example is tactile-maze learning, for which H.M. showed 75 percent savings 2 years later. In this case as well, he indicated that he did not remember any earlier experience with this test (Milner 1962; Sidman, Stoddard & Mohr 1968; Milner, Corkin & Teuber 1968).

More recently, when in his sixties, H.M. learned to use a wheelchair and walking frame after he broke his ankle, but he could not remember why he used them. And after learning a mental rotation skill with abstract figures presented on a computer over a period of a month and becoming quite good at recognizing letters presented in a variety of orientations, he still had no idea at the beginning of each session what the computer was or what would be done with it (Ogden & Corkin 1991). Similar examples include those of other amnesic patients who learned to play new tunes on the piano despite no indication of remembering where or when they had learned them (Luria 1976; Starr & Phillips 1970).

2. It is well known that verbal reports of normal humans about their own cognition can be strikingly inaccurate, e.g., how they solved a problem, what or how they learned, or even what they detected or perceived. This is why trained psychologists aware of this dissociation pay much more attention to what humans actually do than what they say they do or say they know. In a review of such effects, Nisbett and Wilson (1977) concluded that, "People often cannot report accurately on the effects of particular stimuli on higher order, inference-based responses. Indeed, sometimes they cannot report on the existence of critical stimuli, sometimes cannot report on the existence of their responses, and sometimes cannot even report that an inferential process of any kind has occurred." (p. 233) For the issue of selective expression, the implication is that much of what is learned by humans may be exhibited but not acknowledged verbally or vice versa.

Striking examples of selective expression in normal humans have been observed through the distinction between direct and indirect tests (sometimes referred to as explicit and implicit tests) of memory (Johnson & Hasher 1987; Richardson-Klavehn & Bjork 1988; Hintzman 1990). If a person is given a list of words to remember, a direct test might be for them to recall all the words they can or to recognize those they studied from among a larger set of words. As an indirect test of memory, persons might be shown a very rapid (in milliseconds) presentation of each word interspersed with presentations of nonwords or words not previously studied and asked to make a judgment as to whether the item presented was a real word or not. While subjects are very accurate in discriminating words from pseudo words, they respond more rapidly to the words that have been studied previously. This facilitated judgment effect occurs even though the studied words might not be correctly recalled or even recognized as having been on the studied list (e.g., Jacoby 1988). In short, a person may deny having seen a word previously presented, yet a change in perceptual efficacy indicates that a memory for that word was acquired.

The variety of indirect tests that can indicate memory when direct tests do not is quite large and varied. For instance, subjects given lists of words that vary in frequency of occurrence can remember the frequencies of occurrence of each word remarkably well, even though their recall of the words is relatively poor. Differences in the subject's age, their standardized achievement scores, or circumstances of study—variables that make a big difference in how well the words are recalled—make little difference in memory for frequency of occurrence (Hasher & Zacks 1984).

Brain-damaged persons with amnesia show more striking selective expression of learning with direct and indirect tests because their responses frequently are comparable to normal subjects in indirect tests of memory, although, of course, they perform much more poorly in direct tests such as recall or recognition. One indirect test assessed learning to read words printed in inverted type (Cohen & Squire 1980). In normal humans, this experience leads to an increase in the reading speed of new materials presented in this way. In an indirect test of this kind, amnesic subjects also increased their reading speed of new material and did so at about the same rate as control subjects. Direct tests assessed reading speed of the words previously presented and also their recognition. The amnesic patients showed a significant impairment in the extra increase usually shown in speed of reading old words actually studied earlier and in recognition of these words (termed *declarative* memory [Cohen & Squire 1980]).

A particularly interesting test of indirect memory suggested by Larry Jacoby (personal communication, 1983) is the extent to which people laugh after hearing a joke they have heard before. People told a familiar joke usually laugh less, or only out of politeness or not at all, and usually with the clear realization of having heard it previously. Jacoby reported that an amnesic patient, when told a joke he had heard several times before (and had laughed at originally), did not laugh even though he claimed that he had never heard the joke before. It was only that it "did not seem funny" to the patient.

The dramatic selective expression of memory exhibited by direct versus indirect tests has generated a great deal of attention, many articles and books, often under different headings such as "explicit memory versus implicit memory" or "conscious versus unconscious memory." The indirect-versus-direct distinction seems preferable because it refers both to differences in experimental operations and to the hypothetical processes believed to be tested in the two situations (Jacoby, Lindsay & Toth 1992).

It has been very tempting, particularly through the implicit versus explicit language, to treat these examples of selective expression as representing the action of separate memory systems. Separate memory systems have frequently been suggested for purposes of theory and are briefly considered next.

MULTIPLE MEMORY SYSTEMS

We should be clear about the issue here. The question is whether different kinds of events and episodes are processed for learning and memory by different systems in the brain, which we take ultimately to mean different arrangements and configurations of processing units such as neurons, synapses between neurons, or events that take place within neurons. There are many other ways of conceptualizing a system. We will not attempt to discuss this general issue except to say that if there actually are separate systems of memory, they could be either independent or interactive. It seems implausible that memory systems would not be in some sense interactive. For instance, separate memory systems for spatial relationships, temporal durations, feeding-related episodes, or events pertinent to reproduction have been suggested. To have so many common attributes involved would seem to require some interaction or interchange of information. It is difficult to imagine, for example, an animal's memory for spatial relationships that does not involve a temporal component representing the time required to go from one place to another, or memory for a feeding episode that would not involve spatial information about where the food is located.

It is easy enough to devise a theory; the trick is to produce one that is credible and useful in accounting for known facts and in predicting new ones. We now mention a sample of reasonable versions of multiple memory systems. These are organized in terms of whether the memory systems are distinguished by a process, source of environmental information, or neuroanatomy.

MEMORY SYSTEMS DISTINGUISHED BY COGNITIVE PROCESS

This category of memory systems has a longer history than others—as long as persons have speculated about their own subjective experiences with learning and memory. Ancient literature and philosophy include a variety of metaphors used to describe experiences with memory. Differences in the metaphors applied sometimes tended to be considered differences in types of memory. A list of these metaphors is presented in Table 12-1, taken from an insightful discussion of this topic by Roediger (1980). These metaphors have linked memory processing to things or events we are more familiar with, and the things and events we are familiar with have changed throughout the years as technology has changed. The most common metaphor for

TABLE 12-1 **Metaphors Used to Describe Memory**

A. Spatial Analogies with Search
Wax tablet (Plato, Aristotle)
Gramophone (Pear 1922)
Aviary (Plato)
House (James 1890)
Rooms in a house (Freud 1924/1952)
Switchboard (John 1972)
Purse (G. A. Miller 1956)
Leaky bucket or sieve (G. A. Miller 1956)
Junk box (G. A. Miller 1963)
Bottle (G. A. Miller, Galanter & Pribram 1960)
Computer program (Simon & Feigenbaum 1964)
Stores (Atkinson & Shiffrin 1968)
Mystic writing pad (Freud 1940/1950)
Workbench (Klatzky 1975)
Cow's stomach (Hintzman 1974)
Pushdown stack (Bernbach 1969)
Acid bath (Posner & Konick 1966)
Library (Broadbent 1971)
Dictionary (Loftus 1977)
Keysort cards (Brown & McNeill 1966)
Conveyor belt (Murdock 1974)
Tape recorder (see Posner & Warren 1972)
Subway map (Collins & Quillian 1970)
Garbage can (Landauer 1975)

B. Other Spatial Theories
Organization theory (Tulving 1962)
Hierarchical networks (G. Mandler 1967)
Associative networks (Anderson & Bower 1973)

C. Other Analogies
Muscle (strength) (Woodworth 1929)
Construction (Bartlett 1932)
Reconstruction of a dinosaur (Neisser 1967)
Levels of processing (Craik & Lockhart 1972)
Signal detection (Bernbach 1967)
Melodies on a piano (Wechsler 1963)
Tuning fork (Lockhart, Craik & Jacoby 1976)
Hologram (Pribram 1971)
Lock and key (Kolers & Palef 1976)

Reprinted from Roediger (1980) with permission of the publisher.

memory today is, of course, the computer. The most advanced instrument for transmitting information among the ancient Greeks was the wax tablet, which at that time was the popular metaphor for memory.

An example of how these metaphors became translated into separate memory systems may be considered in terms of the distinction between episodic and semantic memories, introduced with great effect and success by Tulving (1972). Tulving introduced this distinction on the basis of a good deal of evidence and reason, but at that time there was little hard, systematic evidence that might demand the distinction scientifically. So in hypothesizing that semantic and episodic memory should be treated separately, Tulving did so, ". . . primarily for the convenience of communication, rather than as an expression of any profound belief about structural or functional separation of the two." (Tulving 1972, 384) By the time Tulving wrote a book on this distinction about 10 years later, research during the interim allowed him to publish a table that included 28 important differences between episodic and semantic memory.

In Tulving's (1972) view, "Semantic memory is the memory necessary for the use of language. It is a mental thesaurus. . . ." (p. 386) In contrast, "Episodic memory receives and stores information about temporally dated episodes or events, and temporal-spatial relations among these events." (p. 385) The meaning of episodic memory—which is also the meaning most often attached to memory in general—is helped by a quote from William James: "Memory requires more than mere dating of the fact in the past. It must be dated in *my* past." (James 1890, 659; from Tulving 1972, 389) As a further clarification, Tulving (1972) noted "The term 'episode' is a somewhat loose synonym of 'occurrence,' and one of its dictionary definitions is that of 'an event that is distinctive and separate although part of a larger series.' Episodic memory is about occurrence of such events." (p. 385) (A competent linguist fluent in several languages, Tulving introduced a variety of significant terms into cognitive psychology.)

The distinction between episodic and semantic memory was made important by a large number of experiments that Tulving conducted or inspired, along with solid reasoning and thought. It is important to realize, however, that not only are various distinctions between types of memory systems plentiful historically and in contemporary psychology, this particular distinction actually has been used by a huge number of philosophers and psychologists since Aristotle. The nature of these precedents has been reviewed (Herrmann 1982; Hintzman 1978; Schacter & Tulving 1982), and a list of these is presented in Table 12-2 (Herrmann 1982).

Some Reasons to Invoke Separate Memory Systems

Unlike many persons who have claimed a distinction among separate memory systems, Tulving analyzed carefully why consideration of multiple systems of memory is worthwhile (Tulving 1985). He felt, first, that because the most consistent facts we know are based on particular instances of memory and may or may not apply to all instances, we would be on safer ground scientifically to limit general conclusions to specific kinds of memory rather than to memory in general. Second, in view of the evolutionary process that has led to such a divergence in physical characteristics, such as structural differences from one part of the brain to the other, it is reasonable to expect that the various brain structures and mechanisms would lead to a corresponding variety in kinds of memory.

Third, Tulving cited apparently separate systems of visual perception as support for the idea that other psychological functions, such as memory, might have separate systems. These include the remarkable phenomenon of "blindsight" observed in humans with significant damage to the visual cortex. These persons claim that they cannot see within a particular portion of their visual field (sometimes nearly all of it), and indeed behave as if they were quite blind in basically all behaviors. Yet they can respond accurately if asked to make a decision about the location of an object presented to them in their blind visual field (Weiskrantz et al. 1974). The experimenter's questioning of the blind person goes something like this: "I am holding an object at a certain distance from the ground. Can you see it?" (The patient replies, "No.") "If you could see it, where would it be?" (The patient points directly to the object.) A similar dissociation of visual perception systems is indicated by the discovery of one critical neural pathway that controls the recognition of objects and another that controls only the location of the objects in space (Young 1988).

Another of Tulving's (1972) reasons for considering multiple memory systems was simply that it is so difficult to imagine how a single system could be controlling such apparently different phenomena as, ". . . perceptual motor adaptations to distorting lenses and their aftereffects . . ." and an affirmative answer to the question of ". . . whether Abraham Lincoln is dead." (p. 386)

It is notable that although Tulving's distinction among episodic memory, semantic memory, and procedural memory (a system he added later [Tulving 1983]) is couched in terms of cognitive processes, Tulving's thinking about the basis of the distinction involves the biological basis of fundamental behaviors. While acknowledging that a separation between memory systems could be conceptualized abstractly on the basis of differential correlation of processes with systems, Tulving views his distinction among memory systems as having a quite different basis. For Tulving, ". . . a more concrete conceptualization—one that refers to the correlation of behavior and thought with brain processes and postulates the verifiable, real assistance of memory systems—is preferable because it points to stronger tests of such existence." (Tulving 1985, 386) Tulving's decisions about memory systems are, in short, made on a psychobiological basis that depends on information about brain and memory in both animals and humans.

TABLE 12-2 **Long-term Memory Classification Schemes Compatible with the Semantic-Episodic Distinction**

Author(s)	Semantic-Memory Term	Episodic-Memory Term
Philosophy		
Aristotle (c. 300 B.C.)	Affection of conception	Affection of perception
Augustine (c. 410)	Of things learned or intuited, and principles	Images of things perceived and of feeling
Aquinas (c. 1260)	Thoughts	Fixed in the past
Abercrombie (1833)	Natural or philosophical association	Local or incidental association
Brown (1858)	Conception	Memory of temporal relations
Bain (1875)	Knowledge	Memory of experiences
Bergson (1912)	Habit memory	True memory
Russell (1912)	Knowledge by description	Knowledge by acquaintance
Broad (1925)	Nonperceptual memory	Perceptual memory
Ryle (1949)	Something learned	Episode
Ayer (1956)	Habit memory	Event memory
Malcolm (1963)	Factual memory	Perceptual memory
Locke (1971)	Factual memory	Personal memory
Langer (1972)	Factual, inductive and object memory	Childhood and biographical memory
Psychology		
Steele (1889)	Logical memory	Circumstantial memory
James (1890)	Knowledge	Memory of one's past
Baker (1896)	Philosophic memory	Circumstantial memory
Wundt (1896)	Cognition	Recognition
Angell (1906)	Habit memory	True memory
McDougall (1923)	Memory in the wide sense	Memory in the narrow sense
Bentley (1925)	Memory from learning	Memory of the past
Carr (1925)	Conception	Personal experiences
Boring, Langfeld & Weld (1935)	Memory for experience and habits	Memory images
Koffka (1935)	Skills	Memory of the past
Reiff & Scheerer (1959)	Memoria	Remembrances
Bruner (1969)	Memory without record	Memory with record
Herrmann (1972)	General language store	Separate event long-term store
Piaget & Inhelder (1973)	Memory in the wide sense	Memory in the narrow sense
Psychiatry		
Schactel (1947)	Practical knowledge	Autobiographical knowledge
Neurology		
Clarparede (1911)	Marginal memory	Egocentric memory
Nielsen (1958)	Categorical	Temporal
Pribram (1969)	Specific	Contextual
Luria (1976)	Habit memory	True memory
Penfield (1975)	Concepts	Experimental record

Reprinted from Herrmann (1982) with permission of the publisher.

A Less Successful Cognitive-Process Distinction among Hypothetical Memory Systems: Short-Term Memory and Long-Term Memory

At various places in this book we have used the terms *short-term retention* and *long-term retention*. The intention has been to apply only an operational distinction to differences in memory effects observed when retention is tested within seconds or minutes after learning (short-term retention) and when tested after longer intervals (long-term retention). Many scientists have gone further and viewed effects observed with these different operations as reflecting qualitatively different types of memory processing, short-term memory and long-term memory. This distinction has fallen from use for lack of empirical evidence or now is used either vaguely or in a sense unrelated to the original meaning.

The conceptual distinction between short-term memory and long-term memory that became popular was really Hebb's (1949), which was more a metaphor than a description of fact. Hebb's theory was that a group or assembly of brain cells activated by a learning episode become interconnected as a consequence and that, for a while, neural impulses reverberate around this cell-assembly circuit. While in the reverberating state this circuit, taken to be the memorial representation of learning, was viewed as particularly susceptible to disruption by electroconvulsive shock or other neurological insult to the brain. In addition, this reverberating circuit was expected to die away gradually unless a sufficient number of essentially identical learning trials occurred. If the reverberation were maintained by sufficient repetitions, however, the permanent interconnections would be established within the cell assembly and eventually among groups of cell assemblies (phase sequences). In this permanent stage, the memorial representation of an episode was presumed to be no longer susceptible to destruction by a temporary physiological aberration in the brain.

This was an easily appreciated system—Hebb was a persuasive writer as well as a visionary neuroscientist. It lent itself quite nicely to a distinction between a short-term memory, in force during a reverberatory phase, and a long-term memory, existing once the interconnections within the cell assembly and phase sequence become permanent. The implication was that we can hold information in a transitory, ephemeral state for a brief period, but without sufficient repetition to transfer it to a more permanent state, certain time-related processes will operate on the memory storage to remove it from our potential use.

Through experimental tests and clinical observation, important functional differences between these two kinds of memory seemed to emerge, and the distinction between short-term and long-term memory was applied widely by theorists. The problem was that the functional differences did not hold up under careful scientific scrutiny. The distinction between short-term memory and long-term memory consequently became less and less useful. It has now essentially disappeared as an explanatory device among scientists of memory, but nevertheless, short-term memory and long-term memory still are frequently cited as different systems in some textbooks. This suggests that it might be useful to sample briefly the findings that led to the distinction and the later events that essentially eliminated its continued use.

Two kinds of clinical evidence helped promote the notion of separate short-term and long-term memory systems. Both will be familiar to you, through this book and others. The first is the phenomenon of retrograde amnesia, made especially dramatic through the extensive study of Russell and Nathan (1946) on a large number of concussion-related casualties in World War II. From this report and literally daily occurrences that are frequent and familiar through the news media, there is absolutely no doubt that memories acquired just prior to acute brain insult involving concussion (or general seizure, but not just any brain damage) are likely to be more susceptible to subsequent retention deficit than memories for more remote events. This retrograde amnesia has been taken as evidence that in the early stages of a memory's existence the neurophysiological representation of a memory is more susceptible to destruction than later. The similarity with Hebb's distinction between an early, ephemeral process underlying short-term memory and a more robust and resistant process underlying long-term memory is unmistakable, and in fact Hebb's notion was based in part on Russell and Nathan's report.

The second clinical effect is the common characteristic of amnesia associated with damage to the temporal regions of the brain and to some extent that associated with advanced alcoholism (Korsakoff's syndrome) or Alzheimer's disease. The major symptom in these cases is, of course, a deficiency in maintaining a normal level of long-term retention for new information. The patient characteristically is unable to retain information for longer than a few minutes after attention has been distracted from the task at hand, despite apparently unimpaired capacity for retrieval of memories acquired prior to the brain damage or disease (the use of "apparently unimpaired" is significant; some evidence suggests as much impairment for old as for new memories [Sanders & Warrington 1971]). Both examples lent themselves to interpretation as a deficiency in transfer from some hypothetical short-term memory store to a long-term memory store or simply as a deficiency in the long-term memory system.

Retrograde Amnesia as Evidence for a Distinction between Short-Term and Long-Term Memory

There is a clear problem with interpreting retrograde amnesia as a failure for information acquired in short-term memory to enter long-term memory: Despite brain insult shortly after learning, the information is not totally unavailable for long-term retention; under the right circumstances, some or all of it can be retrieved. We have seen this in several experiments with animals presented earlier in this book (see chapters 8 and 9)—instances in which the effects of an amnestic treatment are alleviated, indicating that the memory was in fact acquired and available. This effect is supported by the frequent clinical observation of spontaneous recovery from retrograde amnesia (albeit incomplete) in humans.

A dramatic experiment with humans has lent similar support (Bickford et al. 1958). In this study the brain was electrically stimulated by means of electrodes implanted there. The memory test was for verbal materials presented just prior to the stimulation (Bickford et al. 1958). The stimulation was expected to induce a deficit in recall of these materials, and it did. In tests given relatively soon after this treatment, the amount of retention was found to be poorer the greater the intensity or duration of stimulation. It was as if little or no memory was acquired if, soon afterwards, a strong current of long duration were applied. Despite the initial retention deficit, however, evidence of retention after longer intervals was strong regardless of the characteristics of the stimulation.

As to the general experimental strategy of studying retrograde amnesia to decide about a distinction between short-term memory and long-term memory, Weiskrantz (1970) suggested that most of the experiments had been directed inappropriately at separating these hypothetical memory processes by establishing a stable length for the interval between learning and brain insult, after which the latter does not influence retention. The far more important interval, said Weiskrantz, is the interval that establishes how long after learning a brain insult can be applied and result in no retention (assuming that no retention is also found for all shorter intervals). Weiskrantz noted that when this interval has been examined closely, it appears that it is so short—on the order of milliseconds—as to be uninteresting in terms of memory processing, although perhaps of interest for sensory registration and perception.

Anterograde Amnesia and Short-Term versus Long-Term Memory

What about the brain-damaged persons for whom there seems to be no long-term retention despite good short-term retention? Although clinical observations of anterograde amnesia initially appear to suggest a failure to transfer information from a short-term to a long-term memory system, other clinical evidence has indicated that information might immediately enter a long-term memory state. Such an outcome immediately questions the need for a separate short-term memory system. The critical clinical evidence was found in one particular brain-damaged patient, K.F., and then in a few other subjects tested by Weiskrantz and Warrington in England. These patients paradoxically had essentially normal long-term retention, despite severe deficits in a variety of short-term retention tests (Warrington & Weiskrantz 1973; Weiskrantz 1970; also L. Weiskrantz & E. K. Warrington, personal communication, 1973). From such evidence Weiskrantz (1970) suggested that what is meant by a short-term memory process may simply be rehearsal activities entered into by humans to accommodate an overload of information destined for long-term storage in any case. If the unique process underlying short-term retention is rehearsal, then it is certainly important for understanding memory in humans, but if it is no more, this process may apply only to human verbal behavior and consequently have little generality. There are more recent indications that patients with K.F.'s symptoms do show impaired long-term retention when this requires phonological processing that simulates processing used for short term retention. This implies that the deficit is more related to phonological processing in general than to length of retention interval (an alternative interpretation in terms of traditional short-term memory has been suggested by Squire et al. 1993).

Cognitive Basis for Short-Term versus Long-Term Memory
Functional dissociations observed in memory processing by normal humans also seemed at one time to support a distinction between a short-term and a long-term memory system. Functional dissociation means that memory associated with one system (e.g., after short intervals) is influenced by a particular variable differently than is memory associated with another system (e.g., after long intervals). If a particular treatment affects short-term retention differently from how it affects long-term retention, we may conclude that there is a short-term memory system that functions differently from a long-term memory system. Functional dissociation is a critical tool for deciding whether there are different memory systems (although it in itself is not sufficient, as we shall see).

Excellent critiques of the functional dissociations claimed for short-term and long-term memory were published several years ago (Clayton 1974; Wickelgren 1973, 1975). The first point noted was that many variables have precisely the same effect on short-term and long-term retention. These include the influence of degree of original learning, retroactive or proactive interference, and the effects of the use of some memory aids (Clayton 1974).

The major point made in these reviews, however, was that the functional dissociations used to support the idea that there are both short-term and long-term memory systems did not make the case; the dissociations claimed could be explained readily by simpler ideas than separate memory systems. For example, essentially all of the functional differences between short-term and long-term retention could be accounted for either on the basis of the peculiar action of specific sensory systems (audition versus vision) or by active rehearsal, which applies primarily to short-term retention (Clayton 1974).

The general conclusion seems to be that if we are to deal with different memory systems, it probably is not useful to do so with most conventional views of short-term memory versus long-term memory, although a distinction in terms of an immediate-memory system that persists for a very brief period (on the order of milliseconds), remains tenable. It is difficult to deny that the different effects observed after short- and long-term retention intervals suggest the operation of different systems (Squire, Knowlton & Musen 1993). Yet their nature, and the distinction between them, can be expected to be different from the older short-term memory and long-term memory uses reviewed in this section. Given recent developments in distinguishing conscious and unconscious memory (e.g., Greenwald 1992; Jacoby et al. 1992), a potentially useful distinction is possible in terms of how long the representation of an episode remains active in conscious memory. We find this distinction strikingly similar to the view of James (1890) although based on much more evidence.

Other Bases for Considering Multiple Memory Systems

Several psychobiological orientations to the study of memory have suggested the existence of multiple memory systems. As examples, we shall consider two rather different approaches.

The first approach does not explicitly deal with separate memory systems in a structured theory. Implicitly, however, it treats individual sensory systems as if they were associated with separate memory systems. The second case illustrates the widespread and perhaps inevitable consideration of anatomically distinct areas of the brain that may correspond to separate memory systems.

Implications of the Ontogenesis of Sensory System Effectiveness and of Learning

All mammals have in common the order in which their sensory systems become functional during development. Detection of tactile and olfactory stimulation occurs first, then taste, then audition, and finally vision (see chapter 7). Most episodes with which we test learning and memory are multimodal, in the sense that more than one sensory system is centrally involved. The animal receives food (gustation, olfaction) if a bell (audition) rings, a startling shock (tactile) may be predicted by a flashing light (vision), an animal follows a particular odor to the tactile comfort of home, and so forth. So, most of our experiments are unlikely to allow us to study memories involving, say, only olfactory events or only visual events. And even if one did observe differences in the characteristics of purely olfactory or purely visual memories, it is hard to determine how much is due to the differences between olfaction and vision and how much to differences between other characteristics of the memories, such as the intensity of the odor and visual event, or their complexity, familiarity, affective consequence, and so forth. It is not an impossible problem experimentally, but it is very difficult to hold constant all factors except the particular sensory system involved.

There is reason to believe, however, that each sensory system might conceivably be accompanied by a relatively unique memory system. One reason is the specialized characteristics of the information processed by each sensory system. For instance, much of vision involves contrast and comparison among simultaneous events whereas for audition, the valuable information is usually sequential (for instance, the speech we hear is in sequential elements of information). Another specialized characteristic is the speed of onset and offset of a sensory event; whereas intense auditory stimuli may reach their peak within milliseconds and disappear almost as quickly, olfactory events are more likely to increase only gradually over time to a maximum and decrease as slowly.

It would not be hard to generate a theory that includes a separate memory system for each sensory system. Implicit and somewhat indirect support for such a theory is found in considering the ontogeny of learning about events from different sensory systems. We refer here to this experimental question: At what age will an animal first learn an episode involving olfaction? or taste? or audition? or vision? You will recall from chapter 7 that this is the sort of question asked in a systematic series of studies by Rudy, Vogt and Hyson (1984). Their answer was that the ontogenetic order of learning involved with different sensory systems was exactly the same as the ontogenetic order of sensory detection with these sensory systems. This might seem unsurprising; an animal could hardly learn about a stimulus it could not detect. But there was an unexpected feature of this evidence: there always seemed to be a lag between the age at which an event could be detected and the eventual age at which that event could be learned in association with another event.

Suppose it were generally true that in order to have the capacity for associative learning, additional development is needed beyond the capacity for detection. There is no reason why that additional development should occur at the same rate in all sensory systems (and one could hardly expect this anyway, given the differences in rate of development of the sensory systems themselves). It would thus be possible, for instance, for visual learning to emerge ontogenetically prior to auditory learning, even though the auditory sense develops before vision in terms of detection. But if there were a single unitary memory system into which all sensory events were funneled for processing toward learning and memory, one would not expect visual learning to precede auditory learning. So long as this hypothetical central memory system functions at an appropriately mature level, sensory detection and registration within any sensory system would be sufficient for learning and memory.

One might, however, speculate further that additional maturation might be needed in the pathways that link a sensory system to the hypothetical central memory system, which could require a certain amount of time beyond the age at which detection takes place. Even so, one would not expect a great deal of variance in the delay between detection capability and learning capability across sensory systems, if there were a single, central memory system. Otherwise—given a substantial lag between sensory detection and learning—we might need to consider the possibility of each sensory system functioning as a separate memory system. Further research in this important area will tell us whether this will be a real requirement.

Separate Memory Systems Associated with Separate Brain Structures

Evidence linking particular brain structures with apparently different kinds of memory has been gathered in several laboratories. Usually the focus has been on memory structures that seem important for one of two alternative kinds of memory. For instance, Mishkin and his colleagues have considered two possible memory systems in monkeys (see chapter 10). One is linked with simple multitrial discrimination learning and referred to as a habit memory system. This system presumably is based on associations between specific stimuli and responses. The other is supposed to control recognition memory, is tested usually with delayed matching-to-sample, and is viewed as an example of higher order organization or representational memory. This system is thought to be controlled by higher order sensory areas of the cortex, including a circuit that involves the limbic system and thalamus as well as the cortex (e.g., Mishkin, Malamut & Bachevalier 1984).

Two other frequently distinguished hypothetical systems are working memory and reference memory (see chapters 5, 6). Working memory, you will recall, operates on recently acquired information, such as which alternatives of a radial maze happen to be rewarded during this particular day. Reference memory deals with more general information, such as food sometimes is found at the ends of particular alleys in this maze. Control over working memory frequently has been hypothesized as residing in the hippocampus (e.g., Olton 1983).

Procedural and declarative memory provide another example. The instance referred to earlier in this chapter was that of amnesic patients who could readily acquire the procedures involved in learning to read with inverted print despite a drastic deficit in memory for what was read. Procedural memory has been linked with the results of indirect tests of memory or implicit memory, discussed earlier, and has been applied by Tulving (1983) as a separate, third system of memory in addition to episodic and semantic memory. Declarative memory, as used by Squire and Cohen (Cohen & Squire 1980; Squire 1987), is similar to episodic memory. Declarative memory is believed by Squire and his colleagues to be controlled by a circuit that involves the medial temporal cortex, including hippocampus and the diencephalic areas of the brain (the locus of control over procedural memory is less certain and probably more diffuse).

A relatively extensive theory of the control of multiple memory systems by discrete neural structures has been proposed by Kesner (1991). Kesner's approach is marked by careful attention to the literature of both human and animal memory, the creation of innovative tests of animal memory to simulate basic features of human memory, and the view that a memory consists of a variety of attributes. He proposes that an acquired memory includes attributes to represent each of five critical features of a learned episode: temporal, spatial, affect, sensory-perceptual, and response attributes. The theory generally is relatively complex, but a full description is not necessary for our purposes, and a few examples will suffice.

Kesner considers how memory attributes interact for higher levels of organization that include contextual control of retrieval and the development of cognitive maps. Analogous to several broad-based theories of memory, a distinction is made between a data-based memory system (the relatively recent facts at hand) and an expectancy-based system (acquired associations that generate expectancies in the face of particular stimuli). Within each of these systems, memory attributes combine in ways that allow empirical testing and indicate similarities with other theories. For instance, interactions among temporal and affect attributes produce moods that can combine with specific knowledge within the expectancy-based memory system, as is assumed in other theories for reference memory or semantic memory. On the other hand, combinations of the sensory-perceptual attributes and response attributes may interact within Kesner's expectancy-based system to become skills, analogous to Mishkin's habit memory or the procedural memory of Squire and Cohen.

A large number of experiments have indicated that particular brain areas are linked with separate aspects of Kesner's memory system. Included are apparent relationships between the hippocampus and attributes for external context, between the amygdala and attributes for internal context, between the caudate nucleus and hippocampus for spatial attributes, and among areas of the motor cortex, brain stem, and cerebellum for the control of skills resulting from the interaction between sensory-perceptual and response attributes.

A good example of the reach of Kesner's theory can be taken from tests of his hypothesis about memories involving temporal attributes. He proposes that such memories are mediated within the expectancy-based memory system by the dorsolateral or medial prefrontal cortex. The evidence to support this begins with the familiar observation that humans with damage to the frontal cortex have difficulty with short-term retention for the temporal order in which events occur. Although these patients may remember which events were presented, they have difficulty remembering their order—which events occurred first and which second, or which is the more or less recent. In other words, although retention of item information is relatively unaffected, retention of order information is drastically impaired. Monkeys with lesions in the dorsolateral prefrontal cortex seem to show a similar deficit in terms of tasks such as delayed matching-to-sample. The delayed matching problem, especially when only a few alternative samples are used, can be solved by simply discriminating the most recent event from the less recent event.

Rats with lesions in the medial prefrontal cortex (which probably serves the same function as the dorsolateral prefrontal cortex in monkeys and humans) also are deficient in memory for temporal order. Some studies have suggested this in terms of retention of specific response sequences or in delayed alternation. A more convincing test for dissociating item and order information in the rat was devised by Kesner and Holbrook (1987). Rats were trained until they learned that in an eight-arm radial maze, once an arm had been visited and the reinforcer (a Froot Loop) consumed, no further reward would be found in that alternative. They then were trained to remember the particular sequence with which they had visited four of the arms in the radial maze. This was assessed with a test in which two of the arms were made available for entry (say, items that were second and third in the previous sequence) and the rat's response was reinforced only if it chose the arm (item) that had occurred earlier in the sequence. Item memory was tested by allowing the animal entry into two alleys, one of which previously had been visited and one of which had not, with reward present only in the latter.

After the rats had become expert at remembering the sequential information and the item information, some of them were given lesions of the medial prefrontal cortex. These animals subsequently showed drastic impairment in remembering the sequence in which they had previously visited the alleys (order information), although they were relatively effective in remembering whether or not they had previously visited a particular alley (item information). Such a result lends significant support to the notion that this area of the prefrontal cortex is selective in its control over retention: retention of order information (as represented by a temporal attribute) is impaired but retention of item information (as represented by a spatial attribute) is spared. In this sense, one aspect of memory is dissociated from another in terms of its control by a particular brain structure.

This sort of dissociation experiment has been used to great advantage by Kesner and others. Kesner has completed several experiments that dissociate in both directions such that one area (e.g., the hippocampus) controls memories involving spatial attributes but not those involving temporal attributes, whereas another (e.g., prefrontal cortex) controls memories involving temporal attributes but not involving spatial attributes—a double dissociation (for another example, see Packard & McGaugh 1992). Such dissociation experiments are difficult to accomplish, but they provide a necessary condition for treating memory systems as if they were separate and perhaps independent.

How Many Memory Systems Really Exist and What Are They?

In one sense the answer to this question is quite simple: we do not know. But, of course, science would not progress very far if puzzles were left with that answer. The answer must be instead, "we do not know yet, so what can we do to find the answer?"

The first thing we must do is develop a sensible perspective on the problem. The proliferation of hypothetical systems or types of memory does not help. That such proliferation is easy enough, with or without evidence, was mentioned earlier and can be emphasized by the observations of two of the leading memory scientists of the past 50 years. Tulving (1972) counted, from an earlier book on memory models (Norman 1970), about 25 types of memory that were seriously discussed. He suggested that 50 such memory types probably could be found in the literature with relatively little effort. Underwood (1972) made an analogous point with reference to the complexity of theories and models of memory:

> *[At one time in the past] . . . it might have been said that most conceptualizations of memory were impoverished or simplistic in that they did not at all reflect the variety of memory phenomena evident even to the casual observer. If an increase in the size of the technical or semitechnical behavioral vocabulary signals escape from conceptual poverty, we have become liberated. Memories now have attributes, organization, and structure; there are storage systems, retrieval systems, and control systems. We have iconic, echoic, primary, secondary, and short-, medium-, and long-term memories. There are addresses, readout rules, and holding mechanisms; memories filled with T-stacks, implicit associational responses, natural-language mediators, images, multiple traces, tags, kernel sentences, markers, relational*

rules, verbal loops, and one-buns. Surely, it is only fitting that the workers in the field of memory should have available such an enormously rich and flexible vocabulary to provide the topic the awe it so rightfully deserves. (Underwood 1972, p. 1)

The implication was that much of the vocabulary and categorization in theories of memory may be unnecessary, and this remains true today. Given our present concern as to whether there is more than a single centralized memory system and that the best estimates of the experts rarely exceed three memory systems (e.g., Tulving 1985), we may infer that most of the memory systems that have been hypothesized have not been supported by the facts.

What sorts of evidence would convince scientists of the existence of any two or more specific memory systems? This issue falls in the realm of another discipline, philosophy of science, and it requires more discussion than we can afford here. There seems to be general agreement, however, that a first step is to establish functional dissociations of the sort illustrated by Kesner's work in the previous section. Functional dissociation, you will recall, means that if we have two learning tasks that are each said to represent different memory systems (e.g., one requiring memory for spatial events and the other memory for order or occurrence), a particular variable or treatment (e.g., drug, brain lesion, or distribution of practice) would affect performance on one of the tasks differently from that on the other task. To supplement the functional dissociation, converging evidence also is needed. This means that for a variety of procedures, experimental evidence associated with a particular memory system should converge in that all lead to the same fundamental conclusions about behavior. Another criterion often used is stochastic independence, which in this context usually means that the likelihood of, say, remembering in one of two ways (e.g., recall versus recognition), is independent of the alternative.

The problem is that even if all these criteria were met, it is still possible to generate a model of memory that could accommodate these facts and yet be based on either a single memory system or multiple memory systems. One approach has been to consider more carefully the mathematical nature of the functional dissociations observed, which seems to lead to more powerful criteria for deciding whether genuinely different memory systems are operating (Dunn & Kirsner 1988).

Another approach, by Jacoby and his colleagues (e.g., Jacoby & Kelley 1991) is directed toward correcting a particularly weak link in the experimental logic for testing the multiplicity of memory systems. The assumption has been that particular kinds of tasks correspond to particular kinds of memory processing. Jacoby points out, however, that there is probably no single task that is process pure in the sense that only one type of memory process is operating in completing the task. One of the great truths in psychology is that behavior is overdetermined; a particular behavioral outcome nearly always can be achieved by any of a number of psychological and biological mechanisms. If we want to study categories such as episodic versus semantic memory, automatic versus voluntary processing, implicit versus explicit memory, conscious versus unconscious information processing, and so forth, we are unlikely to find a memory test that does not include at least some aspect of each of the two alternative processes. What Jacoby has accomplished, with good effectiveness despite the difficulty of the problem, is to isolate process differences within a task. The details and results of Jacoby's procedures would require too extensive a description for our purposes, but the success of his approach is mentioned as a point of encouragement toward eventual solution of how the memory process generally is structured.

CHAPTER SUMMARY

A central issue in deciding about the structure of memory is whether a single memory process operates relatively uniformly throughout the brain and for all experiential circumstances. There are many alternatives to this, but they all rest on the notion that separate systems of memory have evolved to accommodate particular ecological challenges and different kinds of information. It is further plausible that if these different systems exist, they may have relatively separate neuroanatomical locations identifiable in terms of established brain structures.

These alternatives do not represent new issues in psychobiology. As examples, this chapter described numerous metaphors (i.e., types of memory systems) that have been offered for memory and the extensive historical precedents for one of the more successful distinctions between hypothetical memory systems (episodic versus semantic). Historical links with other hypothetically separate memory systems are equally easy to detect: for procedural and declarative memory, there is the old question of whether verbal learning and memory have characteristics different from learning and memory involving primarily motoric behavior; and for autonomic versus voluntary or implicit versus explicit memory, there are clear links with the ancient issues of unconscious versus conscious thoughts and behaviors. What has made the debate more interesting today and made more plausible the notion of multiple memory systems is the array of impressive instances of selective expression that seem, according to many scientists, to be understandable only in terms of the action of separate memory systems. It now seems clear that different classes of information are primarily processed in different, identifiable locations in the brain and have different functional characteristics (i.e., are affected differently by variation in the conditions of acquisition, postacquisition and requirements for retention). The task before us is to achieve clearer definition of classes of information and relevant brain locations, and broader identification of functional differences.

Brief consideration was given to the criteria one might use to decide about the number of memory systems that actually exist and to understand instances of selective expression. For the latter it now seems evident that the identification of particular memory tests as a pure representation of the action of a separate memory system (e.g., an implicit memory task or an explicit memory task) is no longer useful because process-pure memory tasks are unlikely. Further advancement probably will require the isolation of process differences within a memory task.

Finally, the issues in this chapter serve also to re-emphasize the importance of understanding the memory processing that takes place after learning has ostensibly been accomplished. It is certainly not that anyone totally understands the acquisition process, and indeed there remains a great deal to be discovered about this learning phase. Yet from our perspective it seems that for a reasonably alert animal or person, learning is almost inevitable, and it is postacquisition factors that determine much, perhaps most, of what is expressed in behavior.

References

Abernathy, E. M. 1940. The effect of changed environmental conditions upon the results of college examinations. *Journal of Psychology,* 10:293–301.

Adams, C. D., & Dickinson, A. 1981. Instrumental responding following reinforcer devaluation. *Quarterly Journal of Experimental Psychology,* 33B:105–22.

Adams, C. D. 1980. Postconditioning devaluation of instrumental reinforcer has no effect on extinction performance. *Quarterly Journal of Experimental Psychology,* 32:447–58.

Aghajanian, G. K., & Bloom, F. E. 1967. The formation of synaptic junctions in developing rat brain: A quantitative electron microscopic study. *Brain Research,* 6:716–27.

Ahlers, S., & Riccio, D. C. 1987. Anterograde amnesia induced by hypothermia in rats. *Behavioral Neuroscience,* 101:333–40.

Alba, J. W., Alexander, S. C., Hasher, L., & Caniglia, K. 1981. The role of context in the encoding of information. *Journal of Experimental Psychology: Human Learning and Memory,* 7:283–92.

Amsel, A. 1958. The role of frustrative nonreward in noncontinuous reward situations. *Psychological Bulletin,* 55:102–19.

———. 1986. Developmental psychobiology and behavior theory: Reciprocating influences. *Canadian Journal of Psychology,* 40:311–42.

Asratian, E. A. 1965. *Compensatory Adaptations, Reflex Activity and the Brain.* New York: Pergamon Press.

Atkinson, R. C., & Shiffrin, R. M. 1968. Human memory: A proposed system and its control processes. In *The Psychology of Learning and Motivation,* eds. K. W. Spence & J. T. Spence Vol. 2, 89–105. New York: Academic Press.

Bachevalier, J. 1991. Cortical versus limbic immaturity; relationship to infantile amnesia. In eds. N. Gunnar and C. A. Nelson, *Developmental Neuroscience,* 24: Hillsdale, NJ: Erlbaum.

Baddeley, A. D. 1990. *Human Memory: Theory and Practice.* Needham Heights, MA: Allyn & Bacon.

Bahrick, H. P., Bahrick, P. O., & Wittlinger, R. P. 1975. Fifty years of memories for names and faces: A cross-sectional approach. *Journal of Experimental Psychology: General,* 104:54–75.

Bahrick, H. P., Clark, S., & Bahrick, P. 1967. Generalization gradients as indicants of learning and retention of a recognition task. *Journal of Experimental Psychology,* 75:464–71.

Bahrick, H. P., & Hall, L. K. 1991. Lifetime maintenance of high school mathematics content. *Journal of Experimental Psychology: General,* 120:20–33.

Bahrick, H. P., & Phelps, E. 1987. Retention of Spanish vocabulary over eight years. *Journal of Experimental Psychology: Learning, Memory and Cognition,* 13:344–49.

Bakner, L., Strohen, K., Nordeen, M., & Riccio, D. C. 1991. Postconditioning recovery from the latent inhibition effect in conditioned taste aversion. *Physiology and Behavior,* 50:1269–72.

Balaz, M. A., Gustin, P., Cachiero, H., & Miller, R. R. 1982. Blocking as retrieval failure: Reactivation of associations to a blocked stimulus. *Quarterly Journal of Experimental Psychology,* 34B:99–113.

Barnes, J. M., & Underwood, B. J. 1959. "Fate" of first-list associations in transfer theory. *Journal of Experimental Psychology,* 58:97–105.

Bartlett, S. C. 1932. *Remembering: A Study in Experimental and Social Psychology.* Cambridge, England: Cambridge University Press.

Beatty, W. W., & Shavalia, D. A. 1980a. Spatial memory in rats: Time course of working memory and effects of anesthetics. *Behavioral and Neural Biology,* 28:454–62.

———. Rat spatial memory: Resistance to retroactive interference at long retention intervals. *Animal Learning & Behavior,* 8:550–52.

Beitel, R. E., & Porter, P. B. 1968. Deficits in short- and long-term retention and impairments in learning induced by severe hypothermia in mice. *Journal of Comparative and Physiological Psychology,* 66:53–59.

Bekerian, D. A., & Bowers, J. M. 1983. Eyewitness testimony: Were we misled? *Journal of Experimental Psychology: Human Learning and Memory,* 9:139–45.

Benson, D. F., & Geschwind, N. 1967. Shrinking retrograde amnesia. *Journal of Neurology, Neurosurgery and Psychiatry,* 30:539–44.

Berger, B., & Stein, L. 1964. Asymmetrical dissociation of learning between scopolamine and Wy4036, a new benzodiazepine tranquilizer. *Psychopharmacologia,* 14:351–58.

Bessemer, D. W., & Stollnitz, F. 1971. Retention of discriminations and an analysis of learning set. In *Behavior of Nonhuman Primates: Modern Research Trends.* eds. A. M. Schrier & F. Stollnitz, Vol. 4, 1–58. New York: Academic Press.

Bickford, R., Mulder, D. W., Dodge, H. W., Svien, H. J., & Rome, H. P. 1958. Changes in memory function produced by electrical stimulation of the temporal lobes in man. *Research Publications of the Association for Research in Nervous and Mental Disease,* 36:227–57.

Bindra, D., Nyman, B., & Wise, J. 1965. Barbiturate-induced dissociation of acquisition and extinction: Role of movement-initiating processes. *Journal of Comparative and Physiological Psychology,* 60:223–28.

Birnbaum, I. S., & Parker, E. S. 1977. *Alcohol and Human Memory*. Hillsdale, N.J.: Erlbaum.

Bjork, R. A., & Woodward, A. E., Jr. 1973. The directed forgetting of individual words in free recall. *Journal of Experimental Psychology*, 99:22–27.

Bliss, T. V. P., & Lomo, T. 1973. Long-lasting potentiation of synaptic transmission in the dentate area of the anesthetized rabbit following stimulation of the perforant path. *Quarterly Journal of Physiology*, 232:331.

Blough, D. S. 1959. Delayed matching in the pigeon. *Journal of the Experimental Analysis of Behavior*, 2:151–60.

Bohus, B. & de Wied, D. 1966. Inhibitory and facilitatory effect of two related peptides on extinction of avoidance behavior. *Science*, 66:318–20.

———. 1981. Actions of ACTH- and MSH-like peptides on learning, performance and retention. In *Endogenous Peptides and Learning and Memory Processes*, eds. J. L. Martinez, R. A. Jensen, R. B. Messing, H. Rigter, & J. L. McGaugh. New York: Academic Press.

Boothe, R. G., Vassdal, E., & Schneck, M. 1986. Experience and development in the visual system: Anatomical studies. In *Developmental Neuropsychobiology*, eds. W. T. Greenough & J. M. Juraska, 295–315. New York: Academic Press.

Borovsky, D., & Rovee-Collier, C. 1990. Contextual constraints on memory retrieval at six months. *Child Development*, 61:1569–83.

Bouton, M. E. 1991. Context and retrieval in extinction and in other examples of interference in simple associative learning. In *Current Topics in Animal Learning: Brain, Emotion, and Cognition*, eds. L. W. Dachowski & C. F. Flaherty. Hillsdale, N.J.: Erlbaum.

Bouton, M. E., & Swartzentruber, D. 1986. Analysis of the associative and occasion-setting properties of contexts participating in a Pavlovian discrimination. *Journal of Experimental Psychology: Animal Behavior Processes*, 12:333–50.

Bower, G. H. 1967. A multi-component theory of the memory trace. In *The Psychology of Learning and Motivation*, eds. K. W. Spence & J. T. Spence. New York: Academic Press.

———. 1978. Interference paradigms for meaningful propositional memory. *American Journal of Psychology*, 91:575–85.

———. 1981. Mood and memory. *American Psychologist*, 36:129–48.

Bower, G. H., Monteiro, K. P., & Gilligan, S. G. 1978. Emotional mood as a context for learning and recall. *Journal of Verbal Learning and Verbal Behavior*, 17:573–85.

Boyd, S. C., & Caul, W. F. 1979. Evidence of state-dependent learning of brightness discrimination in hypothermic mice. *Physiology and Behavior*, 23:147–53.

Bransford, J. D., & Johnson, M. L. 1972. Contextual prerequisites for understanding: Some investigations of comprehension and recall. *Journal of Verbal Learning and Verbal Behavior*, 11:717–20.

Braun, J. J., Meyer, P. M., & Meyer, D. R. 1966. Sparing of a brightness habit in rats following visual decortication. *Journal of Comparative and Physiological Psychology,* 61:79–82.

Bresnahan, E. E., & Routtenberg, A. 1980. Medial forebrain bundle stimulation during learning and subsequent retention disruption. *Physiological Psychology,* 8:112–19.

Brown, J. 1958. Some tests of the decay theory of immediate memory. *Quarterly Journal of Experimental Psychology,* 10:10–21.

Brown, R., & McNeill, D. 1966. The "tip-of-the-tongue" phenomenon. *Journal of Verbal Learning and Verbal Behavior,* 5:325–77.

Brush, F. R. 1971. Retention of aversively motivated behavior. In *Aversive Conditioning and Learning,* ed. F. R. Brush. New York: Academic Press.

Bures, J., & Buresova, O. 1963. Cortical spreading depression as a memory disturbing factor. *Journal of Comparative and Physiological Psychology,* 56:268–72.

Burr, D. E. S., & Thomas, D. R. 1972. The effect of proactive inhibition upon the post-dicrimination generalization gradient. *Journal of Comparative and Physiological Psychology,* 81:441–48.

Buschke, H. 1974. Spontaneous remembering after recall failure. *Science,* 184:579–81.

Campbell, B. A., & Alberts, J. R. 1979. Ontogeny of long-term memory for learned taste aversions. *Behavioral and Neural Biology,* 25:139–56.

Campbell, B. A., Hayne, H., & Richardson, R., eds. 1992. *Attention and Information Processing in Infants and Adults: Perspectives from Human and Animal Research.* Hillsdale, N.J.: Erlbaum.

Campbell, B. A., & Jaynes, J. 1966. Reinstatement. *Psychological Review,* 73:478–80.

Campbell, B. A., Misanin, J. R., White, B. C., & Lytle, L. D. 1974. Species differences in ontogeny of memory: Indirect support for neural maturation as a determinant of forgetting. *Journal of Comparative and Physiological Psychology,* 87:193–202.

Campbell, B. A., & Spear, N. E. 1972. Ontogeny of memory. *Psychological Review,* 79:215–36.

Capaldi, E. D. 1971. Memory and learning: A sequential viewpoint. In *Animal Memory,* eds. W. K. Honig & P. H. R. James. New York: Academic Press.

Capaldi, E. J., Viveiros, D. M., & Davidson, J. L. 1981. Deprivation, stimulus intensity and incentive factors in the control of instrumental responding. *Journal of Experimental Psychology: Animal Behavior Processes,* 7:140–49.

Carr, H. A. 1925. *Psychology: A Study of Mental Activity.* New York: Longmans, Green.

Catania, A. C. 1984. *Learning.* Englewood Cliffs, N.J.: Prentice Hall.

———. 1987. Behavior analysis and behavior synthesis in the extrapolation from animal to human behavior. In *Animal Models of Human Behavior,* ed. G. C. L. Davey, 51–69. New York: Wiley.

Cermak, L. S. 1982. The long and short of it in amnesia. In *Human Memory and Amnesia*, ed. L. S. Cermak, 43–60. Hillsdale, N.J.: Erlbaum.
Cermak, L. S., & Butters, N. 1972. The role of interference and encoding in the short-term memory deficits of Korsakoff patients. *Neuropsychologia*, 10:89–95.
Cermak, L. S., & Reale, L. 1978. Depth of processing and retention of words by alcoholic Korsakoff patients. *Journal of Experimental Psychology: Human Learning and Memory*, 4:165–74.
Chen, W. J., Lariviere, N. A., Heyser, C., Spear, L. P., & Spear, N. E. 1991. Age-related differences in sensory conditioning. *Developmental Psychobiology*, 24:307–25.
Chiszar, D. A., & Spear, N. E. 1969. Stimulus change, reversal learning, and retention in the rat. *Journal of Comparative and Physiological Psychology*, 69:190–95.
Christiansen, R. E., & Ochalek, K. 1983. Editing misleading information from memory: Evidence for the coexistence of original and postevent information. *Memory and Cognition*, 11:467–75.
Chute, D. L., & Wright, D. C. 1973. Retrograde state-dependent learning. *Science*, 180:878–80.
Ciszewski, W. A., & Flaherty, C. F. 1977. Failure of a reinstatement treatment to influence negative contrast. *American Journal of Psychology*, 90:219–29.
Clayton, K. N. 1974. The distinction between long- and short-term memory. Report Series of the Department of Psychology, Vanderbilt University.
Cohen, J. S., Galgan, R., & Fuerst, D. 1986. Retrospective and prospective short-term memory in delayed response tasks in rats. *Animal Learning and Behavior*, 14:38–50.
Cohen, N. J., & Squire, L. R. 1980. Preserved learning and retention of pattern-analyzing skill in amnesia: Dissociation of "knowing how" and "knowing that." *Science*, 210:207–9.
Collins, A. M., & Loftus, E. F. 1975. A spreading-activation theory of semantic processing. *Psychological Review*, 82:407–28.
Columbo, M., & D'Amato, M. R. 1986. A comparison of visual and auditory short-term memory in monkeys *(Cebus apella)*. *Quarterly Journal of Experimental Psychology*, 38B:425–48.
Colwill, R. M., & Rescorla, R. A. 1985. Postconditioning devaluation of a reinforcer affects instrumental responding. *Journal of Experimental Psychology: Animal Behavior Processes*, 11:120–32.
———. 1990. Effect of reinforcer devaluation on discriminative control of instrumental behavior. *Journal of Experimental Psychology: Animal Behavior Processes*, 16:40–47.
Concannon, J. T., & Carr, M. 1982. Pretest epinephrine injections reverse DDC-induced retrograde amnesia. *Physiology and Behavior*, 9:443–48.

Cook, R. G., Brown, M. F., & Riley, D. A. 1985. Flexible memory processing by rats: Use of prospective and retrospective information in the radial maze. *Journal of Experimental Psychology: Animal Behavior Processes,* 11:453–69.

Corby, J., Caza, P. A., & Spear, N. E. 1982. Ontogenetic changes in the effectiveness of home nest odor as a conditioned stimulus. *Behavioral and Neural Biology,* 35:354–67.

Corkin, S., Cohen, N. J., Sullivan, E. V., Clegg, R. A., Rosen, T. J., & Ackerman, R. H. 1985. Analyses of global memory impairments of different etiologies. *Annals of the New York Academy of Sciences,* 444:10–40.

Cotton, J. W., & Jensen, G. D. 1963. Successive acquisitions and extinctions in a T-maze. *Journal of Experimental Psychology,* 65:546–51.

Coulombe, O., & White, N. M. 1980. The effect of post-training lateral hypothalamic stimulation on aversive and appetitive classical conditioning. *Physiology and Behavior,* 25:267–72.

Coulter, X., Collier, A., & Campbell, B. A. 1976. Long-term retention of Pavlovian fear conditioning by infant rats. *Journal of Experimental Processes: Animal Behavior Processes,* 2:48–56.

Cowan, W. M. 1985. The development of the brain. *Scientific American,* 241:112–133.

Craik, R. I. M., & Tulving, E. 1975. Depth of processing and the retention of words in episodic memory. *Journal of Experimental Psychology: General,* 104:268–94.

Crespi, L. P. 1942. Quantitative variation of incentive and performance in the white rat. *American Journal of Psychology,* 55:467–517.

D'Amato, M. R. 1973. Delayed matching and short-term memory in monkeys. In *The Psychology of Learning and Motivation: Advances in Theory and Research,* ed. G. H. Bower, Vol. 7, 227–69. New York: Academic Press.

D'Amato, M. R., & O'Neill, W. 1971. Effect of delayed-interval illumination on matching behavior in the capuchin monkey. *Journal of the Experimental Analysis of Behavior,* 15:327–33.

D'Amato, M. R., & Salmon, D. P. 1984. Processing and retention of complex auditory stimuli in monkeys *(Cebus apella). Canadian Journal of Psychology,* 38:237–55.

Davies, R. 1991. You're not getting older, you're getting nosier, 1:35–36. *New York Times Review of Books,* May 12, 1991.

Davis, J. C., & Okada, R. 1971. Recognition and recall of positively forgotten items. *Journal of Experimental Psychology,* 89, 181–86.

Dekeyne, A., & Deweer, B. 1990. Interaction between competing memories in the rat: Contextual pretest cuing reverses control of behavior by testing context. *Animal Learning and Behavior,* 18:1–12.

Delamater, A. R., & LoLordo, V. M. 1991. Event revaluation procedures and associative structures in Pavlovian conditioning. In *Current Topics in Animal Learning: Brain, Emotion and Cognition,* eds. L. Dachowski & C. F. Flaherty, 55–94. Hillsdale, N.J.: Erlbaum.

Desiderato, O., Butler, B., & Meyer, C. 1966. Changes in fear generalization gradients as a function of delayed testing. *Journal of Experimental Psychology,* 72:678–82.

Detterman, D. K. 1975. The Von Restoff effect and induced amnesia: Production by manipulation of sound intensity. *Journal of Experimental Psychology: Human Learning and Memory,* 1:614–28.

Detterman, D. K., & Ellis, N. R. 1972. Determinants of induced amnesia in short-term memory. *Journal of Experimental Psychology,* 95:380–86.

Deutsch, J. A., Hamburg, M. D., & Dahl, H. 1966. Anticholinesterase-induced amnesia and its temporal aspects. *Science,* 151:221–23.

DeVietti, T. L., & Holliday, J. J. 1972. Retrograde amnesia produced by ECS after reactivation of a consolidated memory trace: A replication. *Psychonomic Science,* 29:137–38.

DeVietti, T. L., & Hopfer, T. M. 1974. Reinstatement of memory in rats: Dependence upon two forms of retrieval deficit following electroconvulsive shock. *Journal of Comparative and Physiological Psychology,* 86:1090–99.

Deweer, B. 1986. Pretest cuing after forgetting of a food-motivated maze task in rats: Synergistic action of context in reinforcement. *Animal Learning and Behavior,* 14:249–56.

Deweer, B., & Sara, S. J. 1984. Background stimuli as a reminder after spontaneous forgetting: Role of duration of cuing and cuing-test interval *Animal Learning and Behavior,* 12:238–47.

Deweer, B., Sara, S. J., & Hars, B. 1980. Contextual cues and memory retrieval in rats: Alleviation of forgetting by a pretest exposure to background stimuli. *Animal Learning and Behavior,* 8:265–72.

deWied, D. 1966. Inhibitory effect of ACTH and related peptides on extinction of conditioned avoidance behavior in rats. *Proceedings of the Society for Experimental Biology and Medicine,* 122:28–32.

———. 1984. Neurohypophyseal hormone influence on learning and memory processes. In *Neurobiology of Learning and Memory,* eds. G. Lynch, J. L. McGaugh, & N. M. Weinberger. New York: Guilford Press.

Dickens, C. 1870. *The Mystery of Edwin Drood.* Oxford: Clarendon Press.

DiMattia, B. V., & Kesner, R. P. 1984. Serial position curves in rats: Automatic versus effortful information processing. *Journal of Experimental Psychology: Animal Behavior Processes,* 10:557–63.

Domjan, M. 1985. Cue-consequence specificity and long-delay learning revised. *Annals of the New York Academy of Sciences,* 443:54–66.

———. 1993. *The Principles of Learning and Behavior,* 3rd ed. Belmont, CA: Wadsworth.

Doris, J. 1991. *The Suggestibility of Children's Recollections.* Washington, D.C.: American Psychological Association.

Doty, R. W. 1984. Some thoughts and some experiments on memory. In *Neuropsychology of Memory,* eds. L. R. Squire & N. Butters, 330–38. New York: Guilford Press.

Drucker-Colin, R. R., & McGaugh, J. L. 1979. *Neurobiology of Sleep and Memory.* New York: Academic Press.

Dudycha, G. J., & Dudycha, M. M. 1941. Childhood memories: A review of the literature. *Psychological Bulletin,* 38:668–82.

Duncan, C. P. 1949. The retroactive effect of electroshock on learning. *Journal of Comparative and Physiological Psychology,* 42:32–44.

Dunn, J. C., & Kirsner, K. 1988. Discovering functionally independent mental processes: The principle of reversed association. *Psychological Review,* 95:91–101.

Ebbinghaus, H. 1913. *Memory: A Contribution to Experimental Psychology,* trans. H. A. Ruger & C. E. Bussanius. New York: Bureau of Publications, Teachers College, Columbia University.

Ebner, D. L., Richardson, R., & Riccio, D. C. 1981. Ovarian hormones and retention of learned fear in rats. *Behavioral and Neural Biology,* 33:45–58.

Edwards, C. A., Miller, J. S., & Zentall, T. R. 1985. Control of pigeons' matching and mismatching performance by instructional cues. *Animal Learning and Behavior,* 13:382–91.

Eich, J. E. 1980. The cue-dependent nature of state-dependent retrieval. *Memory and Cognition,* 8:157–73.

Eich, J. E., Weingartner, H., Stillman, R. C., & Gillin, J. C. 1975. State-dependent accessibility of retrieval cues in the retention of a categorized list. *Journal of Verbal Learning and Verbal Behavior,* 14:408–17.

———. 1985. Context, memory, and integrated item/context imagery. *Journal of Experimental Psychology: Learning, Memory and Cognition,* 11:764–70.

Ekstrand, B. R. 1967. The effect of sleep on memory. *Journal of Experimental Psychology,* 75:64–72.

———. 1972. To sleep, perchance to dream (about why we forget). In *Human Memory: Festschrift in Honor of Benton J. Underwood,* eds. C. P. Duncan, L. Sechrest, & A. W. Melton. New York: Appleton-Century-Crofts.

Ellis, H. E. 1985. On the importance of mood intensity and encoding demands in memory: Commentary on Hasher, Rose, Zacks, Sanft and Doren. *Journal of Experimental Psychology: General,* 114:392–95.

Ellis, H. C., Thomas, R. L., McFarland, A. D., & Lane, J. W. 1985. Emotional mood states and retrieval in episodic memory. *Journal of Experimental Psychology: Learning, Memory and Cognition,* 11:363–70.

Erdelyi, M. H., & Becker, J. 1974. Hypermnesia for pictures: Incremental memory for pictures but not words in multiple recall trials. *Cognitive Psychology,* 6:159–71.

Essman, W. B., & Sudak, F. N. 1963. Effect of hypothermia on the establishment of a conditioned avoidance response in mice. *Journal of Comparative and Physiological Psychology,* 56:366–69.

Estes, W. K. 1959. The statistical approach to learning theory. In *Psychology: A Study of Science,* ed. S. Koch, Vol. 2. New York: McGraw-Hill.

———. 1973. Memory and conditioning. In *Contemporary Approaches to Conditioning and Learning*, eds. F. J. McGuigan & D. B. Lumsden, 265–86. Washington, D.C.: Winston.

Eysenk, M. W. 1977. *Human Memory: Theory, Research and Individual Differences*. New York: Pergamon Press.

Fagen, J. W., & Rovee-Collier, C. 1983. Memory retrieval: A time-locked process in infancy. *Science*, 222:1349–51.

Feigley, D. A., & Spear, N. E. 1970. Effect of age and punishment condition on long-term retention by the rat of active- and passive-aviodance learning. *Journal of Comparative and Physiological Psychology*, 73:515–26.

Fernandez, A., & Glenberg, M. 1985. Changing environmental context does not reliably affect memory. *Memory and Cognition*, 13:333–45.

Fifer, W. P. 1987. Neonatal preference for mother's voice. In *Perinatal Development: A Psychobiological Perspective*, eds. N. A. Krasnegor, E. M. Blass, M. A. Hofer, & W. P. Smotherman, 111–44. Orlando, Fla. Academic Press.

Finger, S., & Stein, D. G. 1982. *Brain Damage and Recovery: Research and Clinical Experience*. New York: Academic Press.

Fishbein, W., ed. 1981. *Sleep, Dreams and Memory*. New York: Spectrum.

Fishbein, W., & Gutwein, B. M. 1977. Paradoxical sleep and memory storage processes. *Behavioral Biology*, 19:425–64.

Flaherty, C. F. 1982. Incentive contrast: A review of behavioral changes following shifts in reward. *Animal Learning and Behavior*, 10:409–40.

———. 1985. *Animal Learning and Cognition*. New York: Knopf.

Flaherty, C. F., & Largen, J. 1975. Within-subjects positive and negative contrast effects in rats. *Journal of Comparative and Physiological Psychology*, 88:653–64.

Fowler, J. M., Sullivan, M. J., & Ekstrand, B. R. 1973. Sleep and memory. *Science*, 179:302–04.

Freedman, J. L., & Loftus, E. F. 1971. Retrieval of words from long-term memory. *Journal of Verbal Learning and Verbal Behavior*, 10:107–15.

Freud, S. 1938. *The Basic Writings of Sigmund Freud*, trans. A. A. Brill. New York: Random House.

Gabriel, M. 1972. Incubation of avoidance produced by generalization to stimuli of the conditioning apparatus. In *Topics in Learning and Performance*, eds. R. F. Thompson & J. F. Voss, 59–84. New York: Academic Press.

Gaffan, D., & Murray, E. A. 1992. Monkeys *(Macaca fascicularis)* with rhinal cortex ablasions succeed in object discrimination learning despite 24-hr intertrial intervals and fail at matching to sample despite double sample presentations. *Behavioral Neuroscience*, 106:30–38.

Gallagher, M. 1982. Naloxone enhancement of memory processes: Effects of other opiate antagonists. *Behavioral and Neural Biology*, 35:375–87.

———. 1984. Neurochemical modulation of memory: A case for opioid peptides. In *Neuropsychology of Memory*, eds. N. Burns & L. Squire. New York: Guilford Press.

Gallagher, M., Bostock, E., & King, R. 1985. Effects of opiate antagonists on spatial memory in young and aged rats. *Behavioral and Neural Biology,* 44:374–88.

Gallagher, M., & Kapp, B. S. 1978. Manipulation of opiate activity in the amygdala alters memory processes. *Life Sciences,* 23:1973–78.

———. 1981. Influence of amygdala opiate sensitive mechanisms, fear-motivated responses, and memory processes for aversive experiences. In *Endogenous Peptides and Learning and Memory Processes,* eds. J. L. Martinez, R. A. Jensen, R. B. Messing, H. Rigter, & J. L. McGaugh. New York: Academic Press.

Garcia, J., & Koelling, R. 1966. Relation of cue to consequence in avoidance learning. *Psychonomic Science,* 4:123–24.

Gardner, E. L., Glick, S. D., & Jarvik, M. E. 1972. ECS dissociation of learning and one-way cross-dissociation with physostigmine and scopolamine. *Physiology and Behavior,* 8:11–15.

Geiselman, R. E., Fisher, R. P., MacKinnon, D. P., & Holland, H. L. 1985. Eyewitness memory enhancement in the police interview: Cognitive retrieval mnemonics versus hypnosis. *Journal of Applied Psychology,* 70:401–12.

———. 1986. Enhancement of eyewitness memory with a cognitive interview. *American Journal of Psychology,* 99:385–401.

Geller, A., & Jarvik, M. E. 1968. The time relations of ECS-induced amnesia. *Psychonomic Science,* 12:169–70.

———. 1970. The role of consolidation in memory. In *Biochemistry of Brain and Behavior,* eds. R. E. Bowman & S. P. Datta. New York: Plenum Press.

Gerson, R., & Hendersen, R. W. 1978. Conditions that potentiate the effects of electroconvulsive shock administered 24 hours after avoidance training. *Animal Learning and Behavior,* 6:346–51.

Gisquet-Verrier, P., & Alexinsky, T. 1986. Does contextual change determine long-term forgetting? *Animal Learning and Behavior,* 14:349–58.

———. 1988. Time-dependent fluctuations of retention performance in an aversively motivated task. *Animal Learning and Behavior,* 16:58–66.

Gisquet-Verrier, P., Dekeyne, A., & Alexinsky, T. 1989. Differential effects of several retrieval cues over time: Evidence for time-dependent reorganization of memory. *Animal Learning and Behavior,* 17:394–408.

Gleitman, H. 1971. Forgetting of long-term memories in animals. In *Animal Memory,* eds. W. K. Honig & P. H. R. James. New York: Academic Press.

Gleitman, H., & Steinman, F. 1964. Depression effect as a function of retention interval before and after shift in reward magnitude. *Journal of Comparative and Physiological Psychology,* 57:158–60.

Godden, D. R., & Baddeley, A. D. 1975. Context-dependent memory in two natural environments: On land and underwater. *British Journal of Psychology,* 66:325–31.

Gold, P. E. 1986. Glucose modulation of memory storage processing. *Behavioral and Neural Biology,* 45:342–49.

———. 1987. Sweet memories. *American Scientist,* 75:151–55.

―――. 1989. Neurobiological features common to memory modulation by many treatments. *Animal Learning and Behavior,* 17:94–100.

Gold, P. E., & King, R. A. 1974. Retrograde amnesia: Storage failure versus retrieval failure. *Psychological Review,* 81:465–69.

Gold, P. E., & VanBuskirk, R. B. 1975. Facilitation of time-dependent memory processes with post-trial epinephrine injections. *Behavioral Biology,* 13:145–53.

―――. 1976a. Effects of post-trial hormone injections on memory processes. *Hormones and Behavior,* 7:509–17.

―――. 1976b. Enhancement and impairment of memory processes with post-trial injections of adrenocorticotrophic hormone. *Behavioral Biology,* 16:387–400.

Gomulicki, B. R. 1953. The development and the present status of the trace theory of memory. *British Journal of Psychology,* 29 (monograph supplement).

Goodwin, D. W., Powell, B., Bremer, D., Hoine, H., & Stern, J. 1969. Alcohol and recall: State-dependent effects in man. *Science,* 163:1358–60.

Gordon, W. C. 1981. Mechanisms of cue-induced retention enhancement. In *Information Processing in Animals: Memory Mechanisms,* eds. N. E. Spear & R. R. Miller, 319–39. Hillsdale, N.J.: Erlbaum.

―――. 1983. The malleability of memory in animals, In *Animal Cognition and Behavior,* ed. R. L. Mellgren. New York: North Holland.

―――. 1989. *Learning and Memory.* Pacific Grove, Calif.: Brooks/Cole.

Gordon, W. C., Flaherty, C. F., & Riley, E. P. 1973. Negative contrast as a function of the interval between preshift and postshift training. *Bulletin of the Psychonomic Society,* 1:25–27.

Gordon, W. C., Frankl, S. E., & Hamberg, J. M. 1979. Reactivation-induced proactive interference in rats. *American Journal of Psychology,* 92:693–702.

Gordon, W. C., & Mowrer, R. R. 1980. The use of an extinction trial as a reminder treatment following CS. *Animal Learning and Behavior,* 8:363–67.

Gordon, W. C., McCracken, K. M., Dess-Beech, N., & Mowrer, R. R. 1981. Mechanisms for the cueing phenomenon: The addition of cueing context to the training memory. *Learning and Motivation,* 12:196–211.

Gordon, W. C., & Spear, N. E. 1973a. The effect of reactivation of a previously acquired memory on the interaction between memories in the rat. *Journal of Experimental Psychology,* 99:349–55.

―――. 1973b. The effects of strychnine on recently acquired and reactivated passive avoidance memories. *Physiology and Behavior,* 10:1071–75.

Gould, J. L. 1986. The locale map of honeybees: Do insects have cognitive maps? *Science,* 232:861–63.

Graefe, T. M., & Watkins, M. J. 1980. Picture rehearsal: An effect of selectively attending to pictures no longer in view. *Journal of Experimental Psychology: Human Learning and Memory,* 6:156–62.

Graf, P., & Schacter, D. L. 1985. Implicit and explicit memory for new associations in normal and amnesic subjects. *Journal of Experimental Psychology: Learning, Memory and Cognition,* 11:501–18.

Graf, P., Squire, L. R., & Mandler, G. 1984. The information that amnesics do not forget. *Journal of Experimental Psychology: Learning, Memory and Cognition,* 10:164–78.

Grant, D. S. 1976. Effect of sample presentation time on long-delay matching in the pigeon. *Learning and Motivation,* 7:580–90.

———. 1981. Short-term memory in the pigeon. In *Information Processing in Animals: Memory Mechanisms,* eds. N. E. Spear & R. R. Miller, 227–56. Hillsdale, N.J.: Erlbaum.

———. 1982. Stimulus control of information processing in rat short-term memory. *Journal of Experimental Psychology: Animal Behavior Processes,* 8:154–64.

———. 1984. Rehearsal in pigeon short-term memory. In *Animal Cognition,* eds. H. L. Roitblat, T. G. Bever, & H. S. Terrace, 99–115. Hillsdale, N.J.: Erlbaum.

———. 1988. Sources of visual interference in delayed matching-to-sample with pigeons. *Journal of Experimental Psychology: Animal Behavior Processes,* 14:368–75.

Grant, D. S., Brewster, R. G., & Stierhoff, K. A. 1983. "Surprisingness" and short-term retention in pigeons. *Journal of Experimental Psychology: Animal Behavior Processes,* 9:63–79.

Grant, D. S., & Roberts, W. A. 1976. Sources of retroactive inhibition in pigeon short-term memory. *Journal of Experimental Psychology: Animal Behavior Processes,* 2:1–16.

Gray, P. 1977. Effect of the estrous cycle on conditioned avoidance in mice. *Hormones and Behavior,* 8:235–41.

Greenwald, A. G. 1992. Unconscious cognition reclaimed. *American Psychologist,* 47:766–79.

Grossman, S. P. 1967. *A Textbook of Physiological Psychology.* New York: Wiley.

Guttman, N., & Kalish, H. I. 1958. Discriminability and stimulus generalization. *Journal of Experimental Psychology,* 51:79–88.

Hamberg, J. M., & Spear, N. E. 1978. Alleviation of forgetting of discrimination learning. *Learning and Motivation,* 9:466–76.

Harlow, H. F. 1959. Learning set and error factor theory. In *Psychology: A Study of Science,* ed. S. Koch, 492–537. New York: McGraw-Hill.

Haroutunian, V., Barnes, E., & Davis, K. L. 1985. Cholinergic modulation of memory in rats. *Psychopharmacology,* 87:266–71.

Hasher, L., & Zacks, R. T. 1984. Automatic processing of fundamental information: The case of frequency occurrence. *American Psychologist,* 39:1372–88.

Hebb, D. O. 1949. *The Organization of Behavior.* New York: Wiley.

Heckelman, S. B., & Spear, N. E. 1967. Supplementary report: The effect of intralist similarity on free learning in children. *Journal of Verbal Learning and Verbal Behavior,* 6:448–51.

Henderson, N. D. 1980. Effects of early experience upon the behavior of animals: The second twenty-five years of research. In *Early Experiences and Early Behavior: Implications for Social Development,* ed. E. C. Simmel, 39–77. New York: Academic Press.

Hendersen, R. W. 1985. Fearful memories: The motivational significance of forgetting. In *Affect, Conditioning and Cognition: Essays on the Determinants of Behavior,* eds. F. R. Brush & J. B. Overmier, 43–53. Hillsdale, N.J.: Erlbaum.

Hendersen, R. W., Patterson, J. M., & Jackson, R. L. 1980. Acquisition and retention of control of instrumental behavior by a cue-signaling air blast: How specific are conditioned anticipations? *Learning and Motivation,* 11:407–26.

Herrmann, D. J. 1982. The semantic-episodic distinction in the history of long-term memory typologies. *Bulletin of the Psychonomic Society,* 20:207–10.

Hill, W. F., Cotton, J. W., Spear, N. E., & Duncan, D. P. 1969. Retention of T-maze learning after varying intervals following partial and continuous reinforcement. *Journal of Experimental Psychology,* 79:584–85.

Hinderliter, C. F., & Misanin, J. R. 1988. Weanling and senescent rats process simultaneously-presented odor and tast differently than young adults. *Behavioral and Neural Biology,* 49:112–17.

Hinderliter, C. F., Webster, T., & Riccio, D. C. 1975. Amnesia induced by hypothermia as a function of treatment-test interval and recooling in rats. *Animal Learning and Behavior,* 3:257–63.

Hintzman, D. L. 1978. *The Psychology of Learning and Memory.* San Francisco: Freeman.

———. 1990. Human learning and memory: Connections and dissociations. *Annual Review of Psychology,* 41:109–39.

Hitchcock, C. L., & Sherry, D. F. 1990. Long-term memory for cache sites in the black-capped chickadee. *Animal Behaviour,* 40:701–12.

Hoffman, H. S., Fleshler, M., & Jensen, P. 1963. Stimulus aspects of aversive controls: The retention of conditioned suppression. *Journal of the Experimental Analysis of Behavior,* 6:575–83.

Hoffmann, H., Hunt, P. S., & Spear, N. E. 1991. Ontogenetic differences in CS palatability following conditioned taste aversion. *Learning and Motivation,* 22:329–52.

Holland, P. C. 1983. Representation-mediated overshadowing and potentiation of conditioned aversions. *Journal of Experimental Psychology: Animal Behavior Processes,* 9:1–13.

———. 1984. Origins of behavior in Pavlovian conditioning. In *The Psychology of Learning and Motivation,* ed. G. Bower, 129–74. New York: Academic Press.

———. 1990. Forms of memory in Pavlovian conditioning. In *Brain Organization and Memory: Cells, Systems and Circuits,* eds. J. L. McGaugh, N. M. Weinberger, & G. Lynch, 78–105. New York: Oxford University Press.

Holland, P. C., & Forbes, D. T. 1982. Control of conditional discrimination performance by CS-evoked event representations. *Animal Learning and Behavior,* 10:249–56.

Holloway, F. A., & Wansley, R. A. 1973a. Multiple retention deficits at periodic intervals after active and passive avoidance learning. *Behavioral Biology,* 9:1–14.

———. 1973b. Multiphasic retention deficits at periodic intervals after passive avoidance learning. *Science,* 180:208–10.

Honey, R. C., Willis, A., & Hall, G. 1990. Context specificity in pigeon autoshaping. *Learning and Motivation,* 21:125–36.

Honig, W. K. 1978. Studies of working memory in the pigeon. In *Cognitive Processes in Animal Behavior,* eds. S. H. Hulse, H. Fowler, & W. K. Honig. Hillsdale, N.J.: Erlbaum.

———. 1984. Contributions of animal memory to the interpretation of animal learning. In *Animal Cognition,* eds. H. L. Roitblat, T. G. Bever, & H. S. Terrace, 29–44. Hillsdale, N.J.: Erlbaum.

Honig, W. K., & Thompson, R. K. R. 1982. Retrospective and prospective processing in animal working memory. In *The Psychology of Learning and Memory,* ed. G. H. Bower, Vol. 16, 239–82. New York: Academic Press.

Howard, R. L., Glendenning, R. L., & Meyer, D. R. 1974. Motivational control of retrograde amnesia: Further explorations and effects. *Journal of Comparative and Physiological Psychology,* 86:187–92.

Howes, D. H., & Solomon, R. L. 1950. A note on McGinnies 'emotionality and perceptual defense.' *Psychological Review,* 57:229–34.

Hubel, D. H., & Weisel, T. N. 1965. Effects of visual deprivation on morphology and physiology of cells in the cat's lateral geniculate body. *Journal of Neurophysiology,* 26:978–92.

Hull, C. L. 1943. *Principles of Behavior.* New York: Appleton-Century-Crofts.

Hunt, J. McV. 1979. Psychological development: Early experience. In *Annual Review of Psychology,* eds. M. R. Rosenzweig & L. W. Porter. Palo Alto, Calif.: Annual Reviews.

Hunt, E., & Love, T. 1972. How good can memory be? In *Coding Processes in Human Memory,* eds. A. W. Melton & E. Martin, 237–60. Washington, D.C.: Winston & Sons.

Hunter, W. S. 1913. The delayed reaction in animals and children. *Behavior Monographs,* 2 (Serial No. 6).

Huppert, F. A., & Piercy, M. 1977. Recognition memory in amnesic patients: A deficit of acquisition? *Neuropsychologia,* 15:643–52.

———. 1978. Dissociation between learning and remembering in organic amnesia. *Nature* (London), 275:317–18.

Hyde, T. S., & Jenkins, J. J. 1973. Recall for words as a function of semantic, graphic and syntactic orienting tasks. *Journal of Verbal Learning and Verbal Behavior,* 12:471–80.

Hyson, R. L., & Rudy, J. W. 1984. Ontogenesis of learning. II. Variation in the rat's reflexive and learned responses to gustatory stimulation. *Developmental Psychobiology,* 17:263–83.

Intraub, H. 1980. Presentation rate and the representation of briefly glimpsed pictures in memory. *Journal of Experimental Psychology: Human Learning and Memory,* 6:1–12.

Introini-Collison, I. B., & McGaugh, J. L. 1986. Epinephrine modulates long-term retention of an aversively motivated discrimination. *Behavioral and Neural Biology,* 45:358–65.

Isaacson, R. L., & Spear, N. E., eds. 1982. *The Expression of Knowledge.* New York: Plenum Press.

Izquierdo, I., & Dias, R. D. 1983. Memory as a state-dependent phenomenon: Role of ACTH and epinephrine. *Behavioral and Neural Biology,* 38:144–51.

Jacobs, B. L., & Sorenson, C. A. 1969. Memory disruption in mice by brief posttrial immersion in hot or cold water. *Journal of Comparative and Physiological Psychology,* 68:239–44.

Jacoby, L. L. 1988. Memory observed and memory unobserved. In *Remembering Reconsidered: Ecological and Traditional Approaches to the Study of Memory,* eds. U. Neisser & E. Winograd, 145–77. Cambridge, England: Cambridge University Press.

Jacoby, L. L., & Brooks, L. R. 1984. Nonanalytic cognition: Memory, perception, and concept learning. In *The Psychology of Learning and Motivation,* ed. G. H. Bower, Vol. 18, 1–47. New York: Academic Press.

Jacoby, L. L., & Craik, F. I. M. 1979. Effects of elaboration of processing at encoding and retrieval: Trace distinctiveness and recovery of initial context. In *Levels of Processing in Human Memory,* eds. L. S. Cermak & F. I. M. Craik. Hillsdale, N.J.: Erlbaum.

Jacoby, L. L., & Kelley, C. M. 1991. Unconscious influences of memory: Dissociations and automaticity. In *The Neuropsychology of Consciousness,* eds. D. Milner & M. Rugg, 201–33. San Diego: Academic Press.

Jacoby, L. L., Lindsay, D. S., & Toth, J. P. 1992. Unconscious influences revealed: Attention, awareness and control. *American Psychologist,* 47:802–9.

Jacoby, L. L., & Witherspoon, D. 1982. Remembering without awareness. *Canadian Journal of Psychology,* 36:300–24.

James, W. 1890. *The Principles of Psychology,* Vol. II. New York: Holt.

Jarrard, L. E., & Moise, S. L. 1971. Short-term memory in the monkey. In *Cognitive Processes of Non-Human Primates,* ed. L. E. Jarrard. New York: Academic Press.

Jenkins, J. B., & Dallenbach, K. M. 1924. Oblivescence during sleep and waking. *American Journal of Psychology,* 35:605–12.

Jensen, G. D., & Cotton, J. W. 1960. Successive acquisitions and extinctions as related to percentage of reinforcement. *Journal of Experimental Psychology,* 60:41–49.

Jensen, L. C., Harris, K., & Anderson, D. C. 1971. Retention following a change in ambient contextual stimuli for six age groups. *Developmental Psychology,* 4:394–99.

Johanson, I. B., & Hall, W. G. 1979. Appetitive learning in 1-day old rat pups. *Science,* 205:419–21.

Johnson, M. K. 1983. A multiple-entry modular memory system. In *The Psychology of Learning and Motivation: Advances in Research Theory,* ed. G. H. Bower, 81–123. New York: Academic Press.
———. 1985. The origin of memories. In *Advances in Cognitive-Behavioral Research and Therapy,* ed. P. C. Kendall, 1–27. New York: Academic Press.
———. 1989. Functional forms of human memory. In *Brain Organization and Memory: Cells, Systems and Circuits,* eds. J. L. McGaugh, N. M. Weinberger, & G. Lynch. New York: Oxford University Press.
Johnson, M. K., & Hasher, L. 1987. Human learning and memory. *Annual Review of Psychology,* 38:631–68.
Johnson, M. K., & Magaro, P. A. 1987. Effects of mood and severity on memory processes in depression and mania. *Psychological Bulletin,* 101:28–40.
Jouvet, M. 1961. Telencephalic and rhombencephalic sleep in the cat. In *Symposium on the Nature of Sleep,* eds. G. Wolstenholme & M. O'Connor. Boston: Little, Brown.
Joy, R. M., & Prinz, P. N. 1969. The effect of sleep-altering environments upon the acquisition and retention of a conditioned avoidance response in the rat. *Physiology and Behavior,* 4:809–14.
Jung, J. 1967. *Verbal Learning.* New York: Holt, Rinehart & Winston.
Kamil, A. C., & Balda, R. P. 1985. Cache recovery and spatial memory in Clark's nutcrackers *(Nucifraga columbiana). Journal of Experimental Psychology: Animal Behavior Processes,* 11:95–111.
Kamin, L. J. 1957. The retention of an incompletely learned avoidance response. *Journal of Comparative and Physiological Psychology,* 50:457–60.
———. 1968. "Attention-like" processes in classical conditioning. In *Miami Symposium on the Prediction of Behavior: Aversive Stimulation,* ed. M. R. Jones, 9–31. Miami, Fla.: University of Miami Press.
Kasprow, W. J., Cachiero, H., Balaz, M. A., & Miller, R. R. 1982. Reminder-induced recovery of associations to an overshadowed stimulus. *Learning and Motivation,* 13:155–56.
Kasprow, W. J., Catterson, D., Schachtman, T. R., & Miller, R. R. 1982. Attenuation of latent inhibition by postacquisition reminder. *Quarterly Journal of Experimental Psychology,* 36B:53–63.
Kaufman, M. A., & Bolles, R. C. 1981. A nonassociative aspect of overshadowing. *Bulletin of the Psychonomic Society,* 18:318–20.
Kendrick, D. F., & Rilling, M. 1984. The role of interpolated stimuli in the retroactive interference of pigeon short-term memory. *Animal Learning and Behavior,* 12:391–401.
Kennedy, W. 1978. *Billy Phelan's Greatest Game.* New York: Penguin Books.
Keppel, G. 1964. Facilitation in short- and long-term retention of paired associates following distributed practice in learning. *Journal of Verbal Learning and Verbal Behavior,* 3:91–111.

———. 1984. Consolidation and forgetting theory. In *Memory Consolidation: Toward a Psychobiology of Cognition*, eds. H. Weingartner & E. S. Parker, 149–62. Hillsdale, N.J.: Erlbaum.

Keppel, G., Postman, L., & Zavortink, B. 1968. Studies of learning to learn: VIII. The influence of maximum amounts of training upon the learning and retention of paired-associate lists. *Journal of Verbal Learning and Verbal Behavior*, 7:790–96.

Keppel, G., & Underwood, B. J. 1962. Proactive inhibition in short-term retention of single items. *Journal of Verbal Learning and Verbal Behavior*, 1:153–61.

Kesner, R. P. 1991. Neurobiological views of memory. In *Learning and Memory: A Biological View*, 2d ed., eds. J. L. Martinez & R. P. Kesner, 499–548. New York: Academic Press.

Kesner, R. P., & Calder, L. D. 1980. Rewarding periaqueductal gray stimulation disrupts long-term memory for passive avoidance learning. *Behavioral and Neural Biology*, 30:237–49.

Kesner, R. P., & Conner, H. S. 1972. Independence of short- and long-term memory: A neural system analysis. *Science*, 176:432–34.

Kesner, R. P., & Doty, R. W. 1968. Amnesia produced in cats by local seizure activity initiated from the amygdala. *Experimental Neurology*, 21:58–68.

Kesner, R. P., & Holbrook, T. 1987. Dissociation of item and order spatial memory in rats following medical prefrontal cortex lesions. *Neuropsychologia*, 25:653–64.

Kesner, R. P., Measom, M. O., Forsman, S. L., & Holbrook, T. H. 1984. Serial-position curves in rats: Order memory for episodic spatial events. *Animal Learning and Behavior*, 12:378–87.

Kesner, R. P., & Novak, J. M. 1982. Serial position curve in rats: Role of the dorsal hippocampus. *Science*, 218:173–75.

Kimble, G. A., Mann, L. I., & Dufort, R. H. 1955. Classical and instrumental eyelid conditioning. *Journal of Experimental Psychology*, 49:407–17.

Kinsbourne, M. 1989. The boundaries of episodic remembering: Comments on the second section. In *Varieties of Memory and Consciousness*, eds. H. L. Roediger & F. I. M Craik. Hillsdale, N.J.: Erlbaum.

Klein, S. B. 1987. *Learning: Principles and Applications*. New York: McGraw-Hill.

Kleinsmith, L. J., & Kaplan, S. 1963. Paired-associate learning as a function of arousal and interpolated intervals. *Journal of Experimental Psychology*, 65:190–93.

Konorski, J. 1959. A new method of physiological investigation of recent memory in animals. *Bulletin de l'Academie Polonaise des Sciences Serie des Sciences Biologiques*, 7:115–17.

———. 1967. *Integrative Activity of the Brain: An Interdisciplinary Approach*. Chicago: University of Chicago Press.

Kopp, R., Bohdanecky, Z., & Jarvik, M. E. 1968. Proactive effect of a single electroconvulsive shock (ECS) on one-trial learning in mice. *Journal of Comparative and Physiological Psychology*, 65:524–27.

Kraemer, P. J. 1984. Forgetting of visual discriminations by pigeons. *Journal of Experimental Psychology: Animal Behavior Processes,* 10:530–42.

Kraemer, P. J., Hoffmann, H., & Spear, N. E. 1988. Attenuation of the CS preexposure effect after a retention interval in preweanling rats. *Animal Learning and Behavior,* 16:185–90.

Kraemer, P. J., Lariviere, N. A., & Spear, N. E. 1988. Expression of a taste aversion conditioned with an odor-taste compound: Overshadowing is relatively weak in weanlings and decreases over a retention interval in adults. *Animal Learning and Behavior,* 16:164–68.

Kraemer, P. J., & Ossenkopp, K. P. 1986. The effects of flavor preexposure and test interval on conditioned taste aversions in rats. *Bulletin of the Psychonomic Society,* 24:219–21.

Kraemer, P. J., Randall, C. K., & Carbari, T. J. 1991. Release from latent inhibition with delayed testing. *Animal Learning and Behavior,* 19:139–45.

Kraemer, P. J., & Roberts, W. A. 1984a. Short-term memory for visual and auditory stimuli in pigeons. *Animal Learning and Behavior,* 12:275–84.

Kraemer, P. J., & Roberts, W. A. 1984b. The influence of flavor preexposure and test interval on conditioned taste aversion in the rat. *Learning and Motivation,* 15:259–78.

Kraemer, P. J., & Spear, N. E. 1993. Retrieval processes and conditioning. In *Animal Cognition: A Tribute to Donald A. Riley,* eds. T. Zentall & W. Maki, Hillsdale, N.J.: Erlbaum.

Krueger, W. D. F. 1929. The effect of overlearning on retention. *Journal of Experimental Psychology,* 12:71–78.

Kucharski, D., & Richter, N., & Spear, N. E. 1985. Conditioned aversion is promoted by memory of CS–. *Animal Learning and Behavior,* 13:143–51.

Lariviere, N. A., Chen, W. J., & Spear, N. E. 1990. The influence of olfactory context on Pavlovian conditioning and its expression in preweanling (16-day old) and adult rats. *Animal Learning and Behavior,* 18:179–90.

Lashley, K. 1950. In search of the engram. In *Symposium of the Society for Experimental Biology,* Number 4, 454–82. Cambridge, England: Cambridge University Press.

Lawrence, D. H. 1963. The nature of a stimulus: Some relations between learning and perception. In *Psychology: A Study of a Science,* ed. S. Koch, 179–212. New York: McGraw-Hill.

Leight, K. A., & Ellis, H. C. 1981. Emotional mood states, strategies and state-dependency in memory. *Journal of Verbal Learning and Verbal Behavior,* 20:251–66.

Lennarts, R. C., & Weinberger, N. M. 1992. Analysis of response systems in Pavlovian conditioning reveals rapidly versus slowly acquired conditioned responses: Support for two factors, implications for behavior and neurobiology. *Psychobiology,* 20:93–119.

Lett, B. T. 1974. Visual discrimination learning with a one-minute delay of reward. *Learning and Motivation,* 5:174–81.
LeVere, T. E. 1984. Recoveries of function after brain damage: Variables influencing retrieval of latent memories. *Physiological Psychology,* 12:73–80.
LeVere, T. E., & Morlock, J. W. 1973. The nature of visual recovery following posterior decortication in the hooded rat. *Journal of Comparative and Physiological Psychology,* 83:62–67.
Levine, S. 1987. Psychobiological consequences of disruption in mother-infant relationships. In *Perinatal Development: A Psychobiological Perspective,* eds. N. Krasnegor, E. Blass, M. Hofer, & W. Smotherman. New York: Academic Press.
Levy, R. A. 1987. A method for the recovery of mishap-related events lost to amnesia. *Aviation, Space and Environmental Medicine,* 58:257–59.
Lewis, D. J. 1979. Psychobiology of active and inactive memory. *Psychological Bulletin,* 86:1054–83.
Light, L. L., & Carter-Sobell, L. 1970. Effects of changed semantic context on recognition memory. *Journal of Verbal Learning and Verbal Behavior,* 9:1–11.
Lindsay, D. S., & Johnson, M. K. 1989. The reversed eyewitness suggestibility effect. *Bulletin of the Psychonomic Society,* 27:111–13.
Linwick, D., Overmier, J. B., Peterson, G. B., & Mertens, M. 1988. Interaction of memories and expectancies as mediators of choice behavior. *American Journal of Psychology,* 101:313–34.
Lisman, S. A. 1974. Alcohol "blackout": State dependent learning? *Archives of General Psychiatry,* 30:46–53.
Loftus, E. F. 1973. Activation of semantic memory. *American Journal of Psychology,* 86:331–37.
———. 1975. Leading questions and the eyewitness report. *Cognitive Psychology,* 7:560–72.
———. 1979. The malleability of human memory. *American Scientist,* 67:312–20.
Loftus, E. F., & Burns, T. E. 1982. Mental shock can produce retrograde amnesia. *Memory and Cognition,* 10:318–23.
Loftus, E. F., & Miller, D. G., & Burns, H. J. 1978. Semantic integration of verbal information into a visual memory. *Journal of Experimental Psychology: Human Learning and Memory,* 4:19–31.
Loftus, E. F., & Palmer, J. C. 1984. Reconstruction of automobile destruction: An example of the interaction between language and memory. *Journal of Verbal Learning and Verbal Behavior,* 13:585–89.
Logue, A. W. 1979. Taste aversion and the generality of the laws of learning. *Psychological Bulletin,* 86:276–96.
LoLordo, V. M. 1979. Selective associations. In *Mechanisms of Learning and Motivation,* eds. A. Dickinson & R. A. Boakes, 367–98. Hillsdale, N.J.: Erlbaum.
Lubow, R. L. 1973. Latent inhibition. *Psychological Bulletin,* 79:398–407.

Luria, A. R. 1968. *The Mind of a Mnemonist.* New York: Basic Books.
———. 1976. *The Neuropsychology of Memory.* New York: Wiley.
Lynch, S., & Yarnell, P. R. 1973. Retrograde amnesia and delayed forgetting after concussion. *American Journal of Psychology,* 86:643–45.
Macht, M. L., Spear, N. E., & Levis, D. J. 1977. State-dependent retention in humans induced by alterations in affective state. *Bulletin of the Psychonomic Society,* 10:415–18.
Mackintosh, N. J. 1975. A theory of attention: Variations in the associability of stimuli with reinforcement. *Psychological Review,* 82:276–98.
Mactutus, C. F., Ferek, J. M., George, C. A., & Riccio, D. C. 1982. Hypothermia-induced amnesia for newly acquired and old reactivated memories: Commonalities and distinctions. *Physiological Psychology,* 10:79–95.
Mactutus, C. F., Ferek, J. M., & Riccio, D. C. 1980. Amnesia induced by hyperthermia: An unusually profound, yet reversible, memory loss. *Behavioral and Neural Biology,* 30:260–77.
Mactutus, C. F., McCutcheon, K., & Riccio, D. C. 1980. Body temperature cues as contextual stimuli: Modulation of hypothermia-induced retrograde amnesia. *Physiology and Behavior,* 25:875–83.
Mactutus, C. F., & Riccio, D. C. 1978. Hypothermia-induced retrograde amnesia: Role of body temperature in memory retrieval. *Physiological Psychology,* 6:18–22.
Mactutus, C. F., Riccio, D. C., & Ferek, J. M. 1979. Retrograde amnesia for old (reactivated) memory: Some anomalous characteristics. *Science,* 204:1319–20.
Mactutus, C. F., Smith, R. L., & Riccio, D. C. 1980. Extending the duration of ACTH-induced memory reactivation in an amnesia paradigm. *Physiology and Behavior,* 24:541–46
Madsen, M. C., & McGaugh, J. L. 1961. The effect of ECS on one-trial avoidance learning. *Journal of Comparative and Physiological Psychology,* 54:522–23.
Maki, W. S. 1979. Pigeons' short-term memories for surprising versus expected reinforcement and nonreinforcement. *Animal Learning and Behavior,* 7:31–37.
Maki, W. S., & Hegvik, D. 1980. Directed forgetting in pigeons. *Animal Learning and Behavior,* 8:567–74.
Maki, W. S., Moe, J., & Bierley, C. 1977. Short-term memory for stimuli, responses and reinforcers. *Journal of Experimental Psychology: Animal Behavior Processes,* 3:156–77.
Malpass, R. S., & Devine, P. G. 1981. Guided memory in eyewitness identification. *Journal of Applied Psychology,* 66:343–50.
Markiewicz, B., Kucharski, D., & Spear, N. E. 1986. Ontogenetic comparison of memory for Pavlovian conditioned aversions in temperature, vibration, odor or brightness. *Developmental Psychobiology,* 19:139–54.
Marks, L. E. 1978. *The Unity of the Senses: Interrelations Among the Modalities.* New York: Academic Press.

Marshall, J. 1991. Lasting impressions: A review of *In the Palaces of Memory*, by George Johnson. *New York Times. Review of Books,* 24 Feb, 11–12.

Martinez, J. L., Jensen, R. A., & McGaugh, J. L. 1981. Attenuation of experimentally-induced amnesia. *Progress in Neurobiology,* 16:155–86.

Martinez, J. L., Jr., Rigter, H., Jensen, R. A., Messing, R. B., Vasquez, B. J., & McGaugh, J. L. 1981. Endorphin and enkephalin effects on avoidance conditioning: The other side of the pituitary-adrenal axis. In *Endogenous Peptides and Learning and Memory Processes,* eds. J. L. Martinez, Jr., R. A. Jensen, R. B. Messing, H. Figter & J. L. McGaugh. New York: Academic Press.

Martinez, J. L., Vasquez, B. J., Rigter, H., Messing, R. B., Jensen, R. A., Liang, K. C., & McGaugh, J. L. 1980. Attenuation of amphetamine-induced enhancement of learning by adrenal demedullation. *Brain Research,* 199:433–43.

McAllister, W. R., & McAllister, D. E. 1963. Increase over time in the stimulus generalization of acquired fear. *Journal of Experimental Psychology,* 65:576–82.

———. 1967. Incubation of fear: An examination of the concept. *Journal of Experimental Research and Personality,* 3:80–90.

McCloskey, M., & Zaragoza, M. 1985. Misleading postevent information and memory for events: Arguments and evidence against memory impairment hypotheses. *Journal of Experimental Psychology: General,* 114:1–16.

McDonough, J. R., Jr., & Kesner, R. P. 1971. Amnesia produced by brief electrical stimulation of amygdala or dorsal hippocampus in cats. *Journal of Comparative and Physiological Psychology,* 77:171–78.

McGaugh, J. L. 1966. Time-dependent processes in memory storage. *Science,* 153:1351–58.

———. 1983. Hormonal influences on memory. *Annual Review of Psychology,* 34:297–323.

———. 1989a. Involvement of hormonal and neuromodulatory systems in the regulation of memory storage. In *Annual Review of Neuroscience,* Vol. 12. Palo Alto, Calif.: Annual Reviews.

———. 1989b. Modulation of memory storage processes. In *Memory: Interdisciplinary Approaches,* eds. P. R. Solomon, G. R. Gochola, C. M. Kelley, & B. R. Stephens. New York: Springer-Verlag.

McGaugh, J. L., Liang, K. C., Bennett, M. C., & Sternberg, D. B. 1984. Adrenergic influences on memory storage: Interaction of peripheral and central systems. In *Neurobiology of Learning and Memory,* eds. G. Lynch, J. L. McGaugh, & N. M. Weinberger. New York: Guilford Press.

———. 1985. Hormonal influences on memory: Interaction of central and peripheral systems. In *Brain Plasticity, Learning and Memory,* eds. B. E. Will, P. Schmitt, & J. C. Dalrymple-Alford. New York: Plenum Press.

McGeoch, J. A. 1932. Forgetting and the law of disuse. *Psychological Review,* 39:352–70.

———. 1935. The conditions of reminiscence. *American Journal of Psychology,* 47:65–89.

———. 1942. *The Psychology of Human Learning: An Introduction.* New York: Longmans, Green.

McGinnies, E. 1949. Emotionality and perceptual defense. *Psychological Review,* 56:244–51.

McGraw, M. B. 1943. *The Neuromuscular Maturation of the Human Infant.* New York: Columbia University Press.

Meddis, R. 1975. On the function of sleep. *Animal Behaviour,* 23:676–91.

Mello, N. 1971. Alcohol effects on delayed matching-to-sample performance by rhesus monkeys. *Physiology and Behavior,* 7:77–101.

Melton, A. W., & Irwin, J. M. 1940. The influence of degree of interpolated learning on retroactive inhibition and the overt transfer of specific responses. *American Journal of Psychology,* 53:173–203.

Melton, A. W., & Von Lackum, W. J. 1941. Retroactive and proactive inhibition in retention: Evidence for a two-factor theory of retroactive inhibition. *American Journal of Psychology,* 54:157–73.

Menzel, E. W. 1973. Chimpanzee spatial memory organization. *Science,* 182:943–45.

Messing, R. B., Jensen, R. A., Vasquez, B. J., Martinez, J. L., Speihler, V. R., & McGaugh, J. L. 1981. Opiate modulation of memory. In *Endogenous Peptides and Learning and Memory Processes,* eds. J. L. Martinez, R. A. Jensen, R. B. Messing, H. Rigter, & J. L. McGaugh. New York: Academic Press.

Metcalfe, J. 1991. Recognition failure and the composite memory trace in CHARM. *Psychological Review,* 98:529–53.

Metzger, R. L., Boschee, P. F., Haugen, T., & Schnobrich, B. L. 1979. The classroom as a learning context: Changing rooms affects performance. *Journal of Educational Psychology,* 71:440–42.

Meyer, D. R. 1972. Access to engrams. *American Psychologist,* 27:124–33.

———. 1984. The cerebral cortex: Its roles in memory storage and remembering. *Physiological Psychology,* 17:81–8.

Meyer, P. N., & Meyer, D. R. 1982. Memory, remembering and amnesia. In *The Expression of Knowledge,* eds. R. L. Isaacson & N. E. Spear. New York: Plenum Press.

Miller, G. A. 1956. The magical number 7 ± 2: Some limits on our capacity for processing information. *Psychological Review,* 63:81–97.

Miller, J. S., Jagielo, J. A., Gisquet-Verrier, P., & Spear, N. E. 1989. Backward excitatory conditioning can determine the role of the CS– in aversion learning. *Learning and Motivation,* 20:115–29.

Miller, J. S., Jagielo, J. A., & Spear, N. E. 1989. Age-related differences in short-term retention of separable elements of an odor aversion. *Journal of Experimental Psychology: Animal Behavior Processes,* 15:194–201.

———. 1990. Changes in the retrievability of associations to elements of a compound CS determine the expression of overshadowing. *Animal Learning and Behavior,* 18:157–61.

———. 1991. Differential effectiveness of various prior cueing treatments on the reactivation and maintenance of memory. *Journal of Experimental Psychology: Animal Behavior Processes,* 17:249–58.

Miller, J. S., McKinzie, D. L., Kraebel, K., & Spear, N. E. 1993. Blocking and overshadowing represent selective memory retrieval rather than selective associations. Paper presented at meetings of the Midwestern Psychological Association, Chicago.

Miller, J. S., Molina, J. C., & Spear, N. E. 1990. Ontogenetic differences in the expression of odor-version learning in 4- and 8-day old rats. *Developmental Psychobiology,* 23:319–30.

Miller, J. S., & Spear, N. E. 1989. Ontogenetic differences in short-term retention of Pavlovian conditioning. *Developmental Psychobiology,* 22:377–87.

Miller, N. E. 1948. Studies of fear as an acquirable drive: 1. Fear as motivation and fear-reduction as reinforcement in the learning of new responses. *Journal of Experimental Psychology,* 38:89–101.

Miller, N. E., & Dollard, J. C. 1941. *Social Learning and Imitation.* New Haven, Conn.: Yale University Press.

Miller, R. R. 1982. Effects of intertrial reinstatement of training stimuli on complex maze learning in rats: Evidence that "acquisition" curves reflect more than acquisition. *Journal of Experimental Psychology: Animal Behavior Processes,* 8:86–109.

Miller, R. R., Ott, C. A., Berk, A. M., & Springer, A. D. 1974. Appetitive memory restoration after electroconvulsive shock in the rat. *Journal of Comparative and Physiological Psychology,* 87:717–23.

Miller, R. R., & Schactman, T. R. 1985. The several roles of context at the time of retrieval. In *Context and Learning,* eds. P. D. Balsam & A. Tomie, 167–94. Hillsdale, N.J.: Erlbaum.

Miller, R. R. & Springer, A. D. 1972. Induced recovery of memory in rats following electroconvulsive shock. *Physiology and Behavior,* 8:645–51.

Milner, B. 1962. Memory disturbances after bilateral hippocampal lesions. In *Cognitive Processing in the Brain,* eds. P. M. Milner & S. Glickman. Princeton, N.J.: Van Nostrand.

Milner, B. S., Corkin, S., & Teuber, H. L. 1968. Further analysis of the hippocampal amnesic syndrome: 14-year follow-up of H.M. *Neuropsychologia,* 6:215–34.

Misanin, J. R., Haigh, J. M., Hinderliter, C. F., & Nagy, Z. M. 1973. Analysis of response competition and nondiscriminated escape training of neonatal rats. *Journal of Comparative and Physiological Psychology,* 85:570–80.

Misanin, J. R., Miller, R. R., & Lewis, D. J. 1968. Retrograde amnesia produced by electroconvulsive shock after reactivation of a consolidated memory trace. *Science,* 160:554–55.

Misanin, J. R., Nagy, Z. M., Keiser, E. F., & Bowden, W. 1971. Emergence of long-term memory in the neonatal rat. *Journal of Comparative and Physiological Psychology,* 77:188–99.

Misanin, J. R., Vonheyn, R. E., Bartlett, S. W., Boulden, W. L., & Hinderliter, C. F. 1979. The effect of hypothermia on memory in rats. *Physiological Psychology,* 7:339–44.

Mishkin, M., & Appenzeller, T. 1987. The anatomy of memory. *Scientific American,* 256:80–89.

Mishkin, M., & Delacour, J. 1975. An analysis of short-term visual memory in the monkey. *Journal of Experimental Psychology: Animal Behavior Processes,* 1:326–34.

Mishkin, M., Malamut, B., & Bachevalier, J. 1984. Memories and habits: Two neural systems. In *Neurobiology of Learning and Memory,* eds. G. Lynch, J. L. McGaugh, & N. M. Weinberger. New York: Guilford Press.

Moise, S. L. 1970. Short-term retention in *Macacca speciosa* following interpolated activity during delayed matching from sample. *Journal of Comparative and Physiological Psychology,* 73:506–14.

Mondadori, C., Waser, P. G., & Huston, J. P. 1977. Time dependent effects of post-trial reinforcement, punishment, or ECS on passive avoidance learning. *Physiology and Behavior,* 18:1103–09.

Morilak, D. A., Orndoff, R. K., Riccio, D. C., & Richardson, R. 1983. Persistence of flavor neophobia as an indicator of state-dependent retention induced by pentobarbitol, stress, and estrus. *Behavioral and Neural Biology,* 38:47–60.

Morris, R. G. M. 1981. Spatial localization does not require the presence of local cues. *Learning and Motivation,* 12:239–60.

Mowrer, O. H. 1960. *Learning Theory and Behavior.* New York: Wiley.

Moye, T. B., & Rudy, J. W. 1985. Ontogenesis of learning. VI. Learned and unlearned responses to visual stimulation in the infant hood rat. *Developmental Psychobiology,* 18:395–409.

Mueller, C. W., Lisman, S. A., & Spear, N. E. 1982. A human memory procedure to investigate drug discriminations and state dissociations simultaneously. In *First International Symposium on Drugs as Discriminative Stimuli,* eds. F. C. Colpaert & J. A. Rosencrans. Amsterdam: Elsevier/North Holland Biomedical Press.

Muller, G. E., & Pilzecker, A. 1900. Experimentelle bietrage zur lehre bom gedachtnisses. *Zeitschrift für Psychologie,* Erganzungaband 1.

Nairne, J. S., & Rescorla, R. A. 1981. Second-order conditioning with diffuse auditory reinforcers in the pigeon. *Learning and Motivation,* 12:65–91.

Nation, J. R., Wrather, D. M., & Mellgren, R. L. 1974. Contrast effects in escape conditioning of rats. *Journal of Comparative and Physiological Psychology,* 86:69–73.

Nisbett, R. E., & Wilson, T. D. 1977. Telling more than we can know: Verbal reports on mental processes. *Psychological Review,* 84:231–59.

Norman, D. A. 1970. *Memory and Attention,* 2d ed. New York: Wiley.

Ogden, J. A., & Corkin, S. 1991. Memories of H.M. In *Memory Mechanisms: A Tribute to G. V. Goddard,* eds. W. C. Abraham, M. C. Corballis, & K. G. White, 195–218. Hillsdale, N.J.: Erlbaum.

Olton, D. S. 1979. Mazes, maps and memory. *American Psychologist,* 34:583–96.

———. 1983. Memory functions and the hippocampus. In *Neurobiology of the Hippocampus,* ed. W. Seifert, 335–73. London: Academic Press.

Olton, D. S., & Samuelson, R. J. 1976. Remembrance of places passed: Spatial memory in rats. *Journal of Experimental Psychology: Animal Behavior Processes,* 2:97–116.

Ornstein, P. A. 1977. Memory development in children. In *Developmental Psychology,* 2d ed., eds. R. Liebert, R. Paulos, & G. Marmor. Englewood Cliffs, N.J.: Prentice-Hall.

Overman, W. H., & Doty, R. W. 1980. Prolonged visual memory in macaques and man. *Neuroscience,* 5:1825–31.

Overmier, J. B., & Seligman, M. E. P. 1967. Effects of inescapable shock upon subsequent escape in avoidance responding. *Journal of Comparative and Physiological Psychology,* 63:28–33.

Overton, D. A. 1964. State-dependent or "dissociated" learning produced with pentobarbitol. *Journal of Comparative and Physiological Psychology,* 57:3–12.

———. 1978. Major theories of state dependent learning. In *Drug Discrimination and State Dependent Learning,* eds. B. T. Ho, D. W. Richards, & D. L. Chute. New York: Academic Press.

———. 1982. Memory retrieval failures produced by changes in drug state. In *The Expression of Knowledge,* eds. R. L. Isaacson & N. E. Spear, 113–40. New York: Plenum Press.

———. 1984. State dependent learning and drug discrimination. In *Handbook of Psychopharmacology,* ed. L. L. Iverson, Vol. 18, 59–127. New York: Plenum Press.

———. 1985. Contextual stimulus effects of drugs and internal states. In *Context and Learning,* eds. P. D. Balsam & A. Tomie, 357–84. Hillsdale, N.J.: Erlbaum.

Packard, M. G., & McGaugh, J. L. 1992. Double dissociation of fornix and caudate nucleus lesions on acquisition of two water maze tasks: Further evidence for multiple memory systems. *Behavioral Neuroscience,* 106:439–46.

Palfai, T., & Chillag, D. 1971. Time-dependent memory deficits produced by pentylenetetrazol (Metrazol): The effects of reinforcer magnitude. *Physiology and Behavior,* 7:439–42.

Paolino, R. M., Quartermain, D., & Miller, N. E. 1966. Different temporal gradients of retrograde amnesia produced by carbon dioxide anesthesia and electroconvulsive shock. *Journal of Comparative and Physiological Psychology,* 62:270–74.

Papousek, H. 1969. Elaboration of conditioned headturning. Paper presented at the XIX International Congress of Psychology, London.

Parsons, P. J., Fagan, T., & Spear, N. E. 1973. Short-term retention of habituation by infant, weanling and adult rats. *Journal of Comparative and Physiological Psychology,* 84:543–45.

Parsons, P. J., & Spear, N. E. 1973. Long-term retention of avoidance learning by immature and adult rats as a function of environmental enrichment. *Journal of Comparative and Physiological Psychology,* 80:297–303.

Payne, D. G. 1987. Hypermnesia and reminiscence in recall: A historical and empirical review. *Psychological Bulletin,* 101:5–27.

Pearce, J. M. 1987. A model for stimulus generalization in Pavlovian conditioning. *Psychological Review,* 94:61–73.

Pearce, J. M., & Hall, G. 1980. A model for Pavlovian learning: Variations in the effectiveness of conditioned but not unconditioned stimuli. *Psychological Review,* 87:532–52.

Pearlman, C., Sharpless, S. K., & Jarvik, M. E. 1961. Retrograde amnesia produced by anesthetic and convulsant agents. *Journal of Comparative and Physiological Psychology,* 54:109–12.

Pelchat, M. L., Grill, H. J., Rozin, P., & Jacobs, J. 1983. Quality of acquired responses to taste by *Rattus norvegicus* depends on type of associative discomfort. *Journal of Comparative Psychology,* 97:140–53.

Perkins, C. C., Jr., & Weyant, R. G. 1958. The interval between training and test trials as determiner of the slope of generalization gradients. *Journal of Comparative and Physiological Psychology,* 51:596–600.

Perlmutter, M. 1984. Continuities and discontinuities in early human memory paradigms, processes, and performance. In *Comparative Perspectives on the Development of Memory,* eds. R. Kail & N. E. Spear, 253–84. Hillsdale, N.J.: Erlbaum.

Peterson, L. R., & Peterson, M. J. 1959. Short-term retention of individual verbal items. *Journal of Experimental Psychology,* 58:193–98.

Pfister, J. P., & Alberts, J. R. 1983. Development of thermotactile controls of huddling in the rat pups. Paper presented at the meeting of the International Society for Developmental Psychobiology.

Pinel, J. P. J., & Cooper, R. M. 1966. Incubation and its implications for the interpretation of the ECS gradient effect. *Psychonomic Science,* 4:123–24.

Pinel, J. P., Malsbury, C. W., & Corcoran, J. E. 1971. The incubation effect in rats: Skin resistance changes after footshock. *Physiology and Behavior,* 6:111–14.

Postman, L. 1976. Interference theory revisited. In *Recall and Recognition,* ed. J. Brown. New York: Wiley.

Postman, L., Stark, K., & Fraser, J. 1976. Temporal changes in interference. *Journal of Verbal Learning and Verbal Behavior,* 7:672–94.

Quartermain, D., & Judge, M. E. 1983. Retrieval enhancement in mice by pretest amphetamine injection after a long retention interval. *Physiological Psychology,* 11:166–72.

Quartermain, D., Judge, M. E., & Jung, H. Amphetamine enhanced retrieval following diverse sources of forgetting. *Physiology and Behavior,* 43:239–41.

Quinton, E. E., & Bloom, A. S. 1977. Effects of *d*-amphetamine and strychnine on cycloheximide and diethyldithiocarbamate-induced amnesia in rats. *Journal of Comparative and Physiological Psychology,* 91:1390–97.

Rand, G., & Wapner, S. 1967. Postural status as a factor in memory. *Journal of Verbal Learning and Verbal Behavior,* 6:268–71.

Rescorla, R. A. 1973. Effect of US habituation following conditioning. *Journal of Comparative and Physiological Psychology,* 82:137–43.

———. 1974. Effective inflation of the unconditioned stimulus value following conditoning. *Journal of Comparative and Physiological Psychology,* 86: 101–6.

———. 1988. Pavlovian conditioning: It's not what you think. *American Psychologist,* 42:151–60.

Rescorla, R. A., Durlach, P. J., & Grau, J. W. 1985. Contextual learning in Pavlovian conditioning. In *Context and Learning,* eds. P. D. Balsam & A. Tomie, 23–56. Hillsdale, N.J.: Erlbaum.

Rescorla, R. A., & Wagner, A. R. 1972. A theory of Pavlovian conditioning: Variations in the effectiveness of reinforcement and nonreinforcement. In *Classical Conditioning II: Current Research and Theory,* eds. A. H. Black & W. F. Prokasy, 64–99. New York: Appleton-Century-Crofts.

Revusky, S. 1971. The role of interference in association over a delay. In *Animal Memory,* eds. W. K. Honig & P. H. R. James. New York: Academic Press.

Ribot, T. A. 1882. *The Diseases of Memory,* trans. J. Fitzgerald. New York: Humboldt Library, No. 46.

Riccio, D. C., Ackil, J., & Burch-Vernon, A. 1992. Forgetting of stimulus attributes: Methodological implications for assessing associative phenomena. *Psychological Bulletin,* 112:433–45.

Riccio, D. C., & Concannon, J. T. 1981. ACTH and the reminder phenomena. In *Endogenous Peptides and Learning and Memory Processes,* eds. J. L. Martinez, R. A. Jensen, R. B. Messing, H. Rigter, & J. L. McGaugh. New York: Academic Press.

Riccio, D. C., Hodges, L. A., & Randall, P. K. 1968. Retrograde amnesia produced by hypothermia in rats. *Journal of Comparative and Physiological Psychology,* 66:618–22.

Riccio, D. C., Richardson, R., & Ebner, D. L. 1984. Memory retrieval deficits based upon altered contextual cues: A paradox. *Psychological Bulletin,* 96:152–65.

Richardson, R., & Campbell, B. A. 1991. The influence of maternal presence on the orienting responses in preweanling rats. *Infant Behavior and Development,* 14:313–34.

Richardson, R., Guanowsky, V., Ahlers, S. T., & Riccio, D. C. 1984. Role of body temperature in the onset of, and recovery from, hypothermia-induced anterograde amnesia. *Physiological Psychology,* 12:125–32.

Richardson, R., & Riccio, D. C. 1986. An examination of a contextual component of memory following recovery from anterograde amnesia in rats. *Physiological Psychology,* 14:75–81.

Richardson, R., Riccio, D. C., Jamis, M., Skozcen, T., & Cabosky, J. 1982. Modification of reactivated memory through "counterconditioning." *American Journal of Psychology,* 95:67–84.

Richardson, R., Riccio, D. C., & Morilak, D. 1983. Anterograde memory loss induced by hypothermia in rats. *Behavioral and Neural Biology,* 37:76–88.

Richardson, R., Riccio, D. C., & Mowrey, H. 1982. Retrograde amnesia for previously acquired Pavlovian conditioning: UCS exposure as a reactivation treatment. *Physiological Psychology,* 10: 384–90.

Richardson, R., Riccio, D. C., & Smoller, D. E. 1987. Counterconditioning of memory in rats. *Animal Learning and Behavior,* 15:321–26.

Richardson, R., Riccio, D. C., & Steele, J. H. 1986. State-dependent retention induced by postacquisition exposure to pentobarbitol or shock-stress in rats. *Animal Learning and Behavior,* 14:73–79.

Richardson, R., Williams, C., & Riccio, D. C. 1984. Stimulus generalization of conditioned taste aversion in rats. *Behavioral and Neural Biology,* 41:41–53.

Richardson-Klavehn, A., & Bjork, R. A. 1988. Measures of memory. *Annual Review of Psychology,* 39:475–544.

Rigter, H., Janssens-Elbertse, R., & van Riezen, H. 1976. Reversal of amnesia by an orally active $ACTH_{4-9}$ analog (Org 2766). *Pharmacology, Biochemistry and Behavior,* 5:53–58.

Robbins, M. J., & Meyer, D. R. 1970. Motivational control of retrograde amnesia. *Journal of Experimental Psychology,* 84:220–25.

Roberts, W. A. 1980. Distribution of trials and intertrial retention in delayed matching-to-sample with pigeons. *Journal of Experimental Psychology: Animal Behavior Processes,* 6:217–37.

Roberts, W. A., & Grant, D. S. 1976. Studies of short-term memory in the pigeon using the delayed matching-to-sample procedure. In *Processes of Animal Memory,* eds. D. L. Medin, W. A. Roberts, & R. T. Davis, 79–112. Hillsdale, N.J.: Erlbaum.

Roberts, W. A., & Kraemer, P. J. 1981. Recognition memory for lists of visual stimuli in monkeys and humans. *Animal Learning and Behavior,* 9:587–94.

———. 1984. Timing variables in delayed matching-to-sample. In *Timing and Time Perception,* eds. J. Gibbon & L. Allan, 335–45. New York: New York Academy of Sciences.

Roberts, W. A., Mazmanian, D. S., & Kraemer, P. J. 1984. Directed forgetting in monkeys. *Animal Learning and Behavior,* 12:29–40.

———. Memory for picture fragments in monkeys and humans. *Canadian Journal of Psychology,* 41:1–19.

Roediger, H. L. 1974. Inhibiting effect of recall. *Memory and Cognition,* 2:261–69.

———. 1980. Memory metaphors in cognitive psychology. *Memory and Cognition,* 8:231–46.

———. 1985. Recall criterion does not affect recall level or hypermnesia: A puzzle for generate/recognize theories. *Memory and Cognition,* 13:1–7.

Roediger, H. L., & Payne, D. G. 1982. Hypermnesia: The role of repeated testing. *Journal of Experimental Psychology: Learning, Memory and Cognition,* 8:66–72.

Roediger, H. L., & Thorpe, L. A. 1978. The role of recall time in producing hypermnesia. *Memory and Cognition*, 6:296–305.

Rohrbaugh, M., & Riccio, D. C. 1968. Stimulus generalization of learned fear in infant and adult rats. *Journal of Comparative and Physiological Psychology*, 66:530–33.

Roitblat, H. L. 1980. Codes and coding processes in pigeon short-term memory. *Animal Learning and Behavior*, 8:341–51.

———. 1981. The meaning of representation in animal memory. *The Behavioural and Brain Sciences*, 5:353–406.

Rose, R. J. 1992. Degree of learning, interpolated tests, and rate of forgetting. *Memory and Cognition*, 20:621–32.

Ross, R. T., & Holland, P. C. 1981. Conditioning of simultaneous and serial feature-positive discriminations. *Animal Learning and Behavior*, 9:293–303.

Rovee-Collier, C. 1984. The ontogeny of learning and memory in human infancy. In *Comparative Perspectives on the Development of Memory*, eds. R. Kail & N. E. Spear. Hillsdale, N.J.: Erlbaum.

———. 1989. The joy of kicking: Memories, motives and mobiles. In *Memory: Interdisciplinary Approaches*, eds. P. R. Solomon, G. R. Goethals, C. M. Kelley, & B. R. Stephens, 151–80. New York: Springer-Verlag.

———. 1990. The "memory system" of prelinguistic infants. *Annals of the New York Academy of Sciences*, 608:517–36.

Rovee-Collier, C., & Hayne, H. 1987. Reactivation of infant memory: Implications for cognitive development. In *Advances in Child Development and Behavior*, ed. H. W. Reese, 185–238. New York: Academic Press.

Rozin, P. 1976. The psychobiological approach to human memory. In *Neural Mechanisms of Learning and Memory*, eds. M. R. Rosenzweig & E. L. Bennett. Cambridge, Mass.: MIT Press.

Rozin, P., & Ree, P. 1972. Long extension of effective CS-US as interval by anesthesia between CS and US. *Journal of Comparative and Physiological Psychology*, 80:43–48.

Rudy, J. W., Vogt, M. B., & Hyson, R. L. 1984. A developmental analysis of the rat's learned reaction to gustatory and auditory stimulation. In *Comparative Perspectives on the Development of Memory*, eds. R. Kail & N. E. Spear, 181–208. Hillsdale, N.J.: Erlbaum.

Runquist, W. N. 1986. Changes in the rate of forgetting produced by recall tests. *Canadian Journal of Psychology*, 40:282–89.

Russell, W. R. 1971. *The Traumatic Amnesias*. London: Oxford Press.

Russell, W. R., & Nathan, P. 1946. Traumatic amnesia. *Brain*, 69:280–300.

Salmon, D. P., & D'Amato, M. R. 1981. Note on delay-interval illumination effects on retention in monkeys. *(Cebus apella). Journal of the Experimental Analysis of Behavior*, 36:381–85.

Saltz, E., & Asdourian, D. 1963. Incubation of anxiety as a function of cognitive differentiation. *Journal of Experimental Psychology*, 66:17–22.

Sanders, H. I., & Warrington, E. K. 1971. Memory for remote events in amnesic patients. *Brain,* 94:661–68.

Sands, S. F., & Wright, A. A. 1980. Primate memory: Rentention of serial list items by a rhesus monkey. *Science,* 209:938–40.

Santi, A., & Roberts, W. A. 1985. Prospective representation: The effects of varied mapping of sample stimuli to comparison stimuli and differential trial outcomes on pigeons' working memory. *Animal Learning and Behavior,* 13:103–8.

Santucci, A., & Riccio, D. C. 1986. Hypothermia-induced anterograde amnesia and its reversal in rats trained on a T-maze escape task. *Physiology and Behavior,* 36:1065–69.

Santucci, A. C., Schroeder, H., & Riccio, D. C. 1990. Homeostatic disruption and memory: Effect of insulin administration in rats. *Behavioral and Neural Biology,* 53:321–33.

Sara, S. J. 1984. Forgetting of a conditioned emotional response and its alleviation by pretest amphetamines. *Physiological Psychology,* 12:17–27.

Sara, S. J., & Deweer, B. 1982. Memory retrieval enhanced by amphetamine after a long retention interval. *Behavioral and Neural Biology,* 36:146–60.

Sara, S. J., & Remacle, J. F. 1977. Strychnine-induced passive avoidance facilitation after electroconvulsive shock or under-training: A retrieval effect. *Behavioral Biology,* 19:465–75.

Saufley, W. H., Otaka, S. R., & Bavaresco, J. L. 1985. Context effects: Classroom tests and context independence. *Memory and Cognition,* 13:522–28.

Saufley, W. H., Jr., & Winograd, E. 1970. Retrograde amnesia and priority instructions in free recall. *Journal of Experimental Psychology,* 85:150–52.

Schacter, D. L. 1983. Amnesia observed: Remembering and forgetting in a natural environment. *Journal of Abnormal Psychology,* 92: 236–42.

———. 1987. Implicit memory: History and current status. *Journal of Experimental Psychology: Learning, Memory and Cognition,* 13:501–18.

Schacter, D. L., & Crovitz, H. F. 1977. Memory function after closed head injury: A review of the quantitative research. *Cortex,* 13:150–76.

Schacter, D. L., & Tulving, E. 1982. Memory, amnesia and the episodic/semantic distinction. In *The Expression of Knowledge,* eds. R. L. Isaacson & N. E. Spear, 33–66. New York: Plenum Press.

Schare, M. L., Lisman, S. A., & Spear, N. E. 1984. The effects of mood variation on state dependent retention. *Cognitive Therapy and Research,* 8:387–407.

Schneiderman, N. 1972. Response system divergencies in aversive classical conditioning. In *Classical Conditioning II: Current Research and Theory,* eds. A. H. Black & W. F. Prokasy, 341–76. New York: Appleton-Century-Crofts.

Schuz, A. 1978. Some facts and hypotheses concerning dendritic spines and learning. In *Architectronics of the Cerebral Cortex,* IBRO Monograph Series, Vol. 3, eds. M. A. B. Brazier & H. Petsche. New York: Raven Press.

Schwartz, B. 1989. *Psychology of Learning and Behavior.* New York: W. W. Norton.

Schwartz, B., & Reilly, R. 1985. Long-term retention of a complex operant in pigeons. *Journal of Experimental Psychology: Animal Behavior Processes,* 11:337–55.

Sechenov, I. M. 1965. *Reflexes of the Brain.* Cambridge, Mass.: MIT Press (originally published 1863).

Seligman, M. E. P., Maier, S. F., & Solomon, R. L. 1971. Unpredictable and uncontrollable aversive events. In *Aversive Conditioning and Learning,* ed. F. R. Brush. New York: Academic Press.

Seybert, J. A., McClanahan, L. G., & Gilliland, J. S. 1982. Retention following appetitive discrimination training: The Kamin effect. *Bulletin of the Psychonomic Society,* 19:37–40.

Seybert, J. A., Vandenberg, A. L., Harvey, R. J., & Budd, J. R. 1979. Retention of an appetitive instrumental behavior: The Kamin effect. *Behavioral and Neural Biology,* 26:266–86.

Shapiro, S., & Erdelyi, N. G. 1974. Hypermnesia for pictures but not words. *Journal of Experimental Psychology,* 103:1218–19.

Shavalia, D. A., Dodge, A. M., & Beatty, W. W. 1981. Time-dependent effects of ECS on spatial memory in rats. *Behavioral and Neural Biology,* 31:261–73.

Sheingold, K., & Tenney, Y. 1982. Memory for a salient childhood event. In *Memory Observed: Remembering in Natural Contexts,* ed. U. Neisser. San Francisco: Freeman.

Shepard, R. N. 1967. Recognition memory for words, sentences and pictures. *Journal of Verbal Learning and Verbal Behavior,* 6:156–63.

———. 1987. Toward a universal law of generalization for psychological science. *Science,* 237:1317–23.

Shettleworth, S. 1983. Memory in food-hoarding birds. *Scientific American,* 248:102–10.

Shettleworth, S. J., & Krebs, J. R. 1982. How marsh tits find their hoards: The roles of site preference and spatial memory. *Journal of Experimental Psychology: Animal Behavior Processes,* 8:354–75.

Shurtleff, D., & Ayres, J. J. 1981. One-trial backward excitatory conditioning in rats: Acquisition, retention, extinction and spontaneous recovery. *Animal Learning and Behavior,* 9:65–74.

Sidman, M., Stoddard, L. T., & Mohr, J. P. 1968. Some additional quantitative observations of immediate memory in a patient with bilateral hippocampal lesions. *Neuropsychologia,* 6:245–54.

Siegel, S. 1983. Wilkie Collins: Victorian novelist as psychopharmacologist. *Journal of the History of Medicine and Allied Sciences,* 38:161–75.

Skinner, B. F. 1950. Are theories of learning necessary? *Psychological Review,* 57:193–216.

Slamecka, N. J. 1985. Ebbinghaus: Some associations. *Journal of Experimental Psychology: Learning, Memory, and Cognition,* 11:414–35.

Smith, G. J., & Spear, N. E. 1981. Role of proactive interference in infantile forgetting. *Animal Learning and Behavior,* 9:371–80.

Smith, S. 1985. Background music and context dependent memory. *American Journal of Psychology,* 98:599–603.

Smith, S. M. 1979. Remembering in and out of context. *Journal of Experimental Psychology: Human Learning and Memory,* 5:460–71.

Smith, S. M., Glenberg, A., & Bjork, R. A. 1978. Environmental context and human memory. *Memory and Cognition,* 6:342–53.

Smith, S. M., & Vela, E. 1991. Incubated reminiscence effects. *Memory and Cognition,* 19:168–76.

Smoller, D. E., Serwatka, J., & Spear, N. E. 1987. Second-order conditioning and "unitization" in the developing rat. Presented at the meeting of the International Society for Developmental Psychobiology.

Smotherman, W. P. 1982. Odor aversion learning by the rat fetus. *Physiology and Behavior,* 29:769–71.

Smotherman, W. P., & Robinson, S. R. 1987. Psychobiology of fetal experience in the rat. In *Perinatal Development: A Psychobiological Perspective,* eds. N. A. Krasnegor, E. M. Blass, M. A. Hofer, & W. P. Smotherman, 39–60. Orlando, Fla.: Academic Press.

———. 1991. Conditioned activation of fetal behavior. *Physiology and Behavior,* 50:73–77.

Spear, N. E. 1967. Retention of reinforcer magnitude. *Psychological Review,* 74:216–34.

———. 1970. Verbal learning and retention. In *Experimental Psychology: Methodology, Psychophysics and Learning,* ed. M. R. D'Amato, 543–638. New York: McGraw-Hill.

———. 1971. Forgetting as retrieval failure. In *Animal Memory,* eds. W. K. Honig & P. H. R. James, 45–109. New York: Academic Press.

———. 1976. Retrieval of memories. In *Handbook of Learning and Cognitive Processes,* Vol. IV: *Attention and Memory,* ed. W. K. Estes, 17–90. Hillsdale, N.J.: Erlbaum.

———. 1978. *The Processing of Memories: Forgetting and Retention.* Hillsdale, N.J.: Erlbaum.

———. 1979. Memory storage factors leading to infantile amnesia. In *The Psychology of Learning and Motivation,* Vol. 13, ed. G. H. Bower, 91–154. New York: Academic Press.

———. 1981. Extending the domain of memory retrieval. In *Information Processing in Animals: Memory Mechanisms,* eds. N. E. Spear & R. R. Miller. Hillsdale, N.J.: Erlbaum.

———. 1984a. The future study of learning and memory from a psychobiological perspective. In *Perspectives in Psychological Experimentation,* eds. V. Sarris & A. Parducci. Hillsdale, N.J.: Erlbaum.

———. 1984b. Behaviors that indicate memory: Levels of expression. *Canadian Journal of Psychology,* 38:348–67.

Spear, N. E. & Gordon, W. C. 1981. Sleep, dreaming and the retrieval of memories. In *Recent Advances in Sleep Research,* Vol. IV: *Learning and Memory,* ed. W. Fishbein, 183–203. New York: Spectrum.

Spear, N. E., & Hyatt, L. W. 1993. How the timing of experience can affect the ontogeny of learning. In *Developmental Time and Timing,* eds. G. Turkewitz & D. Devenny. Hillsdale, N.J.: Erlbaum.

Spear, N. E., McKinzie, D. L., & Arnold, H. M. 1993. Suggestions from the infant rat about brain dysfunction and memory. In *The Memory System of the Brain,* ed. J. Delacour. River Edge, N.J.: World Scientific Publishing.

Spear, N. E., & Mueller, C. W. 1984. On the meaning of consolidation during storage and retrieval. In *Memory Consolidation: Toward a Psychobiology of Cognition,* eds. H. Weingartner & E. S. Parker, 111–47. Hillsdale, N.J.: Erlbaum.

Spear, N. E., & Parsons, P. J. 1976. Alleviation of forgetting by reactivation treatment: A preliminary analysis of the ontogeny of memory processing. In *Processes of Animal Memory,* eds. D. Medin, W. Roberts, & R. Davis, 135–66. Hillsdale, N.J.: Erlbaum.

Spear, N. E., & Rudy, J. W. 1991. Tests of learning and memory in the developing rat. In *Developmental Psychobiology: Current Methodological and Conceptual Issues,* eds. H. N. Shair, G. A. Barr, & M. A. Hofer, 84–113. New York: Oxford University Press.

Spear, N. E., Smith, G. J., Bryan, R. G., Gordon, W. C., Timmons, R., & Chiszar, D. A. 1980. Contextual influences on the interaction between conflicting memories in the rat. *Animal Learning and Behavior,* 8:273–81.

Spence, K. W. 1956. *Behavior Theory and Conditioning.* New Haven, Conn.: Yale University Press.

Springer, A. D. 1975. Vulnerability of skeletal and autonomic manifestation of memory in the rat. *Journal of Comparative and Physiological Psychology,* 88:890–903.

Squire, L. R. 1987. *Memory and Brain.* New York: Oxford University Press.

———. 1992. Memory and the hippocampus: A synthesis from findings with rats, monkeys and humans. *Psychological Review,* 99:195–231.

Squire, L. R., & Cohen, N. 1979. Memory and amnesia: Resistance to disruption develops for years after learning. *Behavioral and Neural Biology,* 25:115–25.

Squire, L. R., & Cohen, N. J. 1984. Human memory and amnesia. In *Neurobiology of Learning and Memory,* eds. G. Lynch, J. L. McGaugh, & N. M. Weinberger. New York: Guilford Press.

Squire, L. R., Knowlton, B., & Musen, G. 1993. The structure and organization of memory. *Annual Review of Psychology,* 44:453–95.

Squire, L. R., & Miller, P. L. 1974. Diminution of anterograde amnesia following electroconvulsive therapy. *British Journal of Psychiatry,* 125:490–95.

Squire, L. R., & Slater, P. C. 1975. Forgetting in very long-term memory as assessed by an improved questionnaire technique. *Journal of Experimental Psychology: Human Learning and Memory,* 104:50–54.

Squire, L. R., & Spanis C. W. 1984. Long gradient of retrograde amnesia in mice: Continuity with the findings in humans. *Behavioral Neuroscience,* 98:345–48.

Starr, A., & Phillips, L. 1970. Verbal and motor memory in the amnesia syndrome. *Neuropsychologia,* 8:75–88.

Stein, J., Ed. 1984. *Random House College Dictionary, Revised Edition.* New York: Random House.

Steinert, P. A., Infurna, R. N., & Spear, N. E. 1980. Long-term retention of a conditioned taste aversion in preweanling and adult rats. *Animal Learning and Behavior,* 8:375–81.

Stern, L. D. 1981. A review of theories of human amnesia. *Memory and Cognition,* 9:247–62.

Stewart, U., Krebs, W. H., & Kaczender, E. 1967. State-dependent learning produced with steroids. *Nature (London),* 216:1223–24.

Stonebraker, T. B. 1981. Retrospective versus prospective processes in delayed matching-to-sample. Unpublished Ph.D. Thesis, Michigan State University.

Stonebraker, T. B., & Rilling, M. 1981. Control of delayed matching-to-sample performance using directed forgetting techniques. *Animal Learning and Behavior,* 9:196–220.

Stroebel, C. F. 1967. Behavioral aspects of circadian rhythms. In *Comparative Psychopathology,* eds. J. Zubin & H. F. Hunt. New York: Grune & Stratton.

Sulin, R. A., & Dooling, D. J. 1974. Intrusion of a thematic idea in retention of prose. *Journal of Experimental Psychology,* 103:255–62.

Summers, W. V., Horton, D. L., & Diehl, V. A. 1985. Contextual knowledge during encoding influences sentence recognition. *Journal of Experimental Psychology: Learning, Memory and Cognition,* 11:771–79.

Sussmann, P. S., & Ferguson, H. B. 1980. Retained elements of early avoidance training and relearning of forgotten operants. *Developmental Psychobiology,* 13:545–62.

Sutherland, R. J., & Dyck, R. H. 1984. Place navigation by rats in a swimming pool. *Canadian Journal of Psychology,* 38:322–47.

Sutherland, R. J., & Linggard, R. 1982. Being there: A novel demonstration of latent spatial learning in the rat. *Behavioral and Neural Biology,* 36:103–07.

Tait, R. W., & Saladin, M. E. 1986. Concurrent development of excitatory and inhibition associations during backward conditioning. *Animal Learning and Behavior,* 14: 133–37.

Thomas, D. A., & Riccio, D. C. 1979. Forgetting of a CS attribute in a conditioned suppression paradigm. *Animal Learning and Behavior,* 7:191–95.

Thomas, D. R. 1981. Studies of long-term memory in the pigeon. In *Information Processing in Animals: Memory Mechanisms,* eds. N. E. Spear & R. R. Miller. Hillsdale, N.J.: Erlbaum.

———. 1985. Contextual stimulus control of operant responding in pigeons. In *Context and Learning,* eds. P. Balsam & A. Tomie. Hillsdale, N.J.: Erlbaum.

———. 1991. Context as a retrieval cue in pigeon long-term memory. In *Memory Mechanisms: A Tribute to G. V. Goddard,* eds. W. C. Abraham, M. C. Corballis, & K. G. White, 329–52. Hillsdale, N.J.: Erlbaum.

Thomas, D. R., & Burr, D. E. S. 1969. Stimulus generalization as a function of the delay between training and testing procedures: A reevaluation. *Journal of the Experimental Analysis of Behavior,* 12:105–09.

Thomas, D. R., & Empedocles, S. 1992. Novelty vs. retrieval cue value in the study of long-term memory in pigeons. *Journal of Experimental Psychology: Animal Behavior Processes,* 18:22–33.

Thomas, D. R., & Lopez, L. J. 1962. The effects of delayed testing on generalization slope. *Journal of Comparative and Physiological Psychology,* 55:541–44.

Thomas, D. R., Windell, B. T., Bakke, I., Kreye, J., Kimose, E. & Aposhyan, H. 1985. I. Long-term memory in pigeons: The role of discrimination problem difficulty assessed by reacquisition measures. II. The role of stimulus modality assessed by generalization slope. *Learning and Motivation,* 16:464–77.

Thompson, C. P. 1982. Memory for unique personal events: The roommate study. *Memory and Cognition,* 10:324–32.

Thompson, C., & Neely, J. E. 1970. Dissociated learning in rats produced by electroconvulsive shock. *Physiology and Behavior,* 5:783–86.

Thompson, R. F. 1986. The neurobiology of learning and memory. *Science,* 233:941–47.

Tinklepaugh, O. L. 1928. An experimental study of representative factors in monkeys. *Journal of Comparative Psychology,* 8:197.

Tolman, E. C. 1932. *Purposive Behavior in Animals and Men.* New York: Century.

———. 1948. Cognitive maps in rats and men. *Psychological Review,* 55:189–208.

———. 1959. Principles of purposive behavior. In *Psychology: A Study of a Science,* Vol. 2: *General Systematic Formulations, Learning and Special Processes,* ed. S. Koch, 92–157. New York: McGraw-Hill.

Tranberg, D. K., & Rilling, M. 1980. Delay-interval illumination changes interfere with pigeon short-term memory. *Journal of Experimental Analysis of Behavior,* 33:39–49.

Trapold, M. A. 1970. Are expectancies based upon different positive reinforcing events discriminably different? *Learning and Motivation,* 1:129–40.

Treichler, R. F. 1984. Long-term retention of concurrent discrimination by monkeys. *Physiological Psychology,* 12:92–96.

Tulving, E. 1967. The effects of presentation and recall of material in free recall learning. *Journal of Verbal Learning and Verbal Behavior,* 6:175–84.

———. 1969. Retrograde amnesia in free recall. *Science,* 164:88–90.

———. 1972. Episodic and semantic memory. In *Organization of Memory,* eds. E. Tulving & W. Donaldson, 382–404. New York: Academic Press.

———. 1974. Cue-dependent forgetting. *American Scientist,* 62:74–82.

———. 1983. *Elements of Episodic Memory*. New York: Oxford University Press.

———. 1985. How many memory systems are there? *American Psychologist,* 40:385–98.

Tulving, E., & Pearlstone, Z. 1966. Availability versus accessibility of information in memory for words. *Journal of Verbal Learning and Verbal Behavior,* 5:381–91.

Tulving, E., & Thomson, D. M. 1973. Encoding specificity and retrieval processes in episodic memory. *Psychological Review,* 80: 352–73.

Uehling, B. S. 1972. Arousal in verbal learning. In *Human Memory: Festschrift in Honor of Benton J. Underwood,* eds. C. P. Duncan, L. Sechrest, & W. A. Melton. New York: Appleton-Century-Crofts.

Underwood, B. J. 1954. Speed of learning and amount retained: A consideration of methodology. *Psychological Bulletin,* 51:276–82.

———. 1957. Interference and forgetting. *Psychological Review,* 64:49–60.

———. 1964. Degree of learning and the measurement of forgetting. *Journal of Verbal Learning and Verbal Behavior,* 3:112–29.

———. 1966. Motor-skills learning and verbal learning: Some observations. In *Acquisition of Skill,* ed. E. A. Bilodeau. New York: Academic Press.

———. 1969. Attributes of memory. *Psychological Review,* 76:559–73.

———. 1972a. Word recognition memory and frequency information. *Journal of Experimental Psychology,* 94:276–83.

———. 1972b. Are we overloading memory? In *Coding Processes in Human Memory,* eds. A. W. Melton & E. Martin. Washington, D.C.: Winston.

———. 1983. *Attributes of Memory.* Glenview, Ill.: Scott, Foresman.

Underwood, B. J., & Ekstrand, B. R. 1966. An analysis of some shortcomings in the interference theory of forgetting. *Psychological Review,* 73:540–49.

Underwood, B. J., Ham, M., & Ekstrand, B. 1962. Cue selection and paired-associate learning. *Journal of Experimental Psychology,* 64:405–9.

Updike, J. 1981. *Rabbit is Rich.* New York: Knopf.

———. 1990. *Rabbit at Rest.* New York: Knopf.

Urcuioli, P. J., & Zentall, T. R. 1986. Retrospective coding in pigeons' delayed matching-to-sample. *Journal of Experimental Psychology: Animal Behavior Processes,* 12:69–77.

Urcuioli, P. M., & Zentall, T. R. 1992. Transfer across delayed discriminations: Evidence regarding the nature of prospective working memory. *Journal of Experimental Psychology: Animal Behavior Processes,* 18:154–73.

Vardaris, R. M., Gaebelein, C., & Riccio, D. C. 1973. Retrograde amnesia from hypothermia-induced brain seizures. *Physiological Psychology,* 1:204–08.

Volokhof, A. A. 1970. The ontogenetic development of higher nervous activity in animals. In *Developmental Neurobiology,* ed. W. A. Himwich. Springfield, Ill.: Charles C. Thomas.

Wagner, A. R. 1981. SOP: A model of automatic memory processing in animal behavior. In *Information Processing in Animals: Memory Mechanisms,* eds. N. E. Spear & R. R. Miller, 233–65. Hillsdale, N.J.: Erlbaum.

Wagner, A. R., & Brandon, S. E. 1989. Evolution of a structured connectionist model of Pavlovian conditioning (AESOP). In *Contemporary Learning Theories: Pavlovian Conditioning and the Status of Traditional Learning Theory*, eds. S. B. Klein & R. R. Mowrer. Hillsdale, N.J.: Erlbaum.

Wagner, A. R., Rudy, J. W., & Whitlow, J. W., Jr. 1973. Rehearsal in animal conditioning. *Journal of Experimental Psychology*, 97:407–26 (Monograph).

Wallace, J., Steinert, P. A., Scobie, S. R., & Spear, N. E. 1980. Stimulus modality and short-term memory in rats. *Animal Learning and Behavior*, 8:10–16.

Wansley, R. A., & Holloway, F. A. 1975. Multiple retention deficits following one-trial appetitive training. *Behavioral Biology*, 14:135–49.

Warrington, E. K. 1985. A disconnection analysis of amnesia. *Annals of the New York Academy of Sciences*, 444:72–77.

Warrington, E. K., & Sanders, H. I. 1971. The fate of old memories. *Quarterly Journal of Experimental Psychology*, 23:432–43.

Warrington, E. K., & Weiskrantz, L. 1968. A new method of testing long-term retention with special reference to amnesic patients. *Nature*, 217:972–74.

———. 1970. Amnesic syndrome: Consolidation or retrieval? *Nature*, 228:628–30.

———. 1973. An analysis of short-term and long-term memory deficits in man. In *The Physiological Basis of Memory*, ed. J. A. Deutsch, 365–95. New York: Academic Press.

———. 1974. The effect of prior learning on subsequent retention in amnesic patients. *Neuropsychologia*, 12:419–28.

———. 1978. Further analysis of the prior learning effect in amnesic patients. *Neuropsychologia*, 16:169–77.

Wasserman, E. A. 1986. Prospection and retrospection as processes of animal short-term memory. In *Theories of Animal Memory*, eds. D. F. Kendrick, M. E. Rilling, & M. R. Denny, 53–75. Hillsdale, N.J.: Erlbaum.

———. 1993. Comparative cognition: Beginning the second century of the study of animal intelligence. *Psychological Bulletin*, 113:211–28.

Watkins, M. J., & Graefe, T. M. 1981. Delayed rehearsal of pictures. *Journal of Verbal Learning & Verbal Behavior*, 20: 276–88.

Watson, J., & Raynor, R. 1920. Conditioned emotional reactions. *Journal of Experimental Psychology*, 3:1–19.

Weingartner, H., & Faillace, L. A. 1971. Alcohol state-dependent learning in man. *Journal of Nervous and Mental Disease*, 153:395–406.

Weingartner, H., Miller, H., & Murphy, D. L. 1977. Mood state-dependent reterieval of verbal associations. *Journal of Abnormal Psychology*, 86:276–84.

Weingartner, H., & Parker, E. S., eds. 1984. *Memory Consolidation: Toward a Psychobiology of Cognition*. Hillsdale, N.J.: Erlbaum.

Weiskrantz, L. 1966. Experimental studies of amnesia. In *Amnesia*, eds. W. C. M. Whitty & O. L. Zangwill, 1–35. London: Butterworths.

———. 1970. A long-term view of short-term memory in psychology. In *Short-Term Changes in Neural Activity and Behavior*, eds. G. Horn & R. A. Hinde. Cambridge, England: Cambridge University Press.

———. 1985. On issues and theories of the human amnesic syndrome. In *Memory Systems of the Brain*, eds. N. M. Weinberger, J. L. McGaugh, & G. Lynch, 380–415. New York: Guilford Press.

———. 1989. Remembering dissociations. In *Varieties of Memory and Consciousness*, eds. H. L. Roediger & F. I. M. Craik. Hillsdale, N.J.: Erlbaum.

Weiskrantz, L., & Warrington, E. K. 1970a. Verbal learning and retention by amnesic patients using partial information. *Psychonomic Science,* 20:210–11.

———. 1970b. A study of forgetting in amnesic patients. *Neuropsychologia,* 8:281–88.

———. 1979. Conditioning in amnesic patients. *Neuropsychologia,* 17:187–94.

Weiskrantz, L., Warrington, E. K., Sanders, M. D., & Marshall, J. 1974. Visual capacity in the hemianopic field following a restricted occipital ablation. *Brain,* 97:709–28.

Wendt, G. R. 1937. Two and one-half year retention of a conditioned response. *Journal of General Psychology,* 17:178–80.

White, N. M., & Milner, P. M. 1992. The psychobiology of reinforcers. *Annual Review of Psychology,* 43:443–71.

Whitely, P. L., & Blankenship, A. B. 1935. The influence of certain conditions prior to learning upon subsequent recall. *Journal of Experimental Psychology,* 19:496–504.

Wickelgren, W. A. 1972. Trace resistance and the decay of long-term memory. *Journal of Mathematical Psychology,* 9:418–55.

———. 1973. The long and short of memory. *Psychological Bulletin,* 80:425–38.

———. 1975. More on the long and short of memory. In *Short-Term Memory*, eds. D. Deutsch & J. A. Deutsch, 66–75. New York: Academic Press.

Wickens, D. D. 1970. Encoding categories of words: An empirical approach to meanings. *Psychological Review,* 77:1–15.

———. 1972. Characteristics of word encoding. In *Coding Processes in Human Memory*, eds. A. W. Melton & E. Martin. Washington, D.C.: H. Winston.

Wickens, D. D., Tuber, D. S., Nield, A. F., & Wickens, C. 1977. Memory for the conditioned response: The effects of potential interference introduced before and after original conditioning. *Journal of Experimental Psychology: General,* 106:47–70.

Winocur, G., & Kinsbourne, A. 1978. Contextual cueing as an aid to Korsakoff amnesics. *Neuropsychologia,* 16:671–82.

Winocur, G., Kinsbourne, M., & Moscovitch, M. 1981. The effect of cuing on release from proactive interference in Korsakoff amnesic patients. *Journal of Experimental Psychology: Human Learning and Memory,* 7:56–65.

Winograd, E., & Soloway, R. M. 1986. On forgetting the locations of things stored in special places. *Journal of Experimental Psychology: General,* 115:366–72.

Wittman, T. K., & DeVietti, T. L. 1980. Heart-rate activity to reminder treatment predicts test performance in rats given ECS following training. *Physiological Psychology,* 8:515–21.

Wittrup, M., & Gordon, W. C. 1982. Alteration of a training memory through cueing. *American Journal of Psychology,* 95:497–508.
Woodward, A. E., Bjork, R. A., & Jongeward, R. H. 1973. Recall and recognition as a function of primary rehearsal. *Journal of Verbal Learning and Verbal Behavior,* 12:608–17.
Wright, D. C., Chute, D. L., & McCollum, G. C. 1974. Reversible sodium pentobarbitol amnesia in one-trial discrimination learning. *Pharmacology, Biochemistry and Behavior,* 2:603–6.
Wright, A. A., Urcuioli, P. J., & Sands, S. F. 1986. Proactive interference in animal memory. In *Theories of Animal Memory,* eds. D. F. Kendrick, M. E. Rilling, & M. R. Denny, 101–25. Hillsdale, N.J.: Erlbaum.
Yates, F. A. 1966. *The Art of Memory.* Chicago: University of Chicago Press.
Yerkes, R. M. 1928. The mind of a gorilla: Part III. Memory. *Comparative Psychology Monographs,* 5:1–92.
Young, A. W. 1988. Functional organization of visual recognition. In *Thought Without Language,* ed. L. Weiskrantz, 78–107. Oxford: Clarendon Press.
Zaragoza, M. S. 1991. Preschool children's susceptibility to memory impairment. In *The Suggestibility of Children's Recollections,* ed. J. Peris, 27–39. Washington, D.C.: American Psychological Association.
Zaragoza, M. S., & Koshmider, J. W. 1989. Misled subjects may know more than their performance implies. *Journal of Experimental Psychology: Learning, Memory and Cognition,* 15:246–55.
Zaragoza, M. S., McCloskey, M., & Jamis, M. 1987. Misleading postevent information and recall of the original event: Further evidence against the memory impairment hypothesis. *Journal of Experimental Psychology: Learning, Memory and Cognition,* 13:36–44.
Zechmeister, E. B., & Nyberg, S. E. 1982. *Human Memory: An Introduction to Research and Theory.* Belmont, Calif.: Wadsworth.
Zentall, T. R. 1970. Effects of context change on forgetting in rats. *Journal of Experimental Psychology,* 86:440–48.
Zentall, T. R., Stern, J. N., & Jackson-Smith, P. 1990. Memory strategies in pigeons' performance of a radial-arm-maze analog task. *Journal of Experimental Psychology: Animal Behavior Processes,* 16:358–71.
Zinkin, S., & Miller, A. J. 1967. Recovery of memory after amnesia induced by electroconvulsive shock. *Science,* 155:102–4.
Zola-Morgan, S. M., & Squire L. R. 1990. The primate hippocampal formation: Evidence for a time-limited role in memory storage. *Science,* 250:288–90.
Zornetzer, S. F., & McGaugh, J. L. 1971. Retrograde amnesia and brain seizures in mice. *Physiology and Behavior,* 7:401–8.

Index

Adrenergic hormones in memory modulation, 224–225
Adrenocorticotrophic hormone (ACTH)
  in memory modulation, 224
  state-dependent effects of, on memory modulation, 227–228
Affective states, memory and, 81–82
Alcohol, state-dependent retention and, 78
Amnesia(s), 213–243
  anterograde, 238–242. *See also* Anterograde amnesia (AA)
  experimentally induced, retrieval deficits in, 259–271
  human
    aspects of, 281–300
    Mishkin's neurobiological model of, 295–297
  infantile, 177, 200–207. *See also* Infantile amnesia
  learning and, 2–3
  memory retrieval by persons with, 272–278
  recovery from
    induced by priming, 276–277
    induced by re-exposure to amnestic agent, 277–278
    test-induced, 273–275
  retrograde, 213–222. *See also* Retrograde amnesia (RA)
  source, 334–335
Amnestic agent, re-exposure to
  recovery from amnesia induced by, 277–278
  in recovery from experimentally induced amnesia, 267–270
Amphetamine, attenuation of forgetting induced by, 250–251
  after brain damage, 256–257
Anterograde amnesia (AA), 238–242
  alleviation of, 270–271
  human, 286–290
    methodological concerns on, 294–295
  short-term versus long-term memory and, 344–345
Associative learning, 302–304
Associative memory, 147
Autonomic learning, 324–325
Aversive events, memory for, 164–165

Backward conditioning, 324
Behavioral development in infancy, features of, 186–187
Behavioral treatments, post-trial, in memory modulation, 228–229
Blocking effect, 320–321
Brain
  damage to, attenuation of forgetting after, 256–259
  development of, features of, 183–186
  memory and, 7–8
  ontogenetic change in, 182–186
  structures of, separate, separate memory systems associated with, 347–350

Caches, memory for, 170–173
Carbon dioxide, retrograde amnesia induced by, 219
Cholinergic agents in memory modulation, 226
Circadian rhythms, memory and, 80
Cognition, short-term retention in animals and, 132–140

395

Cognitive basis for short-term versus long-term memory, 345
Cognitive dispositions contributing to retention and forgetting, developmental differences in, 197–200
Cognitive maps, 168–170
Cognitive process, memory systems distinguished by, 337–345
Conditional discrimination, 58–59
Conditioned stimulus (CS)
  expression of learning and, 325
  representations of, 308–309
Conditioning
  backward, 324
  basic, 44–46
    contextual influences on, 59–61
    external contextual stimuli controlling expression of, 70–71
  Pavlovian, misconceptions about, 303–304
Consolidation, forgetting and, 86–87
Context
  attributes of, new, induction of, memory modulation by, 233–234
  basic conditioning and, 59–61
  definition of, 54–55
  forgetting and, 53–83
  internal, 56
  learning, physical presence of, context effect and, 67–68
  learning and, 54–55, 59–61
  linguistic, 56
  meaning of, sharpening, 55–56
  memory and, 55
    issues in relationship between, 56–59
    Smith experiments on, 65–69
  in memory retrieval, 61–63
  remembering, 69–70
  retention and, 53–59
Contextual change effect, 63–74
  in deep-sea diving, 69–70
  generality of, 69–74
    limits to, 72–74
  how word is perceived/encoded and, 67
  human memory and, 64–65
  novelty of test context and, 66–67
  physical presence of learning context and, 67–68
  in retention, 56–57
Contextual stimuli
  external, controlling expression of basic conditioning, 70–71
  forgetting and, 297
Contiguity in basic learning, 303
Contrast effects on memory, 163–164
Control groups in measurement of memory, 19–21
Correspondence assumption, 12
Cuing, prior, to alleviate forgetting
  in animals, 247–250, *252–253*
  in humans, 254–255

Decay of memory, 86–87
Decrement, generalized, 57
Delayed alteration in short-term retention assessment, 146
Delayed matching-to-sample in short-term retention assessment, 112–114
Delayed response test in short-term retention assessment, 110–112
Descartes on memory, 5
Discrimination, conditional, 58–59
Dissociation as research strategy in psychobiology of memory, 292–293
Drugs, attenuation of forgetting induced by, 250–251

Ebbinghaus, Herman, on memory processing, 8, *9*
Electroconvulsive shock (ECS), retrograde amnesia induced by, 214–216
Emotional states, memory and, 81–82
Engrams, 256
Epinephrine
  in memory modulation, 223–224
  state-dependent effects of, on memory modulation, 227–228
Experience, early
  nonspecific, significance of, 188–189
  with specific learning, 189–190
Explicit memory, 290–292
Expression of learning
  induced, 315–323. *See also* Induced expression
  selective, 323–327. *See also* Selective expression of learning

Female reproductive cycle, memory and, 80–81
Flavor attributes, forgetting, 158–159
Forgetting
  absence of, in early laboratory tests with animals, 28–29
  alleviation of
    after brain damage, 256–259
    in animals, 247–253, *252–253*
      drugs in, 250–251
      prior cuing in, 247–250, *252–253*
    in humans, 251, 254–255
      prior cuing in, 254–255
      spontaneous, 255
  in animals, 96–100
  cognitive dispositions contributing to, developmental differences in, 197–200
  consolidation and, 86–87
  context and, 53–83
  direct, 137–140
  in everyday life, 297–299
  of interoceptive attributes, 158–159
  over time, everyday, 32–36
  rate of, content of memory and, 129–132
  recovery from, 245–279. *See also* Forgetting, alleviation of
  retention and, 16
  retention interval filled with relative inactivity and, 31–51
  sources of, 24–25, 53–107
    context as, 53–83. *See also* Context
    interference as, 85–107
  as steady decline
    exceptions to, 39–46
    generality of, 36–38
  of stimulus attributes by humans, 159–160
  time and, 27–52
  understanding, orientation for, 29–31

Galen on memory, 5
Generalization gradients and memory for conflicting stimuli, 161–162
Generalized decrement, 57
Growth, infantile amnesia and, 207

Hormones
  changes in, in female reproductive cycle, memory and, 80–81
  in memory modulation, 223–225
Hypermnesia, 39–46
  basic conditioning as, 44–46
  incubation as, 42–44
  reminiscence as, 39–40
Hyperthermia, retrograde amnesia induced by, 220, *221*
Hypothermia, retrograde amnesia induced by, 219–220

Identity matching, retroactive interference and, 118–119
Implicit memory, 290–292
Incubation, 42–44
Induced expression, 315–323
  blocking effect in, 320–321
  latent inhibition in, 321–322
  overshadowing in, 316–320
  selective expression and, basis of, 332–334
Infantile amnesia, 177, 200–207
  growth and, 207
  memory content and, 203–207
  theoretical issues in, 202–203
Infants, expression of learning in, 326–327
Inhibition, latent, 321–322
Interference, 85–107
  action of, 85–86
  alternatives to, 86–87
  in animals, 96–100
  in anterograde amnesia in humans, 287–290
  forgetting and, 297–298
  mechanisms and features of, 89–96
  mix-up mechanism of, 90
  nonspecific, in animal memory, 100–102
  proactive, 88, 93–96
    in short-term retention, 121–126
      from prior processing of particular samples, 123–126
      sources of, 122–123
  response competition in, 90–91
  retroactive, 87–88, 92–93
    nonspecific, illumination as example of, 115–117
    sensory modality and, 117–119
    in short-term retention, 114–119

Interference *(cont.)*
  similarity as cornerstone of, 88–89
Internal context, 56
Interoceptive attributes, forgetting of, 158–159

James, William
  on mnemonic techniques, 4
  on trait of retentiveness, 4, 8

Kamin effect on retention, 46–49
Korsakoff's syndrome, retrograde amnesia in, 283–284
Kraemer experiments on proactive interference in animals, 98–100

Latent inhibition, 321–322
Learning
  about schedules of reinforcement, ontogenetic differences in, systematic analysis of, 196–197
  associative, 302–304
  autonomic, 324–325
  capacity for
    emergence of, 191–193
    ontogenetic change in, 191–200
  context and, 54–55, 59–61
  context for, physical presence of, context effect and, 67–68
  developmental changes in, assessing, 179–181
  earliest onset of specific instances of, 194–196
  expression of
    induced, 315–323. *See also* Induced expression
    selective, 323–327. *See also* Selective expression of learning
  memory and, 2
    conceptual distinctions between, 2–4
  memory established by, 302–311
  memory retrieval and, similarity between, 312–315
  ontogenesis of, implications of, for multiple memory systems, 346–347
  ontogeny of, 178–182
  principles of, memory and, 301–329
  representations and memories and, 305–310
  retention and, 14–16
  significance of, during development, 188–190
  somatic, 324–325
  specific, early experience with, 189–190
  theories of, theories of memory and, 311–329
Levorphanol in memory modulation, 226
Linguistic context, 56
Long-term retention, short-term memory distinguished from, 342–343
  anterograde amnesia and, 344–345
  cognitive basis for, 345
  retrograde amnesia as evidence for, 343–344

Magnitude of reinforcement principle, 163
Maps, cognitive, 168–170
Marijuana, state-dependent retention and, 78
Matching, identity, retroactive interference and, 118–119
Matching-to-sample
  delayed, in short-term retention assessment, 112–114
  symbolic, retroactive interference and, 118–119
Memory(ies)
  acquisition of, memory retrieval and, similarity between, 312–315
  animal, nonspecific interference in, 100–102
  associative, 147
  for attributes of reinforcers or unconditioned stimuli, 162–165
  available and expressed, dissociation between, 21–24
  for aversive events, 164–165
  brain and, 7–8
  for caches, 170–173
  circumstances and, 30–31
  for conflicting stimuli, generalization gradients and, 161–162
  content of, infantile amnesia and, 203–207
  context and, 55

Memory(ies) *(cont.)*
    issues in relationship between, 56–59
    novelty of test context and, 66–67
    Smith experiments on, 65–69
  decay of, 86–87
  definitions of, 10–14
  development of
    foundations of, 182–187
    general issues in, 181–182
  developmental changes in, assessing, 179–181
  early ideas about, 4–10
  explicit and implicit, 290–292
  expression of, 16–21
  facilitation of
    by induced sleep, 105–106
    by REM sleep, 104–105
  fifty-year, 32–34
  human, contextual change effect and, 64–65
  learning and, 2
    conceptual distinctions between, 2–4
  learning principles and, 301–329
  malleability of, in humans, 234–236
    interpretation of, 236–238
  malleable and modulated, 237–238
  measurement of, 17–21
    control groups in, 19–21
    different methods of, different conclusions from, 22–23
    features of, 23–24
    principles of, 18–19
    recall in, 17–18
    recognition in, 17–18
    relearning in, 18
  metaphors used to describe, 338*t*
  modulation of, 222–234
    hormonal, 223–225
    by induction of new contextual attributes, 233–234
    neurotransmitters in, 225–227
    for old memories, 231–233
    pharmacological, 222–223
    post-trial behavioral treatments on, 228–229
    postacquisition state-dependent effects on, 227–228
    through reinforcement, 229–231
  monkey and human, comparison of, 143–147
  ontogeny of, 178–182
  overt representation for, 119–121
  as process, 11–12, 13–14
  processing of
    art of, 6
    developmental change in, 177–211
    science of, 7–10
  psychobiology of, dissociation as research strategy in, 292–293
  as representation, 12–13
  retrieval of. *See* Retrieval
  in short-term retention, content of, 126–132
    prospective and retrospective, 127–129
    rate of forgetting and, 129–132
  significance of, during development, 188–190
  sleep and, 102–106
  spatial, 165–174. *See also* Spatial memory
  state-dependent, 77–79
  stimulus attributes and, 151–165
  storage capacity for, ontogenetic change in, 191–193
  structure of, 331–353
  study of
    early, 8–10
    increased breadth in, 10
    systematic experiments on, first, 8–10
  theories of, theories of learning and, 311–329
  uses of term, 11–12
Memory dissociation, endogenous states and, 80–83
Memory representation(s), 302–311. *See also* Representation(s)
Method of loci, 5
Metrazol, retrograde amnesia induced by, 219
Mishkin's neurobiological model of human amnesia, 295–297
Mnemonics
  James on, 4
  origin on, 5–6
Mood, memory and, 81–82
Morris maze, 168–170
Motivation, forgetting and, 299

Motoric learning, 324–325
Multiple memory systems, 337
  alternatives of, 331–334
  distinguished by cognitive process, 337–345
  implications of ontogenesis of sensory system effectiveness and of learning for, 346–347
  quantity and nature of, 350–352
  separate
    associated with separate brain structures, 347–350
    reasons to invoke, 339–340
Myelin in brain development, 184

Naloxone in memory modulation, 226
Negative transfer after brain damage, 258
Neurons in brain development, 184–186
Neurotransmitters in memory modulation, 225–227

Opiate agonist in memory modulation, 226
Opiate antagonists in memory modulation, 226
Overshadowing, 316–320
Overt representation for memory, 119–121

Pavlovian conditioning, misconceptions about, 303–304
Pentobarbital, retrograde state-dependent effect of, 227
Pharmacological agents in memory modulation, 222–223
Plato on memory, 4
Potassium chloride, retrograde amnesia induced by, 219
Priming, recovery from amnesia induced by, 276–277
Proactive interference, 88, 93–96
  in short-term retention, 121–126
    from prior processing of particular samples, 123–126
    sources of, 122–123
Process, memory as, 11–12, 13–14

Radial maze task, 165–166
Rapid-eye-movement (REM) sleep, 103

  in normal sleep, memory facilitated by, 104–105
Recall
  in measurement of memory, 17–18
  of pictures and words, improvement in, over time, 40–42
Recognition in measurement of memory, 17–18
Recovery from retrograde amnesia, 263–270
Rehearsal
  animal memory and, 133–137
  of pictures by monkey and human, 145–146
Reinforcement
  memory modulation through, 229–231
  schedules of, learning about, ontogenetic differences in, systematic analysis of, 196–197
Reinforcers
  attributes of, memory for, 162–165
  in recovery from experimentally induced retrograde amnesia, 264–267
  representations of, 306–308
Relearning in measurement of memory, 18
Remembering
  memory acquisition and, similarity between, 312–315
  of unique personal events, 34–35, *35, 36*
  verbal reports of, misleading nature of, 21–22
Reminiscence, 39–40
Representation(s), 302–311
  of conditioned stimulus, 308–309
  further evidence and comment on, 309–310
  learning and, 305–310
  memory as, 12–13
  overt, for memory, 119–121
  of unconditioned stimulus or reinforcer, 306–308
Reproductive cycle, female, memory and, 80–81
Retention
  cognitive dispositions contributing to, developmental differences in, 197–200
  context and, 53–59
  contextual change effect in, 56–57
  fluctuations in, repeated, 49–50, *51*

Retention *(cont.)*
    forgetting and, 16
    functions of, multiphasic, 49–50, *51*
    increases in, 39–46
    learning and, 14–16
    long-term, 342–343. *See also* Long-term retention
    ontogeny of, 200–207
        theoretical issues in, 202–203
    short-term, 109–149, 342–343. *See also* Short-term retention
    state-dependent, 48, 74–79
        drug-induced, principles of, 79
        experimental analysis of, 75–77
        in humans, 77–79
        variables affecting, 76–77
    temporarily impaired, 46–49
Retention interval, forgetting and, 31–51
Retrieval, 16
    context in, 61–63
    deficits in
        in experimentally induced amnesia, 259–271
        retrograde amnesia from, 259–260
    memory acquisition and, similarity between, 312–315
    by persons with amnesia, 272–278
    sleep promoting, in human infants, 106
Retrieval phenomena, 245–279. *See also* Forgetting, alleviation of
Retroactive interference, 87–88, 92–93
    nonspecific, illumination as example of, 115–117
    sensory modality and, 117–119
    in short-term retention, 114–119
Retrograde amnesia (RA), 213–222
    alleviation of, spontaneous, 263–270
    as evidence for distinction between short-term and long-term memory, 343–344
    experimentally induced, 214
        characteristics of, 216–222
        interval between amnestic agent and retention test in, 217–218
        interval between training and amnestic agent in, 216–217
        retrieval deficits in, 259–271
        time and, 260–262
        type of amnestic agent in, 218–222

growth of, over time, 260–262
    in humans, 282–286
    length of interval between training and amnestic agent and, 262–263
    recovery from, 263–270
    retrieval impairment and, 259–260

Sechenov, I. M., on memory processing, 7
Selective expression of learning, 323–327
    in autonomic learning, 324–325
    backward conditioning in, 324
    breadth of, 334–337
    induced expression and, basis of, 332–334
    in infants, 326–327
    nature of conditioned stimulus and, 325
    in somatic learning, 324–325
    unconditioned stimulus and, 325–326
Sensory modality
    for learning, forgetting rate and, 129–132
    retroactive interference and, 117–119
Sensory systems effectiveness, ontogenesis of, implications of, for multiple memory systems, 346–347
Short-term retention, 109–149
    in animals, cognition and, 132–140
    assessment of, 109–114
        associative memory in, 147
        delayed alteration in, 146
        delayed matching-to-sample technique in, 112–114
        by delayed response test, 110–112
    in humans, 140–143
        capacity of, 141
        duration of, 141–143
    long-term memory distinguished from, 342–343
        anterograde amnesia and, 344–345
        cognitive basis for, 345
        retrograde amnesia as evidence for, 343–344
    memory in, content of, 126–132
        prospective and retrospective, 127–129
        rate of forgetting and, 129–132
    monkey and human, comparison of, 143–147
    proactive interference in, 121–126
        from prior processing of particular samples, 123–126

Short-term retention *(cont.)*
  sources of, 122–123
  retroactive interference in, 114–119
Similarity as cornerstone of interference theory, 88–89
Sleep
  active, 103
  function of, 103–104
  induced, memory aided by, 105–106
  memory and, 102–106
  paradoxical, 103
  promoting memory retrieval in human infants, 106
  rapid-eye-movement, 103
    in normal sleep, memory facilitated by, 104–105
    stages of, 103
Smith experiments of effects of simple context on human memory, 65–69
Somatic learning, 324–325
Source amnesia, 334–335
Spatial memory, 165–174
  cognitive maps and, 168–170
  historical note on, 173–174
  memory for caches and, 170–173
  Morris maze and, 168–170
  radial maze task and, 165–166
State-dependent retention (SDR), 74–79
  drug-induced, principles of, 79
  experimental analysis of, 75–77
  in humans, 77–79
  variables affecting, 76–77
Stimulus(i)
  attributes of
    forgetting of, by humans, 159–160
    interoceptive, forgetting of, 158–159
    memory for, 154–160
  conditioned
    expression of learning and, 325
    representations of, 308–309
  conflicting, memory for, generalization gradients and, 161–162
  contextual, external, controlling expression of basic conditioning, 70–71
  generalization of, 152–154
  unconditioned
    expression of learning and, 325–326
    memory for attributes of, 162–165
    representations of, 306–308
Storage, 16
Strychnine in memory modulation, 222–223
Surprising event, memory disruption induced by, 220–222
Switching, 70–71
Symbolic matching-to-sample, retroactive interference and, 118–119

Thermoregulatory disturbances, retrograde amnesia induced by, 219–220, *221*
Tip-of-the-tongue (TOT) effect, 246
Training stimulus, exposure to, in recovery from experimentally induced retrograde amnesia, 267

Unconditioned stimulus (US)
  expression of learning and, 325–326
  memory for attributes of, 162–165
  representations of, 306–308
Unlearning, 92